The Handbook of Alcohol Use

Understandings from Synapse to Society

The Handbook of Alcohol Use

Understandings from Synapse to Society

Edited by

Daniel Frings
Centre for Addictive Behaviours Research,
School of Applied Sciences, London South Bank University

Ian P. Albery
Centre for Addictive Behaviours Research,
School of Applied Sciences, London South Bank University

ELSEVIER

ACADEMIC PRESS
An imprint of Elsevier

Academic Press is an imprint of Elsevier
125 London Wall, London EC2Y 5AS, United Kingdom
525 B Street, Suite 1650, San Diego, CA 92101, United States
50 Hampshire Street, 5th Floor, Cambridge, MA 02139, United States
The Boulevard, Langford Lane, Kidlington, Oxford OX5 1GB, United Kingdom

Notices
Knowledge and best practice in this field are constantly changing. As new research and experience broaden our understanding, changes in research methods, professional practices, or medical treatment may become necessary.

Practitioners and researchers must always rely on their own experience and knowledge in evaluating and using any information, methods, compounds, or experiments described herein. In using such information or methods they should be mindful of their own safety and the safety of others, including parties for whom they have a professional responsibility.

To the fullest extent of the law, neither the Publisher nor the authors, contributors, or editors, assume any liability for any injury and/or damage to persons or property as a matter of products liability, negligence or otherwise, or from any use or operation of any methods, products, instructions, or ideas contained in the material herein.

British Library Cataloguing-in-Publication Data
A catalogue record for this book is available from the British Library

Library of Congress Cataloging-in-Publication Data
A catalog record for this book is available from the Library of Congress

ISBN: 978-0-12-816720-5

Publisher: Nikki Levy
Editorial Project Manager: Sara Pianavilla
Production Project Manager:
Swapna Srinivasan
Cover Designer: Christian J. Bilbow

Typeset by MPS Limited, Chennai, India

Dedications

For the latest two distractions, Anica Starkey Albery and George Neculai Starkey Albery. And in memory of two influential others, John Albery and Neculai Tunariu, who have recently gone to join my father Philip John Starkey elsewhere. Thank you, both.

—Ian P. Albery, October 2020

For my parents, Angela and Michael Frings, for providing more support than they know, and for Louise, Katherine and Annabelle Frings for bringing a touch of joy and laughter to each and every day. Thank you all.

—Dan Frings, October 2020

Contents

List of contributors

Dominic Abrams Centre for the Study of Group Processes, School of Psychology, University of Kent, United Kingdom

Ian P. Albery Centre for Addictive Behaviours Research, London South Bank University, London, United Kingdom

Georgina Bartlett Centre for Addictive Behaviours Research, Division of Psychology, School of Applied Sciences, London South Bank University, London, United Kingdom

Leah M. Bouchard, AM School of Social Work, Virginia Commonwealth University, Richmond, VA, United States

James Cane School of Psychology and Life Sciences, Canterbury Christ Church University, Canterbury, Kent, United Kingdom

Gabriele Caselli Studi Cognitivi, Milano, Italy; Department of Psychology, Sigmund Freud University, Milano, Italy

Karen G. Chartier School of Social Work, Virginia Commonwealth University, Richmond, VA, United States; Department of Psychiatry, School of Medicine, Virginia Commonwealth University, Richmond, VA, United States

Dean Connolly Institute of Psychiatry, Psychology and Neuroscience, King's College London, UK; Barts Health NHS Trust, London, United Kingdom

Amber Copeland Department of Psychology, University of Sheffield, Sheffield, United Kingdom

W. Miles Cox School of Psychology, Bangor University, Bangor, Gwynedd, United Kingdom

Phoenix R. Crane Department of Psychological Sciences, Texas Tech University, Lubbock, TX, United States

Shane Darke National Drug & Alcohol Research Centre, University of New South Wales, Sydney, NSW, Australia

Emma L. Davies Faculty of Health and Life Sciences, Oxford Brookes University, United Kingdom

Fabien D'Hondt Univ. Lille, Inserm, CHU Lille, U1172 - LilNCog - Lille Neuroscience & Cognition, F-59000, Lille, France; CHU Lille, Clinique de Psychiatrie, CURE, Lille, France; Centre National de Ressources et de Résilience (CN2R), Lille, France

Angelo M. DiBello Department of Psychology, City University of New York, Brooklyn College, Brooklyn, NY, United States

Genevieve A. Dingle School of Psychology, The University of Queensland, Brisbane, Australia

Daniel Donkor Lead Clinical Psychologist, Turning Point, London, United Kingdom

Katie Drax School of Psychological Science, University of Bristol, Bristol, United Kingdom

Catharine E. Fairbairn Department of Psychology, University of Illinois at Urbana-Champaign, Champaign, IL, United States

Jason A. Ferris Centre for Health Services Research, The University of Queensland, Brisbane, QLD, Australia

Matt Field Department of Psychology, University of Sheffield, Sheffield, United Kingdom

Anthony M. Foster Department of Psychological Sciences, Texas Tech University, Lubbock, TX, United States

Daniel Frings Centre for Addictive Behaviours Research, School of Applied Sciences, London South Bank University

Julie Gawrylowicz Division of Psychology and Forensic Science, School of Applied Sciences, Abertay University, Dundee, United Kingdom

Paramabandhu Groves Camden and Islington NHS Foundation Trust, London, United Kingdom

Catherine Haslam School of Psychology, The University of Queensland, Brisbane, Australia

Nick Heather Division of Psychology, Northumbria University, Newcastle upon Tyne, United Kingdom

Derek Heim Department of Psychology, Edge Hill University, Ormskirk, West Lancashire, United Kingdom; Liverpool Centre for Alcohol Research, Liverpool Health Partners, Liverpool Science Park, Liverpool, United Kingdom

Tim Hopthrow Centre for the Study of Group Processes, School of Psychology, University of Kent, United Kingdom

Hirotaka Imada Centre for the Study of Group Processes, School of Psychology, University of Kent, United Kingdom

Isabella Ingram School of Psychology, The University of Wollongong, Wollongong, Australia

Andrew Jones Department of Psychology, University of Liverpool, Liverpool, United Kingdom; Liverpool Centre for Alcohol Research, University of Liverpool, Liverpool, United Kingdom

Dahyeon Kang Department of Psychology, University of Illinois at Urbana-Champaign, Champaign, IL, United States

Peter J. Kelly School of Psychology, The University of Wollongong, Wollongong, Australia

Eric Klinger Division of Social Sciences, University of Minnesota, Morris, MN, United States

Emmanuel Kuntsche Centre for Alcohol Policy Research, La Trobe University, Australia; Institute of Psychology, Eötvös Loránd University, Budapest, Hungary

Sandra Kuntsche Centre for Alcohol Policy Research, La Trobe University, Australia

Jan Larkin School of Psychology, Turning Point, London, United Kingdom

Tran H. Le Department of Psychological Sciences, Texas Tech University, Lubbock, TX, United States

Kristen P. Lindgren School of Social Work, Virginia Commonwealth University, Richmond, VA, United States; Department of Psychiatry, School of Medicine, Virginia Commonwealth University, Richmond, VA, United States

Giovanni Mansueto Studi Cognitivi, Milano, Italy; Department of Psychology, Sigmund Freud University, Milano, Italy; Maastricht University Medical Center, Department of Psychiatry & Psychology, University of Maastricht, Maastricht, The Netherlands; Maastricht University, The Netherlands; Department of Health Sciences, University of Florence, Firenze, Italy

Raffaella Margherita Milani University of West London, Psychology and Addiction Studies, London, United Kingdom

Pierre Maurage UCLouvain, Louvain Experimental Psychopathology Research Group (LEP), Louvain-la-Neuve, Belgium

Rebecca Monk Department of Psychology, Edge Hill University, Ormskirk, West Lancashire, United Kingdom; Liverpool Centre for Alcohol Research, Liverpool Health Partners, Liverpool Science Park, Liverpool, United Kingdom

James Morris Centre for Addictive Behaviours Research, School of Applied Sciences, London South Bank University, United Kingdom

Antony C. Moss Centre for Addictive Behaviours Research, School of Applied Sciences, London South Bank University, United Kingdom

Marcus R. Munafò Medical Research Council (MRC) Integrative Epidemiology Unit at the University of Bristol, United Kingdom; School of Psychological Science, University of Bristol, United Kingdom

Clayton Neighbors Department of Psychology, University of Houston, Houston, TX, United States

Luisa Perrino University of West London, Psychology and Addiction Studies, London, United Kingdom

Kirsten P. Peterson Department of Psychiatry and Behavioral Sciences, University of Washington, Seattle, WA, United States

Cheneal Puljevic Centre for Health Services Research, The University of Queensland, Brisbane, QLD, Australia; School of Public Health, The University of Queensland, Brisbane, QLD, Australia

Robin Room Centre for Alcohol Policy Research, La Trobe University, Australia; Centre for Social Research on Alcohol and Drugs, Department of Public Health Sciences, Stockholm University, Stockholm, Sweden

Benjamin Rolland Université de Lyon, UCBL, INSERM U1028, CNRS UMR5292, Centre de Recherche en Neuroscience de Lyon (CRNL), Bron, France; Service Universitaire d'Addictologie de Lyon (SUAL), CH Le Vinatier, Bron, France

Abigail Rose Department of Psychology, University of Liverpool, Liverpool, United Kingdom; Liverpool Centre for Alcohol Research, University of Liverpool, Liverpool, United Kingdom

Dinkar Sharma School of Psychology, University of Kent, Canterbury, Kent, United Kingdom

Sunny H. Shin School of Social Work, Virginia Commonwealth University, Richmond, VA, United States; Department of Psychiatry, School of Medicine, Virginia Commonwealth University, Richmond, VA, United States

Marcantonio M. Spada Division of Psychology, School of Applied Sciences, London South Bank University, London, United Kingdom

Tom Stafford Department of Psychology, University of Sheffield, Sheffield, United Kingdom

Amelia E. Talley Department of Psychological Sciences, Texas Tech University, Lubbock, TX, United States

Miyuki Fukushima Tedor Department of Criminology, Anthropology, and Sociology, Cleveland State University, Cleveland, OH, United States

Adam R. Winstock Global Drug Survey, London, United Kingdom; University College London, London, Australia

Ahnjili Zhuparris Global Drug Survey, London, United Kingdom

Preface

For many years, different disciplines have taken different approaches to the study of alcohol use—some focused on the micro, some on the macro and with a diverse set in-between. Perhaps as an outcome of this, it often feels as if these various strands work in isolation rather than collaboratively, and at times can be downright confrontational. This complex backdrop also features people researching and practicing who often hold different understandings and objectives. The result? A rich but messy and too-often segregated research and practice landscape.

The concept of this book stemmed from our feeling that while the richness (and maybe the mess) are positive, the division and segregation are not. Indeed, from our own perspective, the more we know about how humans "work"—both behaviorally and psychologically—the less defendable the idea of a single "truth" about alcohol becomes. This also implies a greater need for synergy, or at least a sense of respectful and productive pluralism. On this basis, this volume is an attempt to bring together a variety of approaches to the topic of alcohol use, highlighting the idea that it can (and must) be understood as a complex multilevel phenomena with causes and effects ranging, as the title suggests, "from synapse to society."

Of course, such an approach does not also assume we all agree—one can (and as writers we ourselves have in other work) argue a given level or perspective perhaps needs more recognition, or that elements of others can be challenged or refuted. This is a healthy debate, which at times you will see played out in the current volume, but care needs to be taken that it does not become polemic. In this way differing understandings can lead the field to be greater than the sum of its parts, and progress to be better made.

This is not an easy thing to aim for. Even with the best of intentions the realpolitik of funding, careers, and treatment priorities are not a natural substrate for such an idealized situation to thrive. However, we are cautiously optimistic that progress can be made—based not least in our experience of similar schisms in other fields. Despite much of our careers being shaped by the study of alcohol, neither of us actually started out with it as a research focus—in fact we both undertook our doctoral training as experimental social psychologists interested in basic psychosocial processes. Social psychology had (and still has) its own divisions, most notably, between experimental lab-based work and more social constructivist approaches. These were historically the cause of much professional, and at times personal, animosity among colleagues. However, the relatively recent rapprochement of these fields has begun to lead to a richer, more effective discipline (and also a more relaxed set of communal coffee breaks for some!). One can argue that this was achieved despite broadly the same pressures toward division which apply to alcohol and addiction.

While we of course don't assume any single volume will create a different research or practice landscape, we hope this one offers readers a chance to see *across* the collection of amazing researchers, practitioners, and those with lived experience that our field collectively possesses. Perhaps it will also inspire us to look a little further beyond our own treatment and researcher niches when searching for answers to our own foci. If this book achieves those aims, even partly, then the effort (some our own, but mostly of the authors you will read) will be wholly worthwhile.

Daniel Frings and Ian P. Albery

October 2020

Acknowledgments

We would like to thank the staff at Elsevier and Academic Press for their extremely well organized and thorough approach to the production of this book. Our thanks go in particular to Emily Ekle and Sara Pianavilla at Elsevier for their enthusiasm and dedication to the project which, we must say, rubbed off on us, "the writers and editors," at times when the book started to take second place to the many other things we have to deal with in our lives. Sorry for being a bit fussy over the cover! Of course, such a book is also not possible without the enthusiasm and commitment of the authors—all of whom worked hard over a very strange year to produce insightful chapters under difficult circumstances. Thanks to you all!

Section 1

Positioning alcohol use and misuse

Chapter 1

Contemplating the micro and macro of alcohol use and misuse to enable meta-understandings

Ian P. Albery and Daniel Frings
Centre for Addictive Behaviours Research, London South Bank University, London, United Kingdom

> *"That's the problem with drinking, I thought, as I poured myself a drink. If something bad happens you drink in an attempt to forget; if something good happens you drink in order to celebrate; and if nothing happens you drink to make something happen."*
>
> Henry Charles Bukowski, b: August 1920, d: March 1994, German-American poet and novelist

This quote says it all. For all of us, whether we be drinkers or non-drinkers, members of certain groups, or (in)experienced participants in our current culture, our relationship with alcohol is complicated and, for some, an overwhelmingly dominant feature of our everyday existence. Not only is alcohol a significantly influential socio-political agent which operates on the international stage, it is one of the most researched areas of activity among individuals covering a vast array of disciplines. This work attempts to answer different questions by using varying methodologies which are housed in disperse theoretical positionings. Geneticists, biologists, social anthropologists, sociologists, historians, geographers, archeologists, pharmacists, psychologists, clinicians of many sorts, physiologists, political scientists, economists, epidemiologists, etc., have all claimed a part of the alcohol and drinking pie for themselves, and produced, or have claimed to produce, meaningful (and sometimes 'definitive') understandings from their relative positions. A quick Google Scholar search[1] with the terms alcohol and drinking alcohol returns a

1. Search conducted on 28th July 2020 at 16:45 GMT

The Handbook of Alcohol Use - Understandings from Synapse to Society.
DOI: https://doi.org/10.1016/B978-0-12-816720-5.00025-6

massive 1.38 million records since the year 2000, c.69k per year over the 19.5 years since that date. Compare this to other salient "drugs" and we find that for gambling there have been c.380k publications since 2000, for heroin 219k, and for cocaine about 707k. Indeed, only smoking (tobacco) outdoes alcohol in terms of the number returned sitting at 2.14 million listed outputs since 2000.

So, we like to study all things alcohol and drinking-related, but why is there this interest? We suppose the answer to this question, whilst encapsulated in the comprehensiveness of Bulowski's musings, is best understood in terms of our cultural and historical relationship not only with C2H5OH[2] use but fundamentally with the "thing" we do to deliver the ethyl alcohol into our bloodstreams i.e. 'the drinking' – the vital behavioral bit of the puzzle. Understanding the chemistry and biochemistry of ethyl alcohol is one thing, getting to grips with why people *choose* to deliver the drug into their bodies is of a totally different order in terms of possible explanation and figuration. This has been the predominant focus of much of the alcohol-related research across a multitude of disciplines over the past century or so, and forms the basis from which the current volume was derived. However, as an introduction to this diverse field, let's begin by taking a look at a rather unsatisfactory and pitted history of our relationship with consuming alcohol. [For a comprehensive examination of the history of alcohol we would highly recommend either Nicholls' (2009) book *The Politics of Alcohol: A History of the Drink Question in England*, Berridge's (2013) *Demons: Our Changing Attitudes to Alcohol, Tobacco, and Drugs* or Hames' (2014) *Alcohol in World History*.]

A (very) brief history of consuming C2H5OH

According to Andrew Curry in his article *Our 9,000-Year Love Affair with Booze* that appeared in *National Geographic* in February 2017, "Alcohol isn't just a mind-altering drink: It has been a prime mover of human culture from the beginning, fueling the development of arts, language, and religion." The earliest evidence for the production of alcoholic beverages comes from around 7000 BCE when corn was domesticated in Jiahu, China (Curry, 2017), with the brewing of beer dating back to the Bronze Age and Mesopotamian civilizations and the Egyptians of the 3rd century BC (Hames, 2014). By the time of the publication of British Doomsday survey in 1086, the significant role of alcohol production was recognized with 130 vineyards being recorded in England (Berridge, 2013). It is clear, therefore, that we have had a significant period of time to develop a liking as well as, at the same, a disliking for "the drink" and its effects on individuals and

2. The structural formula for ethyl alcohol which is the main active ingredient found in alcoholic beverages.

cultures (see Nicholls, 2009). Although referred to extensively in popular literature and religious and political discourse, the academic pursuit for understanding why is it that drinking alcohol is so very important for us humans is a more recent advance. It really only dates back a couple of hundred years and was developed further by the founding of a number influential specialized journals in the US and UK; most particularly the Journal of Inebriety (1987–14, US) and the British Journal of Inebriety (later the British Journal of Addiction and then Addiction (1903 to date)). [For those interested in accessing some of the earlier writings associated with alcohol use and related interventions (and indeed for other drugs), we recommend exploring Daniel Malieck's (2020) two volume edited series entitled *Drugs, Alcohol and Addiction in the Long Nineteenth Century*.]

Over the years, people have conceptualized the drinking of alcohol and, importantly, the effects that consumption brings in varying ways. During the 18th century in the UK, excessive alcohol consumption was a culturally acceptable thing to do, common across the whole of society, and "....drink was built into the fabric of social life – it played a part in nearly every public and private ceremony, commercial bargain and craft ritual" (Berridge, 2013, p. 32). This said, at this time drinking patterns varied according to where people dwelled with urban dwellers consuming more than rural dwellers, and the prominence of the pub or inn as a gathering point for, largely lower class, people and groups (e.g. trade unions) came to the fore (Nicholls, 2009). This time also saw indications that the drinking of alcohol was starting to become associated with what those "in power" deemed problematic outcomes. William Hogarth's 1751 engravings, "Gin Lane" and "Beer Street", encapsulate these observations with alcohol (mis)use now seen as a problem of urbanization and of the lower classes in particular. Just looking at these engravings gives the impression that drinking is related to all sorts of problems for both the individual and more generally for society as a whole (e.g. crime, child neglect, laziness, etc.). With this type of propaganda, it is of little surprise that society's attitude towards alcohol use and misuse started to develop, and the central response to use of alcohol more organized. Some saw excessive drinking as a moral flaw (which we're sure was not what Hogarth intended) and that drinking was contrary to *our* presumed shared values.

Social movements, such as *temperance*, took hold in the early 19th century in the UK and elsewhere, particularly the US. Berridge (2013) identifies a number of phases in the development of the movement. The early phase (1830s) was characterized by groups opposed to the consumption of spirits and not beer or wine, and comprised the clergy and middle/upper class members. Soon the movement developed into one including an active working class membership, at which point the mantra became one of *teetotalism* and the pledge-making of complete abstinence. The UK movement was influenced by activities in the US such as the 1846 Maine Law which banned the production and sale of alcoholic beverages and also the impression that social movements could lead to legislative policy intervention - they are not merely directed at the individuals. To this end, the United Kingdom Alliance was founded in 1853 with its aim of taking temperance into the political world of legislative influence. For this group the most effective way to address the drinking problem was through political public reform not personal reform per se. Were they successful? Not really in terms of legislation, and the temperance movement was declining by the time of the outbreak of the First World War in 1914.

The US experience of temperance was very similar to that in the UK with the development of a movement based on abstention from spirits funded by well-to-do individuals and its broadening into a more working class group with dreams of political influence. The difference seems to be that in the US the political was, to some extent, achieved with prohibition legislated in thirteen states. By the time of the assassination of Archduke Franz Ferdinand in June 1914 (and the world plummeting into bloody conflict), the temperance movement in the US was on the up largely through the influence of the Anti Saloon League pressure group. And what did this increasing influence at a time of national crisis (i.e. war) culminate in? Advocates of the movement may have claimed the passing of the 18th amendment to the US Constitution which prohibited the making, selling, or transporting of alcohol drinks in January 1919, and the implementation of the amendment via the Volstead Act (1919). Irrespective, by 1920 alcohol use was essentially prohibited in the US and this would last until its repeal by the passing of the 21st Amendment in 1933 which effectively passed alcohol legislation back to the States themselves. Of note, the US was not the only country to go this way – a number of Scandinavian countries adopted prohibition even before the war (Iceland and Finland) and Canada and Norway instituted partial prohibition subsequently.

The next major theme for understanding our relationship with alcohol is rooted in the medicalisation of the behavior and more specifically the classification of excessive drinking as a disease. This understanding of alcohol use and misuse began in the mid-19th century, and was really popularized after the Second World War as an alternative to the arguably Victorian concept of "the addict" as weak and morally flawed as a "bad" person (the moral model). It continues today as the brain disease model. Over the years this approach has manifested itself in the development and adoption of classification systems for the identification of alcohol dependence, substance use disorders and the like (e.g. Diagnostic and Statistical Manuel of Mental Disorders (DSM) and the International Classification for Diseases (ICD)), and "treatments" based on these disorders. This has served to create a binary understanding relating the outcomes associated with one's drinking behavior to a biological system that is or is not functioning normally. In other words, you either have the disease or you don't. For the US National Institute of Drug Abuse (NIDA) addiction is an acquired disease of the brain (Leshner, 1997) and should be studied and treated or intervened with as such (Volkow, Koob, & McLellan, 2016). For those who endorse this account, not only does the scientific evidence support this claim but it is also useful at a more socio-political level – ensuring that "alcoholics" are seen not as at fault for their drinking but because they have the disease that effectively compels them to drink excessively even if they know that it is bad for them. This outright "nailing of your opinion to the mast" has not been adopted by UK and European bodies (e.g. Public Health England, 2016), where the focus has been more on questioning whether the (brain) disease model is the most appropriate specification in terms of the scientific evidence base (see Field, Heather, & Wiers, 2019; Heim, 2014; Lewis, 2015; Peele, 2016), the given socio-political environment (e.g. Hall, Carter, & Barnett, 2017; Heather, 2017), and whether alternatives might be more apposite (e.g. Fenton & Wiers, 2017; Heather & Segal, 2017; Matthews, 2017; Wiers & Verschure, 2021). To get a detailed understanding of the debate concerning disease-framed versus alternative positions of addiction (and alcohol misuse) take a look at the special issue *Is addiction a disease? Testing and refining Marc Lewis' critique of the Brain Disease Models of Addiction* edited by Anke Smoek and Steve Matthews that appeared in *Neuroethics* in 2017 (Smoek & Matthews, 2017). With such a (long) history of the disease approach it is of no surprise that descriptors such as "alcoholism" or "alcoholic" have become rooted in lay framing and language (Khadjesari et al., 2019) and also among those involved in intervening with those with problems related to their addictive behavior (e.g. Avery, Avery, Mouallem, Demner, & Cooper, 2020; Barnett, O'Brien, Hall, & Carter, 2020).

Beginning in the 1970s, calls for a reappraisal of how alcohol consumption and its effects were thought of were made. The idea was that understandings of alcohol use as an issue should not just be focussed on those who have the "disease" but was a matter of significance for all. In other words, alcohol use and the effects of that use should be looked at in the population as a whole and not just be concerned with the few people who experience the most severe consequences (see Edwards, 1994; see Babor et al., 2010). From this perspective, we should start to adopt a more public health understanding by asking questions concerned with why and how people drink across the full spectrum of use and, importantly, what can be done to minimize any harms associated with use that is deemed harmful or potentially harmful. With this approach the wider community, irrespective of pattern of drinking, stepped more into the spotlight of research focus and policy advocacy. The number of people with drinking issues were no longer just those who were in treatment and, seemingly, dependent. Both academics and practitioners started to measure drinking rates in community samples, identifying potentially at risk drinking behaviors and drinking populations as well as thinking about how to develop interventions with aimed at reducing potential harms for the individual and society as a whole (see Room, Babor, & Rehm, 2005). And with that type of understanding, what sorts of things do we now know?

How much do we consume?

According to the *Global Status Report on Alcohol and Health 2018* (World Health Organization, 2018), global per capita alcohol consumption is increasing making it the most popular used substance for recreation. There has been an increase in the volume of pure alcohol (ethanol) consumed by those 15 years of age and older from about 5.9 L per person per year in 2005 to 6.5 L per person per year in 2016, and this is projected to increase to about 7.6 L in 2030 (Manthey et al., 2019). Modeling has also shown that these increases are likely to be most prevalent in so-called low to middle income areas (Livingston & Callinan, 2019). Latest estimates from the WHO (2018) report is that in 2016 about 43% of world's population had consumed an alcohol beverage in the last twelve months but this general figure masks real differences across continents and countries. For example, in the European WHO area 59.9% of over 15 year-olds had consumed alcohol in the past month, a figure fairly consistent with that attributable to the Americas (54.1%) (e.g. Argentina, Brazil, Cost Rica, El Salvador, etc.) and the Western Pacific Region (53.8%) (Australia, Japan, New Zealand, Singapore, etc.). In other words, over a half of people in these areas aged 15 years or older drink alcohol. Indeed, if one excludes the 2.9% figure attributable to the Eastern Mediterranean Region (e.g. Bahrain, Egypt, Djibouti, Egypt, etc.), the range for population current drinkers is 32.2% (African Region) to 59.9% (European Region). That the proportion of the people who consume alcohol is large is highlighted further by country specific figures. For example, over three quarters of the Australian population aged 18 years and over drink alcohol (c.77% for 2017–18) (Australian Bureau of Statistics, 2018). But what are the implications of this?

So, we drink. So what?

There are a number of ways to approach this question. We could ask why is it that people appear to enjoy drinking alcohol and generate answers concerning how behavior has become more or less associated in lay terms with more positive expectations (e.g. social lubricant, sociability, friendliness, attractiveness, popularity, to fit in with my group, to name a few). Alternatively, we could ask, why is it the some people want to stop or cut down on their drinking, and cannot very easily in some instances? And therein lies the dilemma faced by policy makers, regulators and those interested in working to balance the enjoyment experienced (and tax revenue gained) against potential and real possible costs. On the one hand, the majority of drinkers do not experience many negative outcomes associated with their drinking, save for the odd hangover here and there and possibly regretting something they might have done whilst under the influence which they would not have dreamed of doing when sober. On the other hand, some drinkers will also experience negative effects associated with their alcohol in the immediate aftermath of a drinking session (e.g. drink-driving, hangover, risk-taking, violence, personal relationships, etc.), or which may accrue over time with repeated drinking. This, of course, points to those who are actually drinking at levels which may be putting them an increased risk of future health-related harm but which is not recognized by the individual themselves as a problem (Morris, Albery, Heather, & Moss, 2020). This comprises a significant number of people. Finally, there are those who through repeated drinking over a period of time have developed a pattern of drinking which places them firmly at an increased risk of experiencing physical and psychological harm associated directly with their alcohol use, the so-called problem drinkers or dependent drinkers.

Much work has been undertaken to estimate the proportion of drinkers who are at an increased risk of experiencing negative health and social outcomes as a result of the drinking behavior. In the UK, the *Alcohol Toolkit Study* (see http://www.alcoholinengland.info/index) was designed to track national patterns of alcohol use using monthly cross-sectional household surveys of representative samples of people aged 16 years and over in England (see Beard et al., 2015 for protocol). It provides a wonderful in-time statement of, among other indices, the proportion of people drinking at hazardous and problematic levels, their engagement with intervention services, and how drinking behaviors are related to use of other substances. It also has the capacity to undertaken relevant analyses to investigate interesting questions concerning, for example, social (in)equalities and alcohol-related harms to others (e.g. Beard et al., 2019; Beynon et al., 2019). Since 2014, we therefore have figures from c.2000 different people every month (over 20k per year) concerning their drinking behavior and drinking motivations and also six month follow up data on (some) of these individuals.

So, what has the *Toolkit* showed in terms of the amount of people showing signs of hazardous or problematic drinking behaviors and who may, or may not, be receiving some form intervention for their drinking? According to the latest available figures at the time of writing, as of June 2020 some 33% of respondents scored greater than four on the AUDIT-C (Bush, Kivlahan, McDonell, Fihn, & Bradley, 1998) and could be considered risky drinkers and 15% scored greater than seven on the full AUDIT (Saunders, Aasland, Babor, De la Fuente, & Grant, 1993) or were drinking hazardously in the previous month (accessed from http://www.alcoholinengland.info/latest-stats, August 24th, 2020). However, these figures are rather unrepresentative of the general trend month-by-month since March 2014 since they concerned the significant increase of use of alcohol during the period of the Covid-19-related lockdown in the UK (beginning in March 2020) (see Jackson, Garnett, Shahab, Oldham, & Brown, 2020). In terms of trends, the toolkit data has shown that on average c.13% of respondents could be classed as hazardous drinkers (see also Beard, West, Michie, & Brown, 2017), circa a quarter higher risk drinkers and 10% regular binge drinkers (de Vocht et al., 2016).

With such levels of consumption it is likely that alcohol consumption poses a "real" public health issue to the extent that such patterns of behavior is detrimental to both short-term and longer term health, social and economic indicators (Balakrishnan, Allender, Scarborough, Webster, & Rayner, 2009). It is estimated that in excess of 3.3 million deaths are attributable to alcohol per year (World Health Organization, 2018). In high income countries this makes alcohol the third leading cause of premature death (Ezzati et al., 2002), ranked the seventh leading cause among 195 countries and territories reviewed in the Global Burden of Disease Study 2016 (see Roth et al., 2018), and costs on average about 2.5% of gross domestic product (Rehm et al., 2009). Not only is alcohol a group 1 carcinogen, it is estimated that 3.5% of cancer deaths are attributable to alcohol consumption (Cogliano et al., 2011), and it is linked to over sixty other diseases that result in premature mortality (e.g. injuries, heart disease, stroke, etc.) (Connor, Haber, & Hall, 2016). In addition, people experience harm because of others' drinking. One estimate is that about 20% of the US population has experienced harm due to somebody else's drinking (Nayak, Patterson, Wilsnack, Karriker-Jaffe, & Greenfield, 2019). For example, it is estimated that more than 50% of sexual assaults in the US have involved pre-assault alcohol consumption by either victim and/or perpetrator (see Gilmore et al., 2018; Ullman, Lorenz, & Kirkner, 2017). In England the Office for National Statistics (2016) report that some 39% of violent crimes in England and 49% in Wales involved a perpetrator believed to be under the influence by the victim. And we could go on into the realms of driving injuries and fatalities, accident and emergency admissions, and so on. What is clear is that in raw terms, alcohol consumption is related to lots of "nasty" negative health and social outcomes and costs us significantly as societies and as individuals in those societies in purely economic terms; costs associated with health and social care, criminal justice, working days lost for productivity, etc.

At a more personal level, for some individuals going without a drink will become problematic in its own right. In other words, some drinkers will become psychologically and physically dependent on drinking alcohol to the extent that *not* drinking is *no longer* an option for self-regulation. How many people are dependent in this way? One estimate for England is that there are over half a million dependent drinkers or 1.34 per hundred people, the vast majority of whom (82%) are not receiving or accessing any form of treatment (Public Health England, 2019). For the US, it is estimated that 5.8% of people over eighteen years of age (14.4 million in total) had alcohol use disorder (AUD) and only c.8% of these were receiving treatment (Substance Abuse & Mental Health Services Administration (SAMHSA), 2018). Taken together, this evidence suggests a significant minority of drinkers are dependent but that the vast majority of these may not be accessing or engagement in any form of intervention.

Is alcohol consumption more or less "dangerous" than other substances like heroin or cocaine? In 2010 the past Chair of the UK Government's Advisory Council on the Misuse of Drugs (David Nutt) and colleagues, convened an independent panel of experts (the Independent Scientific Committee on Drugs) and other invited specialists to score twenty drugs (including alcohol, tobacco, cocaine, heroin, etc.) on 16 harm-related physical, social and psychological evaluation criteria. These criteria usefully reflected either harms produced in the user themselves, such as dependence, loss of relationships, drug-related deaths, or those harms that affect others around the user, including crime, economic cost and familial adversities. In other words, the data enabled comparisons between drugs in terms of harms experienced by the individual user, harms produced on others and also the combined effect of these harms. Nutt and colleagues showed that for harms related to the individual, alcohol ranked fourth most harmful behind crack cocaine, heroin and methamphetamine; for harms to others alcohol ranked first (by a significant margin); and for overall harm alcohol again was argued to be the most harmful drug (see Nutt, King, & Phillips, 2010). But are these findings specific to the UK context? It seems not – at least in Europe. The pattern is the same in the Netherlands (van Amsterdam, Opperhuizen, Koeter, & van den Brink, 2010) and in the European Union (EU) more generally (van Amsterdam, Nutt, Phillips, & van den Brink, 2015). In terms of the latter, a group of 40 drug experts representing 21 EU member states, undertook a similar exercise using the same multi-criteria decision analysis model utilized by Nutt et al. They found a similar pattern of results with alcohol, heroin and crack the most harmful and in that order of magnitude. Whatever way we look at, it seems that alcohol use and misuse can be a massive harm-related burden for the individual user but also has huge implications for others around them in the general population. Thus, it seems vital that we understand *why* we drink.

The need to understand "why" we drink

To this point, it seems clear that many, many people around the world drink alcohol. Equally apparent is that while the vast majority of these drinkers will reap primarily pleasure from their "indulgence", a significant proportion of those people will have at some point experienced some form of negative consequence from their drinking, or drink at levels that increased their relative risks of experiencing such outcomes, and a much smaller proportion will experience more serious effects. As we have also seen, the harm-related cost to health and social services for addressing the needs of people who are experiencing either acute or chronic effects of their consumption behavior is staggering, and the economic costs (e.g. lost work days, etc.), equally disconcerting. In addition, it is clear that alcohol use produces significant harms for both the individual and the wider community in which the individual exists, more so than for other so-called drugs of dependence. On this basis it seems eminently reasonable to ask why people choose to drink alcohol in the ways they do in different situations or contexts and as function of their drinking career? What motivates individuals to consume what they consume? We need, in effect, to provide an understanding of *drinking behavior* because this behavior is both the *result* of our motives and thinking patterns and, at the same time, acts as *the stimulus* for developing these needs and thoughts. It is also the "thing" that produces (and is produced by) both the benefits and the harms noted above for the individual and for the society in which the individual operates.

It is to these sorts of questions that authors in the current volume have turned their attention. As you browse the contents page we hope that it becomes fairly self-evident that answers can take many forms and be approached from many different angles, perspectives and positions. To aid the reader we have attempted to, in effect, group the contributions according to a nomenclature for a series of distinct sections concentrating first on the positioning of alcohol use, and then asking questions generated from within the body and mind, and subsequently with a focus on the individual, the group, culture and what such questions may mean for taking theory into practice. The authors in this volume have explored a number of questions using perspectives and approaches to allow for either a more micro (bottom-up) or a more macro (top-down) understanding of alcohol use and misuse. Why is this important? Because when thinking about why people drink what they drink, when they drink and the whole decisional framework which guides such reasoning, potential explanations can take many forms, each of which have equivalent meaningful value. The point is to attain a reasonable understanding of, for example, why a person gets into a car after drinking a bucket load of beer and drives the short distance to their home? To get to grips with such behaviors requires questions posed from numerous perspectives and ones that can be usefully synthesized as part of the wider puzzle. We could ask, for instance: What are the pharmacological effects of alcohol as influencing behavioral choice on a purely biological level? How do people "think" (or not) about their alcohol use and what cognitive systems do they use? Are people motivated to do what they do, or is it just habit? Are behavioral norms and group identity important – and how do they affect (and are affected by) individuals? Does our cultural experience affect our relationship with drinking-related behaviors? And so on, *ad infinitum*, because an answer to one question should always generate further related questions. The first twenty chapters in this volume take a glance at these types of questions and issues incorporating either a spotlight on more biological processes, individual-based factors, those that position behavior and associated beliefs operating as a function of group processes, or those that more broadly function within parameters based on culture. The book is structured to enable the reader to move from more micro-understandings to more macro-conceptualizations. For example, you will encounter chapters that ask how different impulsive and reflective cognitive systems are useful for understanding drinking, how exposure to drinking norms plays a part, the role of spirituality in alcohol use and misuse, how messaging is related to problem recognition, whether groups make different decisions under the influence of alcohol, the role of identity processes in drinking and alcohol misuse, what effects alcohol has on our social thinking which guide our interpersonal functioning, whether witnesses to crime are reliable and accurate after drinking, what difficult to reach populations of drinkers have to say about use and misuse, and the relationship between drinking, ethnicity and adolescence.

On top of these types of questions, and the chapters which point to some answers, we *must* then tackle the issue of what we do with these understandings? At the forefront of most people's minds is invariably the observation that alcohol use is, at one at the same time, beneficial and harmful for some individuals some of the time. How these lay understandings are used depends really on what one is trying to achieve. For example, the drinks industry may want to encourage certain type of drinkers to select their particular brand to consume on a night out with friends, and supermarkets and other outlets may want to maximize through-sales through discounted prices and offers. In contrast, Public Health England, the US National Institute of Health and other bodies, might want to develop relevant effective and sensitive public health messages, while those involved in the criminal justice system might want to understand the relationship between alcohol and weekend evening crime. At a more proximal level, those responsible for developing, implementing and evaluating group-based and individual treatment programmes might want to know how best to maximize *recovery* in their clients. Chapters 21–25 focus of these types of issues and broadly point to how theory and evidence can be usefully embedded in the response we make to overcoming alcohol-related harms.

By the time you arrive at Chapter 26 we hope you are starting to ask yourself how micro and macro approaches interact to play out in terms of understanding drinking use and abuse from different common perspectives. The final chapter directly does this by comparing predominant understandings from disease-based and psychosocial approaches to arrive at a positioned synthesis which usefully sets the agenda for future explorations of questions concerned with *why* and *how* do we drink?

It was our intention that each of the chapters are stand alone to the extent that the reader is enabled to dip in and out of the book at different points depending on their needs and interests. The book does not have to be read sequentially from cover to cover but can be read as distinct sections addressing a different focus of understanding. In other words, reading order doesn't matter.

We hope you enjoy what you read, and that it helps inform your thinking and practice in an eclectic and novel way – understanding alcohol as something which makes its impacts felt, as the cover suggests, from 'Synapse' to 'Society'.

References

Australian Bureau of Statistics. (2018). *National health survey: First results, 2017–18*. Canberra: Australian Bureau of Statistics.

Avery, J. J., Avery, J. D., Mouallem, J., Demner, A. R., & Cooper, J. (2020). Physicians' and attorneys' beliefs and attitudes related to the brain disease model of addiction. *The American Journal on Addictions*.

Babor, T., Caetano, R., Casswell, S., Edwards, G., Giesbrecht, N., Graham, K., ... Homel, R. (2010). *Alcohol research and public policy: No ordinary commodity* (2nd ed.). Oxford: Oxford University Press.

Balakrishnan, R., Allender, S., Scarborough, P., Webster, P., & Rayner, M. (2009). The burden of alcohol-related ill health in the United Kingdom. *Journal of Public Health, 31*(3), 366–373.

Barnett, A., O'Brien, K., Hall, W., & Carter, A. (2020). Support for the psychosocial, disease and brain disease models of addiction: A survey of treatment providers' attitudes in Australia, the UK, and US. *Journal of Substance Abuse Treatment*, 108033.

Beard, E., Brown, J., West, R., Acton, C., Brennan, A., Drummond, C., ... Walmsley, M. (2015). Protocol for a national monthly survey of alcohol use in England with 6-month follow-up: 'The Alcohol Toolkit Study'. *BMC Public Health, 15*(1), 230.

Beard, E., West, R., Michie, S., & Brown, J. (2017). Association between smoking and alcohol-related behaviours: A time–series analysis of population trends in England. *Addiction, 112*(10), 1832–1841.

Beard, E., Brown, J., West, R., Kaner, E., Meier, P., & Michie, S. (2019). Associations between socio-economic factors and alcohol consumption: A population survey of adults in England. *PLoS One, 14*(2), e0209442.

Beynon, C., Bayliss, D., Mason, J., Sweeney, K., Perkins, C., & Henn, C. (2019). Alcohol-related harm to others in England: A cross-sectional analysis of national survey data. *BMJ Open, 9*(5), e021046.

Berridge, V. (2013). *Demons: Our changing attitudes to alcohol, tobacco, and drugs*. Oxford: Oxford University Press.

Bush, K., Kivlahan, D. R., McDonell, M. B., Fihn, S. D., & Bradley, K. A. (1998). The AUDIT alcohol consumption questions (AUDIT-C): an effective brief screening test for problem drinking. *Archives of Internal Medicine, 158*(16), 1789–1795.

Cogliano, V. J., Baan, R., Straif, K., Grosse, Y., Lauby-Secretan, B., El Ghissassi, F., ... Galichet, L. (2011). Preventable exposures associated with human cancers. *Journal of the National Cancer Institute, 103*(24), 1827–1839.

Connor, J. P., Haber, P. S., & Hall, W. D. (2016). Alcohol use disorders. *The Lancet, 387*(10022), 988–998.

Curry, A. (2017). Our 9,000-year love affair with booze. *National Geographic*, 30–53.

de Vocht, F., Heron, J., Angus, C., Brennan, A., Mooney, J., Lock, K., ... Hickman, M. (2016). Measurable effects of local alcohol licensing policies on population health in England. *Journal of Epidemiology and Community Health, 70*(3), 231–237.

Edwards, G. (1994). *Alcohol policy and the public good*. USA: Oxford University Press.

Ezzati, M., Lopez, A. D., Rodgers, A., Vander Hoorn, S., Murray, C. J., & Comparative Risk Assessment Collaborating Group. (2002). Selected major risk factors and global and regional burden of disease. *The Lancet, 360*(9343), 1347–1360.

Fenton, T., & Wiers, R. W. (2017). Free will, black swans and addiction. *Neuroethics, 10*(1), 157–165.

Field, M., Heather, N., & Wiers, R. W. (2019). Indeed, not really a brain disorder: Implications for reductionist accounts of addiction. *Behavioral and Brain Sciences*, 42.

Gilmore, A. K., Walsh, K., Badour, C. L., Ruggiero, K. J., Kilpatrick, D. G., & Resnick, H. S. (2018). Suicidal ideation, posttraumatic stress, and substance abuse based on forcible and drug-or alcohol-facilitated/incapacitated rape histories in a national sample of women. *Suicide and Life-Threatening Behavior*, *48*(2), 183–192.

Hall, W., Carter, A., & Barnett, A. (2017). Disease or developmental disorder: Competing perspectives on the neuroscience of addiction. *Neuroethics*, *10*(1), 103–110.

Hames G. *Alcohol in world history*, 2014. Routledge, London.

Heather, N. (2017). Q: Is addiction a brain disease or a moral failing? A: Neither. *Neuroethics*, *10*(1), 115–124.

Heather, N., & Segal, G. (Eds.), (2017). *Addiction and choice: Rethinking the relationship*. Oxford University Press.

Heim, D. (2014). Addiction: Not just brain malfunction (Letter). *Nature*, *507*, 40.

Jackson, S. E., Garnett, C., Shahab, L., Oldham, M., & Brown, J. (2020). Association of the Covid-19 lockdown with smoking, drinking, and attempts to quit in England: An analysis of 2019-2020 data. *medRxiv*.

Khadjesari, Z., Stevenson, F., Toner, P., Linke, S., Milward, J., & Murray, E. (2019). 'I'm not a real boozer': A qualitative study of primary care patients' views on drinking and its consequences. *Journal of Public Health*, *41*(2), e185–e191.

Leshner, A. I. (1997). Addiction is a brain disease, and it matters. *Science*, *278*, 45–47.

Lewis, M. (2015). *The biology of desire: Why addiction is not a disease*. UK: Hachette.

Livingston, M., & Callinan, S. (2019). Examining Australia's heaviest drinkers. *Australian and New Zealand Journal of Public Health*, *43*(5), 451–456.

Malieck's. (2020). *Drugs, alcohol and addiction in the long nineteenth century*.

Manthey, J., Shield, K. D., Rylett, M., Hasan, O. S., Probst, C., & Rehm, J. (2019). Global alcohol exposure between 1990 and 2017 and forecasts until 2030: A modelling study. *The Lancet*, *393*(10190), 2493–2502.

Matthews, S. (2017). Chronic automaticity in addiction: Why extreme addiction is a disorder. *Neuroethics*, *10*(1), 199–209.

Morris, J., Albery, I. P., Heather, N., & Moss, A. C. (2020). Continuum beliefs are associated with higher problem recognition than binary beliefs among harmful drinkers without addiction experience. *Addictive Behaviors*, *105*, 106292-106292.

Nayak, M. B., Patterson, D., Wilsnack, S. C., Karriker-Jaffe, K. J., & Greenfield, T. K. (2019). Alcohol's secondhand harms in the United States: New data on prevalence and risk factors. *Journal of Studies on Alcohol and Drugs*, *80*(3), 273–281.

Nicholls, J. (2009). The politics of alcohol: A history of the drink question in England. Manchester: Manchester University Press.

Nutt, D. J., King, L. A., & Phillips, L. D. (2010). Drug harms in the UK: A multicriteria decision analysis. *The Lancet*, *376*(9752), 1558–1565.

Office for National Statistics. (2016). *Crime in England and Wales, 2016*. Retrieved July 29, 2020, from https://www.ons.gov.uk/peoplepopulationandcommunity/crimeandjustice/bulletins/crimeinenglandandwales/2015-07-16.

Peele, S. (2016). People control their addictions: No matter how much the "chronic" brain disease model of addiction indicates otherwise, we know that people can quit addictions—with special reference to harm reduction and mindfulness. *Addictive Behaviors Reports*, *4*, 97–101.

Public Health England. (2016). *Health matters: Harmful drinking and alcohol dependence*. Retrieved August 12, 2020, from https://www.gov.uk/government/publications/health-matters-harmful-drinking-and-alcohol-dependence/health-matters-harmful-drinking-and-alcohol-dependence.

Public Health England. (2019). *Health matters: Identifying and offering brief advice to tobacco and alcohol users*. Retrieved September 5, 2020, from https://publichealthmatters.blog.gov.uk/2019/03/21/health-matters-identifying-and-offering-brief-advice-to-tobacco-and-alcohol-users/.

Rehm, J., Mathers, C., Popova, S., Thavorncharoensap, M., Teerawattananon, Y., & Patra, J. (2009). Global burden of disease and injury and economic cost attributable to alcohol use and alcohol-use disorders. *The Lancet*, *373*(9682), 2223–2233.

Room, R., Babor, T., & Rehm, J. (2005). Alcohol and public health. *The Lancet*, *365*(9458), 519–530.

Roth, G. A., Abate, D., Abate, K. H., Abay, S. M., Abbafati, C., Abbasi, N., ... Abdollahpour, I. (2018). Global, regional, and national age-sex-specific mortality for 282 causes of death in 195 countries and territories, 1980–2017: A systematic analysis for the Global Burden of Disease Study 2017. *The Lancet*, *392*(10159), 1736–1788.

Saunders, J. B., Aasland, O. G., Babor, T. F., De la Fuente, J. R., & Grant, M. (1993). Development of the alcohol use disorders identification test (AUDIT): WHO collaborative project on early detection of persons with harmful alcohol consumption-II. *Addiction*, *88*(6), 791–804.

Snoek, A., & Matthews, S. (2017). Introduction: Testing and refining Marc Lewis's critique of the brain disease model of addiction. *Neuroethics*, *10*(1), 1–6.

Substance Abuse and Mental Health Services Administration (SAMHSA). (2018). *Key substance use and mental health indicators in the United States: Results from the 2016 National Survey on Drug Use and Health (HHS Publication No. SMA 17-5044, NSDUH Series H-52)*. Rockville, MD: Center for Behavioral Health Statistics and Quality. Substance Abuse and Mental Health Services Administration, Retrieved from https://www.samhsa.gov/data..

Ullman, S. E., Lorenz, K., & Kirkner, A. (2017). Alcohol's role in social reactions to sexual assault disclosures: A qualitative study of informal support dyads. *Journal of Interpersonal Violence*, 0886260517721172.

van Amsterdam, J., Nutt, D., Phillips, L., & van den Brink, W. (2015). European rating of drug harms. *Journal of Psychopharmacology*, *29*(6), 655–660.

van Amsterdam, J., Opperhuizen, A., Koeter, M., & van den Brink, W. (2010). Ranking the harm of alcohol, tobacco and illicit drugs for the individual and the population. *European Addiction Research*, *16*(4), 202–207.

Volkow, N. D., Koob, G. F., & McLellan, A. T. (2016). Neurobiologic advances from the brain disease model of addiction. *New England Journal of Medicine*, *374*(4), 363–371.

Wiers, R. W., & Verschure, P. (2021). Curing the broken brain model of addiction: Neurorehabilitation from a systems perspective. *Addictive Behaviors*, 106602.

World Health Organization, *Global status report on alcohol and health* 2016, World Health Organization, Geneva.

Chapter 2

The world's favorite drug: What we have learned about alcohol from over 500,000 respondents to the Global Drug Survey

Emma L. Davies[1], Cheneal Puljevic[2,3], Dean Connolly[4,5], Ahnjili Zhuparris[6], Jason A. Ferris[2] and Adam R. Winstock[6,7]
[1]Faculty of Health and Life Sciences, Oxford Brookes University, United Kingdom, [2]Centre for Health Services Research, The University of Queensland, Brisbane, QLD, Australia, [3]School of Public Health, The University of Queensland, Brisbane, QLD, Australia, [4]Institute of Psychiatry, Psychology and Neuroscience, King's College London, UK, [5]Barts Health NHS Trust, London, United Kingdom, [6]Global Drug Survey, London, United Kingdom, [7]University College London, London, Australia

Introduction

The Global Drug Survey (GDS) is an independent research organization that runs the world's largest anonymous annual web survey of drug use. The purpose of GDS is to understand new trends in drug use, and to use these data to inform harm reduction measures that make drug use safer, regardless of the legal status of the drug. It is important to note that GDS refers to the name of the organization, which has subsidiary activities, as well as the survey itself. Between GDS2012 and GDS2020 over 650,000 people completed the survey and alcohol is, unsurprisingly, the most common drug that respondents use – around 98% of respondents report having ever used alcohol and around 80–90% report last year use of alcohol in each survey.

This chapter will draw on GDS alcohol findings from GDS2015–2020. We will begin by outlining GDS methods, and the structure of the survey, and will then consider the utility of non-probability samples in exploring alcohol use, before considering the alcohol-related research areas that we have explored over the last five years. An overview of the topics covered, papers published on the topic and approximate Ns are given in Table 2.1

The Handbook of Alcohol Use - Understandings from Synapse to Society.
DOI: https://doi.org/10.1016/B978-0-12-816720-5.00022-0

TABLE 2.1 Overview of GDS alcohol content discussed in this chapter, Ns and papers published.

Year	Topic	N	Chapter section	Publication
2015	Normative misperceptions	9820	6.2	Garnett et al. (2015)
2015	Harms from others' drinking	63,725	5	Bellis et al. (2015)
2015	Getting drunk and the tipping point	61,043	4.1	Davies, Cooke, Maier, Winstock, & Ferris (2020)
2015	Pre-drinking	64,485	4.2	Ferris, Puljević, Labhart, Winstock, & Kuntsche (2019), Labhart, Ferris, Winstock, & Kuntsche (2017)
2015	Motivations for reducing drinking	72,209	6.1	Davies, Conroy, Winstock, & Ferris (2017)
2016	Emotions and types of drinking	29,836	4.3	Ashton, Bellis, Davies, Hughes, & Winstock (2017)
2017	Sources of support for reducing drinking	82,190	6.2.1	Davies, Maier, Winstock, & Ferris (2019)
2018	Alcohol labeling	75,969	6.2.3	Davies, Foxcroft, Puljević, Ferris, & Winstock (under review), Winstock, Holmes, Ferris, & Davies (2020)
2018/ 2019	Comparisons between cisgender and trans respondents	118,157	7	Connolly et al. (2020)
2019/ 2020	Frequency of getting drunk and feeling regret	2019: 88,604 and 2020: 51,433	4.2	Papers in preparation (Winstock, Barratt, et al., 2020)

Although the area of the survey's focus has changed each year, typically building on previous results, there is a consistent set of questions that are included within the core alcohol section, which is offered to all those who have used alcohol in the last 12 months. These include the 10 item Alcohol

Use Disorders Identification Test (AUDIT), questions on whether the participants would like to use less alcohol next year, whether they would like help and if so whether they plan to seeking help to use less, as well as questions on whether they have sought emergency medical treatment following the use of alcohol.

A brief summary of the areas explored are given below before we describe in more detail the findings from each of our discreet research projects within this chapter. In GDS2015 we sought to explore the amount of alcohol needed to reach different stages of intoxication (Davies et al., 2020). The following year in GDS2016 we explored the commonly-cited myth that different types of alcohol might lead to different emotional effects (Ashton et al., 2017). In GDS2017 we added detail regarding the consistent finding that 30–40% of GDS participants who report drinking alcohol wish to drink less in the next 12 months. The GDS also covers questions relating to harm from alcohol and ways to reduce this harm. In sections on harm reduction, we focus on what factors would lead people to think about cutting down (GDS2015) and what kind of help they would like to do so from (GDS2017). We discuss interventions, both at an individual level, for example in the use of online self-help tools (e.g. the free Drinks Meter app / drinksmeter.com) and at a population level in terms of product/container health warning labeling (GDS2018). Interventions may benefit from tailored content, and thus during GDS2019 and GDS2020 we have explored drinking and regrets.

After a brief history of GDS, we start the chapter looking at findings about drinking prevalence, and then experiences of intoxication, before moving on the consequences of drinking and interventions to reduce associated harms. Finally, we reflect on what GDS has learned about alcohol so far, while setting out our vision for future research into the world's favorite drug.

GDS history and methods

The first iteration of GDS - before it was called GDS – began in collaboration with MixMag, a dance music magazine, when Dr Adam Winstock began collecting data from people who use drugs in the United Kingdom (U.K.) in 1999 (see Fig. 2.1). In 2011, reborn as the Global Drug Survey, our annual survey stepped beyond the initial focus on club drug use to engage with the wider populations and tribes who used drugs. GDS surveys follow a unique naming convention whereby the survey name (e.g. GDS2020) is based on the year the associated report was released and not on the year data collection commenced (e.g. November 2019). GDS2012 was the first in this new series of surveys but was only available in English, but GDS2013 was translated into seven languages. Since inception, GDS has not received funding from the alcohol, tobacco or cannabis industries. Many of the people working with GDS volunteer their time, or their time is supported by their host

FIGURE 2.1 Examples of MixMag covers from the early days of Global Drug Survey.

institution, for example through university-funded research time. Other sources of funding include that received from media organizations, government and non-governmental organizations, and consultancy work.

GDS treats participants as experts in their own experiences. The data that participants share with GDS is used to inform harm reduction tools, such as the Highway Code (see https://www.globaldrugsurvey.com/brand/the-highway-code/), and safer use limits (see http://saferuselimits.co/?LMCL = b8uKmA). GDS recruits people through media partners and harm reduction partners who promote the annual survey through their distribution means, including Facebook, Twitter and other social media. In GDS2012, 22,000 people took part, from four English speaking countries (AU, UK, USA and NZ) and this number increased to 135,000 in GDS2018 from over 50 countries when the survey was translated into 19 languages. GDS2020 received over 110,000 respondents and to date almost 900,000 people have taken part in our surveys. GDS does struggle to retain participants for the full duration of the survey. If a respondent reports last year/last month use of a number of different drugs, then this means they are directed to all questions relevant to that drug, which can make the survey feel arduous.

The opportunistic nature of recruitment into GDS delivers a large but non-probability sample and initially many journal reviewers and editors were critical about the sample composition. With over 60 publications to the group's name however, and focusing on those areas here, non-probability samples are useful complements to more representative surveys such as household surveys, meaning that GDS has become an increasingly recognized source of drug information. Seminal papers on new and emerging drugs trends such the use of darknet drug markets (Barratt, Ferris, & Winstock, 2014) and novel drugs such as mephedrone and Synthetic Cannabinoid Receptor Agonists (Winstock & Barratt, 2013) have been produced. GDS data can be used to its greatest effect when we segment populations of people who use drugs to identify dose-response relationship between consumption, risk and pleasure. For example, looking at peripheral neuropathy with nitrous users (Winstock & Ferris, 2019), maculopathy with poppers (Davies, Borschmann, et al., 2017), and ketamine bladder (Winstock, Mitcheson, Gillatt, & Cottrell, 2012).

GDS stresses to our media and research partners as well as academic publications that GDS is not representative of the populations of the countries in which the participants reside. The strength of GDS is that it taps into more hidden populations of people who use drugs, and unlike national probabilistic surveys, GDS is able to reach large numbers of people who use a variety of drugs. Each year, the GDS drug screen module asked participants which of over 150 different drugs they have used. The list includes common drugs (alcohol, tobacco, cannabis and cocaine), more traditional drugs (ayahuasca, kava and betel nut) as well as new and emerging psychoactive substances (NPS, NBome etc.). The drug screen module has allowed GDS experts to respond to changes in drug supplies through the dark web and explore the emergence of trends such as inhaling alcohol (Winstock, Winstock, & Davies, 2020), the use of ayahuasca (Lawn et al., 2017), the recreational use of nitrous oxide (Kaar et al., 2016), and the characteristics of methamphetamine 'cooks' (Puljević et al., under revision). While this data set is therefore not intended to be representative, analysis have shown that GDS recruits people similar in demographic characteristics to people who reported alcohol use from representative surveys undertaken in the U.S., Australia, and Switzerland (Barratt et al., 2017).

Drinking prevalence and patterns in the GDS

Alcohol is treated like any other drug with the annual survey. An initial screen identifies if respondents have ever consumed the drug, and then if they have used it in the last 12 months. Those who have used within the last 12 months are then offered the opportunity to complete a more detailed section concerning that drug, looking at key issues such as frequency of use, amount used, acute harms and source of purchase. We use standardized measures that are consisted across the years. In the alcohol section, other than days used in the last year and month, respondents are always presented with the 10 item AUDIT (Babor, Higgins-Biddle, Saunders, & Monteiro, 2001). AUDIT is scored from 0 to 40 and then categorized: 0–7 = low risk, 8–15 = increasing risk 16–19 = higher risk; 20+ = possible dependence. In GDS2020, 99% of the sample said they had 'ever' used alcohol, and 96.3% had used it in the last year. Of those, we have full AUDIT scores for 90,646 respondents. Table 2.2 illustrates how participants scored on the AUDIT in GDS2020. Nearly half were classified as low risk drinkers according to AUDIT. Larger proportions of women aged 25 and over were classified as low risk compared to other groups. A larger proportion of men aged 25 and over are classified as possibly dependent compared to other groups.

One of the greatest assets of the GDS is the large numbers of respondents from countries around the world. When comparing respondents from different countries, it is important to keep in mind that these are not representative samples of people who drink in each country and in part reflect the variation in mean age of different country samples. Nonetheless, some interesting differences in country-level AUDIT scores are observed, which largely, reflect cultural patterns of drinking observed in other studies. Fig. 2.2 displays the median AUDIT score for each country where there were at least 250 respondents to GDS2020 (which includes the Balkan region capturing– Albania; Bosnia and Herzegovina; Bulgaria; Croatia; Kosovo; Macedonia; Serbia; Slovenia). The data presented in Fig. 2.2 is also categorized by sex. Respondents from Denmark had the highest median AUDIT score of 12, followed by Scotland with 11. Respondents from Argentina, Romania and Russian Federation had the lowest median AUDIT score of 6.

TABLE 2.2 AUDIT scores in the GDS2020 sample by gender and age group with percentages rounded to one decimal place.

	Low risk (0–7) N (%)	Increasing risk (8–15) N (%)	Higher risk (16–19) N (%)	Possible dependence (20+) N (%)
All	40,843 (45.1)	36,105 (39.8)	8001 (8.8)	5697 (6.3)
Men <25	10,294 (38.6)	12,131 (45.5)	2558 (9.6)	1692 (6.3)
Women <25	6189 (43.8)	5996 (42.4)	1185 (8.4)	761 (5.4)
Men 25+	14,281 (44.5)	12,244 (38.2)	3122 (9.7)	2413 (7.5)
Women 25+	9564 (57.3)	5339 (32.0)	1050 (6.3)	730 (4.4)

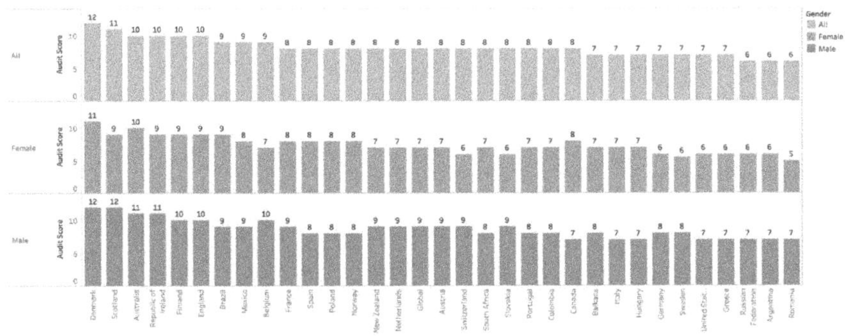

FIGURE 2.2 Median AUDIT scores for GDS2020 respondents by country and sex, presented in rank order of 'all.'

Getting drunk

Reaching your tipping point

An important feature of GDS is that it acknowledges that people get pleasure from taking drugs, including alcohol. Many people around the world really like drinking to intoxication, or drunkenness, as means unwinding or enhancing social occasions (de Visser, Wheeler, Abraham, & Smith, 2013; Measham & Brain, 2005). Understanding more about how much alcohol people need to drink to get drunk, is a good way to start thinking about how to help them do this more safely.

In GDS2015, participants were asked about three different stages of intoxication: 'feeling the effects' of alcohol, being 'as drunk as you would like to be' and 'the tipping point – starting to feel more drunk than you want to be' (Davies et al., 2020). To explore these three stages, respondents indicated their usual drink type: wine; beer, cider or lager; spirits and alcopop/coolers (i.e. pre-mixed single container) and then what a typical sized drink was for them (sizes presented were as follows; wine = small wine 125 mL, medium wine 175 mL, large wine 200 mL or other; beer/cider/lager = small 300 mL, medium 400 mL, large 500 mL / other; spirit = small 30 mL, large 60 mL or other; alcopops = small 350 mL large 700 mL or other). Respondents where then presented with the following scenario: "Imagine you were drinking just this type of drink and not using any other drugs. How many drinks would it take for you to reach the three stages of intoxication?" Respondents then answered: "Over the last 12 months, how often have you reached each of these stages of intoxication?" We applied alcohol by volume (ABV) to each drink size using estimates for each product (wine = 12%, beer = 4.5%, spirits = 40% and alcopops = 5%) and then converted this volume into mass representing 10 g of alcohol per 100 milliliters of the beverage.

We compared the grams of alcohol that were reported to the stated guidelines for low risk consumption in each included country (see Table 2.3). What was striking was that the amount of alcohol typically consumed to reach what respondents considered an ideal level of intoxication was almost double the upper limit recommended in most countries. The average amount of alcohol to be 'as drunk as you like' was 88 g for men and 70 g for women, compared to a maximum of 40 g recommend by many countries. Moreover, these average amounts were still substantially higher than the 60 g of alcohol in a single session that is considered to be heavy episodic drinking (HED) by the WHO (2018). For example, in Austria, the daily alcohol consumption guidelines for females are 16 g of pure alcohol (Eurocare, 2016), but on average, female respondents indicated needing 26.32 g of alcohol to feel the effects and 51.70 g to deem themselves as being as drunk as they would like to be (3.3 times the Austrian guidelines). Moreover, males in Austria on average reported that they needed 33.01 g of alcohol to feel the effects and 69.99 g to be as drunk as they would like to be (almost 3 times the guidelines). Strikingly, even to simply feel the effects of alcohol, not to be drunk, the amounts reported by some respondents approach the WHO HED level. For example, female respondents from the Netherlands on average needed 42.49 g of alcohol and male respondents needed 48.11 g to feel the effects. Some respondents needed to drink in excess of weekly country guidelines, in a single session, to reach their tipping point. For example, In the UK, the average amount of alcohol to reach the tipping point was 113.20 g for females and 144.13 g for males on a background of a weekly recommended 112 g of alcohol (Department of Health, 2016).

Respondents were also asked where they did most of their drinking (at home on your own, at home with partner/family, at house parties, at pubs or bars, at clubs). House parties were the most frequently chosen drinking location (34.1%), followed by pubs/bars (31.8%), at home with partner/family (19.5%), clubs (8.2%) and drinking at home alone (6.4%) (Davies, Cooke, Maier, Ferris, & Winstock, in preparation). Tipping point consumption was highest in clubs (136.66 g), followed by house parties (131.41 g) and pubs (128.32 g) and lower at home alone (126.02 g) and at home with partner or family (110.70 g).

We have also explored tipping point consumption in relation to the type of drink preferred by respondents. Respondents who consumed alcopops (134.11 g) and wine (133.01 g) reported the highest tipping point consumption (Davies et al., in preparation). However, it is also important to note that people may drink alcohol alongside other drugs and this may influence how the tipping point is experienced. People may also consume alcohol with energy drinks, which may increase feelings of arousal and increase the amount of alcohol that is consumed before the tipping point is reached (Peacock, Bruno, Ferris, & Winstock, 2017).

TABLE 2.3 Comparison of daily and/or weekly low risk drinking guidelines in grams of pure alcohol between countries included in the study.

	Daily		Weekly		Mean grams female			Mean grams male		
Country	Female	Male	Female	Male	Feel effects	As drunk as you want to be	Tipping point	Feel effects	As drunk as you want to be	Tipping point
Australia	20	20			33.37	77.22	109.44	40.20	99.8	149.38
Austria	16	24	112	168	26.32	51.70	86.98	33.01	69.99	117.42
Belgium	–	–	100	100	36.31	75.76	109.40	43.70	99.72	149.57
Brazil	20	30			43.65	84.60	133.71	49.57	103.85	172.26
Canada	27	40.7	136	204	33.57	78.50	113.77	36.62	93.52	137.90
Denmark	12	24	84	168	36.75	72.60	120.14	41.20	106.33	172.40
France	20	30	140	210	34.99	76.22	115.74	37.79	90.56	140.98
Greece	20–32	30–48			37.06	69.30	99.00	51.26	93.55	139.72
Hungary	17	34	–	–	32.70	65.45	102.65	39.65	85.23	137.99
Republic of Ireland	–	–	110	170	39.76	84.56	119.04	49.42	109.85	159.11
Italy	20	36	–	–	34.67	69.82	109.26	35.62	76.60	120.99
Netherlands	20	30			42.49	94.63	136.05	48.11	116.22	174.66

(*Continued*)

TABLE 2.3 (Continued)

	Daily		Weekly		Mean grams female			Mean grams male		
Country	Female	Male	Female	Male	Feel effects	As drunk as you want to be	Tipping point	Feel effects	As drunk as you want to be	Tipping point
New Zealand	20	30	100	150	36.30	79.92	112.62	46.43	112.11	164.89
Poland	20	40	140	280	33.92	81.21	112.55	37.61	95.29	142.32
Portugal	10 – 24	10 – 24			35.13	68.70	108.09	46.04	93.26	153.01
Spain	–	–	110	170	32.61	66.28	96.19	36.41	80.82	118.17
Sweden	10	20	–	–	28.04	64.53	102.77	33.68	89.31	142.06
Switzerland	20–24	30–36	–	–	32.31	62.32	98.22	37.79	80.05	129.64
UK	–	–	112	112	34	79.14	113.2	40.43	99.74	144.13
United States	42	56	98	196	33.17	73.13	104.94	34.88	87.06	128.84
Germany	12	24			25.26	49.89	84.53	32.92	70.71	121.73

Information gathered from multiple sources (Eurocare, 2016; Furtwaengler & de Visser, 2013; Kalinowski & Humphreys, 2016; WHO, 2018).

Twenty percent of the sample reached their tipping point at least once a month, meaning that they were more intoxicated than they actually wanted to be. This gives us a useful place to direct/ target interventions. The experience of reaching the tipping point is generally experienced as psychologically and physically unpleasant (e.g. Burgess, Cooke, & Davies, 2019). Given the volume of alcohol that respondents said they consumed to be as drunk as they would like to be, it may be controversial to encourage people to 'only' drink that much and not reach their tipping point (Davies et al., 2020). Tipping point drinking is associated with both acute and chronic harms to the drinker and those around them (Laslett et al., 2010). As such, reducing the number of occasions an individual reaches tipping point has the potential to reduce a range of harms.

Enjoying and regretting getting drunk

GDS2019 started to explore respondents' experiences of getting drunk and feelings of regret as one possible avenue to reducing HED. They were presented with the following text:

> We would like to know how often you get drunk and how often you enjoy it.
> On approximately how many days did you get drunk last year?

When we released the data in May 2019, the British press (e.g. Boyd, 2019; Marsh, 2019) were quick to pick up on the finding that respondents from the UK reported getting drunk on average 51 times a year – so about once a week - and this was more than respondents from all the other included countries. Fig. 2.3 shows the mean number of times that respondents reported getting drunk. The USA and Canada come second and third to the UK, while respondents from Chile, Portugal and Germany report getting drunk on far fewer occasions.

Regardless of the definitions used, simply knowing that respondents get drunk a certain number of times may not on its own be a useful starting point when considering ways to reduce alcohol consumption. This could be particularly tricky when we consider the study discussed in the previous section that also found that 65.6% of respondents got 'as drunk as they would like to be' on a monthly or weekly basis (Davies et al., 2020). Thus, in GDS2019, we also asked respondents to estimate how many of those times they really enjoyed getting drunk and how many times they regretted it. Fig. 2.4 shows the same countries, but this time the number of times participants really enjoyed or regretted getting drunk is expressed as a percentage of the total number of times they reported getting drunk. Here we can see that German respondents reported they regretted a greater percentage of the times they got drunk whereas Danish respondents reported that they regretted a smaller percentage of time they got drunk. Comparing this to Fig. 2.2, it can be seen that there is a

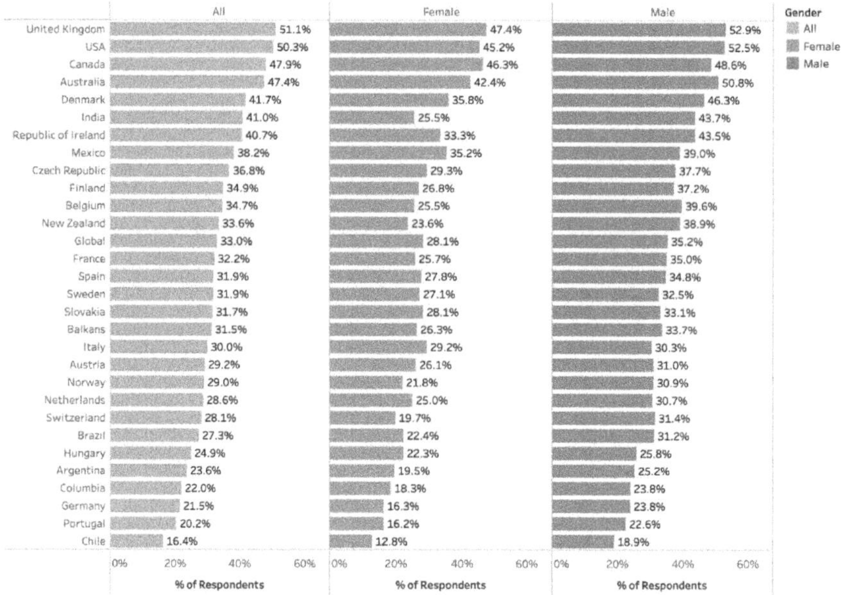

FIGURE 2.3 Mean number of times drunk in the last year by country and sex in GDS2019 presented in rank order of 'All.'

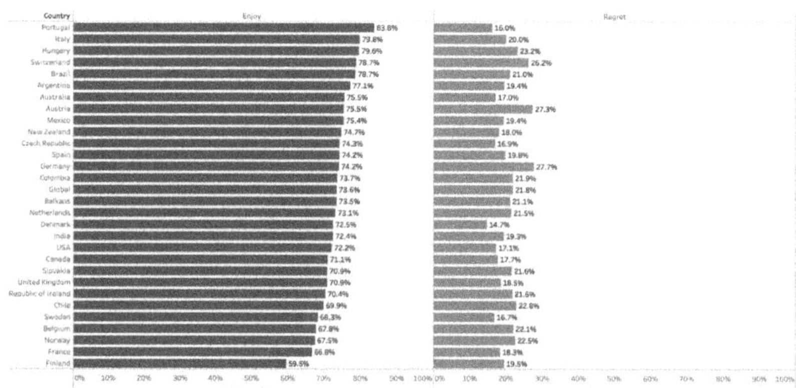

FIGURE 2.4 Percentage of times GDS2019 respondents enjoyed and regretted getting drunk by country presented in rank order of 'enjoy.'

possible relationship between frequency of drunkenness and regrets or enjoyment. For example looking at the UK, the percentage of times that respondents regret getting drunk is relatively low, even though they reported getting drunk the most, whereas those from Chile get drunk the least, but regretted a larger proportion of these occasions.

Overall, the 2019 data showed that in the global sample our respondents enjoyed getting drunk 73.55% of the time and regretted it 21.80% of the time. People were not required to ensure that their responses to these questions added up to the number of times they said they got drunk, which is why these figures do not add up to 100%. It is possible that sometimes people neither really enjoy nor regret getting drunk— perhaps they are ambivalent about it. However, if people regret getting drunk around one-fifth of the times that they do it, this could be another useful avenue for encouraging them to reduce their alcohol consumption.

Regrets in GDS2020

In GDS2020 we asked the same question about how many times people got drunk and how many times they regretted it. However, a more detailed definition of 'getting drunk' was provided in this survey. Respondents were presented with the following text:

> First of all how many times did you get drunk in the last 12 months (we define drunk as having drunk so much that your physical and mental facilities are impaired to the point your balance/speech may be effected, you are unable focus on clearly on things and that your conversation and behaviours are disinhibited).

The reported number of times drunk per year was considerably lower; for example those from UK (capturing England, Scotland, Wales and Northern Ireland) reported getting drunk an average of 33 times compared to 51 times the previous year. However, they were still the top country followed closely by Australia (Mean = 31.78) and Denmark (Mean = 31.32), and overall there was no change in the pattern of results by country. When looking at the percentage of times that respondents regret getting drunk, we observed some surprising country differences (see Fig. 2.5). It appears that those from Colombia, Argentina and Mexico, regret getting drunk a lot more than respondents from other countries. When we analyzed this data we were struck by these differences. It appears that these countries also report fewer mean occasions when they get drunk (Colombia = 11.16, Argentina, = 13.44, Mexico = 16.67). The differences could therefore reflect public acceptability of drunkenness. However, we also considered the way that our definition of drunkenness was translated into Spanish and how this may have been interpreted by respondents. Issues with precise translation are another challenge faced when delivering the same survey questions across different languages and cultures.

In GDS2020 we asked people to tell us their top three reasons for feeling regret after getting drunk. With the new definition of getting drunk, we observed a higher percentage of regretful occasions; respondents said they regretted getting drunk an average of 32.75% of the time, while 28.2% never regretted it and 14% of respondents said they regretted getting drunk every

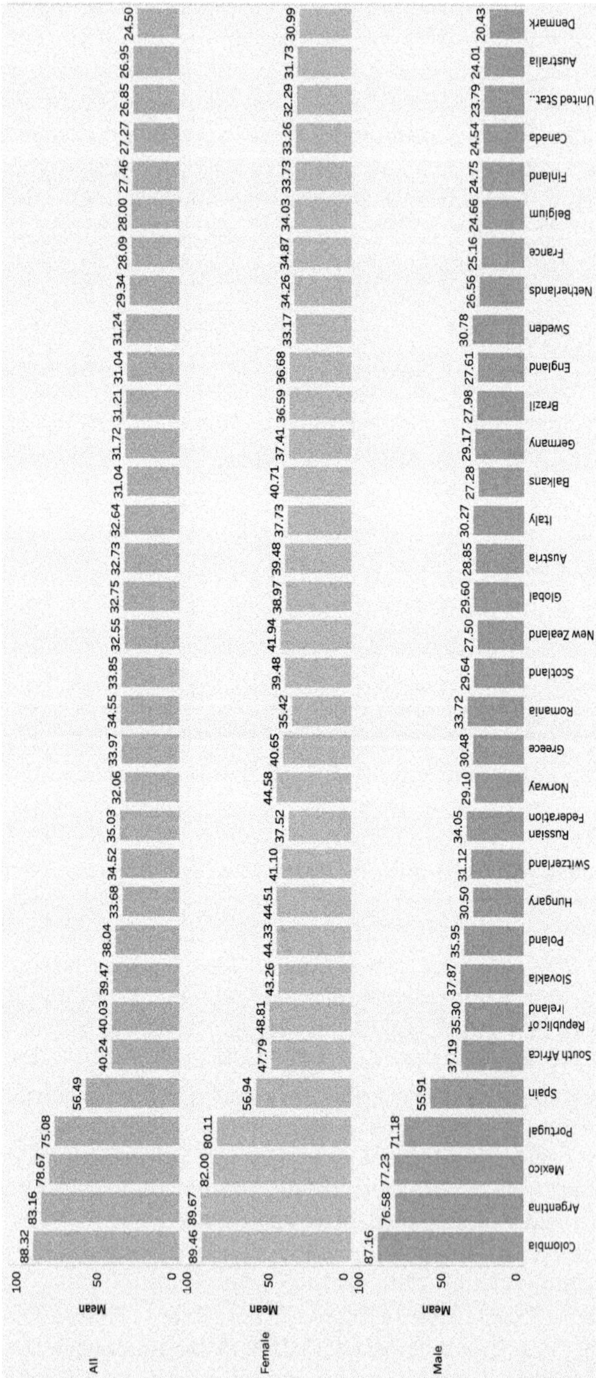

FIGURE 2.5 Percentage of times drunk that were regretted by country in GDS2020 in rank order of all.

time. The most commonly selected reasons for regretting getting drunk were having a hangover (74.6%), saying something they would not normally say (42%) and feelings of increased anxiety the next day (31.1%). The proportion of respondents who selected these reasons was compared by country (Fig. 2.6). Unsurprisingly, hangovers were a common reason for regret across sample. Respondents from Northern European countries reported higher proportions of feeling anxious the following day.

A focus on anticipated regret – the emotions and cognitions that may be experienced if behavior is not changed – has been explored in relation to alcohol reduction (Cooke, Sniehotta, & Schuz, 2007). Studies have posited that encouraging people to think about the possible regrets they may have the next day may be one way to encourage them to drink less. However, such studies rarely consider the broader consequences of drinking that might be regretted – instead they ask people the extent to which they will regret getting drunk (Davies & Joshi, 2018). Furthermore, a previous study suggested that those who experienced more regrets had a higher level of optimism about their susceptibility to alcohol related health harms (Davies & Joshi, 2018), highlighting that this approach needs to be applied with caution. Our GDS2020 findings provide a cornerstone to develop more targeted anticipated regret interventions by exploring socio-demographic factors associated with the top three regrets that are selected.

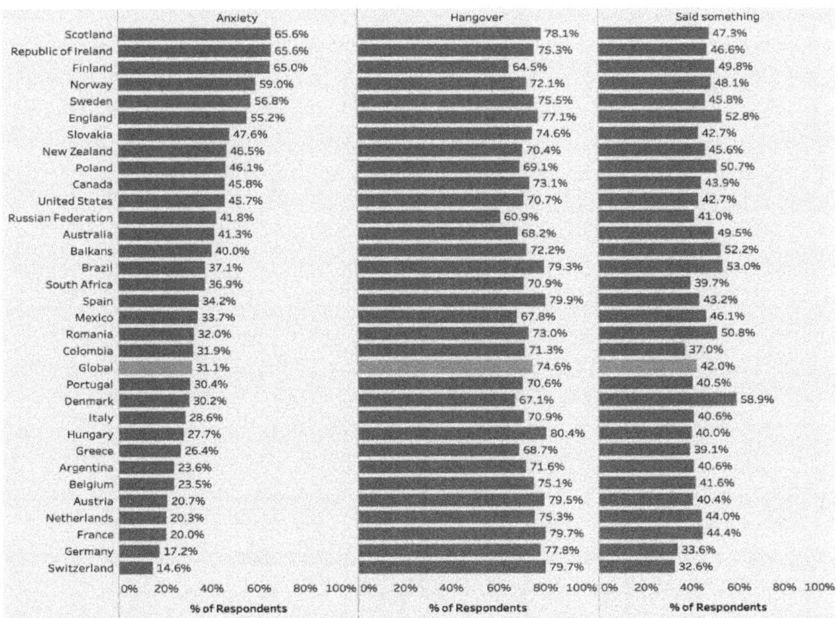

FIGURE 2.6 Top three reasons for regret in GDS2020 sample compared by country and ranked by proportion reporting anxiety.

Emotions and drink type

Of course, regret is not the only emotion associated with drinking alcohol. GDS2015 respondents were asked to self-report the types of alcohol they consumed and which emotions (energized, relaxed, sexy, confident, tired, aggressive, ill, restless and tearful) they associated with these drinks (Ashton et al., 2017). Positive emotions such as energy, confidence and feeling sexy were associated with drinking spirits, while red wine and beer were associated with feeling relaxed. Spirts were also associated with feeling more aggressive, ill, restless and tearful compared to other drink types. Respondents who scored 20 + on AUDIT reported feeling a greater range of both positive and negative emotions from their drinking (Ashton et al., 2017). Knowledge of the drink types and demographic characteristics associated with negative emotions, such as aggression, which may lead to violent incidents, can also inform targeted interventions to reduce harm to others as well as the drinker themselves.

Pre-loading

As discussed in "Reaching your tipping point" section, respondents who did most of their drinking in clubs were among those who reached their tipping point most frequently (Davies et al., in preparation). However, across many countries many people begin their night out by drinking at home before heading out to pubs and clubs. This serves the purpose of saving money, but is also an important time for socializing with friends away from busy nightlife settings (Atkinson & Sumnall, 2017; Davies & Paltoglou, 2019). This practice, often referred to as pre-loading or pre-drinking, has been associated with increased overall alcohol consumption during a night out, as well as increased experiences of negative consequences such as fights and accidents (Hughes, Anderson, Morleo, & Bellis, 2008; Miller et al., 2016).

The country-level effects of drinking and drink prices on pre-loading behaviors were explored in 65,126 GDS2015 respondents from 25 countries (Labhart et al., 2017). The estimated percentage of pre-drinkers per country ranged from 17.7% among respondents in Greece, to 85.4% among those from Ireland. The eight countries with the highest percentages of pre-drinkers were either English speaking (e.g. Ireland, Canada, New Zealand, UK) or Nordic (e.g. Norway, Denmark, Finland, Sweden), while the eight countries with the lowest percentages were mostly Southern and Eastern European (e.g. Greece, Hungary, Poland, Switzerland, Italy, Belgium), or Latin American (Brazil, Mexico). Across all countries, we found that the higher the prevalence of current drinkers, the higher the percentage of pre-drinkers. In addition, an interaction between the prevalence of heavy drinkers (those who reported drinking 60 or more grams of pure alcohol on at least one occasion at least monthly) and each country's ratio of on premise versus off-premise drink prices was found. In countries with a low price ratio (e.g. Norway, we found a higher prevalence of heavy drinkers, and a higher percentage of pre-drinkers). The opposite effect was observed in countries with high price ratios (Labhart et al., 2017).

Further analysis of these data investigated the role of sex and age on preloading behaviors among this sample (Ferris et al., 2019). Results suggested that males were more likely to engage in pre-drinking than females, other than for respondents in Canada and Denmark, where females were more likely to pre-load (Ferris et al., 2019). This gender difference may reflect findings from other studies showing that females are more likely to pre-load to socialize and get ready for the night out together (Atkinson & Sumnall, 2017), or as an opportunity to match the intoxication levels of their male counterparts (Paves, Pedersen, Hummer, & Labrie, 2012). Interestingly, while the GDS analyzes also suggested that the probability of pre-loading decreased after age 21 for most respondents, there also appeared to be an increase in the probability of pre-drinking after age 30 among respondents from Brazil, Canada, Ireland, New Zealand, England and the United States (Ferris et al., 2019). While younger respondents may pre-load to save money or get intoxicated earlier, it is possible that these pre-drinkers aged in their thirties are enjoying a drink at home with friends before going out for dinner (Ritchie, Ritchie, & Ward, 2009).

Consequences

Alongside patterns in drinking behaviors discussed in "Getting drunk" section, GDS also collects data on the negative impacts of drinking alcohol. For example, each year respondents are asked if they have had to seek emergency medical treatment as a result of their drinking. Fortunately, only a small proportion (2%) of the sample have had this experience, but there are gender and age differences observed (see Fig. 2.7). When split further by age females under the age of 25 (3.4%) were more likely to have sought treatment than to their male counterpart (2.8%) and compared to those over the age of 25 years (males 1.3%; females 1.2%).

It is important to recognize that harms are also experienced by people around the drinker (Laslett et al., 2010, 2011). GDS respondents were asked about their experiences of harm from others' drinking in 2015 (Bellis et al., 2015). The question posed was as follows: 'In the last 12 months have you been negatively affected by someone else's drinking in any of the following ways: (1) physically assaulted by someone who was drunk; (2) sexually harassed or assaulted by someone who was drunk; (3) called names or insulted by someone who was drunk; (4) injured accidentally by someone who was drunk; (5) had property damaged by someone who was drunk; (6) involved in a traffic accident caused by a drunk driver or pedestrian; (7) kept awake by drunken noise.' Overall, 9.2% of men and 4.7% of women reported

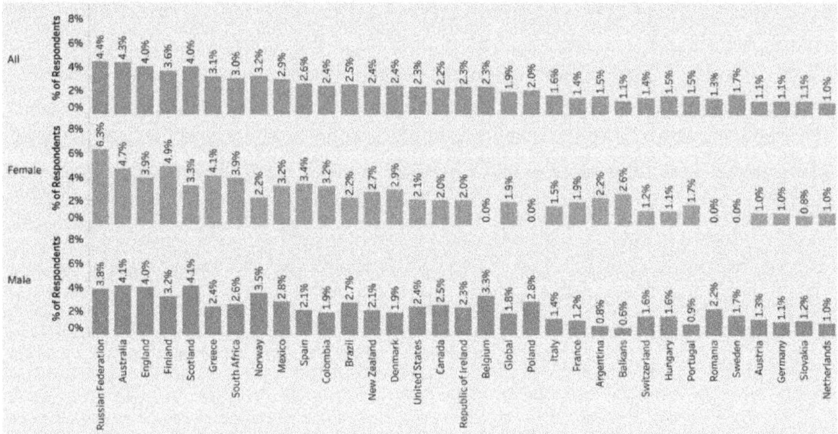

FIGURE 2.7 Percentage of respondents seeking emergency medical treatment by country and gender in GDS2020 in rank order of 'all.'

experiencing physical assault, and 15.3% of women and 2.5% of men reported sexual assault or harassment (Bellis et al., 2015).

Reducing harms

Cutting down on alcohol

In this chapter so far, we have discussed a selection of GDS studies exploring the experience of drinking and drunkenness, and some of the negative consequences of drinking alcohol. With 20% of respondents reaching their tipping point at least monthly, and around 20% of drunken occasions being regretted, it is clear that there is potential for reducing alcohol related harms, without necessarily reducing the enjoyment that people get from drinking. In order to understand what might lead respondents to think about drinking less, we explored a range of possible experiences which might motivate people to think about cutting down (Davies, Conroy, et al., 2017). Respondents viewed the following list of 13 possible experiences and asked to select their top three in order of importance.

1. Social embarrassment/humiliation;
2. Being sexually assaulted /taken advantage of;
3. Sexual regret (e.g. ending up in bed with someone);
4. Getting injured in an accident;
5. Being unable to remember the night before;
6. Seeking emergency medical treatment;
7. Physical health condition related to/worsened by alcohol;
8. Mental health condition related to/worsened by alcohol;

9. Concerns raised by partner /friends about what you are like when you are drunk;
10. Negative impact on education/study/work;
11. Involved in violent incident;
12. Trouble with the police;
13. Financial worries.

Within the whole sample, the physical health item (7) was one of the most commonly selected experiences that would lead the respondents to think about reducing their alcohol consumption. However, there were some gender and country differences observed. For example, female respondents were more likely to select the sexual assault item than male respondents. Respondents from Germany and Northern European countries were more likely to select social embarrassment/humiliation, whereas respondents from Southern Europe were more likely to pick injuries and violence. Those from the United States were more likely to pick the item about being in trouble with the police and those from Poland and Greece picked financial issues more often (Davies, Conroy, et al., 2017). Such differences are interesting when we think about patterns of drinking observed in the GDS sample, as well as cultural differences in drinking patterns more broadly. They suggest brief interventions to reduce drinking could be enhanced by a focus on the most demographically relevant experience that is likely to motivate someone to reduce their drinking. Harm reduction messages, including those contained in digital interventions, and information on alcohol product labels could be similarly targeted.

Interventions

Individual level interventions

In GDS2017, 34.8% of respondents said they would like to drink less in the following 12 months, which is in line with the proportion who say this each year of the survey. This is a sizeable group of people, and the GDS2017 data suggested that respondents in higher AUDIT categories were those more likely to say they want to drink less in the next year (Davies et al., 2019). For example, 56.4% of those in the AUDIT 16–19 group (higher risk drinkers) and 69.4% of those in the AUDIT 20+ group (possibly dependent drinkers) said yes to this question, compared to 21.8% in the 0–7 group (low risk) and 40.0% in the 8–15 (increasing risk) group. In general, respondents from heavier drinking countries were also more likely to say they wanted to cut down. However, in total only 7.6% of respondents wanted help to reduce their drinking. This is not to say that those who do not want help will be unsuccessful, but it is important to acknowledge that individuals may not wish to seek help as they are worried about feeling stigmatized (Khadjesari, Stevenson, Godfrey, & Murray, 2015). There can also be considerable delays in treatment seeking rates in those with alcohol use disorders (Chapman, Slade, Hunt, & Teesson, 2015), and financial barriers to treatment seeking (Schuler, Puttaiah, Mojtabai, & Crum, 2015).

We explored the preferred sources of support for help to reduce drinking in the 2118 respondents who said they would like help (Davies et al., 2019). They were asked *'which of the following would you be most likely to use to get help with your drinking?'* They could select one of the following options: self-help tool (online or via app); counseling via email; counseling via phone; counseling via Skype/live video; counseling at a family doctor (GP); counseling or therapy at a specialist doctor; alternative therapy. Only a small number picked counseling via email (N = 102), phone (N = 62) and Skype/live video (N = 30) and so these were combined into a category named' non-face-to-face counseling'. There were two important differences, which related to the selection of digital tools compared to face to face counseling or therapy with a specialist. Respondents with low risk drinking patterns, who were educated and not taking a prescribed medication for a mental health condition were more likely to select online tools. On the other hand, being in the higher AUDIT categories and taking a prescribed medication for a mental health condition were associated with preferring the support of a specialist counsellor (Davies et al., 2019).

Digital tools and e-health

These are important findings in a landscape where digital tools such as websites, apps and wearables are being rapidly developed due to their potential to engage more people outside clinical settings and to reach large numbers of people relatively cheaply (Kaner et al., 2017). However, even though there are a large number of alcohol apps on the market, only a minority have a focus on improving health, and few contain recognized behavior change techniques (Crane, Garnett, Brown, West, & Michie, 2015). Until recently, there was little evidence to suggest that digital tools were effective in reducing alcohol consumption. However, a recent systematic review suggested that participants who were using a digital tool reduced their drinking by up to three UK units of alcohol (24 g) compared with control participants (Kaner et al., 2017). Our findings highlight the importance of ensuring access to good quality face to face support for heavier drinkers with co-morbid mental health issues. Online tools offering screening and brief advice should signpost such drinkers to specialist treatment services, which must continue to receive sufficient funding in order to help those at most risk (Davies et al., 2019).

One possible issue with engaging drinkers who would benefit from reducing their drinking is that often people compare their drinking behaviors more favorably to others. GDS data suggests that many respondents underestimated the amount of alcohol they consumed compared to others

(Garnett et al., 2015). This misperception was common in Caucasian respondents, those under the age of 25, males, those from the UK, as well as those less well educated and unemployed. Drinkers may also believe their own behavior is not as bad as others when they are drunk (Davies, Lewis, & Hennelly, 2018). These kinds of issues pose a challenge for the reach and impact of individual level interventions.

GDS has developed a digital intervention – The Drinks Meter (see www.drinksmeter.com) – which attempts to counter misperceptions about drinking. Drinks Meter is a free tool based on identification and brief advice, which also provides people with normative information about how their drinking compares to other people with similar demographic/geographic characteristics. This resource has been has been highly rated by users (Milward et al., 2016). In a pilot trial, which compared this app to another app and to a control group, we actually found that all groups significantly decreased their drinking over four week period (Davies, Lonsdale, Hennelly, Winstock, & Foxcroft, 2017). The pilot trial had a number of limitations, including the possibility of demonstrating the mere measurement effect on reported alcohol reduction, as well as being insufficiently powered. Drinks Meter has recently been updated and has new behavior change techniques and a new study of its impact will be undertaken.

A further GDS app, also tested in our pilot trial was OneTooMany (see Fig. 2.8; onetoomany.co). On the OneTooMany website people are asked to respond to 20 questions about embarrassing situations that they may have experienced while drinking. Situations include posting an embarrassing photo on social media, being sick in public, or getting into fights. The website asks participants to indicate whether each of the 20 experiences have occurred 'in the last month', 'in the last year' or 'never/not in the last year'. On completion, the participant is presented with an alcohol related social embarrassment (*ARSE*) score (ranging from 0 to 40). The app uses light-hearted language to provide feedback on the associated risks and consequences of one's score and signposts to other services. In a qualitative study we found that this humorous approach might have costs as well as benefits. Young adults said that some of the embarrassing consequences of drinking were seen as a badge of honor, however many thought that using humor to get the message across could be effective (Davies, Law, Hennelly, & Winstock, 2017).

Population level interventions

The limitations of using individual approaches, such as apps, is that people have to acknowledge and decide they want to cut down and make changes to their behavior in a strongly 'alcogenic' environment (Hill, Foxcroft, & Pilling, 2018). Population approaches, such as alcohol product labeling may be advantageous in promoting messages to a wide audience of people who

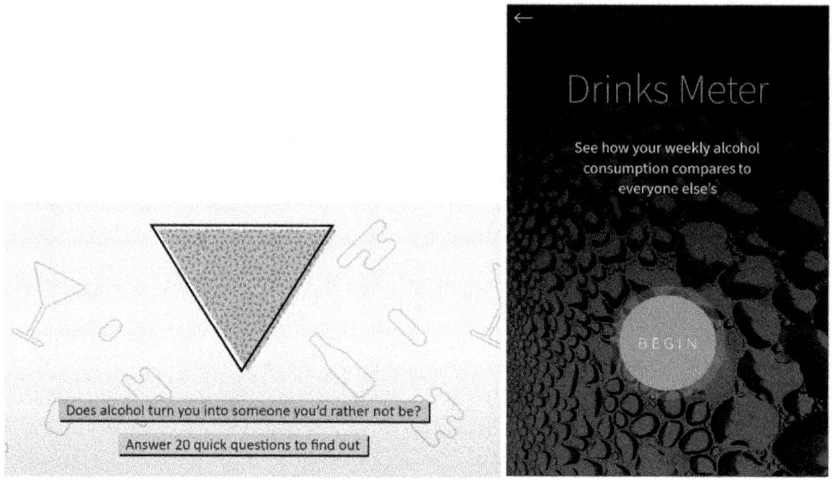

FIGURE 2.8 Screen shots of Drinks Meter and OneTooMany apps.

drink alcohol. The United States first introduced mandatory labels in 1989, which included information about the risks of driving while drunk and about drinking in pregnancy. However, while these messages were successful in raising awareness of such risks (Kaskutas & Greenfield, 1992; Mazis, Morris, & Swasy, 1991) there was little evidence that they were actually able to change behaviors (Stockwell, 2006). In recent years, there has been a resurgence of interest in the possibilities of communicating risk information on labels, and research has begun to focus on more specific messaging, such as that about the links between alcohol and cancer – for which levels of awareness appear to be low in the general population (Blackwell, Drax, Attwood, Munafò, & Maynard, 2018).

In GDS2018, we included seven health information labels that were developed from a review of the literature (relating to heart disease, liver, cancer, calories, violence, taking two days off and the myth of benefits to moderate drinking – see Fig. 2.9). Respondents were asked if the information was new to them, if they believed it, if it was personally relevant and if it would make them would make them consider drinking less (Winstock, Holmes, et al., 2020). A sample of 75,696 respondents from 29 countries was included in this study.

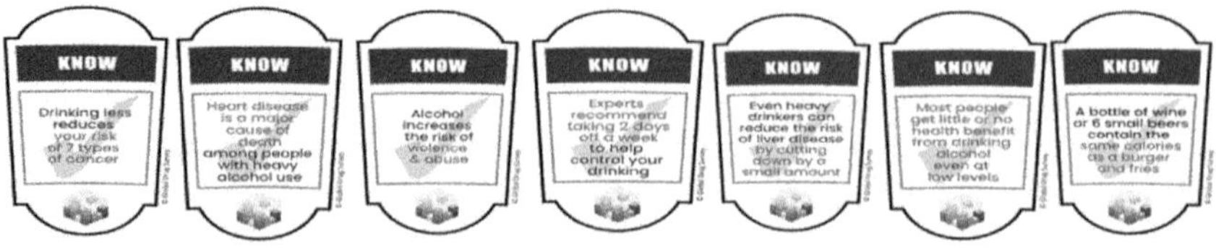

FIGURE 2.9 The seven alcohol labels included in GDS2018.

When it came to how 'new' the information on the labels was, 61.8% said the cancer message was new, compared to only 11.2% for the violence message. The message about violence was also the most believable (89.4%) and the most relevant (40.1%) message in the sample. This is an interesting finding, perhaps reflecting that the GDS sample often witness or experience violent behavior when they are drinking alcohol. The least believable message (62.3%) was the one about the myths of benefits to moderate drinking. Perhaps this reflects that there are often media stories promoting the health benefits of drinking red wine, and that people want this information to be true, as it supports their continued alcohol consumption. However, it was also rated the least relevant (15.1%) message and the one least likely to make respondents consider drinking less (14.2%). The message about cancer was the one that most respondents (39.6%) said it would make them consider drinking less. The liver message was in second place with 31.0% saying it would make them consider drinking less. New, believable and personally relevant information on product labels was associated with potential behavior change (Winstock, Holmes, et al., 2020).

The salience of the cancer message was one of the most important findings of this study. Not only was it more likely to change behavior, but also it was the least well known of all the seven messages. Given that alcohol was first categorized as a Group 1 carcinogen by the International Agency for Research on Cancer (IARC) in 1988 (IARC, 1988), it is worrying that this knowledge is not well known. We acknowledge, and indeed further qualitative studies are underlining (Davies et al., in preparation), that people may well not wish to see messages about the links between alcohol and cancer on their products, but we believe that people have a right to accurate information about the products they consume. The issue with current product labels is that there is wide variability across the world in what is included. In many countries the alcohol industry self-regulate, meaning that seemingly pro-health messages, such as 'drink responsibly' are presented. Further analysis of the GDS data on alcohol labels has shown considerable variability in levels of awareness of the information that was presented in different countries. For example, lower levels of awareness for all messages were observed in Colombia, Poland, Mexico, Brazil, and higher levels in Finland, Scotland, Germany (Davies et al., under review).

Advocating for trans people who use alcohol

In GDS we continue to strive to represent under researched populations of drug users, but we have not always got this right. Up until GDS2017, gender was assessed by a single question and around 65% of the sample reported being male. However, in 2017, GDS responded to some helpful participant feedback which suggested how we could improve the way we record gender, to be more inclusive of transgender (trans) respondents (those whose lived gender identity differs from their birth-assigned gender).[1] From GDS2018 a two-stage approach to assessing gender was adopted. The first question assesses participants' lived gender identity with the following options: 'male', 'female', 'non-binary', 'different identity'. The second question seeks to understand each participant's birth-assigned gender, with response options 'male' or 'female'. While 'non-binary' and 'different identity' are considered exclusively trans identities, the combination of responses to these questions allows us to determine which of those disclosing 'male' or 'female' gender identities are trans. For example, those who report female gender identity and male birth-assigned gender are classified as trans women.

With 1710 and 1799 trans respondents to GDS2018 and GDS2019 respectively, we believe that we are now reporting on the largest sample of trans people in the alcohol literature, which puts us in a unique position to understand and advocate for trans people who use alcohol. Early work has sought to compare alcohol use and dependence between five gender groups (cis women, cis men, trans women, trans men and non-binary people) responding to GDS2018. Given that non-binary refers to individuals whose gender identity exists beyond the binary categories of 'male' and 'female', it was decided that 'different identity' likely represented a collection of different labels for the same concept. As such, these groups were combined to increase statistical power. We found that last-year alcohol use was common among all gender groups (87.9–94.9%) but that non-binary people (AOR 0.42) and trans men (AOR 0.43) were half as likely as cis women to have used alcohol in the preceding year (Connolly et al., under review). Conversely, among those who have used alcohol, trans people were significantly more likely to report probable alcohol dependence (AUDIT ≥ 20). This was most significant for trans women (AOR 2.24) and non-binary people (AOR 3.28), highlighting the importance of disaggregating analysis for different subgroups of trans participants (Connolly et al., under review).

This work was followed up with a study comparing the same gender groups on their intention to reduce their alcohol use and to seek help to do so. We were able to combine GDS2018 and GDS2019 datasets to give a total sample of 185,055 (2579 trans) participants (Connolly et al., 2020). We found no differences between trans and cis respondents on the intention to use less alcohol. However, among those seeking to reduce their alcohol use, trans (particularly non-binary) respondents were more likely to want help to do so −10.5–14% vs 7.9–8.5% (Connolly et al., 2020). While we acknowledge that this work is introductory, we are motivated to understand the reasons why trans people are more likely to be alcohol dependent and to need help to reduce their use. We are specifically targeting our recruitment

1. Cisgender (cis) individuals are those whose lived gender identity matches that assigned to them at birth.

towards such minority groups to increase the diversity of our sample and give a voice to marginalized groups, often omitted from alcohol research.

Reflections and conclusions

This chapter has provided an overview of what we have learned so far about alcohol from over 500,000 GDS respondents from countries around the world. The majority of GDS participants receive an AUDIT score in the low risk drinking category, however the distribution of AUDIT scores varies by respondents' country of residence with median scores ranging from 6 to 12. As described, it is important to be cautious when making country comparisons within the GDS sample, as respondents are not representative of the general population, but it seems that the country differences we observe often fall in line with those observed in population studies.

Results from GDS presented in this chapter have many important implications for reducing alcohol related harms. For example, the finding that 20% of respondents reach their tipping point, an undesirable level of consumption, on a frequent basis is an opportunity for targeted interventions to encourage people to cut down without a losing the pleasure they get from drinking. Interventions that take into account the positive emotions associated with drinking are much more likely to hit their mark than those that simply warn of the risks and harms, which often people are aware of. Our labeling studies suggest that people are aware of many of the harms associated with drinking alcohol, but that they are not aware of the association between alcohol and cancers.

GDS has a rapidly expanding research profile; the team has published >60 academic papers in total, with alcohol experts drawing on our data to describe patterns and trends worldwide (Gage, 2020; Nutt, 2020; The Lancet, 2018). However, as we reflect on the strengths and implications of our body of work on alcohol so far, we acknowledge that there are many improvements we can make to our survey questions and to the diversity of drug users with whom we engage. Our sample is predominantly white, well educated, and from western countries; respondents must be literate and have internet access. An example of one area where some inroads have been made pertains to the inclusivity of different gender groups within the sample. However, we must do more to partner with organizations in a broader number of countries, in a number of other languages, in order to be a truly global survey. We are striving to do this and welcome collaboration and input in order to get better.

A major strength of the GDS research team is the ability to design, pilot and translate the large survey, recruit large numbers and then rapidly and report on this data each year. In 2020 this was put to the test when we chose to respond to the COVID-19 pandemic with a special edition of the survey. We recognized that the pandemic would have a significant impact on people's drug use, and particularly their alcohol consumption. We developed a survey to address the impact of lockdown conditions on drug use, with a particular focus on mental health and relationships. We found that around about a third of people reported drinking earlier in the day and although many people were drinking more frequently during lockdown due to boredom and having more time on their hands, many people had reduced their drinking, and were experiencing benefits to their physical and mental health as a result (Winstock, Davies, et al., 2020).

In the last eight years more than 500,000 people have completed the GDS specialist section on alcohol. Supported by granular details on demographics, lifestyle and mental health, we are able to explore novel areas using a unique and very large international dataset. Using the AUDIT each year, we have explored diverse questions that can be usefully explored using a non-probability sample, focusing on analyzes between different populations of drinkers. As the same survey is completed within the same time frame, using the same methodology across different regions we are able to explore cultural and legislative impacts upon drinking. Because we are self-funded, we can move quickly to focus on areas of public health importance and support areas relevant to policy.

To date our work has confirmed the existence of normative perceptions within diverse populations of heavy drinkers and have confirmed the potential utility of feedback using this information to nudge people's drinking behaviors (www.drinksmeter,com). We have collaborated with public health experts to highlight that those heavier drinkers who do themselves them greatest harm also have a significant adverse effects upon others in their community. Differential access and pricing between shops and bars has informed our work on the role of pre-drinking in excessive consumption in some regions.

Combined use with energy drinks and the role of excessive alcohol in the reporting of ketamine bladder symptoms demonstrate the importance of researching alcohol in the context of other drug use and showcase our ability to look at the negative consequences of the use of alcohol in combination with other substances. Work exploring how much people drink to get drunk and how different types of beverages impact on people's emotions allows us to start a dialogue with heavier drinkers to raise awareness of the risk of consuming more potent forms of alcohol such as spirits and challenge the current marketing that alcohol brands are allowed to exploit.

In more recent years we have focused on determining the motivations for people who want to drink less and identity the methods by which these groups would like to receive help. Our work on the impact of alcohol health warning labels and a focus on regret when drinking will hopefully inform future public health interventions and digital messaging to support and inform people to drink less but still have a good time. GDS's mission is to help people use drugs regardless of the legal status of the drugs and to facilitate honest conversation about drug use. Our work on alcohol demonstrates this commitment.

References

Ashton, K., Bellis, M. A., Davies, A. R., Hughes, K., & Winstock, A. R. (2017). Do emotions related to alcohol consumption differ by alcohol type? An international cross-sectional survey of emotions associated with alcohol consumption and influence on drink choice in different settings. *BMJ Open*, *7*(10), e016089. Available from: https://doi.org/10.1136/bmjopen-2017-016089. Available from: http://bmjopen.bmj.com/content/7/10/e016089.abstract.

Atkinson, A. M., & Sumnall, H. (2017). 'Isn't it mostly girls that do pre-drinks really?' Young men and women's accounts of pre-loading in the UK. *Drugs: Education, Prevention and Policy*, 1–10. Available from: https://doi.org/10.1080/09687637.2017.1377154.

Babor, T., Higgins-Biddle, J. C., Saunders, J. B., & Monteiro, M. G. (2001). *The alcohol use disorders identification test: Guidelines for use in primary care*.

Barratt, M. J., Ferris, J. A., & Winstock, A. R. (2014). Use of Silk Road, the online drug marketplace, in the United Kingdom, Australia and the United States. *Addiction*, *109*(5), 774–783. Available from: https://doi.org/10.1111/add.12470.

Barratt, M. J., Ferris, J. A., Zahnow, R., Palamar, J. J., Maier, L. J., & Winstock, A. R. (2017). Moving on from representativeness: testing the utility of the Global Drug Survey. *Substance Abuse: Research and Treatment*. Available from: https://doi.org/10.1177/1178221817716391.

Bellis, M. A., Quigg, Z., Hughes, K., Ashton, K., Ferris, J. A., & Winstock, A. (2015). Harms from other people's drinking: an international survey of their occurrence, impacts on feeling safe and legislation relating to their control. *BMJ Open*, *5*(12). Available from: https://doi.org/10.1136/bmjopen-2015-010112.

Blackwell, A. K. M., Drax, K., Attwood, A. S., Munafò, M. R., & Maynard, O. M. (2018). Informing drinkers: Can current UK alcohol labels be improved? *Drug & Alcohol Dependence*, *192*, 163–170. Available from: https://doi.org/10.1016/j.drugalcdep.2018.07.032.

Boyd, C. (2019). Britons get drunk more often than anyone in world: UK tops major global survey followed by the US, Canada and Australia. *Mail Online*. <https://www.dailymail.co.uk/health/article-7031677/UK-adults-drunk-world.html>.

Burgess, M., Cooke, R., & Davies, E. L. (2019). My own personal hell: Approaching and exceeding thresholds of too much alcohol. *Psychology & Health*. Available from: https://doi.org/10.1080/08870446.2019.1616087.

Chapman, C., Slade, T., Hunt, C., & Teesson, M. (2015). Delay to first treatment contact for alcohol use disorder. *Drug and Alcohol Dependence*, *147*, 116–121. Available from: https://doi.org/10.1016/j.drugalcdep.2014.11.029.

Connolly, D., Davies, E. L., Lynskey, M., Barratt, M. J., Maier, L., Ferris, J., ... Gilchrist, G. (2020). Comparing intentions to reduce substance use and willingness to seek help among transgender and cisgender participants from the Global Drug Survey. *Journal of Substance Abuse Treatment*, *112*, 86–91. Available from: https://doi.org/10.1016/j.jsat.2020.03.001.

Connolly, D., Davies, E. L., Lynskey, M., Maier, L. J., Ferris, J., Winstock, A., & Gilchrist, G. (under review). Differences in alcohol and other drug use and dependence between transgender and cisgender participants from the 2018 Global Drug Survey.

Cooke, R., Sniehotta, F., & Schuz, B. (2007). Predicting binge-drinking behaviour using an extended TPB: Examining the impact of anticipated regret and descriptive norms. *Alcohol and Alcoholism*, *42*(2), 84–91. Available from: https://doi.org/10.1093/alcalc/agl115.

Crane, D., Garnett, C., Brown, J., West, R., & Michie, S. (2015). Behavior change techniques in popular alcohol reduction apps: Content analysis. *Journal of Medical Internet Research*, *17*(5). Available from: https://doi.org/10.2196/jmir.4060, Article e118.

Davies, A. J., Borschmann, R., Kelly, S. P., Ramsey, J., Ferris, J., & Winstock, A. R. (2017). The prevalence of visual symptoms in poppers users: A global survey. *BMJ Open Ophthalmology, 1*(1). Available from: https://doi.org/10.1136/bmjophth-2016-000015, e000015-e000015.

Davies, E. L., Conroy, D., Winstock, A. R., & Ferris, J. A. (2017). Motivations for reducing alcohol consumption: An international survey exploring experiences that may lead to a change in drinking habits. *Addictive Behaviors, 75*, 40–46. Available from: https://doi.org/10.1016/j.addbeh.2017.06.019.

Davies, E. L., Cooke, R., Maier, L. J., Ferris, J., & Winstock, A. (in preparation). Association between drinking location, drink preference and levels of alcohol intoxication: An exploratory international survey of people who drink alcohol in 21 countries.

Davies, E. L., Cooke, R., Maier, L. J., Winstock, A. R., & Ferris, J. A. (2020). Drinking to excess and the tipping point: An international study of alcohol intoxication in 61,000 people. *International Journal of Drug Policy, 83*, 102867. Available from: https://doi.org/10.1016/j.drugpo.2020.102867

Davies, E. L., Foxcroft, D. R., Puljević, C., Ferris, J., & Winstock, A. (under review). Global comparisons of responses to alcohol health warning labels: A cross sectional study of people who drink alcohol from 29 countries.

Davies, E. L., & Joshi, M. S. (2018). "Here's to a night of drunken mistakes": Exploring experiences, regrets, and optimism in young adult drinkers. *Substance Use & Misuse, 53*(13), 2174–2183. Available from: https://doi.org/10.1080/10826084.2018.1461227.

Davies, E. L., Law, C., Hennelly, S. E., & Winstock, A. R. (2017). Acceptability of targeting social embarrassment in a digital intervention to reduce student alcohol consumption: A qualitative think aloud study. *Digital Health, 3*. Available from: https://doi.org/10.1177/2055207617733405, 2055207617733405.

Davies, E. L., Lewis, E.-B. C., & Hennelly, S. E. (2018). "I am quite mellow but I wouldn't say everyone else is": How UK students compare their drinking behaviour to their peers'. *Substance Use and Misuse*. Available from: https://doi.org/10.1080/10826084.2017.1416403.

Davies, E. L., Lonsdale, A. J., Hennelly, S. E., Winstock, A. R., & Foxcroft, D. R. (2017). Personalized digital interventions showed no impact on risky drinking in young adults: A pilot randomized controlled trial. *Alcohol and Alcoholism*, 1–6. Available from: https://doi.org/10.1093/alcalc/agx051.

Davies, E. L., Maier, L. J., Winstock, A. R., & Ferris, J. A. (2019). Intention to reduce drinking alcohol and preferred sources of support for help: An international cross sectional study. *Journal of Substance Abuse Treatment*. Available from: https://doi.org/10.1016/j.jsat.2019.01.011.

Davies, E. L., & Paltoglou, A. E. (2019). Public self-consciousness, pre-loading and drinking harms among university students. *Substance Use & Misuse*. Available from: https://doi.org/10.1080/10826084.2018.1536720.

de Visser, R. O., Wheeler, Z., Abraham, C., & Smith, J. A. (2013). "Drinking is our modern way of bonding": Young people's beliefs about interventions to encourage moderate drinking. *Psychology & Health, 28*(12), 1460–1480. Available from: https://doi.org/10.1080/08870446.2013.828293.

Department of Health. (2016). *UK chief medical officers' low risk drinking guidelines 2016*. <https://www.gov.uk/government/uploads/system/uploads/attachment_data/file/545937/UK_CMOs__report.pdf>.

Eurocare. (2016). *European report on alcohol policy*. Alliance: E. A. P. Available from: https://www.eurocare.org/publications.php.

Ferris, J. A., Puljević, C., Labhart, F., Winstock, A., & Kuntsche, E. (2019). The role of sex and age on pre-drinking: An exploratory international comparison of 27 countries. *Alcohol and Alcoholism*, *54*(4), 378–385. Available from: https://doi.org/10.1093/alcalc/agz040.

Furtwaengler, N. A. F. F., & de Visser, R. O. (2013). Lack of international consensus in low-risk drinking guidelines. *Drug and Alcohol Review*, *32*(1), 11–18. Available from: https://doi.org/10.1111/j.1465-3362.2012.00475.x.

Gage, S. (2020). *Say why to drugs*. Hodder & Stoughton.

Garnett, C., Crane, D., West, R., Michie, S., Brown, J., & Winstock, A. (2015). Normative misperceptions about alcohol use in the general population of drinkers: A cross-sectional survey. *Addictive Behaviors*, *42*, 203–206. Available from: https://doi.org/10.1016/j.addbeh.2014.11.010.

Hill, K. M., Foxcroft, D. R., & Pilling, M. (2018). "Everything is telling you to drink": Understanding the functional significance of alcogenic environments for young adult drinkers. *Addiction Research & Theory*, *26*(6), 457–464. Available from: https://doi.org/10.1080/16066359.2017.1395022.

Hughes, K., Anderson, Z., Morleo, M., & Bellis, M. A. (2008). Alcohol, nightlife and violence: The relative contributions of drinking before and during nights out to negative health and criminal justice outcomes. *Addiction*, *103*(1), 60–65. Available from: https://doi.org/10.1111/j.1360-0443.2007.02030.x, [Record #4610 is using a reference type undefined in this output style.].

Kaar, S. J., Ferris, J., Waldron, J., Devaney, M., Ramsey, J., & Winstock, A. R. (2016). Up: The rise of nitrous oxide abuse. An international survey of contemporary nitrous oxide use. *Journal of Psychopharmacology*, *30*(4), 395–401. Available from: https://doi.org/10.1177/0269881116632375.

Kalinowski, A., & Humphreys, K. (2016). Governmental standard drink definitions and low-risk alcohol consumption guidelines in 37 countries. *Addiction*, *111*(7), 1293–1298. Available from: https://doi.org/10.1111/add.13341.

Kaner, E. F. S., Beyer, F. R., Garnett, C., Crane, D., Brown, J., Muirhead, C., ... Michie, S. (2017). Personalised digital interventions for reducing hazardous and harmful alcohol consumption in community-dwelling populations. *Cochrane Database of Systematic Reviews*, *9*, Cd011479. Available from: https://doi.org/10.1002/14651858.CD011479.pub2.

Kaskutas, L., & Greenfield, T. K. (1992). First effects of warning labels on alcoholic beverage containers. *Drug Alcohol Depend*, *31*(1), 1–14.

Khadjesari, Z., Stevenson, F., Godfrey, C., & Murray, E. (2015). Negotiating the 'grey area between normal social drinking and being a smelly tramp': A qualitative study of people searching for help online to reduce their drinking. *Health Expectations*, *18*(6), 2011–2020. Available from: https://doi.org/10.1111/hex.12351.

Labhart, F., Ferris, J. A., Winstock, A., & Kuntsche, E. (2017). The country-level effects of drinking, heavy drinking and drink prices on pre-drinking: An international comparison of 25 countries. *Drug and Alcohol Review*, *36*(6), 742–750. Available from: https://doi.org/10.1111/dar.12525.

Laslett, A. M., Catalano, P., Chikritzhs, T., Dale, C., Doran, C., Ferris, J. A., ... Matthews, S. (2010). *The range and magnitude of alcohol's harm to others*. A. E. a. R. Foundation. Available from: http://www.fare.org.au/wp-content/uploads/research/The-Range-and-Magnitude-of-Alcohols-Harm-to-Others.pdf.

Laslett, A. M., Room, R., Ferris, J. A., Wilkinson, C., Livingston, M., & Mugavin, J. (2011). Surveying the range and magnitude of alcohol's harm to others in Australia. *Addiction*, *106*(9), 1603–1611. Available from: https://doi.org/10.1111/j.1360-0443.2011.03445.x.

Lawn, W., Hallak, J. E., Crippa, J. A., Dos Santos, R., Porffy, L., Barratt, M. J., ... Morgan, C. J. A. (2017). Well-being, problematic alcohol consumption and acute subjective drug effects in past-year ayahuasca users: A large, international, self-selecting online survey. *Scientific Reports*, *7*(1), 15201. Available from: https://doi.org/10.1038/s41598-017-14700-6.

Marsh, S. (2019). Britons get drunk more often than 35 other nations, survey find. *The Guardian*. Available from: https://www.theguardian.com/society/2019/may/15/britons-get-drunk-more-often-than-35-other-nations-survey-finds.

Mazis, M. B., Morris, L. A., & Swasy, J. L. (1991). An evaluation of the alcohol warning label: Initial survey results. *Journal of Public Policy & Marketing*, *10*(1), 229–241. Available from: https://doi.org/10.1177/074391569101000116.

Measham, F., & Brain, K. (2005). 'Binge' drinking, British alcohol policy and the new culture of intoxication. *Crime, Media, Culture*, *1*(3), 262–283. Available from: https://doi.org/10.1177/1741659005057641.

Miller, P., Droste, N., De Groot, F., Palmer, D., Tindall, J., Busija, L., ... Wiggers, J. (2016). Correlates and motives of pre-drinking with intoxication and harm around licensed venues in two cities [Article]. *Drug and Alcohol Review*, *35*(2), 177–186. Available from: https://doi.org/10.1111/dar.12274.

Milward, J., Khadjesari, Z., Fincham-Campbell, S., Deluca, P., Watson, R., & Drummond, C. (2016). User preferences for content, features, and style for an app to reduce harmful drinking in young adults: Analysis of user feedback in app stores and focus group interviews. *JMIR mHealth uHealth*, *4*(2), e47. Available from: https://doi.org/10.2196/mhealth.5242.

Nutt, D. (2020). *Drink? The new science of alcohol and your health*. Yellow Kite.

Paves, A. P., Pedersen, E. R., Hummer, J. F., & Labrie, J. W. (2012). Prevalence, social contexts, and risks for prepartying among ethnically diverse college students. *Addictive Behaviors*, *37*(7), 803–810. Available from: https://doi.org/10.1016/j.addbeh.2012.03.003.

Peacock, A., Bruno, R., Ferris, J., & Winstock, A. (2017). Energy drink use frequency among an international sample of people who use drugs: Associations with other substance use and well-being. *Drug Alcohol Depend*, *174*, 70–79. Available from: https://doi.org/10.1016/j.drugalcdep.2017.01.010.

Puljević, C., Zahnow, R., Benfer, I., Winstock, A., Maier, L. J., Barratt, M. J., & Ferris, J. A. (under revision). Patterns of methamphetamine production among an international sample of methamphetamine 'cooks.' *Drug and Alcohol Review*.

Ritchie, C., Ritchie, F., & Ward, R. (2009). A good night out: Alcohol-related behaviours in young adults. *Worldwide Hospitality and Tourism Themes*, *1*(2), 169–193. Available from: https://doi.org/10.1108/17554210910962549.

Schuler, M. S., Puttaiah, S., Mojtabai, R., & Crum, R. M. (2015). Perceived barriers to treatment for alcohol problems: A latent class analysis. *Psychiatric Services*, *66*(11), 1221–1228. Available from: https://doi.org/10.1176/appi.ps.201400160.

Stockwell, T. (2006). *A review of research into the impacts of alcohol warning labels on attitudes and behaviour*. C. f. A. R. o. BC. <https://www.uvic.ca/research/centres/cisur/assets/docs/report-impacts-alcohol-warning-labels.pdf>.

The Lancet. (2018). Changing the conversation to make drug use safer. *Lancet*, *391*(10134), 1965. Available from: https://doi.org/10.1016/s0140-6736(18)31075-4.

WHO. (2018). *Global status report on alcohol and health 2018*.

Winstock, A. R., & Barratt, M. J. (2013). Synthetic cannabis: A comparison of patterns of use and effect profile with natural cannabis in a large global sample. *Drug Alcohol Depend*, *131*(1–2), 106–111. Available from: https://doi.org/10.1016/j.drugalcdep.2012.12.011.

Winstock, A. R., Barratt, M. J., Maier, L. J., Villa-Llera, C., Zhuparris, A., Davies, E. L., ... Ferris, J. A. (2020). *Global drug survey 2020 key findings report.*

Winstock, A. R., Davies, E. L., Gilchrist, G., Zhuparris, A., Ferris, J. A., Maier, L. J., & Barratt, M. J. (2020). *Global drug survey special edition on Covid-19 interim report 02/06/20.* <https://www.globaldrugsurvey.com/global-drug-survey-special-edition-on-covid-19/>.

Winstock, A. R., & Ferris, J. A. (2019). Nitrous oxide causes peripheral neuropathy in a dose dependent manner among recreational users. *Journal of Psychopharmacology, 34*(2), 229–236. Available from: https://doi.org/10.1177/0269881119882532.

Winstock, A. R., Holmes, J., Ferris, J. A., & Davies, E. L. (2020). Perceptions of alcohol health warning labels in a large international cross sectional survey of people who drink alcohol. *Alcohol & Alcoholism*. Available from: https://doi.org/10.1093/alcalc/agz099.

Winstock, A. R., Mitcheson, L., Gillatt, D. A., & Cottrell, A. M. (2012). The prevalence and natural history of urinary symptoms among recreational ketamine users. *BJU International, 110*(11), 1762–1766. Available from: https://doi.org/10.1111/j.1464-410X.2012.11028.x.

Winstock, A. R., Winstock, C., & Davies, E. L. (2020). Inhaling alcohol vapour or mist: An international study of use, effects and harms. *International Journal of Drug Policy, 85*, 102920. Available from: https://doi.org/10.1016/j.drugpo.2020.102920.

Chapter 3

Transparency and replication in alcohol research

Katie Drax[1] and Marcus R. Munafò[2,3]
[1]*School of Psychological Science, University of Bristol, Bristol, United Kingdom,* [2]*Medical Research Council (MRC) Integrative Epidemiology Unit at the University of Bristol, United Kingdom,* [3]*School of Psychological Science, University of Bristol, United Kingdom*

Introduction

All stakeholders of scientific research take steps to ensure the quality of the research that is produced. Funders, regulators, researchers, research institutions and journals use a range of measures to reduce the risk of false, inaccurate or unreliable discoveries. However, although various quality control measures exist there is evidence that they may be suboptimal. Over the last 15 years, research on practices that influence research quality has increased. This applications of the scientific method to methodological issues is called meta-research, or "research on research" (Ioannidis, 2018, p. 1). One of the earliest examples is Rosenthal's (1966) work on experimenter effects.

The growing interest in the factors that contribute to research quality has been described in several ways, such as the 'open science' or 'evidentiary value' movement. Others have referred to a 'reproducibility crisis' (Finkel, Eastwick, & Reis, 2015; Nelson, Simmons, & Simonsohn, 2018). The majority of the debate has focused on the biomedical sciences (Jarvis & Williams, 2016), but has also extended to economics (Angrist & Pischke, 2010), biomechanics (Knudson, 2017), computational neuroscience (Miłkowski, Hensel, & Hohol, 2018) political science (Clark & Golder, 2014), artificial intelligence (Hutson, 2018) and beyond.

This growing discussion and demand for better research practices suggests there are genuine problems with research quality in many scientific disciplines. Understanding this will require a focus on both the factors that contribute to research quality, including current incentive structures and research culture, in order to develop approaches that address these and ultimately serve to improve the quality and efficiency of research. Here we provide an overview of current evidence in relation to both these issues.

The Handbook of Alcohol Use - Understandings from Synapse to Society.
DOI: https://doi.org/10.1016/B978-0-12-816720-5.00005-0

What is the evidence that research quality is suboptimal?

In 2005, John Ioannidis argued that most published research results may be false under certain conditions. He argued that findings are more likely to be false if many research efforts are biased, have low statistical power, and test associations or effects that are probably not true. Whilst Ioannidis argued from first principles, there have since been several empirical reports that a relatively small proportion of the published literature is reproducible. The pharmaceutical industry raised concerns about the low success they observed when attempting to replicate published findings from the academic community (Begley & Ellis, 2012; Prinz, Schlange, & Asadullah, 2011), whilst an attempt to replicate 100 published findings in the psychology literature reported a replication rate of around 40% (Open Science Collaboration, 2015). Researchers themselves report difficulties in reproducing experiments. In a survey of 1576 researchers 62–87%, depending on their discipline, said they had failed to reproduce someone else's experiment. 41–64% said they had failed to reproduce their own (Baker, 2016).

There are many potential causes of low replication rates. Some could be outside of researchers' control. Findings of true phenomena that are highly variable or context-dependent are difficult to replicate – chance will be responsible at times, as will honest human error. However, there is empirical evidence for some of the conditions described by Ioannidis that are within researchers' control – for example, average statistical power across a range of biomedical domains appears to be around 20%, far lower than the 80% that is considered the conventional minimum (Button et al., 2013; Dumas-Mallet, Button, Boraud, Gonon, & Munafò, 2017). Hundreds of researchers across numerous research areas, career stages and research locations admit to performing or observing potentially biased practices in anonymous surveys, sometimes referred to as questionable research practices (QRPs). QRPs have been reported to be common across a range of disciplines, including psychology (John, Loewenstein, & Prelec, 2012), health professions education (Artino, Driessen, & Maggio, 2019), electrical brain stimulation (Héroux, Loo, Taylor, & Gandevia, 2017), ego depletion (Wolff, Baumann, & Englert, 2018), ecology and evolution (Fraser, Parker, Nakagawa, Barnett, & Fidler, 2018) and management (Banks et al., 2016). These irreplicable results and admissions of poor practice indicate research is problematic. The specific practices that undermine research quality are discussed below and summarized in Fig. 3.1.

What are the factors that contribute to research quality?

Analytical flexibility

Researchers must make many decisions when analyzing data: which outliers to exclude, which statistical test to use, which covariates to include, and so on. Often several equally defensible choices exist. Gelman and Loken (2014)

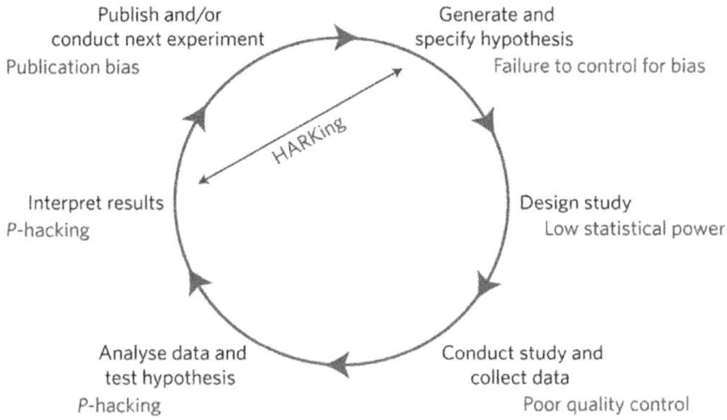

FIGURE 3.1 Threats to reproducible science. An idealized version of the hypothetico-deductive model of the scientific method is shown. Various potential threats to this model exist (indicated in red), including lack of replication, hypothesizing after the results are known (HARKing), poor study design, low statistical power, analytical flexibility, p-hacking, publication bias and lack of data sharing. Together these will serve to undermine the robustness of published research and may also impact on the ability of science to self-correct.

described this analytical flexibility as the 'garden of forking paths.' A garden where there are many legitimate paths we can take, each with a different result at the end, and where unplanned choices will probably be informed by the data. Importantly, the results from these different analyzes can support different interpretations and conclusions from the data. Silberzahn et al. (2018) tasked multiple researchers to answer the same research question by analyzing the same dataset. The 29 teams used a wide range of different analytical strategies. 20 produced a P-value $<.05$ and the estimated odds ratios ranged from 0.89 to 2.93 (Median = 1.31). This highlights the flexibility available in a dataset and how this flexibility makes it dangerous to determine the presence or absence of an effect based on P-values. The problem of flexibility is also apparent in other fields – for example, Carp (2012) found that 207 unique analytical strategies were in a sample of 241 functional magnetic resonance imaging (fMRI) studies. Essentially, almost no two studies used the same analytical pipeline.

Researchers, consciously or not, can use this analytical flexibility to capitalize on chance findings. One way this can be done is p-hacking. This occurs when data is reanalyzed multiple times but only the analyzes that produce the "best" result are reported. This could involve testing one hypothesis many ways using different analytical strategies, or subsets of the data, or testing many hypotheses (Simonsohn, Nelson, & Simmons, 2014). Simmons, Nelson, and Simonsohn (2011) demonstrated how relatively simple p-hacking, such as analyzing multiple outcomes or conditions and reporting one, inflated the number of false positive findings. Critically, many of the researchers surveyed by John et al. (2012) considered such behavior to be acceptable, indicating they were either unaware or unconcerned that p-hacking may damage the quality of their research.

Another QRP is to construct a hypothesis for the observed results and present this hypothesis as if it was formulated *a priori* – a phenomenon known as hypothesizing after results are known (HARKing; Kerr, 1998). This means that exploratory research, where data are used to *generate* predictions, is presented as confirmatory research, where data are used to *test* predictions (Nosek, Ebersole, DeHaven, & Mellor, 2018). HARKing blurs the distinction between exploratory and confirmatory research (and arguably devalues the importance of genuine, hypothesis-generating exploratory research).

Cognitive biases

Biased research will yield biased results. The risk from financial conflicts of interest (COIs) is well documented in the biomedical research (see Box 3.1),

BOX 3.1 Issues in alcohol research: Conflicts of interest

One source of bias that is particularly relevant to alcohol research is financial conflicts of interest (COIs) – for example through the involvement of the alcohol industry in research. A COI occurs when there is a "risk that professional judgment or actions regarding a primary interest will be unduly influenced by a secondary interest" (Institute of Medicine (US) Committee on Conflict of Interest in Medical Research Education and Practice, 2009, p. 46). The secondary interest could be financial, professional or social. Comparisons of results from studies with and without financial COIs consistently highlights the risk of bias from COIs, which is well documented in biomedical research. Lundh, Lexchin, Mintzes, Schroll, and Bero (2017) concluded that industry-sponsored studies of drugs or medical devices are more likely to yield confirmatory results than non-industry sponsored studies, even though their designs suggested no obvious differences in risk of bias. Concerns about industry involvement are well-documented in the alcohol literature, and included the potential for the industry to introduce bias, strategically use research for its own ends, award funding without adequate peer review, attack research (and researchers) whose work does not further its own ends, and encourage secrecy (McCambridge & Mialon, 2018). Despite these widely and frequently voiced anxieties there are few studies that directly examine the biasing effects of alcohol industry funding and the industry's practices. Addressing this evidence gap is essential, particularly given that the little evidence that does exist is mixed (Avery et al., 2016; Casswell, 2013; McCambridge & Hartwell, 2015; McCambridge, Hawkins, & Holden, 2014). Without empirical evidence none of these concerns can be effectively acted on by. However, it is important not to neglect other types of COIs. Alcohol research is a controversial area and as such alcohol researchers may be especially vulnerable to personal of cognitive conflicts of interest.

but researchers may be less aware of the cognitive biases that may influence their interpretation and presentation of their own and others' data. Humans are subject to confirmation bias – we tend to try to confirm our expectations or beliefs, rather than refute them (Nickerson, 1998), and researchers are no different. Researchers are still prone to reject contradictory evidence and present or interpret evidence in favor of their preferred hypothesis. Panagiotou and Ioannidis (2012) asked researchers to how likely it was that the true effect size of a heterogenous meta-analysis was larger than the meta-analytic result. They compared seven methodologists, uninvolved in the research area, to 16 primary authors of research in that area. Methodologists were less likely to believe that a strong association existed than were the six authors who had published significant findings in that field themselves. Tilburt et al. (2010) had 882 conventional and 679 complementary and alternative medicine (CAM) practitioners interpret results from two hypothetical CAM trials. One showed improvement in patients who received CAM alongside conventional treatment, the other did not. After seeing the effective trial, 65–84% convectional practitioners and 76–95% CAM practitioners were willing to recommend them, depending on the CAM treatment in question. After seeing the ineffective trial, 3–9% conventional practitioners and 20–77% CAM practitioners were willing to recommend them. Practitioner's intentions to recommend CAM depended on their prior beliefs about the treatment.

Another inherent cognitive bias, related to confirmation bias, is apophenia – our tendency to see associations between unrelated things and patterns in randomness. For example, we can see faces where none exist, on clouds, the moon, cars, houses, and even toast (Liu et al., 2014) and can believe that past random events can influence future ones (Gilovich, Vallone, & Tversky, 1985). A 'streak' of heads in a coin toss changes how likely we think it is that the next toss will be tails. Researchers can be similarly misled – they may interpret chance findings as evidence of their hypothesis. This means apophenia will have more influence the more chance events there are to misinterpret. Researchers will be at greater risk of apophenia if they conduct research that is likely to yield chance events – for example testing unlikely hypotheses, data mining or failing to control for multiple comparisons. Whilst scientific training protects against these cognitive biases to some extent, it cannot do so perfectly, not least because these biases are ubiquitous and unconscious. Instead, we need robust procedures and tools to safeguard against them and prevent us from fooling ourselves.

Sample size and statistical power

Statistical power is the probability that a statistical test will correctly identify a true effect or association (i.e., reject the null hypothesis when it is false). It depends on multiple factors including the true effect size, the probability of getting a false positive (α), sample size, and measurement variance (Gelman & Carlin, 2014). Power ($1 - \beta$) is the complement of the false negative rate (β), the probability that a test will not detect a true effect (Cohen, 1992). Critically, with lower power the proportion of statistically significant findings that are true positives rather than false positives declines (Button et al., 2013). Low power also inflates the estimates of true effect sizes – smaller studies will be imprecise and give a wider range of effect size estimates, but if a threshold is applied for declaring significance (and which in turn influences publication) only those studies that generate large effect sizes will be published (Ioannidis, 2008). There is empirical evidence that statistical power is much lower on average than the 80% considered the conventional minimum across a range of disciplines, including psychology (Cohen, 1962; Sedlmeier & Gigerenzer, 1989), cognitive neuroscience (Szucs & Ioannidis, 2017), neuroscience (Button et al., 2013), and biomedicine (Dumas-Mallet et al., 2017; Moher, Dulberg, & Wells, 1994).

Inadequate statistical training

Misunderstandings about statistics appear to be widespread among researchers. Lang and Altman (2015) reviewed 17 studies that evaluated statistics in medical, anesthesia, dermatology, psychiatry, urology, surgical and psychology journals. All found that many articles contain errors in the conduct, interpretation and reporting of statistical tests, and related methodological errors. These errors did not always invalidate the study's conclusions but, as Nelson et al. (2018) point out, they may indicate that the authors of the studies lack basic statistical knowledge or training. This explanation would be unsurprising since misunderstanding about even basic statistical concepts of *P*-values, confidence intervals and standard error bars appear to be widespread are (Belia, Fidler, Williams, & Cumming, 2005; Gigerenzer, 2018).

Lack of replication

Replication is the primary means by which the robustness of reported findings is evaluated. These can be 'direct' or 'conceptual' (Lebel, Berger, Campbell, & Loving, 2017). Direct replications attempt to repeat a previous experimental procedure as closely as possible, while conceptual replications attempt to repeat a previous study using different methods (Schmidt, 2009). So, a replication's place on the spectrum depends on how similar it is to the initial study. Both types of replication are important as each provides unique information about the initial study. Direct replication confirms the robustness of findings generated by a specific study procedure or design (Zwaan, Etz, Lucas, & Donnellan, 2017), while conceptual replications can demonstrate the generalizability of a finding and the limits of any underlying theory. However, conceptual replications cannot say anything about the existence of a previous finding under its original conditions (Lebel et al., 2017). Given that the method of replication determines what can be inferred about the initial finding, both direct and conceptual replications have a role.

Despite their essential role, replications are rare in many fields, especially direct replications. In a random sample of 269 empirical biomedical articles only 1.5% were replications, 51.7% were novel, 1.5% contained replicated and novel findings, and 45.2% were unclear or did not specify (Iqbal, Wallach, Khoury, Schully, & Ioannidis, 2016). Overall only 3% of the 269 articles contained clear replications, although unidentified replications could mean the true number is higher. However, citation analysis of the 269 articles found that only 3.1% were subsequently subjected to a replication attempt. The prevalence of replications in other fields is also very low. Makel, Plucker, and Hegarty (2012) estimated that around 2% psychology papers published in the 1990s were direct or conceptual replications. Their estimate for papers published in the 2010s was around 2.7%. Similarly, no direct replications were found in 302 behavioral ecology papers (Kelly, 2006) and 30 human factors papers (Jones, Derby, & Schmidlin, 2010). Both studies found conceptual replications to be far more common suggesting an imbalance of direct and conceptual replications.

Lack of transparency

Transparency is essential for replication and evaluation. If details of the methods, materials or data relating to a study are confusing, inaccurate, selective or inaccessible it is difficult to replicate the study without the original authors' help and judge the quality of the evidence. The importance of transparency makes assessments of reporting quality alarming. Researchers in several of the QRP surveys listed above admitted to not reporting certain outcomes. Other studies have assessed reporting quality of articles with reporting checklists or by comparing study protocols and articles. Assessments from numerous fields exist, from music-based interventions (Robb et al., 2018) otorhinolaryngology (Hendriksma, Joosten, Peters, Grolman, & Stegeman, 2017) to health professions education research (Cook, Levinson, & Garside, 2011). All found the reporting of their respective samples to be wanting. A systematic review of five studies comparing protocols and publications of randomized clinical trials found that between 40% and 62% of trials changed, introduced or omitted at least one primary outcome (Dwan, Gamble, Williamson, & Kirkham, 2013).

Selective and inaccurate reporting continues despite the availability of multiple reporting guidelines for a range of disciplines and study designs.

These are readily accessible through the Enhancing the QUAlity and Transparency of health Research (EQUATOR) Network (http://www.equator-network.org/). HARKing and p-hacking make it difficult to evaluate analysis methods or replicate them on different data, and yet we know these practices occur thanks to researchers' self-admission (e.g. Héroux et al., 2017) and discrepancies between study protocols and final publications (e.g. Goldacre et al., 2019). Poor reporting could be unconscious or conscious. Unconscious bad reporting could result from cognitive biases, such as confirmation bias and apophenia. In contrast, deliberate poor reporting can be seen when researchers 'spin' their results, which can impact readers' interpretations (Boutron et al., 2014).

A combination of factors – p-hacking, low statistical power, HARKing, lack of replication, lack of transparency – will all conspire to undermine the robustness of published findings. A scientific field with high bias, low power and unlikely relationships will be littered with false and inaccurate findings. Without replication it will struggle to self-correct and "unconfirmed genuine discoveries and unchallenged fallacies" (Ioannidis, 2012, p. 649) will remain.

What is the role of incentives and research culture?

Some of the problems discussed above may appear to have simple solutions. There could be more replication studies, for example. Researchers could report their methods and analysis strategies completely, or at least in enough detail to allow replication. Reporting all tested hypotheses and results could minimize deliberate HARKing and p-hacking. Specifying analyzes before seeing the data ('preregistration') could control unconscious p-hacking and HARKing. Better training and collaborating with statisticians could reduce statistical errors. Studies could be designed to be adequately powered. Why, then, do these problems persist if they are harmful to the progress of science and people have identified them? One explanation is that the existing research culture sustains researchers' problematic behavior and creates barriers to reforms.

Publication bias

Publication is the main way of disseminating findings and drives career success in academia (Balsmeier & Pellens, 2014; van Dijk, Manor, & Carey, 2014). This incentivizes researchers to produce 'publishable' manuscripts. Here publication bias – the publication, or non-publication, of research depending on the nature and direction of the results (Sterne, Egger, & Moher, 2011) – is an issue. Such bias hides legitimate results and distorts the academic record. In turn, any meta-analyzes that synthesize the published literature will produce a biased estimate of the average effect size (Sterne et al., 2011). The evidence for publication bias is considerable. Most findings in numerous fields are statistically significant – they are estimated to make up 75–95% of the biological and social science literature (Cristea & Ioannidis, 2018; Dwan et al., 2013; Fanelli, 2010). This suggests non-significant or 'null' findings that do not support the tested hypothesis are not published, and graphical and formal tests of small study bias, which may arise because of publication bias against null results, confirm this in many cases.

Two main mechanisms contribute to publication bias (1) journals rejecting manuscripts reporting null results, and (2) researchers not submitting them in the first place. A review of 570 scientific journals found that, on average, journals rejected 62% of submissions they received in 2014 (Da Silva, 2015). Unlike selective reporting, selective publication is not necessarily a bad thing. Choosing not to publish poorly designed studies would prevent untrustworthy results from entering the literature. Certainly, we expect editors and peer reviewers to act as gatekeepers. However, declining to publish results simply because they are deemed uninteresting (even if the question is important and the methodology robust) introduces bias. At the same time, researchers admit to not submitting null results (Fraser et al., 2018; Héroux et al., 2017; John et al., 2012). Scherer, Ugarte-Gil, Schmucker, and Meerpohl (2015) investigated why researchers leave some of their studies in the "file-drawer" (Rosenthal, 1979), reviewing 24 surveys. All asked authors why they had not published studies at least two years after presenting them at a biomedical conference. Some cited null results (4.4%), insufficiently important results (7.8%) and expectation of journal rejection (11.2%) as a reason for non-publication. Lack of time and/or resources made up about 50% of all reported reasons. The other most frequently cited reasons were insufficient English fluency (22%), study incomplete (17%) and publishing being a low priority (17%) or not an intention (19%). Of course, researchers may be unwilling to make publishing a priority because they believe the study is unpublishable. Alternatively, they may not think publication of null results will benefit their career.

Older editorial policies and surveys identified a clear bias against null results (Devaney, 2001; Neuliep & Crandall, 1990; Rosenthal, 1979). Today this bias is either smaller or less overt. A major review of publication bias stated: "we are not currently aware of explicit journal instructions to authors that may be a cause of publication bias" (Song et al., 2010, p. 43). Furthermore, several journals now have special sections exclusively for null findings (Matosin, Frank, Engel, Lum, & Newell, 2014). However, the lack of expressly biased editorial policies does not prove the process is unbiased. Peer reviewers and editors could unconsciously prefer significant results, although two studies found that journals are equally likely to publish positive and null submissions (Olson et al., 2002; van Lent, IntHout, & Out, 2015). However, the submitted null studies could differ from positive submissions. They may be of particularly high quality or clinical importance. Emerson et al. (2010) found support for this hypothesis: they submitted almost identical studies, except for their results being positive or null results, to two orthopedic journals. Studies with null results were more likely to be rejected, had more errors identified, and received lower scores for methodological validity, despite having identical methods to the positive studies.

Studies may also go unpublished even without biased editorial practices. Researchers' own biases and interests could discourage publication. For example, researchers seek to support a hypothesis they have a vested interest to abandon or avoid contradictory findings. Editorial policies may encourage publication bias, but so may the unconscious bias of editors and reviewers, and the decisions made by researchers themselves, which in turn may be shaped by current incentives.

Emphasis on novelty

Scientific culture's focus on novelty is most obvious in the absence of replication studies. Like publication bias against null results, editorial policies may play a role. Few editorial policies are overtly anti-replication, but novelty is often favored. A review found that only 1% of 1151 psychology journal policies stated that they did not accept replications, but 33% emphasized the novelty of submissions (Martin & Clarke, 2017). There is evidence that editorial policies have become less overtly biased against replications (Easley, Madden, & Gray, 2013; Hensel, 2019), but an emphasis on novelty creates an implicit bias against replication studies, since they are inherently less original if they use a previous method. Ottoline Leyser says: "We're encouraged to do groundbreaking research, but what's groundbreaking for? You break ground in order to build something, and if all you do is groundbreaking you end up with lots of holes in the ground." (as cited in Munafò, 2017). This is not to say that groundbreaking research should not be done. Novelty is essential for innovation, but we must balance high-risk exploratory work with corrective, confirmatory replication work. Otherwise, we cannot distinguish between chance findings and genuine scientific discovery and develop robust, accurate theories.

Research evaluation

Researchers can achieve professional, financial and social advancement through securing jobs, promotions, tenure, prizes, higher salaries and better research resources, such as funding or personnel. Individuals are incentivized to pursue the things that will grant them these achievements. How hiring, promotion, funding and tenure committees evaluate individuals shapes their decisions. In other words, research evaluation contributes to incentive structures. For example, positive results are more likely to be cited than null results (Duyx, Urlings, Swaen, Bouter, & Zeegers, 2017). Citation bias has the potential to distort funding, hiring, tenure and promotion decisions because these committees often use citation counts in their assessments (Hammarfelt, 2017). This creates a disincentive for research to write up null results, which they know will be less likely to be cited.

Among many other things, academic achievement follows from publication in high impact factor journals and citations. If, as the evidence suggests, publication and citations are biased towards positive results researchers will be incentivized to achieve and publish these results over others for maximum benefit. It is notable that the widespread concerns about research quality stemmed in part from concerns raised by the pharmaceutical industry. This may reflect differences in incentive structures. The industry has clear financial incentives for getting the 'right' answer – developing an effective treatment to profit from – whereas academics are incentivized to publish and get cited over accurate and true results.

Emphasis on narrative

The incentives for researchers to get positive and novel findings implicitly create pressure to present inconclusive results as conclusive. Strong and consistent results are easier to make sense of than inconsistent ones, but the reality of science if often messy. The published literature, however, does not fully reflect this. Selective reporting can suppress null and confusing results, spin can misrepresent them, and HARKing can transform them into positive ones. Indeed, junior researchers are often encouraged to adopt persuasive and engaging writing styles (Bem, 2003; Jordan & Zanna, 2007). Some argue that rhetoric provides 'context' (Singleton, 1995), does not 'turn heads' (Greenhalgh, 1995) or invites excitement and debate (Junger, 1995). While this may be true, authors who pursue a readable, exciting story may ignore or simplify 'uninteresting' and complicated details. We need to encourage researchers to fully and accurately represent their work, not simply tell good stories (Funder et al., 2014).

Potential solutions

If science really is in "crisis", as some have argued, then why is progress still being made? Rather than viewing science as in crisis, perhaps a better perspective is to think about how it can be made to work even better – by preventing waste, improving efficiency, and accelerating progress. One consequence of the recent debate around reproducibility is that there are now many initiatives being introduced with the aim of improving science – from new journal submission formats such as Registered Reports, to the growth in large-scale collaborations. What is lacking, however, is evidence. It is not yet clear whether these initiatives improve matters. Below we discuss some of the major initiatives that are currently ongoing, and they are summarized in Table 3.1 (Box 3.2).

TABLE 3.1 Actions to combat threats to research quality.

Theme	Proposal	Examples of initiatives/ potential solutions (extent of current adoption)	Stakeholder(s)
Methods	Protecting against cognitive biases	All of the initiatives listed below (* to ****) Blinding (**)	J, F
	Improving methodological training	Rigorous training in statistics and research methods for future researchers (*) Rigorous continuing education in statistics and methods for researchers (*)	I, F
	Independent methodological support	Involvement of methodologists in research (**) Independent oversight (*)	F
	Collaboration and team science	Multi-site studies/distributed data collection (*) Team-science consortia (*)	I, F
Reporting and dissemination	Promoting study pre-registration	Registered Reports (*) Open Science Framework (*)	J, F
	Improving the quality of reporting	Use of reporting checklists (**) Protocol checklists (*)	J
	Protecting against conflicts of interest	Disclosure of conflicts of interest (***) Exclusion/containment of financial and non-financial conflicts of interest (*)	J
Reproducibility	Encouraging transparency and open science	Open data, materials, software and so on (* to **) Pre-registration (**** for clinical trials, * for other studies)	J, F, R
Evaluation	Diversifying peer review	Preprints (* in biomedical/ behavioral sciences, **** in physical sciences) Pre- and post-publication peer review, for example, Publons, PubMed Commons (*)	J
Incentives	Rewarding open and reproducible practices	Badges (*) Registered Reports (*) Transparency and Openness Promotion guidelines (*) Funding replication studies (*) Open science practices in hiring and promotion (*)	J, I, F

Estimated extent of current adoption: *, <5%; **, 5–30%; ***, 30–60%; ****, >60%. Abbreviations for key stakeholders: J, journals/publishers; F, funders; I, institutions; R, regulators.

BOX 3.2 Differences in alcohol research fields: clinical and preclinical

The amount that animal research can tell us about alcohol-related phenomena in humans is an ongoing area of controversy. Out of 101 articles published in six top life science journals, 27 led to at least one published randomized trial. Five were translated into clinical use up to 20 years after publication (Contopoulos-Ioannidis, Ntzani, & Ioannidis, 2003). One reason for this relatively poor level of translational success may be the robustness of both preclinical and clinical research. In other words, to improve translational throughput, various threats to the robustness of clinical and preclinical research must be tackled. There are differences in how widely rigorous practices are applied to the two fields. For example, efforts to eliminate selective reporting are better implemented in clinical fields – preregistration is common and enforced by major journals and other organization such as the Centre for Evidence-Based Medicine Outcome Monitoring Project (http://compare-trials.org/). In preclinical research preregistration is rarer, increasing the risk of selective reporting and making it harder to identify. In addition, scope for data sharing differ. Preclinical research, particularly animal research, faces far fewer ethical issues when sharing data than clinical research, which may require complex anonymization processes and may not be possible if identification is possible. These examples underline how attempts to improve the quality of alcohol research will need to be field or method dependent; there is no one-size-fits-all solution. On the other hand, all fields can learn examples of best practice from each other.

Sharing data and materials

Authors can share their data and materials, assuming this is done ethically and legally, and can be achieved either by making data available on request or archiving on a repository. Some journals and funders require or encourage data sharing, and various methods exist for doing this, including supplementary materials or platforms like institutional repositories and third-party services such as GitHub and the OSF. Public sharing is superior to sharing on request: it is more consistent with FAIR (findable, accessible, interoperable, reusable; Heringa et al., 2016) principles of data sharing and prevents the data from becoming inaccessible through loss or difficulty contacting authors (Vines et al., 2014). Sharing raw data and materials, including analysis code, could improve the evaluation of research quality. Others can reanalyze the data and assess materials' quality. This may increase the likelihood of errors being detected and corrected and encourage researchers to engage in more rigorous practices to avoid errors in the first place (Munafò et al., 2017). Data and materials also provide information not included in the main article and thereby improve reporting indirectly.

However, data and materials sharing remains uncommon in many disciplines or restricted to availability on request. Data sharing remains rare, even in areas like genome-wide association studies, where data sharing norms are supposedly strong (Thelwall et al., 2019). Often, authors do not provide outputs 'on request' even if the journal requires them to. Vanpaemel, Vermorgen, Deriemaecker, and Storms (2015) requested data from 394 papers published in four American Psychological Association (APA) journals in 2012. At the time, APA policy mandated that authors make their materials and data available on request. Only 38% of authors provided their data, while 41% did not reply and 18% were unwilling or claimed to be unable to share. Efforts to retrieve data from articles in the British Medical Journal (Naudet et al., 2018; Rowhani-Farid & Barnett, 2016) and 516 biological articles (Vines et al., 2014) were similarly unsuccessful. Attempts to retrieve materials are far fewer. One attempt contacted authors of economics papers who offered to share materials on request at their own discretion (it was not a condition of the journal). Only 44% of the 200 authors provided their materials and 36% did not respond (Krawczyk & Reuben, 2012). Sharing 'on request' is clearly inadequate – it requires original authors to be contactable, willing and able to share their data. Publicly sharing data and materials on a repository overcomes these problems. Unfortunately, public sharing is rare and good quality public sharing even rarer. Researchers found 18.3% of 104 biomedical articles discussed their data availability or publicly shared some of it (Wallach, Boyack, & Ioannidis, 2018). It is unclear how much of the data is FAIR since some articles conducted secondary analyzes on pre-existing datasets. Even if all the datasets are publicly accessible 18.3% is a low proportion. The situation is similar in the social sciences. Hardwicke, Wallach, Kidwell, and Ioannidis (2019) randomly sampled social science papers published from 2014 to 2017. Of 103 relevant papers, six claimed their data were available and three their analysis scripts. Only two datasets were reusable, and two analysis scripts were accessible. Public data has problems and so does on request sharing'. The quality of sharing materials was no better; 15% of 96 relevant articles claimed their materials were available, but two had broken links.

Routine sharing of data and materials on repositories in a way that adheres to FAIR principles remains rare, despite encouragement from funders and publishers. While there are ethical and regulatory issues to address when sharing data, these are typically not insurmountable (although there will be exceptions). Other valid concerns include lack of resources and training in preparing data and materials for sharing, concerns about how the data might be reused or interpreted, fear of others identifying errors, and inadequate citation standards for non-traditional outputs (Hardwicke & Ioannidis, 2018; Houtkoop et al., 2018). However, sharing data and materials also makes it more likely that data are well-curated, allowing researchers themselves to be able to return to a dataset years later and make sense of them rapidly. In other words, there are both selfless and selfish reasons for data and materials sharing (Markowetz, 2015).

Preregistration and registered reports (RRs)

Preregistration, or prospective registration, allows researchers to state their planned research methods and analysis strategy in a protocol before they collect or analyze their data. Pre-specifying the analysis strategy before seeing the data prevents p-hacking and HARKing, whether conscious or unconscious, as the data cannot inform analytical choices. Preregistration does not limit researchers to their pre-specified analyzes; they can do as many analyzes as they wish. However, it ensures confirmatory and exploratory analyzes are transparently reported as such (or at least, in principle, allows reviewers to check this), and guarantees a distinction between hypothesis testing and generation (Nosek et al., 2018).

Preregistration is common in clinical trials and systematic reviews of health-related outcomes. The Cochrane Collaboration, which began in 1993, has always encouraged protocols for systematic reviews (Chalmers, 1993). Since 2005, the International Committee of Medical Journal Editors (ICMJE) member journals requires clinical trials to be publicly registered for publication (De Angelis, 2004). For medical studies, several preregistration platforms exist, including ClinicalTrials.gov and the ISRCTN registry. However, there are other platforms, such as the Open Science Framework (OSF; see Box 3.3) or the International Prospective Register of Systematic Reviews (PROSPERO) that support preregistration. Preregistrations allow others to avoid duplication of ongoing or planned research, identify unpublished studies, identify selective reporting and evaluate the impact of any

BOX 3.3 The Open Science Framework

The Open Science Framework (OSF; http://help.osf.io) is a free, open source repository that researchers can use for managing collaborations, sharing data and files, and preregistering study protocols. It supports persistent project pages with multiple sub-components and assigns Digital Object Identifiers (DOIs) and copyright licenses to these. This creates a centralized location to upload, license, cite and discover all research outputs. Access to the pages and components can kept private or shared publicly. This enables researchers to link their outputs to their papers and for others to cite non-paper outputs. Preregistrations can be made for new projects or connected to an existing one. All are made public either immediately or after an embargo period of up to four years. Preregistrations can only be withdrawn, not deleted, and after withdrawal basic details about the preregistration, including the title, reason for withdrawal and contributors, remain on the OSF. This guarantees that preregistrations remain on public record.

deviations from the protocol on the results. All these anticipated benefits depend on preregistrations being adhered to. Evaluations find mixed impacts of preregistrations on reported outcomes. Kaplan and Irvin (2015) identified fewer positive results in clinical trials published after 2000, than those published before. A finding supported by Papageorgiou, Xavier, Cobourne, and Eliades (2018). In contrast, two other studies of clinical trials find less conclusive differences in the number of positive results and size of effect estimates between preregistered and unregistered studies (Dechartres, Ravaud, Atal, Riveros, & Boutron, 2016; Odutayo et al., 2017). Since none of these studies assessed adherence to preregistration the inclusion of all 'registered' studies regardless of the quality of adherence may mask an existing effect. Preliminary evidence supports this explanation because preregistered studies seem to frequently deviate from their preregistrations (Claesen, Gomes, Tuerlinckx, & Vanpaemel, 2019), although much less than unregistered studies (Chan et al., 2017). Even if bias continues to affect results because preregistrations are not followed, other benefits of preregistration still stand, such as allowing others to identify deviations from the study protocol.

A stronger version of preregistration is Registered Reports (RRs), a journal submission format that began at *Cortex* in 2013 (Chambers, 2013). An RR is an empirical article that undergoes a two-stage peer review process. In Stage 1, the protocol is reviewed before data collection. In Stage 2, the complete manuscript is reviewed again after data collection and analysis. Journals must offer in-principal acceptance to manuscripts which pass Stage 1. Stage 1 manuscripts with in-principle acceptance cannot be rejected based on any outcomes observed in Stage 2 (https://cos.io/rr/). The two-stage peer review process gives RRs all the advantages of preregistration and peer review and encourages a focus on the importance of the research question, and the robustness of the methodology. Researchers get feedback on their research question, rationale and method before they start data collection, which should strength methodology and rigor. The post-study peer review also checks that researchers have followed the preregistered protocol and justified any deviations. Given that in-principle acceptance is offered before the results are known, this should disincentivize problematic practices like p-hacking and HARKing.

RRs are a relatively new format, and the evidence for their effectiveness limited. Certainly, the speed of uptake of RRs by journals indicates they are popular and feasible. Moreover, evidence as to their impact on publication outputs is emerging. If RRs minimize publication bias, there should be a higher prevalence of neutral (i.e., non-significant or null) results in RRs than conventional article formats. Preliminary evidence supports this; Allen and Mehler (2019) analyzed 113 published biomedical and psychological RRs and found that 61% of the 296 hypotheses tested were not supported. This is higher than the 9–25% estimated in conventional article formats (Fanelli,

2010). However, the cause of these differences is unclear; RRs could be less vulnerable to p-hacking, HARKing, selective submission, editorial biases, and so on, or RRs could tackle more unlikely hypotheses. Understanding this will require further research.

Protocol preregistration has a long history in medical research, particularly in clinical trials and systematic reviews, but is much less common in other disciplines and sub-disciplines. However, platforms such as the OSF and journal formats such as RRs now allow much more widespread adoption of preregistration. These vary in their level of stringency, and scope for deviation (e.g., whether there is any editorial oversight to the process, and the extent to which eventual publication is guaranteed). Ultimately, further research will be required as to which approach(es) to preregistration work best and offer the greatest benefits in terms of the quality of research outputs, and the fewest downsides. Importantly, this may differ across disciplines and sub-disciplines.

Large-scale collaboration

Collaborations bring networks of researchers across multiple sites, and countries. These are a long-standing feature of science, but there is an increasing number of large-scale collaborations working on projects using common study protocols and pooling data across sites. Co-authorship and collaboration have increased since the 1980s (Larivière, Gingras, Sugimoto, & Tsou, 2014), although large-scale multisite collaborations remain rare. Teams of 1–10 authors account for over 98% of patents, articles and code repositories (Wu, Wang, & Evans, 2019). They are most commonplace in physics and genetics (Austin, Hair, & Fullerton, 2012). Notable examples include the Human Genome Project and the Large Hadron Collider, while genomics projects (e.g., genome-wide association studies; GWAS) now routinely proceed via large-scale collaboration.

Recently, large-scale collaborations have become more popular in other disciplines, with projects like ManyBabies (https://osf.io/rpw6d/), ManyPrimates (https://manyprimates.github.io/) and ManyClasses (https://www.manyclasses.org/). Collaborations offer a solution to several potential problems that may contribute to poor reproducibility, such as low statistical power (collaboration can serve to increase sample size beyond what a single group could achieve) and data sharing (collaboration requires data to be shared across sites, thereby reducing barriers to eventually sharing publicly). In genomics, the growth of GWAS consortia enabled researchers to collect and harmonize huge amounts of genotypic and phenotypic data, leading well-powered studies, and highly replicable findings (Ioannidis, Tarone, & McLaughlin, 2011).

Collecting data across multiple sites can also support large-scale replication projects. Each site acts as a separate direct replication attempt because the methods are standardized while the samples and context vary. If participating labs yield different results this may provide additional understanding about the effect. Even if individual studies do not have adequate power for a replication the analyzes on the combined data will contain more variation and be more generalizable than results from a single site (Moshontz et al., 2018). If collaborations share or combine data collected at multiple sites all collaborators must standardize their study design, materials, conduct, analysis and terminology. Guidelines or standardized operating procedures, sharing data and sharing materials are therefore essential. Evidence about the quality and impact of such guidelines is uncertain (Austin et al., 2012) but they may improve reporting. A description, detailed enough for replication, already exists and could lead to more complete reporting of methods in publications. The internal sharing of data and materials may also make public sharing easier. Again, little evidence exists on how sharing practices differ between collaborative and independent research.

One barrier to large-scale collaboration is governance. Coordinating and providing adequate resources for collecting, sharing and storing data across site is vital for success; otherwise this may prevent or discourage participation (Budin-Ljøsne et al., 2013). Organizers must consider the feasibility of collaboration for a specific research effort to avoid failure. Increased infrastructure and guidance to assist collaborations will make governance less effortful. Such as the development of platforms like StudySwap (https://osf.io/view/StudySwap/) and the Psychological Science Accelerator (https://psysciacc.org/). Another consideration is the appropriateness of the research question – this approach may be better suited to confirmatory research than exploratory research, for example. Smaller teams may be more likely to challenge existing scientific ideas; novelty seems to diminish as team sizes increase (Wu et al., 2019). However, incentives against conducting replications do not seem to prevent participation in large-scale replication studies – several disciplines use large-scale collaborations for replications, such as the Reproducibility Project: Psychology (2015), Reproducibility Project: Cancer Biology (Errington et al., 2014) and the Many Labs 1 project (Klein et al., 2014).

Stakeholders

Journal and funder policies can strongly influence research quality. Editorial decisions can contribute to publication bias, or reward p-hacking, while a focus on novelty by journals and funders could discourage replications. Journal's emphasis on narrative may encourage, or demand, incomplete reporting of a study's methods. However, if the policies and behavior of stakeholders such as journals and funders can increase problematic practices, they can also increase rigorous ones. For example, researchers aiming to publish in ICMJE journals must preregister their clinical trial prior to data collection, since this is typically mandatory for publication. Indeed, several journals and funders have adopted initiatives intended to improve research quality, such as reporting checklists and data sharing requirements.

Journals can also encourage complete reporting. Most journals advise authors to describe their methods in enough detail to allow another, independent researcher to repeat it, but beyond this most journals simply trust authors to do this. Additionally, other factors, such as word limits, may act against this Journals can do much to improve transparency. Requiring the use of reporting checklists might help – articles published in journals that endorse the use of reporting guidelines are better reported than those in journals that do not (Turner et al., 2012).

In general, policies will only be effective if they are enforced. Preregistration increased immediately after the introduction of the ICMJE policy (Zarin, Tse, & Ide, 2005), and led to further policies in the US and other countries to support and mandate trial preregistration (Zarin, Tse, Williams, & Rajakannan, 2017), but even after these changes many journals fail to comply with the ICMJE policy. Gopal et al. (2018) assessed 487 clinical trials published between 2010 and 2015 in medical specialty society journals. All journals endorsed the ICMJE policy, but 9.7% of trials were unregistered and 22.6% were registered after data collection started. Stakeholders must balance the strictness of their policies against the potential quality of their adherence and unintended consequences.

Journals and funders can also support better research practices with infrastructure. A stakeholder that requires data sharing could provide guidance, support training, and/or offer a repository. One such funder is the Wellcome Trust – it requires data sharing and supports this financially: "We will fund any justified costs for delivering the plan as part of funding the research" (Wellcome Trust, 2017). The publication formats that journals offer (e.g., Registered Reports) could improve research quality. Providing infrastructure makes better research practices easier, reducing their burden on researchers. They complement policies that incentivize or mandate certain practices; infrastructure makes adherence possible.

Funders have a major role in implementing potential solutions. Funding can be ring-fenced for replication studies, or meta-research activity, and rigorous practices could be incentivized by making funding conditional on preregistration and data sharing. Some funders are already supporting initiatives to improve research. The Laura and John Arnold Foundation funded the launch of the Center for Open Science (COS) in 2013 (Center for Open Science, n.d.). To date, the Foundation has donated over $21.5 million to support COS's operation, activities and research, including its large-scale replication attempts. Other funding agencies also support replications. In

2016 the Netherlands Organisation for Scientific Research awarded €3 million to support replication studies (Netherlands Organisation for Scientific Research, 2016). And a consortium of funders and other stakeholders in the UK supported the establishment of the UK Reproducibility Network (ukrn.org) in 2019.

Conclusion

There is always room to improve the quality of research, and efforts to do so are now becoming more coordinated and widespread. Efforts to improve transparency and replication are developing, but these efforts are not enough alone. It is vital that incentivizes for researchers are better aligned with what is likely to generate the best science. Current incentives may reward questionable research practices, leading to the "natural selection of bad science" (Smaldino & McElreath, 2016). The last ten years have seen rapid growth in studies investigating the scale of the problem, in terms of the reproducibility and robustness of scientific research. The focus now is turning towards solutions – identifying approaches that may improve research quality and, critically, evaluating whether these are effective. We have identified problems and begun to understand their causes. Now we need to solve them.

References

Allen, C., & Mehler, D. M. A. (2019). Open science challenges, benefits and tips in early career and beyond. *PLoS Biology*, *17*(5), e3000246. Available from: https://doi.org/10.1371/journal.pbio.3000246.

Angrist, J. D., & Pischke, J.-S. (2010). The credibility revolution in empirical economics: How better research design is taking the con out of econometrics. *SSRN*. Available from: https://doi.org/10.2139/ssrn.1639809.

Artino, A. R., Driessen, E. W., & Maggio, L. A. (2019). Ethical shades of gray: International frequency of scientific misconduct and questionable research practices in health professions education. *Academic Medicine*, *94*(1), 76–84. Available from: https://doi.org/10.1097/ACM.0000000000002412.

Austin, M. A., Hair, M. S., & Fullerton, S. M. (2012). Research guidelines in the era of large-scale collaborations: An analysis of genome-wide association study consortia. *American Journal of Epidemiology*, *175*(9), 962–969. Available from: https://doi.org/10.1093/aje/kwr441.

Avery, M.R., Droste, N., Giorgi, C., Ferguson, A., Martino, F., Coomber, K., & Miller, P. (2016). *Mechanisms of influence: Alcohol industry submissions to the inquiry into fetal alcohol spectrum disorders*. Available from: https://doi.org/10.1111/dar.12399.

Baker, M. (2016). 1,500 scientists lift the lid on reproducibility. *Nature*, *533*(7604), 452–454. Available from: https://doi.org/10.1038/533452a.

Balsmeier, B., & Pellens, M. (2014). Who makes, who breaks: Which scientists stay in academe? *Economics Letters*, *122*(2), 229–232. Available from: https://doi.org/10.1016/j.econlet.2013.11.033.

Banks, G. C., O'Boyle, E. H., Pollack, J. M., White, C. D., Batchelor, J. H., Whelpley, C. E., ... Adkins, C. L. (2016). Questions about questionable research practices in the field of management: A guest commentary. *Journal of Management*, *42*(1), 5–20. Available from: https://doi.org/10.1177/0149206315619011.

Begley, C. G., & Ellis, L. M. (2012). Drug development: Raise standards for preclinical cancer research. *Nature*, *483*(7391), 531–533. Available from: https://doi.org/10.1038/483531a.

Belia, S., Fidler, F., Williams, J., & Cumming, G. (2005). *Researchers misunderstand confidence intervals and standard error bars*. Available from: https://doi.org/10.1037/1082-989X.10.4.389.

Bem, D. J. (2003). Writing the empirical journal article. In J. M. Darley, M. P. Zanna, & H. L. Roediger, III (Eds.), *The compleat academic: A practical guide for the beginning social scientist* (2nd ed., pp. 171–201). Washington, DC: American Psychological Association.

Boutron, I., Altman, D. G., Hopewell, S., Vera-Badillo, F., Tannock, I., Ravaud Isabelle Boutron, P., ... du Parvis, P. (2014). Impact of spin in the abstracts of articles reporting results of randomized controlled trials in the field of cancer: The SPIIN randomized controlled trial. *Journal of Clinical Oncology*, *32*, 4120–4126. Available from: https://doi.org/10.1200/JCO.2014.56.7503.

Budin-Ljøsne, I., Isaeva, J., Knoppers, B. M., Tassé, A. M., Shen, H.-Y., Mccarthy, M. I., & Harris, J. R. (2013). Data sharing in large research consortia: Experiences and recommendations from ENGAGE. *European Journal of Human Genetics*, *22*, 317–321. Available from: https://doi.org/10.1038/ejhg.2013.131.

Button, K. S., Ioannidis, J. P. A., Mokrysz, C., Nosek, B. A., Flint, J., Robinson, E. S. J., & Munafò, M. R. (2013). Power failure: Why small sample size undermines the reliability of neuroscience. *Nature Reviews Neuroscience*, *14*(5), 365–376. Available from: https://doi.org/10.1038/nrn3475.

Carp, J. (2012). The secret lives of experiments: Methods reporting in the fMRI literature. *NeuroImage*, *63*(1), 289–300. Available from: https://doi.org/10.1016/j.neuroimage.2012.07.004.

Casswell, S. (2013). Vested interests in addiction research and policy. Why do we not see the corporate interests of the alcohol industry as clearly as we see those of the tobacco industry? *Addiction*, *108*(4), 680–685. Available from: https://doi.org/10.1111/add.12011.

Center for Open Science. (n.d.). *A brief history of COS*. In the beginning. Retrieved June 30, 2019, from <https://cos.io/about/brief-history-cos-2013-2017/>.

Chalmers, I. (1993). The cochrane collaboration: Preparing, maintaining, and disseminating systematic reviews of the effects of health care. *Annals of the New York Academy of Sciences*, *703*(1 Doing More Go), 156–165. Available from: https://doi.org/10.1111/j.1749-6632.1993.tb26345.x.

Chambers, C. D. (2013). Registered reports: A new publishing initiative at Cortex. *Cortex*, *49* (3), 609–610. Available from: https://doi.org/10.1016/J.CORTEX.2012.12.016.

Chan, A.-W., Pello, A., Kitchen, J., Axentiev, A., Virtanen, J. I., Liu, A., & Hemminki, E. (2017). Association of trial registration with reporting of primary outcomes in protocols and publications. *JAMA*, *318*(17), 1709–1711. Available from: https://doi.org/10.1001/jama.2017.13001.

Claesen, A., Gomes, S.L.B.T., Tuerlinckx, F., & Vanpaemel, W. (2019). *Preregistration: Comparing dream to reality*. Available from: https://doi.org/10.31234/osf.io/d8wex.

Clark, W. R., & Golder, M. (2014). Big data, causal inference, and formal theory: Contradictory trends in political science? *PS - Political Science and Politics*, *48*(1), 65–70. Available from: https://doi.org/10.1017/S1049096514001759.

Cohen, J. (1962). The statistical power of abnormal-social psychological research: A review. *The Journal of Abnormal and Social Psychology*, *65*(3), 145–153. Available from: https://doi.org/10.1037/h0045186.

Cohen, J. (1992). Statistical power analysis. *Current Directions in Psychological Science, 1*(3), 98–101. Available from: https://doi.org/10.1111/1467-8721.ep10768783.

Contopoulos-Ioannidis, D. G., Ntzani, E. E., & Ioannidis, J. P. A. (2003). Translation of highly promising basic science research into clinical applications. *The American Journal of Medicine, 114*, 477–484. Available from: https://doi.org/10.1016/S0002-9343(03)00013-5.

Cook, D. A., Levinson, A. J., & Garside, S. (2011). Method and reporting quality in health professions education research: A systematic review. *Medical Education, 45*(3), 227–238. Available from: https://doi.org/10.1111/j.1365-2923.2010.03890.x.

Cristea, I. A., & Ioannidis, J. P. A. (2018). P values in display items are ubiquitous and almost invariably significant: A survey of top science journals. *PLoS One, 13*(5), e0197440. Available from: https://doi.org/10.1371/journal.pone.0197440.

Da Silva, R. (2015). *Selecting for impact: New data debunks old beliefs*. Retrieved June 30, 2019, from Frontiers Blog website: <https://blog.frontiersin.org/2015/12/21/4782/>.

De Angelis, C. (2004). Clinical trial registration a statement from the international committee of medical journal editors special report. *Issue of the New England Journal of Medicine, 351*, 1337–1338. Available from: https://doi.org/10.1161/01.CIR.0000158823.53941.BE.

Dechartres, A., Ravaud, P., Atal, I., Riveros, C., & Boutron, I. (2016). *Association between trial registration and treatment effect estimates: A meta-epidemiological study*. Available from: https://doi.org/10.1186/s12916-016-0639-x.

Devaney, T. A. (2001). Statistical significance, effect size, and replication: What do the journals say? *The Journal of Experimental Education, 69*(3), 310–320. Available from: https://doi.org/10.1080/00220970109599490.

Dumas-Mallet, E., Button, K. S., Boraud, T., Gonon, F., & Munafò, M. R. (2017). Low statistical power in biomedical science: A review of three human research domains. *Royal Society Open Science, 4*(2), 160254. Available from: https://doi.org/10.1098/rsos.160254.

Duyx, B., Urlings, M. J. E., Swaen, G. M. H., Bouter, L. M., & Zeegers, M. P. (2017). Scientific citations favor positive results: A systematic review and meta-analysis. *Journal of Clinical Epidemiology, 88*, 92–101. Available from: https://doi.org/10.1016/J.JCLINEPI.2017.06.002.

Dwan, K., Gamble, C., Williamson, P. R., & Kirkham, J. J. (2013). Systematic review of the empirical evidence of study publication bias and outcome reporting bias - An updated review. *PLoS One, 8*(7), e3081. Available from: https://doi.org/10.1371/journal.pone.0066844.

Easley, R. W., Madden, C. S., & Gray, V. (2013). A tale of two cultures: Revisiting journal editors' views of replication research. *Journal of Business Research, 66*, 1457–1459. Available from: https://doi.org/10.1016/j.jbusres.2012.05.013.

Emerson, G. B., Warme, W. J., Wolf, F. M., Heckman, J. D., Brand, R. A., & Leopold, S. S. (2010). Testing for the presence of positive-outcome bias in peer review. *Archives of Internal Medicine, 170*(21), 1934–1939. Available from: https://doi.org/10.1001/archinternmed.2010.406.

Errington, T. M., Iorns, E., Gunn, W., Tan, F. E. L., Lomax, J., & Nosek, B. A. (2014). An open investigation of the reproducibility of cancer biology research. *ELife, 3*. Available from: https://doi.org/10.7554/eLife.04333.

Fanelli, D. (2010). "Positive" results increase down the hierarchy of the sciences. *PLoS One, 5* (4), e10068. Available from: https://doi.org/10.1371/journal.pone.0010068.

Finkel, E. J., Eastwick, P. W., & Reis, H. T. (2015). Best research practices in psychology: Illustrating epistemological and pragmatic considerations with the case of relationship science. *Journal of Personality and Social Psychology, 108*(2), 275–297. Available from: https://doi.org/10.1037/pspi0000007.

Fraser, H., Parker, T., Nakagawa, S., Barnett, A., & Fidler, F. (2018). Questionable research practices in ecology and evolution. *PloS One*, *13*(7), e0200303. Available from: https://doi.org/10.1371/journal.pone.0200303.

Funder, D. C., Levine, J. M., Mackie, D. M., Morf, C. C., Sansone, C., Vazire, S., & West, S. G. (2014). Improving the dependability of research in personality and social psychology: Recommendations for research and educational practice. *Personality and Social Psychology Review*, *18*(1), 3–12. Available from: https://doi.org/10.1177/1088868313507536.

Gelman, A., & Carlin, J. (2014). Beyond power calculations: Assessing type S (sign) and type M (magnitude) errors. *Perspectives on Psychological Science*, *9*(6), 641–651. Available from: https://doi.org/10.1177/1745691614551642.

Gelman, A., & Loken, E. (2014). The statistical crisis in science. *American Scientist*, *102*(6), 460. Available from: https://doi.org/10.1511/2014.111.460.

Gigerenzer, G. (2018). Statistical rituals: The replication delusion and how we got there. *Advances in Methods and Practices in Psychological Science*, *1*(2), 198–218. Available from: https://doi.org/10.1177/2515245918771329.

Gilovich, T., Vallone, R., & Tversky, A. (1985). The hot hand in basketball: On the misperception of random sequences. *Cognitive Psychology*, *17*(3), 295–314. Available from: https://doi.org/10.1016/0010-0285(85)90010-6.

Goldacre, B., Drysdale, H., Dale, A., Milosevic, I., Slade, E., Hartley, P., ... Mahtani, K. R. (2019). COMPare: A prospective cohort study correcting and monitoring 58 misreported trials in real time. *Trials*, *20*(1), 118. Available from: https://doi.org/10.1186/s13063-019-3173-2.

Gopal, A. D., Wallach, J. D., Aminawung, J. A., Gonsalves, G., Dal-Ré, R., Miller, J. E., & Ross, J. S. (2018). Adherence to the International Committee of Medical Journal Editors' (ICMJE) prospective registration policy and implications for outcome integrity: A cross-sectional analysis of trials published in high-impact specialty society journals. *Trials*, *19*(1). Available from: https://doi.org/10.1186/s13063-018-2825-y.

Greenhalgh, T. (1995). Commentary: Scientific heads are not turned by rhetoric. *BMJ (Clinical Research Ed.)*, *310*(6985), 987–988. Available from: https://doi.org/10.1136/bmj.310.6985.987.

Hammarfelt, B. (2017). Recognition and reward in the academy. *Aslib Journal of Information Management*, *69*(5), 607–623. Available from: https://doi.org/10.1108/AJIM-01-2017-0006.

Hardwicke, T. E., & Ioannidis, J. P. A. (2018). Populating the Data Ark: An attempt to retrieve, preserve, and liberate data from the most highly-cited psychology and psychiatry articles. *PLoS One*, *13*(8), e0201856. Available from: https://doi.org/10.1371/journal.pone.0201856.

Hardwicke, T. E., Wallach, J. D., Kidwell, M. C., & Ioannidis, J. P. A. (2019). An empirical assessment of transparency and reproducibility-related research practices in the social sciences (2014–2017). *In MetaArXiv*. Available from: https://doi.org/10.31222/osf.io/6uhg5.

Hendriksma, M., Joosten, M. H. M. A., Peters, J. P. M., Grolman, W., & Stegeman, I. (2017). Evaluation of the quality of reporting of observational studies in otorhinolaryngology - Based on the STROBE statement. *PLoS One*, *12*(1), e0169316. Available from: https://doi.org/10.1371/journal.pone.0169316.

Hensel, P. G. (2019). Supporting replication research in management journals: Qualitative analysis of editorials published between 1970 and 2015. *European Management Journal*, *37*(1), 45–57. Available from: https://doi.org/10.1016/j.emj.2018.03.004.

Heringa, J., Dumon, O., van der Lei, J., Sansone, S.-A., Brookes, A. J., Dillo, I., ... Wilkinson, M. D. (2016). The FAIR Guiding Principles for scientific data management and stewardship. *Scientific Data*, *3*(2), 160018. Available from: https://doi.org/10.1038/sdata.2016.18.

Héroux, M. E., Loo, C. K., Taylor, J. L., & Gandevia, S. C. (2017). Questionable science and reproducibility in electrical brain stimulation research. *PLoS One*, *12*(4). Available from: https://doi.org/10.1371/journal.pone.0175635.

Houtkoop, B. L., Chambers, C., Macleod, M., Bishop, D. V. M., Nichols, T. E., & Wagenmakers, E.-J. (2018). Data sharing in psychology: A survey on barriers and preconditions. *Vermorgen, Deriemaecker & Storms*, *1*(1), 70–85. Available from: https://doi.org/10.1177/2515245917751886.

Hutson, M. (2018). Artificial intelligence faces reproducibility crisis. Unpublished code and sensitivity to training conditions make many claims hard to verify. *Science*, *359*(6377), 725–726. Available from: https://doi.org/10.1126/science.359.6377.725.

Institute of Medicine (US) Committee on Conflict of Interest in Medical Research Education and Practice. (2009). Principles for identifying and assessing conflicts of interest. In B. Lo & M. J. Field (Eds.), *Conflict of interest in medical research, education, and practice* (pp. 44–61). Available from: https://doi.org/10.17226/12598.

Ioannidis, J. P. A. (2005). Why most published research findings are false. *PLoS Medicine*, *2*(8), e124. Available from: https://doi.org/10.1371/journal.pmed.0020124.

Ioannidis, J. P. A. (2008). Why most discovered true associations are inflated. *Epidemiology*, *19*(5), 640–648. Available from: https://doi.org/10.1097/EDE.0b013e31818131e7.

Ioannidis, J. P. A. (2012). Why science is not necessarily self-correcting. *Perspectives on Psychological Science*, *7*(6), 645–654. Available from: https://doi.org/10.1177/1745691612464056.

Ioannidis, J. P. A. (2018). Meta-research: Why research on research matters. *PLoS Biology*, *16*(3). Available from: https://doi.org/10.1371/journal.pbio.2005468.

Ioannidis, J. P. A., Tarone, R., & McLaughlin, J. K. (2011). The false-positive to false-negative ratio in epidemiologic studies. *Epidemiology (Cambridge, Mass.)*, *22*(4), 450–456. Available from: https://doi.org/10.1097/EDE.0b013e31821b506e.

Iqbal, S. A., Wallach, J. D., Khoury, M. J., Schully, S. D., & Ioannidis, J. P. A. (2016). Reproducible research practices and transparency across the biomedical literature. *PLoS Biology*, *14*(1), 1002333. Available from: https://doi.org/10.1371/journal.pbio.1002333.

Jarvis, M. F., & Williams, M. (2016). Irreproducibility in preclinical biomedical research: Perceptions, uncertainties, and knowledge gaps. *Trends in Pharmacological Sciences*, *37*(4), 290–302. Available from: https://doi.org/10.1016/j.tips.2015.12.001.

John, L. K., Loewenstein, G., & Prelec, D. (2012). Measuring the prevalence of questionable research practices with incentives for truth telling. *Psychological Science*, *23*(5), 524–532. Available from: https://doi.org/10.1177/0956797611430953.

Jones, K. S., Derby, P. L., & Schmidlin, E. A. (2010). An investigation of the prevalence of replication research in human factors. *Human Factors*, *52*(5), 586–595. Available from: https://doi.org/10.1177/0018720810384394.

Jordan, C.H., & Zanna, M.P. (2007). Not all experiments are created equal. In R. J. Sternberg, H. L. Roediger III, & D. F. Halpern (Eds.), *Critical thinking in psychology* (pp. 160–176). Available from: https://doi.org/10.1017/CBO9780511804632.011.

Junger, D. (1995). The rhetoric of research. Embrace scientific rhetoric for its power. *BMJ (Clinical Research Ed.)*, *311*(6996), 61. Available from: https://doi.org/10.1136/bmj.311.6996.61b.

Kaplan, R. M., & Irvin, V. L. (2015). Likelihood of null effects of large NHLBI clinical trials has increased over time. *PLoS One*, *10*(8), e0132382. Available from: https://doi.org/10.1371/journal.pone.0132382.

Kelly, C. D. (2006). Replicating empirical research in behavioral ecology: How and why it should be done but rarely ever is. *The Quarterly Review of Biology*, *81*(3), 221–236. Available from: https://doi.org/10.1086/506236.

Kerr, N. L. (1998). HARKing: Hypothesizing after the results are known. *Personality and Social Psychology Review*, *2*(3), 196–217. Available from: https://doi.org/10.1207/s15327957pspr0203_4.

Klein, R. A., Ratliff, K. A., Vianello, M., Adams, R. B., Bahník, Š., Bernstein, M. J., ... Nosek, B. A. (2014). Investigating variation in replicability: A "many labs" replication project. *Social Psychology*, *45*(3), 142–152. Available from: https://doi.org/10.1027/1864-9335/a000178.

Knudson, D. (2017). Confidence crisis of results in biomechanics research. *Sports Biomechanics*, *16*(4), 425–433. Available from: https://doi.org/10.1080/14763141.2016.1246603.

Krawczyk, M., & Reuben, E. (2012). Accountability in research policies and quality assurance (un)available upon request: Field experiment on researchers' willingness to share supplementary materials (un)available upon request: Field experiment on researchers' willingness to share supplementary materials. *Accountability in Research*, *19*, 175–186. Available from: https://doi.org/10.1080/08989621.2012.678688.

Lang, T. A., & Altman, D. G. (2015). Basic statistical reporting for articles published in biomedical journals: The "Statistical Analyses and Methods in the Published Literature" or the SAMPL guidelines. *International Journal of Nursing Studies*, *52*(1), 5–9. Available from: https://doi.org/10.1016/j.ijnurstu.2014.09.006.

Larivière, V., Gingras, Y., Sugimoto, C.R., & Tsou, A. (2014). *Team size matters: Collaboration and scientific impact since 1900*. Available from: https://doi.org/10.1002/asi.23266.

Lebel, E. P., Berger, D., Campbell, L., & Loving, T. J. (2017). *Falsifiability is not optional*. Available from: https://doi.org/10.1037/pspi0000106.

Liu, J., Li, J., Feng, L., Li, L., Tian, J., & Lee, K. (2014). Seeing Jesus in toast: Neural and behavioral correlates of face pareidolia. *Cortex*, *53*, 60–77. Available from: https://doi.org/10.1016/J.CORTEX.2014.01.013.

Lundh, A., Lexchin, J., Mintzes, B., Schroll, J. B., & Bero, L. (2017). Industry sponsorship and research outcome. *The Cochrane Database of Systematic Reviews*, *2*(2), MR000033. Available from: https://doi.org/10.1002/14651858.MR000033.pub3.

Makel, M. C., Plucker, J. A., & Hegarty, B. (2012). Replications in psychology research: How often do they really occur? *Perspectives on Psychological Science*, *7*(6), 537–542. Available from: https://doi.org/10.1177/1745691612460688.

Markowetz, F. (2015). Five selfish reasons to work reproducibly. *Genome Biology*, *16*(1), 274. Available from: https://doi.org/10.1186/s13059-015-0850-7.

Martin, G. N., & Clarke, R. M. (2017). Are psychology journals anti-replication? A snapshot of editorial practices. *Frontiers in Psychology*, *8*, 523. Available from: https://doi.org/10.3389/fpsyg.2017.00523.

Matosin, N., Frank, E., Engel, M., Lum, J. S., & Newell, K. A. (2014). Negativity towards negative results: A discussion of the disconnect between scientific worth and scientific culture. *Disease Models & Mechanisms*, *7*(2), 171–173. Available from: https://doi.org/10.1242/dmm.015123.

McCambridge, J., & Hartwell, G. (2015). Has industry funding biased studies of the protective effects of alcohol on cardiovascular disease? A preliminary investigation of prospective cohort studies. *Drug and Alcohol Review*, *34*(1), 58–66. Available from: https://doi.org/10.1111/dar.12125.

McCambridge, J., Hawkins, B., & Holden, C. (2014). Vested Interests in Addiction Research and Policy. The challenge corporate lobbying poses to reducing society's alcohol problems: insights from UK evidence on minimum unit pricing. *Addiction*, *109*(2), 199–205. Available from: https://doi.org/10.1111/add.12380.

McCambridge, J., & Mialon, M. (2018). Alcohol industry involvement in science: A systematic review of the perspectives of the alcohol research community. *Drug and Alcohol Review, 37*(5), 565–579. Available from: https://doi.org/10.1111/dar.12826.

Miłkowski, M., Hensel, W. M., & Hohol, M. (2018). Replicability or reproducibility? On the replication crisis in computational neuroscience and sharing only relevant detail. *Journal of Computational Neuroscience, 45*(3), 163–172. Available from: https://doi.org/10.1007/s10827-018-0702-z.

Moher, D., Dulberg, C. S., & Wells, G. A. (1994). Statistical power, sample size, and their reporting in randomized controlled trials. *Journal of the American Medical Association, 272*(2), 122–124. Available from: https://doi.org/10.1001/jama.272.2.122.

Moshontz, H., Campbell, L., Ebersole, C. R., Ijzerman, H., Urry, H. L., Forscher, P. S., ... Chartier, C. R. (2018). The psychological science accelerator: Advancing psychology through a distributed collaborative network. *Advances in Methods and Practices in Psychological Science, 1*(4), 501–515. Available from: https://doi.org/10.1177/2515245918797607.

Munafò, M.R. (2017). Marcus Munafò: "There's this conspiracy of silence around how science really works". Psychologist, 30, 46–49, Retrieved from: <https://issuu.com/thepsychologist/docs/psy1217preview>.

Munafò, M. R., Nosek, B. A., Bishop, D. V. M., Button, K. S., Chambers, C. D., Percie Du Sert, N., ... Ioannidis, J. P. A. (2017). A manifesto for reproducible science. *Nature Human Behaviour, 1*(1), 1–9. Available from: https://doi.org/10.1038/s41562-016-0021.

Naudet, F., Sakarovitch, C., Janiaud, P., Cristea, I., Fanelli, D., Moher, D., & Ioannidis, J. P. A. (2018). Data sharing and reanalysis of randomized controlled trials in leading biomedical journals with a full data sharing policy: Survey of studies published in the BMJ and PLOS Medicine. *BMJ (Online), 360*, 400. Available from: https://doi.org/10.1136/bmj.k400.

Nelson, L. D., Simmons, J., & Simonsohn, U. (2018). Psychology's renaissance. *Annual Review of Psycholgy, 69*(September 2017), 17.1–17.24. Available from: https://doi.org/10.1146/annurev-psych-122216-011836.

Netherlands Organisation for Scientific Research. (2016, July 16). *NWO makes 3 million available for Replication Studies pilot.* Retrieved June 30, 2019, from <https://www.nwo.nl/en/research-and-results/programmes/replication + studies/background>.

Neuliep, J. W., & Crandall, R. (1990). Editorial bias against replication research. *Journal of Social Behavior and Personality, 5*(4), 85–90. Retrieved from: https://search.proquest.com/openview/ecff1f2487c66017c85a0ead234c9168/1?cbl = 1819046&pq-origsite = gscholar.

Nickerson, R. S. (1998). Confirmation bias: A ubiquitous phenomenon in many guises. *In Review of General Psychology, 2.* Retrieved from: <http://psy2.ucsd.edu/~mckenzie/nickersonConfirmationBias.pdf>.

Nosek, B. A., Ebersole, C. R., DeHaven, A. C., & Mellor, D. T. (2018). The preregistration revolution. *Proceedings of the National Academy of Sciences of the United States of America, 115*(11), 201708274. Available from: https://doi.org/10.1073/pnas.1708274114.

Odutayo, A., Emdin, C. A., Hsiao, A. J., Shakir, M., Copsey, B., Dutton, S., ... Hopewell, S. (2017). Association between trial registration and positive study findings: Cross sectional study (Epidemiological Study of Randomized Trials-ESORT). *BMJ (Clinical Research Ed.), 356*, j917. Available from: https://doi.org/10.1136/bmj.j917.

Olson, C. M., Rennie, D., Cook, D., Dickersin, K., Flanagin, A., Hogan, J. W., ... Pace, B. (2002). Publication bias in editorial decision making. *Journal of the American Medical Association, 287* (21), 2825–2828. Available from: https://doi.org/10.1001/jama.287.21.2825.

Open Science Collaboration. (2015). Estimating the reproducibility of psychological science. *Science, 349*(6251). Available from: https://doi.org/10.1126/science.aac4716, aac4716–aac4716.

Panagiotou, O. A., & Ioannidis, J. P. A. (2012). Primary study authors of significant studies are more likely to believe that a strong association exists in a heterogeneous meta-analysis compared with methodologists. *Journal of Clinical Epidemiology*, *65*(7), 740–747. Available from: https://doi.org/10.1016/j.jclinepi.2012.01.008.

Papageorgiou, S. N., Xavier, G. M., Cobourne, M. T., & Eliades, T. (2018). Registered trials report less beneficial treatment effects than unregistered ones: A meta-epidemiological study in orthodontics. *Journal of Clinical Epidemiology*, *100*, 44–52. Available from: https://doi.org/10.1016/J.JCLINEPI.2018.04.017.

Prinz, F., Schlange, T., & Asadullah, K. (2011). Believe it or not: How much can we rely on published data on potential drug targets? *Nature Reviews Drug Discovery*, *10*(9). Available from: https://doi.org/10.1038/nrd3439-c1, 712–712.

Robb, S. L., Hanson-Abromeit, D., May, L., Hernandez-Ruiz, E., Allison, M., Beloat, A., ... Wolf, E. (2018). Reporting quality of music intervention research in healthcare: A systematic review. *Complementary Therapies in Medicine*, *38*, 24–41. Available from: https://doi.org/10.1016/j.ctim.2018.02.008.

Rosenthal, R. (1966). *Experimenter effects in behavioral research.* Retrieved from <https://psycnet.apa.org/record/1967-09647-000>.

Rosenthal, R. (1979). The file drawer problem and tolerance for null results. *Psychological Bulletin*, *86*(3), 638–641. Available from: https://doi.org/10.1037/0033-2909.86.3.638.

Rowhani-Farid, A., & Barnett, A. G. (2016). Has open data arrived at the British Medical Journal (BMJ)? An observational study. *BMJ Open*, *6*(10), e011784. Available from: https://doi.org/10.1136/bmjopen-2016-011784.

Scherer, R. W., Ugarte-Gil, C., Schmucker, C., & Meerpohl, J. J. (2015). Authors report lack of time as main reason for unpublished research presented at biomedical conferences: A systematic review. *Journal of Clinical Epidemiology*, *68*(7), 803–810. Available from: https://doi.org/10.1016/J.JCLINEPI.2015.01.027.

Schmidt, S. (2009). Shall we really do it again? The powerful concept of replication is neglected in the social sciences. *Review of General Psychology*, *13*(2), 90–100. Available from: https://doi.org/10.1037/a0015108.

Sedlmeier, P., & Gigerenzer, G. (1989). Do studies of statistical power have an effect on the power of studies? *Psychological Bulletin*, *105*. Available from: https://doi.org/10.1037/0033-2909.105.2.309.

Silberzahn, R., Uhlmann, E. L., Martin, D. P., Anselmi, P., Aust, F., Awtrey, E., ... Nosek, B. A. (2018). Many analysts, one data set: Making transparent how variations in analytic choices affect results. *Advances in Methods and Practices in Psychological Science*. Available from: https://doi.org/10.1177/2515245917747646.

Simmons, J. P., Nelson, L. D., & Simonsohn, U. (2011). False-positive psychology: Undisclosed flexibility in data collection and analysis allows presenting anything as significant. *Psychological Science*, *22*(11), 1359–1366. Available from: https://doi.org/10.1177/0956797611417632.

Simonsohn, U., Nelson, L. D., & Simmons, J. P. (2014). P-curve: A key to the file-drawer. *Journal of Experimental Psychology: General*, *143*(2), 534–547. Available from: https://doi.org/10.1037/a0033242.

Singleton, A. J. (1995). The rhetoric of research. Encourage spin: It provides context. *BMJ (Clinical Research Ed.)*, *311*(6996), 61. Available from: https://doi.org/10.1136/bmj.311.6996.61a.

Smaldino, P. E., & McElreath, R. (2016). The natural selection of bad science. *Royal Society Open Science*, *3*(9), 160384. Available from: https://doi.org/10.1098/rsos.160384.

Song, F., Parekh, S., Hooper, L., Loke, Y. K., Ryder, J., Sutton, A. J., ... Harvey, I. (2010). Dissemination and publication of research findings: An updated review of related biases. *Health Technology Assessment*, *14*(8), 1–220. Available from: https://doi.org/10.3310/hta14080.

Sterne, J.A.C., Egger, M., & Moher, D. (Eds.). (2011). Chapter 10: Addressing reporting biases. In J. P. T. Higgins, & S. Green (Eds.), *Cochrane handbook for systematic reviews of intervention* (Version 5). Retrieved from: <https://handbook-5-1.cochrane.org/chapter_10/table_10_1_a_definitions_of_some_types_of_reporting_biases.htm>.

Szucs, D., & Ioannidis, J. P. A. (2017). Empirical assessment of published effect sizes and power in the recent cognitive neuroscience and psychology literature. *PLoS Biology*, *15*(3), e2000797. Available from: https://doi.org/10.1371/journal.pbio.2000797.

Thelwall, M., Munafo, M., Mas-Bleda, A., Stuart, E., Makita, M., Weigert, V., ... Kousha, K. (2019). Is useful research data usually shared? An investigation of genome-wide association study summary statistics. *BioRxiv*, 622795. Available from: https://doi.org/10.1101/622795.

Tilburt, J. C., Miller, F. G., Jenkins, S., Kaptchuk, T. J., Clarridge, B., Bolcic-Jankovic, D., ... Curlin, F. A. (2010). Factors that influence practitioners' interpretations of evidence from alternative medicine trials. *Medical Care*, *48*(4), 341–348. Available from: https://doi.org/10.1097/MLR.0b013e3181ca3ee2.

Turner, L., Shamseer, L., Altman, D. G., Weeks, L., Peters, J., Kober, T., ... Moher, D. (2012). Consolidated standards of reporting trials (CONSORT) and the completeness of reporting of randomised controlled trials (RCTs) published in medical journals. *Cochrane Database of Systematic Reviews* (11). Available from: https://doi.org/10.1002/14651858.MR000030.pub2.

van Dijk, D., Manor, O., & Carey, L. B. (2014). Publication metrics and success on the academic job market. *Current Biology*, *24*(11), R516–R517. Available from: https://doi.org/10.1016/J.CUB.2014.04.039.

van Lent, M., IntHout, J., & Out, H. J. (2015). Peer review comments on drug trials submitted to medical journals differ depending on sponsorship, results and acceptance: A retrospective cohort study. *BMJ Open*, *5*(9), e007961. Available from: https://doi.org/10.1136/bmjopen-2015-007961.

Vanpaemel, W., Vermorgen, M., Deriemaecker, L., & Storms, G. (2015). Are we wasting a good crisis? The availability of psychological research data after the storm. *Collabra*, *1*(1). Available from: https://doi.org/10.1525/collabra.13.

Vines, T. H., Albert, A. Y. K., Andrew, R. L., Débarre, F., Bock, D. G., Franklin, M. T., ... Rennison, D. J. (2014). The availability of research data declines rapidly with article age. *Current Biology*, *24*(1), 94–97. Available from: https://doi.org/10.1016/j.cub.2013.11.014.

Wallach, J. D., Boyack, K. W., & Ioannidis, J. P. A. (2018). Reproducible research practices, transparency, and open access data in the biomedical literature, 2015–2017. *PLoS Biology*, *16*(11), e2006930. Available from: https://doi.org/10.1371/journal.pbio.2006930.

Wellcome Trust. (2017). Data, software and materials management and sharing policy. Retrieved June 19, 2019, from <https://wellcome.ac.uk/funding/guidance/data-software-materials-management-and-sharing-policy>.

Wolff, W., Baumann, L., & Englert, C. (2018). Self-reports from behind the scenes: Questionable research practices and rates of replication in ego depletion research. *PLoS One*, *13*(6). Available from: https://doi.org/10.1371/journal.pone.0199554.

Wu, L., Wang, D., & Evans, J. A. (2019). Large teams develop and small teams disrupt science and technology. *Nature*, *566*(7744), 378–382. Available from: https://doi.org/10.1038/s41586-019-0941-9.

Zarin, D. A., Tse, T., & Ide, N. C. (2005). Trial registration at ClinicalTrials.gov between May and October 2005. *The New England Journal of Medicine*, *353*. Available from: https://doi.org/10.1056/nejmsa053234.

Zarin, D. A., Tse, T., Williams, R. J., & Rajakannan, T. (2017). Update on trial registration 11 years after the ICMJE policy was established. *The New England Journal of Medicine*, *376*. Available from: https://doi.org/10.1056/NEJMsr1601330.

Zwaan, R. A., Etz, A., Lucas, R. E., & Donnellan, M. B. (2017). Making replication mainstream. *Behavioral and Brain Sciences*, *41*, 1–61. Available from: https://doi.org/10.1017/S0140525X17001972.

Section 2

Within the body and mind

Chapter 4

Alcohol and mental health: Co-occurring alcohol use and mental health disorders

Raffaella Margherita Milani and Luisa Perrino
University of West London, Psychology and Addiction Studies, London, United Kingdom

The prevalence of co-occurring alcohol use and mental health disorders

There is a strong linkage between alcohol use and mental health, with a wide range of mental health disorders being more prevalent in people who drink problematically. However, determining the prevalence of comorbid Alcohol Use Disorders (AUD) and Mental Health Disorders (MHD) is challenging because of the wide variation in the definitions, measurements, and instruments used to assess whether individuals met diagnostic criteria for AUD and any specific mental disorder (Anker & Kushner, 2019; Boden & Fergusson, 2011).

Mood disorders and Anxiety are particularly common in people with AUD (Kushner et al., 2012). The prevalence of depression in people seeking treatment for AUD ranges from 50 to 70% (Conner, Pinquart, & Gamble, 2009). A meta-analysis of 16 cross-sectional and longitudinal studies investigating the link between AUD and Major Depression (MD), confirmed that the presence of either condition doubles the risks of the second disorder, even after controlling for variations of measures of AUD and MD (Boden & Fergusson, 2011). Subjective measures of depression symptoms in the general population support the clinical findings. A survey based on 5828 respondents to the Health Survey for England found that the risk of alcohol dependence (determined by the amount of alcohol consumed) as well as the experience of alcohol dependence are significantly associated with higher levels of self-rated depression (Churchill & Farrell, 2017).

Research into the intersection between anxiety disorders (AD) and AUD found that up to 50% of individuals receiving treatment for problematic alcohol use also met diagnostic criteria for one or more AD (Chan, Dennis, &

The Handbook of Alcohol Use - Understandings from Synapse to Society.
DOI: https://doi.org/10.1016/B978-0-12-816720-5.00023-2

Funk, 2008; Kushner et al., 2005). Similarly, a synthesis of the major epidemiological studies showed that the risk for meeting diagnostic criteria for alcohol dependence more than doubled among individuals with an AD compared to those with no AD (Kushner, Krueger, Frye, & Peterson, 2008). Individuals with social anxiety (SA) seem particularly vulnerable to develop AUD (Buckner, Heimberg, Ecker, & Vinci, 2013). In the National Epidemiologic Survey on Alcohol and Related Conditions (NESARC) in USA, 48% of individuals with a lifetime diagnosis of Social Anxiety Disorder (SAD) also met criteria for a lifetime diagnosis of an AUD (Grant et al., 2005). People with an AUD and lifetime history of SAD generally experience more severe alcohol dependence and report more major depressive episodes, less peer social support, and lower occupational status than patients without SAD (Buckner et al., 2013). Research on the co-existence of AUD and Obsessive-Compulsive Disorders (OCD) is relatively scarce in comparison to other subtypes. However, the development of the Obsessive–Compulsive Drinking Scale (Anton et al., 1996) signifies the existence of an overlap between OCD and AUD. Also, occurrence of obsessive–compulsive symptoms has been commonly reported among alcohol dependent patients (Lima, Pechansky, Fleck, & De Boni, 2005). A cross-sectional study by Gentil et al. (2009) on 630 OCD patients from seven Brazilian university services, compared patients with and without AUD comorbidity. Out of the overall sample, 7.5% presented AUD comorbidity. Although the prevalence is lower than in other subtypes of AD, comorbidity showed clinical features that deserve special attention from mental health professionals, such as increased risk for suicidality, higher comorbidity with generalized anxiety and somatization disorders, and compulsive sexual behavior.

An issue in estimating and interpreting the prevalence of comorbid AUD and AD is that various subtypes (i.e., social phobia disorder, panic disorder, and generalized anxiety disorder) are often present at the same time in the same individual (Kushner et al., 2012). Another question is whether subtypes of anxiety disorders have a unique association with AUD, or whether each subtype individually contribute a similar increase in the overall risk for AUD. Modeling analysis on the NESARC database (N 43,093) was used to explore the relationship between risk for alcohol misuse and the shared versus unique components of several anxiety and depressive disorders. This analysis showed a strong positive relationship between risk for DSM-IV alcohol dependence and the shared components of the anxiety and depression diagnoses. However, the analysis also showed no relationship between risk for alcohol dependence and the unique components of those diagnoses. These findings are consistent with the idea that all anxiety and mood disorders contribute to general "negative emotionality", which, in turn, correlates with the risk for alcohol dependence (Kushner et al., 2012). These results support the development of a novel integrated "transdiagnostic" therapeutic protocol that focuses on common processes underlying multiple disorders, for mood and anxiety disorders (Vujanovic et al., 2017).

Post-traumatic stress disorder (PTSD) is also highly associated with alcohol dependence (Suh & Ressler, 2018). Particularly vulnerable groups are individuals who have been victim of childhood trauma (Brady & Back, 2012) and women affected by domestic violence (Kaysen et al, 2007). In addition, women have been found to be more likely to have experienced sexual abuse than men in both AUD and MHD clinical and community samples (Drapalski, Bennett, & Bellack, 2011; Gearon, Nidecker, Bellack, & Bennett, 2003). Veterans are also particularly vulnerable to this comorbidity. In a nationally representative sample of Veterans in US, one of every five Veterans with AUD also screened positive for PTSD (Norman, Haller, Hamblen, Southwick, & Pietrzak, 2018). The prevalence is even higher among Veterans seeking care, with up to two-thirds of those with AUD also having a diagnosis of PTSD (Seal et al., 2011). A high rate of AUD was also found in UK Veterans. For example, a recent UK study by Murphy and Turgoose (2019) investigated alcohol misuse and mental health in 403 treatment-seeking veterans, in comparison to the Armed Forces and the general population. They found that although both military samples reported significantly higher levels of AUD than the general population, treatment-seeking veterans were significantly more likely to report alcohol dependence and alcohol related harm than the two comparison groups.

Alcohol is also the most common substance of abuse amongst people with Bipolar Disorders, in a meta-analysis of 78 studies of comorbid bipolar disorder and substance use disorder, it was found that alcohol use was at 42%, followed by cannabis (20%), illicit drugs (17%), cocaine and amphetamine (11%) (Hunt, Malhi, Cleary, Lai, & Sitharthan, 2016). With regard to psychosis, the comorbidity of schizophrenia and AUDs is particularly problematic, as it is associated with depression, suicidality, medication nonadherence, chronic physical problems, homelessness, aggression, violence, incarceration, and high rates of hospitalization (e.g. Hunt, Large, Cleary, Lai, & Saunders, 2018). Individuals with schizophrenia spectrum disorders have three times the risk of heavy alcohol use relative to the general population (Hartz et al., 2014). One meta-analysis of individuals with schizophrenia found a lifetime prevalence of AUD of 24.3% and one American study reported that 36.4% of 404 participants had experienced AUD before their first episode of psychosis. A rarer but clinically significant psychotic disorder is alcohol-induced psychotic disorder (AIPD), which can occur with acute intoxication, alcohol withdrawal, as well as in patients with chronic alcohol use disorder (Jordaan & Emsley, 2014). A review of 21 studies found 0.4% lifetime prevalence of this disorder in the general population and 4.0% in patients with alcohol dependence (Engelhard, Touquet, Tansens, & De Fruyt, 2015). Although relatively rare, AIPD is a serious condition and is associated with high comorbidity with other psychiatric disorders, high re-hospitalization, mortality rates and suicidal behavior (Jordaan & Emsley, 2014).

Alcohol Use Disorders also co-occur at high prevalence with borderline personality disorder (BPD) and antisocial personality disorders (ASPD) (Helle, Watts, Trull, & Sher, 2019). In a recent review (Trull et al., 2018), of those individuals who met diagnostic criteria for BPD, 46%–49% also met diagnostic criteria for current AUD, and 59% for lifetime AUD. Among the general population or clinical samples of individuals with a current diagnosis of AUD or alcohol dependence, the prevalence of a BPD diagnosis was approximately 12%–17%. In the same population, ASPD diagnoses were slightly more prevalent than BPD diagnoses, ranging from 19% to 22%. However, the prevalence of AUD among those diagnosed with ASPD was as high as 68%.

The overlap between Attention Deficit Hyperactive Disorder (ADHD) and substance use disorders in general have been long documented (Magon & Müller, 2012). Data on adult ADHD comorbidity among individuals with AUD are limited, few studies have indicated that adult ADHD is comparatively low among individuals with AUD compared to those who use other substances (van de Glind, van Emmerik-van Oortmerssen, Carpentier, & Levin, 2013). Vice versa, the incidence of AUD in adults with ADHD has been found to be 33–44% (Rasmussen & Gillberg, 2000). While, in a German study of 91 adults with alcohol dependence, 20.9% (WURS-k) or 23.1% (DSM-IV diagnostic criteria) of the patients showed evidence of retrospective ADHD in childhood (Ohlmeier et al., 2008).

Finally, increased attention has recently been given to alcohol-related dementia in the elderly population. For example, a UK cohort study of people with a mean age of 56 found that drinking above 32 UK units of alcohol per week was associated with greater global impairment in cognitive function, as well as in memory and executive function 10 years later (Sabia et al., 2014), these data suggest that alcohol-related dementia represents an under-recognized mental disorder with both clinical and public mental health implications (Rao, 2014).

In conclusion, there is abundant evidence that the co-occurrence of AUD and MHD is highly prevalent and is associated with increased vulnerability, high level of risk to self and others, greater psychological and physical impairment and poor prognosis. Thus, failing to meet the needs of this population leads to serious consequences for the individual and society as a whole, it is therefore paramount that the health and social care sectors treat comorbidity as the norm, rather than the exception.

Etiological theories: what comes first?

There are three main models that explain the etiology of comorbid mental health disorders (MHD) and substance use disorders (SUD): (1) The secondary substance use disorder models, which suggests that MHD cause SUD;

(2) The secondary mental health disorders model, which implies that SUD cause MHD; (3) the common risk factor model, which suggests that there might be shared neurological and psychosocial vulnerabilities that increase the risk of both MHD and SUD. This section will define each model in the context of alcohol use disorders (AUD).

The secondary substance use disorder model

If MHD leads to AUD, by definition, a temporal association should be observed with the former preceding the latter. However, research on the order of onset produced inconclusive results. One limitation of this line of evidence is that the temporal sequence of the disorders does not necessarily imply causality (Anker & Kushner, 2019). In addition, it is difficult to establish the exact start of either MHD or AUD because both disorders develop gradually, hence data on order of onset are not very helpful to determine causality, especially in regard to schizophrenia or bipolar disorders (Mueser, Drake, & Wallach,1998). However, research on anxiety disorders (AD) has produced some supportive evidence of this direction of causality. For example, Kushner, Sher, and Beitman (1990) have shown that the onset of AD preceded alcohol misuse in up to three-quarters of individuals who had both conditions, subsequent studies demonstrated that this is true especially for those who had social anxiety disorders SAD (Buckner, et al., 2013). Grant et al. (2005) also found that the AD persisted following a period of abstinence from alcohol, indicating that it was an independent diagnosis. There are three explanatory models for the observed causal link: the "self-medication hypothesis" (Khantzian, 2013; Quitkin, Rifkin, Kaplan, & Klein, 1972), "tension reduction" (Conger, 1956) and "stressresponse dampening" (Sher & Levenson, 1982). These three models are based on the concept that people with AD attempt to relieve negative consequences of these conditions by drinking alcohol to cope with their symptoms, the "negative reinforcement" (an unpleasant state is successfully taken away in response to drinking) eventually leads to the later onset of AUD (Smith & Randall, 2019). Many studies investigating motivations for using alcoholsupport this hypothesis (see Anker & Kushner, 2019; Smith & Randall, 2012 for a review on the topic), however, most laboratory studies did not find a direct impact of alcohol on the physiological response among those with AD (see Tran & Smith, 2008). One possible explanation for these seemingly incongruent results is that a person's expectations about alcohol's effects can motivate drinking independently of alcohol's actual physiological effects, these expectations influence the likelihood of drinking to cope which in turn increases the risk of excessive drinking (e.g., Abrams & Kushner, 2004). In line with this explanation, men with elevated anxiety regarding heterosexual interactions who were told that alcohol enhances social performance reported less anxiety after drinking before a heterosexual social interaction than men who were told that alcohol impairs social, performance (Keane & Lisman, 1980). Also, men with SA who held stronger tension reduction expectancies reported less anticipatory social anxiety than men who expected less tension reduction from drinking (Abrams & Kushner, 2004). Finally, individuals with AD who reported drinking to cope had a fivefold increased risk for developing alcohol dependence within 3 years; in contrary, people with AD who did not drink to cope showed the same level of risk for developing alcohol dependence as people with no anxiety disorders (Menary, Kushner, Maurer, & Thuras, 2011).

Buckner et al. (2013) proposed a biopsychosocial model for the comorbidity of substance use and social anxiety. Fig. 4.1 is an adaptation of this

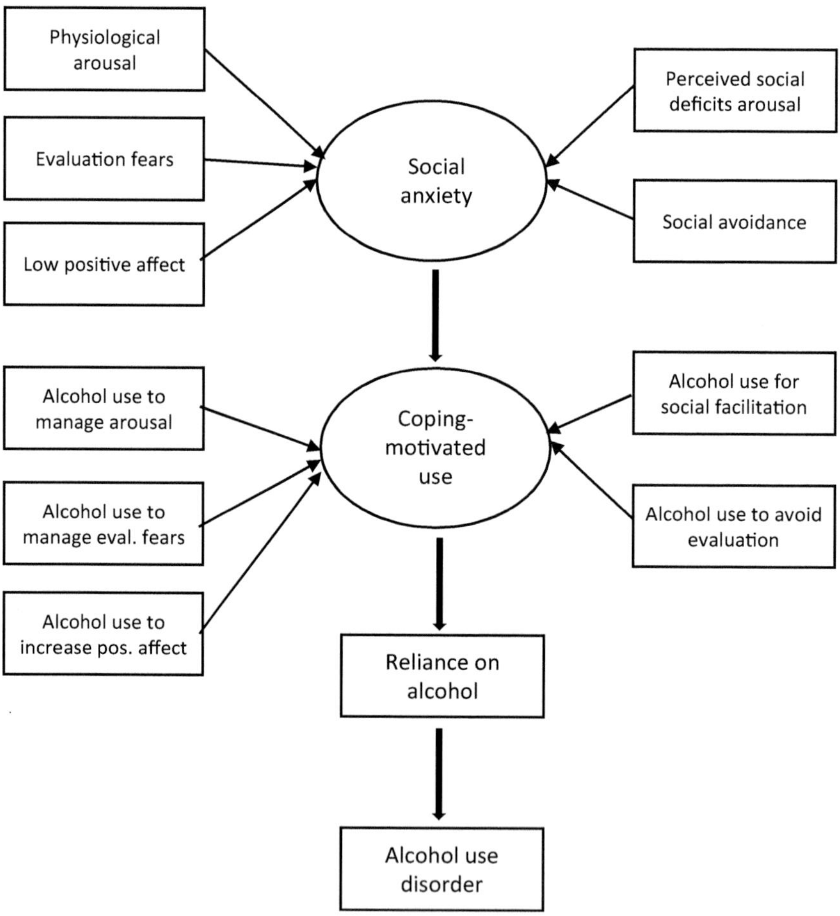

FIGURE 4.1 Proposed model of the relationship between social anxiety and substance used disorders. *Credit: Adapted from: Buckner, J. D., Heimberg, R. G., Ecker, A. H., & Vinci, C. (2013). A biopsychosocial model of social anxiety and substance use.* Depression and Anxiety, 30*(3), 276–284.*

model applied to alcohol use. The graph illustrates that socially anxious individuals may use alcohol to manage various components of social anxiety, for example to cope with unpleasant affective states as well as to increase positive affect (Abrams, Kushner, & Reinertsen, 2002). Some may use alcohol to avoid negative evaluation by their peers (Byers, Yaffe, Covinsky, Friedman, & Bruce, 2010), some may use it to enhance enjoyment during social events (Alden & Wallace, 1995). Finally, the original model suggests that some socially anxious individuals may use substances to help decrease physiological arousal, for example, a study on people with social anxiety found that cannabidiol (CBD) decreased heart rate and decreased self-reported state of social anxiety prior to a speech task (Bergamaschi, Queiroz, Chagas, de Oliveira, & De Martinis, 2011). However, as previously reported (Abrams & Kushner, 2004), the experience of anxiety attenuation following alcohol consumption seems to be determined more by individuals' expectancies, believes and motivations rather than the actual physiological response.

Research has shown that alcohol expectancies mediate alcohol consumption also in people with PSTD who have experienced trauma. A study by Nishith, Mueser, and Morse (2019) compared a clinical sample of individuals with severe mental illness (SMI), PSTD and comorbid AUD with a sample of patients with similar mental health diagnosis but no AUD. They found that compared to people with SMI, PTSD, but no alcohol use disorder, those who had co-occurring AUD endorsed more positive expectancies for the effects of alcohol on increasing social and sexual behavior, and the experience of power and pleasure, but not for the effects on reducing tension and promoting relaxation. The authors suggest that AUD in individuals with SMI and PTSD may be related to attempts to cope with specific symptom clusters of PTSD, such as feelings of numbness and avoidance.

The "alleviation of dysphoria" model has been studied mainly in the context of bipolar disorders and schizophrenia (Mueser et al. 1998). This model holds that people with severe mental illness start drinking alcohol to alleviate the feelings of sadness, gloom, inadequacy, discontent, isolation, and boredom. Consistently with this model, Laudet, Magura, Vogel, and Knight (2004) compared reasons for using substances in individuals suffering from bipolar disorder, schizophrenia, and depression. Overall, they found that alcohol was the most often cited as "substances used first" (65%). Those diagnosed with a bipolar disorder were significantly more likely to cite wanting to fit in with peers as the reason to start using alcohol. Counterintuitively, those with a primary diagnosis of schizophrenia showed a significantly lower likelihood of citing emotional or mental issues as a reason to start using drugs and alcohol in comparison to the other two groups. The role of alcohol as social lubricant for people with severe mental health disorders was demonstrated also by Thornton et al. (2012). Their study showedthat reasons for using substances varied according to substance and mental disorder. As shown in Table 4.1, overall, alcohol was primarily used to

TABLE 4.1 Percentage of study 5 participants endorsing reasons for tobacco, alcohol and cannabis use, collected via free response.

	Substance					
	Tobacco (n = 99)		Alchol (n = 81)		Cannabis (n = 77)	
Main reasons for substance use	Pyschotic disorder (n = 56)	Depression (n = 43)	Pyschotic disorder (n = 46)	Depression (n = 37)	Pyschotic disorder (n = 47)	Depression (n = 30)
Social						
To be social/gives me a social life	0%	7.0%	21.7%	29.7%	6.4%	26.7%
Peer pressure, to be a part of a group	3.6%	2.3%	2.2%	0%	2.1%	3.3%
Its available	3.6%	7.0%	2.2%	0%	8.5%	10.0%
To celebrate	0%	0%	4.3%	2.7%	0%	0%
Pleasure						
To relieve boredom	21.4%	20.9%	8.7%	8.1%	8.5%	0%
To feel good, to make me feel happy	10.7%	7.0%	13.0%	18.9%	21.3%	16.7%
To relax, give me a mellow mood	10.7%	11.6%	10.9%	13.5%	31.9%	33.3%
To get drunk or high, I like the effect, to have fun	7.1%	7.0%	13.0%	13.5%	29.8%	26.7%
I like the taste, good with a meal	3.6%	7.0%	10.9%	10.8%	4.3%	0%

Copying						
Cravings, addiction, habit	62.5%	48.8%	2.2%	8.1%	10.6%	16.7%
Relieve tension and stress, calm me	26.8%	27.9%	15.2%	18.9%	6.4%	23.3%
Take away sad feelings, cheer me up, loneliness	0%	4.7%	28.3%	16.2%	4.3%	10.0%
Block everything out, escape reality	0%	0%	19.6%	13.5%	8.5%	6.7%
Illness						
Help side effects of medication	0%	2.3%	4.3%	0%	0%	0%
Negative affect relief, stop me from being suicidal	0%	0%	6.5%	10.8%	2.1%	3.3%
Get away from hallucinations and paranoia	0%	0%	4.3%	0%	4.3%	0%
Pain management	0%	0%	0%	0%	4.3%	3.3%

Credit: Taken from: Thornton, L. K., Baker, A. L., Lewin, T. J., Kay-Lambkin, F. J., Kavanagh, D., Richmond, R., ... & Johnson, M. P. (2012). Reasons for substance use among people with mental disorders. *Addictive Behaviors, 37*(4), 427–434.

cope (79%), and for social motives (75%). Interestingly, "To be social/gives me a social life" was cited much more frequently by participants with psychosis (21.7%) as opposed to those with depression (6.4%), for whom cannabis was the preferred social lubricant. In addition, for the psychosis group, to "Take away sad feelings, cheer me up, loneliness" was the most frequently cited coping motive (28.3%). In line with these findings, Drake, Wallach, Alverson, and Mueser (2002) proposed that the emphasis on biological and pharmacological factors in the literature on "dual diagnosis" has diverted attention from important psychosocial issues. The authors suggest that factors such as social networks, expectancies of drug effects, boredom, dysphoria, unemployment, and poverty "are critically important in the presentation, development and course of substance abuse and in the process of helping people attain sobriety, stable abstinence and recovery" (p. 100).

Studies into gender differences suggested that women are more prone to drink to cope with symptoms of AD (negative reinforcement) (Norberg, Norton, Olivier, & Zvolensky, 2010) whereas men are more likely to drink to enhance their experience (positive reinforcement) (Peltier et al, 2019). Recent research also demonstrated gender differences in stress-related alcohol use might be partly related to the role of ovarian hormones in regulating stress-response (see Peltier et al., 2019 for a review on gender differences in stress-related alcohol use).

In conclusion, there is evidence to support the secondary AUD model, however, this should be taken with caution as it is associated with at least two limitations: the analyses often rely on retrospective self-reported data and findings derive from clinical samples can inflate prevalence estimates of self-medication, especially if alcohol-dependent individuals are evaluated during acute alcohol withdrawal (Mueser et al., 1998). Despite these limitations, this line of research suggests that interventions for co-occurring AUD and AD, especially PTSD, should be gender sensitive and consider people's alcohol expectancies and reasons to drink.

The secondary mental health disorders model

The second hypothesis proposes that AUD can induce MHD via biological, psychological, or social processes. For example, Boden and Ferguson's (2011) metanalysis found that the most plausible causal association between AUD and major depression (MD) is the one in which AUD increase the risk of MD, rather than vice versa. Churchill and Farrell's (2017) study on 5828 respondents from the Health Survey for England (HSE), confirmed the same direction of causality. They also found that higher levels of depression were associated with intensity (the volume of alcohol consumed) as opposed to frequency of alcohol consumption. There is some evidence that gender might moderate order of onset, whereby depression is often an antecedent of drinking problems among women but is experienced as a consequence of drinking in men (Schutte et al., 1995; Churchill & Farrell, 2017). AUD has also been found to precipitate or exacerbate anxiety disorders (AD) and psychosis. The section below illustrates some of the biological and mechanisms and neurological structures underpinning these causal links.

Biological and neurological mechanisms

One explanation of the biological mechanism through which AUD can cause MD is that alcohol exposure may generatemetabolic changes that also increase the risk of MD. For instance, McEachin, Keller, Saunders, and McInnis (2008) found evidence that exposure to ethanol leads to reductions in the production of MTHFR (methylenetetrahydrofolate reductase), an enzyme related to folate metabolism. Reduced folate levels have, in turn, been linked to increased risks of MD, indicating a possible causal link between AUD and MD through decreased MTHFR production. Another stream of research focuses on the effects that alcohol consumption has on the neurocognitive processes underlying MD. For Instance, trait rumination has been noted to be prevalent in those who suffer with depression (Mandell, Siegle, Shutt, Feldmiller, & Thase, 2014). Mandell et al. (2014) suggest that it is a risk factor towards more intense and harder to treat depressions. Trait rumination is the tendency to engage in sustained and repetitive thinking regarding negative thoughts about events that have happened in the past. The cognitive processes that have been suggested to be important to rumination are automatic attention to negative information, and difficulty disengaging from negative information. Therefore, it is hypothesized there is a lack of cognitive control mechanisms in place to aid regulation of attention, emotion, and emotional processing (Menke, 2019). Mandell et al. (2014) examined this set of mechanisms using 29 adults with a diagnosis of MD. The participants completed an FMRI protocol, self-report questionnaires (10 measures on rumination, emotional control, and intrusiveness) and qualitative data from clinical interviews. The study found that depressed individuals had primarily greater sustained amygdala activity and that related areas within the brain such as the hippocampus, dorsal lateral pre frontal cortex, anterior insula, medial frontal gyrus and posterior cingulate were activated depending on the type of rumination. However, notably the higher amygdala activation was most important as this can connote poorer emotional control, higher attention to stimuli that trigger negative emotional responses and dysfunctional control in response to internal feelings which may be ruminated upon. This may cause more emotional discomfort and distress for the individual. In people with chronic AUD, the amygdala is impaired in its function due to plastic changes dictated by gene expression such as down regulation of oxyreductases (Dager et al., 2015). This is important for energy stores and metabolism in the brain. With chronic alcohol use these functions are diminished suggesting reduced neuronal energy stores and additionally higher oxidative damage in the brain. In turn chronic alcohol use can lead to reduced neurogenesis which affects plasticity and therefore an individual's response to novel and stressful conditions (Kryger & Wilce, 2010). In consideration of this damage through alcohol use a circular issue may occur where stimuli become more stressful, emotional regulation becomes increasingly more difficult, and therefore this leads to more reliance of alcohol and its effects of dampening the amygdala when intoxicated (Roberto, Gilpin, & Siggins, 2012). Therefore, an already dysfunctional hyperactive or hyperreactive amygdala (as seen in dual diagnosis cases) will be further compromised through use of alcohol in attempt to self-medicate rumination, sadness, to cope with anxiety or depression symptoms.

In reference to anxiety disorders, there is evidence that chronic alcohol dependence results in an overall GABA deficiency that may induce anxiety (Smith & Randall, 2012). Withdrawal periods also can induce changes in the brain, which can include excessive activity (i.e., hyperexcitability) of certain brain systems (i.e., the limbic system and the norepinephrine system) (Kushner et al., 1990), both of which are involved in triggering panic attacks (Graeff & Del-Ben, 2008). Repeated withdrawal episodes can lead to neural adaptation that makes the drinker more susceptible to anxiety and exacerbates stress-induced negative affect when alcohol intake stops (Breese, Sinha, & Heilig, 2011). This explains why people with alcohol dependence who are recently abstinent report increased feelings of anxiety, panic, and phobic-like behaviors in the short term, and symptoms of autonomic activity (i.e., sympathetic activation, such as increased heart rate and faster/shallower breathing) and persistent anxiety across prolonged withdrawal.

The amygdala has been signified as one of the most supported regions that shows hyperactivity or hyperreactivity in people with AUD during fMRI and PET neuroimaging (Niciu & mason, 2014). Withdrawal induced anxiety is part of the functional rebound changes from an excess of GABA from chronic use of alcohol and subsequent high glutamatergic expression. Considering that the Amygdala is primarily GABAergic, the disinhibition of downstream brain regions can be problematic for the individual who has chronically used or is dependent on alcohol. Downstream brain regions that innervate the central amygdala are outlined by Pitkanen (2000) and include the ventral tegmental area (important for reward and production of forebrain dopamine), the locus coeruleus (important for stress response) and the medial pre frontal cortex (mPFC). The mPFC has been outlined as critical in processing emotionally salient information and facilitates behavioral responses to cues. Deregulation of this area has been implicated in addiction and in other neuropsychiatric disorders such as schizophrenia, depression, mood, and anxiety disorders (Stamatakis et al., 2014).

In reference to psychosis, alcohol can precipitate psychotic symptoms during acute intoxication, withdrawal, or chronic use (Archibald, Brunette, Wallin, & Green, 2019). In one study in emergency departments, 18.9% of those with a diagnosis of substance-induced psychosis had alcohol as the primary substance (Caton et al., 2005), patients with alcohol-related psychosis have a 5%–30% risk of developing a chronic schizophrenia-like syndrome (Glass, 1989). In chronic alcohol dependent patients, lack of thiamine is a common condition. Thiamine deficiency is known to lead to Wernicke-Korsakoff syndrome, which is characterized by neurological findings on examination and a confusional-apathetic state (Perälä et al., 2010).

Psychosocial factors

From a psychosocial perspective, it can be argued that both anxiety and depression can be caused by the social and financial sequalae of alcohol dependence, for example loss of employment, financial difficulties, family breakdown, homelessness, ill health and isolation (e.g. Foster, Powell, Marshall, & Peters, 1999). However, studies that have accounted for the possible influence of a range of life circumstances in the causal link between AUD and major depression have found that these links persist even after controlling for social and environmental factors (Hasin & Grant, 2002; Paljärvi et al., 2009; Sihvola, et al., 2008).On the contrary, there is support evidence for life stressors to generate anxiety disorders. There are least two ways that can explain this causal link: first, the consistent presence of life stressors can intensify anxiety symptoms among already vulnerable individuals. Second, as explained in the earlier section, alcohol use in the presence of stress stimuli may interfere with extinction-based learning necessary for normal adaptation to stressors. Thus, AUD can lead to anxiety through a combination of greater levels of life stress coupled with poor coping skills (Smith & Randall, 2012).

The common risk factors model

Recent research provides increasing support for the perspective that AUD and co-occurring MHD share underlying, mutually exacerbating, neurological and psychosocial processes.

Common biological risk factors have received considerable support in the context of Borderline Personality Disorders (BPD) and Antisocial Personality Disorders (ASPD). BPD and ASPD tend to relate similarly to AUD in terms of impulsivity, negative affect, and externalizing correlates; this commonality has been linked to the sharing of general personality traits, particularly antagonism and impulsivity (disinhibition) (Helle et al., 2019). For example, using a multivariate behavioral genetic twin design, Slutske et al. (2002) found that the genetic variance associated with impulsivity, novelty seeking, and aggression, accounted for 40% of the genetic variance in alcohol dependence. These findings support the notion that the overlap of impulsivity and AUD originates from shared genetic mechanisms.

Bornovalova, et al. (2013) have demonstrated the same for AUD and BPD. This common genetic mechanism appears to generate externalizing behavior and psychopathology generally, including AUD, other substance use disorder, conduct disorder, and antisocial behavior (Helle et al., 2019).

Genetic research has also found evidence of increased risks of both AUD and major depression (MD) among individuals with specific genotypes (Boden & Fergusson, 2011). For instance, studies by Wang et al. (2004) and Luo et al. (2005) found that variants of the muscarinic acetylcholine receptor M2 (CRHM2) gene are related to increased risks of both disorders. Similarly, several polymorphisms (genetic variations) of the brain-derived neurotrophic factor (BDNF) protein correlate with co-occurring schizophrenia and alcohol dependence but not with alcohol dependence alone, suggesting that these polymorphisms may contribute to a specific vulnerability to these co-occurring disorders (Hartz et al., 2017).

From a psycho-social perspective, trauma is a risk factor for both MHD and SUD, including AUD. Rates of trauma exposure in psychiatric inpatients range from 53% to 100% (McFarlane, Bookless, & Air, 2001), while about 90% of individuals with SMI (severe mental illness) report having experienced at least one traumatic event, most of whom have been multiply traumatized (Goodman, Dutton, & Harris, 1997; Mueser et al., 1998). As illustrated in the epidemiological section, rates of AUD among people with PTSD is high. There is growing evidence of the shared neurobiological mechanisms that link AUD and PTSD. Neuroimaging studies have found that dysregulation in the hippocampus and the amygdala are implicated in both PTSD and AUD (Logue, et al., 2018; Norman, et al., 2012). The amygdala has been shown to be reduced in size within children who endured early life stress and/or trauma such as physical abuse, low socioeconomic status, and neglect (Hanson et al., 2015). Additionally, these structural changes have been identified in individuals who have survived a life-threatening illness or worked in critical care with life threatening or terminal illness and whom display PTSD symptoms from their ordeal (Matsuoka, Yamawaki, Inagaki, Akechi, & Uchitomi, 2003; Stevens, et al., 2017). Hyperactive and/or hyper-reactive activity in the amygdala (Gilpin & Weiner, 2017) have been shown in many studies concerning PTSD in combat veterans and interpartner violence studies (Poirier, Cordero, & Sandi, 2013). Furthermore, women who have undergone intimate partner violence and who suffer with PTSD showed hyperactivation in the amygdala when exposed to fearful faces (Fonzo, et al., 2010). Similar to individuals diagnosed with PTSD, people who are diagnosed with AUD exhibit functional and structural changes in relation to the amygdala. Lower Amygdala volume has been reported in individuals with AUD (Dager, et al., 2015) and has been associated with higher alcohol drinking up to 6 months after imaging. However, to date there is a paucity of neuro imaging studies that investigate individuals with comorbid PTSD and AUD. One study by Nikolova, Knodt, Radtke, and Hariri (2016) used blood-oxygen-level-dependent functional magnetic resonance imaging to explore the relationship between alcohol use and levels of stress in a sample of 759 undergraduate students and demonstrated that problem drinking was highest in the context of stress. The study also showed that participants with higher levels of problem drinking displayed either high threat-related reactivity of the amygdala combined with low reward-related activity of the ventral striatum (VS) or low threat-related reactivity of the amygdala combined with high reward-related activity of the VS. These results suggest that the relationship between neural activity and stress-related AUD may not be simply related to activity in one brain region, but rather may depend on convergent or divergent (re)activity in multiple brain regions. Semple et al. (2000) used positron emission tomography to compare regional blood flow (rCBF) in patients with PTSD, alcohol and cocaine misuse at rest and during an auditory continuous performance task (ACPT). They found higher rCBF in the right amygdala and left parahippocampal gyrus, and lower blood flow in the frontal cortical regions for individuals with comorbid PTSD and alcohol or cocaine misuse in comparison to healthy controls, however one limitation of this study was that there were no PTSD-only and AUD-only comparison groups. A recent line of research has proposed that medial prefrontal cortex subregion (mPFC) projections to extended amygdala nuclei control fear and drug-seeking behaviors, and that dysregulation of these top-down PFC projections may lead to the abnormal fear conditioning that characterises PTSD and the compulsive drug-seeking behavior in AUD (Peters, Kalivas, & Quirk, 2009). It has been suggested that the medial prefrontal cortex (mPFC) is impaired over time with excessive drinking and these impairments are similar to those seen in research regarding repeated stress. Accordingly, Holmes et al. (2012) examined the effects of excessive alcohol exposure on mice and found that there was a diminished capacity of the mPFC to mediate fear extinction. Below is a description of the fear/addiction circuitry to illustrate the connection. The mPFC is included in the pre-frontal cortex (PFC) and therefore is a part of this network. It has been suggested to be integral in working with the amygdala which is influenced by the Hypothalamus Pituitary Axis (HPA) Axis and other fear circuitry. This circuitry is important in dampening emotional responses to fear, and its dysregulation plays a part in self-medication using alcohol to cope with internal and external stressors that are present for individuals who suffer with PTSD, see Fig. 4.2 (Suh & Ressler, 2018).

The above model is taken from Suh & Ressler, (2018) and it shows the fear and addiction circuitry that is discussed in their review of common biological mechanisms of AUD and PTSD. The PFC and amygdala are mutually connected and the amygdala projects to the Nucleus Acumens via glutamatergic innervations. All areas illustrated above receive projections from dopamine neurons in the ventral tegmental area (VTA). The major components of the HPA include the paraventricular nucleus (PN) of the hypothalamus and the pituitary and adrenal glands.

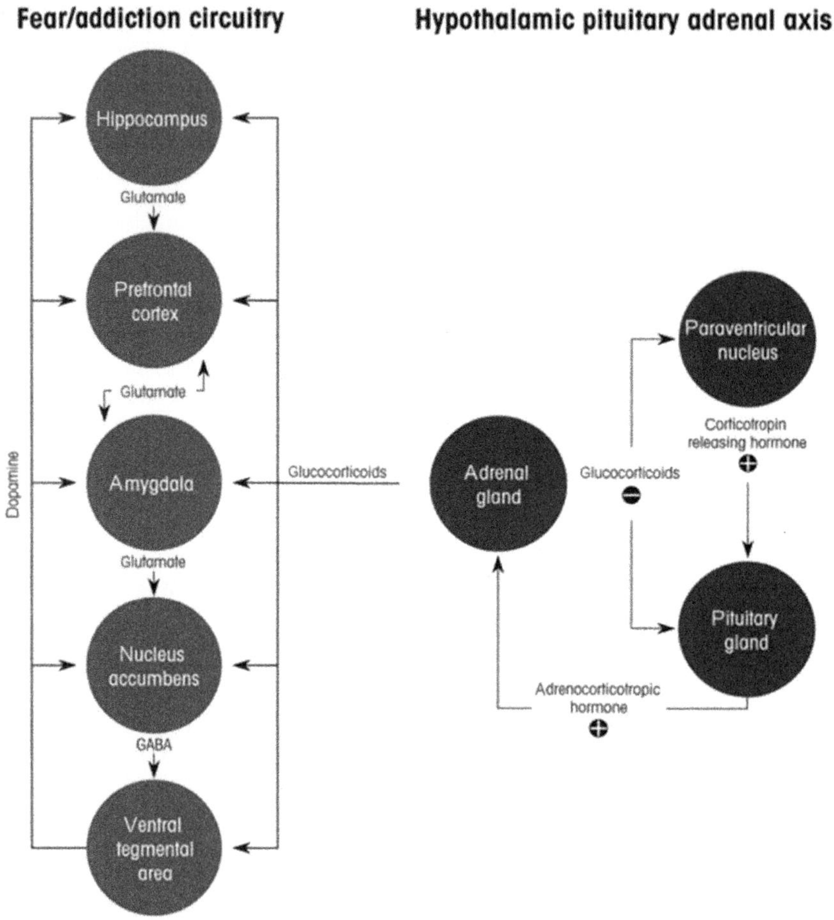

FIGURE 4.2 Interactions between the fear/addiction neural circuitry and the hypothalamic pituitary adrenal (HPA) axis. *Credit: Suh, J., & Ressler, K. J. (2018). Common biological mechanisms of alcohol use disorder and post-traumatic stress disorder.* Alcohol Research: Current Reviews, 39*(2), 131–145.*

Corticotropin releasing hormone (CRH) from the PN stimulates release of adrenocorticotropic hormone (ACTH) from the anterior pituitary into the venal system. ATCH induces glucocorticoid release from the adrenal glands. Glucocorticoids mediate negative feedback regarding the HPA axis and directs it to reduce the stress response. Furthermore, Glucocorticoids affect the fear / addiction circuitry via their own receptors which can trigger physiological, cellular and molecular changes which in turn causes genetic alterations (epigenetic changes).

In summary, stress is a likely common neurobiological link between the processes of substance use disorders, including AUDand anxiety disorders. Stress responses are mediated through the HPA axis, which in turn can influence brain circuits that control motivation. Higher levels of stress have been shown to reduce activity in the prefrontal cortex and increase responsivity in the striatum, which leads to decreased behavioral control, increased impulsivity, and increased compulsive behaviors. Early life stress, isolation, trauma and chronic stress can also cause long-term alterations in the HPA axis, which affects limbic brain circuits that are involved in motivation, learning, and adaptation, which are impaired in individuals with AUD and MHD.

Scientists are also beginning to understand the ways that genetic and environmental factors interact at the molecular level. Chronic stress caused by social factors such as isolation, homelessness, financial difficulties, trauma, or drug and alcohol exposure can induce stable changes that affect how genetic information is read and acted on by cells in the body (see Fig. 4.3 and Wong, Mill, & Fernandes, 2011; for a review on epigenetics in addiction). These alterations contribute to the development of MHD and addiction. However, there is also evidence that some of these changes can be reversed with interventions or environmental alteration (Guintivano & Kaminsky, 2016).

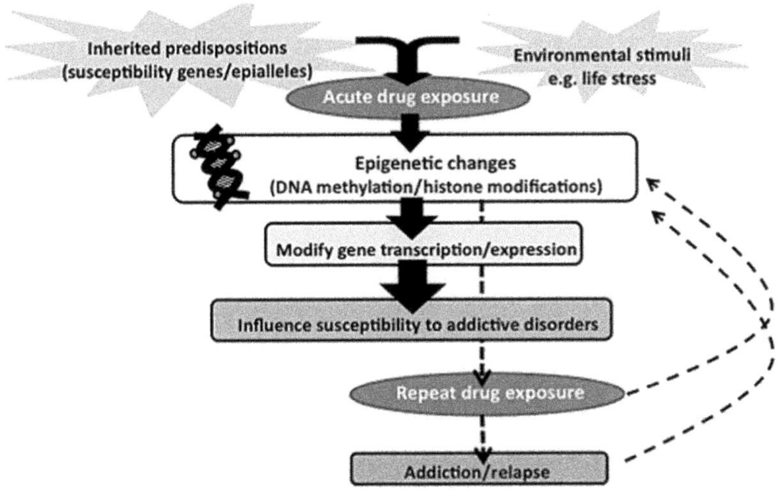

FIGURE 4.3 The proposed relationship between inherited predispositions, environmental factors, exposure to addictive substances and vulnerability to addictive disorders. When exposed to adverse environmental stimuli, individuals carrying susceptibility genes or epialleles predisposing to addictive behaviors may have an increased risk of developing addiction. Acute substance use may produce enduring alterations in gene expression via epigenetic changes that influence susceptibility to addictive disorders. Enhanced vulnerability to substances of abuse will then feed back into increased risk of future drug use (as shown by the dashed arrow) that bring about further modifications to the epigenome and gene expression. *Credit: Taken from: Wong, C. C. Y., Mill, J., & Fernandes, C. (2011). Drugs and addiction: An introduction to epigenetics.* Addiction, 106*(3), 480–489.*

Conclusions and treatment considerations

In conclusion, there is evidence to support all three main theoretical models of co-occurring AUD and MHD. However, it is becoming clear that the interaction between the two conditions is complex and, in many cases, bidirectional, with one reinforcing the other in a cyclic fashion (e.g. Suh & Ressler, 2018). Although it is important to try and disentangle the interaction between AUD and MHD, ultimately, regardless of the etiological model, these disorders are strongly associated. Thus, treatment must address both the MHD symptoms and AUD in an integrated fashion. Research into the common underlying mechanisms indicates that interventions should aid individuals with such comorbidity develop skills to cope with the consequences of trauma and with stress.The evidence presented in this chapter also suggests that women are more likely to use alcohol to deal with symptoms of anxiety and stress in comparison to men, they are also more likely to have been victim of sexual abuse, they tend to display more severe psychiatric symptoms and more severe AUD related complications (see Gearon et al., 2011; Peltier et al, 2019). As a result, women have a greater number of service needs, especially for treatment related to family and trauma issues (Grella, 2003). Therefore, it is recommended that treatment interventions should be gender sensitive.

The strong connection between mental and alcohol use disorders indicates that transdiagnostic therapeutic protocols might be the way forward. The interplay between the psychological and biological factors imply that therapeutic approaches may require a combination of pharmacological and psychosocial interventions. Finally, the complex and multiple needs of individuals with "dual diagnosis" can only be met if treatment and policy interventions adopt a joint and coordinated approach.

References

Abrams, K., & Kushner, M. G. (2004). The moderating effects of tension-reduction alcohol outcome expectancies on placebo responding in individuals with social phobia. *Addictive Behaviors*, *29*(6), 1221–1224. Available from https://doi.org/10.1016/j.addbeh.2004.03.020.

Abrams, K., Kushner, M., & Reinertsen, K. (2002). Effects of alcohol on anxiety-relevant cognitions in individuals with social phobia. *Cognitive Behaviour Therapy*, *31*(3), 97–110. Available from https://doi.org/10.1080/165060702320337979.

Alden, L. E., & Wallace, S. T. (1995). Social phobia and social appraisal in successful and unsuccessful social interactions. *Behaviour Research and Therapy*, *33*(5), 497–505. Available from https://doi.org/10.1016/0005-7967(94)00088-2.

Anker, J. J., & Kushner, M. G. (2019). Co-occurring alcohol use disorder and anxiety: Bridging psychiatric, psychological, and neurobiological perspectives. *Alcohol Research: Current Reviews*, *40*(1). Available from https://doi.org/10.35946/arcr.v40.1.03.

Anton, R. F., Moak, D. H., & Latham, P. (1996). The obsessive compulsive drinking scale: A new method of assessing outcome in alcoholism treatment studies. *Arch Gen Psychiatry*, *53*, 225–231.

Archibald, L., Brunette, M. F., Wallin, D. J., & Green, A. I. (2019). Alcohol use disorder and schizophrenia or schizoaffective disorder. *Alcohol Research: Current Reviews*, *40*(1), 51–59. Available from https://doi.org/10.35946/arcr.v40.1.06.

Bergamaschi, M. M., Queiroz, R. H. C., Chagas, M. H. N., de Oliveira, D. C. G., De Martinis, B. S., et al. (2011). Cannabidiol reduces the anxiety induced by simulated public speaking in treatment-naive social phobia patients. *Neuropsychopharmacology*, *36*(6), 1219–1226. Available from https://doi.org/10.1038/npp.2011.6.

Boden, J. M., & Fergusson, D. M. (2011). Alcohol and depression. *Addiction*, *106*(5), 906–914. Available from https://doi.org/10.1111/j.1360-0443.2010.03351.

Brady, K. T., & Back, S. E. (2012). Childhood trauma, posttraumatic stress disorder, and alcohol dependence. *Alcohol Research: Current Reviews*, *34*(4), 408–413.

Breese, G. R., Sinha, R., & Heilig, M. (2011). Chronic alcohol neuroadaptation and stress contribute to susceptibility for alcohol craving and relapse. *Pharmacology & Therapeutics*, *129* (2), 149–171. Available from https://doi.org/10.1016/j.pharmthera.2010.09.007.

Buckner, J. D., Heimberg, R. G., Ecker, A. H., & Vinci, C. (2013). A biopsychosocial model of social anxiety and substance use. *Depression and Anxiety*, *30*(3), 276–284. Available from https://doi.org/10.1002/da.22032.

Byers, A. L., Yaffe, K., Covinsky, K. E., Friedman, M. B., & Bruce, M. L. (2010). High occurrence of mood and anxiety disorders among older adults: The national comorbidity survey replication. *Archives of General Psychiatry*, *67*(5), 489–496. Available from https://doi.org/10.1001/archgenpsychiatry.2010.35.

Caton, C. L., Drake, R. E., Hasin, D. S., Dominguez, B., Shrout, P. E., Samet, S., & Schanzer, W. B. (2005). Differences between early-phase primary psychotic disorders with concurrent substance use and substance-induced psychoses. *Archives of General Psychiatry*, *62*(2), 137–145. Available from https://doi.org/10.1001/archpsyc.62.2.137.

Chan, Y. F., Dennis, M. L., & Funk, R. R. (2008). Prevalence and comorbidity of major internalizing and externalizing problems among adolescents and adults presenting to substance abuse treatment. *Journal of Substance Abuse Treatment*, *34*(1), 14–24. Available from https://doi.org/10.1016/j.jsat.2006.12.031.

Churchill, S. A., & Farrell, L. (2017). Alcohol and depression: Evidence from the 2014 health survey for England. *Drug and Alcohol Dependence*, *180*, 86–92. Available from https://doi.org/10.1016/j.drugalcdep.2017.08.006.

Conger, J. J., & Alcoholism. (1956). Theory, problem, and challenge. II: Reinforcement theory and the dynamics of alcoholism. *Quarterly Journal of Studies on Alcohol*, *17*, 296–305. PMID: 13336262.

Conner, K. R., Pinquart, M., & Gamble, S. A. (2009). Meta-analysis of depression and substance use among individuals with alcohol use disorders. *Journal of Substance Abuse Treatment*, *37*(2), 127–137. Available from https://doi.org/10.1016/j.jsat.2008.11.007.

Dager, A. D., McKay, D. R., Kent, J. W., Curran, J. E., Knowles, E., Sprooten, E., ... Glahn, D. (2015). Shared genetic factors influence amygdala volumes and risk for alcoholism. *Neuropsychopharmacology*, *40*(2), 412–420. Available from https://doi.org/10.1038/npp.2014.187.

Drake, R. E., Wallach, M. A., Alverson, H. S., & Mueser, K. T. (2002). Psychosocial aspects of substance abuse by clients with severe mental illness. *J Nerv Ment Dis*, *190*(2), 100–106. Available from 10.1097/00005053-200202000.

Drapalski, A., Bennett, M., & Bellack, A. (2011). Gender differences in substance use, consequences, motivation to change, and treatment seeking in people with serious mental illness. *Substance Use & Misuse*, *46*(6), 808–818. Available from https://doi.org/10.3109/10826084.2010.538460.

Engelhard, C. P., Touquet, G., Tansens, A., & De Fruyt, J. (2015). Alcohol-induced psychotic disorder: A systematic literature review. *Tijdschrift voor Psychiatrie*, *57*(3), 192–201.

Fonzo, G. A., Simmons, A. N., Thorp, S. R., Norman, S. B., Paulus, M. P., & Stein, M. B. (2010). Exaggerated and disconnected insular-amygdalar blood oxygenation level-dependent response to threat-related emotional faces in women with intimate-partner violence posttraumatic stress disorder. *Biological Psychiatry*, *68*(5), 433–441. Available from https://doi.org/10.1016/j.biopsych.2010.04.028.

Foster, J. H., Powell, J. E., Marshall, E. J., & Peters, T. J. (1999). Quality of life in alcohol-dependent subjects: A review. *Quality of Life Research*, *8*(3), 255–261. Available from https://doi.org/10.1023/A:1008802711478.

Garfinkel, S. N., Abelson, J. L., King, A. P., Sripada, R. K., Wang, X., Gaines, L. M., & Liberzon, I. (2014). Impaired contextual modulation of memories in PTSD: An fMRI and psychophysiological study of extinction retention and fear renewal. *Journal of Neuroscience*, *34*(40), 13435–13443. Available from https://doi.org/10.1523/JNEUROSCI.4287-13.2014.

Gearon, J. S., Nidecker, M., Bellack, A., & Bennett, M. (2003). Gender difference in drug use behavior in people with serious mental illnesses. *The American Journal on Addictions*, *12*, 229–241.

Gentil, A. F., de Mathis, M. A., Torresan, R. C., Diniz, J. B., Alvarenga, P., do Rosário, M. C., ... Miguel, E. C. (2009). Alcohol use disorders in patients with obsessive-compulsive disorder: The importance of appropriate dual-diagnosis. *Drug and Alcohol Dependence*, *100* (1–2), 173–177.

Glass, I. B. (1989). Alcoholic hallucinosis: A psychiatric enigma–2. Follow-up studies. *British Journal of Addiction*, *84*(2), 151–164. Available from https://doi.org/10.1111/j.1360-0443.1989.tb00564.x.

van de Glind, G., van Emmerik-van Oortmerssen, K., Carpentier, P. J., Levin, F. R., Koeter, M. W., Barta, C., & van den Brink, W. (2013). The international ADHD in substance use disorders prevalence (IASP) study: Background, methods and study population. *International Journal of Psychiatric Research*, *22*(3), 232–244. Available from https://doi.org/10.1002/mpr.1397.

Goodman, L. A., Dutton, M. A., & Harris, M. (1997). The relationship between violence dimensions and symptom severity among homeless, mentally ill women. *Journal of Traumatic Stress*, *10*, 51–70.

Graeff, F. G., & Del-Ben, C. M. (2008). Neurobiology of panic disorder: From animal models to brain neuroimaging. *Neuroscience and Biobehavioral Reviews*, *32*, 1326–1335.

Grella, C. (2003). Effects of gender and diagnosis on addiction history, treatment utilization, and psychosocial functioning among a dually-diagnosed sample in drug treatment. *Journal of Psychoactive Drugs, SARC Supplement*, *1*, 169–179.

Grant, B. F., Hasin, D. S., Blanco, C., Stinson, F. S., Chou, S. P., Goldstein, R. B., ... Huang, B. (2005). The epidemiology of social anxiety disorder in the United States: Results from the national epidemiologic survey on alcohol and related conditions. *The Journal of Clinical Psychiatry*, *66*(11), 1351–1361. Available from https://doi.org/10.4088/JCP.v66n1102.

Guintivano, J., & Kaminsky, Z. A. (2016). Role of epigenetic factors in the development of mental illness throughout life. *Neuroscience Research, 102*, 56–66. Available from https://doi.org/10.1016/j.neures.2014.08.003.

Hanson, J. L., Nacewicz, B. M., Sutterer, M. J., Cayo, A. A., Schaefer, S. M., Rudolph, K. D., ... Davidson, R. J. (2015). Behavioral problems after early life stress: Contributions of the hippocampus and amygdala. *Biological Psychiatry, 77*(4), 314–323. Available from https://doi.org/10.1016/j.biopsych.2014.04.020.

Hartz, S. M., Pato, C. N., Medeiros, H., Cavazos-Rehg, P., Sobell, J. L., Knowles, J. A., ... Pato, M. T. (2014). Comorbidity of severe psychotic disorders with measures of substance use. *JAMA Psychiatry, 71*(3), 248–254. Available from https://doi.org/10.1001/jamapsychiatry.2013.3726.

Hartz, S. M., Horton, A. C., Oehlert, M., Carey, C. E., Agrawal, A., Bogdan, R., et al. (2017). Association between substance use disorder and polygenic liability to schizophrenia. *Biological psychiatry, 82*(10), 709–715.

Hasin, D. S., & Grant, B. F. (2002). Major depression in 6050 former drinkers: Association with past alcohol dependence. *Archives of General Psychiatry, 59*(9), 794–800. Available from https://doi.org/10.1001/archpsyc.59.9.794.

Helle, A. C., Watts, A. L., Trull, T. J., & Sher, K. J. (2019). Alcohol use disorder and antisocial and borderline personality disorders. *Alcohol Research: Current Reviews, 40*(1). Available from https://doi.org/10.35946/arcr.v40.1.05.

Hunt, G. E., Large, M. M., Cleary, M., Lai, H. M. X., & Saunders, J. B. (2018). Prevalence of comorbid substance use in schizophrenia spectrum disorders in community and clinical settings, 1990–2017: Systematic review and meta-analysis. *Drug and Alcohol Dependence, 191*, 234–258. Available from https://doi.org/10.1016/j.drugalcdep.2018.07.011.

Hunt, G. E., Malhi, G. S., Cleary, M., Lai, H. M. X., & Sitharthan, T. (2016). Prevalence of comorbid bipolar and substance use disorders in clinical settings. *Journal of Affective Disorders, 206*, 331–349. Available from https://doi.org/10.1016/j.jad.2016.07.011.

Jordaan, G. P., & Emsley, R. (2014). Alcohol-induced psychotic disorder: A review. *Metabolic Brain Disease, 29*(2), 231–243. Available from https://doi.org/10.1007/s11011-013-9457-4.

Kaysen, D., Dillworth, T. M., Simpson, T., Waldrop, A., Larimer, M. E., & Resick, P. A. (2007). Domestic violence and alcohol use: trauma-related symptoms and motives for drinking. *Addictive Behaviors, 32*(6), 1272–1283. Available from https://doi.org/10.1016/j.addbeh.2006.09.007.

Keane, T. M., & Lisman, S. A. (1980). Alcohol and social anxiety in males: Behavioral, cognitive, and physiological effects. *Journal of Abnormal Psychology, 89*(2), 213–223. Available from https://doi.org/10.1037/0021-843X.89.

Khantzian, E. J. (2013). Addiction as a self-regulation disorder and the role of self-medication. *Addiction, 108*(4), 668–669.

Kryger, R., & Wilce, P. A. (2010). The effects of alcoholism on the human basolateral amygdala. *Neuroscience, 167*(2), 361–371.

Kushner, M. G., Abrams, K., Thuras, P., Hanson, K. L., Brekke, M., & Sletten, S. (2005). Follow-up study of anxiety disorder and alcohol dependence in comorbid alcoholism treatment patients. *Alcoholism: Clinical and Experimental Research, 29*(8), 1432–1443. Available from https://doi.org/10.1097/01.alc.0000175072.17623.f8.

Kushner, M. G., Krueger, R., Frye, B., & Peterson, J. (2008). Epidemiological perspectives on co-occurring anxiety disorder and substance use disorder. In S. H. Stewart, & P. J. Conrod (Eds.), *Anxiety and substance use disorders* (pp. 3–17). Boston, MA: Springer. Available from https://doi.org/10.1007/978-0-387-74290-8_1.

Kushner, M. G., Sher, K. J., & Beitman, B. D. (1990). The relation between alcohol problems and the anxiety disorders. *The American Journal of Psychiatry*, *147*(6), 685–695. Available from https://doi.org/10.1176/ajp.147.6.685.

Kushner, M. G., Wall, M. M., Krueger, R. F., Sher, K. J., Maurer, E., Thuras, P., & Lee, S. (2012). Alcohol dependence is related to overall internalizing psychopathology load rather than to particular internalizing disorders: Evidence from a national sample. *Alcoholism: Clinical and Experimental Research*, *36*(2), 325–331. Available from https://doi.org/10.1111/j.1530-0277.2011.01604.x.

Laudet, A. B., Magura, S., Vogel, H. S., & Knight, E. L. (2004). Perceived reasons for substance misuse among persons with a psychiatric disorder. *American Journal of Orthopsychiatry*, *74* (3), 365–375. Available from https://doi.org/10.1037/0002-9432.74.3.365.

Lima, A. F., Pechansky, F., Fleck, M. P., & De Boni, R. (2005). Association between psychiatric symptoms and severity of alcohol dependence in a sample of brazilian men. *The Journal of Nervous and Mental Disease*, *193*(2), 126–130. Available from https://doi.org/10.1097/01.nmd.0000152818.38001.2c.

Logue, M. W., van Rooij, S. J. H., Dennis, E. L., Davis, S. L., Hayes, J. P., Stevens, J. S., & Morey, R. A. (2018). Smaller hippocampal volume in posttraumatic stress disorder: A multisite ENIGMA-PGC study: Subcortical volumetry results from posttraumatic stress disorder consortia. *Biological Psychiatry*, *83*(3), 244–253. Available from https://doi.org/10.1016/j.biopsych.2017.09.006.

Magon, R., & Müller, U. (2012). ADHD with comorbid substance use disorder: Review of treatment. *Advances in Psychiatric Treatment*, *18*(6), 436–446. Available from https://doi.org/10.1192/apt.bp.111.009340.

Mandell, D., Siegle, G. J., Shutt, L., Feldmiller, J., & Thase, M. E. (2014). Neural substrates of trait ruminations in depression. *Journal of Abnormal Psychology*, *123*(1), 35–48. Available from https://doi.org/10.1037/a0035834.

Matsuoka, Y., Yamawaki, S., Inagaki, M., Akechi, T., & Uchitomi, Y. (2003). A volumetric study of amygdala in cancer survivors with intrusive recollections. *Biological Psychiatry*, *54* (7), 736–743. Available from https://doi.org/10.1016/S0006-3223(02)01907-8.

McEachin, R. C., Keller, B. J., Saunders, E. F., & McInnis, M. G. (2008). Modeling gene-by-environment interaction in comorbid depression with alcohol use disorders via an integrated bioinformatics approach. *BioData Mining*, *1*(1), 2. Available from https://doi.org/10.1186/1756-0381-1-2.

McFarlane, A. C., Bookless, C., & Air, T. (2001). Posttraumatic stress disorder in a general psychiatric inpatient population. *Journal of Traumatic Stress*, *14*, 633–645. Available from https://doi.org/10.1023/A:1013077702520.

Menary, K. R., Kushner, M. G., Maurer, E., & Thuras, P. (2011). The prevalence and clinical implications of self-medication among individuals with anxiety disorders. *Journal of Anxiety Disorders*, *25*(3), 335–339. Available from https://doi.org/10.1016/j.janxdis.2010.10.006.

Menke, A. (2019). Is the HPA axis as target for depression outdated, or is there a new hope? *Frontiers in Psychiatry*, *10*, 101. Available from https://doi.org/10.3389/fpsyt.2019.00101.

Mueser, K. T., Drake, R. E., & Wallach, M. A. (1998). Dual diagnosis: A review of etiological theories. *Addictive Behaviors*, *23*(6), 717–734. Available from https://doi.org/10.1016/S0306-4603(98)00073-2.

Mueser, K. T., Goodman, L. A., Trumbetta, S. L., Rosenberg, S. D., Osher, F. C., Vidaver, R., & Foy, D. W. (1998). Trauma and posttraumatic stress disorder in severe mental illness. *Journal of Consulting and Clinical Psychology*, *66*, 493–499.

Murphy, D., & Turgoose, D. (2019). Exploring patterns of alcohol misuse in treatment-seeking UK veterans: A cross-sectional study. *Addictive Behaviors*, *92*, 14–19. Available from https://doi.org/10.1016/j.addbeh.2018.11.044.

Niciu, M. J., & Mason, G. F. (2014). Neuroimaging in alcohol and drug dependence. *Current Behavioral Neuroscience Reports*, *1*(1), 45–54. Available from https://doi.org/10.1007/s40473-013-0005-7.

Nikolova, Y. S., Knodt, A. R., Radtke, S. R., & Hariri, A. R. (2016). Divergent responses of the amygdala and ventral striatum predict stress-related problem drinking in young adults: Possible differential markers of affective and impulsive pathways of risk for alcohol use disorder. *Molecular Psychiatry*, *21*(3), 348–356. Available from https://doi.org/10.1038/mp.2015.85.

Nishith, P., Mueser, K. T., & Morse, G. A. (2019). Alcohol expectancies in persons with severe mental illness and posttraumatic stress disorder. *Cogent Medicine*, *6*(1), 1635805. Available from https://doi.org/10.1080/2331205X.2019.1635805.

Norberg, M. M., Norton, A. R., Olivier, J., & Zvolensky, M. J. (2010). Social anxiety, reasons for drinking, and college students. *Behavior Therapy*, *41*(4), 555–566. Available from https://doi.org/10.1016/j.beth.2010.03.002.

Norman, S. B., Haller, M., Hamblen, J. L., Southwick, S. M., & Pietrzak, R. H. (2018). The burden of co-occurring alcohol use disorder and PTSD in U.S. military Veterans: Comorbidities, functioning, and suicidality. *Psychology of Addictive Behaviors*, *32*(2), 224–229. Available from https://doi.org/10.1037/adb0000348.

Norman, S. B., Myers, U. S., Wilkins, K. C., Goldsmith, A. A., Hristova, V., Huang, Z., ... Robinson, S. K. (2012). Review of biological mechanisms and pharmacological treatments of comorbid PTSD and substance use disorder. *Neuropharmacology*, *62*(2), 542–551. Available from https://doi.org/10.1016/j.neuropharm.2011.04.032.

Ohlmeier, M. D., Peters, K., Te Wildt, B. T., Zedler, M., Ziegenbein, M., Wiese, B., ... Schneider, U. (2008). Comorbidity of alcohol and substance dependence with attention-deficit/hyperactivity disorder (ADHD). *Alcohol and Alcoholism (Oxford, Oxfordshire)*, *43*(3), 300–304. Available from https://doi.org/10.1093/alcalc/agn014.

Paljärvi, T., Koskenvuo, M., Poikolainen, K., Kauhanen, J., Sillanmäki, L., & Mäkelä, P. (2009). Binge drinking and depressive symptoms: A 5-year population-based cohort study. *Addiction*, *104*(7), 1168–1178. Available from https://doi.org/10.1111/j.1360-0443.2009.02577.x.

Peltier, M. R., Verplaetse, T. L., Mineur, Y. S., Petrakis, I. L., Cosgrove, K. P., Picciotto, M. R., & McKee, S. A. (2019). Sex differences in stress-related alcohol use. *Neurobiology of Stress*, *10*, 100149. Available from https://doi.org/10.1016/j.ynstr.2019.100149.

Perälä, J., Kuoppasalmi, K., Pirkola, S., Härkänen, T., Saarni, S., Tuulio-Henriksson, A., ... Suvisaari, J. (2010). Alcohol-induced psychotic disorder and delirium in the general population. *The British Journal of Psychiatry*, *197*(3), 200–206. Available from https://doi.org/10.1192/bjp.bp.109.070797.

Peters, J., Kalivas, P. W., & Quirk, G. J. (2009). Extinction circuits for fear and addiction overlap in prefrontal cortex. *Learning & Memory*, *16*(5), 279–288. Available from https://doi.org/10.1101/lm.1041309.

Pitkanen, A. (2000). Connectivity of the rat amygdaloid complex. The amygdala, a functional analysis. *Dental Journal of Waste Medical University*, *21*(3), 164–176.

Poirier, G. L., Cordero, M. I., & Sandi, C. (2013). Female vulnerability to the development of depression-like behavior in a rat model of intimate partner violence is related to anxious temperament, coping responses, and amygdala vasopressin receptor 1a expression. *Frontiers in Behavioral Neuroscience*, *7*, 35. Available from https://doi.org/10.3389/fnbeh.2013.00035.

Quitkin, F. M., Rifkin, A., Kaplan, J., & Klein, D. F. (1972). Phobic anxiety syndrome complicated by drug dependence and addiction. A treatable form of drug abuse. *Archives of General Psychiatry*, *27*, 159–162. PMID: 5042823.

Rao, T. (2014). The role of community nursing in providing integrated care for older people with alcohol misuse. *British Journal of Community Nursing*, *19*(2), 80–84. Available from https://doi.org/10.12968/bjcn.2014.19.2.80.

Rasmussen, P., & Gillberg, C. (2000). Natural outcome of ADHD with developmental coordination disorder at age 22 years: A controlled, longitudinal, community-based study. *Journal of the American Academy of Child and Adolescent Psychiatry*, *39*(11), 1424–1431. Available from https://doi.org/10.1097/00004583-200011000-00017.

Roberto, M., Gilpin, N. W., & Siggins, G. R. (2012). The central amygdala and alcohol: Role of γ-aminobutyric acid, glutamate, and neuropeptides. *Cold Spring Harbor Perspectives in Medicine*, *2*(12), a012195.

Sabia, S., Elbaz, A., Britton, A., Bell, S., Dugravot, A., Shipley, M., ... Singh-Manoux, A. (2014). Alcohol consumption and cognitive decline in early old age. *Neurology*, *82*(4), 332–339. Available from https://doi.org/10.1212/WNL.0000000000000063.

Seal, K. H., Cohen, G., Waldrop, A., Cohen, B. E., Maguen, S., & Ren, L. (2011). Substance use disorders in Iraq and Afghanistan veterans in VA healthcare, 2001–2010: Implications for screening, diagnosis and treatment. *Drug and Alcohol Dependence*, *116*(1–3), 93–101. Available from https://doi.org/10.1016/j.drugalcdep.2010.11.027.

Schutte, K. K., Moos, R. H., & Brennan, P. L. (1995). Depression and drinking behavior among women and men: A three-wave longitudinal study of older adults. *Journal of Consulting and Clinical Psychology*, *63*(5), 810–822. Available from https://doi.org/10.1037/0022-006X.63.

Semple, W. E., Goyer, P. F., McCormick, R., Donovan, B., Muzic, R. F., Jr, Rugle, L., et al. (2000). Higher brain blood flow at amygdala and lower frontal cortex blood flow in PTSD patients with comorbid cocaine and alcohol abuse compared with normals. *Psychiatry*, *63* (1), 65–74. Available from https://doi.org/10.1080/00332747.2000.11024895.

Sher, K. J., & Levenson, R. W. (1982). Risk for alcoholism and individual differences in the stress-response-dampening effect of alcohol. *Journal of Abnormal Psychology*, *91*, 350–367. PMID: 7142573.

Sihvola, E., Rose, R. J., Dick, D. M., Pulkkinen, L., Marttunen, M., & Kaprio, J. (2008). Early-onset depressive disorders, predict the use of addictive substances in adolescence: A prospective study of adolescent Finnish twins. *Addiction*, *103*(12), 2045–2053. Available from https://doi.org/10.1111/j.1360-0443.2008.02363.x.

Smith, J. P., & Randall, C. L. (2012). Anxiety and alcohol use disorders: Comorbidity and treatment considerations. *Alcohol Research: Current Reviews*, *34*(4), 414–431.

Stamatakis, A. M., Sparta, D. R., Jennings, J. H., McElligott, Z. A., Decot, H., & Stuber, G. D. (2014). Amygdala and bed nucleus of the stria terminalis circuitry: Implications for addiction-related behaviors. *Neuropharmacology*, *76 Pt B*(0 0), 320–328. Available from https://doi.org/10.1016/j.neuropharm.2013.05.046.

Stevens, J. S., Kim, Y. J., Galatzer-Levy, I. R., Reddy, R., Ely, T. D., Nemeroff, C. B., ... Ressler, K. J. (2017). Amygdala reactivity and anterior cingulate habituation predict PTSD symptom maintenance after acute civilian trauma. *Biological Psychiatry*, *81*(12), 1023–1029. Available from https://doi.org/10.1016/j.biopsych.2016.11.015.

Suh, J., & Ressler, K. J. (2018). Common biological mechanisms of alcohol use disorder and post-traumatic stress disorder. *Alcohol Research: Current Reviews*, *39*(2), 131–145.

Thornton, L. K., Baker, A. L., Lewin, T. J., Kay-Lambkin, F. J., Kavanagh, D., Richmond, R., ... Johnson, M. P. (2012). Reasons for substance use among people with mental disorders. *Addictive Behaviors*, *37*(4), 427–434. Available from https://doi.org/10.1016/j.addbeh.2011.11.039.

Tran, G. Q., & Smith, J. P. (2008). Comorbidity of social anxiety and alcohol use disorders: Review of psychopathology research findings. In S. H. Stewart, & P. J. Conrod (Eds.), *Anxiety and substance use disorders: The vicious cycle of comorbidity* (pp. 59–79). New York, NY: Springer.

Trull, T. J., Freeman, L. K., Vebares, T. J., Choate, A. M., Helle, A. C., & Wycoff, A. M. (2018). Borderline personality disorder and substance use disorders: An updated review. *Borderline Personality Disorder and Emotion Dysregulation*, *5*, 15–27.

Vujanovic, A. A., Meyer, T. D., Heads, A. A., Stotts, A. L., Villarreal, Y. R., & Schmitz, J. M. (2017). Cognitive-behavioral therapies for depression and substance use disorders: An overview of traditional, third-wave, and transdiagnostic approaches. *The American Journal of Drug and Alcohol Abuse*, *43*(4), 402–415. Available from https://doi.org/10.1080/00952990.2016.1199697.

Wong, C. C. Y., Mill, J., & Fernandes, C. (2011). Drugs and addiction: An introduction to epigenetics. *Addiction*, *106*(3), 480–489. Available from https://doi.org/10.1111/j.1360-0443.2010.03321.x.

Further reading

Anthenelli, R. M. (2010). Focus on: Comorbid mental health disorders. *Alcohol Research & Health*, *33*(1–2), 109–117.

Ashwick, R., Syed, S., & Murphy, D. (2018). Exploring demographics and health as predictors of risk-taking in UK help-seeking veterans. *Healthcare*, *6*(2), 58. Available from https://doi.org/10.3390/healthcare6020058.

Bacon, A. K., & Ham, L. S. (2010). Attention to social threat as a vulnerability to the development of comorbid social anxiety disorder and alcohol use disorders: An avoidance-coping cognitive model. *Addictive Behaviors*, *35*(11), 925–939. Available from https://doi.org/10.1016/j.addbeh.2010.06.002.

Brower, K. J., Aldrich, M. S., Robinson, E. A., Zucker, R. A., & Greden, J. F. (2001). Insomnia, self-medication, and relapse to alcoholism. *American Journal of Psychiatry*, *158*(3), 399–404. Available from https://doi.org/10.1176/appi.ajp.158.3.399.

Buckner, J. D., & Heimberg, R. G. (2010). Drinking behaviors in social situations account for alcohol-related problems among socially anxious individuals. *Psychology of Addictive Behaviors*, *24*(4), 640. Available from https://doi.org/10.1037/a0020968.

Carrigan, M. H., & Randall, C. L. (2003). Self-medication in social phobia: A review of the alcohol literature. *Addictive Behaviors*, *28*(2), 269–284. Available from https://doi.org/10.1016/S0306-4603(01)00235-0.

Crum, R. M., Brown, C., Liang, K. Y., & Eaton, W. W. (2001). The association of depression and problem drinking: Analyses from the Baltimore ECA follow-up study. *Addictive Behaviors*, *26*(5), 765–773. Available from https://doi.org/10.1016/S0306-4603(00)00163-5.

Darvishi, N., Farhadi, M., Haghtalab, T., & Poorolajal, J. (2015). Alcohol-related risk of suicidal ideation, suicide attempt, and completed suicide: A meta-analysis. *PLoS One*, *10*(5). Available from https://doi.org/10.1371/journal.pone.0126870, Article e0126870.

Driessen, M., Schulte, S., Luedecke, C., Schaefer, I., Sutmann, F., Ohlmeier, M., ... the TRAUMAB-Study Group. (2008). Trauma and PTSD in patients with alcohol, drug, or dual dependence: A multi-center study. *Alcoholism: Clinical and Experimental Research, 32*(3), 481–488. Available from https://doi.org/10.1111/j.1530-0277.2007.00591.x.

Gilpin, N. W., & Koob, G. F. (2008). Neurobiology of alcohol dependence: Focus on motivational mechanisms. *Alcohol Research & Health, 31*(3), 185.

Grella, C. E. (2003). Effects of gender and diagnosis on addiction history, treatment utilization, and psychosocial functioning among a dually-diagnosed sample in drug treatment. *Journal of Psychoactive Drugs, 35*(Suppl. 1), 169–179.

Harris, K. M., & Edlund, M. J. (2005). Self-medication of mental health problems: New evidence from a national survey. *Health Services Research, 40*(1), 117–134. doi:10.1111/j.1475-6773.2005.00345.x.

Hussong, A. M., Galloway, C. A., & Feagans, L. A. (2005). Coping motives as a moderator of daily mood-drinking covariation. *Journal of Studies on Alcohol and Drugs, 66*(3), 344–353. Available from https://doi.org/10.15288/jsa.2005.66.344.

Koskinen, J., Löhönen, J., Koponen, H., Isohanni, M., & Miettunen, J. (2009). Prevalence of alcohol use disorders in schizophrenia: A systematic review and meta-analysis. *Acta Psychiatrica Scandinavica, 120*(2), 85–96. Available from https://doi.org/10.1111/j.1600-0447.2009.01385.x.

Lehman, A. F., Meyers, C. P., & Corty, E. (2000). Assessment and classification of patients with psychiatric and substance abuse syndromes. *Psychiatric Services, 51*(9), 1119–1125. Available from https://doi.org/10.1176/appi.ps.51.9.1119.

McManus, S., Bebbington, P., Jenkins, R., & Brugha, T. (Eds.), (2016). *Mental health and wellbeing in England: Adult psychiatric morbidity survey 2014*. Leeds: NHS Digital.

Price, J. L., & Wayne, C. (2010). Neurocircuitary of mood disorders. *Neuropsychopharmacology, 1*(35), 164–176.

Quigley, B. M., Houston, R. J., Antonius, D., Testa, M., & Leonard, K. E. (2018). Alcohol use moderates the relationship between symptoms of mental illness and aggression. *Psychology of Addictive Behaviors, 32*(7), 770–778. Available from https://doi.org/10.1037/adb0000390.

Sjöholm, L. K., Kovanen, L., Saarikoski, S. T., Schalling, M., Lavebratt, C., & Partonen, T. (2010). CLOCK is suggested to associate with comorbid alcohol use and depressive disorders. *Journal of Circadian Rhythms, 8*(1), 1. doi:10.1186/1740-3391-8-1.

Stankewicz, H. A., Richards, J. R., & Salen, P. (2018). *Alcohol related psychosis. StatPearls [Internet]*. StatPearls Publishing.

Swendsen, J. D., Tennen, H., Carney, M. A., Affleck, G., Willard, A., & Hromi, A. (2000). Mood and alcohol consumption: An experience sampling test of the self-medication hypothesis. *Journal of Abnormal Psychology, 109*(2), 198–204. Available from https://doi.org/10.1037/0021-843X.109.2.198.

Thomas, S. E., Randall, C. L., & Carrigan, M. H. (2003). Drinking to cope in socially anxious individuals: A controlled study. *Alcoholism: Clinical and Experimental Research, 27*(12), 1937–1943.

Yuodelis-Flores, C., & Ries, R. K. (2015). Addiction and suicide: A review. *The American Journal on Addictions, 24*(2), 98–104. Available from https://doi.org/10.1111/ajad.12185.

Chapter 5

The pharmacological understandings of alcohol use and misuse

Abigail Rose[1,2] and Andrew Jones[1,2]
[1]*Department of Psychology, University of Liverpool, Liverpool, United Kingdom,* [2]*Liverpool Centre for Alcohol Research, University of Liverpool, Liverpool, United Kingdom*

Introduction: addiction as a biological model (a 'brain disease')

Historically, addiction has been blamed on the individual, their poor choices, deviant characteristics, and weak will. The effect this has had on the public's perception of addiction, a reluctance of funding bodies to support addiction research, and the impact such negative stigma has on the addict and their family should not be underestimated. However, as behavioral sciences and neuroscience advanced, we began to identify and map the various effects alcohol (or ethanol) and other substances had on the brain. Our understanding of the neurobiology of addiction (more specifically alcohol use and misuse) was founded on influential animal models (e.g. Crews & Boettiger, 2009; Jentsch & Taylor, 1999; Olmstead, 2006). However, they are limited in their predictive utility, and are unable to fully capture the human condition (Field & Kersbergen, 2019; Koob & Volkow, 2010). Therefore, there has been considerable resources focused on brain imaging research in humans such as functional Magnetic Resonance Imaging (fMRI) and Positron Emission Tomography (PET) (Fowler, Volkow, Kassed, & Chang, 2007), in the hopes of progressing our understanding.

Imaging the structure and function of the brain led to the dominant view of alcohol use disorders ('addiction') by researchers and medical professionals as a *brain disease*. First suggested in 1997 by Alan Leshner of the National Institute of Drug Abuse (Leshner, 1997), the central tenant of labeling addiction as a brain disease is that the excessive and long-term use of psychoactive drugs causes persuasive and enduring adaptations to the brain's functioning and structure. This conceptualisation had numerous perceived

The Handbook of Alcohol Use - Understandings from Synapse to Society.
DOI: https://doi.org/10.1016/B978-0-12-816720-5.00007-4

benefits, such as allowing the medicalization of substance misuse (and the benefits of insurance coverage, and dedicated services for substance use/mental health (Smith, 2017) and the removal of stigma from the substance user). Arguably, it is these biological changes that are the key to addiction. As these changes affect the brain circuits which cause 'normal' behaviors to go awry in addiction, leading to issues of compulsive craving, inability to control behavior or make rational decisions. It is these changes that have also led to addiction being termed a '*chronic relapsing disorder*', whereby these long term brain adaptations make relapse and continued drug use more likely.

The concept of addiction as a disease is a contentious issue. Many argue that, although brain adaptations do occur in response to the presence of alcohol, the drinker still has some control over their symptoms. For instance, someone with an alcohol use disorder (AUD) can reduce their drinking which will result in their AUD-symptoms diminishing, unlike someone with cancer or dementia. There are many articles on this (e.g. Barnett, Hall, Fry, Dilkes-Frayne, & Carter, 2018; Lewis, 2018) but for the remainder of this chapter we will refer to brain adaption models (BAM).

Following a period of focus on BAM, debate has grown around the importance of these theories and the (over) reliance on animal research to help us understand addiction. There are a number of reviews and commentaries on these topics which the interested reader should seek out (e.g. Field & Kersbergen, 2019; Hall, Carter, & Forlini, 2015; Lewis, 2018). However, if these brain changes are key in understanding addiction, then AUD poses a substantial challenge. While most drugs of abuse, such as cocaine and opiates, have a relatively narrow range of effects on the brain, the pharmacological actions of alcohol use and misuse are numerous, interactive and complex. Acute intoxication by alcohol (ethanol) causes a cascading change in different neurotransmitter actions across multiple brain regions/sites. Chronic usage is thought to involve neuroplasticity in different brain circuits, as well as dysregulation of various neurotransmitter systems. Because of these direct and indirect, acute and chronic effects to multiple neurotransmitters (including but not limited to dopamine, endogenous opioids, GABA, glutamate, noradrenalin, serotonin, stress hormones) (Abrahao, Salinas, & Lovinger, 2017), a full discussion of all of these systems is beyond the scope of this chapter. Instead we have identified some of the major systems affected by alcohol and which have attracted research which has developed our understanding of alcohol behavior and AUD.

It is important to remember that the neurotransmitter systems and pathways discussed in this chapter are not uniquely associated with alcohol (or other substances with abuse potential), nor do they perfectly predict subsequent behavioral outcomes (for example, there is no alcohol specific impairment pathway or neurotransmitter). Alcohol's acute and chronic effects manifest by influencing brain circuitry that has developed to respond to reward, motivation, emotion, learning, and memory (among other things); key processes that help shape us as individuals regardless of whether or not we consume alcohol. The way in which alcohol influences these circuits, the way our brain responds and adapts to the presence of alcohol, may play a key role in the development of AUD. However, it is not the only element that is important. AUDs develop from a complex combination of neural responses, cognitive and behavioral processes (discussed below), genetics (Tawa, Hall, & Lohoff, 2016), environmental and social experiential factors (Sher, Grekin, & Williams, 2005).

The aim of this chapter is to introduce you to some of the key neurotransmitter systems affected by alcohol, discuss the possible psychological and/or behavioral correlates of these neuroadaptations, and how these may contribute to the development of AUD. As a theoretical example, we will outline an influential BAM which attempts to show how multiple adaptations across several systems leads to addiction, and some of the animal and human research which has influenced this field. Importantly, any theoretical assertion needs to help us understand key factors within addiction, so we will also briefly discuss how brain adaptions may help explain phenomena such as relapse and withdrawal. We will also describe some of the main pharmacotherapy approaches to AUD, and how these may work through action on the neurotransmitter systems highlighted at the start of the chapter. Overall, the chapter should give you a good grounding on alcohol's basic neurochemical effects and highlight some of the issues which show that BAMs, in isolation, cannot provide a complete understanding of alcohol behavior and AUD.

Broad pharmacological effects of alcohol

Alcohol acts upon a widespread and interacting group of neurotransmitters which may in part account for its diverse behavioral effects. Although often referred to as a Central Nervous System depressant, at lower doses alcohol has more of a stimulant effect which can produce euphoria and psychomotor activation, but at higher doses sedation and reduced psychomotor activation occurs. Additionally, alcohol has clear biphasic effects; as the levels of blood alcohol increase drinkers often experience more stimulating, positive reinforcing effects of alcohol. As blood alcohol decreases, sedative and depressant effects are more likely to be experienced. Individual differences in the experience of these biphasic effects (e.g. susceptibility to stimulant and/or and insensitivity to sedative effects) may increase or decrease drinking behavior and thus risk of alcohol-related harm (Hendler, Ramchandani, Gilman, & Hommer, 2013; King, Houle, de Wit, Holdstock, & Schuster, 2002). Below we discuss the primary candidate neurotransmitters and metabolites associated with alcohol use, and their behavioral correlates following acute and chronic drinking.

Dopamine

Dopamine (DA) is perhaps the most widely researched neurotransmitter in relation to alcohol use. Dopamine is primarily synthesized in the substantia nigra and the ventral tegmental area (VTA) and stored in the striatum. The mesocorticolimbic dopamine system covers DA pathways which project to and from the VTA and compromises two pathways: the *mesolimbic pathway* which projects from the VTA to the limbic forebrain, especially the nucleus accumbens, but also involves the amygdala, hippocampus, and the bed nucleus of the stria terminalis; and the *mesocortical pathway* which projects from the VTA to the prefrontal cortex (Gonzales, Job, & Doyon, 2004). The mesocorticolimbic system is crucial in determining functions related to our survival (e.g. food and water intake, sexual behavior) but is also affected by alcohol and other substance use. When we drink, alcohol causes a dose-dependent, transient increase of firing in DA neurones in the VTA, which in turn increases the release of DA in the projected regions of the nucleus accumbens and prefrontal cortex (Brodie & Appel, 1998). Alcohol consumption also increases DA activity indirectly via effects on GABAergic neurons and opioid receptors within the nucleus accumbens. These effects relate to acute alcohol consumption, if drinking becomes a chronic behavioral condition the responses of the DA (and other neurotransmitter) systems change, often displaying reduced or opposing responses through neuroadaptation. These are discussed more below but suffice to say, the mesocorticolimbic system is thought to be key in the development of addictive behaviors.

Behavioral effects: Historically, DA was primarily implicated in the *positive, rewarding* aspect of acute alcohol intoxication, and was termed the 'reward' neurotransmitter: if a stimulus triggered DA release, it would be perceived as rewarding by the individual. However, more contemporary theories suggest that this is an over-simplification; research demonstrates that rewarding experiences are still sought out in the absence of DA activity (Koob, 1992). Interestingly, different neuronal systems may be more or less important depending on the progression of alcohol use. For instance, there is some suggestion that DA is key in the development of alcohol use, but perhaps not as important in the maintenance of drinking behavior (Gianoulakis, 2001).

So rather than DA being a simple proxy of reward, it may be involved in determining current motivational states. Over time and repeated exposure, we associate certain cues with alcohol (e.g. the sight of our local bar) through processes of classical-conditioning (i.e. associative learning). Eventually, mere exposure to these cues can also trigger DA release *independently* of alcohol ingestion. So DA may act as a teaching signal for reward prediction (e.g. DA activity may increase in the alcohol-related context, alerting the individual to its availability). DA may also be involved in establishing memories of rewarding experiences which could help determine the reward status of alcohol and how to behave in future alcohol contexts (Berridge, 2012).

Robinson and Berridge (Robinson & Berridge, 1993; 2008) developed the seminal Incentive Sensitization theory which places DA at the heart of understanding addiction, arguing that DA plays a vital role in the attribution of *incentive salience*. According to this theory, as our alcohol use escalates, we desire alcohol more, and this state of *wanting* is due to the incentive salience we place on alcohol and alcohol-related cues. The Incentive Sensitization theory argues that the DA-mediated process of incentive salience, is the driving force in addiction, causing the user to compulsively want the drug in the absence of liking the drug. This theory may help us to understand the compulsive nature of addictive drinking: even when an individual claims to dislike alcohol and blames alcohol for health, personal and financial problems they may still want alcohol (known as the addiction paradox) (Dennis, 2017). It may also explain why individuals can relapse after long periods of abstinence as this model argues that the hypersensitive dopaminergic system is a long-term neuroadaptation.

Alcohol use disorders are also thought to involve changes to cognitive processes and activation of D1 and D2 dopamine receptors in the prefrontal cortex directly mediates our Executive Cognitive Functions (Logue & Gould, 2014). These higher order, complex functions are thought to be key in goal-directed behaviors, and involve the stopping of inappropriate responses (known as *inhibitory control*), our memory capacity (known as *updating*) and cognitive flexibility (known as shifting (Miyake et al., 2000)). Some studies have suggested an 'inverted-U' shaped function between DA release and executive cognitive functions, in that there is an optimum range of DA activity and that too much or too little activity has a detrimental impact on performance. Early animal research showed that memory impairments were related to DA depletion (but not disruption of other neurotransmitters (Brozoski, Brown, Rosvold, & Goldman, 1979)). More recently research has moved away from the 'inverted-U' hypothesis; DA regulation is thought to vary considerably across receptor regions and cognitive domains (Floresco, 2013) so there is not a 'one-size fits all' function. No matter what the specific relationship is between DA and executive cognitive functions, we know that these processes can be impaired within AUD populations.

Overall, DA is key to the brain's reward and control systems. The nature of dopaminergic activity within the mesocorticolimbic system in response to drinking may be crucial in determining alcohol's reward value, attributing incentive salience to alcohol and alcohol-related cues, and establishing response habits (George, Le Moal, & Koob, 2012). It may also impair the ability to implement goal-directed actions, making it more difficult to overcome the 'wanting' of alcohol, and contribute to some of the other cognitive impairments we see during the development and treatment of AUD.

Opioids

There are three types of endogenous opioid peptides: β-endorphins, enkephalins, and dynorphins which work through three G-protein coupled opioid receptor subtypes: mu (μ), delta (δ), kappa (Ƙ) (Darcq & Kieffer, 2018). The strength with which a neurotransmitter binds to a receptor is called the 'binding affinity'. β-endorphins have almost equal binding affinity to μ and δ receptor subtypes, enkephalins have greatest affinity with δ-receptors, and dynorphins selectively bind to Ƙ-receptors (Le Merrer, Becker, Befort, & Kieffer, 2009).

The cell bodies which synthesize β-endorphins are primarily located in the hypothalamic arcuate nucleus, and the β-endorphin fibers from this region regulate key brain regions associated with alcohol and substance use, including the nucleus accumbens, ventral tegmental area, amygdala, hippocampus, and frontal cortex (Pastor, Font, Miquel, Phillips, & Aragon, 2011). Administration of μ-receptor agonists increases activity of dopaminergic neurons within the VTA, and can increase the release and metabolism of DA in the nucleus accumbens and the prefrontal cortex. This suggests that the endogenous opioid system, especially the μ-opioid system (which can be activated by both β-endorphins and enkephalins), is key in regulating the mesolimbic dopamine system (Herz, 1997). It is not surprising, therefore, that alcohol-related opioid activity is important in determining alcohol's rewarding effects.

Alcohol can influence opioidergic activity through several mechanisms including opioid synthesis, release, metabolism, and receptor density and binding (Gianoulakis, 2001). Acute alcohol increases the release of β-endorphins from several brain regions, with increases from the pituitary and hypothalamus being mediated by alcohol-induced increases of corticotropin releasing hormone from the hypothalamus. Acute alcohol administration also activates μ- and δ-receptors within the mesolimbic DA system (Font, Lujan, & Pastor, 2013). Animal ethanol administration studies have indicated that μ-receptors in the VTA regulates dopaminergic activity of the mesocorticolimbic system in response to ethanol, and that both μ- and δ-receptors play a key role in the function of the nucleus accumbens and prefrontal cortex (Mendez & Morales-Mulia, 2008).

Behavioral effects: Endogenous opioids contribute to alcohol-related behavior because of their role in mediating alcohol-induced reward and positive reinforcement, through the modulation of DA (discussed above, and see Vengeliene, Bilbao, Molander, & Spanagel, 2008). Administration of opioid receptor antagonists decreases ethanol self-administration in animals (Ulm, Volpicelli, & Volpicelli, 1995) and humans with AUD as well as frequency of relapse (Mendez & Morales-Mulia, 2008).

The evidence regarding the role of dynorphin in alcohol behavior is less consistent than that for β-endorphins. However, Ƙ-opioid receptors have a regulatory role on several other neurotransmitter systems within the brain's motivation circuitry. For instance, at a pre-synaptic level, Ƙ-receptors regulate DA, GABA, serotonin and glutamate inputs to the nucleus accumbens (Kissler et al., 2014). In addition, there is a significant density of Ƙ-receptors in the central nucleus of the amygdala, an area known to be involved in addiction. Some findings suggest that chronic alcohol use leads to an upregulation of the *dynorphinergic system* (Kissler et al., 2014) which is associated with the increase in dysphoria and other negative emotional states (e.g. anxiety) often observed in those with chronic, severe AUD and withdrawal. Therefore, the *dynorphinergic system may contribute to alcohol use through negative reinforcement processes.*

Overall, dopaminergic and opioidergic systems interact to determine the salience of alcohol and alcohol related cues, and to establish the rewarding and positive reinforcing effects of drinking. Therefore the activity of these two systems likely plays a major motivational role in both social and harmful alcohol use.

GABA & glutamate

Both GABA (the brain's major inhibitory neurotransmitter) and glutamate (the brain's major excitatory neurotransmitter) are essential amino acids and are key in regulating brain function and metabolism. This is because neurons tend to have one of two 'normal' states, some neurons continually fire at a given rate and this rate can either be decreased (e.g. by GABA) or increased (e.g. by glutamate), other neurons don't fire unless they are excited (e.g. by glutamate). Primarily, alcohol is described as a GABA agonist, and is thought to alter the balance between glutamate and GABA (Valenzuela, 1997).

$GABA_A$ receptors are ionotropic (ligand-gated) and can be composed of number of subunits (α, β, γ, δ, ε, θ, and π), although most consist of two $\alpha 1$, two $\beta 2$ and one $\gamma 2$ (Lobo & Harris, 2008). Intoxicating levels of alcohol activate $GABA_A$ receptors (although very low levels of alcohol are only able to activate a restricted type of $GABA_A$ receptor) (Vengeliene et al., 2008).

There are two $GABA_A$ receptor-mediated alcohol actions on the central nervous system, and these are some of the most widely researched mechanisms due to the high number of $GABA_A$ receptors in the system (Kumar et al., 2009). Firstly, alcohol causes a direct pre-synaptic increase in GABA release which is thought to modulate $GABA_A$ receptors across the amygdala, hippocampus and cerebellum (Criswell, Ming, Kelm, & Breese, 2008). Secondly, indirect effects of acute alcohol consumption on GABA are thought to act through an increase in neurosteroid levels in the brain, which enhance the effects of GABA (Enoch, 2008). Although it is well-established that alcohol can increase $GABA_A$ function, it is important to realize that some research is inconsistent. Some studies have failed to find an effect of intoxication on $GABA_A$ function, and others show that alcohol only influences $GABA_A$ activity in certain brain regions (Valenzuela, 1997). Due to this it is likely that other inhibitory neurotransmitters are also involved in alcohol's behavioral effects (e.g. glycine) (Valenzuela, 1997).

Glutamate binds to ionotropic (as well as G-protein coupled) receptors, divided into three classes: AMPA, Kainate and NMDA. These ionotropic receptors are responsible for the majority of fast-acting excitatory signals in the CNS (Gonzales & Jaworski, 1997). Similarly to GABA receptors, glutamate receptors are made up of sub-units and the ability of alcohol to affect these receptors will depend on sub-unit composition. Unlike the AMPA and Kainate receptors, which only need the presence of glutamate to fire, the NMDA receptor requires both glutamate and another depolarizing stimulus. Due to this need for more than one event, NMDA receptor activity plays a key role in learning and memory (Rezvani, 2006), and is vital during critical development stages (e.g. feotal development and adolescence).

In terms of glutamate, NMDA receptors have received the most focus within addiction research as they are inhibited even at low doses of alcohol. Studies have shown that alcohol reduces the function of NMDA receptors and also disrupts NMDA-induced neuronal electro-activity and neurotransmitter (e.g. acetycholine, dopamine, noradrenalin) release (Gonzales & Jaworski, 1997).

Behavioral effects: $GABA_A$ is thought to underlie many of the behavioral effects of acute alcohol use including anxiolytic, sedative, hypnotic, motor co-ordination, pro-aggressive action and impairment of cognitive functioning (Lobo & Harris, 2008). Indeed, the description of alcohol as a CNS depressant is believed mainly to be due to its acute excitation of GABA and inhibition of glutamate activity (Mirijello et al., 2015). Early links between the role of GABA and these behavioral effects where established when it was observed that the behavioral effects of acute alcohol administration are similar to those caused by benzodiazepines (which also modulate $GABA_A$ receptors and are often used as a first line treatment for alcohol withdrawal). Specific $GABA_A$ receptors are sensitive to differing levels of alcohol intoxication, which may help to explain the broad range of behavioral effects caused by alcohol (Kumar et al., 2009). A number of knock-out and knock-in animal models (whereby certain genes are inactivated, or genetic material is added) have shown that targeting $GABA_A$ receptors can impact various behavioral effects of intoxication, including hyperactivity, motor-impairment, and anxiolytic effects (Lobo & Harris, 2008) as well as decreasing self-administration (Stephens, Pistovcakova, Worthing, Atack, & Dawson, 2005). As may be expected, chronic alcohol use can produce adaptations of $GABA_A$ receptor functioning, possibly through downregulation of the $\alpha 1$ subunit (Koob, 2013; Mhatre, Pena, Sieghart, & Ticku, 1993).

GABA may also be linked to memory consolidation and executive functioning deficits. If alcohol is consumed prior to memory encoding, $GABA_A$ disrupts the coding of new information in the hippocampus which impairs memory consolidation (McGaugh, 2004). This suggests that GABA may play a key role in reported memory loss ('blackouts') during heavy episodic drinking sessions (Lee, Roh, & Kim, 2009). Human imaging data also demonstrates that sober binge drinkers can have significantly lower rates of GABA in the anterior cingulate cortex (ACC: a key area for executive functioning), and significant correlations have been found between GABA in the ACC and motor inhibition and switching behavior (Silveri et al., 2014).

Overall, given the opposing actions of GABA and glutamate, it is essential that these are balanced. However, alcohol disrupts this balance by increasing GABA (inhibition) and decreasing glutamate (excitation). At high levels of intoxication this disruption can result in serious depressant effects including respiratory failure and death. Behaviorally, GABA and glutamate have a broad range of effects, particularly the common side-effects of acute alcohol intoxication. Furthermore, they may also play a direct role in modulating consumption and potential memory impairments following heavy episodic drinking (bingeing). In line with DA, there is also evidence for involvement in impairments of cognitive functions, further demonstrating the broad range of neurotransmitter actions caused by alcohol intoxication.

Corticotrophin releasing hormone and glucocorticoids

Alcohol triggers release of corticotropin-releasing hormone (CRH, a peptide hormone, also known as corticotropin-releasing factor) from the hypothalamus, a region which controls multiple hormonal activities related to stress responses as well as other bodily processes (Stephens & Wand, 2012). CRH cascades down to release adrenocorticotropic hormone from the pituitary which then stimulates the release of cortisol (corticosterone in rodents) from the adrenal cortex. This system is commonly known as the Hypothalamic-Pituitary-Adrenal (HPA) axis. Cortisol is often described as the 'stress hormone' as it is released in response to physical and psychological stressors. However, it is important to note that *arousing* stimuli, whether from positive or negative sources, can activate the HPA axis (Rose, Shaw, Prendergast, & Little, 2010).

Under normal circumstances the HPA axis is a *negative feedback loop* , with the release of cortisol feeding back to stop the release of CRH. The neurocircuitry underpinning stress responses involve interactions between the brain stem (e.g. VTA, dorsal raphe, locus coeruleus, substantia nigra), limbic regions (e.g. amygdala, hypothalamus, thalamus), insular and anterior cingulate cortex, regions of the prefrontal cortex, ventral and dorsal striatum, and sensory and motor cortices. These pathways help process alcohol and stressful stimuli and regulate responses to them (Wemm & Sinha, 2019). For example, CRH regulates the extended amygdala (located beneath the basal ganglia), which in turn manages neural responses to stress and other negative emotions (e.g. anxiety).

Behavioral effects: Animal studies suggest that cortisol has some reinforcing properties itself, as rats will self-administer corticosterone to achieve plasma concentrations in the range of 1 - 1.5 μM (similar to those that occur during stressful experiences) (Piazza et al., 1993).

Cortisol activity may contribute to increased risk of harmful drinking. Non-dependent drinkers with a family history of AUD show heightened cortisol responses and greater alcohol consumption following exposure to stress (Brkic, Soderpalm, & Soderpalm Gordh, 2015). Compared with light social drinkers, heavy social drinkers can display a blunted cortisol response to a moderate (0.8 g/kg) dose of alcohol (King, Munisamy, de Wit, & Lin, 2006).

As well as being a potential risk factor for harmful drinking, cortisol activity changes as AUD develop (Stephens & Wand, 2012). Within dependent drinkers, both self-reported craving and plasma cortisol levels were greater in response to alcohol cues and alcohol consumption, relative to a control group (Hammarberg, Jayaram-Lindstrom, Beck, Franck, & Reid, 2009). Compared with controls, abstinent patients reported greater craving and anxiety following guided stress and alcohol imagery scripts. However, greater cortisol levels were only found following alcohol exposure in the patients (increased cortisol responses were limited to stress exposure in controls) (Sinha et al., 2009).

Despite these findings most research has suggested that chronic alcohol use results in a blunted cortisol response (Koob & Schulkin, 2018). Pratt and Davidson (Pratt & Davidson, 2009) measured salivary cortisol and alcohol consumption following a stress procedure in AUD participants. Compared with a control condition, blunted cortisol response to stress was associated with increased drinking. Similarly, Junghanns et al (Junghanns et al., 2003) demonstrated that a blunted cortisol response predicted early relapse following abstention.

These findings suggest that cortisol may be involved in determining drinking behavior via several mechanisms. For instance, if alcohol consumed in close temporal proximity to a stressful event reduces the stress-induced cortisol release, we may drink to achieve alcohol's anxiolytic effects (negative reinforcement). In contrast, if there are some positive reinforcing aspects to alcohol induced cortisol activity, then we may drink more to overcome the blunted cortisol response that develops from chronic alcohol consumption. However, we would argue that there are enough inconsistencies in this area to suggest that as drinking becomes heavier, cortisol activity becomes dysfunctional (not necessarily hyporeactive) (Rose et al., 2010).

Overall, the relationship between alcohol behavior and cortisol activity is complex, with HPA function both influencing, and being influenced by, drinking behavior. This relationship may also involve both positive and negative reinforcement processes, with cortisol playing an important role during alcohol withdrawal (discussed below).

Acetaldehyde

As well as alcohol's direct effects on neurotransmitters, its metabolism can also influence our response to alcohol and risk of alcohol harm. While alcohol's metabolism is not a key aspect in the prominent BAMs, it is worth providing a brief overview as it has also informed the development of pharmacotherapeutic treatments.

Although alcohol is metabolized through several pathways, the most common is via the enzymes alcohol dehydrogenase (ADH) and aldehyde dehydrogenase (ALDH2). ADH metabolizes alcohol into *acetaldehyde*, a carcinogen which is highly toxic, especially to the *liver where the majority of alcohol metabolism takes place* (Guo & Ren, 2010). From this, ALDH breaks down *acetaldehyde* to *acetate*, which is then metabolized to water and carbon dioxide before being excreted.

Some people have an ALDH2 deficiency which results in a build-up of acetaldehyde, leading to a number of unpleasant and potentially dangerous side effects including facial flushing, nausea and tachycardia. Approximately 36% of East Asian populations possess this ALDH2 deficiency which is often associated withlower alcohol use or abstinence (Brooks, Enoch, Goldman, Li, & Yokoyama, 2009). There are two types of ALDH2 deficiency, one in which the build-up of acetaldehyde is higher and often results in people not consuming alcohol due to the adverse effects, and one in which the adverse effects are not as significant. In these people, alcohol consumption is possible but is linked with a significantly higher risk of developing serious health problems, such as esophageal cancer (Brooks et al., 2009).

Behavioral effects: At small doses acetaldehyde is thought to cause stimulation and positive reinforcement, indicated by the finding that animals (rats) will reliably self-administer acetaldehyde (sometimes at greater levels than alcohol) (Brown, Amit, & Rockman, 1979), and are more likely to consume alcohol after being injected with acetaldehyde (Myers, Ng, Marzuki, Myers, & Singer, 1984). Although there are some inconsistences in the evidence base, these types of finding suggest that acetaldehyde has considerable motivational properties. The effects are biphasic, however, and also include sedation, a loss of consciousness and impaired ability to co-ordinate movements at higher doses (Quertemont, Tambour, & Tirelli, 2005). Some have observed that greater doses of acetaldehyde contributes to poor memory consolidation and 'blackouts' (Quertemont & Tambour, 2004) and so maybe involved in some of the negative effects commonly reported with binge-drinking (Marino & Fromme, 2016). Rapid accumulation of acetaldehyde can lead to unpleasant and aversive effects, which has led to the development of the pharmacotherapy Disulfiram (discussed below).

Brain adaptations: a theoretical framework

In the previous section we outlined some of the key neurotransmitters, their interactions, and behavioral correlates, highlighting the complexity of alcohol's effects. Any theoretical framework that seeks to help us understand AUD and addictive behavior needs to acknowledge this complexity. One particularly influential BAM has been developed by Koob and colleagues. A thorough overview of this model is beyond the scope of this chapter, but this section will highlight some of the key aspects of this BAM in relation to alcohol use. Koob has a large number of comprehensive articles for the interested reader (e.g. Koob, 2009; Koob & Le Moal, 2001, 2008b; Koob & Schulkin, 2018; Koob & Volkow, 2010).

Koob argues that addiction develops through a three-stage cycle: binge/intoxication, withdrawal/negative affect, and preoccupation/anticipation. This cycle becoming progressively worse as alcohol use increases. Koob also claims that early stages of alcohol use are governed more by impulsive behavior (acting in response to internal/external cues with little regard to potential negative consequences) and positive reinforcement processes. As alcohol use becomes more frequent and heavier, a series of brain adaptations results in deficits of the reward system and cognitive impairments which leads to compulsive behavior (persisting in a behavior despite being aware of adverse consequences). Such compulsive drinking is governed by negative reinforcement processes (i.e. removal of negative emotional and physical states). This proposal fits with the finding that neurotransmission of dopamine and opioids, associated more with reward and positive reinforcement, become depleted as drinking becomes more dependent (Gianoulakis, 2001). Once drinking becomes compulsive, individuals may be motivated to drink in an attempt to avoid the negative state produced by hypoactive opioidergic and dopaminergic systems (among other neurotransmitter systems).

According to this model, the progression from positive to negative reinforcement develops from an *allostatic dysregulation* of the brain's reward system, and later allostatic dysregulation of multiple neuronal systems. In its 'normal' healthy state, the brain works to maintain system homeostasis (a state of equilibrium at a given set-point which allows systems to function well). Given the significant effects alcohol can have on the brain's neuronal functioning, it seems reasonable within this framework that the brain will counteract these effects in an attempt to reinstate homeostasis. For instance, a homeostatic or counter-adaptation response might be to inhibit dopamine activity.

Allostasis is a more complex state than homeostasis, and is defined as 'stability through change', whereby stability can only be maintained by shifting the set point. Unlike homeostasis, which works through a negative feedback mechanism (George et al., 2012) (i.e. the output will inhibit the original activating stimulus), allostasis works through a feedforward mechanism, with frequent re-evaluations resulting in constant adjustment of the system's set-points. Eventually an allostatic load is reached which can result in negative, pathological states, which drives the individual to drink more in an attempt to alleviate this state (negative reinforcement).

Koob et al. proposed that brain adaptations during the development of AUD includes both within- and between-system changes. A within-system neuroadaptation describes when the direct response to alcohol administration changes in order to reduce alcohol's effect, for instance reduced GABA function (Koob, 2013). Another example would be reduced response of monoamines (e.g. dopamine and serotonin) within the nucleus accumbens. This adaptation could reduce the positive reinforcing effects of alcohol and, if this adaptation continues when alcohol is not present, may contribute to the experience of withdrawal. As drinking continues, between-system adaptations also occur, whereby brain systems not directly involved in the rewarding effects of alcohol become dysregulated via persistent activation of the reward system.

The extended amygdala is described as a key region which integrates neural arousal-stress systems with hedonic processing systems. Koob (2013) suggests that this is a vital between-system in the development of the opponent/adaptive processes seen in AUD. As outlined above, evidence shows that CRF function within the extend amygdala and HPA axis becomes increasingly dysfunctional as AUD develops, with higher (neurotoxic) levels of cortisol present during alcohol withdrawal. Koob argues that the increased activity of the brains stress systems (which would also include dynorphin activity) significantly contributes to the heightened anxiety and negative states experienced during withdrawal.

Although Koob and colleagues do not discount the role of cognitive impairments, incentive salience and other factors highlighted in alternative models, their primary argument is that AUDs are a reward deficit disorder and that the withdrawal syndrome is a major barrier to achieving abstinence. Both within- and between-system adaptations reduce reward function thus producing the dysphoric state often observed in those with severe AUDs and during times of withdrawal (Koob, 2013). Although increased drinking may initially be due to dysfunction of one system, as AUD becomes more severe, many more systems are impaired resulting in chronic, life-debilitating alcohol use.

Koob and colleague's work on this adaptation model over many years has led to a detailed theoretical framework from which to study drinking behavior and make predictions about development of AUD and treatment outcomes (e.g. Koob, 2003, 2009, 2013, 2015; Volkow, Koob, & McLellan, 2016). However, that is not to conclude that this BAM, or others, do not have their critics. There are numerous papers that have highlighted issues with inconsistent evidence, absence of predicative validity, and failure to take into account the important role of other factors (e.g. environment). We would encourage the reader to seek these out (e.g. Hall et al., 2015; Heather et al., 2018).

The role of brain adaptations in key aspects of addiction

Alcohol use disorders are commonly referred to as a chronically relapsing disorder, with individuals experiencing several cycles of alcohol use, abstinence, and relapse. Relapse is one of the major challenges AUD, which can be up to 70% within 6 months of receiving treatment (Raistrick, Heather, & Godfrey, 2006). Below we briefly describe three major triggers for dependent and non-dependent alcohol consumption (priming, cues, and stress), and the potential neuropharmacological mechanisms by which these triggers exert their effect. Additionally, we will highlight particular adaptations believed to support the maintenance of drinking behavior and which are significantly related to relapse risk (tolerance and withdrawal).

Priming

'Priming' describes the process whereby initial administration of a substance (e.g. alcohol) can stimulate motivation to continue self-administration, perhaps to excessive levels. Anecdotal evidence suggests that an initial 'slip drink' may precipitate relapse in individuals trying to abstain from drinking or a binge drinking episode in current drinkers. Stewart et al.(1984) positive affective, motivational-incentive theory, suggests that substances produce positive effects via direct actions on the central nervous system (e.g. an increase in dopamine activity), and that these actions underlie motivation to continue substance use. Particularly in the short-term, senitization to a substance's positive effects could result in a priming dose transiently motivating drinking behavior (Stewart & de Wit, 1987). Several studies have found that priming is associated with the subjective positive effects of alcohol (Rose & Duka, 2006; Rose & Grunsell, 2008), indicating that priming may work through positive reinforcement.

As outlined above, β-endorphin activity is related to alcohol's positive effects and in vitro alcohol exposure to the pituitary gland or hypothalamus triggers the release of β-endorphin in a dose-dependent manner, with lower concentrations (similar to a priming dose) producing the greatest release and this effect only lasting for a limited period (15–20 minutes) (Gianoulakis, 2001). Therefore, it is likely that alcohol's effect on the DA and opioid system underlie its ability to 'prime' individuals. Indeed, although not specific to alcohol, several studies have found that DA agonists and DA antagonists trigger and block drug-induced relapse respectively, and that the mesocorticolimbic pathways are key in this process (Stewart, 2008).

Cues

Through associative learning processes (e.g. classical and instrumental conditioning), cues/stimuli which often co-occur with alcohol and drinking episodes can become conditioned stimuli, alerting the individual to the possible availability of alcohol. These cues, e.g. the sight of a local bar or a bottle of your favorite wine on a shop shelf, can trigger alcohol seeking and consumption independently of the pharmacological effects of alcohol (e.g. priming).

A variety of studies have shown that the opioid system may be important in cue-induced alcohol behavior. Animals can show a conditioned place preference (CPP), for environments that have previously been associated with alcohol and its effects. Lesions of the β-endorphin fibers innervating the nucleus accumbens can facilitate the extinction of the CPP when animals are placed in the environment in an alcohol free state. Opioid antagonists (e.g. naltrexone) can reduce cue-induced relapse in animals (Liu & Weiss, 2002) and can increase periods of abstinence in humans (O'Malley et al., 1992). Dopamine has also been implicated in this area. In humans, reduced DA-D2 receptors have been associated with increased neural activation within the anterior cingulate and regions of the prefrontal cortex in response to alcohol (compared with control) stimuli. Additionally, correlations were found between decreased DA-D2 receptors and reported craving in detoxified AUD patients, and craving was predictive of relapse risk (Heinz et al., 2004, 2010). Imaging studies have shown that, compared with control cues, alcohol cues trigger greater activity in the anterior cingulate, medial prefrontal cortex and putamen in AUD patients relate to controls. Interestingly, the degree of activation in these areas predicted craving and was positively related to alcohol intake when patients relapsed, even though craving was not (Grusser et al., 2004).These areas have also been highlighted as important in other substance-induced relapse (e.g. cocaine) as well as the basolateral amygdala (BLA), the hippocampus, and the core of the nucleus accumbens (Stewart, 2008).

Stress

The link between stress and alcohol consumption was originally made by the tension-reduction hypotheses (Cappell & Herman, 1972). Stress increases anxiety and so alcohol is consumed to ameliorate this negative state, i.e. self-medication. If this chain of events occurs when someone is abstinent, this is called stress-induced reinstatement/relapse (Mason, Shaham, Weiss, & Le, 2009). Individuals with AUD demonstrate altered stress responses, such as a dysfunction in the HPA axis and the neural circuits that mediate behavioral responses to stressors. These adaptations may make elevated stress and anxiety a key symptom of AUD (particularly withdrawal) (Koob, 2015).

Stress increases the release of CRH/CRF, which stimulates the production of adrenocorticotropic hormones (ACTH), which in turn stimulates the synthesis of cortisol and glucocorticoids. Long term alcohol use is thought to attenuate cortisol response to stressors (see Errico, Parsons, King, & Lovallo, 1993). Highlighting this, Sinha et al. (Sinha et al., 2011) demonstrated that lack of stress (and cue-induced) cortisol responses distinguished alcohol-dependent patients from controls. In animal models, CRF activity has been implicated in stress-induced alcohol relapse (Le et al., 2000), with Liu & Weiss (2002) finding that a CRF antagonist blocked relapse following foot shock (an animal model of stress induction). Animal models have also found that the noradrenalin agonist lofexidine can block stress-induced relapse, and that the noradrenalin antagonist can yohimbine can trigger alcohol seeking (Le, Harding, Juzytsch, Funk, & Shaham, 2005). Given noradrenalin's role in psychiatric disorders, such as major depression and stress-induced depression (Seki, Yoshida, & Jaiswal, 2018), it is perhaps not surprising that alcohol use via negative reinforcement processes involves this neurotransmitter.

This brief section shows that specific mechanisms of alcohol use may involve both shared and unique neurotransmitters and brain regions. It is important to keep in mind, however, that there can be variation in the response to the biological systems affected by stress, cues, and alcohol, with factors such as AUD severity, duration and stressful life events playing a role (Brady & Sonne, 1999; Sillaber & Henniger, 2004).

Tolerance

As we drink more frequently, often we will find that the subjective effects of intoxication are less extreme. This tolerance may increase the frequency with which we drink and/or the quantity of alcohol we consume, in an attempt to experience alcohol's reinforcing subjective effects. The neurochemical basis of tolerance mainly covers changes to the neurotransmitters outlined above. For instance, tolerance to GABA-/glutamate related behavioral effects (sedation, motor-co-ordination and cognitive impairment) have been observed following long-term alcohol use in experimental animal studies (Gonzales & Jaworski, 1997; Silvers, Tokunaga, Mittleman, & Matthews, 2003). Additionally, DA release is inversely related to the frequency of heavy drinking (Urban et al., 2010), suggesting tolerance involves blunted DA responses. In line with BAMs, tolerance can be described as an increase in reward thresholds; we have to drink more in order to activate reward pathways. Tolerance further complicates our understanding of AUD, as it can be moderated by environment. Consuming alcohol in unfamiliar contexts (without conditioned cues) are often stronger in both humans and animals (Birak, Higgs, & Terry, 2011; Mccusker & Brown, 1990), highlighting the importance of associative learning mentioned above. Furthermore, the tolerance of GABA systems due to alcohol can make treating the alcohol withdrawal syndrome with GABA agonists (such as Benzodiazepines) difficult as the therapeutic effects of these drugs can be reduced via mechanisms of cross-tolerance (Liang & Olsen, 2014).

Withdrawal

The alcohol withdrawal syndrome (AWS) usually develops 6–24 hours after someone has stopped drinking or significantly reduced their alcohol intake. AWS can range from mild to severe and is often characterized by negative mood states including apathy, agitation and anxiety, low mood, irritability and depression (Trevisan, Boutros, Petrakis, & Krystal, 1998). Physically the individual is likely to feel nausea, tremors, hypertension and tachycardia. Cognitively, confusion and a lack of concentration are common. At the more extreme end, hallucinations, seizures, delirium tremens and coma are possible and must be medically managed (Mirijello et al., 2015). Some physical symptoms often decrease over the first few days of abstinence and other mild-moderate symptoms start to improve after one - two weeks. However, there can also be a protracted AWS which lasts for many months after drinking has ceased. The protracted AWS may involve persistence of symptoms at lower levels and is often focused more on psychological symptoms, e.g. depression, anhedonia, anxiety (Heilig, Egli, Crabbe, & Becker, 2010).

Withdrawal is often seen as a key factor in AUD, either through helping maintain drinking to avoid withdrawal or as a trigger to remove withdrawal during a period of abstinence. During withdrawal, neurotransmission of all the systems outlined above becomes dysfunctional. Those systems associated with positive reinforcement (e.g. dopamine, opioid, serotonin) show reduced activity, and those systems associated with negative reinforcement (e.g. adrenocorticotropic hormone, cortisol, and amygdala CRF) show increased activity (Koob & Le Moal, 2008a).

As withdrawal is associated with heightened feelings of stress and anxiety, it is not surprising that the HPA axis is involved. However, from an evolutionary point of view it has been argued that stress states are often associated with imminent threat. In this situation energy is directed to make quick fight/flight responses, and the midbrain may inhibit activity within the prefrontal cortex (which requires energy and time to make complete complex executive functions) (Arnsten, 2009). Although useful in immediate threat situations, this neuronal environment might help explain why it can be so difficult for some individuals to engage with psychosocial treatments and make rational decisions about their behavior during withdrawal.

Animal studies have shown that corticosterone levels are high in the brain and plasma following alcohol withdrawal (Little et al., 2008). However, interestingly, while plasma levels returned to normal levels within about 24 hours, brain levels continued to be high even after 2 months of abstinence (equivalent to around 6 years in humans) especially within the hippocampus and prefrontal cortex (Sengupta, 2013). This prolonged increased cortisol activity during withdrawal may play an important role in the cognitive impairments observed during this time. Prolonged, elevated levels of glucocorticoids induce neuronal changes and are neurotoxic. In humans, more severe cognitive deficits were found in patients who had higher cortisol levels during alcohol withdrawal (Errico et al., 2002; Keedwell et al., 2001). It is possible, that these cognitive impairments could be avoided, or at least reduced. In animal studies, administration of a glucocorticoid receptor antagonist (mifepristone) just before alcohol withdrawal blocked the memory deficits usually observed after 1–2 weeks of abstinence (Jacquot et al., 2008).

Similarly to cortisol, glutamate is also neurotoxic at elevated levels. As suggested by Koob and colleagues and confirmed by some animal models (Koob, 2014; Clapp et al., 2008), while acute alcohol consumption inhibits glutamate activity, chronic consumption results in counter-adaptations including an increased number of NMDA receptors (Gilpin & Koob, 2008). When someone with severe AUD abstains, the increased NMDA activity may contribute to cognitive impairments via neuronal death and withdrawal seizures via hyperexcitability (Gonzales & Jaworski, 1997).

The anhedonia and dysphoria often felt during withdrawal likely involves the dopaminergic, serotonergic, and opioidergic systems. For instance, reduced activity within the mesolimbic system has been linked with reduced positive reinforcement as alcohol use becomes more chronic (tolerance), the negative moods often experienced by those trying to abstain, and increased craving for alcohol (George et al., 2012). Animal studies show that both DA and serotonin activity remains inhibited during alcohol withdrawal (Koob, 2013). Within humans, imaging research has shown lower numbers of D2 DA receptors in those with severe AUDs, and these reduced levels persist through withdrawal (Volkow et al., 2002). Reduced receptors combined with lower extracellular DA levels may result in the anhedonia observed during withdrawal: patients cannot find pleasure in alcohol or natural reinforcers as the brain's reward circuitry is impaired (Koob, 2013).

Dynorphins (opioid peptides with a preference for binding to κ receptors) are widely distributed in the central nervous system, and are involved in regulating pain and neuroendocrine function, appetitive behavior and stress response (Schwarzer, 2009). Dynorphins are thought to mediate negative affective states and trigger dysphoria. Dopamine can trigger dynorphin release which in turn reduces both dopaminergic and glutamatergic activity within the mesolimbic dopamine system and nucleus accumbens and increases CRF in neural stress pathways (Koob et al., 2014). Together, this suggests that dynorphins may play a role decreased positive reinforcement and increased negative reinforcement processes as AUD develops.

In summary, the neural context of withdrawal contributes to a psychological state whereby the individual experiences significant stress and dysphoria, an inability to find pleasure, and an impaired ability to make decisions. Withdrawal involves a complex interaction between multiple neurotransmitter systems and brain regions. From this context, it is not difficult to understand why withdrawal is associated with a high risk of relapse, with individuals drinking in an attempt to remove/ameliorate negative affect. However, we should always keep in mind the significant number of people who do not relapse, or those who relapse once the withdrawal syndrome has subsided.

How are drug treatments developed

Brain adaptation models of addiction have contributed to the rapid identification of key neurotransmitters involved in the addiction cycle, and their observable cognitive and behavioral manifestations. The primary goal of medication development is to identify these therapeutic targets and create effective compounds (Litten et al., 2012). If we are able to identify candidate neurotransmitters or enzymes which contribute to lower thresholds for relapse (through increases in incentive salience or decreases in cognitive control, for example), then we may be able to develop and synthesize pharmacological (drug) treatments to target these neurotransmitters.

However, only a small number of medications are approved for the treatment of alcohol dependence, with more currently being investigated 'off-label' and some currently under development. At first glance, this small number may seem surprising, but it is worth noting that drug development is a slow and expensive process often taking more than 10 years and billions of pounds/dollars. Furthermore, the most commonly used drugs for treating alcohol dependence (disulfiram, naltrexone and acamprosate) were FDA approved before or around the same time as the BAM of addiction came to prominence. The success of pharmacological treatments for AUD is heavily debated, given that a key promise of BAMs were greater number and more effective treatments (Swift & Aston, 2015). As we have seen the pharmacological profile of alcohol use and misuse is complex (not to mention the effects of environmental and genetic factors), which in turn contributes to highly heterogeneous AUDs.

As our understanding of the neurotransmitter profile of alcohol use and misuse improves it may help us to understand the mechanisms underlying treatment efficacy/effectiveness. This section shall provide an overview of the pharmacotherapies licensed for treatment of AUD, as well as some that are commonly used off-label. It is worth noting that despite the prominent focus of research on DA's role in alcohol behavior, there are currently no treatments which are focused primarily on dopaminergic activity. Again, this highlights the complexities of the neurotransmitter profile of alcohol but may also be partly explained by inconsistent results (Ma & Zhu, 2014). Both animal and human studies have shown that DA agonists (e.g. bromocriptine) and DA antagonists (e.g. tiapride) are (or are not) associated with reducing alcohol consumption and symptoms of AUD (e.g. craving, anxiety) (Bender et al., 2007; Lawford et al., 1995; Naranjo, Dongier, & Bremner, 1997; Shaw et al., 1994; Weiss, Mitchiner, Bloom, & Koob, 1990).

Naltrexone/naloxone/nalmefene: opioid antagonists

Naloxone, naltrexone and nalmefene are all non-selective opioid receptor antagonists; they activate all three key opioid receptor subtypes, although naltrexone and naloxone have a higher affinity with the μ receptor (HERZ 1997). Given the earlier discussion of the specific roles different opioid receptors may play in determining alcohol use, it is perhaps not surprising that antagonists of the μ and δ opioid receptor subtypes appear to be more effective in reducing drinking behavior compared with antagonists of the κ receptor subtype.

In humans with AUD, naltrexone can decrease compulsive drinking behavior and frequency of relapse (Mendez & Morales-Mulia, 2008). Naltrexone is thought to exert its therapeutic effect by blocking μ-opioid receptors within the mesolimbic dopamine system. By doing this naltrexone may reduce the rewarding effects of alcohol, leading to reduced cravings and continued abstinence (therefore it is working through reducing positive reinforcement). For example, Helstrom et al. (2016 provided Naltrexone to alcohol dependent patients in a residential treatment program and demonstrated that during treatment, craving scores decreased faster compared with individuals who declined Naltrexone. An obvious limitation in the strength of this finding is the lack of randomization and the increased craving levels at baseline in individuals who accepted Naltrexone. Further support of Naltrexone's efficacy comes from observed improvement in short-term treatment outcomes (including relapse) (Anton et al., 2001), however various null results have also been published (Gastpar et al., 2002). Overall, quantitative syntheses of the available evidence suggest that injectable naltrexone reduces heavy drinking days by approximately 5% (4.6%: 95% CIs 0.56%–8.5%), but has no effect on abstinence (Jonas et al., 2014).

Nalmefene is a partial agonist on κ-receptors, with animal studies suggesting this dampens the acute rewarding and positive reinforcing effects of alcohol, by reducing activation in the mesolimbic DA system. It was approved for the recommendation of the reduction of alcohol consumption in patients with alcohol dependence who drink at high risk levels on a daily basis (> 60 g of alcohol if male, >40 g if female). Meta-analyses have demonstrated that nalmefene can be effective in the reduction of alcohol consumption, including the number of heavy drinking days at 6 months and total alcohol consumption at six months follow-up (Palpacuer et al., 2015). However, the decision to recommend nalmefene has been criticized based on a lack of critical evidence in the specific population for which it was approved and a lack of randomized controlled trials comparing it to naltrexone: a drug with similar clinical effectiveness but less expensive (Naudet, Fitzgerald, & Braillon, 2016).

Opioid-based treatments provide a good example of how individual factors may influence how effective a treatment is. Risk of developing AUD involves a large heritability component (~ 50% (Verhulst, Neale, & Kendler, 2015)), and genetic studies have identified several polymorphisms which may increase risk of developing AUD through a variety of psychopharmacological mechanisms. For instance, there is a functional polymorphism

(Asn40Asp) of the OPRM1 gene, which increases binding of β-endorphins to μ-opioid receptor subtypes in response to alcohol ingestion. This has the effect of increasing the positive reinforcing effects of alcohol, and thus its abuse potential. Animal studies have also shown that this variant results in an increase of approximately 200% extracellular dopamine in response to ethanol administration (Ramchandani et al., 2011). This is much greater than the ~20–50% increase often observed in animal ethanol studies (Doyon et al., 2003). In human studies, patients with the Asn40Asp variant had better outcomes associated with naltrexone treatment than those without the variant (e.g. Anton et al., 2008). Although candidate gene research has produced some interesting findings, their validity has been questioned and research is moving more towards gene-wide association research (Duncan, Ostacher, & Ballon, 2019).

Acamprosate

Acamprosate affects glutamate and GABA neurotransmission. Although its precise mechanism of action is not certain, its effect on glutamate and GABA maybe indirect, with mechanisms of effect occurring via action on neuronal calcium channels, and there is some evidence that Acamprosate can indirectly increase DA activity within the nucleus accumbens(Kalk & Lingford-Hughes, 2014). After 21 days of acamprosate treatment, participants with AUD seeking to control their intake (but not achieve total abstinence) displayed a reduced alcohol priming effect and no associated increase in cortisol, but no effect was found on cue reactivity (Hammarberg et al., 2009). Several meta-analysis have demonstrated that Acamprosate is superior to placebo across various outcomes including abstinent days, complete abstinence and non-drinking days (Kranzler & Van Kirk, 2001; Mason & Lehert, 2012). The efficacy of Acamprosate is thought to be similar to Naltrexone, with increased efficacy when these two drugs are combined (Boothby & Doering, 2005). Evidence from animal models suggests that acamprosate does not influence alcohol-induced reward (unlike the effects of Naltrexone) but rather reduces alcohol's negative reinforcing effects when consumed during the descending phase of the blood alcohol when the pharmacological effects of alcohol are 'wearing off'. The effect of Acamprosate on NMDA and $GABA_A$ receptor function decreases glutamate during alcohol withdrawal and subjectively its use is associated with decreased anxiety, arousal and insomnia (Hammarberg et al., 2009). Again, this suggests that its therapeutic efficacy may be working via attenuating alcohol's negative reinforcing effects. In some human studies, however, acamprosate does not seem to influence subjective or psychomotor alcohol-related effects (Brasser, McCaul, & Houtsmuller, 2004), and others have suggested the effects of acamprosate on subjective effects are 'subtle' (Kalk & Lingford-Hughes, 2014).

Baclofen

Baclofen is a γ-aminobutyric acid B ($GABA_B$) receptor agonist used as an anti-spasticity agent since the 1970s which has recently attracted interest as a pharmacotherapy for AUD. One appealing aspect of baclofen is that it is excreted largely through the kidneys, so is a potential pharmacotherapy for some of the most high-need AUD patients (Owens et al., 2017). For instance those with alcohol-related liver disease cannot take naltrexone or disulfiram, and acamprosate should be avoided in those with renal impairment. Therefore, baclofen was highlighted as a potential pharmacotherapy for high-need patients and/or those who have already failed to respond to other pharmacotherapies.

$GABA_B$ receptors are prolific n the limbic system, a key area for regulating emotion. The stimulation of these receptors inhibits the release of excitatory amino acids (glutamate, aspartate), as well as decreasing serotonin and noradrenaline, and DA activity within the mesolimbic dopamine system (Johnson, 2005). Treatments that activate this system may therefore have multiple actions including reducing the reinforcing and rewarding effects of drinking, negative emotion (e.g. anxiety) and alcohol withdrawal (Brennan, Leung, Gagliardi, Rivelli, & Muzyk, 2013).

Both pre-clinical (i.e. animal) and human studies have shown that baclofen reduces alcohol intake (for a review see Rose & Jones, 2018). Although the psychological mechanisms by which baclofen's therapeutic effects occurs are unclear, its pharmacological profile suggests that it may work through affecting mood and alcohol reinforcement processes. However, recent meta-analyses of clinical randomised control trials have found that baclofen performs no better than placebo (Bschor, Henssler, Muller, & Baethge, 2018; Rose & Jones, 2018).

Glucocorticoid antagonists

Some initial small trials have shown therapeutic benefit of cortisol antagonism. When mifepristone (a glucocorticoid Type II receptor antagonist) was given to non-treatment seeking AUD participants, craving was reduced in a laboratory cue reactivity assessment, and this decrease predicted lower self-reported alcohol consumption during follow-up (Vendruscolo et al., 2015). Given the neurotoxic effects of prolonged cortisol activity and the cognitive impairments this can result in (e.g. learning new skills, executive function, attention and memory (Donoghue et al., 2016)), glucocorticoids antagonists given during withdrawal might prevent some of these. By reducing the cognitive impairments observed during withdrawal it might allow the patient to engage more with psychosocial treatments and, therefore, improve their efficacy.

Disulfiram

Disulfiram (trade name Antabuse) was the first medication approved by the FDA for the treatment of alcohol-dependence, but is considered a controversial treatment. The mechanism of action is to block the enzyme aldehyde dehydrogenase following alcohol consumption, which leads to the accumulation of acetaldehyde. This rapid accumulation causes unpleasant physical symptoms including nausea and vomiting (Swift, 1999). Although these physical effects are thought to play a key role in treatment, the anticipation of these unpleasant effects is also thought to influence the decision to consume alcohol (a psychological deterrent). Meta-analyses have demonstrated that disulfiram is successful at reducing primary treatment-outcomes (ranging from total abstinence to time to first heavy drinking day). However, these effects are largely driven by open-label trials, as blinded RCT designs demonstrated no superiority over controls (Skinner, Lahmek, Pham, & Aubin, 2014). This suggests that the psychological effects of disulfiram play a key role in its efficacy, as patients would be aware of these effects in an open-label trial.

Comparing the effectiveness of different drug treatments

There has been considerable research into the effectiveness of pharmacotherapy for AUD in humans, which can range from; individual-case studies, prospective cohort studies, open label and Randomised Controlled trials (RCTs). One of the most influential analyses on the effectiveness of pharmacotherapy for AUD was a meta-analysis published in 2014. In this study they included adults with AUD who were prescribed an FDA-approved medication or any of 23 off-label medications over a period of 12 weeks (Jonas et al., 2014). They only included RCTs in which pharmacotherapy was compared with a placebo or other medication. In total they included 95 RCTs in their analysis with the majority of studies examining acamprosate, disulfiram or naltrexone. However, there was a large number of off-label drugs (including buspirone, citalopram, fluoxetine etc.). They also examined different possible outcomes, such as return to any drinking, return to heavy drinking, % of drinking days, quality of life, and mortality. The meta-analyses main finding was that there was moderate evidence for acamprosate and naltrexone reducing the likelihood of returning to drinking (numbers needed to treat ranging from 12 to 20). However, the strength of evidence for any established pharmacotherapeutic treatments improving overall quality of life or reducing mortality was considered low, and for many outcomes there was an insufficient number of studies. In relation to off-label medications, there was improvement in consumption outcomes for Nalmefene and Topiramate.

More recently a meta-analysis examined the effects of Nalmefene, naltrexone, acamprosate, baclofen or Topiramate on total-alcohol consumption in non-abstinent adults diagnosed with alcohol dependence or AUDs (Palpacuer et al., 2018). This analysis was timely given nalmefene's approval for pharmacologically controlled drinking (e.g. those who may want to control their drinking rather than be abstinent) by the Europeans Medicine Agency. Network meta-analysis allows for direct comparisons within individual RCTs (e.g. treatment vs control), as well as indirect comparisons across multiple trials. They included 32 placebo controlled RCTs and demonstrated that all drugs reduced total alcohol consumption compared to placebo, with Topiramate demonstrating superiority.

Summary

There is no doubt that alcohol and other substances have direct effects on neuroactivity within the brain, there is also no doubt that persistent alcohol use can lead to functional (e.g. dopamine, opioid, GABA) and structural (e.g. prefrontal cortex) changes within the brain, and that these can contribute to the development of AUD. However, in isolation these effects cannot explain why AUD develops. For instance, the positive reinforcing and rewarding experience of enhanced DA and opioid activity in response to alcohol consumption occurs in both light and heavy drinkers, but not all drinkers develop AUD. Globally, 5–10% of individuals over the age of 15 years consumed alcohol within the past year (these rates are much higher - over 50% - in countries within the Western Pacific, Western Europe, and North America), yet global rates of AUD are 1.4% (approximately 107 million people) (Ritchie & Roser, 2019). This is obviously a significant number of people who require support and treatment (and very likely an underestimation of the true prevalence rate of AUD), but if we were to accept the brain adaptation models and the notion of addiction as a disease, in isolation, this number should be much higher. Additionally, rates of AUD are highest within the 25–34 year age bracket (Ritchie & Roser, 2019), showing that most people do recover from AUD, yet the brain disease framework emphasizes long-term neuroadaptations which make recover increasingly difficult. Furthermore, evidence suggests that after periods of abstinence the persuasive structure and function of brain changes are partially reversible (Buhler & Mann, 2011). Our experience of alcohol intoxication and our risk of developing AUD is the result of complex interactions between neural responses, cognitive and behavioral processes, genetics, environment, social and experiential factors. Alcohol harm is a major public health issue, if we are to reduce the rates of hazardous drinking and AUDs (i.e. prevention) and develop more efficacious treatments, research funding needs to reflect the true nature of alcohol use.

References

Abrahao, K. P., Salinas, A. G., & Lovinger, D. M. (2017). Alcohol and the brain: Neuronal molecular targets, synapses, and circuits. *Neuron*, *96*(6), 1223–1238. Available from https://doi.org/10.1016/j.neuron.2017.10.032.

Anton, R. F., Moak, D. H., Latham, P. K., Waid, L. R., Malcolm, R. J., Dias, J. K., & Roberts, J. S. (2001). Posttreatment results of combining naltrexone with cognitive-behavior therapy for the treatment of alcoholism. *Journal of Clinical Psychopharmacology*, *21*(1), 72–77.

Anton, R. F., Oroszi, G., O'Malley, S., Couper, D., Swift, R., Pettinati, H., & Goldman, D. (2008). An evaluation of mu-opioid receptor (OPRM1) as a predictor of naltrexone response in the treatment of alcohol dependence. *Archives of General Psychiatry*, *65*(2), 135–144. Available from https://doi.org/10.1001/archpsyc.65.2.135.

Arnsten, A. F. T. (2009). Stress signalling pathways that impair prefrontal cortex structure and function. *Nature Reviews Neuroscience*, *10*(6), 410–422. Available from https://doi.org/10.1038/nrn2648.

Barnett, A. I., Hall, W., Fry, C. L., Dilkes-Frayne, E., & Carter, A. (2018). Drug and alcohol treatment providers' views about the disease model of addiction and its impact on clinical practice: A systematic review. *Drug and Alcohol Review*, *37*(6), 697–720. Available from https://doi.org/10.1111/dar.12632.

Bender, S., Scherbaum, N., Soyka, M., Ruther, E., Mann, K., & Gastpar, M. (2007). The efficacy of the dopamine D2/D3 antagonist tiapride in maintaining abstinence: A randomized, double-blind, placebo-controlled trial in 299 alcohol-dependent patients. *The International Journal of Neuropsychopharmacology*, *10*(5), 653–660. Available from https://doi.org/10.1017/S1461145706007164.

Berridge, K. C. (2012). From prediction error to incentive salience: Mesolimbic computation of reward motivation. *The European Journal of Neuroscience*, *35*(7), 1124–1143. Available from https://doi.org/10.1111/j.1460-9568.2012.07990.x.

Birak, K. S., Higgs, S., & Terry, P. (2011). Conditioned tolerance to the effects of alcohol on inhibitory control in humans. *Alcohol and Alcoholism*, *46*(6), 686–693. Available from https://doi.org/10.1093/alcalc/agr084.

Boothby, L. A., & Doering, P. L. (2005). Acamprosate for the treatment of alcohol dependence. *Clinical Therapeutics*, *27*(6), 695–714. Available from https://doi.org/10.1016/j.clinthera.2005.06.015.

Brady, K. T., & Sonne, S. C. (1999). The role of stress in alcohol use, alcoholism treatment, and relapse. *Alcohol Research & Health*, *23*(4), 263–271.

Brasser, S. M., McCaul, M. E., & Houtsmuller, E. J. (2004). Alcohol effects during acamprosate treatment: A dose-response study in humans. *Alcoholism-Clinical and Experimental Research*, *28*(7), 1074–1083. Available from https://doi.org/10.1097/01.Alc.0000130802.07692.29.

Brennan, J. L., Leung, J. G., Gagliardi, J. P., Rivelli, S. K., & Muzyk, A. J. (2013). Clinical effectiveness of baclofen for the treatment of alcohol dependence: A review. *Clinical Pharmacology*, *5*, 99–107. Available from https://doi.org/10.2147/CPAA.S32434.

Brkic, S., Soderpalm, B., & Soderpalm Gordh, A. (2015). A family history of Type 1 alcoholism differentiates alcohol consumption in high cortisol responders to stress. *Pharmacology, Biochemistry, and Behavior*, *130*, 59–66. Available from https://doi.org/10.1016/j.pbb.2014.12.008.

Brodie, M. S., & Appel, S. B. (1998). The effects of ethanol on dopaminergic neurons of the ventral tegmental area studied with intracellular recording in brain slices. *Alcoholism:*

Clinical and Experimental Research, *22*(1), 236–244. Available from https://doi.org/10.1111/j.1530-0277.1998.tb03644.x.

Brooks, P. J., Enoch, M. A., Goldman, D., Li, T. K., & Yokoyama, A. (2009). The alcohol flushing response: An unrecognized risk factor for esophageal cancer from alcohol consumption. *PLoS Medicine*, *6*(3), e50. Available from https://doi.org/10.1371/journal.pmed.1000050.

Brown, Z. W., Amit, Z., & Rockman, G. E. (1979). Intraventricular self-administration of acetaldehyde, but not ethanol, in naive laboratory rats. *Psychopharmacology (Berl)*, *64*(3), 271–276. Available from https://doi.org/10.1007/bf00427509.

Brozoski, T. J., Brown, R. M., Rosvold, H. E., & Goldman, P. S. (1979). Cognitive deficit caused by regional depletion of dopamine in prefrontal cortex of rhesus monkey. *Science*, *205*(4409), 929–932. Available from https://doi.org/10.1126/science.112679.

Bschor, T., Henssler, J., Muller, M., & Baethge, C. (2018). Baclofen for alcohol use disorder-a systematic meta-analysis. *Acta Psychiatr Scand*, *138*(3), 232–242. Available from https://doi.org/10.1111/acps.12905.

Buhler, M., & Mann, K. (2011). Alcohol and the human brain: A systematic review of different neuroimaging methods. *Alcoholism-Clinical and Experimental Research*, *35*(10), 1771–1793. Available from https://doi.org/10.1111/j.1530-0277.2011.01540.x.

Cappell, H., & Herman, C. P. (1972). Alcohol and tension reduction. A review. *Quarterly Journal of Studies in Alcohol*, *33*(1), 33–64.

Clapp, P., Bhave, S. V., & Hoffman, P. L. (2008). How adaptation of the brain to alcohol leads to dependence: a pharmacological perspective. *Alcohol Res Health*, *31*(4), 310–339.

Crews, F. T., & Boettiger, C. A. (2009). Impulsivity, frontal lobes and risk for addiction. *Pharmacology, Biochemistry, and Behavior*, *93*(3), 237–247. Available from https://doi.org/10.1016/j.pbb.2009.04.018.

Criswell, H. E., Ming, Z., Kelm, M. K., & Breese, G. R. (2008). Brain regional differences in the effect of ethanol on GABA release from presynaptic terminals. *Journal of Pharmacology and Experimental Therapeutics*, *326*(2), 596–603. Available from https://doi.org/10.1124/jpet.107.135418.

Darcq, E., & Kieffer, B. L. (2018). Opioid receptors: Drivers to addiction? *Nature Reviews Neuroscience*, *19*(8), 499–514. Available from https://doi.org/10.1038/s41583-018-0028-x.

Dennis, F. (2017). Conceiving of addicted pleasures: A 'modern' paradox. *The International Journal on Drug Policy*, *49*, 150–159. Available from https://doi.org/10.1016/j.drugpo.2017.07.007.

Donoghue, K., Rose, A., Coulton, S., Milward, J., Reed, K., Drummond, C., & Little, H. (2016). Double-blind, 12 month follow-up, placebo-controlled trial of mifepristone on cognition in alcoholics: The MIFCOG trial protocol. *BMC Psychiatry*, *16*, 40. Available from https://doi.org/10.1186/s12888-016-0757-1.

Doyon, W. M., York, J. L., Diaz, L. M., Samson, H. H., Czachowski, C. L., & Gonzales, R. A. (2003). Dopamine activity in the nucleus accumbens during consummatory phases of oral ethanol self-administration. *Alcoholism-Clinical and Experimental Research*, *27*(10), 1573–1582. Available from https://doi.org/10.1097/01.Alc.0000089959.66222.B8.

Duncan, L. E., Ostacher, M., & Ballon, J. (2019). How genome-wide association studies (GWAS) made traditional candidate gene studies obsolete. *Neuropsychopharmacology*, *44*(9), 1518–1523. Available from https://doi.org/10.1038/s41386-019-0389-5.

Enoch, M. A. (2008). The role of GABA(A) receptors in the development of alcoholism. *Pharmacology Biochemistry and Behavior*, *90*(1), 95–104. Available from https://doi.org/10.1016/j.pbb.2008.03.007.

Errico, A. L., Parsons, O. A., King, A. C., & Lovallo, W. R. (1993). Attenuated cortisol response to biobehavioral stressors in sober alcoholics. *Journal of Studies on Alcohol, 54*(4), 393–398. Available from https://doi.org/10.15288/jsa.1993.54.393.

Errico, A. L., King, A. C., Lovallo, W. R., & Parsons, O. A. (2002). Cortisol dysregulation and cognitive impairment in abstinent male alcoholics. *Alcohol Clin Exp Res*. Available from https://doi.org/10.1097/01.alc.0000025885.23192.ff.

Field, M., & Kersbergen, I. (2019). Are animal models of addiction useful? *Addiction*. Available from https://doi.org/10.1111/add.14764.

Floresco, S. B. (2013). Prefrontal dopamine and behavioral flexibility: Shifting from an "inverted-U" toward a family of functions. *Frontiers in Neuroscience, 7*. Available from https://doi.org/10.3389/fnins.2013.00062, 62-62.

Font, L., Lujan, M. A., & Pastor, R. (2013). Involvement of the endogenous opioid system in the psychopharmacological actions of ethanol: The role of acetaldehyde. *Frontiers in Behavioral Neuroscience, 7*. Available from https://doi.org/10.3389/fnbeh.2013.00093, 93.

Fowler, J. S., Volkow, N. D., Kassed, C. A., & Chang, L. (2007). Imaging the addicted human brain. *Science & Practice Perspectives, 3*(2), 4–16.

Gastpar, M., Bonnet, U., Boning, J., Mann, K., Schmidt, L. G., Soyka, M., ... Croop, R. (2002). Lack of efficacy of naltrexone in the prevention of alcohol relapse: Results from a German multicenter study. *Journal of Clinical Psychopharmacology, 22*(6), 592–598.

George, O., Le Moal, M., & Koob, G. F. (2012). Allostasis and addiction: Role of the dopamine and corticotropin-releasing factor systems. *Physiology & Behavior, 106*(1), 58–64. Available from https://doi.org/10.1016/j.physbeh.2011.11.004.

Gianoulakis, C. (2001). Influence of the endogenous opioid system on high alcohol consumption and genetic predisposition to alcoholism. *Journal of Psychiatry & Neuroscience, 26*(4), 304–318.

Gilpin, N. W., & Koob, G. F. (2008). Neurobiology of alcohol dependence focus on motivational mechanisms. *Alcohol Research & Health, 31*(3), 185–195.

Gonzales, R. A., & Jaworski, J. N. (1997). Alcohol and glutamate. *Alcohol Health & Research World, 21*(2), 120–127.

Gonzales, R. A., Job, M. O., & Doyon, W. M. (2004). The role of mesolimbic dopamine in the development and maintenance of ethanol reinforcement. *Pharmacology & Therapeutics, 103*(2), 121–146. Available from https://doi.org/10.1016/j.pharmthera.2004.06.002.

Grusser, S. M., Wrase, J., Klein, S., Hermann, D., Smolka, M. N., Ruf, M., ... Heinz, A. (2004). Cue-induced activation of the striatum and medial prefrontal cortex is associated with subsequent relapse in abstinent alcoholics. *Psychopharmacology, 175*(3), 296–302.

Guo, R., & Ren, J. (2010). Alcohol and acetaldehyde in public health: From marvel to menace. *International Journal of Environmental Research and Public Health, 7*(4), 1285–1301. Available from https://doi.org/10.3390/ijerph7041285.

Hall, W., Carter, A., & Forlini, C. (2015). Brain disease model of addiction: Misplaced priorities? *Lancet Psychiatry, 2*(10), 867. Available from https://doi.org/10.1016/S2215-0366(15)00417-4.

Hammarberg, A., Jayaram-Lindstrom, N., Beck, O., Franck, J., & Reid, M. S. (2009). The effects of acamprosate on alcohol-cue reactivity and alcohol priming in dependent patients: A randomized controlled trial. *Psychopharmacology (Berl), 205*(1), 53–62. Available from https://doi.org/10.1007/s00213-009-1515-6.

Heather, N., Best, D., Kawalek, A., Field, M., Lewis, M., Rotgers, F., ... Heim, D. (2018). Challenging the brain disease model of addiction: European launch of the addiction theory network. *Addiction Research & Theory*, *26*(4), 249–255. Available from https://doi.org/10.1080/16066359.2017.1399659.

Heilig, M., Egli, M., Crabbe, J. C., & Becker, H. C. (2010). Acute withdrawal, protracted abstinence and negative affect in alcoholism: are they linked? *Addiction Biology*, *15*(2), 169–184. Available from https://doi.org/10.1111/j.1369-1600.2009.00194.x.

Heinz, A., Beck, A., Mir, J., Grüsser, S. M., Grace, A. A., & Wrase, J. (2010). Alcohol craving and relapse prediction: Imaging studies. In K. G. Kuhn CM (Ed.), *Advances in the neuroscience of addiction* (2nd ed.). Boca Raton (FL): CRC Press/Taylor & Francis.

Heinz, A., Siessmeier, T., Wrase, J., Hermann, D., Klein, S., Grusser, S. M., ... Bartenstein, P. (2004). Correlation between dopamine D(2) receptors in the ventral striatum and central processing of alcohol cues and craving. *The American Journal of Psychiatry*, *161*(10), 1783–1789. Available from https://doi.org/10.1176/appi.ajp.161.10.1783.

Helstrom, A. W., Blow, F. C., Slaymaker, V., Kranzler, H. R., Leong, S., & Oslin, D. (2016). Reductions in alcohol craving following naltrexone treatment for heavy drinking. *Alcohol and Alcoholism*, *51*(5), 562–566. Available from https://doi.org/10.1093/alcalc/agw038.

Hendler, R. A., Ramchandani, V. A., Gilman, J., & Hommer, D. W. (2013). Stimulant and sedative effects of alcohol. *Current Topics in Behavioral Neurosciences*, *13*, 489–509. Available from https://doi.org/10.1007/7854_2011_135.

Herz, A. (1997). Endogenous opioid systems and alcohol addiction. *Psychopharmacology (Berl)*, *129*(2), 99–111. Available from https://doi.org/10.1007/s002130050169.

Jacquot, C., Croft, A. P., Wang, G., Prendergast, M. A., Mulholland, P., Shaw, S. G., & Little, H. J. (2008). Effects of the glucocorticoid antagonist. mifepristone, on the consequences of withdrawal from long term alcohol consumption. *Alcohol Clin Exp Res*, *32*, 2107–2116. Available from https://doi.org/10.1111/j.1530-0277.2008.00799.x.

Jentsch, J. D., & Taylor, J. R. (1999). Impulsivity resulting from frontostriatal dysfunction in drug abuse: Implications for the control of behavior by reward-related stimuli. *Psychopharmacology*, *146*(4), 373–390. Available from https://doi.org/10.1007/Pl00005483.

Johnson, B. A. (2005). Recent advances in the development of treatments for alcohol and cocaine dependence: Focus on topiramate and other modulators of GABA or glutamate function. *CNS Drugs*, *19*(10), 873–896. Available from https://doi.org/10.2165/00023210-200519100-00005.

Jonas, D. E., Amick, H. R., Feltner, C., Bobashev, G., Thomas, K., Wines, R., ... Garbutt, J. C. (2014). Pharmacotherapy for adults with alcohol use disorders in outpatient settings a systematic review and meta-analysis. *JAMA-Journal of the American Medical Association*, *311* (18), 1889–1900. Available from https://doi.org/10.1001/jama.2014.3628.

Junghanns, K., Backhaus, J., Tietz, U., Lange, W., Bernzen, J., Wetterling, T., ... Driessen, M. (2003). Impaired serum cortisol stress response is a predictor of early relapse. *Alcohol and Alcoholism*, *38*(2), 189–193. Available from https://doi.org/10.1093/alcalc/agg052.

Kalk, N. J., & Lingford-Hughes, A. R. (2014). The clinical pharmacology of acamprosate. *British Journal of Clinical Pharmacology*, *77*(2), 315–323. Available from https://doi.org/10.1111/bcp.12070.

Keedwell, P. A., Poon, L., Papadopolous, A. S., Marshall, J., & Checkley, S. A. (2001). Salivary cortisol measurements during a medically assisted withdrawal. *Addict Biol*, *6*, 247–257. Available from https://doi.org/10.1080/13556210120056580.

King, A., Munisamy, G., de Wit, H., & Lin, S. (2006). Attenuated cortisol response to alcohol in heavy social drinkers. *International Journal of Psychophysiology*, *59*(3), 203–209. Available from https://doi.org/10.1016/j.ijpsycho.2005.10.008, doi:S0167-8760(05)00264-3 [pii].

King, A. C., Houle, T., de Wit, H., Holdstock, L., & Schuster, A. (2002). Biphasic alcohol response differs in heavy versus light drinkers. *Alcoholism: Clinical and Experimental Research*, *26*(6), 827–835.

Kissler, J. L., Sirohi, S., Reis, D. J., Jansen, H. T., Quock, R. M., Smith, D. G., & Walker, B. M. (2014). The one-two punch of alcoholism: Role of central amygdala dynorphins/kappa-opioid receptors. *Biological Psychiatry*, *75*(10), 774–782. Available from https://doi.org/10.1016/j.biopsych.2013.03.014.

Koob, G. F. (1992). Drugs of abuse: Anatomy, pharmacology and function of reward pathways. *Trends in Pharmacological Sciences*, *13*(5), 177–184.

Koob, G. F. (2003). Alcoholism: Allostasis and beyond. *Alcoholism: Clinical and Experimental Research*, *27*(2), 232–243.

Koob, G. F. (2009). Neurobiological substrates for the dark side of compulsivity in addiction. *Neuropharmacology*, *56*(S1), 18–31. Available from https://doi.org/10.1016/j.neuropharm.2008.07.043, doi:S0028-3908(08)00328-6 [pii].

Koob, G. F. (2013). Theoretical frameworks and mechanistic aspects of alcohol addiction: Alcohol addiction as a reward deficit disorder. *Behavioral Neurobiology of Alcohol Addiction*, *13*, 3–30. Available from https://doi.org/10.1007/7854_2011_129.

Koob, G. F. (2015). Addiction as a stress surfeit disorder. *Biological Psychiatry*, *77*, 9.

Koob, G. F., Buck, C. L., Cohen, A., Edwards, S., Park, P. E., Schlosburg, J. E., & George, O. (2014). Addiction as a stress surfeit disorder. *Neuropharmacology*, *76*, 370–382. Available from https://doi.org/10.1016/j.neuropharm.2013.05.024.

Koob, G. F., & Le Moal, M. (2001). Drug addiction, dysregulation of reward, and allostasis. *Neuropsychopharmacology*, *24*(2), 97–129. Available from https://doi.org/10.1016/S0893-133X(00)00195-0.

Koob, G. F., & Le Moal, M. (2008a). Addiction and the brain antireward system. *Annual Review of Psychology*, *59*, 29–53. Available from https://doi.org/10.1146/annurev.psych.59.103006.093548.

Koob, G. F., & Le Moal, M. (2008b). Review. Neurobiological mechanisms for opponent motivational processes in addiction. *Philosophical Transactions of the Royal Society of London. Series B, Biological Science*, *363*(1507), 3113–3123. Available from https://doi.org/10.1098/rstb.2008.0094, doi:C54412M472226253 [pii].

Koob, G. F., & Schulkin, J. (2018). Addiction and stress: An allostatic view. *Neuroscience and Biobehavioral Reviews*. Available from https://doi.org/10.1016/j.neubiorev.2018.09.008.

Koob, G. F., & Volkow, N. D. (2010). Neurocircuitry of addiction (vol 35, pg 217, 2010). *Neuropsychopharmacology*, *35*(4). Available from https://doi.org/10.1038/Npp.2010.4, 1051-1051.

Koob, G. F. (2014). Chapter 3 - Neurocircuitry of alcohol addiction: synthesis from animal models. In E. V. Sullivan (Ed.), *Handbook of Clinical Neurology* (125, pp. 33–54). Adolf Pfefferbaum. Available from https://doi.org/10.1016/B978-0-444-62619-6.00003-3.

Kranzler, H. R., & Van Kirk, J. (2001). Efficacy of naltrexone and acamprosate for alcoholism treatment: A meta-analysis. *Alcoholism-Clinical and Experimental Research*, *25*(9), 1335–1341. Available from https://doi.org/10.1111/j.1530-0277.2001.tb02356.x.

Kumar, S., Porcu, P., Werner, D. F., Matthews, D. B., Diaz-Granados, J. L., Helfand, R. S., & Morrow, A. L. (2009). The role of GABA(A) receptors in the acute and chronic effects of ethanol: A decade of progress. *Psychopharmacology*, *205*(4), 529–564. Available from https://doi.org/10.1007/s00213-009-1562-z.

Lawford, B. R., Young, R. M., Rowell, J. A., Qualichefski, J., Fletcher, B. H., Syndulko, K., ... Noble, E. P. (1995). Bromocriptine in the treatment of alcoholics with the D2 dopamine receptor A1 allele. *Nature Medicine*, *1*(4), 337–341.

Le, A. D., Harding, S., Juzytsch, W., Funk, D., & Shaham, Y. (2005). Role of alpha-2 adrenoceptors in stress-induced reinstatement of alcohol seeking and alcohol self-administration in rats. *Psychopharmacology*, *179*(2), 366–373. Available from https://doi.org/10.1007/s00213-004-2036-y.

Le, A. D., Harding, S., Juzytsch, W., Watchus, J., Shalev, U., & Shaham, Y. (2000). The role of corticotrophin-releasing factor in stress-induced relapse to alcohol-seeking behavior in rats. *Psychopharmacology*, *150*(3), 317–324. Available from https://doi.org/10.1007/s002130000411.

Lee, H., Roh, S., & Kim, D. J. (2009). Alcohol-induced blackout. *International Journal of Environmental Research and Public Health*, *6*(11), 2783–2792. Available from https://doi.org/10.3390/ijerph6112783.

Le Merrer, J., Becker, J. A., Befort, K., & Kieffer, B. L. (2009). Reward processing by the opioid system in the brain. *Physiological Reviews*, *89*(4), 1379–1412. Available from https://doi.org/10.1152/physrev.00005.2009.

Leshner, A. I. (1997). Addiction is a brain disease, and it matters. *Science*, *278*(5335), 45–47.

Lewis, M. (2018). Brain change in addiction as learning, not disease. *New England Journal of Medicine*, *379*(16), 1551–1560. Available from https://doi.org/10.1056/NEJMra1602872.

Liang, J., & Olsen, R. W. (2014). Alcohol use disorders and current pharmacological therapies: The role of GABA(A) receptors. *Acta Pharmacologica Sinica*, *35*(8), 981–993. Available from https://doi.org/10.1038/aps.2014.50.

Litten, R. Z., Egli, M., Heilig, M., Cui, C. H., Fertig, J. B., Ryan, M. L., ... Noronha, A. (2012). Medications development to treat alcohol dependence: A vision for the next decade. *Addiction Biology*, *17*(3), 513–527. Available from https://doi.org/10.1111/j.1369-1600.2012.00454.x.

Little, H. J., Croft, A. P., O'Callaghan, M. J., Brooks, S. P., Wang, G., & Shaw, S. G. (2008). Selective increases in regional brain glucocorticoid: A novel effect of chronic alcohol. *Neuroscience*, *156*(4), 1017–1027. Available from https://doi.org/10.1016/j.neuroscience.2008.08.029.

Liu, X., & Weiss, F. (2002). Additive effect of stress and drug cues on reinstatement of ethanol seeking: Exacerbation by history of dependence and role of concurrent activation of corticotropin-releasing factor and opioid mechanisms. *Journal of Neuroscience*, *22*(18), 7856–7861.

Lobo, I. A., & Harris, R. A. (2008). GABA(A) receptors and alcohol. *Pharmacology, Biochemistry, and Behavior*, *90*(1), 90–94. Available from https://doi.org/10.1016/j.pbb.2008.03.006.

Logue, S. F., & Gould, T. J. (2014). The neural and genetic basis of executive function: Attention, cognitive flexibility, and response inhibition. *Pharmacology, Biochemistry,and Behavior*, *123*, 45–54. Available from https://doi.org/10.1016/j.pbb.2013.08.007.

Ma, H., & Zhu, G. (2014). The dopamine system and alcohol dependence. *Shanghai Archives of Psychiatry*, *26*(2), 61–68. Available from https://doi.org/10.3969/j.issn.1002-0829.2014.02.002.

Marino, E. N., & Fromme, K. (2016). Early onset drinking predicts greater level but not growth of alcohol-induced blackouts beyond the effect of binge drinking during emerging adulthood. *Alcoholism-Clinical and Experimental Research*, *40*(3), 599–605. Available from https://doi.org/10.1111/acer.12981.

Mason, B. J., & Lehert, P. (2012). Acamprosate for alcohol dependence: A sex-specific meta-analysis based on individual patient data. *Alcoholism-Clinical and Experimental Research*, *36*(3), 497–508. Available from https://doi.org/10.1111/j.1530-0277.2011.01616.x.

Mason, B. J., Shaham, Y., Weiss, F., & Le, A. D. (2009). Stress, alcohol craving, and relapse risk: Mechanisms and viable treatment targets. *Alcohol*, *43*(7), 541–543. Available from https://doi.org/10.1016/j.alcohol.2009.09.024.

Mccusker, C. G., & Brown, K. (1990). Alcohol-predictive cues enhance tolerance to and precipitate craving for alcohol in social drinkers. *Journal of Studies on Alcohol*, *51*(6), 494–499. Available from https://doi.org/10.15288/jsa.1990.51.494.

McGaugh, J. L. (2004). The amygdala modulates the consolidation of memories of emotionally arousing experiences. *Annual Review of Neuroscience*, *27*, 1–28. Available from https://doi.org/10.1146/annurev.neuro.27.070203.144157.

Mendez, M., & Morales-Mulia, M. (2008). Role of mu and delta opioid receptors in alcohol drinking behaviour. *Current Drug Abuse Reviews*, *1*(2), 239–252.

Mhatre, M. C., Pena, G., Sieghart, W., & Ticku, M. K. (1993). Antibodies specific for Gaba(a) receptor alpha-subunits reveal that chronic alcohol treatment down-regulates alpha-subunit expression in rat-brain regions. *Journal of Neurochemistry*, *61*(5), 1620–1625.

Mirijello, A., D'Angelo, C., Ferrulli, A., Vassallo, G., Antonelli, M., Caputo, F., ... Addolorato, G. (2015). Identification and management of alcohol withdrawal syndrome. *Drugs*, *75*(4), 353–365. Available from https://doi.org/10.1007/s40265-015-0358-1.

Miyake, A., Friedman, N. P., Emerson, M. J., Witzki, A. H., Howerter, A., & Wager, T. D. (2000). The unity and diversity of executive functions and their contributions to complex "frontal lobe" tasks: A latent variable analysis. *Cognitive Psychology*, *41*(1), 49–100.

Myers, W. D., Ng, K. T., Marzuki, S., Myers, R. D., & Singer, G. (1984). Alteration of alcohol drinking in the rat by peripherally self-administered acetaldehyde. *Alcohol*, *1*(3), 229–236.

Naranjo, C. A., Dongier, M., & Bremner, K. E. (1997). Long-acting injectable bromocriptine does not reduce relapse in alcoholics. *Addiction*, *92*(8), 969–978.

Naudet, F., Fitzgerald, N., & Braillon, A. (2016). Nalmefene for alcohol dependence: a NICE decision? *Lancet Psychiatry*, *3*(12), 1104–1105. Available from https://doi.org/10.1016/S2215-0366(16)30356-X.

Olmstead, M. C. (2006). Animal models of drug addiction: Where do we go from here? *Quarterly Journal of Experimental Psychology*, *59*(4), 625–653. Available from https://doi.org/10.1080/17470210500356308.

O'Malley, S. S., Jaffe, A. J., Chang, G., Schottenfeld, R. S., Meyer, R. E., & Rounsaville, B. (1992). Naltrexone and coping skills therapy for alcohol dependence. A controlled study. *Archives of General Psychiatry*, *49*(11), 881–887. Available from https://doi.org/10.1001/archpsyc.1992.01820110045007.

Owens, L., Thompson, A., Rose, A., Gilmore, I., Pirmohamed, M., & Richardson, P. (2017). A prospective cohort study examining the effectiveness of baclofen in the maintenance of abstinence in alcohol use disorder patients attending a joint liver and alcohol treatment clinic. *Alcohol*, *62*, 11–15. Available from https://doi.org/10.1016/j.alcohol.2016.12.005.

Palpacuer, C., Duprez, R., Huneau, A., Locher, C., Boussageon, R., Laviolle, B., & Naudet, F. (2018). Pharmacologically controlled drinking in the treatment of alcohol dependence or alcohol use disorders: A systematic review with direct and network meta-analyses on nalmefene, naltrexone, acamprosate, baclofen and topiramate. *Addiction*, *113*(2), 220–237. Available from https://doi.org/10.1111/add.13974.

Palpacuer, C., Laviolle, B., Boussageon, R., Reymann, J. M., Bellissant, E., & Naudet, F. (2015). Risks and benefits of nalmefene in the treatment of adult alcohol dependence: A systematic literature review and meta-analysis of published and unpublished double-blind randomized controlled trials. *PLoS Medicine*, *12*(12). Available from https://doi.org/10.1371/journal.pmed.1001924, e1001924.

Pastor, R., Font, L., Miquel, M., Phillips, T. J., & Aragon, C. M. G. (2011). Involvement of the beta-endorphin neurons of the hypothalamic arcuate nucleus in ethanol-induced place preference conditioning in mice. *Alcoholism-Clinical and Experimental Research, 35*(11), 2019–2029.

Piazza, P. V., Deroche, V., Deminiere, J. M., Maccari, S., Le Moal, M., & Simon, H. (1993). Corticosterone in the range of stress-induced levels possesses reinforcing properties: Implications for sensation-seeking behaviors. *Proceedings of the National Academy of Sciences of the United States of America, 90*(24), 11738–11742.

Pratt, W. M., & Davidson, D. (2009). Role of the HPA axis and the A118G polymorphism of the mu-opioid receptor in stress-induced drinking behavior. *Alcohol and Alcoholism, 44*(4), 358–365. Available from https://doi.org/10.1093/alcalc/agp007.

Quertemont, E., & Tambour, S. (2004). Is ethanol a pro-drug? The role of acetaldehyde in the central effects of ethanol. *Trends in Pharmacological Sciences, 25*(3), 130–134.

Quertemont, E., Tambour, S., & Tirelli, E. (2005). The role of acetaldehyde in the neurobehavioral effects of ethanol: A comprehensive review of animal studies. *Progress Neurobiology, 75*(4), 247–274. Available from https://doi.org/10.1016/j.pneurobio.2005.03.003.

Raistrick, D., Heather, N., & Godfrey, C. (2006). *Review of the effectiveness of treatment for alcohol problems*. London: Department of Health.

Ramchandani, V. A., Umhau, J., Pavon, F. J., Ruiz-Velasco, V., Margas, W., Sun, H., ... Heilig, M. (2011). A genetic determinant of the striatal dopamine response to alcohol in men. *Molecular Psychiatry, 16*(8), 809–817. Available from https://doi.org/10.1038/mp.2010.56.

Rezvani, A. H. (2006). Involvement of the NMDA system in learning and memory. In E. D. Levin, & J. J. Buccafusco (Eds.), *Animal models of cognitive impairment*. Boca Raton (FL).

Ritchie, A., & Roser, M. (2019). Alcohol consumption. Retrieved 15/08/19 <https://ourworldindata.org/alcohol-consumption>.

Robinson, T. E., & Berridge, K. C. (1993). The neural basis of drug craving: An incentive-sensitisation theory of addiction. *Brain Research Reviews, 18*, 247–291.

Robinson, T. E., & Berridge, K. C. (2008). The incentive sensitization theory of addiction: Some current issues. *Philosophical Transactions of the Royal Society B-Biological Sciences, 363*(1507), 3137–3146. Available from https://doi.org/10.1098/rstb.2008.0093.

Rose, A. K., & Duka, T. (2006). Effects of dose and time on the ability of alcohol to prime social drinkers. *Behavioural Pharmacology, 17*(1), 61–70.

Rose, A. K., & Grunsell, L. (2008). The subjective, rather than the disinhibiting, effects of alcohol are related to binge drinking. *Alcoholism-Clinical and Experimental Research, 32*(6), 1096–1104. Available from https://doi.org/10.1111/j.1530-0277.2008.00672.x, doi: ACER672 [pii].

Rose, A. K., & Jones, A. (2018). Baclofen: Its effectiveness in reducing harmful drinking, craving, and negative mood. A meta-analysis. *Addiction, 113*(8), 1396–1406. Available from https://doi.org/10.1111/add.14191.

Rose, A. K., Shaw, S. G., Prendergast, M. A., & Little, H. J. (2010). The importance of glucocorticoids in alcohol dependence and neurotoxicity. *Alcoholism-Clinical and Experimental Research, 34*(12), 2011–2018. Available from https://doi.org/10.1111/j.1530-0277.2010.01298.x.

Schwarzer, C. (2009). 30 years of dynorphins - New insights on their functions in neuropsychiatric diseases. *Pharmacology & Therapeutics, 123*(3), 353–370.

Seki, K., Yoshida, S., & Jaiswal, M. K. (2018). Molecular mechanism of noradrenaline during the stress-induced major depressive disorder. *Neural Regeneration Research, 13*(7), 1159–1169. Available from https://doi.org/10.4103/1673-5374.235019.

Sengupta, P. (2013). The laboratory rat: Relating its age with human's. *International Journal of Preventive Medicine*, *4*(6), 624–630.

Shaw, G. K., Waller, S., Majumdar, S. K., Alberts, J. L., Latham, C. J., & Dunn, G. (1994). Tiapride in the prevention of relapse in recently detoxified alcoholics. *British Journal of Psychiatry*, *165*(4), 515–523. Available from https://doi.org/10.1192/bjp.165.4.515.

Sher, K. J., Grekin, E. R., & Williams, N. A. (2005). The development of alcohol use disorders. *Annual Review of Clinical Psychology*, *1*, 493–523. Available from https://doi.org/10.1146/annurev.clinpsy.1.102803.144107.

Sillaber, I., & Henniger, M. S. (2004). Stress and alcohol drinking. *Annals of Medicine*, *36*(8), 596–605. Available from https://doi.org/10.1080/07853890410018862.

Silveri, M. M., Cohen-Gilbert, J., Crowley, D. J., Rosso, I. M., Jensen, J. E., & Sneider, J. T. (2014). Altered anterior cingulate neurochemistry in emerging adult binge drinkers with a history of alcohol-induced blackouts. *Alcoholism-Clinical and Experimental Research*, *38*(4), 969–979. Available from https://doi.org/10.1111/acer.12346.

Silvers, J. M., Tokunaga, S., Mittleman, G., & Matthews, D. B. (2003). Chronic intermittent injections of high-dose ethanol during adolescence produce metabolic, hypnotic, and cognitive tolerance in rats. *Alcoholism-Clinical and Experimental Research*, *27*(10), 1606–1612. Available from https://doi.org/10.1097/01.Alc.0000090141.66526.22.

Sinha, R., Fox, H. C., Hong, K. A., Bergquist, K., Bhagwagar, Z., & Siedlarz, K. M. (2009). Enhanced negative emotion and alcohol craving, and altered physiological responses following stress and cue exposure in alcohol dependent individuals. *Neuropsychopharmacology*, *34*, 1198–1208. Available from https://doi.org/10.1038/npp.2008.78, doi:npp200878 [pii].

Sinha, R., Fox, H. C., Hong, K. I., Hansen, J., Tuit, K., & Kreek, M. J. (2011). Effects of adrenal sensitivity, stress- and cue-induced craving, and anxiety on subsequent alcohol relapse and treatment outcomes. *Archives of General Psychiatry*, *68*(9), 942–952. Available from https://doi.org/10.1001/archgenpsychiatry.2011.49.

Skinner, M. D., Lahmek, P., Pham, H., & Aubin, H. J. (2014). Disulfiram efficacy in the treatment of alcohol dependence: A meta-analysis. *PLoS One*, *9*(2), e87366. Available from https://doi.org/10.1371/journal.pone.0087366.

Smith, D. E. (2017). Medicalizing the opioid epidemic in the U.S. in the era of health care reform. *Journal of Psychoactive Drugs*, *49*(2), 95–101. Available from https://doi.org/10.1080/02791072.2017.1295334.

Stephens, D. N., Pistovcakova, J., Worthing, L., Atack, J. R., & Dawson, G. R. (2005). Role of GABAA alpha5-containing receptors in ethanol reward: The effects of targeted gene deletion, and a selective inverse agonist. *European Journal of Pharmacology*, *526*(1–3), 240–250. Available from https://doi.org/10.1016/j.ejphar.2005.09.031.

Stephens, M. A., & Wand, G. (2012). Stress and the HPA axis: Role of glucocorticoids in alcohol dependence. *Alcohol Research*, *34*(4), 468–483.

Stewart, J. (2008). Psychological and neural mechanisms of relapse. *Philosophical Transactions of the Royal Society B-Biological Sciences*, *363*(1507), 3147–3158. Available from https://doi.org/10.1098/rstb.2008.0084.

Stewart, J., & de Wit, H. (1987). Reinstatement of drug-taking behaviour as a method of assessing incentive motivational properties of drugs. In M. A. Bozarth (Ed.), *Methods of assessing the reinforcing properties of abused drugs* (pp. 211–227). New York: Springer-Verlag.

Stewart, J., de Wit, H., & Eikelboom, R. (1984). Role of unconditioned and conditioned drug effects in the self-administration of opiates and stimulants. *Psychological Review*, *91*, 251–268.

Swift, R. M. (1999). Drug therapy for alcohol dependence. *The New England Journal of Medicine*, *340*(19), 1482–1490. Available from https://doi.org/10.1056/NEJM199905133401907.

Swift, R. M., & Aston, E. R. (2015). Pharmacotherapy for alcohol use disorder: Current and emerging therapies. *Harvard Review of Psychiatry*, *23*(2), 122–133. Available from https://doi.org/10.1097/Hrp.0000000000000079.

Tawa, E. A., Hall, S. D., & Lohoff, F. W. (2016). Overview of the genetics of alcohol use disorder. *Alcohol and Alcoholism*, *51*(5), 507–514. Available from https://doi.org/10.1093/alcalc/agw046.

Trevisan, L. A., Boutros, N., Petrakis, I. L., & Krystal, J. H. (1998). Complications of alcohol withdrawal - Pathophysiological insights. *Alcohol Health & Research World*, *22*(1), 61–66.

Ulm, R. R., Volpicelli, J. R., & Volpicelli, L. A. (1995). Opiates and alcohol self-administration in animals. *Journal of Clinical Psychiatry*, *56*(Suppl. 7), 5–14.

Urban, N. B. L., Kegeles, L. S., Slifstein, M., Xu, X. Y., Martinez, D., Sakr, E., ... Abi-Dargham, A. (2010). Sex differences in striatal dopamine release in young adults after oral alcohol challenge: A positron emission tomography imaging study with [C-11]raclopride. *Biological Psychiatry*, *68*(8), 689–696. Available from https://doi.org/10.1016/j.biopsych.2010.06.005.

Valenzuela, C. F. (1997). Alcohol and neurotransmitter interactions. *Alcohol Health and Research World*, *21*(2), 144–148.

Vendruscolo, L. F., Estey, D., Goodell, V., Macshane, L. G., Logrip, M. L., Schlosburg, J. E., ... Mason, B. J. (2015). Glucocorticoid receptor antagonism decreases alcohol seeking in alcohol-dependent individuals. *The Journal of Clinical Investigation*, *125*(8), 3193–3197. Available from https://doi.org/10.1172/JCI79828.

Vengeliene, V., Bilbao, A., Molander, A., & Spanagel, R. (2008). Neuropharmacology of alcohol addiction. *British Journal of Pharmacology*, *154*(2), 299–315. Available from https://doi.org/10.1038/bjp.2008.30.

Verhulst, B., Neale, M. C., & Kendler, K. S. (2015). The heritability of alcohol use disorders: A meta-analysis of twin and adoption studies. *Psychological Medicine*, *45*(5), 1061–1072. Available from https://doi.org/10.1017/S0033291714002165.

Volkow, N. D., Koob, G. F., & McLellan, A. T. (2016). Neurobiologic advances from the brain disease model of addiction. *The New England Journal of Medicine*, *374*(4), 363–371. Available from https://doi.org/10.1056/NEJMra1511480.

Volkow, N. D., Wang, G. J., Maynard, L., Fowler, J. S., Jayne, B., Telang, F., ... Pappas, N. (2002). Effects of alcohol detoxification on dopamine D2 receptors in alcoholics: A preliminary study. *Psychiatry Research*, *116*(3), 163–172.

Weiss, F., Mitchiner, M., Bloom, F. E., & Koob, G. F. (1990). Free-choice responding for ethanol versus water in alcohol preferring (P) and unselected wistar rats is differentially modified by naloxone, bromocriptine, and methysergide. *Psychopharmacology*, *101*(2), 178–186. Available from https://doi.org/10.1007/Bf02244123.

Wemm, S. E., & Sinha, R. (2019). Drug-induced stress responses and addiction risk and relapse. *Neurobiological Stress*, *10*, 100148. Available from https://doi.org/10.1016/j.ynstr.2019.100148.

Chapter 6

Learning from the dead: How death provides insights into alcohol-related harm

Shane Darke
National Drug & Alcohol Research Centre, University of New South Wales, Sydney, NSW, Australia

Introduction

Why study drug-related death? In particular, why study alcohol-related death? Why not simply focus upon the living? There are a number of cogent reasons why we should study the dead. Firstly, each alcohol-related death represents a tragedy for the decedent, their family and friends. To understand how, and why, these people died is worthy of our attention. More broadly, however, the dead have much to teach the living. They provide us with information on the types of harms that the living face with alcohol, they provide us with information on the toxicology of alcohol-related death, and on the circumstances that cause serious harm. Death may be the sharp-end of alcohol-related problems, but it is a sharp end that reflects the broader harms to the individual and society. Indeed, much of the data provided by decedents would not be available to us in any other way.

All such deaths are preventable, and the overall aim is to use this information to reduce the number of such deaths and, more broadly, to reduce the burden of disease contributed by alcohol. The extensive work done in the past few decades examining illicit drug-related death has had a major impact, changing the way we think about issues such as opioid overdose and psychostimulant toxicity, and influencing the way in which we respond to these events (e.g. Darke & Duflou, 2016; Darke, Duflou, & Torok, 2010; Darke, Kaye, & Duflou, 2017). The study of alcohol-related death may prove as fruitful.

There are two complementary methods of studying alcohol-related death: epidemiology and forensic science. The epidemiology of alcohol-related death provides important data on the extent to which alcohol impacts upon premature death in a society, and what kinds of deaths it incurs. This informs

The Handbook of Alcohol Use - Understandings from Synapse to Society.
DOI: https://doi.org/10.1016/B978-0-12-816720-5.00020-7

us of the general contours of alcohol-related harm. Forensic studies examine the coronial records of cases of alcohol-related death, and contain granular information on case characteristics, toxicology, organ system pathology, and the circumstances of death. Taken together, these two methods provide powerful insights into alcohol-related behaviors and disease.

What the epidemiology of alcohol-related death tells us

The epidemiology of alcohol-related death indicates clearly that the global impact of alcohol use and abuse upon mortality worldwide is substantial. Indeed, alcohol use disorders account for 10% of all deaths amongst working age people (Stahre, Roeber, Kanny, Brewer, & Zhang, 2014; Whiteford et al., 2013). More broadly, this suggests a serious burden of disease among the living.

What is important, however, is whether it can be demonstrated that changes in drinking rates amongst a country's population are associated with changes in its all-cause mortality. Such data clearly would provide important clues on how to reduce alcohol-related harms. While these data concern the deceased, they are proxies for how a population's drinking affects its overall health. It is possible, of course, that increases in alcohol consumption may *improve* population health if these increases reflect increases in moderate consumption and if such consumption reduced the risk for factors such as cardiovascular disease. The epidemiological evidence, however, suggests increases in alcohol consumption do indeed impair population health. Broadly speaking, for each 1 L per capita increase in alcohol consumption there is a 1% increase in all-cause mortality (Gmel, Rehm, & Frick, 2001; Her & Rehm, 1998; Norström, 2001; Norström & Ramstedt, 2005; Razvodovsky, 2008).

Upon closer inspection, however, these data provide more clues to public health, as the strength of the association varies markedly by region. While the 1% per 1 L association is seen in southern Europe, the figure is closer to 3% in north America, eastern Europe and northern Europe. Why should this be so? It is likely we are seeing markers here for harmful *behaviors*. Thus, a strong possibility is that these differences reflect the extent to which a culture that has a general pattern of drinking to intoxication, with attendant risk.

All-cause mortality data provide a broad-brush snapshot of population health. Equally important is what these figures tell us about *how* people die (toxicity, disease, trauma, suicide) and about specific harms brought about by alcohol.

Alcohol toxicity

A blood alcohol concentration of ≥0.30 g/100 mL alcohol induces marked respiratory depression. While the minimum fatal concentration is generally considered to be >0.40 g/100 mL, fatal concentrations vary markedly with alcohol tolerance (Baselt, 2014). Acute alcohol toxicity may also result in death due to aspiration pneumonia (due to inhalation of alcohol-induced vomitus whilst unconscious).

Curiously, there are few population studies of national alcohol consumption and alcohol toxicity mortality rates (Norström & Ramstedt, 2005; Poikolainen, Leppänen, & Vuori, 2002; Razvodovsky, 2008, 2009; Stickley et al., 2007). These suggest that a 1% per capita increase in alcohol consumption is associated with a 0.4% increase in deaths due to alcohol toxicity. Importantly, this association is strongest with spirits which, given the high blood alcohol concentrations likely to be involved, makes clinical sense. The authors of these studies appear to imply, however, that the results reflect binge drinking, which carries an implication of non-regular consumption. The forensics data does not support this view. We will return to this issue below.

Disease

Alcohol is known to be associated with a range of diseases and conditions, including cardiomyopathy, ischemic and hypertensive heart disease, stroke, liver cirrhosis and Korsakoff psychosis (US Department of Health & Human Services, 2000). Unlike the proximal effects of alcohol, such as alcohol toxicity or traumatic injury, there is likely to be substantial lag times between changes in population alcohol consumption and the incidence of death due to alcohol-related disease. Despite this, there is evidence to link death rates due to ischemic heart with population alcohol use, at least in countries with higher rates of harmful drinking (Norström & Ramstedt, 2005; Razvodovsky, 2009, 2010, 2013). In Russia, a country with high rates of spirit consumption, it has been estimate that a 1 L per capita increase in an consumption is associated with a 4–5% increase in cardiovascular mortality (Razvodovsky, 2009, 2010). Moreover, in a natural experiments during the 1980s anti-alcohol campaign in the Soviet Union, alcohol consumption declined by 25% and cardiovascular mortality by 9% (Norström & Ramstedt, 2005).

Another way of looking at this is the estimated proportion of disease deaths attributable to alcohol, a marker for broader societal harm. It is estimated that 3–5% of all cancer deaths are alcohol-related, as are half of deaths due to liver cirrhosis (Nelson et al., 2013; Rehm & Shield, 2014; Rehm, Samokhvalov, & Shield, 2013). In Russia, it has been estimated that a fifth of fatal strokes are alcohol-related, as are 30–40% of deaths due to ischemic heart disease (Razvodovsky, 2013; 2014).

Traumatic death

An association between alcohol use and violence is well recognized, and may reflect the disinhibition, emotional lability or reduced cognitive functioning associated with alcohol intoxication (Darke, 2010). Homicide (which includes manslaughter and murder) is a good marker for broader societal violence. Does an increase in national alcohol consumption increase levels of interpersonal violence and, thus, homicide rates? The evidence is quite clear: in periods when per capita consumption increases, so do homicide rates. Conversely, when consumption declines, so do homicide rates (Mann, Zalcman, Smart, Rush, & Suurvali, 2006; Norström & Ramstedt, 2005; Pridemore, 2002; Razvodovsky, 2003; Rossow, 2001, 2004; Strickley & Razvodovsky, 2012). An increase of 1 L per capita alcohol consumption is associated with increases in homicide rates. The strength of this association varies by country, but in all cases it is substantial: 16% (northern Europe), 10% (mid-Europe), 6–7% (north America, Russia, southern Europe). In eastern Europe, the effect is strongest for spirits, for northern Europe and north America, the effect is strongest for beer, and in southern Europe for wine. Reflecting the epidemiology of both alcohol consumption and of violence, the association is stronger amongst males.

Alcohol-related trauma is not restricted to interpersonal violence. There is a strong association between alcohol consumption and accidental traumatic injury. National data indicate that total consumption increases fatal accident risk for motor vehicle accidents, falls and other traumatic injury (Landberg, 2010; Norström & Ramstedt, 2005; Rehm & Shield, 2014; Skog, 2001a, 2001b). Globally, one in seven of all injury deaths are alcohol-related (Rehm & Shield, 2014; Shield, Gmel, Patra, & Rehm, 2012).

Suicide

An association between alcohol and suicide is well documented (Darke, Duflou & Torok, 2009b). It is, however, far more complex than death due to alcohol toxicity, or even alcohol-related violence, as heavy alcohol users have high rates of mood disorders and suicidality (Darvishi, Farhadi, Haghtalab, & Poorolajal, 2015; Heather, Peters, & Stockwell, 2001). Alcohol may also result in impulsive suicidal behaviors that might not otherwise occur, and some people may use alcohol to increase their courage to attempt suicide.

An association between the amount of alcohol consumed by a population and their suicide rate has been well demonstrated (Caces & Harford, 1998; Landberg, 2008; Lester, 1995; Mäkelä, 1996; Nemtsov, 2003; Norström & Ramstedt, 2005; Ramstedt, 2001, 2005). Given that there are many more suicide attempts than completions (Mościcki, 2001), we would expect a far larger increase in suicide attempts as alcohol consumption rates increase. These population level studies, however, show remarkable regional variation. An 1 L increase in annual per capita alcohol consumption has been associated with increases in suicide rates of 3% (France), 4% (Canada), 6–8% (eastern Europe) and 7–13% (Russia, Sweden). The strongest association is with spirits, and in countries where spirits predominate.

What forensic studies tells us

Epidemiological studies give us an idea as to the types of harms associated with alcohol, and how they relate to global consumption. They can tell us nothing, however, of the characteristics of decedents, and the circumstances in which they die. In contrast, fine-grained forensic data completes the picture of alcohol-related death, and the broader harms such cases represent.

Who dies?

The average person who dies from alcohol toxicity may be characterized a single male, aged in their late 40s (Below & Lignitz, 2003; Darke, Duflou, Torok, & Prolov, 2013a; 2013b; Jones & Holmgren, 2003; Jones, Kugelberg, Holmgren, & Ahlner, 2011; Nordrum, Eide, & Jørgensen, 2000; Sjögren, Eriksson, & Ahlm, 2000). Moreover, this demographic profile applies to those who die from high range alcohol deaths due to causes other than toxicity. While a great deal of media attention is given to young binge drinkers, the evidence is clear. These are not the people who comprise the majority of deaths. It is the older drinker who is at most risk.

It was noted earlier that the epidemiological data relating alcohol consumption to toxicity deaths has been interpreted to reflect binge drinking. The forensic evidence is clear. These cases are not typically binge drinkers. These are people with long histories of dependent, regular, heavy drinking. A person does not attain a blood alcohol concentration in excess of 0.40 mg/L by irregular binge drinking. Such an individual would be unconscious well before they achieved such a concentration. To achieve such a concentration, a high dependence for alcohol must have developed after a pattern of sustained, regular heavy drinking. Consistent with this profile, no seasonal or weekday variations are seen in high range alcohol deaths. These are not weekend bingers. Indeed, almost all alcohol toxicity decedents are known to have long-standing alcohol problems, as do three quarters of high range deaths due to other causes. They were also likely to be in poor health prior to death, with a range of alcohol-related pathologies, as may be seen from autopsies findings (see below).

Despite clear forensic evidence that the average alcohol-related death has long-standing alcohol dependence, with all the attendant problems this entails, very few are in treatment for alcohol dependence at the time of death.

What was their toxicology?

The toxicology of those who die an alcohol-related death gives us crucial information that is not available in epidemiological data. It tells us how much alcohol was in the person's blood when they died, and whether other drugs were also present. While the average blood alcohol concentration of an alcohol toxicity death is in the vicinity of 0.40 g/100 mL, survival has been reported in cases with concentrations in excess of 1.0 g/100 mL (Below & Lignitz, 2003; Darke et al., 2013a, 2013b; Jones & Holmgren, 2003; Jones et al., 2011; Nordrum et al., 2000; Sjögren et al., 2000). Moreover, deaths due to other causes (e.g. traumatic accident) occur with alcohol concentrations well over that deemed fatal. These are people who had tolerance so high they could survive "fatal" blood alcohol concentrations, but died through disease or trauma. We cannot thus simply look at a blood alcohol concentration and infer that a person had a toxic amount in their blood at the time of death. This is a finding that is also true of other drugs, such as heroin and methamphetamine (Darke & Duflou, 2016; Darke et al., 2017).

Toxicology may tell use more important details of the circumstances of death. By examining the urine/blood ratio of alcohol concentrations we can determine if the person was still absorbing alcohol or had reached the post-absorptive phase of alcohol metabolism. The overwhelming majority of toxicity deaths occur in the absorptive phase of alcohol metabolism at the time of death. Typically, these are people in whom blood alcohol concentrations were still *increasing* at the time of death, even if they were not still actively drinking.

The role of polydrug use is a crucial one for drug toxicity across all major drug classes. Lower alcohol concentrations are frequently seen in cases where death is attributed to multiple drug toxicity involving the combined effects of alcohol and other central nervous system depressants, such as opioids or the benzodiazepines. In such circumstances, the combined respiratory depressant effects may be such that a blood alcohol concentration below 0.30 g/100 mL may prove fatal.

How did they die?

Toxicity: Most alcohol toxicity deaths are of a socially isolated individual who is drinking at home alone (Darke et al., 2013a). The epidemiological data most closely ties spirits drinking to alcohol toxicity deaths. The forensic data are consistent with these findings: fatal cases of alcohol toxicity are overwhelmingly spirit drinkers. Indeed, a substantial proportion drink denatured alcohol, as the cheapest possible option. The regular drinking of alcohol with the highest alcohol content is the quickest, cheapest way to achieve and maintain a high blood alcohol concentration. The question that arises here is what was different about that particular day? These are people for whom a blood alcohol concentration of >0.30 g/100 mL (or even 0.40 g/100 mL) was, in all probability, a daily occurrence. Why did they die on that day? This is a question that also arises in relation to other drug-related death, as the pattern of regular, dependent use (with a presumed high tolerance) is also the norm (Darke et al., 2010, 2017). It remains a mystery, but one possible answer may be emerge from the organ system pathology of cases (discussed below).

Trauma: As we have seen, an epidemiological link between alcohol consumption and homicide is well demonstrated. When we examine the forensic data, the reasons for this become apparent (Abrams, Leon, Tardiff, Marzuk, & Sutherland, 2007; Darke, 2010; Darke & Duflou, 2008; Darke, Duflou, & Torok, 2009a; Kuhns, Wilson, Clodfelter, Maguire, & Ainsworth, 2011). Looking at homicide victims, alcohol the most commonly observed substance, present in 40–50% of cases, and a third are intoxicated at the time of death. Moreover, alcohol is present in half of offenders, the majority of whom were intoxicated at the time of their offence (Darke, 2010; Kuhns, Exum, Clodfelter, & Bottia, 2014).

Alcohol clearly places a person at greater risk of being a homicide victim or offender. Why should this be so? One common scenario is of people drinking together, followed by an argument, a physical altercation and a fatality. Another is of two intoxicated males coming across each other on the street, and exchange words that result in violence. In both scenarios alcohol-induced disinhibition increases the risk of an altercation. To an extent, the similarities between offenders and victims reflects the fact that two intoxicated people are fighting, in which one lives and one dies. It could have easily been the reverse. Male homicide deaths involving alcohol are most likely to occur on the street or in pubs, where random interactions of alcohol affected individuals are more likely to occur. Females are most likely to be a victim of domestic violence in their home. In this case, alcohol may increase interpersonal tension, with a violent result. These scenarios are in no way a "blame the victim" narrative. What they indicate is that when violence occurs, alcohol is frequently present and increases the risk of it occurring. Unlike toxicity deaths, where there is no pattern across weekdays, homicide case are more likely to occur and to involve alcohol on the weekend. In this case, weekend binge drinking would appear to play a substantial role.

The marked impairment of perceptual, cognitive and motor functions that occur in alcohol intoxication also manifests in traumatic accidents (Bellis, Bolster, & Doyle, 2009; Darke et al., 2013b; Ehmke, du Toit-Prinsloo, & Saayman, 2014; Kelly, Darke, & Ross, 2004; Loftus & Dada, 1992; Nordrum et al., 2000; Sjögren et al., 2000). Motor vehicle accidents are prominent in traumatic death, and alcohol is present in the blood of a third to half of drivers killed in fatal accidents. Alcohol is also present in a high proportion of pedestrian fatalities. Alcohol is also highly prevalent in deaths due to falls, fire and drowning, seen in similar proportions to those of motor vehicle accident fatalities. Acute intoxication may also contribute to death from positional asphyxia (in which a comatose individual sustains a posture that obstructs breathing) (Benomran & Hassan, 2011; Byard, Wick, & Gilbert, 2008; Darke et al., 2013b).

Suicide: The toxicology of completed suicide provides clues to the observed epidemiological association of alcohol consumption with completed suicide. Alcohol is prominent in such cases. Indeed, the levels of alcohol seen amongst completed suicides are comparable to those seen in homicides (Cherpitel, Borges, & Wilcox, 2004; Crombie, Pounder, & Dick, 1998; Darke, Duflou, & Torok, 2009b; Dhossche, Rich, Ghani, & Isacsson, 2001; Shields, Hunsaker, Hunsaker, & Ward, 2006). Approximately 40% of cases have alcohol in their blood at the time of their suicide. Moreover, the levels detected are not trivial, with medians in the vicinity of 0.10 g/100 mL, which equates to approximately 5 standard drinks, and has been observed to range up to 0.40 g/100 mL (equivalent to some 20 drinks). The high presence of alcohol is observed in cases of self-poisoning and suicide by violent means.

How might alcohol influence the occurrence of a suicide? Alcohol-induced disinhibition, anger and aggression may lead to an impulsive suicide that my otherwise not have occurred. This is analogous to the externalized violence seen in many cases of alcohol-related homicide. Alternately, in a planned suicide alcohol is frequently used to build up the courage to make an attempt. The high levels of major depression and dysthymia seen amongst alcohol dependent individual (Darvishi et al., 2015; Heather et al., 2001) are also of relevance, a mood disorder being a risk factor for both attempts and completions. Alcohol intoxication in combination with a mood disorder will increase risk. What should be borne in mind is that completions are a marker for the far larger number of attempts, which may carry significant morbidity to the individual (e.g. anoxic brain damage after an attempted hanging).

What was their state of health?

Alcohol is associated with a range of diseases and conditions (US Department of Health and Human Services, 2000). Moreover, as we have seen, and despite time lags in the development of such conditions, a number of pathologies have been associated with national consumption. Coronial cases provide clues as to why this is so, and the extent of the problem. In cases of sudden or unnatural death, autopsies are typically conducted with an examination of all major organ systems. Most importantly, they are also conducted in cases where the direct cause of death was not due to alcohol-related disease (e.g. death due to trauma). Such data provide crucial data on the health of alcohol users that is not available by other means. They may be seen as snapshot of the living, particularly of those who are alcohol dependent.

Unfortunately, this is an opportunity that has rarely been utilized. In the one study I am aware of that has presented such detailed data, we examined sudden or unnatural deaths involving high blood alcohol concentrations (≥0.30 g/100 mL) (Darke et al., 2013b). Deaths due to alcohol-related disease constituted 13% of cases. Remarkably high levels of serious alcohol-related disease were observed, however, amongst those who did *not* die due to disease. Taking deaths due to traumatic accident as an illustration, liver cirrhosis and severe fatty liver were each diagnosed in 21%, chronic pancreatitis in 14%, cerebellar atrophy in a 9%, and alcohol-related cardiomyopathy in 6%. These are high levels of serious disease which, if the person has not died due to misadventure, may well have eventually killed them. The typical profile of these cases was of a dependent, heavy alcohol user. The clinical implication for the broader population of living, dependent alcohol users is that significant proportions will present with serious underlying alcohol-related. Such levels of disease might plausibly increase the risk of death in the presence of a high alcohol concentration, through mechanisms such as an increased risk for cardiac arrhythmia, or an impaired ability to metabolize alcohol due to liver disease.

What alcohol-related death has taught us

What then have we learnt from alcohol-related death? Firstly, that the amount a society drinks has major implications for its mortality, in terms of toxicity, disease, trauma and suicide. As has been emphasized throughout this chapter, death is a marker for the morbidity and burden of disease contributed by alcohol more broadly. The forensic data confirm the epidemiology by illustrating the role alcohol plays in mortality. The implications for public health are stark. If per capita consumption can be reduced (by whatever means) then we will see fewer deaths, and a lower burden of disease, due to alcohol toxicity, homicide, alcohol-related disease, traumatic accident and suicide.

These studies also tell us that it is the older, dependent user who is most at risk. Such an individual is likely to have a range of serious alcohol-related health problems, and is very unlikely to be enrolled in any form of treatment programme. Contrary to a great deal of media focus on youth binge drinking, it is the high volume, regular older drinker who should be the a major target for specialized intervention. This not to belittle efforts to intervene with the young. We must, however, be aware of what these data tell us about the demographics of risk. Getting a higher proportion of those with alcohol-related problems to enroll in treatment is crucial. Currently, it is estimated that an average of 18 years elapse between the onset of an alcohol use disorder and the first seeking of treatment (Chapman, Slade, Hunt, & Teesson, 2015). This is clinically unacceptable. Early intervention is always good intervention, and a great deal of harm might be averted if this period were to be substantially shortened. Those who are treating alcohol-dependent patients, whether in drug treatment or in general medical settings, need to be aware of the levels of disease that this group is likely to experience. Regular check-ups and scans for liver, heart and pancreatic disease, as well as cognitive impairment appear prudent. This is a group that is also at high risk for suicide. Again, screening for suicide history, mood, ideation and intent is good clinical practice in any high risk population.

The forensic data tells us something about the immediate risk from alcohol toxicity. The person who is unconscious is still at risk, despite that fact that they are no longer drinking. Their blood alcohol concentration may still be rising. Leaving them to "sleep it off" may be to consign them to a premature death. To reduce the risk of aspiration pneumonia or positional asphyxia, the person should be placed in the recovery position and regularly monitored. Many alcohol-related deaths I have reviewed would have been prevented had these simple interventions occurred.

These are not easy problems to solve. If they were, given the long history of alcohol consumption, we would have solved them already. We do, however, know a great deal more on which to build solutions. Death tells us much about life. By closely studying alcohol-related death, we can learn much on how to provide the living with a better quality of life, and a lower risk of premature death.

References

Abrams, R. C., Leon, A. C., Tardiff, K., Marzuk, P. M., & Sutherland, K. (2007). "Gray murder": Characteristics of elderly compared with nonelderly homicide victims in New York City. *American Journal of Public Health, 97*, 1666–1670.

Baselt, R. C. (Ed.), (2014). *Disposition of toxic drugs and chemicals in man (10th ed.)*. California: Biomedical Publications.

Bellis, M., Bolster, M. A., & Doyle, C. T. (2009). The role of alcohol in deaths presenting to the coroner's service in Cork City and County. *Irish Medical Journal, 102*, 13–15.

Below, E., & Lignitz, E. (2003). Cases of fatal poisoning in post-mortem examinations at the Institute of Forensic Medicine in Greifswald - Analysis of five decades of post-mortems. *Forensic Science International, 133*, 125–131.

Benomran, F. A., & Hassan, A. I. (2011). An unusual accidental death from positional asphyxia. *American Journal of Forensic Medicine and Pathology, 32*, 31–34.

Byard, R. W., Wick, R., & Gilbert, J. D. (2008). Conditions and circumstances predisposing to death from positional asphyxia in adults. *Journal of Forensic and Legal Medicine, 15*, 415–419.

Caces, F. E., & Harford, T. (1998). Time series analysis of alcohol consumption and suicide mortality in the United States, 1934–1987. *Journal of Studies on Alcohol, 59*, 455–461.

Chapman, C., Slade, T., Hunt, C., & Teesson, M. (2015). Delay to first treatment contact for alcohol use disorder. *Drug and Alcohol Dependence, 147*, 116–121.

Cherpitel, C. J., Borges, G. L., & Wilcox, H. C. (2004). Acute alcohol use and suicidal behavior: A review of the literature. *Alcoholism: Clinical and Experimental Research, 28*, 18S–28S.

Crombie, I. K., Pounder, D. J., & Dick, P. H. (1998). Who takes alcohol prior to suicide? *Journal of Clinical Forensic Medicine, 5*, 65–68.

Darke, S. (2010). The toxicology of homicide offenders and victims: A review. *Drug and Alcohol Review, 29*, 202–215.

Darke, S., & Duflou, J. (2008). Toxicology and circumstances of death of homicide victims in New South Wales, Australia 1996–2005. *Journal of Forensic Sciences, 53*, 447–451.

Darke, S., & Duflou, J. (2016). The toxicology of heroin-related death: Estimating survival times. *Addiction, 111*, 1607–1613.

Darke, S., Duflou, J., & Torok. (2010). The comparative toxicology and major organ pathology of fatal methadone and heroin toxicity cases. *Drug and Alcohol Dependence, 106*, 1–6.

Darke, S., Duflou, J., & Torok, M. (2009a). Drugs and violent death: Comparative toxicology of homicide and non-substance toxicity suicide victims. *Addiction, 104*, 1000–1005.

Darke, S., Duflou, J., & Torok, M. (2009b). Toxicology and circumstances of completed suicide by means other than overdose. *Journal of Forensic Sciences*, *54*, 490–494.

Darke, S., Duflou, J., Torok, M., & Prolov, T. (2013a). Toxicology, circumstances and pathology of deaths from acute alcohol toxicity. *Journal of Forensic and Legal Medicine*, *20*, 1122–1125.

Darke, S., Duflou, J., Torok, M., & Prolov, T. (2013b). Characteristics, circumstances and toxicology of sudden or unnatural deaths involving very high range alcohol concentrations. *Addiction*, *108*, 1411–1417.

Darke, S., Kaye, S., & Duflou, J. (2017). Rates, characteristics and circumstances of methamphetamine-related death in Australia: A national 7 year study. *Addiction*, *112*, 2191–2201.

Darvishi, N., Farhadi, M., Haghtalab, T., & Poorolajal, J. (2015). Alcohol-related risk of suicidal ideation, suicide attempt, and completed suicide: A meta-analysis. *PLoS One*, *10*, e0126870.

Dhossche, D. M., Rich, C. L., Ghani, S. O., & Isacsson, G. (2001). Patterns of psychoactive substance detection from routine toxicology of suicides in Mobile, Alabama, between 1990 and 1998. *Journal of Affective Disorders*, *64*, 167–174.

Ehmke, U., du Toit-Prinsloo, L., & Saayman, G. (2014). A retrospective analysis of alcohol in medico-legal autopsied deaths in Pretoria over a 1 year period. *Forensic Science International*, *245*, 7–11.

Gmel, G., Rehm, J., & Frick, U. (2001). Methodological approaches to conducting pooled cross-sectional time series analysis: The example of the association between all-cause mortality and per capita alcohol consumption for men in 15 European states. *European Addiction Research*, *7*, 128–137.

Heather, N., Peters, T. J., & Stockwell, T. (Eds.), (2001). *International handbook of alcohol dependence and problems*. Chichester: John Wiley Sons.

Her, M., & Rehm, J. (1998). Alcohol and all-cause mortality in Europe 1982–1990: A pooled cross-section time-series analysis. *Addiction*, *93*, 1335–1340.

Jones, A. W., & Holmgren, P. (2003). Urine/blood ratios of ethanol in deaths attributed to acute alcohol poisoning and chronic alcoholism. *Forensic Science International*, *135*, 206–212.

Jones, A. W., Kugelberg, F. C., Holmgren, A., & Ahlner, J. (2011). Drug poisoning deaths in Sweden show a predominance of ethanol in mono-intoxications, adverse drug–alcohol interactions and poly-drug use. *Forensic Science International*, *206*, 43–51.

Kelly, E., Darke, S., & Ross, J. (2004). A review of drug use and driving: Epidemiology, impairment, risk factors and risk perceptions. *Drug and Alcohol Review*, *23*, 319–344.

Kuhns, J. B., Exum, M. L., Clodfelter, T. A., & Bottia, M. C. (2014). The prevalence of alcohol-involved homicide offending: A meta-analytic review. *Homicide Studies*, *18*, 251–270.

Kuhns, J. B., Wilson, D. B., Clodfelter, T. A., Maguire, E. R., & Ainsworth, S. A. (2011). A meta-analysis of alcohol toxicology study findings among homicide victims. *Addiction*, *106*, 62–72.

Landberg, J. (2008). Alcohol and suicide in Eastern Europe. *Drug and Alcohol Review*, *27*, 361–373.

Landberg, J. (2010). Population drinking and fatal injuries in Eastern Europe: A time-series analysis of six countries. *European Addiction Research*, *16*, 43–52.

Lester, D. (1995). The association between alcohol consumption and suicide and homicide rates: A study of 13 nations. *Alcohol and Alcoholism*, *30*, 465–468.

Loftus, I. A., & Dada, M. A. (1992). A retrospective analysis of alcohol in medicolegal postmortems over a period of five years. *American Journal of Forensic Medicine and Pathology*, *13*, 248–252.

Mäkelä, P. (1996). Alcohol consumption and suicide mortality by age among Finnish men, 1950–1991. *Addiction, 91*, 101–112.

Mann, R. E., Zalcman, R. F., Smart, R., Rush, B. R., & Suurvali, H. (2006). Alcohol consumption, Alcoholics Anonymous membership and homicide mortality rates in Ontario, 1968 to 1991. *Alcoholism: Clinical & Experimental Research, 30*, 1743–1751.

Mościcki, E. K. (2001). Epidemiology of completed and attempted suicide: Toward a framework for prevention. *Clinical Neuroscience Research, 1*, 310–323.

Nelson, D. E., Jarman, D. W., Rehm, J., Greenfield, T. K., Rey, G., Kerr, W. C., & Naimi, T. S. (2013). Alcohol-attributable cancer deaths and years of potential life lost in the United States. *American Journal of Public Health, 103*, 641–648.

Nemtsov, A. (2003). Suicides and alcohol consumption in Russia, 1965–1999. *Drug and Alcohol Dependence, 71*, 161–168.

Nordrum, I., Eide, T. J., & Jørgensen, L. (2000). Alcohol in a series of medico-legally autopsied deaths in northern Norway 1973–1992. *Forensic Science International, 110*, 127–137.

Norström, T. (2001). Per capita alcohol consumption and all-cause mortality in 14 European countries. *Addiction, 96*(Suppl. 1), 113–128.

Norström, T., & Ramstedt, M. (2005). Mortality and population drinking: A review of the literature. *Drug and Alcohol Review, 24*, 537–547.

Poikolainen, K., Leppänen, K., & Vuori, E. (2002). Alcohol sales and fatal alcohol poisonings: A time-series analysis. *Addiction, 97*, 1037–1040.

Pridemore, W. A. (2002). Vodka and violence: Alcohol consumption and homicide rates in Russia. *American Journal of Public Health, 92*, 1921–1930.

Ramstedt, M. (2001). Alcohol and suicide in 14 European countries. *Addiction, 96*(Suppl. 1), 59–75.

Ramstedt, M. (2005). Alcohol and suicide at the population level—The Canadian experience. *Drug And Alcohol Review, 24*, 203–208.

Razvodovsky, Y. E. (2003). Association between distilled spirits consumption and violent mortality rate. *Drugs: Education, Prevention & Policy, 3*, 235–250.

Razvodovsky, Y. E. (2008). All-cause mortality and fatal alcohol poisoning in Belarus, 1970–2005. *Drug and Alcohol Review, 27*, 562–565.

Razvodovsky, Y. E. (2009). Alcohol poisoning and cardiovascular mortality in Russia, 1956–2005. *Alcoholism, 45*, 27–41.

Razvodovsky, Y. E. (2010). Beverage-specific alcohol sale and cardiovascular mortality in Russia. *Journal of Environmental and Public Health*, 253853.

Razvodovsky, Y. E. (2013). Alcohol-attributable fraction of ischemic heart disease mortality in Russia. *ISRN Cardiolog*, Article ID 287869.

Razvodovsky, Y. E. (2014). Fraction of stroke mortality attributable to alcohol consumption in Russia. *Adicciones, 26*, 126–133.

Rehm, J., & Shield, K. D. (2014). Alcohol and mortality: Global alcohol-attributable deaths from cancer, liver cirrhosis, and injury in 2010. *Alcohol Research: Current Reviews, 35*, 174.

Rehm, J., Samokhvalov, A. V., & Shield, K. D. (2013). Global burden of alcoholic liver diseases. *Journal of Hepatology, 59*, 160–168.

Rossow, I. (2001). Alcohol and homicide: A cross-cultural comparison of the relationship in 14 European countries. *Addiction, 96*(Suppl. 1), 77–92.

Rossow, I. (2004). Alcohol consumption and homicides in Canada, 1950–1999. *Contemporary Drug Problems, 31*, 541–559.

Shield, K. D., Gmel, G., Patra, J., & Rehm, J. (2012). Global burden of injuries attributable to alcohol consumption in 2004: A novel way of calculating the burden of injuries attributable to alcohol consumption. *Population Health Metrics, 10*, 9.

Shields, L. B. E., Hunsaker, D. M., Hunsaker, J. C., & Ward, M. K. (2006). Toxicologic findings in suicide. A 10-year retrospective review of Kentucky medical examiner cases. *American Journal of Forensic Medical Pathology*, *27*, 106–112.

Sjögren, H., Eriksson, A., & Ahlm, K. (2000). Role of alcohol in unnatural deaths: A study of all deaths in Sweden. *Alcoholism: Clinical and Experimental Research*, *24*, 1050–1056.

Skog, O. J. (2001a). Alcohol consumption and overall accident mortality in 14 European countries. *Addiction*, *96*(Suppl. 1), 35–47.

Skog, O. J. (2001b). Alcohol consumption and mortality rates from traffic accidents, accidental falls, and other accidents in 14 European countries. *Addiction*, *96*(Suppl. 1), 49–58.

Stahre, M., Roeber, J., Kanny, D., Brewer, R. D., & Zhang, X. (2014). Contribution of excessive alcohol consumption to deaths and years of potential life lost in the United States. *Preventing Chronic Disease*, *11*, E109.

Stickley, A., Leinsalu, M., Andreev, E., Razvodovsky, Y., Vågerö, D., & McKee, M. (2007). Alcohol poisoning in Russia and the countries in the European part of the former Soviet Union, 1970–2002. *European Journal of Public Health*, *17*, 444–449.

Strickley, A., & Razvodovsky, Y. (2012). The effects of beverage type on homicide rates in Russia, 1970–2005. *Drug and Alcohol Review*, *31*, 257–262.

US Department of Health and Human Services. (2000). *10th special report to the US congress on alcohol and health*. Bethesda, MD: National Institute on Alcohol Abuse and Alcoholism.

Whiteford, H. A., Degenhardt, L., Rehm, J., Baxter, A. J., Ferrari, A. J., Erskine, H. E., & Burstein, R. (2013). Global burden of disease attributable to mental and substance use disorders: Findings from the Global Burden of Disease Study 2010. *Lancet*, *382*, 1575–1586.

Section 3

The individual

Chapter 7

Levels of cognitive understanding: Reflective and impulsive cognition in alcohol use and misuse

Dinkar Sharma[1] **and James Cane**[2]
[1]*School of Psychology, University of Kent, Canterbury, Kent, United Kingdom,* [2]*School of Psychology and Life Sciences, Canterbury Christ Church University, Canterbury, Kent, United Kingdom*

The influences that guide a person to use and misuse alcohol are complex and involve a number of different facets including social, situational, and environmental aspects (see Borsari, Murphy, Barnett, 2007; Clapper, Martin, & Clifford, 1994; Melotti et al., 2011; Simons, 2003). Whilst these factors can play a large part in guiding one to consume, or even avoid, alcohol, fundamentally it is the cognitive processing of these situational, environmental, and societal factors that leads to specific behavioral responses and decisions to engage with, or avoid, alcohol or alcohol-related situations (see Tiffany & Conklin, 2000). Some of these cognitive processes we can be aware of, and involve us appraising situations or making, and reflecting on, explicit decisions to engage with alcohol or alcohol-related situations, however others are impulsive, or automatic, and can occur without conscious awareness and these can relate to our goals, motivations or previous experiences with alcohol. In this chapter, we will explore and discuss the interaction between these different cognitive processes and specifically focus on the interplay between reflective and impulsive processing of alcohol-related situations, objects and environments and related emotions and how processing of these factors may lead to different behavioral outcomes. We will also explore how researchers have explored these underlying cognitive processes and the research that has helped guide our understanding of the cognitive processing of alcohol-related situations.

Ostensibly all human behavior involves some form of interaction between attention, memory, and decision processes. In relation to alcohol, specific alcohol responses based on our previous experiences with alcohol and in

The Handbook of Alcohol Use - Understandings from Synapse to Society.
DOI: https://doi.org/10.1016/B978-0-12-816720-5.00018-9

alcohol-related situations are stored in our memory, and are thought to develop through positive or negative reinforcement mechanisms (see Cooper, Frone, Russell, & Mudar, 1995; Farber, Khavari, & Douglass, 1980). Evidence suggests that associations and knowledge structures created through these conditioning processes subsequently guide our attention towards or away from alcohol-related situations or objects, these may in-turn lead to impulsive behavioral responses, but we may also be able to make reflective decisions to interact, or not, with the environment, social situation, or specific alcohol-related objects based on the feelings and thoughts that manifest from these underlying cognitive processes. Evidence of such cognitive processing comes from empirical studies showing that those who have higher levels of alcohol consumption have a greater predisposition of attention towards alcohol-related objects – that is, there is some form of attentional orientation to, or attentional capture of, alcohol-related objects over objects unrelated to alcohol (see Cox, Fadardi, & Pothos, 2006; Hallgren & McCrady, 2013; Hobson, Bruce, & Butler, 2013). Commonly termed *attentional bias* this attention-related phenomenon is reported to be stronger in those with a history of alcohol abuse compared to heavy, light or social drinkers (see Cox et al., 2006). Furthermore, alcohol attentional biases have also been shown to be a predictor of treatment outcome, with those who show greater levels of attentional distraction from alcohol-related stimuli having poorer treatment outcomes (i.e. relapsed during treatment, did not maintain outpatient contact, or failed to complete a treatment program; see Cox, Hogan, Kristian, & Race, 2002).

Empirical studies have employed a variety of methods to explore attentional bias in relation to alcohol. The most common method being an adapted version of the emotional Stroop task (Williams, Matthews, & MacLeod, 1996) often called the addiction-Stroop task (see Cane, Sharma, & Albery, 2009). In this task, alcohol-related words (e.g. beer, alcohol, vodka) and words unrelated to alcohol (e.g. mouse, bike, phone) are presented in different colored inks. Participants in these tasks have to identify the color of the ink of the words as quickly and accurately as possible, whilst trying to ignore the words, or the context of the words, themselves. Rooted in the assumptions of classic Stroop task effects (see MacLeod, 1991; Stroop, 1935) whereby color-words conflict with color-naming, it is assumed that *if* the alcohol-related words distract or 'grab' attention then this should lead to slower color-naming of those words. Thus, an *attentional bias* for addiction-related words is thought to be denoted when the color-naming of addiction-related words is slower than the color-naming of neutral words. Such effects have been shown across a number of alcohol-related studies providing evidence of effects indicative of attentional bias for alcohol-related stimuli (e.g. Duka & Townshend, 2004; Field, Duka et al., 2007; Sharma, Albery, & Cook, 2001; see Cox et al., 2006 for a review). The modified Stroop task has proved beneficial in identifying differences in attentional bias for alcohol stimuli between in-treatment abstaining drinkers and those who have high alcohol drinking consumption and those with low alcohol drinking consumption, where those who are currently undergoing treatment show the greatest distractability from alcohol related words over neutral words (see Lusher, Chandler, & Ball, 2004; Sharma, Albery, & Cook, 2001). Similarly, in a study relating to college drinkers, the modified Strop task has highlighted differences in alcohol attentional bias in relation to drinking *intensity* rather than drinking frequency or drinking-related problems, with those who had a recent binge-drinking episode showing greater attentional bias for alcohol stimuli (Hallgren & McCrady, 2013). Thus, the modified Stroop task has proved effective in not only identifying attentional bias in relation to alcohol, but has also proved effective in differentiating between the attentional bias shown in different groups, either who are currently consuming alcohol, or those with a history of alcohol use and abuse.

A further development of the modified version of the addiction Stroop task by McKenna and Sharma (2004) has proved effective in identifying immediate effects on attention which happen during stimulus presentation and 'lingering' effects on attention which occur on trials following the critical stimulus presentation. Measured using a sequence involving a single addiction-related word followed by a number of counterbalanced neutral words, the attention-grabbing effects of stimuli are characterized by slower color-naming during the presentation of the alcohol-related word (also called the 'fast effect'). In contrast, attentional-holding effects are characterized by slower color-naming on neutral stimuli that immediately follow the alcohol-related word – often referred to as the 'slow effect' or 'carryover' effect. These slow effects are thought to represent the difficulty to disengage attention from the stimuli or rumination over the concepts relating to the stimuli (see Cane et al., 2009; Sharma & Money, 2010; Waters, Sayette, & Wertz, 2003; Waters, Sayette, Franken, & Schwartz, 2005). It has been proposed that the fast effects represent impulsive bottom-up stimulus responses stemming from the salience and low-level properties of the stimuli grabbing ones attention and the slow effects represent the more reflective top-down response regulation or disruption of inhibitory regulation and failure to disengage attention from the stimulus or concepts relating to the stimulus (see Cane, Sharma, & Albery, 2009). Through these changes to the modified Stroop task, the task has been further developed to distinguish between different aspects of cognition and attention in relation to alcohol use and misuse. Indeed, research has shown that both fast, immediate attention-grabbing effects, and slow effects, can be present in relation to substance use (see Cane, Sharma, & Albery, 2009), and in relation to alcohol both fast and slow effects of alcohol have been shown to be evident using this modified task (Clarke, Sharma, & Salter, 2015). Furthermore, Clarke et al. (2015) found that the slow effects, but not fast effects, were positively correlated with increased drinking levels in both social drinkers and in-treatment drinkers. Thus, there is emerging evidence that differentiating between these fast and slow effects of attention, may be theoretically, and potentially, practically important.

Dual-task paradigms are conceptually similar to Stroop task paradigms, in that slowing down on one task is a product of reactions to specific stimuli. However, Waters and Green (2003) suggest that the dual-task procedure they used provides stronger evidence for attentional bias effects than the Stroop task and the visual probe task (see below) because, unlike the Stroop task, responses are more likely to represent active shifts in visuo-spatial attention towards addiction-related stimuli. Dual-task paradigms, as the name suggests, involve two concurrent tasks. In one task the user is presented with alcohol-related or neutral stimuli, and in a second task participants complete a reaction time task which is cognitively demanding. As with the Stroop task, slowing down on the reaction time task indicates that attention is being captured by the alcohol-related stimulus. For instance, Waters and Green (2003) adopted a dual-task paradigm in a group of abstinent alcoholics and a group of control subjects. For their dual-task procedure, the reaction time task required participants to respond to odd and even numbers shown centrally on a screen and for the secondary addiction-related task they asked participants to respond to words (alcohol and neutral words) and non-words 'out of the corner of their eye'. Using this task, they found that abstaining alcoholics were slowed on the odd-even task when the peripheral cues were alcohol-related words compared to when the peripheral words were neutral, thus indicating that attention was allocated to alcohol stimuli to a greater extent than neutral stimuli.

Whilst the Stroop task and dual-task paradigms has proved effective in identify effects of attentional orientation or capture in relation to alcohol, they only provide an indication of covert attention processes, other tasks are thought to be a better direct measure visuo-spatial attention as they monitor where visual attention is allocated at particular points in time (i.e. overt attention) – these tasks include tasks such as the visual-probe (or dot-probe) task, and eye-tracking methodology. In the visual-probe task, two stimuli (images or words) are displayed simultaneously adjacent to each other for a short period of time on a screen (commonly below 1 s). One of the stimuli is alcohol-related (e.g. the word 'beer' or an image of a glass of wine) and the other is neutral (e.g. the word 'brick' or the image of a shoe). After the stimuli presentation a probe (usually either one dot or two dots, or an arrow in certain orientation) replaces the position of one of the stimuli. The participants' task is to respond as quickly and as accurately as possible to the nature of probe shown (e.g. the direction of the arrow or the number of dots). It is expected that respondents would be quicker to respond to probes that are presented in the area where their attention has been directed than areas to which attention has been drawn away from. For instance, if respondents' attention is grabbed by an alcohol-related stimuli they should be quicker to respond to probes which replace those alcohol-related stimuli. Thus, an alcohol-related attentional bias in the visual probe task is indicated by faster response times when probes replace alcohol-related stimuli, compared with response times when probes replace neutral stimuli. It has been argued that the visual probe task is a fairly direct measurement of visuo-spatial attention as visual attention has to be given to the area of the stimulus before the probe can be correctly and readily detected (Field, 2006). Furthermore, the task has been consistent in revealing effects which are indicative of attentional bias for alcohol-related stimuli across a number of studies (e.g. Duka & Townshend, 2004; Field, Mogg, Zetteler, & Bradley, 2004; Miller & Fillmore, 2010). Furthermore, recent studies have shown evidence that visuo-spatial orientation to alcohol stimuli using the visual probe task is positively correlated with increased craving (Field, Mogg, & Bradley, 2005).

Research using the visual probe task has also provided interesting findings that suggest a differentiation between impulsive and reflective processes. By varying the duration to which pairs of stimuli are presented it is possible to disentangle between immediate shifts in attention to stimuli and later shifts in attention that occur once the stimuli have been further processed, these are thought to represent impulsive and reflexive responses respectively. Responses to probes after short stimulus durations (commonly <500 ms) are thought to represent immediate 'attention grabbing' effects, whilst responses to probes after longer stimulus durations (commonly >2000 ms) are thought to represent the maintenance of attention on, or inability to disengage from, a stimulus (Bradley, Mogg, Wright, & Field, 2003). Shorter stimulus durations thus correspond to bottom-up stimulus salience responses and longer stimulus durations correspond to the engagement of, or interruption of, top-down regulation of control. These are comparable with the fast and slow effects shown in the Stroop task described previously. Thus, the visual probe task, like the addiction Stroop task, is not only an effective measure of attentional bias but has the potential to distinguish between fast and slow, 'lingering' effects of attentional bias.

Eye-Movement technology has also been used to examine whether visuo-spatial attention is directly given to alcohol-related objects. Some studies have employed this in conjunction with versions of the visual probe task (see above) to corroborate that attention is directed to particular stimuli before responding to the probe (see Miller & Fillmore, 2010) and others have employed eye-tracking with natural scenes containing alcohol-related stimuli. One such study was conducted by Roy-Charland et al., 2017 who across two experiments recorded eye-movement patterns across natural scenes containing either alcohol objects or being absent of alcohol-related objects. In one experiment, participants self-determined the time the images were presented for and were given no direction on the reasons for viewing the images, and in a second experiment the available time for viewing the scenes was limited and participants were specifically asked to memorize aspects of the image for a future recall task. In Experiment 1 there was no evidence of a link between alcohol-related attentional bias and levels of alcohol consumption, even amongst those who reported high levels of drinking. However, in Experiment 2 a positive correlation was identified between the number of shifts into and out of alcohol-related areas of interest and levels of annual alcohol consumption, with greater shifts of attention to these areas being associated with higher levels of consumption. The authors posit that the attentional biases to alcohol-related objects can occur where there is certainty of attentional focus in a particular environment. These findings build on earlier findings that have generally shown evidence of greater attention being given to alcohol objects in natural scenes in those who have a heavy versus light drinking patterns, especially where there are high levels of craving alcohol (see Hobson, Bruce, & Butler, 2013).

In contrast to paradigms purporting to measure visuo-spatial attention, the Go/No-Go task is believed to specifically tap inhibitory-control mechanisms (see Eaglem, Barry, & Robbins, 2008). The measurement of inhibitory control is believed to be important as it is thought to play a role in the development and maintenance of drug use and misuse behaviors (see de Wit, 2009; Fillmore, 2003; Goldstein & Volkow, 2002). The task requires that participants press a designated key when a 'go' symbol is presented as rapidly as possible but withhold their response when a 'no-go' symbol is presented. In alcohol-related studies, participants are typically required to initiate responses to non-alcohol related images of drinks (e.g. a water bottle, bottle of cola) and withhold responses to images of alcohol-related drinks (e.g. a bottle of beer, a bottle of wine). The number of initiated responses to alcohol-related objects (false alarms) is thought to represent problems in inhibitory control. Studies adopting this task have identified poorer inhibitory control in those who have high levels of drinking compared to those with lower levels of drinking (see Ahmadi et al., 2013; Easdon et al., 2005) and furthermore that these indications of poorer performance on the Go/NoGo are related to dysfunction in specific brain regions related to response inhibition (see Ahmadi et al., 2013),

Using these tasks has highlighted the potential underlying cognitive processes that drive behavioral responses in relation to alcohol and alcohol-related situations and environments. Largely, these cognitive processes, once developed, are deemed to be implicit in their nature and impulsive—that is out of our explicit control (see Tiffany, 1990). This is in contrast to cognitive processes which are explicit in their nature, including short and long-terms goals, explicit views and reasoning about alcohol, alcohol use, and alcohol-related situations. In the following section we will discuss how the implicit/impulsive responses to alcohol and alcohol-related situations and environments have been modeled using dual-process models and how these models help us to understand how these cognitive components relate to behaviors, thoughts and feelings that often accompany repeated substance use and misuse.

Dual-process models

Dual-process models have been developed to explain the activation of behavioral representations and influences on behavioral outcomes across different areas of psychology (see Bargh & Chartrand, 1999; Strack & Deutsch, 2004). In general, these models have attempted to describe the interaction between impulsive and reflective processes, where the former are based on associations and representations that are triggered by stimuli (i.e. as a 'bottom-up' process) and are thought to be fast, and the latter reflective processes are processes that are goal-directed, propositional and rule-based and involve reasoning processes (i.e. involving top-down processes; see Barrett, Tugade, & Engle, 2004) and are thought to be slow in nature. In these models, behavior is explained by the interaction of these processes and the moment-to-moment balance of these stimulus-driven and propositional/rule-based components (see Barrett et al., 2004; Palfai, 2006). In everyday terms, the stimulus-driven aspects relate to associations triggered by specific objects or situations, for instance seeing an off-licence on a high street might trigger pleasurable feelings relating to previous drinking experiences. In contrast, the reflective processes guide behaviors in line with propositional reasoning, for instance a person might have the intention to abstain from drinking and will likely reason about the benefits or costs of walking into the off-licence to buy a drink, potentially concluding that this would be a bad idea. Thus, these two distinct processes can be congruous (e.g. the triggering positive feelings about drinking, and reasoning that drinking is good), or they can be incongruous (e.g. the triggering of positive feelings about drinking, but reasoning that drinking would be a bad idea). These dual-process models seek to explain some of the phenomena that have been identified in empirical studies relating to the impulsive responses to stimuli versus the reflective aspects of cognition. These models commonly specify that the attention to, and subsequent perception of, stimuli can trigger automatic internal representations of knowledge structures and internal-goal states. The knowledge structures can be anything that one might already have knowledge about relating to the stimuli-specific context. For instance, knowledge structures can relate to simple memories (e.g. recalling a time when you had a good time with friends when drinking, or when you had a really bad hangover after drinking), or associations derived through, often repeated, logical thinking or assumptions, even if there is no direct experience of those events (e.g. repeatedly being told by a friend that drinking makes them feel good). The propositional route can comprise of reasoning relating to specific goals to which a person is driven to achieve. For instance, one might have the intention to give up drinking and so would have the goal to avoid alcohol-related situations or the consumption of alcohol. In contrast, a person might have the goal to increase their sociability at a party, and therefore may aim to drink alcohol to achieve this goal. It is believed that environmental cues can trigger both the associations and propositional reasoning that can ultimately lead to related thoughts and feelings, and behavioral responses (see Bargh & Chartrand, 1999; Barrett et al., 2004). For instance, the smell of alcohol might trigger memories of previous drinking situations and increase the propensity to drink.

One of the earliest dual-process models specifically developed to explain drug use behavior and that incorporates the idea of an interaction between impulsive and reflective cognitive components is the Cognitive Model of Drug Urges and Drug-Use Behavior proposed by Tiffany (1990). In this model drug use is primarily controlled by automatic processes, which are fast and of which we are not consciously aware of, but is accompanied with non-automatic aspects, such as drug-related urges, which we are consciously aware of and take effort to control. One important aspect of Tiffany's model is that drug-use behaviors that have become automatic will have little influence on the processing of other behaviors or cognitions, and have little or no influence on processes relating to executive function. These responses are therefore reflexive rather than reflective. Such automatic processes are developed through consistent pairings between the drug-stimulus and a response, but can be mediated by the effects of the drug itself, (e.g. alcohol). Tiffany suggests five key properties of these automatic processes:

1. There is little conscious awareness of these processes directly.
2. They become less variable and faster the more they are repeated.
3. The stimulus alone can elicit the response—i.e they are "*stimulus bound*".
4. They require minimal effort or attention.
5. They are not under our explicit control.

Because of their automatic nature on other aspects of cognition, these processes have very little impact on working memory, or on working memory capacity, which can be used for the processing of other stimuli, cognitive inputs or behaviors. Furthermore, when automatic processes are interrupted (e.g. when drinking alcohol is not possible), the non-automatic processes relating to drug-use are likely to be more prominent, i.e. there may be greater craving or explicit thoughts about the drug itself (see Tiffany, 1990).

Wiers et al. (2007) developed a similar dual-process model that specifies how the reflective processes might inhibit the automatic associative processes involved in alcohol use, and how this might change at different life stages (e.g. during adolescence versus adulthood). Through their model, Wiers et al. (2007) that addictive behaviors result from an imbalance between implicit appetite responses towards the consumption of a substance and the self-regulatory control mechanisms available to inhibit these implicit appetitive responses. In their model they specified three particular components: the explicit attitude related to the consumption of a particular substance; the implicit appetitive response tendency for consuming the substance; and the inhibitory control that one can exert over implicit appetitive responses. The latter inhibitory control has the possibility of influencing the implicit appetitive responses, as a form of self-regulation, however this is reliant on their being sufficient motivation to engage those mechanisms and fundamentally the ability to put those processes into play. Wiers et al. highlight evidence that shows that motivational influences to control drinking behavior are often weak during adolescence, where there is little consideration of any issues with their drinking behavior. In contrast, later life comes with the increased probability of the experience of problematic outcomes as a result of drinking, and so the motivation to regulate drinking becomes stronger later in adult life. Furthermore, given that one would need the ability to engage in self-regulation, and this can sometimes be tempered as a results of previous problematic drinking, especially in cases where this has resulted in neurological adaptations or damage affecting inhibitory control mechanisms. This model is therefore important in highlighting the variation in control that the reflective self-regulatory processes have on the implicit, impulsive processes at different stages in the face of non-problematic, and problematic drinking.

More recently, Moss and Albery (2009) proposed an alternative dual-process model drawing from both (i) myopia theory (Steele & Josephs, 1990), which suggests diminished processing capacity after alcohol consumption leading to the processing of only the most salient cues in a situation, and (ii) alcohol-expectancy theory, which posits that expectations of alcohol effects predict behavioral outcomes even in the absence of alcohol (i.e. when a placebo is consumed or when primed with alcohol cues; see Friedman, McCarthy, Förster, Markus, 2005 for an example). Building on previous models, Moss and Albery suggest that mental representations and alcohol expectancies, are triggered by drug-related cues, however the influence that these cues have on behavior is controlled by propositional reasoning, the controlled goal-directed reflective processes. Importantly, their model suggests two particular stages, a pre-consumption stage and a post-consumption stage. In the pre-consumption stage, whilst the associations that are triggered may be many (especially in the case of heavy-drinkers) the propositional reasoning component is able to control the representations that may lead to behavioral outcomes. However, in the post-consumption stage the effortful cognitive processing of other stimuli is disrupted and control processes become disrupted, and therefore these automatically derived mental representations are more likely to influence behaviors. Indeed, evidence from studies has indeed shown that alcohol consumption can lead to impairment of cognitive function, including aspects involved in reasoning (see Dawson & Reid, 1997; Moss & Albery, 2009). Therefore, Moss and Albery's model allows us to understand specifically how alcohol influences the determination of a behavioral outcomes in those who drink alcohol.

A neural network approach to dual-process models

Theoretical models of addiction suggest that attentional bias is a contributor to the development and maintenance of substance abuse. Dual process models suggest that behavior is guided by both impulsive and reflective processes. Such models also indicate that alcohol consumption results in a reduced influence from propositional processes (e.g. Moss & Albery, 2009).

It is clear from the above discussion that dual process models provide a general framework for understanding substance abuse. One drawback of such models is that they do not provide an explicitly computational model. This is important to enable the field to work with complex interacting mechanisms that not only reproduce behavioral outcomes but also are clear about the underlying assumptions. Here we try to make such links with the cognitive literature where these models are more common. The underlying mechanisms described in dual process models have parallels in neural network models. Here we draw attention to the processing of information in a bottom-up (automatic or reflexive) or top-down (proactive or reflective) manner. Such network models have not been described in the addiction literature, however, it is possible to do so. Here we provide a brief description largely to draw parallels with how negative salient stimuli are implemented in neural network models particularly as there is evidence that part of the effects of addictive substances is related to their negative affect. In this literature the general framework for impulsive and reflexive systems is often described as involving cognitive control (Braver, 2012). Cognitive control is the ability to flexibly guide behavior in line with our goals or intentions and in particular to help in situations of otherwise compelling response tendencies or what is also called prepotent tendency. Such a definition has been used in the general cognitive literature to describe behaviors as simple as saying a word to more complex behaviors as crossing the road or stopping at a traffic light.

Cognitive control is fundamental to all forms of higher cognitive function (also known as executive functions) including language planning, problem solving, and decision making. However, to study this scientifically it helps to have a simple example that can be used in the laboratory. The most popular task used to study cognitive control is the original Stroop task which is probably the most robust phenomena in psychology. As described earlier, the Stroop task has also been modified to study salient stimuli that includes emotional and alcohol related stimuli (Cox et al., 2006; Phaf & Kan, 2007; Williams et al., 1996). To capture the many findings discovered using the Stroop task we first describe a general neural network model (see Cohen, Dunbar, & McClelland, 1990) and then show how it can be extended to salient stimuli, particularly alcohol related stimuli. Although we focus on the Stroop task here a similar approach has been taken for modeling the findings from the dot-probe task using emotionally salient stimuli (see Frewen, Dozois, Joanisse, & Neufeld, 2008).

In the Stroop task how is it that when asked to name the ink color of a word one is able to ignore the word (the prepotent or default response) and respond to the ink color? Network models have been used to capture the processes that we think the brain uses to do this task. The basic model provides a simple associative framework where there are connections from input stimuli to output responses and with information flowing initially in a bottom-up fashion from input to output (see Fig. 7.1). Often a hidden layer is used to associatively

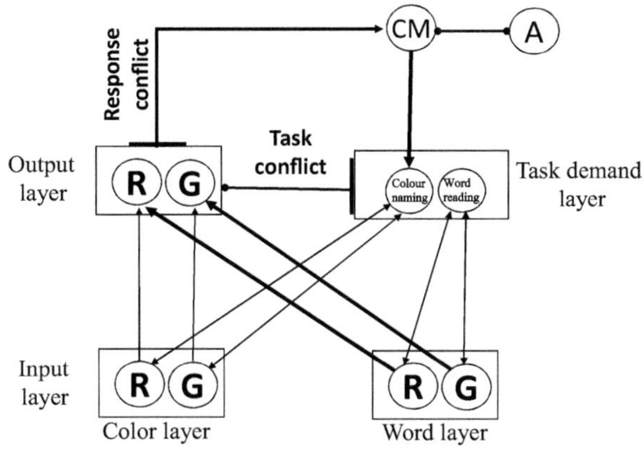

FIGURE 7.1 A network model adapted from Wyble et al. (2008) and Kalanthroff et al. (2015). Response conflict triggers additional top-down activation via the conflict monitoring unit (CM) to color naming as in Botvinick et al. (2001). Task conflict is represented as the inhibitory connection between the task demand layer and the output layer. When a unit (circles) is activated within a layer (rectangles) that unit inhibits other units within its layer. R = red, G = green, A = alcohol or affectively relevant stimuli.

connect the inputs to the outputs, however, to simplify description, this layer will remain hidden to show the direct connections from input to output (Cohen, Dunbar, & McClelland, 1990; Cohen & Huston 1994).

In this network model when a word (e.g. a word CHAIR, or GREEN) is presented (irrespective of which color the word is written in) the default response is to read the word (say 'chair' or 'green'). This is commonly represented in the model as a stronger association between the word inputs and the response output (indicated by thicker lines in Fig. 7.1). The stronger association indicating that greater attention is given to this aspect of processing. So how is it that when asked to respond to the color in which a word is written we are able to overcome this default response? The extra feature needed is supplied by the task demand layer. The task demand layer allows the task instructions (aka task goals) to have an influence along the ink color processing pathway. Such instructions or goals are thought to be a key function of our central executive system and located in the prefrontal cortex (Cohen & Servan-Schreiber, 1992; Zhao et al., 2014). This top-down influence ("name the ink color") can help to override the activity of the default response (respond to the word). In this simple model the Stroop effect is thought to be the result of response competition, that is, competition between the color units in the output layer. Typically competition is implemented by inhibitory connections between the units within each layer. Inclusion of the task demand layer highlights one mechanism of proactive control, that is, one way that the information processing pathways can be influenced in a top-down manner by deliberate strategic thinking.

More recently there has been interest in more automatic top-down control mechanisms. In particular the trial by trial adjustments in cognitive control that can take place during the performance of a task (Botvinick, Braver, Barch, Carter, & Cohen, 2001; Braver, 2012). In the Stroop task there has been an emphasis on understanding how an incongruent trial (e.g. the word RED printed in the ink color green) can lead to speeding up on a subsequent incongruent trial (also referred to as the Grattan effect, sequential congruency effect, or conflict adaptation effect) (Botvinick et al, 2001; Gratton, Coles, & Donchin, 1992). Here we will refer to this finding as the sequential congruency effect (SCE). A dominant explanation of the sequential congruency effect is the conflict monitoring hypothesis which suggests that there is a conflict monitoring (CM) unit that detects the level of competition in the output layer (see Fig. 7.1) and subsequently increases activation of the color naming task goal in the task demand layer (Botvinick et al., 2001). Increasing the activation of the color naming unit simulates increased attention to the task goal whilst at the same time shifting attention away from the word reading. This top-down control mechanism is thought to result in the response conflict on subsequent incongruent trials being reduced and thus speeding up performance.

Although early models emphasized response conflict as the main source of conflict, recent models suggest there is also competition between the color naming and word reading units in the task demand layer. This competition is referred to as task conflict (Goldfarb & Henik, 2007). The consequence of task conflict is that it leads to a general inhibition of responses in the output layer (see Fig. 7.1; Kalanthroff, Avnit, Henik, Davelaar, & Usher, 2015; Kalanthroff, Davelaar, Henik, Goldfarb, & Usher, 2018). The introduction of task conflict helps to explain several unexpected findings. (i) A reversed facilitation effect. Usually congruent stimuli (e.g. the word GREEN printed in the ink color green) are faster to respond to than control stimuli, however, under certain conditions (e.g. when top-down control is reduced) even a congruent word can take longer to respond to than a non-word (Goldfarb & Henik, 2007; Kalanthroff et al., 2015). This is thought to be because any word (even a congruent word) can activate task conflict in the task demand layer resulting in a general slowdown of responses. (ii) Initially it was thought that conflict monitoring indicated activity in the dorsal anterior cingulate cortex (dACC). However, MacLeod and MacDonald (2000) have highlighted that both congruent and incongruent trials activate the dACC. As both congruent and incongruent trials both include words one suggestion is that the dACC is activated by task conflict rather than response conflict. (iii) More recent work provides further support that task conflict can be triggered in a top-down manner by priming goals proactively. Sharma (2018) showed that words that had earlier been studied for an upcoming memory task took longer to respond to than words that were not studied. It is thought that studying words results in greater top-down activation of the word reading task demand unit which in turn increases task conflict leading to a general slowdown in performance.

In summary this model provides an established framework to understand how we can selectively attend to ink color and ignore the word even when the word is the default response. Such a mechanism can be generalized to other behaviors that are triggered by emotional inputs. There is considerable evidence that emotionally negative stimuli produce longer color naming responses than neutral stimuli (i.e. the emotional Stroop effect). Initially models assumed that negative or threat related stimuli had their influence on response competition. For example, Matthews and Harley (1996) explored different ways in which threatening stimuli could be implemented in a neural network model. Their main suggestion was to include additional threat units in the input word layer and the output layer as well as adding stronger connections between these input-output threat units relative to other non-threat word units. Activating threat output units would result in greater competition between the threat unit and the other color units in the output layer which could explain the attentional bias to threat stimuli. Adding alcohol inputs that have stronger connections to alcohol units in the output layer would also be consistent with the general finding of an attentional bias to alcohol. It would also be consistent with the general conclusion that threat and alcohol related stimuli automatically capture attention particularly in groups who are emotionally vulnerable.

Research using negative emotional stimuli indicates not only the fast automatic capture of attention but also slow effects indicative of perseveration onto subsequent stimuli (McKenna & Sharma, 2004; Phaf & Kan, 2007). This slow effect has also been reported for addiction related stimuli (Cane, Sharma, & Albery, 2009; Clarke et al., 2015). Wyble, Sharma, and Bowman (2008) have suggested that the slow effect could be modeled if it is assumed that negative stimuli reduce top-down cognitive control. This was implemented in their model by adding reciprocal inhibitory connections between the conflict monitoring unit and threat input units (see Fig. 7.1). Thus in the presence of a threat word proactive control is inhibited allowing subsequent words to more strongly influence color naming performance. Further support that negative stimuli reduce top-down cognitive control comes from the work of Padmala, Bauer, and Pessoa (2011) who show that the sequential congruency effect (an index of top-down cognitive control) is reduced for negative stimuli. This approach is synonymous with other approaches that highlight that negative stimuli draw on cognitive resources to either facilitate performance, when task relevant, or interfere with performance, when task irrelevant (see Pessoa, 2017). A straightforward extension of the Wyble et al. (2008) model would allow alcohol related stimuli (in a similar way to negative stimuli) to inhibit the conflict monitoring unit. A recent finding suggests this line of inquiry is promising. Sharma (2017) has shown that the sequential congruency effect is also reduced by alcohol related stimuli in a group of heavy drinkers.

A lot of further work is required to fully explore the consequences of alcohol related stimuli in reducing top-down control. For example, an important question is related to the representation of goals in the task demand layer. It would be interesting to investigate how positive and negative alcohol expectancies could affect both response conflict and task conflict. Equally important would be to model the effects of individual differences, the effect of alcohol priming as well as any differences for different substances of abuse. Neural network models could provide the vehicle to explicitly implement the underlying mechanisms, which is important for testing complex models that involve many interactive elements.

References

Ahmadi, A., Pearlson, G. D., Meda, S. A., Dager, A., Potenza, M. N., Rosen, R., ... Stevens, M. C. (2013). Influence of alcohol use on neural response to go/no-go task in college drinkers. *Neuropsychopharmacology*, *38*(11), 2197–2208. Available from: https://doi.org/10.1038/npp.2013.119.

Bargh, J. A., & Chartrand, T. L. (1999). The unbearable automaticity of being. *American Psychologist*, *54*, 462–479.

Barrett, L. F., Tugade, M. M., & Engle, R. W. (2004). Individual differences in working memory capacity and dual-process theories of the mind. *Psychological Bulletin*, *130*(4), 553–573.

Borsari, B., Murphy, J. G., & Barnett, N. P. (2007). Predictors of alcohol use during the first year of college: Implications for prevention. *Addictive Behaviors*, *32*(10), 2062–2086. Available from: https://doi.org/10.1016/j.addbeh.2007.01.017.

Botvinick, M. M., Braver, T. S., Barch, D. M., Carter, C. S., & Cohen, J. D. (2001). Conflict monitoring and cognitive control. *Psychological Review*, *108*, 624–652. Available from: https://doi.org/10.1037/0033-295X.108.3.624.

Bradley, B. P., Mogg, K., Wright, T., & Field, M. (2003). Attentional bias in drug dependence: Vigilance for cigarette-related cues in smokers. *Psychology of Addictive Behaviors*, *17*(1), 66–72. Available from: https://doi.org/10.1037/0893-164X.17.1.66.

Braver, T. S. (2012). The variable nature of cognitive control: A dual mechanisms framework. *Trends in Cognitive Sciences*, *16*, 106–113. Available from: https://doi.org/10.1016/j.tics.2011.12.010.

Cane, J. E., Sharma, D., & Albery, I. P. (2009). The addiction Stroop task: Examining the fast and slow effects of smoking and marijuana-related cues. *Journal of Psychopharmacology*, *23*, 510–519. Available from: https://doi.org/10.1177/0269881108091253.

Clapper, R. L., Martin, C. S., & Clifford, P. R. (1994). Personality, social environment, and past behavior as predictors of late adolescent alcohol use. *Journal of Substance Abuse*, *6*(3), 305–313. Available from: https://doi.org/10.1016/S0899-3289(94)90491-X.

Clarke, S. P., Sharma, D., & Salter, D. (2015). Examining fast and slow effects for alcohol and negative emotion in problem and social drinkers. *Addiction Research & Theory*, *23*(1), 24–33. Available from: https://doi.org/10.3109/16066359.2014.922961.

Cohen, J. D., Dunbar, K., & McClelland, J. L. (1990). On the control of automatic processes: A parallel distributed processing account of the Stroop effect. *Psychological Review*, *97*, 332–361. Available from: https://doi.org/10.1037/0033-295X.97.3.332.

Cohen, J. D., & Servan-Schreiber, D. (1992). Context, cortex and dopamine: A connectionist approach to behavior and biology in schizophrenia. *Psychological Review*, *99*, 45–77. Available from: https://doi.org/10.1037/0033-295X.99.1.45.

Cohen J. D., and Huston T. A., 1994, Progress in the use of interactive models for understandingattention and performance. In: Umilta' C. and Botvinick M. M., (Eds.), *Attention and performance XV*. Cambridge, MA: MIT Press, 453–476.

Cooper, M. L., Frone, M. R., Russell, M., & Mudar, P. (1995). Drinking to regulate positive and negative emotions: A motivational model of alcohol use. Journal of Personality and Social Psychology, 69(5), 990–1005. Available from: https://doi.org/10.1037/0022-3514.69.5.990.

Cox, W. M., Fadardi, J. S., & Pothos, E. M. (2006). The Addiction-Stroop test: Theoretical considerations and procedural recommendations. *Psychological Bulletin, 132*(3), 443–476. Available from: https://doi.org/10.1037/0033-2909.132.3.443.

Cox, W. M., Hogan, L. M., Kristian, M. R., & Race, J. H. (2002). Alcohol attentional bias as a predictor of alcohol abusers' treatment outcome. *Drug and Alcohol Dependence, 68*(3), 237–243. Available from: https://doi.org/10.1016/S0376-8716(02)00219-3.

Dawson, D., & Reid, K. (1997). Fatigue, alcohol and performance impairment. *Nature, 388*, 235. Available from: https://doi.org/10.1038/40775.

de Wit, H. (2009). Impulsivity as a determinant and consequence of drug use: A review of underlying processes. *Addiction Biology, 14*(1), 22–31. Available from: https://doi.org/10.1111/j.1369-1600.2008.00129.x.

Duka, T., & Townshend, J. M. (2004). The priming effect of alcohol pre-load on attentional bias to alcohol-related stimuli. *Psychopharmacology, 176*, 353–362. Available from: https://doi.org/10.1007/s00213-004-1906-7.

Eagle, D. M., Bari, A., & Robbins, T. W. (2008). The neuropsychopharmacology of action inhibition: Cross-species translation of the stop-signal and go/no-go tasks. *Psychopharmacology, 199*(3), 439–456. Available from: https://doi.org/10.1007/s00213-008-1127-6.

Easdon, C., Izenberg, A., Armilio, M. L., Yu, H., & Alain, C. (2005). Alcohol consumption impairs stimulus- and error-related processing during a go/no-go task. *Cognitive Brain Research, 25*(3), 873–883. Available from: https://doi.org/10.1016/j.cogbrainres.2005.09.009.

Farber, P. D., Khavari, K. A., & Douglass, F. M. (1980). A factor analytic study of reasons for drinking: Empirical validation of positive and negative reinforcement dimensions. *Journal of Consulting and Clinical Psychology, 48*(6), 780–781. Available from: https://doi.org/10.1037/0022-006X.48.6.780.

Field, M. (2006) Attentional biases in drug abuse and addiction: cognitive mechanisms, causes, consequences, and implications. In Munafo M., & Albery I.P. (Eds.), *Cognition and Addiction*. Oxford, UK: Oxford University Press, pp. 73–99.

Field, M., Duka, T., Eastwood, B., Child, R., Santarcangelo, M., & Gayton, M. (2007). Experimental manipulation of attentional biases in heavy drinkers: do the effects generalise? *Psychopharmacology, 192*(4), 593–608. Available from: https://doi.org/10.1007/s00213-007-0760-9.

Field, M., Mogg, K., & Bradley, B. P. (2005). Craving and cognitive biases for alcohol cues in social drinkers. *Alcohol and Alcoholism, 40*(6), 504–510. Available from: https://doi.org/10.1093/alcalc/agh213.

Field, M., Mogg, K., Zetteler, J., & Bradley, B. P. (2004). Attentional biases for alcohol cues in heavy and light social drinkers: The roles of initial orienting and maintained attention. *Psychopharmacology, 176*, 88–93. Available from: https://doi.org/10.1007/s00213-004-1855-1.

Fillmore, M. T. (2003). Drug abuse as a problem of impaired control: Current approaches and findings. *Behavioral and Cognitive Neuroscience Reviews, 2*(3), 179–197. Available from: https://doi.org/10.1177/1534582303257007.

Frewen, P. A., Dozois, D. J. A., Joanisse, M. F., & Neufeld, R. W. J. (2008). Selective attention to threat versus reward: Meta-analysis and neural-network modeling of the dot-probe task. *Clinical Psychology Review, 28*, 307–337. Available from: https://doi.org/10.1016/j.cpr.2007.05.006.

Friedman, R. S., McCarthy, D. M., Förster, J., & Denzler, M. (2005). Automatic effects of alcohol cues on sexual attraction. *Addiction, 100*(5), 672–681. Available from: https://doi.org/10.1111/j.1360-0443.2005.01056.x.

Goldfarb, L., & Henik, A. (2007). Evidence for task conflict in the Stroop effect. *Journal of Experimental Psychology: Human Perception and Performance, 33*, 1170–1176. Available from: https://doi.org/10.1037/0096-1523.33.5.1170.

Goldstein, R. Z., & Volkow, N. D. (2002). Drug addiction and its underlying neurobiological basis: Neuroimaging evidence for the involvement of the frontal cortex. *The American Journal of Psychiatry, 159*(10), 1642–1652.

Gratton, G., Coles, M. G. H., & Donchin, E. (1992). Optimizing the use of information: Strategic control of activation of responses. *Journal of Experimental Psychology: General, 121*, 480–506. Available from: https://doi.org/10.1037/0096-3445.121.4.480.

Hallgren, M. S., & McCrady, B. S. (2013). Interference in the alcohol Stroop task with college student binge drinkers. *Journal of Behavioral Health, 2*(2), 112–119. Available from: https://doi.org/10.5455/jbh.20130224082728.

Hobson, J., Bruce, G., & Butler, S. H. (2013). A flicker change blindness task employing eye tracking reveals an association with levels of craving not consumption. *Journal of Psychopharmacology, 27*(1), 93–97. Available from: https://doi.org/10.1177/0269881112447990.

Kalanthroff, E., Avnit, A., Henik, A., Davelaar, E. J., & Usher, M. (2015). Stroop proactive control and task conflict are modulated by concurrent working memory load. *Psychonomic Bulletin & Review, 22*, 869–875. Available from: https://doi.org/10.3758/s13423-014-0735-x.

Kalanthroff, E., Davelaar, E. J., Henik, A., Goldfarb, L., & Usher, M. (2018). Task conflict and proactive control: A computational theory of the Stroop task. *Psychological Review, 125*(1), 59–82. Available from: https://doi.org/10.1037/rev0000083.

Lusher, J., Chandler, C., & Ball, D. (2004). Alcohol dependence and the alcohol Stroop paradigm: Evidence and issues. *Drug and Alcohol Dependence, 75*(3), 225–231. Available from: https://doi.org/10.1016/j.drugalcdep.2004.03.004.

MacLeod, C. M. (1991). Half a century of research on the Stroop effect: An integrative review. *Psychological Bulletin, 109*, 163–203. Available from: https://doi.org/10.1037/0033-2909.109.2.163.

MacLeod, C. M., & MacDonald, P. A. (2000). Interdimensional interference in the Stroop effect: Uncovering the cognitive and neural anatomy of attention. *Trends in Cognitive Sciences, 10*, 383–391. Available from: https://doi.org/10.1016/S1364-6613(00)01530-8.

Matthews, G., & Harley, T. A. (1996). Connectionist models of emotional distress and attentional bias. *Cognition and Emotion, 10*(6), 561–600. Available from: https://doi.org/10.1080/026999396380060.

McKenna, F. P., & Sharma, D. (2004). Reversing the emotional Stroop effect reveals that it is not what it seems: The role of fast and slow components. *Journal of Experimental Psychology, 30*, 382–392. Available from: https://doi.org/10.1037/0278-7393.30.2.382.

Melotti, R., Heron, J., Hickman, M., Macleod, J., Araya, R., & Lewis, G. (2011). Adolescent alcohol and tobacco use and early socioeconomic position: The ALSPAC birth cohort. *Pediatrics, 127*(4), e948–e955. Available from: https://doi.org/10.1542/peds.2009-3450.

Miller, M. A., & Fillmore, M. T. (2010). The effect of image complexity on attentional bias toward alcohol-related images in adult drinkers. *Addiction (Abingdon, England), 105*(5), 883–890. Available from: https://doi.org/10.1111/j.1360-0443.2009.02860.x.

Moss, A. C., & Albery, I. P. (2009). A dual process model of the alcohol-behaviour link for social drinking. Psychological Bulletin., *135*(4), 516–530.

Padmala, S., Bauer, A., & Pessoa, L. (2011). Negative emotion impairs conflict-driven executive control. *Frontiers in Psychology*, *2*, 192. Available from: https://doi.org/10.3389/fpsyg.2011.00192.

Palfai, T. P. (2006). Automatic processes in the self-regulation of addictive behaviours. In Wiers R. W. & Stacy A. W. (Eds.), *Handbook of implicit cognition and addiction*. Thousand Oaks, California: Sage, pp. 413–414, n26. Available from: http://doi.org/10.4135/9781412976237.

Pessoa, L. (2017). Cognitive-motivational interactions: Beyond boxes-and-arrows models of the mind-brain. *Motivation Science*, *3*(3), 287–303. Available from: https://doi.org/10.1037/mot0000074.

Phaf, R. H., & Kan, K. (2007). The automaticity of emotional Stroop: A meta-analysis. *Journal of Behavior Therapy and Experimental Psychiatry*, *38*, 184–199.

Roy-Charland, A., Plamondon, A., Homeniuk, A. S., Flesch, C. A., Klein, R. M., & Stewart, S. H. (2017). Attentional bias toward alcohol-related stimuli in heavy drinkers: Evidence from dynamic eye movement recording. *The American Journal of Drug and Alcohol Abuse*, *43*(3), 332–340. Available from: https://doi.org/10.1080/00952990.2016.1209511.

Sharma, D. (2017). The variable nature of cognitive control in a university sample of young adult drinkers. *Journal of Applied Social Psychology*, *47*, 118–123. Available from: https://doi.org/10.1111/jasp.12416.

Sharma, D. (2018). Priming can affect naming colours using the study test procedure. Revealing the role of task conflict. *Acta Psychologica*, *189*, 19–25. Available from: https://doi.org/10.1016/j.actpsy.2016.11.004.

Sharma, D., Albery, I. P., & Cook, C. (2001). Selective attentional bias to alcohol related stimuli in problem drinkers and non-problem drinkers. *Addiction*, *96*(2), 285–295. Available from: https://doi.org/10.1046/j.1360-0443.2001.96228512.x.

Sharma, D., & Money, S. (2010). Carryover effects to addiction-associated stimuli in a group of marijuana and cocaine users. *Journal of Psychopharmacology*, *24*, 1309–1316. Available from: https://doi.org/10.1177/0269881109350079.

Simons, J. S. (2003). Differential prediction of alcohol use and problems: The role of biopsychological and social-environmental variables. *The American Journal of Drug and Alcohol Abuse*, *29*(4), 861–879. Available from: https://doi.org/10.1081/ADA-120026265.

Steele, C. M., & Josephs, R. A. (1990). Alcohol myopia. Its prized and dangerous effects. *The American Psychologist*, *45*(8), 921–933. Available from: https://doi.org/10.1037//0003-066x.45.8.921.

Strack, F., & Deutsch, R. (2004). Reflective and impulsive determinants of social behavior. *Personality and Social Psychology Review*, *8*, 220–247.

Stroop, J. R. (1935). Studies of interference in serial verbal reactions. *Journal of Experimental Psychology*, *18*(6), 643–662. Available from: https://doi.org/10.1037/h0054651.

Tiffany, S. T. (1990). A cognitive model of drug urges and drug-use behavior: Role of automatic and nonautomatic processes. *Psychological Review*, *97*(2), 147–168.

Tiffany, S. T., & Conklin, C. A. (2000). A cognitive processing model of alcohol craving and compulsive alcohol use. *Addiction*, *95*(8s2), 145–153. Available from: https://doi.org/10.1046/j.1360-0443.95.8s2.3.x.

Waters, A. J., Sayette, M. A., Franken, I. H. A., & Schwartz, J. E. (2005). Generalizability of carry-over effects in the emotional Stroop task. *Behavior Research & Therapy*, *43*, 715–732.

Waters, A. J., Sayette, M. A., & Wertz, J. M. (2003). Carry-over effects can modulate emotional Stroop effects. *Cognition & Emotion*, *17*, 501–509.

Waters, H., & Green, M. (2003). A demonstration of attentional bias, using a novel dual task paradigm, towards clinically salient material in recovering alcohol abuse patients? *Psychological Medicine*, *33*, 491–498. Available from: https://doi.org/10.1017/S0033291702007237.

Wiers, R. W., Bartholow, B. D., van den Wildenberg, E., Thush, C., Engels, R. C. M. E., Sher, K. J., ... Stacy, A. W. (2007). Automatic and controlled processes and the development of addictive behaviors in adolescents: A review and a model. *Pharmacology Biochemistry and Behavior*, *86*(2), 263–283. Available from: https://doi.org/10.1016/j.pbb.2006.09.021.

Williams, J. M. G., Mathews, A., & MacLeod, C. (1996). The emotional Stroop task and psychopathology. *Psychological Bulletin*, *120*(1), 3–24. Available from: https://doi.org/10.1037/0033-2909.120.1.3.

Wyble, B., Sharma, D., & Bowman, H. (2008). Strategic regulation of cognitive control by emotional salience: A neural network model. *Cognition and Emotion*, *22*(6), 1019–1051. Available from: https://doi.org/10.1080/02699930701597627.

Zhao, Y., Tang, D., Hu, L., Zhang, L., Hitchman, G., Wang, L., & Chen, A. (2014). Concurrent working memory task decreases the Stroop interference effect as indexed by the decreased theta oscillations. *Neuroscience*, *262*, 92–106. Available from: https://doi.org/10.1016/j.neuroscience.2013.12.052.

Chapter 8

Social cognition in severe alcohol use disorder

Fabien D'Hondt[1,2,3], Benjamin Rolland[4,5] and Pierre Maurage[6]
[1]Univ. Lille, Inserm, CHU Lille, U1172 - LilNCog - Lille Neuroscience & Cognition, F-59000, Lille, France, [2]CHU Lille, Clinique de Psychiatrie, CURE, Lille, France, [3]Centre National de Ressources et de Résilience (CN2R), Lille, France, [4]Université de Lyon, UCBL, INSERM U1028, CNRS UMR5292, Centre de Recherche en Neuroscience de Lyon (CRNL), Bron, France, [5]Service Universitaire d'Addictologie de Lyon (SUAL), CH Le Vinatier, Bron, France, [6]UCLouvain, Louvain Experimental Psychopathology Research Group (LEP), Louvain-la-Neuve, Belgium

Introduction

Severe Alcohol Use Disorder (SAUD; DSM-5; American Psychiatric Association, 2013) is a highly prevalent chronic disorder, lifetime prevalence being around 3% worldwide (World Health Organisation, 2018). It is centrally characterized by a compulsion to seek and consume alcohol, together with impaired control over consumption, despite the associated negative consequences (Koob & Volkow, 2016). Alcohol is considered as the most harmful drug when considering the joint deleterious consequences for the consumer and relational, familial as well as societal environments (Nutt, King, & Phillips, 2010). During the last decades, neuroimaging studies have evidenced structural and functional cerebral impairments in patients with SAUD (Bühler & Mann, 2011; Rolland, Dricot, Creupelandt, Maurage, & De Timary, 2019; Volkow, Fowler, & Wang, 2003). These findings strongly contributed to the emergence of the most influential approach of SAUD in (neuro)psychology, namely the dual-process models. The main proposal of these models is that efficient decision-making in everyday life situations is determined by the equilibrium between a "reflective system" (mostly relying on frontal regions and responsible for the deliberative and controlled responses) and a "reflexive/impulsive system" (mostly relying on striatal/limbic regions and initiating the automatic/appetitive behaviors): when confronted with appetitive stimulations (e.g., rewarding substance, food, or sexual cues), the automatic activation of the impulsive system (which is

The Handbook of Alcohol Use - Understandings from Synapse to Society.
DOI: https://doi.org/10.1016/B978-0-12-816720-5.00004-9

adaptive and needed, as it is the key factor for initiating actions) will be modulated by the reflective system (allowing to consciously decide whether the stimulation should be approached or avoided, according to the context). In this view, the emergence and persistence of alcohol-related disorders are thought to be generated by an imbalance between those systems, the under-activation of the reflective system resulting in reduced executive control and memory abilities, while the over-activation of the impulsive system induces an increased automatic reactivity toward alcohol cues (Stacy & Wiers, 2010): individuals presenting SAUD will thus present, when confronted with alcohol-related stimuli, a double impairment increasing consumption risk, as they will simultaneously show a stronger attraction towards these stimuli (indexed for example by exacerbated craving) and a lower ability to regulate such attraction (due to reduced frontal control). Indeed, evidence shows that recently detoxified patients with SAUD present, when compared to controls, increased responses of the striatum and limbic regions to alcohol-related cues (Braus et al., 2001; Grüsser et al., 2004; Heinz et al., 2007; Wrase et al., 2007), this effect being correlated with alcohol craving (Wrase et al., 2007) and increased relapse risk (Braus et al., 2001; Grüsser et al., 2004). There is also strong evidence for alterations of frontal and prefrontal regions in patients with SAUD (Moselhy, Georgiou, & Kahn, 2001) that can be linked to their frequently described cognitive deficits (Stavro, Pelletier, & Potvin, 2013), including executive functions (Brion, D'Hondt, Pitel, et al., 2017) and particularly inhibition (Noël et al., 2001).

Despite significant theoretical and experimental advances in our understanding of the disease, relapse rate among detoxified SAUD patients remains very high—at least 50% in the months following treatment (Krampe, Stawicki, Hoehe, & Ehrenreich, 2007; Mckay, Franklin, Patapis, & Lynch, 2006; Moos & Moos, 2006). This suggests that current therapeutic settings, including medication and psychotherapy, have quite low efficiency. Several new research avenues have been recently proposed in the treatment of addiction, including innovative drugs (e.g., De Ternay et al., 2019), neurostimulation (e.g., Diana et al., 2017), behavioral approaches (e.g., Volkow & Morales, 2015) or emotion-focused therapy (e.g., Herman & Duka, 2018). Among them, there is a growing interest in cognitive remediation (Holmes, Craske, & Graybiel, 2014; Keshavan, Vinogradov, Rumsey, Sherrill, & Wagner, 2014) and efforts are made to identify neurocognitive mechanisms that should be targeted by these interventions (Franken & van de Wetering, 2015). In keeping with this goal, we recently proposed that the priority of cognitive training should be given to impairments observed early after substance withdrawal and for which a clear link with early dropout or relapse has been made (Rolland, D'Hondt, et al., 2019). Actually, using a systematic literature search, we found that the impairments related to early relapse concerned long-term memory, impulsivity/inhibition, and higher-order executive functions (e.g., decision making) in SAUD. This result fits well with the dual-process framework, which suggests that neuropsychological training programs should primarily aim at diminishing the activation of the impulsive system and/or increasing the activation of the reflective system. However, we further proposed that this approach should be individually tailored, given the possible heterogeneity of patients' profiles regarding those deficits. Indeed, it appears that not all patients show cognitive dysfunctions at the early stage of the detoxification process (Alarcon, Nalpas, Pelletier, & Perney, 2015). In addition, recent evidence even suggests that these deficits could also be due to frequent psychiatric comorbidities such as depression or anxiety rather than SAUD *per se* (D'Hondt et al., 2018). Moreover, beyond the disequilibrium between the impulsive system and the reflective system as proposed by dual-process models, the previously mentioned review also underlined the need to consider other categories of impairments, and centrally the emotional and interpersonal abilities of patients with SAUD.

Up to now, dual-process models applied to the field of substance use disorders have neglected emotional and interpersonal difficulties in their conceptualization of the disease (but see Noël, Brevers, & Bechara, 2013). Actually, research on this topic is more recent and fragmented than the literature on cognitive impairments in SAUD (Bora & Zorlu, 2017; Castellano et al., 2015; Le Berre, Fama, & Sullivan, 2017; Onuoha, Quintana, Lyvers, & Guastella, 2016; Sanvicente-Vieira et al., 2017). Yet, negative emotions and interpersonal conflicts are reported, at the clinical or self-reported levels, as the main reasons for relapse among patients with excessive alcohol consumption (Marlatt, 1996; Shafiei, Fatemeh Hoseini, Bibak, & Azmal, 2014; Zywiak, Westerberg, Connors, & Maisto, 2003). Social support also appears essential for patients to maintain abstinence at mid- and long-term (Gordon & Zrull, 1991; Hunter-Reel, McCrady, & Hildebrandt, 2009), suggesting that attention should be paid to the ability of patients to establish and maintain satisfactory emotional life and interpersonal relationships. Accordingly, the aim of the present chapter is to propose an overview of current research on social cognition, i.e. the psychological processes that contribute to the capacity to deal with information from others and ourselves (Green, Horan, & Lee, 2015). To this end, the findings of studies comparing detoxified patients with SAUD and healthy controls are presented according to four topics: (i) *emotional experience*, i.e. the physiological and subjective reactivity to affectively-laden stimuli, and *emotion regulation*, i.e. the ability to control emotional experience; (ii) *perception of social cues*, i.e. the decoding of emotional facial, body and/or voice expression; (iii) *theory of mind*, i.e. the use of social signals to infer mental states of others and predict their behaviors; (iv) complex social cognition abilities, i.e. skills that integrate several social cognition components such as *empathy* and *social emotions processing*. Finally, this chapter ends by specifying several research avenues that may be considered in the coming years, particularly the social cognition abilities of patients with SAUD that are either not sufficiently understood or remain absolutely unexplored.

Emotional experience and emotion regulation

Emotional experience corresponds to the collection of responses that are elicited by affectively-laden stimuli. These emotional responses are thought to find their origin in the activation of a set of brain structures that constitutes the "affective brain system", including the amygdala, the ventral striatum, the insula, the anterior cingulate cortex (ACC), the medial and lateral parts of the orbitofrontal cortex (OFC), the hypothalamus and regions of the midbrain and brainstem that are involved in autonomic control (Barrett & Bar, 2009; Lindquist, Satpute, Wager, Weber, & Barrett, 2016; Lindquist, Wager, Kober, Bliss-Moreau, & Barrett, 2012; Rudrauf et al., 2008; 2009). These brain regions contribute to analyzing the affective significance of external and internal stimuli and are then involved in the allocation of attentional resources towards these stimuli as well as in the initiation of visceral and musculoskeletal responses (Rudrauf et al., 2009). Feelings are considered as subjective mental experiences of these emotional responses (Damasio & Carvalho, 2013).

Clinical observations of patients with SAUD frequently report difficulties in identifying, discriminating, and communicating one's own feelings (Evren et al., 2008; Taieb et al., 2002; Thorberg, Young, Sullivan, & Lyvers, 2009; Uzun, 2003), a phenomenon that has been defined as alexithymia (Parker, Keefer, Taylor, & Bagby, 2008; Sifneos, 1973). Independently of SAUD, studies on alexithymia investigating autonomic reactivity and subjective responses to emotionally-laden stimuli typically report a decoupling between these two measures in individuals with high alexithymia (Connelly & Denney, 2007; Friedlander, Lumley, Farchione, & Doyal, 1997; Martin & Pihl, 1986; Nandrino et al., 2012; Rabavilas, 1987; Stone & Nielson, 2001). Interestingly, a subjective/physiological dissociation has also recently been observed in patients with SAUD, these individuals showing an altered generation of autonomic signals associated with affectively-laden stimuli, as revealed by reduced heart rate and skin conductance reactivity to both positive and negative emotional stimuli, while they did not differ from healthy controls regarding subjective reports (Carmona-Perera, Sumarroca-Hernández, Santolaria-Rossell, Pérez-García, & Reyes del Paso, 2018). The exact mechanism sustaining this weak correspondence between subjective and physiological responses remains to be understood.

Nevertheless, several neuroimaging studies report disturbances in brain activation during emotion processing among patients with SAUD. A seminal study by Wrase et al. (2007) revealed that anticipation of nonalcohol-related reward in SAUD was associated with reduced striatal activity, suggesting a decreased activity of the reward system towards naturally appetitive stimulations. Heinz et al. (2007) found that the experience of positive and negative stimuli was rather linked to increased activity in affective brain regions: patients with SAUD showed, compared to healthy controls, stronger brain responses in the ACC, medial OFC, ventral striatum, and thalamus in response to positive (compared to neutral) stimuli, and in the medial OFC in response to negative (compared to neutral) stimuli. Interestingly, Heinz et al. (2007) also observed that the increased activity in the ventral striatum and thalamus for positive vs neutral stimuli was associated with a lower relapse risk at 6 months. In an fMRI study, Gilman and Hommer (2008) further revealed that only patients with SAUD displayed higher brain activation in response to negative compared to positive images presented concomitantly with neutral or soft beverages, notably in some affective brain regions (insular cortex and inferior frontal gyrus) and in some areas involved in visual recognition. Patients also displayed stronger responses to negative images than healthy controls within the ventral visual stream. This increased brain activity was reduced when pictures were presented together with alcohol-related stimuli, suggesting that these cues are likely to modify the emotional experience. Actually, this study suggests that the stronger experience of negative emotions is blunted by alcohol-related stimuli, providing a cerebral counterpart to a phenomenon frequently described among patients with SAUD, namely the coping strategy consisting of using alcohol to reduce the unpleasant effects of negative emotions, which are critical in relapse (Marlatt, 1996; Shafiei et al., 2014; Zywiak et al., 2003).

Emotion regulation abilities have received little interest in the field of SAUD. These abilities refer to the psychological processes by which individuals influence emotional experience and expression (Gross, 1998). Several types of emotion regulation strategies have been described, having distinct impacts on wellbeing and social functioning. Among the five types described by Gross (1998), Petit et al. (2015) found, using the Emotion Regulation Interview (ERI, Werner, Goldin, Ball, Heimberg, & Gross, 2011), that response modulation (i.e. the modulation of emotional experience once responses have been generated) and attentional deployment (i.e. directing the focus of attention towards a given aspect of a situation) were more used by patients compared to controls, while the opposite pattern was found for cognitive change (i.e. reappraising the meaning of a situation). Interestingly, results suggested that prolonged abstinence increased the use of cognitive change and that craving was higher with greater use of response modulation, these two strategies being supposed to be respectively linked to higher and lower levels of well-being and social functioning (Gross, 1998; Gross & John, 2003; John & Gross, 2004). These findings, although preliminary, suggest that emotion regulation strategies should be assessed among patients with SAUD to determine those who use strategies that might promote abstinence and those who should benefit from a reorientation toward these strategies.

In sum, studies investigating *emotional experience* and *emotion regulation* in SAUD are relatively sparse. Regarding *emotional experience*, they appear to confirm the clinical observations suggesting that patients with SAUD display altered subjective, physiological, and cerebral responses to emotional stimuli by showing: (i) increased level of alexithymia (Evren et al., 2008; Taieb et al., 2002; Thorberg et al., 2009; Uzun, 2003) and dissociation between physiological and subjective responses to emotional stimuli (Carmona-Perera et al., 2018); (ii) reduced activation of the ventral striatum in the anticipation of non-alcoholic reward (Wrase et al., 2007); (iii) increased brain responses of the affective brain system and the visual areas to affectively-laden stimuli (Gilman & Hommer, 2008; Heinz et al., 2007). The increased brain responses could reflect a protective factor when they are observed in response to positive stimuli and can be reduced by the presence of alcohol-related cues when stimuli are negative (Gilman & Hommer, 2008). Together with results showing stronger processing of alcohol-related stimuli by the brain reward system, these findings may explain why patients show a reduced interest for any other activity that may contribute to their well-being by leading to the emergence of positive emotions. Finally, SAUD is associated with *emotion dysregulation*, and abstinence appears associated with a shift toward the use of more adaptative emotion regulation strategies.

Perception of social cues

Perception of social cues refers to the ability to decode emotional signals expressed by others through their faces, voices, or body postures. In particular, *emotional facial expression (EFE) processing* has a crucial role in social interactions (Frith, 2009) and is the ability that has received the more attention in the field of social cognition in SAUD (Bora & Zorlu, 2017; Castellano et al., 2015; D'Hondt, Campanella, Kornreich, Philippot, & Maurage, 2014; de Lima Osório & Donadon, 2014). The very first studies revealed that individuals with SAUD overestimate the intensity of EFE, have difficulties in identifying them (particularly the negative emotions), and are not conscious of their deficit (Oscar-Berman, Hancock, Mildworf, Hutner, & Weber, 1990; Philippot et al., 1999). Numerous researches were then conducted and confirmed those findings [see Bora & Zorlu (2017) and Castellano et al. (2015) for meta-analyses]. Among them, some have shown that difficulties in basic EFE decoding extend towards situations requiring subtler emotion decoding abilities such as when mild emotional intensity is expressed or when several EFE are mixed (D'Hondt, de Timary, Bruneau, & Maurage, 2015; Frigerio, Burt, Montagne, Murray, & Perrett, 2002), patients needing more emotional intensity to correctly identify facial expressions (D'Hondt et al., 2015). Furthermore, evidence suggests that deficits in EFE decoding, which are linked to the interpersonal problems frequently encountered by patients suffering from SAUD (Kornreich et al., 2002), may not be due to a more general impairment for face processing (Maurage, Campanella, Philippot, Martin, & de Timary, 2008) and are not associated with anxiety or depression levels (e.g., Freeman et al., 2018). In addition, these deficits worsen during the disease course (Freeman et al., 2018; Townshend & Duka, 2003), persist at least in the first months of abstinence

(Foisy et al., 2007, 2005; Kornreich et al., 2015) and appear to predict relapse/dropout (Rupp et al., 2017).

Several studies investigated the cerebral correlates of those deficits using neuroimaging or electrophysiology. The first fMRI study by Salloum et al. (2007) revealed that, while patients with SAUD did not differ from controls in their ability to discriminate between low- and high-intensity EFE, they showed globally reduced brain activations compared to healthy controls in response to these stimuli, particularly in the ACC during negative EFE processing. Moreover, Marinkovic et al. (2009) found that, contrary to healthy participants, patients did not show stronger activation in the amygdala and hippocampus when viewing happy or sad faces relative to neutral expressions. Finally, lower performance in recognizing fearful faces among patients with SAUD compared to controls was found to be associated with reduced activations of the OFC and the insula, this effect being even enhanced among patients with repeated previous detoxification stays (O'Daly et al., 2012). Electrophysiological studies using the event-related potential (ERP) technique, owing to its high temporal resolution, are particularly useful to track the sequence of cerebral activations related to the different stages of information processing. The ERP study by Maurage, Campanella, Philippot, Pham, and Joassin (2007) assessed the ability to detect rare pictures of EFE among frequently presented photographs of neutral faces, and showed globally delayed and/or reduced brain activations in patients compared to healthy controls, all along the information processing stream. Importantly, deficits began as early as the visual processing stage (as indexed by a delayed P100 component), a result that was further confirmed during an EFE discrimination task, independently of comorbid depression (Maurage, Campanella, Philippot, de Timary, et al., 2008). Evidence also suggests that deficits specific to negative EFE (anger) processing are found at later stages related to attention (N2b/P3a complex) and decision making (P3b; Maurage, Campanella, Philippot, Vermeulen, et al., 2008).

Deficits observed for EFE processing have been extended to the *processing of body postures* (Maurage et al., 2009) and *prosody* (patterns of language intonation, Maurage et al., 2009; Monnot, Nixon, Lovallo, & Ross, 2001; Uekermann, Daum, Schlebusch, & Trenckmann, 2005), therefore suggesting a generalized deficit in SAUD for the perception of social cues (Maurage et al., 2009). Furthermore, in everyday life, emotional signals coming from others are most frequently integrated to form a unified and coherent representation of their affective state (Campanella & Belin, 2007; Collignon et al., 2010; Müller, Cieslik, Turetsky, & Eickhoff, 2012). This *crossmodal integration* is beneficial to decode the emotion expressed: it is easier to identify an emotion expressed simultaneously by two modalities (face and voice) than the same emotion expressed by only one modality (face or voice). It has been found that patients with SAUD did not present this facilitation effect for crossmodal conditions (Brion, D'Hondt, Lannoy, et al., 2017;

Maurage et al., 2007). This impairment has been particularly evidenced for negative emotions and is linked to alterations at face (N170) and voice (N2) perceptive processing stages (Maurage, Philippot, et al., 2008). An fMRI study further revealed that in patients with SAUD compared to healthy controls, the activity of the cerebral network sustaining crossmodal integration, including inferior occipital, middle frontal, and superior parietal areas, was lower and also presented reduced functional connectivity with brain regions involved in unimodal processing (Maurage, Joassin, et al., 2013).

To sum up, the deficits of SAUD patients to process their own emotions extend to the identification of others' emotions. In particular, difficulties in *EFE processing* are now well-established (Bora & Zorlu, 2017; Castellano et al., 2015) and may rely on perturbations starting at the early visual stage of information processing (Maurage, Campanella, Philippot, de Timary, et al., 2008; Maurage, Philippot, et al., 2007), potentially due to alterations in the affective brain system (Marinkovic et al., 2009; O'Daly et al., 2012; Salloum et al., 2007). Even though their cerebral correlates remain unknown, deficits in the perception of social cues also concern *emotional prosody* and *body posture* (Maurage et al., 2009; Monnot et al. 2001; Uekermann et al. 2005). Finally, evidence also shows deficits in emotional crossmodal processing (Brion, D'Hondt, Lannoy, et al., 2017; Maurage, Campanella, et al., 2007; Maurage, Joassin, et al., 2013; Maurage, Philippot, et al., 2008). The strong impairment of patients with SAUD to decode social cues probably limits their ability to understand others' affective states. This may explain the difficulties of patients in interpersonal relationships, and in particular, the reduction of interpersonal bonds and their frequent social isolation (D'Hondt et al., 2014).

Theory of mind

Difficulties in social interactions may also rely on *Theory of Mind* (ToM) impairments, which have been well-documented in SAUD (Bora & Zorlu, 2017; Onuoha et al., 2016; Sanvicente-Vieira et al., 2017). Even though its definition is still debated (Schaafsma, Pfaff, Spunt, & Adolphs, 2015), ToM can be broadly defined as the ability to infer the mental states of others, regarding either their thoughts (cognitive subcomponent) or their emotions (affective subcomponent), to anticipate their behaviors and correctly react to them (Premack & Woodruff, 1978; Shamay-Tsoory et al., 2007). One of the first works on this topic was conducted by Uekermann, Channon, Winkel, Schlebusch, and Daum (2007) who used mentalistic questions related to the perspectives of protagonists and understanding of jokes during a task assessing humor processing and found reduced performances of patients with SAUD compared to controls. A large variety of paradigms were used by following studies to measure ToM abilities in SAUD and despite this heterogeneity, coherent results have been obtained (Sanvicente-Vieira et al., 2017), as suggested by two recent meta-analyses showing strong ToM deficits (Bora & Zorlu, 2017; Onuoha et al., 2016). In particular, Bosco, Capozzi, Colle, Marostica, and Tirassa (2014) found that patients were impaired both for first-order (i.e., understanding an individual's beliefs about an external event) and second-order ToM (i.e., understanding an individual's beliefs about others' beliefs). The authors observed that patients with SAUD had even more difficulties in understanding the mental states of others (third-person ToM) than their own (first-person ToM) and at the allocentric perspective rather than at the egocentric perspective (i.e. when the mental states of others were represented independently of self or not, respectively). However, while Maurage, de Timary, Tecco, Lechantre, and Samson (2015) confirmed through the use of false-belief tasks that deficits mostly concerned third-person ToM, they also observed that only just under the half of patients with SAUD in their study presented a significant ToM impairment, underlining the heterogeneity of patients' profiles.

Furthermore, several studies explored ToM through the use of the Reading the Mind in the Eyes test (RMET; Baron-Cohen, Wheelwright, Hill, Raste, & Plumb, 2001) in which participants are required to identify the affective mental state of others from pictures of human individuals' eyes. Even though contradictory findings exist (Kornreich et al., 2011; Mátyássy, Kelemen, Sáközi, Janka, & Kéri, 2006), several studies found lower performances for patients with SAUD compared to controls (Maurage, Grynberg, Noël, Joassin, Hanak, et al., 2011; Nandrino et al., 2014; Thoma, Winter, Juckel, & Roser, 2013). In particular, with the aim to investigate both the cognitive and affective ToM subcomponents within the same patients' sample, Nandrino et al. (2014) used the Versailles-Situational Intention Reading test (cognitive ToM; Bazin et al., 2009) and the RMET (affective ToM), and found that patients were only impaired for affective ToM. This result was recently confirmed in a study in which we used the Movie for Assessment of Social Cognition task (Dziobek et al., 2006) allowing us to distinguish the assessment of cognitive and affective ToM within the same paradigm (Maurage et al., 2016). This task is particularly interesting in that it is based on short movies depicting the social interactions of four characters during dinner, and thus allows examining ToM abilities in a situation that is close to everyday life social interactions. Results showed that patients with SAUD had a significantly lower global performance than healthy controls and thus confirmed previous findings revealing deficits for third-person ToM, but in a more ecological situation. Moreover, subscales analyses further showed that these reduced ToM abilities concern the capacity to infer others' affective mental states, the ability to infer other's cognitive mental states being preserved. In sum, there is clear evidence that ToM is impaired in SAUD and the most recent studies suggest that this deficit may specifically concern the ability of patients to infer others' mental states.

Complex social cognition

Empathy

Empathy can be defined as a complex capacity requiring to share and understand other individuals' cognitive or affective perspectives and to propose a verbal or behavioral answer adapted to the emotions, feelings, or thoughts they expressed (Decety & Jackson, 2004; Green et al., 2015). As such, empathy relies on both ToM and *experience sharing* abilities, which elicit the activation of brain regions involved in the behavior of the person we are looking at, and include *motor resonance* (i.e. the activation of the motor system emerging from the simple observation of another person performing an action) and *affect sharing* (i.e. the activation of the affective brain system emerging from the observation of another person expressing an emotional state) (Green et al., 2015). The work by Martinotti, Nicola, Di Tedeschi, Cundari, and Janiri (2009) used the Empathy Quotient (EQ), a self-reported questionnaire, and revealed that patients with SAUD had a significantly lower level of empathy than healthy controls. Recent evidence suggests that these empathy deficits could be due to decreased cortical thickness in cerebral regions that have been linked to empathy (notably frontal regions, insula, and precuneus) (Schmidt et al., 2017). The heterogeneity in the ways empathy is conceived probably limits our understanding of deficits in patients (e.g., Thoma, Friedmann, & Suchan, 2013; Thoma, Winter, et al., 2013). However, a separate assessment of affective and cognitive empathy, which was performed by Maurage, Grynberg, Noël, Joassin, Philippot, et al. (2011) by analyzing subscales' scores of the Interpersonal Reactivity Index (IRI) and the EQ questionnaires, revealed that patients were specifically impaired for affective empathy, and thus that they had difficulties to detect and feel others' emotional states but remained able to efficiently share and understand others' non-emotional mental states (e.g. intentions; thoughts). Interestingly, this impairment was not associated with anxiety or depression levels but was significantly correlated with alexithymia and difficulties in interpersonal relationships. More recently, Grynberg, Maurage, and Nandrino (2017) used the Condensed and Revised Multifaceted Empathy Test (Edele, Dziobek, & Keller, 2013) in which participants are told to select one label among four to describe the affective state associated with the presented picture (40 photographs of people, 20 in a positive affective state and 20 in a negative one) and to rate on a Likert-type scale how much they are likely to share the affective state of the person in the picture. While patients did not differ from controls regarding affective sharing, they were significantly impaired in affective labeling, suggesting that empathy impairments could be mostly related to difficulties in understanding affective states. Again, these results were not significantly correlated with anxiety or depression. As a whole, in line with the results related to studies investigating ToM, it appears that difficulties in empathy among patients with SAUD mostly concern its affective subcomponent, are not related to the frequent comorbidities and may impact the quality of social interactions.

Social emotions processing

Ostracism, considered as the negative emotional experience that derives from the fact to be ignored and excluded by others, can be considered as social pain. This is, therefore, a process that is triggered by interpersonal interactions, an emotional experience induced by inference regarding others' behaviors and mental states. Patients suffering from SAUD are more likely to feel ostracized than healthy individuals and even than people suffering from other psychiatric disorders, as SAUD appears to be a particularly stigmatized condition (Schomerus et al., 2011). The fMRI study by Maurage et al. (2012) used the Cyberball paradigm (Williams & Jarvis, 2006), an online ball-tossing game in which the participant is excluded, to investigate social exclusion processing in SAUD. Patients with SAUD did not present a significantly higher exclusion feeling score than healthy controls. However, in line with the results obtained by studies investigating emotional experience in SAUD, patients showed increased activation within some regions of the affective brain system (insula and ACC), suggesting an increased emotional reactivity to social rejection. The authors also reported reduced activations in the ventrolateral PFC during the social exclusion and interpreted this result as a difficulty to regulate the emotional responses related to social exclusion.

Social emotions, either negative or positive, can also result from *social norms* transgressions (Tangney, Stuewig, & Mashek, 2007; Treeby, Prado, Rice, & Crowe, 2016). *Shame* and *guilt* are two examples of negative social emotions that have recently been explored in SAUD (Grynberg, de Timary, Van Heuverswijn, & Maurage, 2017), capitalizing on data linking higher shame levels with relapse (Wiechelt & Sales, 2001), and guilt with psychological distress (Randles & Tracy, 2013). Grynberg, de Timary, et al. (2017) compared guilt and shame-proneness between patients with SAUD and healthy controls in specific situations and in general, using the Test of Self-Conscious Affect-3 (TOSCA-3) (Tangney, Dearing, Wagner, & Gramzow, 2000) and the Personal Feelings Questionnaire-2 (PFQ-2) (Harder & Zalma, 1990), respectively. They found that patients with SAUD presented increased contextualized guilt-proneness (e.g., when a colleague is penalized for an error you made at work) while no significant differences were found for uncontextualized situations nor for shame-proneness in both cases. This result, which was not influenced by anxiety or depression levels, suggested, therefore, that patients with SAUD are more likely to have a negative evaluation of their own behavior when it transgresses social norms.

Humor constitutes an example of a positive emotion triggered by the transgression of social norms. This complex phenomenon notably involves ToM abilities and the capacity to use *social knowledge* to detect the incongruent element that creates a humoristic situation. Uekermann et al. (2007) found that SAUD patients were less likely than healthy controls to select the funny punchlines ending of written jokes that involved interpersonal relationships, the performance in this humor detection task being associated with the executive (working memory) and ToM abilities. Interestingly, Schmidt et al. (2016) found that patients with SAUD have difficulties to correctly understand sarcasm, and Amenta, Noël, Verbanck, and Campanella (2013) showed that these individuals are less likely than healthy controls to detect irony in written scenarios, this latter result being significantly correlated with the social skills subscale of the EQ. Because sarcasm and irony understanding requires one to detect and interpret emotional signals from people involved in interpersonal relationships, these results suggest a reduced social knowledge regarding rules sustaining social interactions, that is linked with reduced ability to infer affective states and affective intentions of others. To sum up, it appears that SAUD patients present a strong sensitivity to ostracism and guilt, suggesting that they are more likely to experience negative emotions when they are directly involved in social situations. Conversely, they have difficulties to understand interactions between other individuals, in particular when they have to focus on emotional signals and consider the rules that cover interpersonal relationships.

Perspectives for future studies and conclusion

Research on social cognition in SAUD is a rising field, finding its relevance notably in the frequently assigned role of emotional and interpersonal difficulties in relapse (Marlatt, 1996; Shafiei et al., 2014; Zywiak et al., 2003). The following picture emerges from the main findings reported in the literature: as compared to healthy controls, recently detoxified patients with SAUD appear to be more sensitive when they are directly involved in interactions with their social environment, as revealed by results from neuroimaging studies investigating emotional experience and studies examining the processing of negative social emotions such as ostracism and guilt, while they appear to be less sensitive to social cues informing about mental states and interpersonal relationships of others, as notably suggested by experimental data on the perception of social cues, ToM, and humor processing. The specificity of these impairments in SAUD appears well-grounded, given the numerous studies suggesting that socio-emotional impairments are not associated with anxiety or depression (but see Kornreich et al., 2016). Therefore, it appears important to implement rehabilitation of social cognition in therapeutic programs, as it could positively impact relapse prevention. Much effort has been made to improve the social cognition abilities of patients suffering from schizophrenia and several programs dedicated to the rehabilitation of social cognition skills are now available. Promising results have been obtained, particularly for the perception of social cues and ToM (Grant, Lawrence, Preti, Wykes, & Cella, 2017), which should encourage scientists and clinicians to further explore this topic in the field of SAUD.

This picture remains too simplistic though, particularly because some social cognition components have received much more interest than others. For instance, numerous studies have examined EFE processing and ToM, while research on emotional experience and regulation or on the perception of other social cues remains sparse (Bora & Zorlu, 2017; Castellano et al., 2015; Le Berre et al., 2017; Onuoha et al., 2016; Sanvicente-Vieira et al., 2017). Even for social cognition components that have been frequently investigated, levels of analysis strongly differ, with substantial data both at the behavioral and cerebral levels regarding EFE processing while only behavioral data are available for ToM. The first obvious perspective is thus to deepen our understanding of the different social cognition components in SAUD. To this end, the use of a coherent theoretical background has to be promoted, considering the heterogeneity of definitions regarding many social cognition abilities such as empathy. In agreement with this idea, the present chapter was largely inspired by the typology of social cognition proposed by Green et al. (2015) who reviewed the literature in schizophrenia. In addition to the social cognition skills mentioned above, further investigations should thus be conducted on experience sharing components, namely motor resonance and affect sharing, that have only been examined by studies on empathy. Indeed, brain activation related to experience sharing may reflexively contribute to understanding the mental states of others (Decety & Grèzes, 2006; Green et al., 2015). Also in the field of schizophrenia, Savla, Vella, Armstrong, Penn, and Twamley (2013) put emphasis on other social cognition components, and notably social knowledge and attributional bias, that should also be investigated in SAUD. Actually, it appears that only one study in SAUD (Maurage, de Timary, et al., 2013) directly investigated social knowledge (i.e. the understanding of the conventions governing social interactions). Using a self-reported questionnaire, this study revealed that patients with SAUD tend to present excessively high standards regarding the behaviors they should have in social contexts, that correlated with their interpersonal difficulties. Conversely, nothing is known in SAUD regarding attributional bias, the tendency to consider that the events of one's life are either due to personal or external (i.e. from others or the situation) factors. Finally, other complex social cognition skills should be investigated such as social problem solving, which requires to perceive social cues that suggest interpersonal conflicts, to infer and understand the cognitive and affective mental states of others, and to generate and choose the strategy that is likely to solve the problem (Schmidt et al., 2016). Indeed, recent evidence suggests that patients with SAUD have difficulties generating and determining effective social solutions for interpersonal conflicts (Schmidt et al., 2016).

The question of whether social cognition deficits exist prior and contribute to the emergence and the maintenance of the disease, or are conversely a consequence of the neurotoxicity of alcohol is of great importance and should also constitute a research priority. Even though most studies have compared recently detoxified patients to healthy controls and no longitudinal study that could help to examine this possible causal link exists, this issue has been considered by investigating individuals at risk of developing the disease (Hill & O'Brien, 2015). For instance, evidence shows that high-risk individuals display, as compared to controls, reduced amygdala volume, a key structure of the affective brain system (Hill et al., 2001). Glahn, Lovallo, and Fox (2007) also found in an fMRI study that individuals with a family history of SAUD presented reduced amygdala activations in response to fearful faces compared to individuals without a family history of alcohol-related problems. High-risk individuals performing the RMET equally well at the behavioral level than controls nevertheless presented reduced responses in brain regions related to ToM (Hill et al., 2007). Together with the few data showing an association between social cognition deficits and relapse (Gilman & Hommer, 2008; Rupp et al., 2017), these results stress the need to further explore whether these impairments are involved in both the development and the maintenance of the disease (Kornreich et al., 2002).

Finally, the possibility that heterogeneity exists regarding social cognition deficits among patients with SAUD should also be investigated. Indeed, data on cognitive functioning clearly indicate that SAUD patients do not form a unitary group, as cognitive deficits would concern around 50% of them (Alarcon et al., 2015). This might also apply to emotional and interpersonal difficulties, as we recently showed a high variability of socio-emotional profiles in a study measuring alexithymia and interpersonal problems in 296 recently-detoxified SAUD patients and 246 healthy controls (Maurage, de Timary, & D'Hondt, 2017). While group comparisons showed that patients overall displayed increased alexithymia levels and more interpersonal problems, a cluster analysis allowed identifying five profiles of patients showing different patterns of socio-emotional difficulties. Importantly, only one group (representing around 25% of the total sample) reported no emotional or interpersonal problems, suggesting that the large majority of patients with SAUD are concerned by social cognition deficits.

This study could be seen as an illustration of what future studies should focus on, that is, the relationships between deficits in social cognition and the clinical and functional outcomes in the patients' daily life. Overall, the impact of alcohol-related cognitive impairments and the risk of post-detox relapse has been insufficiently explored so far, including with respect to social cognition (Rolland, D'Hondt et al., 2019). In addition, the relationship between the performance in social cognition among patients with SAUD on the one hand, and their degrees of autonomy, self-confidence, metacognition, or quality of life, on the other hand, is a real issue that warrants sustained investigation. Confirming such associations would greatly support the need for developing remediation training programs in social cognition for patients with SAUD, and these training programs would also make more sense for patients and addiction specialists, as the improvement in social cognition would translate into very practical benefits for patients with SAUD. It appears, therefore, important to further explore the existence of different profiles of patients as a function of social cognition components. These research perspectives should contribute to our understanding of the links between social cognition difficulties and SAUD, and may be particularly helpful to refine an individualized approach of neuropsychological training programs dedicated to relapse-related impairments.

References

Alarcon, R., Nalpas, B., Pelletier, S., & Perney, P. (2015). MoCA as a screening tool of neuropsychological deficits in alcohol-dependent patients. *Alcoholism: Clinical and Experimental Research*, *39*(6), 1042–1048. Available from https://doi.org/10.1111/acer.12734.

Amenta, S., Noël, X., Verbanck, P., & Campanella, S. (2013). Decoding of emotional components in complex communicative situations (irony) and its relation to empathic abilities in male chronic alcoholics: An issue for treatment. *Alcoholism: Clinical and Experimental Research*, *37*(2), 339–347. Available from https://doi.org/10.1111/j.1530-0277.2012.01909.x.

American Psychiatric Association. (2013). *Diagnostic and statistical manual of mental disorders* (5th ed.). American Psychiatric Association. Available from https://doi.org/10.1176/appi.books.9780890425596.

Baron-Cohen, S., Wheelwright, S., Hill, J., Raste, Y., & Plumb, I. (2001). The "Reading the mind in the eyes" test revised version: A study with normal adults, and adults with Asperger syndrome or high-functioning autism. *Journal of Child Psychology and Psychiatry, and Allied Disciplines*.

Barrett, L. F., & Bar, M. (2009). See it with feeling: Affective predictions during object perception. *Philosophical Transactions of the Royal Society B: Biological Sciences*, *364*(1521), 1325–1334. Available from https://doi.org/10.1093/acprof:oso/9780195395518.003.0042.

Bazin, N., Brunet-Gouet, E., Bourdet, C., Kayser, N., Falissard, B., Hardy-Baylé, M.-C., & Passerieux, C. (2009). Quantitative assessment of attribution of intentions to others in schizophrenia using an ecological video-based task: A comparison with manic and depressed patients. *Psychiatry Research*, *167*(1–2), 28–35. Available from https://doi.org/10.1016/J.PSYCHRES.2007.12.010.

Bora, E., & Zorlu, N. (2017). Social cognition in alcohol use disorder: A meta-analysis. *Addiction*, *112*(1), 40–48. Available from https://doi.org/10.1111/add.13486.

Bosco, F. M., Capozzi, F., Colle, L., Marostica, P., & Tirassa, M. (2014). Theory of mind deficit in subjects with alcohol use disorder: An analysis of mindreading processes. *Alcohol and Alcoholism*, *49*(3), 299–307. Available from https://doi.org/10.1093/alcalc/agt148.

Braus, D. F., Wrase, J., Grüsser, S., Hermann, D., Ruf, M., Flor, H., ... Heinz, A. (2001). Alcohol-associated stimuli activate the ventral striatum in abstinent alcoholics. *Journal of Neural Transmission*, 887–894.

Brion, M., D'Hondt, F., Lannoy, S., Pitel, A.-L., Davidoff, D. A., Maurage, P., ... Maurage, P. (2017). Crossmodal processing of emotions in alcohol-dependence and Korsakoff syndrome. *Cognitive Neuropsychiatry*, *22*(5), 436–451. Available from https://doi.org/10.1080/13546805.2017.1373639.

Brion, M., D'Hondt, F., Pitel, A.-L., Lecomte, B., Ferauge, M., de Timary, P., & Maurage, P. (2017). Executive functions in alcohol-dependence: A theoretically grounded and integrative exploration. *Drug and Alcohol Dependence, 177*, 39–47. Available from https://doi.org/10.1016/j.drugalcdep.2017.03.018.

Bühler, M., & Mann, K. (2011). Alcohol and the human brain: A systematic review of different neuroimaging methods. *Alcoholism: Clinical and Experimental Research, 35*(10), 1771–1793. Available from https://doi.org/10.1111/j.1530-0277.2011.01540.x.

Campanella, S., & Belin, P. (2007). Integrating face and voice in person perception. *Trends in Cognitive Sciences, 11*, 535–543. Available from https://doi.org/10.1016/j.tics.2007.10.001.

Carmona-Perera, M., Sumarroca-Hernández, X., Santolaria-Rossell, A., Pérez-García, M., & Reyes del Paso, G. A. (2018). Blunted autonomic responses to emotional stimuli in alcoholism: Relevance of impulsivity. *Adicciones, 31*, 221–232. Available from https://doi.org/10.20882/adicciones.1146.

Castellano, F., Bartoli, F., Crocamo, C., Gamba, G., Tremolada, M., Santambrogio, J., ... Carrà, G. (2015). Facial emotion recognition in alcohol and substance use disorders: A meta-analysis. *Neuroscience and Biobehavioral Reviews, 59*, 147–154. Available from https://doi.org/10.1016/j.neubiorev.2015.11.001.

Collignon, O., Girard, S., Gosselin, F., Saint-Amour, D., Lepore, F., & Lassonde, M. (2010). Women process multisensory emotion expressions more efficiently than men. *Neuropsychologia, 48*(1), 220–225. Available from https://doi.org/10.1016/j.neuropsychologia.2009.09.007.

Connelly, M., & Denney, D. R. (2007). Regulation of emotions during experimental stress in alexithymia. *Journal of Psychosomatic Research, 62*(6), 649–656. Available from https://doi.org/10.1016/j.jpsychores.2006.12.008.

D'Hondt, F., Campanella, S., Kornreich, C., Philippot, P., & Maurage, P. (2014). Below and beyond the recognition of emotional facial expressions in alcohol dependence: From basic perception to social cognition. *Neuropsychiatric Disease and Treatment, 10*, 2177–2182. Available from https://doi.org/10.2147/NDT.S74963.

D'Hondt, F., de Timary, P., Bruneau, Y., & Maurage, P. (2015). Categorical perception of emotional facial expressions in alcohol-dependence. *Drug and Alcohol Dependence, 156*, 267–274. Available from https://doi.org/10.1016/j.drugalcdep.2015.09.017.

D'Hondt, F., Lescut, C., Maurage, P., Menard, O., Gibour, B., Cottencin, O., ... Rolland, B. (2018). Psychiatric comorbidities associated with a positive screening using the Montreal Cognitive Assessment (MoCA) test in subjects with severe alcohol use disorder. *Drug and Alcohol Dependence, 191*(May), 266–269. Available from https://doi.org/10.1016/j.drugalcdep.2018.07.009.

Damasio, A. R., & Carvalho, G. B. (2013). The nature of feelings: Evolutionary and neurobiological origins. *Nature Reviews Neuroscience, 14*(2), 143–152. Available from https://doi.org/10.1038/nrn3403.

de Lima Osório, F., & Donadon, M. (2014). Recognition of facial expressions by alcoholic patients: A systematic literature review. *Neuropsychiatric Disease and Treatment, 10*, 1655. Available from https://doi.org/10.2147/ndt.s65376.

De Ternay, J., Naassila, M., Nourredine, M., Louvet, A., Bailly, F., Sescousse, G., ... Rolland, B. (2019). Therapeutic prospects of cannabidiol for alcohol use disorder and alcohol-related damages on the liver and the brain. *Frontiers in Pharmacology, 10*, 627. Available from https://doi.org/10.3389/fphar.2019.00627.

Decety, J., & Grèzes, J. (2006). The power of simulation: Imagining one's own and other's behavior. *Brain Research, 1079*(1), 4–14. Available from https://doi.org/10.1016/j.brainres.2005.12.115.

Decety, J., & Jackson, P. L. (2004). The functional architecture of human empathy. *Behavioral and Cognitive Neuroscience Reviews, 3*. Available from https://doi.org/10.1177/1534582304267187.

Diana, M., Raij, T., Melis, M., Nummenmaa, A., Leggio, L., & Bonci, A. (2017). Rehabilitating the addicted brain with transcranial magnetic stimulation. *Nature Reviews Neuroscience, 18* (11), 685–693. Available from https://doi.org/10.1038/nrn.2017.113.

Dziobek, I., Fleck, S., Kalbe, E., Rogers, K., Hassenstab, J., Brand, M., ... Convit, A. (2006). Introducing MASC: A movie for the assessment of social cognition. *Journal of Autism and Developmental Disorders, 36*(5), 623–636. Available from https://doi.org/10.1007/s10803-006-0107-0.

Edele, A., Dziobek, I., & Keller, M. (2013). Explaining altruistic sharing in the dictator game: The role of affective empathy, cognitive empathy, and justice sensitivity. *Learning and Individual Differences, 24*, 96–102. Available from https://doi.org/10.1016/j.lindif.2012.12.020.

Evren, C., Sar, V., Evren, B., Semiz, U., Dalbudak, E., & Cakmak, D. (2008). Dissociation and alexithymia among men with alcoholism. *Psychiatry and Clinical Neurosciences, 62*(1), 40–47. Available from https://doi.org/10.1111/j.1440-1819.2007.01775.x.

Foisy, M.-L., Kornreich, C., Fobe, A., D'Hondt, L., Pelc, I., Hanak, C., ... Philippot, P. (2007). Impaired emotional facial expression recognition in alcohol dependence: Do these deficits persist with midterm abstinence? *Alcoholism: Clinical and Experimental Research, 31*(3), 404–410. Available from https://doi.org/10.1111/j.1530-0277.2006.00321.x.

Foisy, M.-L., Philippot, P., Verbanck, P., Pelc, I., Van Der Straten, G., & Kornreich, C. (2005). Emotional facial expression decoding impairment in persons dependent on multiple substances: Impact of a history of alcohol dependence. *Journal of Studies on Alcohol, 66*(5), 663–681. Available from https://doi.org/10.15288/jsa.2005.66.673.

Franken, I. H. A., & van de Wetering, B. J. M. (2015). Bridging the gap between the neurocognitive lab and the addiction clinic. *Addictive Behaviors, 44*, 108–114. Available from https://doi.org/10.1016/j.addbeh.2014.11.034.

Freeman, C. R., Wiers, C. E., Sloan, M. E., Zehra, A., Ramirez, V., Wang, G. J., & Volkow, N. D. (2018). Emotion recognition biases in alcohol use disorder. *Alcoholism: Clinical and Experimental Research, 42*(8), 1541–1547. Available from https://doi.org/10.1111/acer.13802.

Friedlander, L., Lumley, M. A., Farchione, T., & Doyal, G. (1997). Testing the alexithymia hypothesis: Physiological and subjective responses during relaxation and stress. *The Journal of Nervous and Mental Disease, 185*(4), 233–239, Retrieved from. Available from http://www.ncbi.nlm.nih.gov/pubmed/9114808.

Frigerio, E., Burt, D. M., Montagne, B., Murray, L. K., & Perrett, D. I. (2002). Facial affect perception in alcoholics. *Psychiatry Research, 113*(1–2), 161–171. Available from https://doi.org/10.1016/S0165-1781(02)00244-5.

Frith, C. (2009). Role of facial expressions in social interactions. *Philosophical Transactions of the Royal Society B: Biological Sciences, 364*(1535), 3453–3458. Available from https://doi.org/10.1098/rstb.2009.0142.

Gilman, J. M., & Hommer, D. W. (2008). Modulation of brain response to emotional images by alcohol cues in alcohol-dependent patients. *Addiction Biology, 13*(3–4), 423–434. Available from https://doi.org/10.1111/j.1369-1600.2008.00111.x.

Glahn, D. C., Lovallo, W. R., & Fox, P. T. (2007). Reduced amygdala activation in young adults at high risk of alcoholism: Studies from the Oklahoma family health patterns project. *Biological Psychiatry, 61*(11), 1306–1309. Available from https://doi.org/10.1016/j.biopsych.2006.09.041.

Gordon, A. J., & Zrull, M. (1991). Social networks and recovery: One year after inpatient treatment. *Journal of Substance Abuse Treatment*, *8*(3), 143–152. Available from https://doi.org/10.1016/0740-5472(91)90005-U.

Grant, N., Lawrence, M., Preti, A., Wykes, T., & Cella, M. (2017). Social cognition interventions for people with schizophrenia: A systematic review focussing on methodological quality and intervention modality. *Clinical Psychology Review*, *56*(June), 55–64. Available from https://doi.org/10.1016/j.cpr.2017.06.001.

Green, M. F., Horan, W. P., & Lee, J. (2015). Social cognition in schizophrenia. *Nature Reviews Neuroscience*, *16*(10), 620–631. Available from https://doi.org/10.1038/nrn4005.

Gross, J. J. (1998). The emerging field of emotion regulation: An integrative review. *Review of General Psychology*, *2*(3), 271–299. Available from https://doi.org/10.1037/1089-2680.2.3.271.

Gross, J. J., & John, O. P. (2003). Individual differences in two emotion regulation processes: Implications for affect, relationships, and well-being. *Journal of Personality and Social Psychology*. Available from https://doi.org/10.1037/0022-3514.85.2.348.

Grüsser, S. M., Wrase, J., Klein, S., Hermann, D., Smolka, M. N., Ruf, M., . . . Heinz, A. (2004). Cue-induced activation of the striatum and medial prefrontal cortex is associated with subsequent relapse in abstinent alcoholics. *Psychopharmacology*, *175*(3), 296–302. Available from https://doi.org/10.1007/s00213-004-1828-4.

Grynberg, D., de Timary, P., Van Heuverswijn, A., & Maurage, P. (2017). Prone to feel guilty: Self-evaluative emotions in alcohol-dependence. *Drug and Alcohol Dependence*, *179*, 78–82. Available from https://doi.org/10.1016/j.drugalcdep.2017.06.030.

Grynberg, D., Maurage, P., & Nandrino, J.-L. (2017). Preserved affective sharing but impaired decoding of contextual complex emotions in alcohol dependence. *Alcoholism: Clinical and Experimental Research*, *41*(4), 779–785. Available from https://doi.org/10.1111/acer.13330.

Harder, D. H., & Zalma, A. (1990). Two promising shame and guilt scales: A construct validity comparison. *Journal of Personality Assessment*, *55*(3–4), 729–745. Available from https://doi.org/10.1080/00223891.1990.9674108.

Heinz, A., Wrase, J., Kahnt, T., Beck, A., Bromand, Z., Grüsser, S. M., . . . Mann, K. (2007). Brain activation elicited by affectively positive stimuli is associated with a lower risk of relapse in detoxified alcoholic subjects. *Alcoholism: Clinical and Experimental Research*, *31*(7), 1138–1147. Available from https://doi.org/10.1111/j.1530-0277.2007.00406.x.

Herman, A. M., & Duka, T. (2018). Facets of impulsivity and alcohol use: What role do emotions play? *Neuroscience and Biobehavioral Reviews* (May), 1–15. Available from https://doi.org/10.1016/j.neubiorev.2018.08.011.

Hill, S. Y., De Bellis, M. D., Keshavan, M. S., Lowers, L., Shen, S., Hall, J., & Pitts, T. (2001). Right amygdala volume in adolescent and young adult offspring from families at high risk for developing alcoholism. *Biological Psychiatry*, *49*(11), 894–905.

Hill, S. Y., Kostelnik, B., Holmes, B., Goradia, D., McDermott, M., Diwadkar, V., & Keshavan, M. (2007). fMRI BOLD response to the eyes task in offspring from multiplex alcohol dependence families. *Alcoholism: Clinical and Experimental Research*, *31*(12), 2028–2035. Available from https://doi.org/10.1111/j.1530-0277.2007.00535.x.

Hill, S. Y., & O'Brien, J. (2015). Psychological and neurobiological precursors of alcohol use disorders in high risk youth. *Current Addiction Reports*, *2*(2), 104–113. Available from https://doi.org/10.1007/s40429-015-0051-1.

Holmes, E. A., Craske, M. G., & Graybiel, A. M. (2014). Psychological treatments: A call for mental-health science. *Nature*, *511*(7509), 287–289. Available from https://doi.org/10.1038/511287a.

Hunter-Reel, D., McCrady, B., & Hildebrandt, T. (2009). Emphasizing interpersonal factors: an extension of the Witkiewitz and Marlatt relapse model. *Addiction*, *104*(8), 1281–1290. Available from https://doi.org/10.1111/j.1360-0443.2009.02611.x.

John, O. P., & Gross, J. J. (2004). Healthy and unhealthy emotion regulation: Personality processes, individual differences, and life span development. *Journal of Personality*. Available from https://doi.org/10.1111/j.1467-6494.2004.00298.x.

Keshavan, M. S., Vinogradov, S., Rumsey, J., Sherrill, J., & Wagner, A. (2014). Cognitive training in mental disorders: Update and future directions. *American Journal of Psychiatry*, *171*(5), 510–522. Available from https://doi.org/10.1176/appi.ajp.2013.13081075.

Koob, G. F., & Volkow, N. D. (2016). Neurobiology of addiction: A neurocircuitry analysis. *The Lancet Psychiatry*, *3*(8), 760–773. Available from https://doi.org/10.1016/S2215-0366(16)00104-8.

Kornreich, C., Blairy, S., Philippot, P., Hess, U., Noël, X., Streel, E., ... Verbanck, P. (2015). Deficits in recognition of emotional facial expression are still present in alcoholics after mid- to long-term abstinence. *Journal of Studies on Alcohol*, *62*(4), 533–542. Available from https://doi.org/10.15288/jsa.2001.62.533.

Kornreich, C., Delle-Vigne, D., Knittel, J., Nerincx, A., Campanella, S., Noel, X., ... Ermer, E. (2011). Impaired conditional reasoning in alcoholics: A negative impact on social interactions and risky behaviors? *Addiction*, *106*(5), 951–959. Available from https://doi.org/10.1111/j.1360-0443.2010.03346.x.

Kornreich, C., Petit, G., Rolin, H., Ermer, E., Campanella, S., Verbanck, P., & Maurage, P. (2016). Decoding of nonverbal language in alcoholism: A perception or a labeling problem? *Psychology of Addictive Behaviors*, *30*(2), 175–183. Available from https://doi.org/10.1037/adb0000147.

Kornreich, C., Philippot, P., Foisy, M.-L., Blairy, S., Raynaud, E., Dan, B., ... Verbanck, P. (2002). Impaired emotional facial expression recognition is associated with interpersonal problems in alcoholism. *Alcohol and Alcoholism*, *37*(4), 394–400. Available from https://doi.org/10.1093/alcalc/37.4.394.

Krampe, H., Stawicki, S., Hoehe, M. R., & Ehrenreich, H. (2007). Outpatient long-term intensive therapy for alcoholics (OLITA): A successful biopsychosocial approach to the treatment of alcoholism. *Dialogues in Clinical Neuroscience*, *9*(4), 399, Retrieved from. Available from https://www.ncbi.nlm.nih.gov/pmc/articles/PMC3202506/.

Le Berre, A.-P., Fama, R., & Sullivan, E. V. (2017). Executive functions, memory, and social cognitive deficits and recovery in chronic alcoholism: A Critical review to inform future research. *Alcoholism: Clinical and Experimental Research*, *41*(8), 1432–1443. Available from https://doi.org/10.1111/acer.13431.

Lindquist, K. A., Satpute, A. B., Wager, T. D., Weber, J., & Barrett, L. F. (2016). The brain basis of positive and negative affect: Evidence from a meta-analysis of the human neuroimaging literature. *Cerebral Cortex*, *26*(5), 1910–1922. Available from https://doi.org/10.1093/cercor/bhv001.

Lindquist, K. A., Wager, T. D., Kober, H., Bliss-Moreau, E., & Barrett, L. F. (2012). The brain basis of emotion: A meta-analytic review. *Behavioral and Brain Sciences*, *35*(03), 121–143. Available from https://doi.org/10.1017/S0140525X11000446.

Marinkovic, K., Oscar-Berman, M., Urban, T., O'Reilly, C. E., Howard, J. A., Sawyer, K., & Harris, G. J. (2009). Alcoholism and dampened temporal limbic activation to emotional faces. *Alcoholism: Clinical and Experimental Research*, *33*(11), 1880–1892. Available from https://doi.org/10.1111/j.1530-0277.2009.01026.x.

Marlatt G.A., Taxonomy of high-risk situations for alcohol relapse: Evolution and development of a cognitive-behavioral model, Addiction 91 (12s1), 1996, 37–49. https://doi.org/10.1046/j.1360-0443.91.12s1.15.x.

Martin, J. B., & Pihl, R. O. (1986). Influence of alexithymic characteristics on physiological and subjective stress responses in normal individuals. *Psychotherapy and Psychosomatics*, *45*(2), 66–77. Available from https://doi.org/10.1159/000287930.

Martinotti, G., Nicola, M., Di Tedeschi, D., Cundari, S., & Janiri, L. (2009). Empathy ability is impaired in alcohol-dependent patients. *American Journal on Addictions*, *18*(2), 157–161. Available from https://doi.org/10.1080/10550490802544391.

Mátyássy, A., Kelemen, O., Sáközi, Z., Janka, Z., & Kéri, S. (2006). Recognition of complex mental states in patients with alcoholism after long-term abstinence. *Alcohol and Alcoholism*. Available from https://doi.org/10.1093/alcalc/agl045.

Maurage, F., de Timary, P., Tecco, J. M., Lechantre, S., & Samson, D. (2015). Theory of mind difficulties in patients with alcohol dependence: Beyond the prefrontal cortex dysfunction hypothesis. *Alcoholism: Clinical and Experimental Research*, *39*(6), 980–988. Available from https://doi.org/10.1111/acer.12717.

Maurage, P., Campanella, S., Philippot, P., Charest, I., Martin, S., & De Timary, P. (2009). Impaired emotional facial expression decoding in alcoholism is also present for emotional prosody and body postures. *Alcohol and Alcoholism*, *44*(5), 476–485. Available from https://doi.org/10.1093/alcalc/agp037.

Maurage, P., Campanella, S., Philippot, P., de Timary, P., Constant, E., Gauthier, S., ... Verbanck, P. (2008). Alcoholism leads to early perceptive alterations, independently of comorbid depressed state: An ERP study. *Neurophysiologie Clinique*, *38*(2), 83–97. Available from https://doi.org/10.1016/j.neucli.2008.02.001.

Maurage, P., Campanella, S., Philippot, P., Martin, S., & de Timary, P. (2008). Face processing in chronic alcoholism: A specific deficit for emotional features. *Alcoholism: Clinical and Experimental Research*, *32*(4), 600–606. Available from https://doi.org/10.1111/j.1530-0277.2007.00611.x.

Maurage, P., Campanella, S., Philippot, P., Pham, T. H., & Joassin, F. (2007). The crossmodal facilitation effect is disrupted in alcoholism: A study with emotional stimuli. *Alcohol and Alcoholism*, *42*(6), 552–559. Available from https://doi.org/10.1093/alcalc/agm134.

Maurage, P., Campanella, S., Philippot, P., Vermeulen, N., Constant, E., Luminet, O., & de Timary, P. (2008). Electrophysiological correlates of the disrupted processing of anger in alcoholism. *International Journal of Psychophysiology*, *70*(1), 50–62. Available from https://doi.org/10.1016/j.ijpsycho.2008.05.572.

Maurage, P., D'Hondt, F., de Timary, P., Mary, C., Franck, N., & Peyroux, E. (2016). Dissociating affective and cognitive theory of mind in recently detoxified alcohol-dependent individuals. *Alcoholism: Clinical and Experimental Research*, *40*(9), 1926–1934. Available from https://doi.org/10.1111/acer.13155.

Maurage, P., de Timary, P., & D'Hondt, F. (2017). Heterogeneity of emotional and interpersonal difficulties in alcohol-dependence: A cluster analytic approach. *Journal of Affective Disorders*, *217*, 163–173. (December 2016). Available from https://doi.org/10.1016/j.jad.2017.04.005.

Maurage, P., de Timary, P., Moulds, M. L., Wong, Q. J. J., Collignon, M., Philippot, P., & Heeren, A. (2013). Maladaptive social self-beliefs in alcohol-dependence: A specific bias towards excessive high standards. *PLoS One*, *8*(3), e58928. Available from https://doi.org/10.1371/journal.pone.0058928.

Maurage, P., Grynberg, D., Noël, X., Joassin, F., Hanak, C., Verbanck, P., ... Philippot, P. (2011). The "Reading the mind in the eyes" test as a new way to explore complex emotions decoding in alcohol dependence. *Psychiatry Research*, *190*(2–3), 375–378. Available from https://doi.org/10.1016/j.psychres.2011.06.015.

Maurage, P., Grynberg, D., Noël, X., Joassin, F., Philippot, P., Hanak, C., ... Campanella, S. (2011). Dissociation between affective and cognitive empathy in alcoholism: A specific deficit for the emotional dimension. *Alcoholism, Clinical and Experimental Research*, *35*(9), 1662–1668. Available from https://doi.org/10.1111/j.1530-0277.2011.01512.x.

Maurage, P., Joassin, F., Pesenti, M., Grandin, C., Heeren, A., Philippot, P., & de Timary, P. (2013). The neural network sustaining crossmodal integration is impaired in alcohol-dependence: An fMRI study. *Cortex*, *49*(6), 1610–1626. Available from https://doi.org/10.1016/j.cortex.2012.04.012.

Maurage, P., Joassin, F., Philippot, P., Heeren, A., Vermeulen, N., Mahau, P., ... de Timary, P. (2012). Disrupted regulation of social exclusion in alcohol-dependence: An fMRI study. *Neuropsychopharmacology*, *37*(9), 2067–2075. Available from https://doi.org/10.1038/npp.2012.54.

Maurage, P., Philippot, P., Joassin, F., Pauwels, L., Pham, T., Alonso Prieto, E., ... Campanella, S. (2008). The auditory-visual integration of anger is impaired in alcoholism: An event-related potentials study. *Journal of Psychiatry and Neuroscience*, *33*(2), 111–122. Available from https://doi.org/10.1016/j.ijpsycho.2008.05.059.

Maurage, P., Philippot, P., Verbanck, P., Noel, X., Kornreich, C., Hanak, C., & Campanella, S. (2007). Is the P300 deficit in alcoholism associated with early visual impairments (P100, N170)? An oddball paradigm. *Clinical Neurophysiology*, *118*(3), 633–644. Available from https://doi.org/10.1016/j.clinph.2006.11.007.

Mckay, J. R., Franklin, T. R., Patapis, N., & Lynch, K. G. (2006). Conceptual, methodological, and analytical issues in the study of relapse. *Clinical Psychology Review*, *26*, 109–127. Available from https://doi.org/10.1016/j.cpr.2005.11.002.

Monnot, M., Nixon, S., Lovallo, W., & Ross, E. (2001). Altered emotional perception in alcoholics: Deficits in affective prosody comprehension. *Alcoholism: Clinical and Experimental Research*, *25*(3), 362–369. Available from https://doi.org/10.1111/j.1530-0277.2001.tb02222.x.

Moos, R. H., & Moos, B. S. (2006). Rates and predictors of relapse after natural and treated remission from alcohol use disorders. *Addiction*, *101*(2), 212–222. Available from https://doi.org/10.1111/j.1360-0443.2006.01310.x.

Moselhy, H. F., Georgiou, G., & Kahn, A. (2001). Frontal lobe changes in alcoholism: A review of the literature. *Alcohol and Alcoholism*, *36*(5), 357–368. Available from https://doi.org/10.1093/alcalc/36.5.357.

Müller, V. I., Cieslik, E. C., Turetsky, B. I., & Eickhoff, S. B. (2012). Crossmodal interactions in audiovisual emotion processing. *NeuroImage*. Available from https://doi.org/10.1016/j.neuroimage.2011.12.007.

Nandrino, J.-L., Berna, G., Hot, P., Dodin, V., Latrée, J., Decharles, S., & Sequeira, H. (2012). Cognitive and physiological dissociations in response to emotional pictures in patients with anorexia. *Journal of Psychosomatic Research*, *72*(1), 58–64. Available from https://doi.org/10.1016/j.jpsychores.2011.11.003.

Nandrino, J.-L., Gandolphe, M.-C., Alexandre, C., Kmiecik, E., Yguel, J., & Urso, L. (2014). Cognitive and affective theory of mind abilities in alcohol-dependent patients: The role of autobiographical memory. *Drug and Alcohol Dependence*, *143*, 65–73. Available from https://doi.org/10.1016/j.drugalcdep.2014.07.010.

Noël, X., Brevers, D., & Bechara, A. (2013). A neurocognitive approach to understanding the neurobiology of addiction. *Current Opinion in Neurobiology, 23*(4), 632–638. Available from https://doi.org/10.1016/j.conb.2013.01.018.

Noël, X., Paternot, J., Van der Linden, M., Sferrazza, R., Verhas, M., Hanak, C., ... Verbanck, P. (2001). Correlation between inhibition, working memory and delimited frontal area blood flow measured by 99m-Tc-Bicisate Spect in alcohol-dependent patients. *Alcohol and Alcoholism, 36*(6), 556–563. Available from https://doi.org/10.1093/alcalc/36.6.556.

Nutt, D. J., King, L. A., & Phillips, L. D. (2010). Drug harms in the UK: A multicriteria decision analysis. *The Lancet, 376*(9752), 1558–1565. Available from https://doi.org/10.1016/S0140-6736(10)61462-6.

O'Daly, O. G., Trick, L., Scaife, J., Marshall, J., Ball, D., Phillips, M. L., ... Duka, T. (2012). Withdrawal-associated increases and decreases in functional neural connectivity associated with altered emotional regulation in alcoholism. *Neuropsychopharmacology, 37*(10), 2267–2276. Available from https://doi.org/10.1038/npp.2012.77.

Onuoha, R. C., Quintana, D. S., Lyvers, M., & Guastella, A. J. (2016). A meta-analysis of theory of mind in alcohol use disorders. *Alcohol and Alcoholism, 51*(4), 410–415. Available from https://doi.org/10.1093/alcalc/agv137.

Oscar-Berman, M., Hancock, M., Mildworf, B., Hutner, N., & Weber, D. A. (1990). Emotional perception and memory in alcoholism and aging. *Alcoholism: Clinical and Experimental Research, 14*(3), 383–393. Available from https://doi.org/10.1111/j.1530-0277.1990.tb00491.x.

Parker, J. D. A., Keefer, K. V., Taylor, G. J., & Bagby, R. M. (2008). Latent structure of the alexithymia construct: A taxometric investigation. *Psychological Assessment, 20*(4), 385–396. Available from https://doi.org/10.1037/a0014262.

Petit, G., Luminet, O., Maurage, F., Tecco, J., Lechantre, S., Ferauge, M., ... de Timary, P. (2015). Emotion regulation in alcohol dependence. *Alcoholism: Clinical and Experimental Research, 39*(12), 2471–2479. Available from https://doi.org/10.1111/acer.12914.

Philippot, P., Kornreich, C., Blairy, S., Baert, I., Den Dulk, A., Le Bon, O., ... Verbanck, P. (1999). Alcoholics' deficits in the decoding of emotional facial expression. *Alcoholism, Clinical and Experimental Research, 23*(6), 1031–1038, https://doi.org/00000374-199906000-00010 [pii].

Premack, D., & Woodruff, G. (1978). Does the chimpanzee have a theory of mind? *Behavioral and Brain Sciences, 1*(04), 515. Available from https://doi.org/10.1017/S0140525X00076512.

Rabavilas, A. D. (1987). Electrodermal activity in low and high alexithymia neurotic patients. *Psychotherapy and Psychosomatics, 47*(2), 101–104. Available from https://doi.org/10.1159/000288004.

Randles, D., & Tracy, J. L. (2013). Nonverbal displays of shame predict relapse and declining health in recovering alcoholics. *Clinical Psychological Science, 1*(2), 149–155. Available from https://doi.org/10.1177/2167702612470645.

Rolland, B., D'Hondt, F., Montègue, S., Brion, M., Peyron, E., D'Aviau de Ternay, J., ... Maurage, P. (2019). A patient-tailored evidence-based approach for developing early neuropsychological training programs in addiction settings. *Neuropsychology Review*. Available from https://doi.org/10.1007/s11065-018-9395-3.

Rolland, B., Dricot, L., Creupelandt, C., Maurage, P., & De Timary, P. (2019). Respective influence of current alcohol consumption and duration of heavy drinking on brain morphological alterations in alcohol use disorder. *Addiction Biology*, e12751. (July 2018). Available from https://doi.org/10.1111/adb.12751.

Rudrauf, D., David, O., Lachaux, J.-P., Kovach, C. K., Martinerie, J., Renault, B., & Damasio, A. R. (2008). Rapid interactions between the ventral visual stream and emotion-related structures rely on a two-pathway architecture. *Journal of Neuroscience*, *28*(11), 2793–2803. Available from https://doi.org/10.1523/JNEUROSCI.3476-07.2008.

Rudrauf, D., Lachaux, J.-P., Damasio, A., Baillet, S., Hugueville, L., Martinerie, J., ... Renault, B. (2009). Enter feelings: Somatosensory responses following early stages of visual induction of emotion. *International Journal of Psychophysiology*, *72*(1), 13–23. Available from https://doi.org/10.1016/J.IJPSYCHO.2008.03.015.

Rupp, C. I., Derntl, B., Osthaus, F., Kemmler, G., Fleischhacker, W. W., Osthaus, F., & Fleischhacker, W. W. (2017). Impact of social cognition on alcohol dependence treatment outcome: Poorer facial emotion recognition predicts relapse/dropout. *Alcoholism: Clinical and Experimental Research*, *41*(12), 2197–2206. Available from https://doi.org/10.1111/acer.13522.

Salloum, J. B., Ramchandani, V. A., Bodurka, J., Rawlings, R., Momenan, R., George, D., & Hommer, D. W. (2007). Blunted rostral anterior cingulate response during a simplified decoding task of negative emotional facial expressions in alcoholic patients. *Alcoholism: Clinical and Experimental Research*, *31*(9), 1490–1504. Available from https://doi.org/10.1111/j.1530-0277.2007.00447.x.

Sanvicente-Vieira, B., Romani-Sponchiado, A., Kluwe-Schiavon, B., Brietzke, E., Araujo, R. B., & Grassi-Oliveira, R. (2017). Theory of mind in substance users: A systematic mini review. *Substance Use & Misuse*, *52*(1), 127–133. Available from https://doi.org/10.1080/10826084.2016.1212890.

Savla, G. N., Vella, L., Armstrong, C. C., Penn, D. L., & Twamley, E. W. (2013). Deficits in domains of social cognition in schizophrenia: A meta-analysis of the empirical evidence. *Schizophrenia Bulletin*, *39*(5), 979–992. Available from https://doi.org/10.1093/schbul/sbs080.

Schaafsma, S. M., Pfaff, D. W., Spunt, R. P., & Adolphs, R. (2015). Deconstructing and reconstructing theory of mind. *Trends in Cognitive Sciences*. Available from https://doi.org/10.1016/j.tics.2014.11.007.

Schmidt, T., Roser, P., Juckel, G., Brüne, M., Suchan, B., & Thoma, P. (2016). Social cognition and social problem solving abilities in individuals with alcohol use disorder. *Journal of Clinical and Experimental Neuropsychology*, *38*(9), 974–990. Available from https://doi.org/10.1080/13803395.2016.1180346.

Schmidt, T., Roser, P., Ze, O., Juckel, G., Suchan, B., & Thoma, P. (2017). Cortical thickness and trait empathy in patients and people at high risk for alcohol use disorders. *Psychopharmacology*, *234*(23–24), 3521–3533. Available from https://doi.org/10.1007/s00213-017-4741-3.

Schomerus, G., Lucht, M., Holzinger, A., Matschinger, H., Carta, M. G., & Angermeyer, M. C. (2011). The stigma of alcohol dependence compared with other mental disorders: A review of population studies. *Alcohol and Alcoholism*. Available from https://doi.org/10.1093/alcalc/agq089.

Shafiei, E., Fatemeh Hoseini, A., Bibak, A., & Azmal, M. (2014). High risk situations predicting relapse in self-referred addicts to Bushehr province substance abuse treatment centers. *International Journal of High Risk Behaviors and Addiction*, *3*(2), 287–292. Available from https://doi.org/10.5812/ijhrba.16381.

Shamay-Tsoory, S. G., Shur, S., Barcai-Goodman, L., Medlovich, S., Harari, H., & Levkovitz, Y. (2007). Dissociation of cognitive from affective components of theory of mind in schizophrenia. *Psychiatry Research*, *149*(1–3), 11–23. Available from https://doi.org/10.1016/j.psychres.2005.10.018.

Sifneos, P. E. (1973). The prevalence of 'alexithymic'characteristics in psychosomatic patients. *Psychotherapy and Psychosomatics*, *22*(2–6), 255–262. Available from https://doi.org/10.1159/000286529.

Stacy, A. W., & Wiers, R. W. (2010). Implicit cognition and addiction: A tool for explaining paradoxical behavior. *Annual Review of Clinical Psychology*, *6*(1), 551–575. Available from https://doi.org/10.1146/annurev.clinpsy.121208.131444.

Stavro, K., Pelletier, J., & Potvin, S. (2013). Widespread and sustained cognitive deficits in alcoholism: A meta-analysis. *Addiction Biology*, *18*(2), 203–213. Available from https://doi.org/10.1111/j.1369-1600.2011.00418.x.

Stone, L. A., & Nielson, K. A. (2001). Intact physiological response to arousal with impaired emotional recognition in alexithymia. *Psychotherapy and Psychosomatics*, *70*(2), 92–102. Available from https://doi.org/10.1159/000056232.

Taieb, O., Corcos, M., Loas, G., Speranza, M., Guilbaud, O., Perez-Diaz, F., ... Jeammet, P. (2002). Alexithymia and alcohol dependence. *Annales de Medecine Interne*, *153*(SUPPL. 3), 1S51–1S60. Available from https://doi.org/10.1016/S0003-4487(01)00134-2.

Tangney, J. P., Dearing, R., Wagner, P. E., & Gramzow, R. (2000). *The test of self-conscious affect-3 (TOSCA-3)*. George Mason University: Fairfax, VA.

Tangney, J. P., Stuewig, J., & Mashek, D. J. (2007). Moral emotions and moral behavior. *Annual Review of Psychology*, *58*(1), 345–372. Available from https://doi.org/10.1146/annurev.psych.56.091103.070145.

Thoma, P., Friedmann, C., & Suchan, B. (2013). Empathy and social problem solving in alcohol dependence, mood disorders and selected personality disorders. *Neuroscience and Biobehavioral Reviews*, *37*(3), 448–470. Available from https://doi.org/10.1016/j.neubiorev.2013.01.024.

Thoma, P., Winter, N., Juckel, G., & Roser, P. (2013). Mental state decoding and mental state reasoning in recently detoxified alcohol-dependent individuals. *Psychiatry Research*, *205*(3), 232–240. Available from https://doi.org/10.1016/j.psychres.2012.08.042.

Thorberg, F. A., Young, R. M., Sullivan, K. A., & Lyvers, M. (2009). Alexithymia and alcohol use disorders: A critical review. *Addictive Behaviors*, *34*(3), 237–245. Available from https://doi.org/10.1016/j.addbeh.2008.10.016.

Townshend, J. M., & Duka, T. (2003). Mixed emotions: Alcoholics' impairments in the recognition of specific emotional facial expressions. *Neuropsychologia*, *41*(7), 773–782. Available from https://doi.org/10.1016/S0028-3932(02)00284-1.

Treeby, M. S., Prado, C., Rice, S. M., & Crowe, S. F. (2016). Shame, guilt, and facial emotion processing: initial evidence for a positive relationship between guilt-proneness and facial emotion recognition ability. *Cognition and Emotion*, *30*(8), 1504–1511. Available from https://doi.org/10.1080/02699931.2015.1072497.

Uekermann, J., Channon, S., Winkel, K., Schlebusch, P., & Daum, I. (2007). Theory of mind, humour processing and executive functioning in alcoholism. *Addiction*, *102*(2), 232–240. Available from https://doi.org/10.1111/j.1360-0443.2006.01656.x.

Uekermann, J., Daum, I., Schlebusch, P., & Trenckmann, U. (2005). Processing of affective stimuli in alcoholism. *Cortex*, *41*(2), 189–194. Available from https://doi.org/10.1016/S0010-9452(08)70893-1.

Uzun, Ö. (2003). Alexithymia in male alcoholics: Study in a Turkish sample. *Comprehensive Psychiatry*, *44*(4), 349–352. Available from https://doi.org/10.1016/S0010-440X(03)00009-9.

Volkow, N. D., Fowler, J. S., & Wang, G. (2003). The addicted human brain : Insights from imaging studies find the latest version : The addicted human brain : Insights from imaging studies. *The Journal of Clinical Investigation*, *111*(10), 1444–1451. Available from https://doi.org/10.1172/JCI200318533.Imaging.

Volkow, N. D., & Morales, M. (2015). The brain on drugs: From reward to addiction. *Cell, 162* (4), 712–725. Available from https://doi.org/10.1016/J.CELL.2015.07.046.

Werner, K. H., Goldin, P. R., Ball, T. M., Heimberg, R. G., & Gross, J. J. (2011). Assessing emotion regulation in social anxiety disorder: The emotion regulation interview. *Journal of Psychopathology and Behavioral Assessment, 33*(3), 346–354. Available from https://doi.org/10.1007/s10862-011-9225-x.

Wiechelt, S. A., & Sales, E. (2001). The role of shame in women's recovery from alcoholism. *Journal of Social Work Practice in the Addictions, 1*(4), 101–116. Available from https://doi.org/10.1300/J160v01n04_07.

Williams, K. D., & Jarvis, B. (2006). Cyberball: A program for use in research on interpersonal ostracism and acceptance. *Behavior Research Methods, 38*(1), 174–180. Retrieved from http://www.ncbi.nlm.nih.gov/pubmed/16817529.

World Health Organisation. (2018). *Global status report on alcohol and health 2018. World Health Organisation*. World Health Organization, https://doi.org/entity/substance_abuse/publications/global_alcohol_report/en/index.html.

Wrase, J., Schlagenhauf, F., Kienast, T., Wüstenberg, T., Bermpohl, F., Kahnt, T., ... Heinz, A. (2007). Dysfunction of reward processing correlates with alcohol craving in detoxified alcoholics. *NeuroImage, 35*(2), 787–794. Available from https://doi.org/10.1016/j.neuroimage.2006.11.043.

Zywiak, W. H., Westerberg, V. S., Connors, G. J., & Maisto, S. A. (2003). Exploratory findings from the reasons for drinking questionnaire. *Journal of Substance Abuse Treatment, 25*(4), 287–292. Available from https://doi.org/10.1016/S0740-5472(03)00118-1.

Chapter 9

Metacognitive therapy for Alcohol Use Disorder: Theoretical foundations and treatment principles

Giovanni Mansueto[1,2,3,4], Gabriele Caselli[1,2] and Marcantonio M. Spada[5]

[1]Studi Cognitivi, Milano, Italy, [2]Department of Psychology, Sigmund Freud University, Milano, Italy, [3]Maastricht University Medical Center, Department of Psychiatry & Psychology, University of Maastricht, Maastricht, The Netherlands, [4]Department of Health Sciences, University of Florence, Firenze, Italy, [5]Division of Psychology, School of Applied Sciences, London South Bank University, London, United Kingdom

The metacognitive perspective of emotional disorders

Research undertaken over the last fifteen years has underlined the possible role of metacognitive beliefs as concern the initiation, perseveration and maintenance of alcohol use (Hamonniere & Varescon, 2018; Spada, Caselli, Nikčević, & Wells, 2015). In this chapter, within the framework of the Self-Regulatory Executive Function (S-REF) model (Wells & Matthews, 1996), we review research on metacognitive beliefs in Alcohol Use Disorder and outline the possible contribution of the Metacognitive Therapy approach to its treatment.

In 1996, Wells and Matthews outlined the Self-Regulatory Executive Function (S-REF) model of emotional disorders integrating information processing research with Beck's schema theory (e.g. Beck, 1991). The S-REF model differs from standard cognitive theories such as Beck's by emphasizing the importance of how people think about, and regulate, their thoughts and cognition, rather than the content and meaning of thoughts (Wells, 2009).

Central to the S-REF model are the processes which monitor, generate and maintain intrusive and biased cognitive experiences (Wells, 2009). The S-REF model posits that psychological disturbance is maintained by the activation of the Cognitive Attentional Syndrome (CAS) under conditions of psychological distress (Wells & Matthews, 1994; 1996). The CAS encompasses repetitive

The Handbook of Alcohol Use - Understandings from Synapse to Society.
DOI: https://doi.org/10.1016/B978-0-12-816720-5.00021-9

negative thinking styles, thought suppression, excessive attention to threat, excessive self-monitoring, and maladaptive coping behaviors such as avoidance (Caselli & Spada, 2015; Wells, 2009). Although the CAS is used to self-regulate, it is problematic because it leads to prolonged negative emotional experience, and difficulties in regulating thoughts and modifying beliefs (Wells, 2009). The activation of the CAS brings an increase of attentional focus toward distress congruent information and feedback loops, which fail to regulate threatening thoughts (Caselli, Martino, Spada, & Wells, 2018). The CAS is activated by beliefs and knowledge about one's thoughts and cognitive processes (e.g. memory, attention) that are metacognitive in nature (Wells, 2009). Metacognitive beliefs are defined as information and beliefs about cognition and ways of controlling it (Flavell, 1979). According to the S-REF model (Wells & Matthews, 1996), two domains of metacognitive beliefs are detrimental: positive metacognitive beliefs about the usefulness of engaging in aspects of the CAS (e.g. 'Worrying about threats means I can be prepared') and negative metacognitive beliefs about thoughts and feelings (e.g. 'If I continue to worry I will lose my mind').

The S-REF model has led to the development of disorder-specific formulations and treatments for different emotional disorders such as, depression, anxiety disorders, post-traumatic stress disorder, obsessive–compulsive disorder, psychosis spectrum disorders (Sellers, Varese, Wells, & Morrison 2017; Sun, Zhu, & So, 2017; Wells, 2009). Metacognitive therapy (MCT), the psychological treatment based on the S-REF model, which aims to reduce the propensity to engage in the CAS and to modify related metacognitive beliefs, has been applied to the treatment of anxiety and depression with notable results (Normann & Morina, 2018).

The metacognitive perspective of addictive behaviors

Over the last fifteen years a wide research base investigating the relationship between CAS components, metacognitive beliefs and addictive behaviors has emerged (Hamonniere & Varescon, 2018; Spada et al., 2015). This is briefly reviewed in the forthcoming sub-sections.

The cognitive attentional syndrome and addictive behaviors

Repetitive negative thinking styles (i.e. dysfunctional and rigid thinking styles that perpetuate the accessibility of intrusions) have been conceptualized as part of the CAS (Wells & Matthews, 1994; 1996). Rumination, worry and desire thinking, are the main types of repetitive negative thinking styles identified in the literature (Borkovec, 1994; Caselli & Spada, 2015; Nolen-Hoeksema & Morrow, 1991). Rumination and worry are characterized by heightened self-focused attention involving persistent, repetitive, and predominantly verbal internal questioning about the causes, meaning, and consequences of one's internal experiences. While rumination is focused on depressive symptoms and their consequences (Nolen-Hoeksema & Morrow, 1991), worry is characterized by an apprehensive expectation of possible negative outcomes in the future (Borkovec, 1994). Desire thinking is a voluntary process involving the elaboration of a desired target at a verbal level (i.e. Verbal Perseveration) and an imaginal level (i.e. Imaginal Prefiguration) (Caselli & Spada, 2015; Kavanagh, May, & Andrade, 2009). The target of desire thinking may be an activity, an object, or a state (Kavanagh, Andrade, & May, 2004; Kavanagh, Andrade, & May, 2005).

It has been shown that rumination is positively related with different forms of addictive behaviors such as, pathological gambling severity (Kause et al., 2018) and number of smoking quit attempt failures (Dovrak, Simons, & Wray, 2011). Moreover, among alcohol users, rumination has been found to be higher in problem drinkers compared with social drinkers (Caselli, Bortolai, Leoni, Rovetto, & Spada, 2008), and to predict drinking status and level of alcohol use at 3, 6 and 12 month follow-up following a brief course of cognitive–behavioral therapy for alcohol abuse (Caselli et al., 2010). It also significantly increases craving (Caselli et al., 2013).

Several studies have also supported the association between high levels of worry and the tendency to use alcohol (e.g. Goldsmith, Tran, Smith, & Howe, 2009; Smith & Book, 2010). Similarly, desire thinking has been found to be positively associated with different forms of addictive behaviors, including nicotine use, gambling, and problematic Internet use, in both clinical and non-clinical samples (Allen, Kannis-Dymand, & Katsikitis, 2017; Caselli & Spada, 2015; Fernie et al., 2014; Spada, Giustina, Rolandi, Fernie, & Caselli, 2014). Desire thinking may lead to detrimental consequences as interference with the regulation of craving, increased levels of craving, and perception of being out of control, increasing accessibility of target-related information, and a consequent escalation in the severity of addictive behaviors (Caselli & Spada, 2015).

The CAS also encompasses thought suppression (i.e. a mental control strategy involving the attempt to keep certain thoughts that may can lead to an increase in the suppressed thought; Wenzlaff & Wegner, 2000). There is evidence to suggest that thought suppression may be associated with addictive behaviors such as smoking and gambling (Spada et al., 2015). A greater use of smoking-related thought suppression in everyday life has been found to be significantly associated with a greater desire to smoke (Erskine et al., 2012), attempts to quit smoking, and number of cigarettes smoked (Erskine, Georgiou, & Kvavilashvili, 2010). Moreover, a similar relationship has been observed between thought suppression and problem gambling (Riley, 2014).

In addition to the above, Spada et al. (2015) have proposed that metacognitive monitoring (i.e. the ability to monitor internal states as a guide to knowing how close one is to resolving discrepancies and achieving the desired state) is likely to be perpetuate engagement in addictive behaviors.

In support of this view, evidence appears to suggest that poor metacognitive monitoring has been associated with perseveration of gambling activity in gambling disorder patients (Spada et al., 2014). In addition, there is also evidence that not attending internally to the change in cognition and emotion (i.e. poor metacognitive monitoring) that occurs during nicotine use might be associated with an excessive use (Spada et al., 2015).

Finally, as proposed by Spada et al. (2015), attentional bias may be considered as a feature of the CAS being a manifestation of the individual's strategic goals of monitoring for personally relevant cues and threats. Attentional bias may contribute to the development and persistence of addictive behaviors, relapse and craving, with evidence showing that among users of different substances (cannabis, tobacco, heroin, cocaine), substance-related attentional bias is directly proportional to the quantity and frequency of the substance use and prospectively predicts the risk of subsequent relapse (Spada et al., 2015).

Metacognitive beliefs and addictive behaviors

Since the early 2000s, two main lines of research have been explored in the relationship between metacognitive beliefs and different kinds of addictive behaviors, such as, nicotine use, gambling, problematic internet use, alcohol use (Hamonniere & Varescon, 2018; Spada et al., 2015). The first line of research has explored generic metacognitive beliefs about cognitive affective experiences in individuals engaging in addictive behavior (Hamonniere & Varescon, 2018). This line of research showed that people who engage in addictive behaviors hold generic metacognitive beliefs, metacognitive beliefs about addiction-related thoughts, and metacognitive beliefs about craving (Hamonniere & Varescon, 2018). These metacognitive beliefs have been found in both clinical and community samples, although they are more prevalent in the former. Among generic metacognitive beliefs, beliefs about uncontrollability and danger, about the need to control thoughts, and a lack of cognitive confidence (i.e. level of confidence in mnemonic and attentional capabilities) seem to be those beliefs most closely associated with addictive behaviors (Hamonniere & Varescon, 2018). Metacognitive beliefs about the need to control thoughts have been found to be a stronger predictor of addictive behavior than the severity of addictive behavior and relapse, while, metacognitive beliefs about uncontrollability and danger of addiction-related thoughts and negative metacognitive beliefs about craving have been found positively correlated with craving severity (Hamonniere & Varescon, 2018). Furthermore, some evidence based on cross-sectional mediation-moderation study designs has proposed that generic metacognitive beliefs might be involved in the relationship between addictive behavior and psychological disorders comorbidity, negative emotions, personality traits and emotion dysregulation (Akbari, 2017; Jauregi, Urbiola, & Estevez, 2016; Mansueto et al.,

2016; Marino et al., 2016; Moneta, 2011; Spada, Langston, Nikčević, & Moneta, 2008).

The second line of research has investigated metacognitive beliefs about cognitive-affective self-regulatory strategies in those engaging in addictive behaviors (Hamonniere & Varescon, 2018). Consistently in this field of research, studies evaluating metacognitive profiling of specific addictive behaviors, such as, smoking, gambling, and online gaming (Caselli et al., 2018; Nikčević, Caselli, Wells, & Spada, 2015; Spada & Caselli, 2017; Spada & Wells, 2008), have identified two main typologies of metacognitive beliefs about addictive behaviors: (a) positive metacognitive beliefs, which refer to the positive effect of engaging in addictive behavior as a means of regulating emotion (e.g. "Gambling helps me when I feel depressed"; "Cigarettes help me to relax") and cognition (e.g. "Gambling helps me to think about something else"; "Cigarettes help me to be more focused"); and (b) negative metacognitive beliefs, which refer to beliefs about the negative impact of behavior on cognitive functioning (e.g. "Smoking will damage my memory capacities"), the uncontrollability of thoughts related to addictive behavior (e.g. "Thoughts about gambling are uncontrollable"), thought-action fusion (e.g. "If I think about gambling, I will go to play"), and the perception of a lack of executive control over behavior (e.g. "I cannot control my urge to smoke") (Hamonniere & Varescon, 2018).

Positive and negative metacognitive beliefs have also been found to play a role in desire thinking (Caselli & Spada, 2015). Positive metacognitive beliefs about desire thinking relate to the usefulness of this thinking style in distracting from negative thoughts and emotions (e.g. "it helps not to be overwhelmed by my worries"), and increasing the sense of control over behavior (e.g. "it helps to avoid bad decisions", "it helps to have a greater control over my decisions"). Negative metacognitive beliefs about desire thinking regard the uncontrollability of target-related thoughts (e.g. "I cannot stop thinking about my desires") and loss of control over desire thinking (e.g. "thinking too much about my desires make me lose control"). Positive metacognitive beliefs are purported to be involved in the initiation of desire thinking when a target-related thought intrudes into awareness whilst negative metacognitive beliefs may lead to the perception of low control once a desire thinking episode has started leading to the escalation of craving (Caselli & Spada, 2015).

Overall, the literature suggests that metacognitive beliefs may contribute to the initiation, perseveration and maintenance of addictive behaviors, promoting harmful thinking styles and dysfunctional coping strategies (the CAS), which in turn will increase the likelihood of engaging in addictive behavior (Hamonniere & Varescon, 2018; Spada et al., 2015). Positive metacognitive beliefs about addictive behaviors may be involved in the initiation of addictive behaviors by motivating people to engage in it, whereas negative metacognitive beliefs about addictive behaviors may be predominantly involved in the perpetuation of these behaviors. When activated, metacognitive beliefs strengthen the perception of failure in self-regulation and the harmful effect of addictive behavior on functioning, promoting repetitive negative thinking styles and negative emotions (Hamonniere & Varescon, 2018).

The cognitive attentional syndrome and metacognitive beliefs in Alcohol Use Disorder

Spada and Wells (2008) were the first to propose that Alcohol Use Disorder (AUD) may be conceptualized using the metacognitive perspective (Spada & Wells, 2004). Since the original study in the field evidence has accrued on the role of both the CAS and metacognitive beliefs in AUD (Caselli et al., 2013; Caselli, Soliani and Spada, 2013b; Caselli et al., 2018; Hamonniere & Varescon, 2018; Spada, Caselli, & Wells, 2013). It has been advocated that metacognitive beliefs lead to the activation of CAS components associated with AUD (e.g. perseverative thinking about alcohol-related intrusions, the monitoring of internal or external alcohol-related cues, and the reduction of adaptive metacognitive monitoring; Spada et al., 2013). Below, CAS components and metacognitive beliefs associated with AUD are described.

The cognitive attentional syndrome and AUD

A growing body of studies have demonstrated that different forms of negative repetitive thinking styles (i.e. desire thinking, rumination and worry) are positively associated with alcohol use in both non-clinical and clinical samples (Caselli et al., 2008; Caselli, Ferla, Mezzaluna, Rovetto, & Spada, 2012; Caselli & Spada, 2015; Goldsmith et al., 2009; Smith & Book, 2010), in experimental research (Caselli et al., 2013; Caselli, Soliani and Spada, 2013; Caselli, Gemelli, Spada, & Wells, 2016; Caselli, Gemelli, & Spada, 2017) and in longitudinal studies (Caselli et al., 2010; Martino et al., 2017; 2019). In a recent longitudinal study involving one hundred and thirty-five AUD patients it was shown that desire thinking predicts binge drinking, craving and relapse at three months follow-up independently from level of alcohol use (Martino et al., 2019). In addition, literature has suggested that the imaginal prefiguration and verbal perseveration components of desire thinking might play different roles in addictive behaviors (Caselli & Spada, 2011; Caselli et al., 2012; Caselli et al., 2015; Martino et al., 2017; 2019). The imaginal prefiguration component of desire thinking appears to be principally predictive of craving levels while the verbal perseveration component appears to be more closely associated with behavioral enactment (i.e. relapse and binge drinking frequency) (Martino et al., 2019). The possible specific relationship between the verbal perseveration component of desire thinking and behavioral enactment has been established in a series of studies showing that only verbal perseveration (and not imaginal prefiguration) is a longitudinal predictor of binge drinking in healthy volunteers (Martino et al., 2017). This construct also predicts levels of alcohol use in clinical populations (Caselli & Spada, 2011), it is the strongest discriminant predictor across the continuum of drinking behavior (Caselli et al., 2012), and in the classification as a problem drinker (Caselli et al., 2015). Martino et al. (2019) proposed that because the verbal perseveration component of desire thinking nullifies the effect of craving levels in predicting the risk of relapse and binge drinking frequency at follow-up, it could be a key mechanism in predicting return to alcohol use over and above the experience of craving.

Moreover, the detrimental interplay between alcohol use and adaptive metacognitive monitoring is also widely accepted (Caselli et al., 2018; Spada et al., 2013). Impairments of attentional functioning have a relevant role in determining alcohol effects (Hull, 1981; Nelson et al., 1998; Steele & Josephs, 1990). Alcohol's pharmacological properties can narrow the perception to immediate cues and reduce the capacity for abstract reasoning (Steele & Josephs, 1990). Additionally, alcohol reduces self-awareness, conceptualized as the ability to attribute self-relevance in encoding information (Hull, 1981) and neuroscientific evidence suggests that alcohol intoxication impairs neurological systems associated to meta-level processing (Nelson et al., 1998). Overall, these processes are likely to play a key role in the effective monitoring of internal states once a drinking episode has started (Spada et al., 2013): an ineffective monitoring of internal states (i.e. "poor metacognitive monitoring") can lead to higher levels of alcohol use because information on emotional change (e.g., feeling relaxed) and proximity to goals of alcohol use (e.g., achieving a greater level of relaxation) that would serve as a stop signal are not attended to. A significant association between poor metacognitive monitoring and alcohol use, and problem drinking, have been found in both community and clinical samples (Spada et al., 2013).

Metacognitive beliefs and AUD

Metacognitive beliefs have been found to significantly discriminate dependent drinkers, problem drinkers and non-problem drinkers (Hamonniere & Varescon, 2018). As concerns general metacognitive beliefs, metacognitive beliefs about the need to control thoughts have been found to predict prospectively levels of alcohol use and relapse at 3, 6, and 12 months in a sample of problem drinkers, and negative metacognitive beliefs have been found to predict alcohol-dependent status (Hamonniere & Varescon, 2018). Additionally, some evidence has suggested that metacognitive beliefs might moderate the effect of anxiety and depression on alcohol dependence (Hamonniere & Varescon, 2018).

Research exploring alcohol-specific metacognitive beliefs in problem drinkers has identified both positive and negative metacognitive belief domains (Hamonniere & Varescon, 2018). Positive metacognitive beliefs about alcohol use are conceptualized as a specific form of outcome expectancy relating to the use of alcohol as a means of controlling cognition and emotion (Spada & Wells, 2008; 2009). Some examples of positive metacognitive beliefs about alcohol use include: "Drinking makes me think more clearly" (problem-solving), "Drinking helps me to control my thoughts" (thought control), "Drinking helps me focus my mind" (attention regulation), "Drinking reduces my self-consciousness" (self-image regulation), "Drinking reduces my anxious feelings" (emotion regulation) (Spada & Wells, 2008). According to the metacognitive perspective such beliefs play a central role in motivating individuals to engage in alcohol use as a means of cognitive-emotional regulation (Spada & Wells, 2006).

Negative metacognitive beliefs about alcohol use concern the perception of lack of executive control over alcohol use (e.g. "My drinking persists no matter how I try to control it"), and the evaluation of the negative impact of alcohol use on cognitive functioning (e.g. "Drinking will damage my mind"). According to the metacognitive perspective such beliefs play a crucial role in the perpetuation of alcohol use by becoming activated during and following a drinking episode, and triggering negative emotional states that compel a person to drink more (Spada & Wells, 2006).

As observed by Spada and Wells (2008) metacognitive beliefs about alcohol use share some similarities and differences, with a relevant cognitive variable involved in the persistence of alcohol use, i.e. outcome expectancies. Positive metacognitive beliefs about alcohol share similarities and differences with positive alcohol outcome expectancies (Spada & Wells, 2008). Positive alcohol outcome expectancies refer to the drinker's perception of the positive outcomes of drinking and have been shown to be associated to alcohol use (Brown, Christiansen, & Goldman, 1987; Christiansen, Smith, Roehling, & Goldman, 1989; Goldman, Del Boca, & Darkes, 1999; Leigh, 1989; Maisto, Connors, & Sachs, 1981). The key similarity between positive metacognitive beliefs about alcohol use and positive alcohol outcome expectancies is that both constructs capture motivations for alcohol use (Spada, Moneta, & Wells, 2007). Although there is a degree of overlap between positive metacognitive beliefs about alcohol use pertaining to emotion regulation and positive alcohol outcome expectancies pertaining to tension reduction and the modulation of negative affect these constructs are not identical - as correlation coefficients between them of around. 50 attest to (Spada, Nikčević, Moneta, & Wells, 2007; Spada & Wells, 2008). As remarked by Spada and Wells (2008) a key difference between positive metacognitive beliefs about alcohol use and positive alcohol outcome expectancies is that items pertaining to the former construct also tap into the effects of alcohol use on cognition (e.g. problem-solving, thought control, attention regulation, and self-image regulation).

As regard negative metacognitive beliefs about alcohol use, those concerning the perception of lack of executive control over alcohol use assessing cognitive confidence in regulating alcohol use might be conceptualized as a form of cognitive self-efficacy belief, while negative metacognitive beliefs about the impact of alcohol use on cognitive functioning are evaluations of the cognitive costs of drinking (Spada & Wells, 2008). As argued by Spada and Wells (2008), these beliefs are related to negative alcohol outcome expectancies which assesses an individual's estimation that a given behavior will lead to specific negative outcomes (Bandura, 1997)

As remarked by Spada and Wells (2008) the distinctions between alcohol outcome expectancies and metacognitive beliefs about alcohol use are relevant given that according to the metacognitive theory of psychopathology the key markers of dysfunction are beliefs pertaining to the metacognitive rather than cognitive domain (Wells, 2000). The relevance of differentiating between alcohol outcome expectancies and metacognitive beliefs about alcohol is confirmed by findings showing that, among a community sample, metacognitive beliefs about alcohol use were an independent contributor to drinking behavior over and above alcohol outcome expectancies (Spada et al., 2007). Finally, metacognitive beliefs about desire thinking appear to play a role in the persistence of alcohol use. Positive correlations between negative metacognitive beliefs about desire thinking and alcohol use, as well as between metacognitive beliefs (both positive and negative) about desire thinking and craving, have been found among patients with diagnosed of AUD (Hamonniere & Varescon, 2018).

A triphasic metacognitive formulation of problem drinking

Taken together, these data support the applicability of the S-REF model to understanding the development and maintenance of AUD. Applying this model to problem drinking, Spada et al. (2013) proposed the triphasic metacognitive formulation of problem drinking across three phases: pre-alcohol use phase, alcohol use phase and post-alcohol use phase (Fig. 9.1).

During the pre-alcohol use phase, alcohol-related triggers, in the form of cravings, images, memories or thoughts, activate positive metacognitive beliefs about extended thinking, leading to desire thinking, rumination, worry or their combination. In turn, the activation of the latter brings to an escalation of cravings and negative affect, strengthening negative metacognitive beliefs about the need to control thoughts and enhancing the likelihood of alcohol use (Spada et al., 2013).

In the alcohol use phase, positive metacognitive beliefs about alcohol use and a reduction in metacognitive monitoring contribute to dysregulation in alcohol use; over the course of time and as the drinking problem escalates in severity, negative metacognitive beliefs about the uncontrollability of alcohol use and alcohol-related thoughts emerge, contributing to the perseveration of dysregulated alcohol use (Spada et al., 2013).

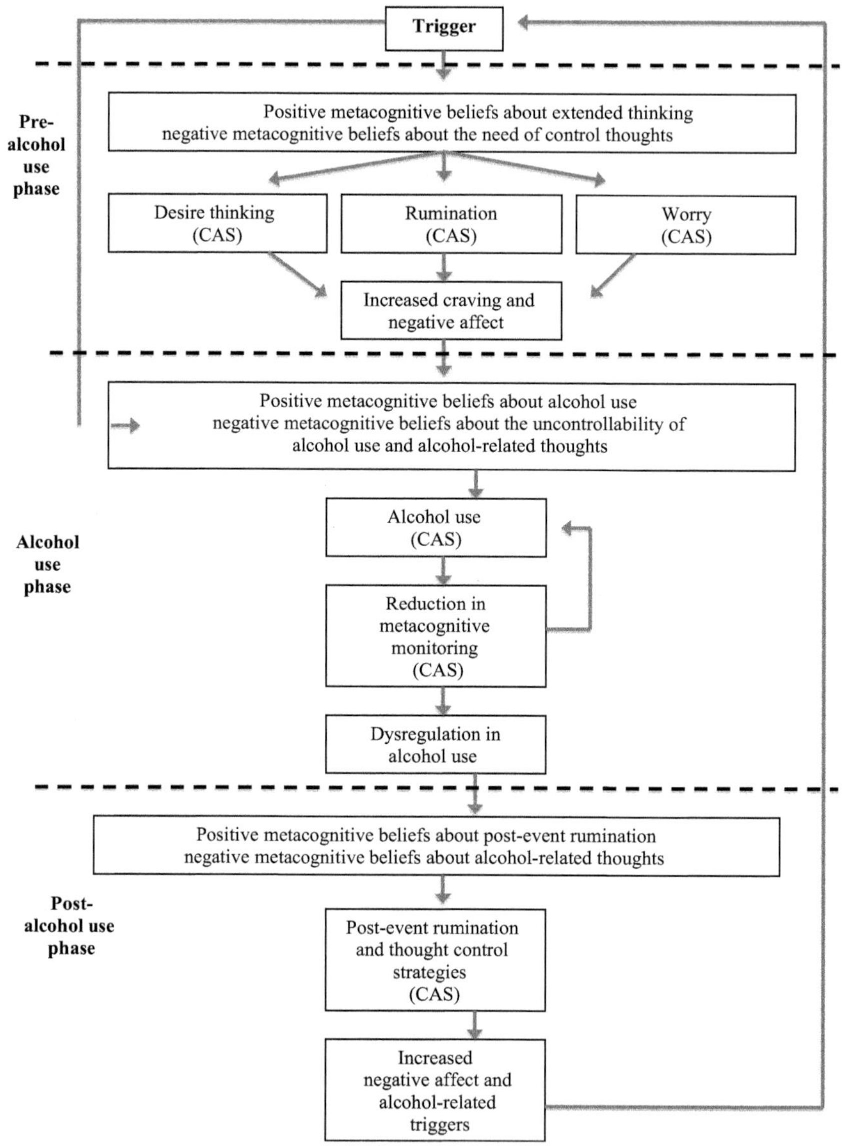

FIGURE 9.1 A triphasic metacognitive formulation of problem drinking. *Adapted from Spada, M. M., Caselli, G., & Wells, A. (2013). A triphasic metacognitive formulation of problem drinking.* Clinical Psychology & Psychotherapy, 20*(6), 494–500.*

Finally, in the post-alcohol use phase following the activation of positive metacognitive beliefs about post-event rumination, the affective, cognitive and physiological consequences of dysregulated alcohol use become the subject of rumination (Spada et al., 2013). This, in turn, leads to a paradoxical increase in negative affect and alcohol-related thoughts, together with the strengthening of negative metacognitive beliefs about such thoughts; intermittent attempts to suppress alcohol-related thoughts increase the likelihood of returning to use alcohol as a means of achieving self-regulation (Spada et al., 2013).

The triphasic metacognitive formulation of problem drinking here described has been supported by empirical data (Hamonniere & Varescon, 2018; Spada et al., 2013).

AUD and the metacognitive perspective: clinical implications

Some clinical implications should be discussed. First, in terms of assessment, information about CAS component associated with AUD (e.g. rumination, worry, desire thinking, the monitoring of internal or external alcohol-related cues, the reduction of adaptive metacognitive monitoring) and related metacognitive beliefs should be gathered during the anamnesis process of AUD (Table 9.1). Secondly, the triphasic metacognitive formulation of AUD may be used to guide the development of an idiosyncratic case conceptualization, as well as, to socialize subjects to the idea that metacognitive beliefs and CAS contribute to the persistence of alcohol use. Thirdly in terms of

TABLE 9.1 Assessment of CAS components and metacognitive beliefs associated with AUD.

Constructs	Instruments
Metacognitive beliefs	Metacognitions questionnaire 30 (MCQ – 30) (Wells 2000; Wells & Cartwright-Hatton 2004)
Metacognitive beliefs about alcohol use	Positive alcohol metacognitions scale (PAMS); negative alcohol metacognitions scale (NAMS) (Spada & Wells, 2008)
Metacognitive beliefs about desire thinking	Metacognitions about desire thinking questionnaire (MDTQ; Caselli & Spada, 2013)
CAS	
Desire thinking	Desire thinking questionnaire (DTQ; Caselli & Spada, 2011)
Rumination	Ruminative responses scale (RRS; Nolen-Hoeksema, 1991)
Worry	Penn state worry questionnaire (PSWQ; Meyer, Miller, Metzger, & Borkovec, 1990)
CAS-Alcohol	Cognitive attentional scale – alcohol (CAS-A) (Caselli et al., 2018)

interventions, reducing the propensity to engage in CAS and modifying related metacognitive beliefs should be considered as therapeutic targets for treatment of AUD. This could be achieved through the use of MCT techniques (Wells, 2000; 2009), which allow for gaining flexible control over attention and thinking style, as Detached Mindfulness (Wells, 2000; 2009), Attention Training Technique (ATT) and Situational Attentional Refocusing (SAR) (Wells, 2000; 2009). Finally, on the basis of the significant relationship found between CAS, metacognitive beliefs and alcohol use in nonclinical samples (Hamonniere & Varescon, 2018; Spada et al., 2013), it should be assumed that the early intervention on metacognitive beliefs and the CAS might help to prevent the more severe forms of alcohol abuse.

MCT as a possible treatment for AUD

Although the CBT has been provided valuable insights in the conceptualization and treatment of AUD some limitations are widely noted. These include: (a) the behavioral component of CBT does not elucidate why only a small proportion of individuals who use alcohol end up losing control over their use (Caselli et al., 2018); (b) the cognitive component of CBT does not establish if irrational beliefs play a causal role in the etiology and development of AUD rather than being an epiphenomenon of this condition (Caselli et al., 2018); and (c) treatment effects for CBT appear to diminish over time, especially at 6–9 month follow-up (Magill & Ray, 2009). As argued by Caselli et al. (2018) these weaknesses of CBT may explain its modest effectiveness on the treatment of AUD when compared to other treatment, such as medical management, treatment as usual, or active psychosocial treatments (Anton et al., 2005; Balldin et al., 2003; Burtscheidt, Wolwer, Schwarz, Strauss, & Gaebel, 2002; Farren, Milnes, Lambe, & Ahern, 2014; Litt, Kadden, Cooney, & Kabela, 2003; Project Match Research Group, 1997; Wetzel et al., 2004; Wolwer et al., 2011).

Drawing on the S-REF model (Wells & Matthews, 1994) it has been proposed that a possible reason for CBT's lack of efficacy might be due to residual symptoms and mechanisms that remain present at a metacognitive level (Spada & Wells, 2008; Spada et al., 2015). More in detail, as proposed by Caselli et al. (2018), the modification of the content of biased cognitive beliefs, which is the main focus of CBT, does not directly modify metacognitive beliefs presumed to be driver of maladaptive cognitive processes (e.g. worry, rumination, desire thinking) as implicated in the S-REF model (Wells & Matthews, 1994).

In a recent study Caselli et al. (2018) conducted the first systematic case series aimed at examining the effects associated with a brief course of MCT in a series of patients with AUD. As reported by authors (Caselli et al., 2018) MCT treatment aimed to promote in patients with AUD a controlled or reduced-risk alcohol use. In order to sustain patient engagement, the controlled or reduced-risk alcohol use might be a pragmatic therapeutic goal, given that, in contrast, abstinence as a therapeutic goal may represent a barrier. Moreover, consistent with the metacognitive framework, directly sustaining a controlled drinking goal is more likely to enhance metacognitive control than would be achieved through abstinence because negative metacognitive beliefs about the uncontrollability of behavior and thoughts need to be tested through controlled behavior (i.e. continued and controlled alcohol use) (Caselli et al., 2018). In this study five patients with primary diagnosis of AUD and without borderline personality disorder and substance use comorbidity, physical withdrawal syndrome, severe cognitive deficits, concurrent psychological or pharmacological treatment were enrolled (Caselli et al., 2018). All AUD patients received MCT protocol for AUD and were evaluated at the baseline, at the end of treatment, and at 3- 6 months of follow-up (Caselli et al., 2018). In the forthcoming sub-sections, the MCT protocol for AUD and findings from the systematic case series (Caselli et al., 2018) are described.

The MCT protocol for AUD

The MCT protocol for AUD (Caselli et al., 2018) consists of 12 weekly sessions of 45–60 min duration and followed the core MCT steps (Wells, 2009) adapted to the metacognitive formulation of AUD (Spada et al., 2013) (Table 9.2).

In the first treatment session an idiosyncratic case formulation based on the metacognitive model of AUD is presented. This emphasizes how dysregulation of drinking behavior can be caused by alterations in self-monitoring and negative metacognitive beliefs about uncontrollability. Then, at the end of the first treatment session Adaptive Self-Monitoring (ASM) is introduced as a method to discover the degree of control patients may have over their alcohol use. ASM is an attentional refocusing strategy that involves the orientation of attentional focus toward goal-progress information as it can give appropriate feedback to the cognitive system on when goals are reached, and ongoing drinking behavior can be moderated or stopped; ASM implies focusing on global self and desired goals during alcohol use or simply counting the number of empty glasses on the table. ASM exercises are practiced in session, as well as, as homework.

In the following seven sessions, treatment focuses on the careful identification of which negative metacognitive beliefs about uncontrollability and/or danger are present and on modifying them. The ASM, controlled drinking experiments, and verbal reattribution are used to modify metacognitive beliefs about uncontrollability of alcohol use. Detached mindfulness techniques (Wells, 2009), postponement of perseverative thinking such as rumination, and verbal reattribution are used to modify metacognitive beliefs about uncontrollability of thinking about alcohol use. Detached mindfulness,

TABLE 9.2 The MCT protocol for AUD.

Sessions	Contents
1	Case formulation and socialization.
2–4	Challenge metacognitive beliefs about the uncontrollability of alcohol use and strengthen adaptive self-monitoring. Metacognitively delivered drinking control experiments. Verbal reattribution strategies.
5–6	Challenge metacognitive beliefs about the uncontrollability and dangerousness of thoughts. Detached mindfulness techniques. Metacognitively delivered exposure and response postponement. Verbal reattribution strategies.
7–8	Challenge "alcoholic brain" beliefs. Evidence examination and mini-survey. Verbal reattribution strategies.
9–10	Challenge positive metacognitive beliefs about alcohol use. Verbal reattribution behavioral experiments.
11–12	Relapse prevention.

Adapted from Caselli, G., Martino, F., Spada, M. M., & Wells, A. (2018). Metacognitive therapy for alcohol use disorder: A systematic case series. *Frontiers in Psychology, 9*, 2019.

metacognitive delivered exposure to thoughts relating to alcohol use with response postponement and verbal reattribution are used to modify beliefs about thought-action fusion. Verbal reattribution, especially the examination of evidence and counterevidence, and mini-surveys are used to modify abnormal brain beliefs.

In the two sessions which follow, positive metacognitive beliefs about alcohol use become the focus of treatment; to counteract these beliefs an analysis of evidence and counterevidence is undertaken to reinforce knowledge about how the desired outcomes could be better achieved in other ways and behavioral experiments are applied to test this.

Finally, in the last two sessions the interventions focus on relapse prevention (i.e. the construction of a replacement plan for situations where using alcohol may take place) and the further reappraisal of metacognitive beliefs (i.e. metacognitive beliefs about the meaning of lapses and relapses) (Caselli et al., 2018).

Preliminary evidence of the efficacy of MCT in the treatment of AUD

Preliminary findings, from a systematic case series including five AUD patients, have suggested that following MCT all AUD cases demonstrated clinically meaningful reductions in weekly alcohol use and number of binge drinking episodes that were upheld at 3 and 6 follow-up in almost all patients

(Caselli et al., 2018). Moreover, compared to baseline, a significant decrease in the degree of conviction in metacognitive beliefs, anxiety, craving, and depression levels were found for all patients at post-treatment and at 3 and 6 months follow-up (Caselli et al., 2018).

These findings suggest that MCT seems to be a feasible treatment for AUD as a primary diagnosis, at least with absence of physical withdrawal syndrome, and when controlled drinking is an accepted or desired treatment goal. Nonetheless, further studies of MCT for AUD on larger samples and randomized designs are required to replicate and confirm these findings, as well as, to determine whether this approach is efficacious and it may provide an alternative to existing treatments (Caselli et al., 2018).

Conclusions

The Self-Regulatory Executive Function (S-REF) model (Wells & Matthews, 1994; 1996) of psychopathology might be applied to the conceptualisation and treatment AUD. Metacognitive beliefs may contribute to the initiation, perseveration and maintenance of alcohol use, promoting the engagement on Cognitive Attentional Syndrome (CAS), which in turn might increase the likelihood of using alcohol as a means of cognitive-affective regulation. The triphasic metacognitive formulation of AUD (Spada, Caselli, & Wells, 2013) may be used to guide the development of an idiosyncratic case. Reducing the propensity to engage in CAS as well as the degree of conviction in metacognitive beliefs may be considered therapeutic goals for treatment of AUD. Preliminary findings (Caselli et al., 2018) suggest that MCT might be an efficacious treatment strategy in treating AUD promoting controlled reduced-risk alcohol use.

References

Allen, A., Kannis-Dymand, L., & Katsikitis, M. (2017). Problematic internet pornography use: The role of craving, desire thinking, and metacognition. *Addictive Behaviors*, *70*, 65–71.

Akbari, M. (2017). Metacognitions or distress intolerance: The mediating role in the relationship between emotional dysregulation and problematic internet use. *Addictive Behaviors Reports*, *6*, 128–133.

Anton, R. F., Moak, D. H., Latham, P., Waid, L. R., Myrick, H., Voronin, K., ... Woolson, R. (2005). Naltrexone combined with either cognitive behavioral or motivational enhancement therapy for alcohol dependence. *Journal of Clinical Psychopharmacology*, *25*, 349–357.

Balldin, J., Berglund, M., Borg, S., Mansson, M., Bendtsen, P., Franck, J., ... Willander, A. (2003). A 6-month controlled naltrexone study: Combined effect with cognitive behavioral therapy in outpatient treatment of alcohol dependence. *Alcoholism: Clinical and Experimental Research*, *27*, 1142–1149.

Bandura, A. (1997). *Self-efficacy: The exercise of control*. New York, USA: Freeman.

Beck, A. (1991). *Cognitive therapy and the emotional disorders*. London: Penguin.

Borkovec, T. D. (1994). The nature, functions and origins of worry. In G. C. L. Davey, & F. Tallis (Eds.), *Worrying: Perspectives on theory, assessment and treatment* (pp. 5–33). New York, USA: Wiley.

Brown, S. A., Christiansen, B. A., & Goldman, M. S. (1987). The alcohol expectancy questionnaire: An instrument for the assessment of adolescent and adult expectancies. *Journal of Studies on Alcohol, 48*, 483–491.

Burtscheidt, W., Wolwer, W., Schwarz, R., Strauss, W., & Gaebel, W. (2002). Out-patient behaviour therapy in alcoholism: Treatment outcome after 2 years. *Acta Psychiatrica Scandinavica, 106*, 227–232.

Caselli, G., Bortolai, C., Leoni, M., Rovetto, F., & Spada, M. M. (2008). Rumination in problem drinkers. *Addiction Research & Theory, 16*, 564–571.

Caselli, G., Canfora, F., Ruggiero, G. M., Sassaroli, S., Albery, I. P., & Spada, M. M. (2015). Desire thinking mediates the relationship between emotional intolerance and problem drinking. *International Journal of Mental Health and Addiction, 13*, 185–193.

Caselli, G., Ferla, M., Mezzaluna, C., Rovetto, F., & Spada, M. M. (2012). Desire thinking across the continuum of drinking behavior. *European Addiction Research, 18*, 64–69.

Caselli, G., Ferretti, C., Leoni, M., Rebecchi, D., Rovetto, F., & Spada, M. M. (2010). Rumination as a predictor of drinking behaviour in alcohol abusers: A prospective study. *Addiction, 105*, 1041–1048.

Caselli, G., Gemelli, A., & Spada, M. M. (2017). The experimental manipulation of desire thinking in alcohol use disorder. *Clinical Psychology & Psychotherapy, 24*, 569–573.

Caselli, G., Gemelli, A., Spada, M. M., & Wells, A. (2016). Experimental modification of perspective on thoughts and metacognitive beliefs in alcohol use disorder. *Psychiatry Research, 244*, 57–61.

Caselli, G., Gemelli, A., Querci, S., Lugli, A. M., Canfora, F., Annovi, C., ... Watkins, E. R. (2013). The effect of rumination on craving across the continuum of drinking behaviour. *Addictive Behaviors, 38*, 2879–2883.

Caselli, G., Martino, F., Spada, M. M., & Wells, A. (2018). Metacognitive therapy for alcohol use disorder: A systematic case series. *Frontiers in Psychology, 9*, 2019.

Caselli, G., Soliani, M., & Spada, M. M. (2013). The effect of desire thinking on craving: An experimental design. *Psychology of Addictive Behaviors, 27*, 301–306.

Caselli, G., & Spada, M. M. (2011). The desire thinking questionnaire: Development and psychometric properties. *Addictive Behaviors, 36*, 1061–1067.

Caselli, G., & Spada, M. M. (2013). The metacognitions about desire thinking questionnaire: Development and psychometric properties. *Journal of Clinical Psychology, 69*(12), 1284–1298.

Caselli, G., & Spada, M. M. (2015). Desire thinking: What is it and what drives it? *Addictive Behaviors, 44*, 71–79.

Christiansen, B. A., Smith, G. T., Roehling, P. V., & Goldman, M. S. (1989). Using alcohol expectancies to predict adolescent drinking behavior after one year. *Journal of Consulting and Clinical Psychology, 57*, 93–99.

Dvorak, R., Simons, J., & Wray, T. (2011). Impulsivity moderates the association between depressive rumination and number of quit attempt failures by smokers. *Addiction Research & Theory, 19*(3), 283–288.

Erskine, J. A., Georgiou, G. J., & Kvavilashvili, L. (2010). I suppress, therefore I smoke: Effects of thought suppression on smoking behavior. *Psychological Sciences, 21*, 1225–1230.

Erskine, J. A., Ussher, M., Cropley, M., Elqindi, A., Zman, M., & Corlett, B. (2012). Effect of thought suppression on desire to smoke and tobacco withdrawal symptoms. *Psychopharmacology, 219*, 205–2011.

Farren, C. K., Milnes, J., Lambe, K., & Ahern, S. (2014). Computerised cognitive behavioural therapy for alcohol use disorder: A pilot randomised control trial. *Irish Journal of Psychological Medicine*, *32*, 237–246.

Fernie, B. A., Caselli, G., Giustina, L., Donato, G., Marcotriggiani, A., & Spada, M. M. (2014). Desire thinking as a predictor of gambling. *Addictive Behaviors*, *39*(4), 793–796.

Flavell, J. H. (1979). Metacognition and cognitive monitoring: A new area of cognitive–developmental inquiry. *American Psychologist*, *34*(10), 906–911.

Goldman, M. S., Del Boca, F. K., & Darkes, J. (1999). Alcohol expectancy theory: The application of cognitive neuroscience. In H. Blane, & K. Leonard (Eds.), *Psychological theories of drinking and alcoholism*. New York: Guilford Press.

Goldsmith, A. A., Tran, G. Q., Smith, J. P., & Howe, S. R. (2009). Alcohol expectancies and drinking motives in college drinkers: Mediating effects on the relationship between generalized anxiety and heavy drinking in negative-affect situations. *Addictive Behaviors*, *34*, 505–513.

Hamonniere, T., & Varescon, I. (2018). Metacognitive beliefs in addictive behaviours: A systematic review. *Addictive Behaviors*, *85*, 51–63.

Jauregui, P., Urbiola, I., & Estevez, A. (2016). Metacognition in pathological gambling and its relationship with anxious and depressive symptomatology. *Journal of Gambling Studies*, *32* (2), 675–688.

Kavanagh, D. J., Andrade, J., & May, J. (2004). Beating the urge: Implications of research into substance-related desires. *Addictive Behaviours*, *29*, 1399-1372.

Kavanagh, D. J., Andrade, J., & May, J. (2005). Imaginary relish and exquisite torture: The elaborated intrusion theory of desire. *Psychological Review*, *112*, 446–467.

Kavanagh, D. J., May, J., & Andrade, J. (2009). Tests of the elaborated intrusion theory of craving and desire: Feature of alcohol craving during treatment for an alcohol disorder. *British Journal of Clinical Psychology*, *48*, 241–254.

Krause, K., Bischof, A., Lewin, S., Guertler, D., Rumpf, H.-J., John, U., & Meyer, C. (2018). Explaining the relation between pathological gambling and depression: Rumination as an underlying common cause. *Journal of Behavioral Addictions*, *7*(2), 384–391.

Leigh, B. C. (1989). In search of the seven dwarves: Issues of measurement and meaning in alcohol expectancy research. *Psychological Bulletin*, *105*, 361–373.

Litt, M. D., Kadden, R. M., Cooney, N. L., & Kabela, E. (2003). Coping skills and treatment outcomes in cognitive-behavioral and interactional group therapy for alcoholism. *Journal of Consulting and Clinical Psychology*, *71*, 118–128.

Mansueto, G., Pennelli, M., De Palo, V., Monacis, L., Sinatra, M., & De Caro, M. F. (2016). The role of metacognition in pathological gambling: A mediation model. *Journal of Gambling Studies*, *32*(1), 93–106.

Magill, M., & Ray, L. A. (2009). Cognitive-behavioral treatment with adult alcohol and illicit drug users: A meta-analysis of randomized controlled trials. *Journal of Studies on Alcohol and Drugs*, *70*, 516–527.

Maisto, S. A., Connors, G. J., & Sachs, P. R. (1981). Expectation as a mediator of alcohol intoxication. *Cognitive Therapy and Research*, *5*, 1–18.

Marino, C., Vieno, A., Moss, A. C., Caselli, G., Nikčević, A. V., & Spada, M. M. (2016). Personality, motives and metacognitions as predictors of problematic Facebook use in university students. *Personality and Individual Differences*, *101*, 70–77.

Martino, F., Caselli, G., Felicetti, F., Rampioni, M., Romanelli, P., Troiani, L., ... Spada, M. M. (2017). Desire thinking as a predictor of craving and binge drinking: A longitudinal study. *Addictive Behaviors*, *64*, 118–122.

Meyer, T. J., Miller, M. L., Metzger, R. L., & Borkovec, T. D. (1990). Development and validation of the penn state worry questionnaire. *Behaviour Research and Therapy*, *28*(6), 487–495.

Martino, F., Caselli, G., Fiabane, E., Felicetti, F., Menchetti, M., Mezzaluna, C., Sassaroli, S., Trevisani, C., Albery, I. P., & Spada, M. M. (2019). Desire thinking as a predictor of drinking status following treatment for Alcohol Use Disorder: A prospective study. *Addictive Behaviors*, *95*, 70–76.

Nelson, T. O., Graf, A., Dunlosky, J., Marlatt, A., Walker, D., & Luce, K. (1994). Effect of acute alcohol intoxication on recall and on judgments of learning during the acquisition of new information. In G. Mazzoni, & T. O. Nelson (Eds.), *Metacognition and Cognitive Neuropsychology, Monitoring and Control Processes*. Erlbaum.

Moneta, G. B. (2011). Metacognition, emotion, and alcohol dependence in college students: A moderated mediation model. *Addictive Behaviors*, *36*(7), 781–784.

Nikčević, A. V., Caselli, G., Wells, A., & Spada, M. M. (2015). The metacognitions about smoking questionnaire: Development and psychometric properties. *Addictive Behaviors*, *44*, 102–107.

Nolen-Hoeksema, S. (1991). *Responses to depression questionnaire*. Unpublished manuscript, Department of Psychology, Stanford University.

Nolen-Hoeksema, S., & Morrow, J. (1991). A prospective study of depression and post-traumatic stress symptoms after a natural disaster: The 1989 Loma Prieta earthquake. *Journal of Personality and Social Psychology*, *61*, 115–121.

Normann, N., & Morina, N. (2018). The efficacy of metacognitive therapy: A systematic review and meta-analysis. *Frontiers in Psychology*, *9*, 2211.

Project Match Research Group. (1997). Project MATCH secondary a priori hypotheses. *Addiction*, *92*, 1671–1698.

Riley, B. (2014). Experiential avoidance mediates the association between thought suppression and mindfulness with problem gambling. *Journal of Gambling Studies*, *30*, 163–171.

Sellers, R., Varese, F., Wells, A., & Morrison, A. P. (2017). A meta-analysis of metacognitive beliefs as implicated in the self-regulatory executive function model in clinical psychosis. *Schizophrenia Research*, *179*, 75–84.

Smith, J. P., & Book, S. W. (2010). Comorbidity of generalized anxiety disorder and alcohol use disorders among individuals seeking outpatient substance abuse treatment. *Addictive Behaviors*, *35*, 42–45.

Spada, M. M., & Caselli, G. (2017). The metacognitions about online gaming scale: Development and psychometric properties. *Addictive Behaviors*, *64*, 281–286.

Spada, M. M., Caselli, G., Nikčević, A. V., & Wells, A. (2015). Metacognition in addictive behaviors: An overview. *Addictive Behaviors*, *44*, 9–15.

Spada, M. M., Caselli, G., & Wells, A. (2013). A triphasic metacognitive formulation of problem drinking. *Clinical Psychology & Psychotherapy*, *20*(6), 494–500.

Spada, M. M., Giustina, L., Rolandi, S., Fernie, B. A., & Caselli, G. (2014). Profiling metacognition in gambling disorder. *Behavioural and Cognitive Psychotherapy*, 1–9.

Spada, M. M., Langston, B., Nikčević, A. V., & Moneta, G. B. (2008). The role of metacognitions in problematic internet use. *Computers in Human Behavior*, *24*(5), 2325–2335.

Spada, M. M., Moneta, G. B., & Wells, A. (2007). The relative contribution of metacognitive beliefs and expectancies to drinking behaviour. *Alcohol and Alcoholism*, *42*, 567–574.

Spada, M. M., Nikčević, A. V., Moneta, G. B., & Wells, A. (2007). Metacognition as a mediator of the relationship between emotion and smoking dependence. *Addictive Behaviors*, *32*, 2120–2129.

Spada, M. M., & Wells, A. (2006). Metacognitions about alcohol use in problem drinkers. *Clinical Psychology and Psychotherapy*, *13*, 138–143.

Spada, M. M., & Wells, A. (2008). Metacognitive beliefs about alcohol use: Development and validation of two self-report scales. *Addictive Behaviors*, *33*(4), 515–527.

Spada, M. M., & Wells, A. (2009). A metacognitive model of problem drinking. *Clinical Psychology & Psychotherapy*, *16*, 383–393.

Steele, C. M., & Josephs, R. A. (1990). Alcohol myopia, its prized and dangerous effects. *American Psychologist*, *45*, 921–933.

Sun, X., Zhu, C., & So, S. H. W. (2017). Dysfunctional metacognition across psycho- pathologies: A meta-analytic review. *European Psychiatry*, *45*, 139–153.

Wells, A. (2000). *Emotional disorders and metacognition: Innovative cognitive therapy*. Chichester, UK: Wiley.

Wells, A. (2009). *Metacognitive therapy for anxiety and depression*. New York: Guilford Press.

Wells, A., & Cartwright-Hatton, S. (2004). A short form of the meta-cognitions questionnaire: Properties of the MCQ-30. *Behavior Therapy*, *42*(4), 385–396.

Wells, A., & Matthews, G. (1994). *Attention and emotion. A clinical perspective*. Hove: Erlbaum.

Wells, A., & Matthews, G. (1996). Modelling cognition in emotional disorder: The S-REF model. *Behaviour Research and Therapy*, *34*, 881–888.

Wenzlaff, R. M., & Wegner, D. M. (2000). Thought suppression. *Annual Review of Psychology*, *51*, 59–91.

Wetzel, H., Szegedi, A., Scheurich, A., Lorch, B., Singer, P., Schlafke, D., ... NeVeR Study Group. (2004). Combination treatment with nefazodone and cognitive-behavioral therapy for relapse prevention in alcohol-dependent men: A randomized controlled study. *Journal of Clinical Psychiatry*, *65*, 1406–1413.

Wolwer, W., Frommann, N., Janner, M., Franke, P. E., Scherbaum, N., Lieb, B., ... Gaebel, W. (2011). The effects of combined acamprosate and integrative behaviour therapy in the outpatient treatment of alcohol dependence: A randomized controlled trial. *Drug Alcohol Depend*, *118*, 417–422.

Further reading

Carpenter, K. M., Schreiber, E., Church, S., & McDowell, D. (2006). Drug Stroop performance: Relationships with primary substance of abuse and treatment outcome in a drug-dependent outpatient sample. *Addictive Behaviors*, *31*, 174–181.

Caselli, G., Fernie, B., Canfora, F., Mascolo, C., Ferrari, A., Antonioni, M., ... Spada, M. M. (2018). The metacognitions about gambling questionnaire: Development and psychometric properties. *Psychiatry Research*, *261*, 367–374.

Cox, W. M., Hogan, L. M., Kristian, M. R., & Race, J. H. (2002). Alcohol attentional bias as a predictor of alcohol abusers' treatment outcome. *Drug and Alcohol Dependence*, *68*, 237–243.

Field, M., & Cox, W. M. (2008). Attentional bias in addictive behaviors: A review of its development, causes and consequences. *Drug and Alcohol Dependence*, *97*, 1–20.

Krause, K., Bischof, A., Lewin, S., Guertler, D., Rumpf, H. J., John, U., & Meyer, C. (2018). Explaining the relation between pathological gambling and depression: Rumination as an underlying common cause. *Journal of Behavioral Addictions*, *7*(2), 384–391.

Mogg, K., Field, M., & Bradley, B. P. (2005). Attentional and approach biases for smoking cues in smokers: An investigation of competing theoretical views of addiction. *Psychopharmacology*, *180*, 333–341.

Sharma, D., Albery, I. P., & Cook, C. (2001). Selective attentional bias to alcohol related stimuli in problem drinkers and non-problem drinkers. *Addiction*, *96*, 285–295.

Spada, M. M., Caselli, G., Slaifer, M., Nikčević, A. V., & Sassaroli, S. (2014). Desire thinking as a predictor of problematic internet use. *Social Science Computer Review*, *32*(4), 474–483.

Waters, A. J., Shiffman, S., Bradley, B. P., & Mogg, K. (2003). Attentional shifts to smoking cues in smokers. *Addiction*, *98*, 1409–1417.

Chapter 10

Promoting problem recognition amongst harmful drinkers: A conceptual model for problem framing factors

James Morris[1], Ian P. Albery[1], Antony C. Moss[1] and Nick Heather[2]
[1]Centre for Addictive Behaviours Research, School of Applied Sciences, London South Bank University, United Kingdom, [2]Division of Psychology, Northumbria University, Newcastle upon Tyne, United Kingdom

Introduction

Amid long-running debates over the disease model of addiction, arguably the most important issue in the context of *alcoholism as disease* relates to the question of stigma. Whilst manifesting in many ways, from the public endorsement of negative stereotypes of alcoholics as dangerous and to blame for their condition (Crisp, Gelder, Goddard, & Meltzer, 2005) to the harmful effects of such beliefs turned inwards, i.e., *self-stigma* (Schomerus, Corrigan, et al., 2011), stigma broadly reflects the social devaluation from owning a stigmatized label. Whilst disease model proponents have defended it on account of removing blame from the person as per attribution theory (Kelley & Michela, 1980), the literature points to a more complex picture (Clark, 2020). For instance, whilst disease model attributions may result in less blame, they are also typically found to be associated with an increased desire amongst the public for social distance and intrapersonal negative effects such as less belief in one's ability to recover; i.e., 'prognostic pessimism' (Kvaale, Haslam, & Gottdiener, 2013).

Drinkers who may be judged as alcoholics—at least in certain contexts—are aware of the implications of owning the stigmatized label, and may respond by rejection of its application via *label avoidance* (Corrigan & Wassel, 2008; Glass, Mowbray, Link, Kristjansson, & Bucholz, 2013). A notable driver of label avoidance is awareness of the *social identity threat* of

The Handbook of Alcohol Use - Understandings from Synapse to Society.
DOI: https://doi.org/10.1016/B978-0-12-816720-5.00026-8

being stigmatised by others irrespective of whether one personally agrees with or adopts the stigmatized identity (Schmader & Major, 2017). Alternatively, identifying oneself as an alcoholic may result in a concomitant lack of belief in one's ability to control drinking (Schomerus, Corrigan, et al., 2011), decreased self-worth (Corrigan, Bink, Schmidt, Jones, & Rüsch, 2016) or a belief that giving up alcohol altogether is the only route to recovery (Cunningham, Sobell, & Chow, 1993; Wallhed Finn, Bakshi, & Andréasson, 2014; Witbrodt, Borkman, Stunz, & Subbaraman, 2015). It seems, therefore, that alcoholic label avoidance reflects the active rejection of a problem drinking identity and its stigma-associated consequences (Glass et al., 2013). As such, stigma has been highlighted as the most pervasive barrier to alcohol treatment (May, Nielsen, & Bilberg, 2019; Speerforck, Schomerus, Matschinger, & Angermeyer, 2017), including the specific threat of the alcoholic label (Khadjesari et al., 2018; Schomerus, Lucht, et al., 2011; Wallhed Finn et al., 2014).

Harmful drinkers as an overlooked population

Many debates about the so called 'failure' of problem drinkers to engage in treatment have overlooked a number of important issues (Young, 2011). In particular, *harmful drinkers* (also described as 'higher risk') represent a specific Alcohol Use Disorder (AUD) group whose drinking is, by definition, causing problems (NICE, 2011) but who do not typically exhibit levels of dependence associated with treatment engagement (Dunne et al., 2018). Indeed, despite outnumbering those with more severe levels of dependency by at least 2:1 (Public Health England, 2019), harmful drinkers have been identified as an important drinking group overlooked by both policy, research and interventions (Khadjesari, Stevenson, Godfrey, & Murray, 2015; Morris, Albery, Heather, & Moss, 2020). The need to focus more on this group is reinforced by the fact that alcohol-related problems are especially concentrated in harmful drinking populations (Public Health England, 2016), for example, making up one in five hospital attendees in England (Roberts et al., 2019). Other work has shown that harmful drinkers are identified as a key group for alcohol industry profits (Bhattacharya et al., 2018) and are targeted in a clandestine manner by marketing campaigns (Maani Hessari et al., 2019).

Harmful drinkers do not tend to engage in alcohol treatment for a number of complex reasons, reflecting both reluctance to seek treatment amongst drinkers with lower dependence severity and services largely failing to account for barriers (Innovative Practice in Alcohol Treatment and Recovery, 2016; Wallhed Finn et al., 2014). In addition to low levels of problem recognition and other stigma-based factors (Morris et al., 2020), additional barriers include the inadequate response by primary care physicians for identification (Albery et al., 1997; Dunne et al., 2018; Oyefeso et al., 2008), a preference to undertake change without help (Cunningham, Sobell, Sobell, Agrawal, & Toneatto, 1993; Saunders, Zygowicz, & D'Angelo, 2006; Wallhed Finn et al., 2014), a belief that help is not necessary (Tucker, Vuchinich, & Rippens, 2004) and that other lifestyle factors are of more relevance (Gunstone, Piggot, Butler, Appleton, & Larson, 2018) and, identity-related threats (Chambers, Canvin, Baldwin, & Sinclair, 2017). Also, harmful drinkers may mistakenly believe Alcoholics Anonymous (AA) is the only support option available (Khadjesari et al., 2018) or that recovery requires lifelong abstinence (Sobell & Sobell, 2011; Witbrodt et al., 2015). It seems that harmful drinkers as exist in a 'gray area' between normal drinking and dependent drinking (Khadjesari et al., 2015), which itself reflects the lack of an explanatory framework to describe the continuum of alcohol use and problems (Morris et al., 2020). Periodic calls have therefore been made to "reframe the widely recognized but poorly understood concept of alcoholism" in order to address this issue (Wilson et al., 2013, p. 8).

Problem recognition and 'othering'

Problem recognition reflects the extent to which drinkers evaluate their own alcohol use as problematic either in terms of potential or actual health and social harms or for dependency and control. Problem recognition can be measured by the extent to which those meeting criteria for harmful or dependent drinking self-appraise their severity or susceptibility to such problems (e.g., Agostinelli, Floyd, Grube, Woodall, & Miller, 2004; Glass, Grant, Yoon, & Bucholz, 2015; Morris et al., 2020). In general, harmful drinkers have been identified as having uniquely low problem recognition characterized by the assessment of their level of alcohol-related harms and problems as similar to non-harmful drinkers (Morris et al., 2020), or the downplaying or rejection of risk for future related problems (Gunstone et al., 2018). It seems, therefore, that low problem recognition may be an important barrier to behavior change (Rickwood, Deane, Wilson, & Ciarrochi, 2005; Schomerus et al., 2018),

Problem recognition is, however, reliant on how drinkers themselves determine what constitutes a 'problem', with societal representations and discourses important factors in how people make sense of such problems and determine their responses (Carter, 2013; Entman, 1993). For instance, the framing of alcohol and addiction problems has been found to be relevant for treatment seeking (Burnette, Forsyth, Desmarais, & Hoyt, 2019) and stigma (Ashford, Brown, & Curtis, 2018; Wiens & Walker, 2015), with a broader literature highlighting important implications of biological attributions in mental health (Haslam & Kvaale, 2015; Pescosolido et al., 2010). Other studies have shown that defensive reactions can be heightened when people feel unable to explain their behaviours. In other words, those facing an *explanatory vacuum* (Oettingen, Grant, Smith, Skinner, & Gollwitzer, 2006) are less likely to respond to information in ways that are conducive to behavior change (Nan, Daily, & Qin, 2018). Little is known, however, about the extent to which the public—or harmful drinkers specifically—endorse or rely on disease or other models of alcohol use and problems to make sense of and evaluate their own drinking (Morris et al., 2020; Young, 2011). Nonetheless, broader research points to the ways in which alcohol users make sense of their alcohol use and determine 'what counts' as problem drinking. For instance, drinkers falling into AUD groups appear to discount or reject the validity of recommended consumption guidelines (Bellis & Jones, 2016), instead emphasizing their ability to gauge and set their own personal limits (Lovatt et al., 2015).

Notably, harmful drinkers appear to emphasize control over their drinking and the meeting of personal responsibilities as exempting them from problem drinking status, and instead draw on stereotypes of the *alcoholic other* as the prototypical benchmark (Khadjesari et al., 2018; Morris et al., 2020; Orford, Martin, & Rolfe, 2009; Wallhed Finn et al., 2014). In contrast to the problematized alcoholic other, harmful drinkers strongly emphasize their own positive experiences of and benefits from alcohol use, downplaying or rejecting the relevance of health harms or risks (Garnett et al., 2015; Gunstone et al., 2018; Orford et al., 2009). This process of *othering* has been identified not only within the alcohol literature (Emslie, Hunt, & Lyons, 2012; Khadjesari et al., 2018; Parke et al., 2018), but also in the context of mental health (Walsh & Foster, 2020), drug policy (Taylor, 2016) and a broader range of socio-cultural processes (Powell & Menedian, 2016). Othering is consistent with the process of separation as per stigma theory in which "labeled persons are placed in distinct categories so as to accomplish some degree of separation of 'us' from 'them'" (Link & Phelan, 2001, p. 367). The cognitive and motivational underpinnings of othering amongst harmful drinkers are not well understood, but have been proposed as a mechanism by which harmful drinkers can maintain low problem recognition by drawing on a binary disease model in which alcohol problems either exist or do not (Morris et al., 2020). As such, harmful drinkers define alcohol problems in accordance with the alcoholic other and in turn draw a stark line between the associated alcoholic stereotypes and their own positive, controlled drinking. In contrast, continuum beliefs—implying all alcohol use and problems lie on a spectrum of severity—have been associated with higher problem recognition amongst harmful drinkers based on the assumption that there is no 'us and them' (Morris et al., 2020).

A conceptual model for problem recognition and framing factors

Fig. 10.1 identifies a conceptual model of problem framing factors and effects on problem recognition amongst harmful drinkers. The model assumes problem recognition as an important first step in behavior change amongst harmful drinkers, whether leading to self-help or help-seeking (Cunningham, Sobell, Sobell, et al., 1993; Morris et al., 2020). Crucially, the model proposes that to facilitate problem recognition, threat control responses must be mitigated. Threat control responses reflect a number of processes identified amongst harmful drinkers and other stigmatised groups whereby an identity threat is minimized or deflected to protect the self-concept (Steele, 1988). As discussed previously, a problem drinking identity poses a number of stigma-related threats and has significant implications for the self in terms of accepting or managing an AUD problem. Othering, therefore, serves to exempt the harmful drinker from the threat of a problem drinking identity and its consequences, in turn maintaining low problem recognition. In this way othering may be seen as a specific process of label avoidance whereby rejection of the alcoholic label is rationalized on the basis of distinguishing the harmful drinker's positive drinking identity from the negative stereotypes of the alcoholic other. As such, othering may reflect a more explicit threat control response which may be triggered when a drinker feels the 'need' to outwardly justify their drinking status as non-problematic (Khadjesari et al., 2018; Parke et al., 2018).

In addition to more explicit threat control processes such as othering, a substantial literature identifies defensive processing responses to personally

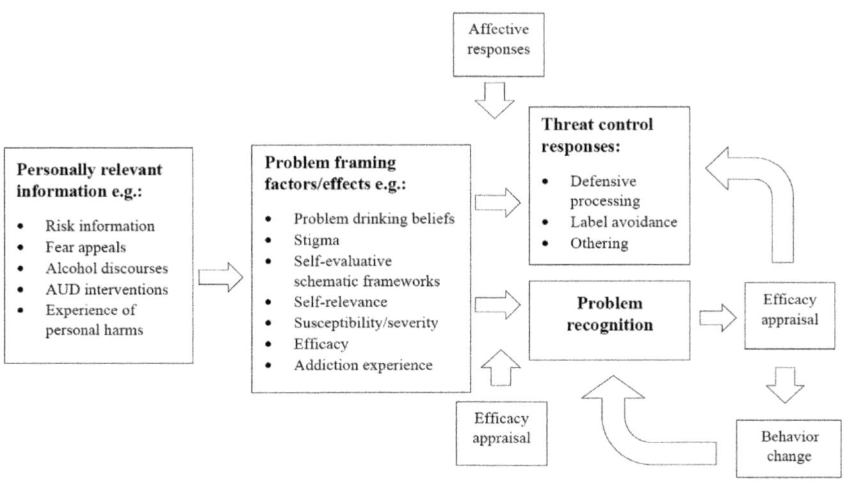

FIGURE 10.1 A conceptual model of problem framing factors and effects on problem recognition for harmful drinkers.

relevant information, particularly in the context of fear appeals attempting to motivate behavior change (Ruiter, Kessels, Peters, & Kok, 2014). Defensive processing broadly reflects cognitive-affective threat control mechanisms such as avoidance, minimization or rejection of relevant information (Yzer, Southwell, & Stephenson, 2012). Such processing has been described as a type of 'attention disengagement process' as commonly seen in response to warnings on tobacco products (e.g., Kessels, Ruiter, Wouters, & Jansma, 2014). A number of studies have identified defensive processing of alcohol-related information, particularly triggered when perceived personal relevance is high, i.e., when drinking at levels that may be judged as problematic in certain contexts (Brown & Locker, 2009; Zhou & Shapiro, 2017). A range of other important mediating or moderating factors for defensive processing have also been proposed including emotional responses (He, 2016) and a range of other dispositional or situational factors, such as self-concept or cultural stereotypes (Nan et al., 2018; Tannenbaum et al., 2015). Emotion-led responses may be particularly important factors in the context of alcohol use, with fear and anxiety identified as key emotions in both the defensive processing literature (So, Kuang, & Cho, 2016) and alcohol studies (Dar-Nimrod, Zuckerman, & Duberstein, 2013).

The proposed model shares conceptual affinity with the Common Sense Model (CSM) of self-regulation (Leventhal & Meyer, 1980) and the Extended Parallel Process Model (EPPM; Tannenbaum et al., 2015; Witte, 1992). That is, as per the CSM, responses of threat control versus problem recognition may be predicted based upon individual-level beliefs or representations about the issue (i.e., alcohol problems). As per the EPPM, efficacy-related beliefs are of particular significance in predicting defensive processing responses. In the proposed model, a number of key framing factors and effects are proposed based on prior research of parallel process models and harmful drinking/addiction findings (e.g., Burnette et al., 2019; Schomerus, Corrigan, et al., 2011; Wiens & Walker, 2015). For example, as per Morris et al. (2020), framing beliefs about problem drinking as a continuum served to enhance problem recognition amongst harmful drinkers compared to control or a binary disease model framed condition. Thus, continuum beliefs appeared to attenuate threat control responses which enable a more accurate and explicit problem recognition appraisal. In this example, addiction experience (such as identifying personal experience or contact with people perceived to have addiction) was found to be a moderating factor, such that those with self-identified addiction experience may already have acknowledged their drinking as problematic or have held stronger pre-existing views about the nature of alcohol problems.

We argued that cognitive and affective representations about alcohol problems have important implications for problem recognition evaluations, particularly in terms of possible implications for perceived severity and/or controllability (Hagger & Orbell, 2003). For instance, under a disease model, 'alcoholism' is perceived as lifelong chronic 'suffering' for which abstinence is the only solution (Miller & Kurtz, 1994; Walters, 2002). This has largely been attributed to the popularity of Alcoholics Anonymous (AA; Flanagan, 2017; Walters, 2002) in which the first of the twelve steps requires one to admit to being "powerless over alcohol" (Alcoholics Anonymous, 2001). Appraising alcohol problems as uncontrollable may lead to lower self-efficacy, a key predictor of threat control responses according to the EPPM (Witte, 1992). Efficacy enhancement has therefore been identified as a crucial component of efforts to motivate behavior change which are certain to result in defensive processing if one lacks belief in their ability to change (Kok, Peters, Kessels, ten Hoor, & Ruiter, 2018; Ruiter et al., 2014). This implies, that to increase the chances of problem recognition, harmful drinkers who actively disassociate themselves from the alcoholic other must believe that problem drinking does not only entail having a disease to which one is powerless over.

As per the Identity-Value Model (Berkman, Livingson, & Kahn, 2017), identity related threats are viewed as particularly important in the context of behavioral self-regulation. Harmful drinkers who place higher positive value on their drinking identity may be more motivated to deflect personally relevant information (Zhou & Shapiro, 2017), particularly when the implication is lifelong abstinence, which in turn reduces the likelihood of problem recognition. For instance, harmful drinkers place significant positive value on the role of alcohol use, particularly relating to social contexts but also for coping, stress management and relaxation (Orford et al., 2009; Parke et al., 2018). As such, problem recognition not only entails the significant threats of stigma, but also the implied requirement of relinquishing their drinking; something highly valued in the context of multiple self-relevant domains including social roles, values, groups and relationships (Sherman & Hartson, 2011). It is these 'adjustments' that may be of particular significance in understanding how identities transition in recovery processes and how such transitions result in longer term change (Best et al., 2016; Frings & Albery 2015, 2016; Frings, Wood, Lionetti, & Albery, 2019). The identity threat posed by mental illness labels has been identified as triggering *identity deflection* as a similar self-protective mechanism (Thoits, 2016). Notably, Thoits (2016) found those with fewer social role identities where more motivated to deflect a mental illness label, further pointing to the protection of the self-concept as a key driver for label avoidance. Indeed, those who deflected a mental illness label reported higher psychological wellbeing even when severity of mental health problems was controlled for.

In summary, harmful drinkers are highly susceptible to the threat to the self-concept from a problem drinking identity, and are highly motivated to maintain low problem recognition via threat control responses both implicitly (e.g., defensive processing) and explicitly for the self (e.g., "I'm not an alcoholic"). Indeed, the threats of a problem drinking identity are acutely present in mainstream narratives around alcohol problems, particularly via the stigma of the alcoholic label (Ashford et al., 2018) as embedded within the disease model of alcohol problems. Harmful drinkers appear to utilize defensive processing responses as a psychological self-protection mechanism to mitigate the fear and anxiety posed by a problem drinking identity (Dar-Nimrod et al., 2013). When facing potential social identity threat from being judged as a potential problem drinker, harmful drinkers seek to ensure that it is not heavy drinking *per se* that defines an alcohol problem, but social transgressions relating to behavior and a failure to adhere to one's responsibilities (Khadjesari et al., 2018; Parke et al., 2018; Schomerus, Lucht, et al., 2011). It seems, therefore, that problem recognition is reliant on providing a self-evaluative process in which multiple threats to the self-concept are mitigated. Thus, the presented model offers a framework for identifying how key problem framing factors refract personally relevant information, in turn shaping problem recognition and subsequent behavioral outcomes.

Real world implications for framing effects and problem recognition

In the proposed model, framing effects may be crucial moderators of behavioral outcomes amongst harmful drinkers, either in terms of maintaining harmful drinking or increasing the likelihood of problem recognition as a crucial first step (Rickwood et al., 2005; Schomerus et al., 2018). Such framing effects may be seen to operate at multiple levels, from that which operates as the broader alcohol discourse through to individual level sense making and interventions. For example, a harmful drinker being informed by their doctor that their consumption levels may be deemed problematic may receive the information framed in a number of ways. As per alcohol brief intervention approaches, such information should be delivered in such a manner that objectively orientates higher levels of consumption as a risk factor for a range of conditions, and with a motivational emphasis on the benefits of reduction, conveyed in a non-confrontational manner. Despite questions over the fidelity of their real world application and effectiveness (McCambridge & Saitz, 2017; O'Donnell et al., 2019), such approaches have been associated with significant reductions in alcohol use in multiple research trials (NICE, 2010), likely mediated by increases in problem recognition. In contrast to such motivationally orientated behavior change techniques, a doctor may simply state that the person "has an alcohol problem", which would likely trigger the patient's own representations of problem drinking, and a semantic interpretation that they are an 'alcoholic'. This will then trigger a defensive, emotion-led response (Dar-Nimrod et al., 2013; Khadjesari et al., 2018).

Separating individual level framing effects from the wider context of alcohol use discourses, however, may be an imprudent task. Individual's sense making draws upon a cultural stock of representations, whereby media representations and common discourses of alcohol use and problems may, for instance, shape associated schemas, categories and stereotypes that "guide individual's processing of information" (Entman, 1993, p. 53). As such, individually targeted interventions will need to work against the cognitive tide when incongruent with broader representations and discourses (Haslam & Kvaale, 2015). Further, persuasion literature highlights the limitations of statistical information (Braddock & Dillard, 2016; Zillmann, 1999), such that objectively highlighting health risks to harmful drinkers may be futile when stigma and identity-related consequences are more salient. However, personal contact has been highlighted as a promising anti-stigma strategy (Corrigan & Wassel, 2008), operating to reduce perceived difference and allaying fear and anxiety led responses to issues such as mental health or addiction problems (Corrigan, Schmidt, et al., 2016; Pettigrew & Tropp, 2008). As such, the use of first person language has been called upon as a key addiction anti-stigma strategy (Hartwell et al., 2020), alongside communicating prognostic optimism, sharing humanizing narratives, and an emphasis on societal rather than individual causes of addiction problems (McGinty & Barry, 2020). Broadly, these strategies may be seen as representative of problem framing factors in the presented conceptual model. That is, framing problems in ways which may reduce stigma, othering, implications of severity and uncontrollability may reduce the threat of problem recognition and thus mitigate the motivation for threat control.

Conclusion

Harmful drinkers are an important AUD group who have been identified as existing in a gray area between 'normal' drinkers and 'alcoholics' as reflective of a commonly enacted false categorization between non-problem versus problem drinkers. This culturally held explanatory vacuum about the continuum of alcohol use and problems is particularly relevant to harmful drinkers who are aware of multiple threats of a problem drinking identity. Notably, stigma persists as a major barrier to alcohol problem recognition and help-seeking, particularly via the social identity threat of the alcoholic label. Harmful drinkers, however, are able and motivated to make a legitimate case for not qualifying as 'alcoholics'. This is primarily achieved by emphasizing their ability to function and perform responsibilities, and as such not experiencing loss of control over their drinking as per common representations of problem drinking. To protect their existing positive drinking identity, harmful drinkers actively reinforce the artificial dividing line between non-problem and problem drinkers by reifying the alcoholic other. In turn, harmful drinkers increase stigma by perpetrating negative stereotypes and separation of the alcoholic outgroup in a bid to protect their own 'non-alcoholic' drinking practices as culturally sanctioned. In this way, harmful drinkers are able to protect the self from the multiple threats of a problem drinking identity and its implications (e.g., lifelong abstinence), as reflected by maintenance of low problem recognition. As such, it is not until the arrival of unequivocal and serious health-related consequences that many heavy drinkers are prompted into change (Adamson, Sellman, & Frampton, 2009; Rohn et al., 2017).

Heightening problem recognition before the onset of tangible health consequences represents an important and under-utilized public health opportunity. The presented conceptual model proposes that such an outcome is dependent on attenuating threat control responses such that relevant information is not dismissed, avoided or manipulated to sustain existing defensive processes. For example, representing alcohol use and problems as a continuum has shown promise in heightening problem recognition via a self-evaluative framework in which the counter-productive stigma and behavioral implications of the alcoholic label are circumvented, and a more logical 'shades of gray' schematic is invoked (Morris et al., 2020). Further work is needed to explore how the mechanisms behind continuum and other aligned models may work to enhance problem recognition, and most importantly, prompt subsequent behavior change.

References

Adamson, S. J., Sellman, J. D., & Frampton, C. M. A. (2009). Patient predictors of alcohol treatment outcome: A systematic review. *Journal of Substance Abuse Treatment*, *36*(1), 75–86. Available from https://doi.org/10.1016/j.jsat.2008.05.007.

Agostinelli, G., Floyd, T. E., Grube, J. W., Woodall, G., & Miller, J. H. (2004). Alcohol problem recognition as a function of own and others' perceived drinking. *Addictive Behaviors*, *29*(1), 143–157. Available from https://doi.org/10.1016/S0306-4603(03)00078-9.

Albery, I. P., Durand, M. A., Heuston, J., Groves, P., Gossop, M., & Strang, J. (1997). Training primary health care staff about alcohol: A study of alcohol trainers in the UK. *Drugs: Education, Prevention and Policy*, *4*(2), 173–186. Available from https://doi.org/10.3109/09687639709017414.

Alcoholics Anonymous. (2001). *Alcoholics Anonymous: The story of how many thousands of men and women have recovered from alcoholism* (4th ed.), Alcoholics Anonymous World Services.

Ashford, R. D., Brown, A. M., & Curtis, B. (2018). Substance use, recovery, and linguistics: The impact of word choice on explicit and implicit bias. *Drug and Alcohol Dependence*, *189*, 131–138. Available from https://doi.org/10.1016/j.drugalcdep.2018.05.005.

Bellis, M., & Jones, L. (2016). *CMO alcohol guidelines review – A summary of the evidence of the health and social impacts of alcohol consumption*. Retrieved from http://www.cph.org.uk/publication/cmo-alcohol-guidelines-review-a-summary-of-the-evidence-of-the-health-and-social-impacts-of-alcohol-consumption/.

Berkman, E., Livingson, J. L., & Kahn, L. E. (2017). Finding the "self" in self-regulation: The identity-value model. *Psychological Inquiry*, *28*(2–3), 76–98. Available from https://doi.org/10.1080/1047840X.2017.1323463.

Best, D., Beckwith, M., Haslam, C., Alexander Haslam, S., Jetten, J., Mawson, E., & Lubman, D. I. (2016). *Overcoming alcohol and other drug addiction as a process of social identity transition: The social identity model of recovery (SIMOR). Addiction Research and Theory*. Taylor & Francis. Available from https://doi.org/10.3109/16066359.2015.1075980.

Bhattacharya, A., Angus, C., Pryce, R., Holmes, J., Brennan, A., & Meier, P. S. (2018). How dependent is the alcohol industry on heavy drinking in England? *Addiction*, *113*(12), 2225–2232. Available from https://doi.org/10.1111/add.14386.

Braddock, K., & Dillard, J. P. (2016). Meta-analytic evidence for the persuasive effect of narratives on beliefs, attitudes, intentions, and behaviors. *Communication Monographs*, *83*(4), 446–467. Available from https://doi.org/10.1080/03637751.2015.1128555.

Brown, S. L., & Locker, E. (2009). Defensive responses to an emotive anti-alcohol message. *Psychology and Health*, *24*(5), 517–528. Available from https://doi.org/10.1080/08870440801911130.

Burnette, J. L., Forsyth, R. B., Desmarais, S. L., & Hoyt, C. L. (2019). Mindsets of addiction: Implications for treatment intentions. *Journal of Social and Clinical Psychology*, *38*(5), 367–394. Available from https://doi.org/10.1521/jscp.2019.38.5.367.

Carter, M. J. (2013). The hermeneutics of frames and framing: An examination of the media's construction of reality. *SAGE Open*, *3*(2), 1–12. Available from https://doi.org/10.1177/2158244013487915.

Chambers, S. E., Canvin, K., Baldwin, D. S., & Sinclair, J. M. A. A. (2017). Identity in recovery from problematic alcohol use: A qualitative study of online mutual aid. *Drug and Alcohol Dependence*, *174*, 17–22. Available from https://doi.org/10.1016/j.drugalcdep.2017.01.009.

Clark, T. W. (2020). Determinism and destigmatization: Mitigating blame for addiction. *Neuroethics*, 1–12. Available from https://doi.org/10.1007/s12152-020-09440-w.

Corrigan, P. W., Bink, A. B., Schmidt, A., Jones, N., & Rüsch, N. (2016). What is the impact of self-stigma? Loss of self-respect and the "why try" effect. *Journal of Mental Health*, *25*(1), 10–15. Available from https://doi.org/10.3109/09638237.2015.1021902.

Corrigan, P. W., Schmidt, A., Bink, A. B., Nieweglowski, K., Al-Khouja, M. A., Qin, S., & Discont, S. (2016). Changing public stigma with continuum beliefs. *Journal of Mental Health*, 1–8. Available from https://doi.org/10.1080/09638237.2016.1207224.

Corrigan, P. W., & Wassel, A. (2008). Understanding and influencing the stigma of mental illness. *Journal of Psychosocial Nursing and Mental Health Services*, Slack Incorporated. Available from https://doi.org/10.3928/02793695-20080101-04.

Crisp, A., Gelder, M., Goddard, E., & Meltzer, H. (2005). Stigmatization of people with mental illnesses: A follow-up study within the Changing Minds campaign of the Royal College of Psychiatrists. *World Psychiatry: Official Journal of the World Psychiatric Association (WPA)*, *4*(2), 106–113, Retrieved from. Available from http://www.ncbi.nlm.nih.gov/pubmed/16633526.

Cunningham, J. A., Sobell, L. C., & Chow, V. (1993). What's in a label? The effects of substance types and labels on treatment considerations and stigma. *Journal of Studies on Alcohol*, Retrieved from. Available from http://www.jsad.com/doi/abs/10.15288/jsa.1993.54.693.

Cunningham, J. A., Sobell, L. C., Sobell, M. B., Agrawal, S., & Toneatto, T. (1993). Barriers to treatment: Why alcohol and drug abusers delay or never seek treatment. *Addictive Behaviors*, *18*(3), 347–353. Available from https://doi.org/10.1016/0306-4603(93)90036-9.

Dar-Nimrod, I., Zuckerman, M., & Duberstein, P. R. (2013). The effects of learning about one's own genetic susceptibility to alcoholism: A randomized experiment. *Genetics in Medicine*, *15*(2), 132–138. Available from https://doi.org/10.1038/gim.2012.111.

Dunne, J., Kimergård, A., Brown, J., Beard, E., Buykx, P., Michie, S., & Drummond, C. (2018). Attempts to reduce alcohol intake and treatment needs among people with probable alcohol dependence in England: A general population survey. *Addiction, 113*(8), 1430–1438. Available from https://doi.org/10.1111/add.14221.

Emslie, C., Hunt, K., & Lyons, A. (2012). Older and wiser? Men's and women's accounts of drinking in early mid-life. *Sociology of Health and Illness, 34*(4), 481–496. Available from https://doi.org/10.1111/j.1467-9566.2011.01424.x.

Entman, R. M. (1993). Framing: Toward clarification of a fractured paradigm. *Journal of Communication, 43*(4), 51–58. Available from https://doi.org/10.1111/j.1460-2466.1993.tb01304.x.

Flanagan, O. (2017). Addiction doesn't exist, but it is bad for you. *Neuroethics, 10*(1), 91–98. Available from https://doi.org/10.1007/s12152-016-9298-z.

Frings, D., & Albery, I. P. (2016). The social identity model of cessation maintenance. In S. Buckingham, & D. Best (Eds.), *Addiction, behavioural change and social identity*. London: Taylor & Francis.

Frings, D., & Albery, I. P. I. P. (2015). The social identity model of cessation maintenance: Formulation and initial evidence. *Addictive Behaviors, 44*, 35–42. Available from https://doi.org/10.1016/j.addbeh.2014.10.023.

Frings, D., Wood, K. V., Lionetti, N., & Albery, I. P. (2019). Tales of hope: Social identity and learning lessons from others in Alcoholics Anonymous: A test of the Social Identity Model of Cessation Maintenance. *Addictive Behaviors, 93*, 204–211. Available from https://doi.org/10.1016/j.addbeh.2019.02.004.

Garnett, C., Crane, D., West, R., Michie, S., Brown, J., & Winstock, A. (2015). Normative misperceptions about alcohol use in the general population of drinkers: A cross-sectional survey. *Addictive Behaviors, 42*, 203–206. Available from https://doi.org/10.1016/j.addbeh.2014.11.010.

Glass, J. E., Grant, J. D., Yoon, H. Y., & Bucholz, K. K. (2015). Alcohol problem recognition and help seeking in adolescents and young adults at varying genetic and environmental risk. *Drug and Alcohol Dependence, 153*, 250–257. Available from https://doi.org/10.1016/j.drugalcdep.2015.05.006.

Glass, J. E., Mowbray, O. P., Link, B. G., Kristjansson, S. D., & Bucholz, K. K. (2013). Alcohol stigma and persistence of alcohol and other psychiatric disorders: A modified labeling theory approach. *Drug and Alcohol Dependence, 133*(2), 685. Available from https://doi.org/10.1016/j.drugalcdep.2013.08.016.

Gunstone, B., Piggot, L., Butler, B., Appleton, A., & Larson, J. (2018). *Drinkaware monitor 2018: Drinking behaviour and moderation*. Retrieved from https://www.drinkaware.co.uk/research/our-research-and-evaluation-reports/drinkaware-monitor-2018-drinking-behaviour-and-moderation/.

Hagger, M. S., & Orbell, S. (2003). A meta-analytic review of the common-sense model of illness representations. *Psychology and Health*. Available from https://doi.org/10.1080/0887044031000081321.

Hartwell, M., Naberhaus, B., Arnhart, C., Ottwell, R., Dunn, K., Rogers, T. C., ... Beaman, J. (2020). The use of person-centered language in scientific research articles focusing on alcohol use disorder. *Drug and Alcohol Dependence, 216*, 108209. Available from https://doi.org/10.1016/j.drugalcdep.2020.108209.

Haslam, N., & Kvaale, E. P. (2015). Biogenetic explanations of mental disorder: The mixed-blessings model. *Current Directions in Psychological Science, 24*(5), 399–404. Available from https://doi.org/10.1177/0963721415588082.

He, X. (2016). *The impact of self-affirmation on defensive processing of health messages: A meta-analysis* (ProQuest dissertations and theses). Retrieved from http://conservancy.umn.edu/handle/11299/181738.

Innovative Practice in Alcohol Treatment and Recovery. (2016). Retrieved from http://www.recovery-partnership.org/uploads/5/1/8/2/51822429/alcohol___innovation_briefing_-_recovery_partnership.pdf.

Kelley, H. H., & Michela, J. L. (1980). Attribution theory and research. *Annual Review of Psychology, 31*(1), 457–501. Available from https://doi.org/10.1146/annurev.ps.31.020180.002325.

Kessels, L. T. E., Ruiter, R. A. C., Wouters, L., & Jansma, B. M. (2014). Neuroscientific evidence for defensive avoidance of fear appeals. *International Journal of Psychology, 49*(2), 80–88. Available from https://doi.org/10.1002/ijop.12036.

Khadjesari, Z., Stevenson, F., Godfrey, C., & Murray, E. (2015). Negotiating the "grey area between normal social drinking and being a smelly tramp": A qualitative study of people searching for help online to reduce their drinking. *Health Expectations, 18*(6), 2011–2020. Available from https://doi.org/10.1111/hex.12351.

Khadjesari, Z., Stevenson, F., Toner, P., Linke, S., Milward, J., & Murray, E. (2018). 'I'm not a real boozer': A qualitative study of primary care patients' views on drinking and its consequences. *Journal of Public Health.* Available from https://doi.org/10.1093/pubmed/fdy067.

Kok, G., Peters, G. J. Y., Kessels, L. T. E., ten Hoor, G. A., & Ruiter, R. A. C. (2018). Ignoring theory and misinterpreting evidence: The false belief in fear appeals. *Health Psychology Review, 12*(2), 111–125. Available from https://doi.org/10.1080/17437199.2017.1415767.

Kvaale, E. P., Haslam, N., & Gottdiener, W. H. (2013). The "side effects" of medicalization: A meta-analytic review of how biogenetic explanations affect stigma. *Clinical Psychology Review.* Available from https://doi.org/10.1016/j.cpr.2013.06.002.

Leventhal, H., & Meyer, D. (1980). *The common sense representation of illness danger* (Vol. 2, pp. 7–30). New York: Pergamon (Medical Psychology). Retrieved from. Available from https://scholar.google.co.uk/scholar?hl = en&as_sdt = 0%2C5&q = Leventhal%2C + Meyer + and + Nerenz + %281980%29&btnG = .

Link, B. G., & Phelan, J. C. (2001). Conceptualizing stigma. *Annual Review of Sociology, 27*(1), 363–385. Available from https://doi.org/10.1146/annurev.soc.27.1.363.

Lovatt, M., Eadie, D., Meier, P. S., Li, J., Bauld, L., Hastings, G., & Holmes, J. (2015). Lay epidemiology and the interpretation of low-risk drinking guidelines by adults in the United Kingdom. *Addiction, 110*(12), 1912–1919. Available from https://doi.org/10.1111/add.13072.

Maani Hessari, N., Bertscher, A., Critchlow, N., Fitzgerald, N., Knai, C., Stead, M., & Petticrew, M. (2019). Recruiting the "Heavy-Using Loyalists of Tomorrow": An analysis of the aims, effects and mechanisms of alcohol advertising, based on advertising industry evaluations. *International Journal of Environmental Research and Public Health, 16*(21), 4092. Available from https://doi.org/10.3390/ijerph16214092.

May, C., Nielsen, A. S., & Bilberg, R. (2019). Barriers to treatment for alcohol dependence. *Journal of Drug and Alcohol Research.* Available from https://doi.org/10.4303/jdar/236083.

McCambridge, J., & Saitz, R. (2017). Rethinking brief interventions for alcohol in general practice. *BMJ (Online)*, 356. Available from https://doi.org/10.1136/bmj.j116.

McGinty, E. E., & Barry, C. L. (2020). Stigma reduction to combat the addiction crisis — Developing an evidence base. *New England Journal of Medicine, 382*(14), 1291–1292. Available from https://doi.org/10.1056/NEJMp2000227.

Miller, W. R., & Kurtz, E. (1994). Models of alcoholism used in treatment: Contrasting AA and other perspectives with which it is often confused. *Journal of Studies on Alcohol, 55*(2), 159–166. Available from https://doi.org/10.15288/jsa.1994.55.159.

Morris, J., Albery, I. P., Heather, N., & Moss, A. C. (2020). Continuum beliefs are associated with higher problem recognition than binary beliefs among harmful drinkers without addiction experience. *Addictive Behaviors, 105*, 106292. Available from https://doi.org/10.1016/j.addbeh.2020.106292.

Nan, X., Daily, K., & Qin, Y. (2018). Relative persuasiveness of gain-vs. loss-framed messages: A review of theoretical perspectives and developing an integrative framework. *Review of Communication*. Available from https://doi.org/10.1080/15358593.2018.1519845.

NICE. (2010). *Alcohol-use disorders: Prevention [PH24]*. Retrieved from https://www.nice.org.uk/guidance/ph24/chapter/Introduction.

NICE. (2011). *Alcohol-use disorders: Diagnosis, assessment and management of harmful drinking and alcohol dependence [CG115]*. The British Psychological Society and The Royal College of Psychiatrists. Retrieved from https://www.nice.org.uk/guidance/cg115/evidence.

O'Donnell, A., Angus, C., Hanratty, B., Hamilton, F. L., Petersen, I., & Kaner, E. (2019). Impact of the introduction and withdrawal of financial incentives on the delivery of alcohol screening and brief advice in English primary health care: An interrupted time−series analysis. *Addiction*. Available from https://doi.org/10.1111/add.14778.

Oettingen, G., Grant, H., Smith, P. K., Skinner, M., & Gollwitzer, P. M. (2006). Nonconscious goal pursuit: Acting in an explanatory vacuum. *Journal of Experimental Social Psychology, 42*(5), 668−675. Available from https://doi.org/10.1016/j.jesp.2005.10.003.

Orford, J., Martin, O., & Rolfe, A. (2009). *Birmingham untreated heavy drinkers project*.

Oyefeso, A., Deluca, P., Drummond, C., Cheeta, S., Perryman, K., Coulton, S., & Phillips, T. (2008). Low identification of alcohol use disorders in general practice in England. *Addiction, 103*(5), 766−773. Available from https://doi.org/10.1111/j.1360-0443.2008.02198.x.

Parke, H., Michalska, M., Russell, A., Moss, A. C., Holdsworth, C., Ling, J., & Larsen, J. (2018). Understanding drinking among midlife men in the United Kingdom: A systematic review of qualitative studies. *Addictive Behaviors Reports, 8*, 85−94. Available from https://doi.org/10.1016/J.ABREP.2018.08.001.

Pescosolido, B. A., Martin, J. K., Long, J. S., Medina, T. R., Phelan, J. C., & Link, B. G. (2010). "A disease like any other"? A decade of change in public reactions to schizophrenia, depression, and alcohol dependence. *American Journal of Psychiatry, 167*(11), 1321−1330. Available from https://doi.org/10.1176/appi.ajp.2010.09121743.

Pettigrew, T. F., & Tropp, L. R. (2008). How does intergroup contact reduce prejudice? Meta-analytic tests of three mediatorsy. *European Journal of Social Psychology, 38*(6), 922−934. Available from https://doi.org/10.1002/ejsp.504.

Powell, J. A., & Menedian, S. (2016). The problem of othering: Towards inclusiveness and belonging. *Othering and Belonging* (1), 14−39, Retrieved from. Available from http://www.otheringandbelonging.org/the-problem-of-othering/.

Public Health England. (2016). *The public health burden of alcohol and the effectiveness and cost-effectiveness of alcohol control policies: An evidence review*. Retrieved from https://www.gov.uk/government/publications/the-public-health-burden-of-alcohol-evidence-review.

Public Health England. (2019). *Health matters: Identifying and offering brief advice to tobacco and alcohol users*. Retrieved September 5, 2019, from https://publichealthmatters.blog.gov.uk/2019/03/21/health-matters-identifying-and-offering-brief-advice-to-tobacco-and-alcohol-users/.

Rickwood, D., Deane, F. P., Wilson, C. J., & Ciarrochi, J. (2005). Young people's help-seeking for mental health problems. *Australian E-Journal for the Advancement of Mental Health, 4*(3), 218−251. Available from https://doi.org/10.5172/jamh.4.3.218.

Roberts, E., Morse, R., Epstein, S., Hotopf, M., Leon, D., & Drummond, C. (2019). The prevalence of wholly attributable alcohol conditions in the United Kingdom hospital system:

A systematic review, meta-analysis and meta-regression. *Addiction*. Available from https://doi.org/10.1111/add.14642.

Rohn, M. C. H., Lee, M. R., Kleuter, S. B., Schwandt, M. L., Falk, D. E., & Leggio, L. (2017). Differences between treatment-seeking and nontreatment-seeking alcohol-dependent research participants: An exploratory analysis. *Alcoholism: Clinical and Experimental Research, 41*(2), 414–420. Available from https://doi.org/10.1111/acer.13304.

Ruiter, R. A. C., Kessels, L. T. E., Peters, G. Y., & Kok, G. (2014). Sixty years of fear appeal research: Current state of the evidence. *International Journal of Psychology, 49*(2), 63–70. Available from https://doi.org/10.1002/ijop.12042.

Saunders, S. M., Zygowicz, K. M., & D'Angelo, B. R. (2006). Person-related and treatment-related barriers to alcohol treatment. *Journal of Substance Abuse Treatment, 30*(3), 261–270. Available from https://doi.org/10.1016/j.jsat.2006.01.003.

Schmader, T., & Major, B. (2017). Stigma, social identity threat, and health. In B. Major, J. F. Dovidio, & B. G. Link (Eds.), *The Oxford Handbook of Stigma, Discrimination, and Health* (Vol. 1, pp. 85–103). Oxford University Press. Available from https://doi.org/10.1093/oxfordhb/9780190243470.013.3.

Schomerus, G., Corrigan, P. W., Klauer, T., Kuwert, P., Freyberger, H. J., & Lucht, M. (2011). Self-stigma in alcohol dependence: Consequences for drinking-refusal self-efficacy. *Drug and Alcohol Dependence, 114*(1), 12–17. Available from https://doi.org/10.1016/j.drugalcdep.2010.08.013.

Schomerus, G., Lucht, M., Holzinger, A., Matschinger, H., Carta, M. G., & Angermeyer, M. C. (2011). The stigma of alcohol dependence compared with other mental disorders: A review of population studies. *Alcohol and Alcoholism, 46*(2), Retrieved from. Available from https://academic.oup.com/alcalc/article/46/2/105/198339.

Schomerus, G., Stolzenburg, S., Freitag, S., Speerforck, S., Janowitz, D., Evans-Lacko, S., … Schmidt, S. (2018). Stigma as a barrier to recognizing personal mental illness and seeking help: A prospective study among untreated persons with mental illness. *European Archives of Psychiatry and Clinical Neuroscience*, 1–11. Available from https://doi.org/10.1007/s00406-018-0896-0.

Sherman, D. K., & Hartson, K. A. (2011). Reconciling self-protection with self-improvement self-affirmation theory. In M. D. Alicke, & C. Sedikides (Eds.), *Handbook of self-enhancement and self-protection*. Guilford Press.

So, J., Kuang, K., & Cho, H. (2016). Reexamining fear appeal models from cognitive appraisal theory and functional emotion theory perspectives. *Communication Monographs, 83*(1), 120–144. Available from https://doi.org/10.1080/03637751.2015.1044257.

Sobell, M. B., & Sobell, L. C. (2011). It is time for low-risk drinking goals to come out of the closet. *Addiction, 106*(10), 1715–1717. Available from https://doi.org/10.1111/j.1360-0443.2011.03509.x.

Speerforck, S., Schomerus, G., Matschinger, H., & Angermeyer, M. C. (2017). Treatment recommendations for schizophrenia, major depression and alcohol dependence and stigmatizing attitudes of the public: Results from a German population survey. *European Archives of Psychiatry and Clinical Neuroscience, 267*(4), 341–350. Available from https://doi.org/10.1007/s00406-016-0755-9.

Steele, C. M. (1988). The psychology of self-affirmation: Sustaining the integrity of the self. *21 Advances in Experimental Social Psychology*. Available from https://doi.org/10.1016/S0065-2601(08)60229-4.

Tannenbaum, M. B., Hepler, J., Zimmerman, R. S., Saul, L., Jacobs, S., Wilson, K., & Albarracín, D. (2015). Appealing to fear: A meta-analysis of fear appeal effectiveness and theories. *Psychological Bulletin, 141*(6), 1178–1204. Available from https://doi.org/10.1037/a0039729.

Taylor, S. (2016). Moving beyond the other: A critique of the reductionist drugs discourse. *Tijdschrift Over Cultuur & Criminaliteit, 6*(1), 100–118. Available from https://doi.org/10.5553/TCC/221195072016006001007.

Thoits, P. A. (2016). "I'm not mentally ill": Identity deflection as a form of stigma resistance. *Journal of Health and Social Behavior, 57*(2), 135–151. Available from https://doi.org/10.1177/0022146516641164.

Tucker, J. A., Vuchinich, R. E., & Rippens, P. D. (2004). A factor analytic study of influences on patterns of help-seeking among treated and untreated alcohol dependent persons. *Journal of Substance Abuse Treatment, 26*(3), 237–242. Available from https://doi.org/10.1016/S0740-5472(03)00209-5.

Wallhed Finn, S., Bakshi, A.-S., & Andréasson, S. (2014). Alcohol consumption, dependence, and treatment barriers: Perceptions among nontreatment seekers with alcohol dependence. *Substance Use & Misuse, 49*(6), 762–769. Available from https://doi.org/10.3109/10826084.2014.891616.

Walsh, D., & Foster, J. (2020). A contagious other? Exploring the public's appraisals of contact with 'mental illness'. *International Journal of Environmental Research and Public Health, 17*(6), 2005. Available from https://doi.org/10.3390/ijerph17062005.

Walters, G. D. (2002). Twelve reasons why we need to find alternatives to alcoholics anonymous. *Addictive Disorders & Their Treatment, 1*(2), 53–59, Retrieved from. Available from https://journals.lww.com/addictiondisorders/Abstract/2002/06000/Twelve_Reasons_Why_We_Need_to_Find_Alternatives_to.3.aspx.

Wiens, T. K., & Walker, L. J. (2015). The chronic disease concept of addiction: Helpful or harmful? *Addiction Research & Theory, 23*(4), 309–321. Available from https://doi.org/10.3109/16066359.2014.987760.

Wilson, G. B., Kaner, E. F. S., Crosland, A., Ling, J., McCabe, K., & Haighton, C. A. (2013). A qualitative study of alcohol, health and identities among UK adults in later life. *PLoS One, 8*(8), e71792. Available from https://doi.org/10.1371/journal.pone.0071792.

Witbrodt, J., Borkman, T. J., Stunz, A., & Subbaraman, M. S. (2015). Mixed methods study of help seekers and self-changers responding to an online recovery survey. *Alcohol and Alcoholism (Oxford, Oxfordshire), 50*(1), 82–88. Available from https://doi.org/10.1093/alcalc/agu077.

Witte, K. (1992). Putting the fear back into fear appeals: The extended parallel process model. *Communication Monographs, 59*(4), 329–349. Available from https://doi.org/10.1080/03637759209376276.

Young, L. B. (2011). Joe Sixpack: Normality, deviance, and the disease model of alcoholism. *Culture & Psychology, 17*(3), 378–397. Available from https://doi.org/10.1177/1354067X11408133.

Yzer, M., Southwell, B. G., & Stephenson, M. T. (2012). *Inducing fear as a public communication campaign strategy*. Retrieved from https://www.semanticscholar.org/paper/Inducing-fear-as-a-public-communication-campaign-Yzer-Southwell/02fc68d2cdd5c9fd8ac0b4d3b6c6a36ee707fb5b.

Zhou, S., & Shapiro, M. A. (2017). Reducing resistance to narrative persuasion about binge drinking: The role of self-activation and habitual drinking behavior. *Health Communication, 32*(10), 1297–1309. Available from https://doi.org/10.1080/10410236.2016.1219931.

Zillmann, D. (1999). Exemplification theory: Judging the whole by some of its parts. *Media Psychology, 1*(1), 69–94. Available from https://doi.org/10.1207/s1532785xmep0101_5.

Chapter 11

A psychological-systems goal-theory model of alcohol consumption and treatment

W. Miles Cox[1] and Eric Klinger[2]
[1]*School of Psychology, Bangor University, Bangor, Gwynedd, United Kingdom,* [2]*Division of Social Sciences, University of Minnesota, Morris, MN, United States*

Alcohol use is widely acknowledged as a prevalent behavior in Western societies, and its overuse often begins early in life. A survey of American high school seniors (12th graders) revealed that during the previous two weeks 28% disclosed having consumed five or more alcoholic drinks consecutively (Terry-McElrath, Stern, & Patrick, 2017).

Whether to take a drink of alcohol is a choice, but not necessarily an easy one. The desire is an expression of motivation, whose intensity is governed by emotion that is evoked by memory of what pleasure or displeasure is likely to be gained by drinking or abstaining. The pleasure, displeasure, or both, constitute the subjective value that the individual places on taking the drink. That and the expected likelihood of particular outcomes determine the individual's choice (consistent with Expectancy X Value Theory; e.g., Nicolai, Moshagen, & Demmel, 2018). In other words, the choice to take that drink entails each of the major psychological systems involved in any choice. In the case of alcohol, however, the value and expected likelihood of the outcome depend substantially on the drinker's previous pattern of consumption, both frequency and volume, and genetics, which can seriously skew a decision in one direction or the other.

The model described here thus presents alcohol use in the context of the individual's larger interrelated psychobiological systems, most prominently motivational processes, but also inextricably related cognitive, emotional, social, and physiological processes. We begin with basic concepts and definitions. Humans, like other animal species, are distinguished from other life forms by the need to detect and pursue the substances and conditions they require for biological survival. We designate as goals the substances and

The Handbook of Alcohol Use - Understandings from Synapse to Society.
DOI: https://doi.org/10.1016/B978-0-12-816720-5.00015-3

conditions that individuals select, and the actions they take to attain them their *goal pursuits*. The internal processes that are specific to choosing and enabling their goal pursuits constitute *motivational* processes, beginning with *commitments* to pursuing each of the respective goals. The model presented here was built on these basic principles (e.g., Cox & Klinger, 2011a; Klinger, 2013; Klinger & Cox, 2011a).

When consuming alcohol becomes one of an individual's goals, it does so in the context of the person's panoply of other goals, which are likely to include important life goals. These are often formed during adolescence and young adulthood (e.g., Shin, Lee, Park, & Seo, 2018), which are also the ages when people begin to decide whether and how to fit the drinking of alcohol into their life patterns. There will be both consistencies and conflicts with the other goals, including trade-offs, in regard to anticipated rewards and losses from consuming alcohol.

As applied to alcohol, the model treats its consumption as a deliberate choice like any other choice. To be clear, the choice is made for the anticipated positive consequences of consumption, not for becoming or remaining addicted, even though that may be an undesired but nevertheless tolerated consequence of use. That is, the choice for or against consumption will be determined in part by a variety of anticipated positively and negatively valued consequences of use and a variety of positively and negatively valued consequences of non-use. Moreover, some choices can become habitual, thus increasing their subsequent frequency.

The central role of emotion in goal choices

The consequences of drinking will be accompanied by emotional responses, which are associated with and perhaps one of the determinants of the subjective value of drinking to the individual. Certainly, many kinds of data now point to the association between emotional arousal and the cues related to an individual's goals (Bock & Klinger, 1986; Klinger, 2013; Nikula, Klinger, & LarsonGutman, 1993). The emotion may be relatively mild, such as the pleasure or displeasure of a flavor, or more significant, such as a changed mood or response to a changed physical state. Certainly a sense of being on track toward goal attainment is associated with positive moods and a sense of failing in goal pursuit leads to negative moods, even depression (Klinger, 1975; Klinger & Cox, 2011a) and unpleasant physical accompaniments, such as headache (Ciere, Visser, Lebbink, Sanderman, & Fleer, 2016). Some unpleasant physical states may, in turn, be determined by physiological changes remaining from previous consumption of alcohol or other substances, changes such as withdrawal experiences. The emotional consequences of use may also arise from social experiences, such as acceptance or rejection by other people. They may arise from alleviation of stress on the job or difficult personal relationships. Some consequences may be powerful enough to override most others, and these might encumber the choice process.

Some consequences come sooner than others. People vary in the extent to which an anticipated delay in the arrival of a welcome consequence reduces its anticipated value for them, presumably in the amount of their anticipated enjoyment or other emotional experiences that they expect to derive from it (*delayed reward discounting*; e.g., Owens et al., 2019). For example, the prospect of finding an attractive job two years from now may be less compelling than the prospect of finding the same one this week. The tendency to discount the value of more distant rewards is a trait also correlated with impulsiveness (Rung & Madden, 2018). If an anticipated long delay before the desired outcome seriously reduces its subjectively experienced value, the person will be less inclined to sacrifice for it the short-term pleasures that may conflict with waiting longer to obtain the anticipated future rewards. Addicted individuals display this kind of delay discounting on average more than other people (Owens et al., 2019; Rung & Madden, 2018), which may contribute to their becoming and remaining addicted.

Alcohol appears to affect people in at least two different kinds of emotional ways. That is, it can promote pleasure in use (reward drinking) and it can relieve negative feelings (relief drinking; Roos, Mann, & Witkiewitz, 2017). Individuals vary in the relative importance of reward and relief in motivating their drinking. These ways, originally proposed by Cox and Klinger (1988), are not mutually exclusive. Motives aligned with drinking for positive emotions include enhancement (of ongoing pleasures) and social (to enjoy the company of others) motives. Motives aligned with drinking to allay negative emotions include conformity (to avoid criticism), and coping (to deal with discomforts and other problems). There is a burgeoning literature around these motive types, which is reviewed later in this chapter.

With regard to negative feelings, evidence suggests a clear link in which individuals' coping motives (strength of desires for ways to assuage problems such as negative emotions) mediate a relationship between anxiety sensitization or depressed mood and problematic consumption of alcohol (Chinneck et al., 2018). Negative emotions are likely related to experiencing undesired events that conflict with personal goals. The rate at which individuals perceive such events as having preceded their drinking episodes is related to patterns of heavy drinking (Fernandes-Jesus et al., 2016). A survey of Korean adolescents (Choi, Park, Kim, & Park, 2017) found that those who reported high levels of self-perceived stress on an average day were significantly more likely to engage in problem drinking. These results do not permit some important distinctions, such as whether the objective events warrant the perceptions or the recall of them or to what extent the events were precipitated by the heavy drinking patterns. It does, however, seem clear that these events entailed the participants' negative emotions and were perceived as leading to drinking episodes. Consistent with this view is the finding that these heavy drinkers also on average reported higher levels of coping motives—ascribing their drinking to allaying perceived problems—and higher levels of various mental health symptoms.

Episodes of low mood or depression typically begin with difficulties in one's goal pursuits that shed doubt on the likelihood of the pursuit's success (Ghassemi, Bernecker, Herrmann, & Brandstätter, 2017; Klinger, 1975, 1977). That triggers an *action crisis* entailing conflict between continuing the pursuit or disengaging from the goal (e.g., Brandstätter, Herrmann, & Schüler, 2013). Battling low mood or depression is a common motivator for drinking episodes. One online cross-cultural study in three nations found a mediational pathway in which self-reported rumination and coping motives linked frequency of depressive symptoms to amount of alcohol respondents typically consumed (Bravo et al., 2018). One kind of event that can depress feeling states is possible loss of close friendships. High self-esteem can be somewhat protective in that situation, whereas low self-esteem can render an individual more vulnerable to feeling threatened. In an experiment (Hamilton & DeHart, 2017) that, in one condition, raised the prospect of possible loss of a best friend's good opinion, thereby reducing the friend's acceptance of the respondent, participants with low implicit self-esteem reported that evening spending more time drinking with friends and consuming more drinks than did participants with high implicit self-esteem and those in the control condition (i.e., no implied threat to the relationship).

Another group that faces awkward social temptations and pressures (*minority stress*) is that of *minority* (i.e., nonheterosexual) women. This group, too, tends toward heavier than average consumption of alcohol, but the amount consumed varies according to the social context. Drinking tends to be especially heavy in groups of exclusively heterosexual companions or of both heterosexual and nonheterosexual companions, as compared with exclusively other nonheterosexual companions (Dworkin, Cadigan, Hughes, Lee, & Kaysen, 2018). The groups that include heterosexual companions presumably present especially awkward situations. It should be noted that neither anxiety nor depression, although unpleasant, is necessarily useless or pathological, provided that it is acute rather than chronic and not overly severe. Both have no doubt evolved as useful adaptations, anxiety in the face of possibly harmful events and depression in consequence of failed goal pursuits (Nesse, 2019; Nesse & Ellsworth, 2009). Anxiety sensitizes one to cues related to what is feared. In that and other senses, anxiety is adaptive (Marks & Nesse, 1994). Depression facilitates disengagement from highly valued goal pursuits, which reduces wasted effort as well as certain risks of harm in the face of opposing factors and can eventually redirect one's undertakings. In that sense, it, too, is adaptive (Keller & Nesse, 2006; Klinger, 1975, 1977; Koppe & Rothermund, 2017; Kotter-Grühn, Scheibe, Blanchard-Fields, & Baltes, 2009; Nesse, 2000, 2001, 2019; Wrosch & Miller, 2009). What eventually terminates depressive episodes is disengagement from hopeless goals and re-engagement with other goals (Eddington, Burgin, & Majestic, 2016; Herrmann, Brandstätter, & Wrosch, 2019; Klinger & Cox, 2011a; Kotter-Grühn et al., 2009; Wrosch, Miller, Scheier, Schulz, & Carver, 2007; Wrosch, Scheier, Miller, Schulz, & Carver, 2003). Excessive use of alcohol can, of course, seriously interfere with successful re-engagement.

Goals, choices, and priorities in cognitive processing

Committing to pursue a goal appears to mobilize and interconnect the relevant systems of the brain, beginning with instating emotional reactions to stimuli associated with the goal and relatedly prioritizing attention to such goal-related cues. One of the best documented examples of such prioritization has been obtained using variations of the Stroop procedure, in which people are shown a sequence of words printed in varying colors and are instructed that at each presentation they are to indicate, as quickly as possible, the color of the font. In the original Stroop procedure, some words on the screen are the names of colors, some of which agree with the color of the font in which the word on the screen is shown but others of which have fonts shown in colors other than the color named on the screen. In the latter case, the perceiver is still required to name the font color, a color other than the color named on the screen. In the latter cases, color naming is reliably delayed by a fraction of a second. In other procedures, the meaning of the word, although irrelevant to color, is associated with one of the perceiver's goals. Then color-naming is also delayed. If that goal is drinking alcohol, as inferred from the perceivers' drinking history, and the displayed word is associated with alcohol, color-naming is similarly delayed (e.g., Cox, Fadardi, & Pothos, 2006), suggesting that the perceiver's previous commitment to drinking alcohol prioritized processing of the alcohol-related word's meaning ahead of the experimentally imposed goal of naming the color of the word's font.

Using a very different method, with an experimental rather than a correlational design and with nonverbal stimuli, Stussi, Ferrero, Pourtois, and Sander (2019) have confirmed the underlying principle. Their results show that even experimental creation of temporary goals through an aversive conditioning procedure temporarily empowers geometric cues for those goals to evoke skin conductance responses that would otherwise have been absent, and such responses were absent after extinguishing the relevancy of those stimuli to the goal.

Interestingly, a small-sample study with problematic drinkers in treatment found that, when the words represented clinically positive change, Stroop interference scores (delay in color-naming with certain classes of words) were weaker for clients who subsequently recovered than they were for those who relapsed (Rettie, Hogan, & Cox, 2018). One possible explanation for this unexpected finding, consistent with the results of Stussi et al., is that those who recovered had met their goal in relation to drinking, thereby desensitizing them to its cues, whereas the relapsed individuals still retained recovery as a goal—acceptable control over drinking—and hence also retained the sensitization to its cues.

Reaction time to alcohol-related questions on the Implicit Association Test is similarly related to amounts of alcohol that a person generally consumes (Lindgren et al., 2018; Montes, Olin, Teachman, Baldwin, & Lindgren, 2018). Other evidence relates the extent to which task-irrelevant stimuli, when alcohol-related, involuntarily distract social drinkers. The results support the automaticity (*involuntariness*) of this *attentional capture* effect of goal-related stimuli, in this instance the goal being alcohol consumption (Brown, Duka, & Forster, 2018; Brown, Forster, & Duka, 2018).

This *attentional bias* for alcohol-related cues is related to drinking in two ways. On the one hand, it is the direct result of having the goal of drinking alcohol. On the other hand, in drawing the person's attention to alcohol-related stimuli, it presumably makes attending to other stimuli less likely or less prominent. As a result, alcohol-related stimuli then play an enlarged role in the person's consciousness. To put this another way, for drinkers, alcohol-related stimuli become more powerful distractions from other stimuli or thoughts. These distractions evidently then increase the likelihood of the person desiring and drinking alcohol (Field & Cox, 2008; Field et al., 2007; Field & Eastwood, 2005). This effect may, of course, conflict with the person's other pursuits.

There may, however, be important individual differences in this distraction effect. Investigators who used a visual probe task rather than the Stroop task to measure attentional bias with adolescent participants reported indications that this attentional biasing in adolescent alcohol use may be present primarily in individuals who also score low on executive control (Van Hemel-Ruiter, de Jong, Ostafin, & Wiers, 2015; Van Hemel-Ruiter, Wiers, Brook, & de Jong, 2016). For drinkers, then, strong executive control could presumably override the distractive power of alcohol stimuli.

There are reasons to believe that the cognitive prioritizing process seen in attentional bias is related to the emotional impact of the goal-related word (e.g., Klinger, 1996). A meta-analysis indeed found evidence of an association between the impact of stimuli to arouse positive emotions and the attentional priority they receive (Pool, Brosch, Delplanque, & Sander, 2016). The authors observed that this association was strengthened when the stimuli were related to the perceiver's goals. The speed of this effect on reaction time is such (see also Brown et al., 2018, for alcohol; Brown et al., 2018, for smoking) that it could not have entailed a full-blown emotional response. It can, therefore, be labeled a *proto-emotional* response that steers attention to cues associated with the respective goals.

Motives for drinking alcohol

As indicated earlier, consumption of alcohol is widespread in western societies. In fact, alcohol use is a major contributor to injuries, mortality, and disease (Rehm et al., 2017); nevertheless, a variety of patterns of both problematic and nonproblematic consumption can be identified (Office of National Statistics, 2017; Pisinger, Holst, Bendtsen, Becker, & Tolstrup, 2017). Whatever the pattern, people consume alcohol because they are *motivated* to do so; that is, by drinking alcohol they attempt to achieve something emotionally important to them.

To account for people's motivation to drink alcohol, Cox and Klinger (1988) formulated a motivational model of alcohol use, which has subsequently undergone several iterations (Cox & Klinger, 1990, 2004, 2011a; see also Cox, Klinger, & Fadardi, 2017a, 2017b). Cooper, Kuntsche, Levitt, Barber, and Wolf (2016) have summarized the following major postulates of the motivational model:

a. People drink alcohol (or use another addictive substance) because they expect that doing so will alter their affect in a desirable way. It will serve either to enhance their positive affect or to reduce their negative affect. The change in affect can, moreover, be achieved either through the direct, pharmacological effects of the alcohol, or through indirect, instrumental effects on other positive and negative incentives in the person's life.

b. People hold beliefs—or expectations—about the effects of drinking alcohol. Regardless of whether these beliefs are accurate, they shape the person's motives for drinking. As indicated earlier, consistent with Value X Expectancy theory (e.g., Nicolai et al., 2018), the people's beliefs about the effects of drinking (i.e., the value that they attribute to it) are combined with their expectations about actually being able to achieve those effects. The multiplicative combination of value and expectancy determine whether a person will decide to imbibe on any particular occasion.

c. People choose (i.e., they make a decision about) whether to consume a drink of alcohol, even though both the decision and the factors affecting it might be neither conscious nor rational. Drinking alcohol, however, is a voluntary act, and the person could decide not to drink, regardless of how difficult that decision might be.

d. Motives for drinking alcohol vary from one individual to another and within a given individual from one point in time to another. For example, one person might drink primarily in an attempt to alleviate negative feelings (e.g., anxiety or depression), whereas another person might drink to enhance ongoing positive feelings (e.g., to enjoy a party even more). A particular individual might initiate a drinking career because of peer approval of drinking. After the drinking has become habitual, he or she might drink to palliate negative feelings during withdrawal (e.g., anxiety, depression, and general malaise).

e. Whereas a variety of variables feed into the motivational pathway leading to the act of drinking, motives for drinking are its most proximal determinant. Other kinds of variables are more distal determinants.

What determines expected affective change from drinking alcohol?

Several categories of variables have an impact on the affective change that a person expects to derive from drinking alcohol. These variables include biological, psychological, sociocultural, and environmental factors. We discuss each of these kinds of factors in turn.

Biological factors. Excessive drinking and problems associated with it tend to run in families (Orford, 1984). This could be due to (a) genetic factors shared among family members, (b) their common environment, or (c) a combination of shared genetic and environmental factors. In an effort to separate the relative contribution of genetic and environmental factors, various studies have compared the relative prevalence of an alcohol use disorder (AUD) among monozygotic and dizygotic twins reared by their biological parents versus those reared by adoptive parents. In a meta-analysis of these studies, Verhulst, Neale, and Kendler (2015) concluded that environmental factors contribute substantially less to the development of an AUD (10% of the shared variance) than do genetic factors (49% of the shared variance).

But what is transmitted genetically that could account for individual differences in affective changes that people expect to derive from drinking alcohol? Research is being conducted to identify variations in the human genome that might make a person susceptible to developing an AUD (e.g., Juraeva et al., 2015; Yan et al., 2014; Ystrom, Kendler, & Reichborn-Kjennerud, 2014). The determinants of genetic risk for developing an AUD are not yet fully understood; nevertheless, some conclusions can be drawn. For instance, the degree to which alcohol affects the neurotransmitters in the brain seems to be partly genetically determined (Tabakoff & Hoffman, 2013). For some people, alcohol strongly reduces anxiety through the release of gamma-aminobutyric acid (GABA). For others, drinking alcohol strongly enhances reward-related stimuli through the release of dopamine (Berridge, 2007).

Another consequence of drinking alcohol that is genetically determined is the alcohol flush reaction (Dickson, James, & Heath, 2006; Ong, Khor, Balasupramaniam, & Say, 2018). It includes various unpleasant bodily reactions in people with a deficiency in aldehyde dehydrogenase (the enzyme that metabolizes acetaldehyde) when they drink alcohol. Deficits in aldehyde dehydrogenase are common among people of East Asian ancestry, but not among people of European ancestry (Dickson et al., 2006). As a consequence, drinking—especially excessive drinking—is less common among East Asian people than among Europeans (Waleewong, Laslett, Chenhall, & Room, 2018).

The various biochemical reactions to alcohol described here affect the value that individual drinkers place on drinking alcohol, either by increasing or by decreasing the degree of reward that a person expects to derive from drinking alcohol. When an individual attributes great value to drinking alcohol, that person will likely find it difficult but not impossible to control his or her drinking.

Finally, in an effort to determine why some individuals are highly motivated to drink alcohol, Newlin and Thomson (1990), see also (Fleming et al., 2015; Schuckit, 2018) reviewed studies that have compared individuals with and without a family history of alcoholism (FH + , FH −). Starting from the premise that alcoholism tends to run in families, they concluded that FH + participants find alcohol more rewarding because it accentuates the pleasurable, excitatory aspects of the initial intoxication and attenuates the feelings of anxiety and depression when alcohol levels in the blood drop.

There are also potentially powerful epigenetic effects—such as traumatic experiences in infancy—that may leave lasting effects on the attractiveness of substance use. A Korean investigation found self-reported early life stress and insecure attachment to be significantly related to drinking alcohol for enhancement and to cope with negative experiences (Jang, Park, Kim, Lee, & Kim, 2019). Interestingly, numerous other investigators have reported that imposing stress on rodent pups, such as separation from mothers during earliest postnatal weeks, had the effect of increasing later consumption of alcohol, opiates, and stimulants as well as conditioned preferences for places associated with the substances (Walters, & Kosten, in press). The infant stress experiences also facilitated reinstatement of use following extinction of the initial addiction (Portero-Tresserra et al., 2018; Walters, & Kosten, in press). Walters and Kosten suggest that the effects of such stress may be attributable to stress-induced methylation (adding methyl groups to DNA segments), which may alter gene function in ways that affect reward-relevant dopamine pathways.

Psychological factors. The psychological variable that has been most often studied in relationship to alcohol use and misuse is personality. In turn, two dimensions of personality have been frequently studied: (a) Behavioral disinhibition and its various dimensions, including impulsivity, reward dependence, and sensation seeking (Loxton, Bunker, Dingle, & Wong, 2015; Mackinnon, Kehayes, Clark, Sherry, & Stewart, 2014; Mikheeva & Tragesser, 2016), and (b) negative emotionality, including anxiety and depression (Mackinnon et al., 2014; Mikheeva & Tragesser, 2016). A drinker who is elevated on behavioral disinhibition is motivated to experience the pleasurable feelings that alcohol can provide (i.e., a positive affective change). Drinkers who are high on negative emotionality are motivated to drink because of the temporarily reduced negative emotions that drinking alcohol brings.

Aluja, Lucas, Blanch, and Blanco (2019) found that among a young (18−30 years old) sample, impulsive-disinhibited personality characteristics were strongly related to both alcohol consumption and drinking-related problems, but that anxiety was unrelated to the alcohol variables being assessed. They concluded that impulsive/disinhibited personality factors in alcohol consumers raise the risk of developing an AUD. Acuff et al. (2018), on the other hand, pointed out that symptoms of depression are common among university students, and they tested the hypothesis that depression among college students is associated with heavy drinking. Among a sample of heavy drinking college students, they found that depressive symptoms predicted alcohol problems related to impaired control (e.g., drinking more than intended) and less reinforcement from nonsubstance sources. These two sets of results together suggest that both behavioral disinhibition and negative emotionality play an important role in young people's alcohol use. Acuff et al.'s (2018) finding that negative emotionality is related to less reinforcement from substance-free activities is particularly relevant for Cox and Klinger's motivational model. A major premise of the model is that drinking alcohol is an attractive way in which people can regulate their affect when they are unable to do so through nonchemical means.

Sociocultural factors. As discussed earlier, the consumption of alcohol and problematic drinking are widespread in western societies. Yet there are wide variations in the drinking patterns of the different countries and regions. One notable difference is the Mediterranean versus the northern European pattern of drinking (e.g., Calafat et al., 2010; Shield, Rehm, Gmel, Rehm, & Allamani, 2013). The Mediterranean pattern is characterized by a prevalence of daily drinkers who consume alcohol with meals. In Mediterranean countries, there is a high tolerance for social drinking, but public drunkenness is ostracized. By contrast, heavy episodic drinking and intoxication characterize the northern European pattern of drinking. At the same time, it should be noted that traditional drinking patterns within particular cultures are to some extent changing. For instance, at the beginning of the 21st century, adolescent alcohol consumption in the Netherlands was at the top of international rankings, whereas nowadays it is found near the bottom of the rankings (de Looze, van Dorsselaer, Saskia, Monshouwer, & Vollebergh, 2017). This dramatic shift in Dutch young people's drinking patterns has been attributed to a substantial increase in Dutch parents' strict, alcohol-specific rule setting. Italy is another example of changing cultural attitudes. Although in Italy drinking in moderation continues to be the norm, heavy alcohol consumption (Laghi, Bianchi, Pompili, Lonigro, & Baiocco, 2019) and alcohol dependence do occur and, in fact, they account for a substantial proportion of the burden of disease in Italy (Shield et al., 2013). Laghi et al. also found (2019) that among Italian adolescents with conformity motives, impairment in social cognition seemed to place the drinkers at risk for heavy episodic drinking, whereas having good social-cognitive skills was protective.

Thus, individual drinkers within these different societies are strongly influenced by the drinking patterns of the society in which they live (e.g.,

Room, 2013). They are directly or indirectly reinforced when they drink like the other people, and they are directly or indirectly censured if their own drinking deviates from the norms of their society. In other words, drinking as other people do is a way to enhance one's positive affect.

Environmental factors. In addition to broad societal attitudes about drinking, environmental factors within a particular society also affect people's expectations of affective change from drinking alcohol. Advertising of alcohol is one such influence. By this, the alcohol industry is, of course, attempting to increase the attractiveness of its products and to persuade the public to purchase them. In many countries, such advertisements are commonplace on television and at sporting events (Gallopel-Morvan et al., 2017; Noel et al., 2017; White et al., 2017), and on social media (Barry et al., 2016; Weaver, Wright, Dietze, & Lim, 2016), and they appear to be effective. For example, higher exposure to alcohol advertising has been shown to lead to both higher alcohol use and binge drinking (e.g., Morgenstern, Li, Li, & Sargent, 2017; Siegel et al., 2016), including drinking among children and adolescents (Carr et al., 2016; Gallopel-Morvan et al., 2017; White et al., 2017). There is, moreover, some evidence that reducing alcohol advertising on television can lead to reduced drinking (White et al., 2017).

Laboratory studies investigating the mechanisms involved in the translation of alcohol advertisements into increased alcohol consumption have revealed some interesting relationships. In a study conducted in their bar laboratory, Stautz et al. (2017) found that exposure to alcohol advertisements led to an increase in positive affect and increased approach but reduced avoidance of alcohol as measured by an adapted version of the Implicit Association Test (Ostafin & Palfai, 2006), although the exposure did not affect the amount of alcohol drunk in an alcohol taste test in comparison with a group exposed to nonalcohol advertisements. In a study to determine how alcohol marketing promotes underage drinking, Courtney, Rapuano, Sargent, Heatherton, and Kelley (2018) used functional magnetic resonance imaging to determine how exposure to alcohol cues is processed in the brain. They found that the alcohol stimuli were processed within the brain's reward system in such a way that the exposure motivates drinking behavior. Also in the laboratory, Bartholow et al. (2018) paired beer brands with the logo of student participants' own university or with some other university to which the participants felt no allegiance. In comparison to the other-university/beer-brand associations, the own-university/beer-brand associations led to increased incentive salience of the beer brand as measured by the P300 component of the event-related potential. These results suggest that marketing beer by associating it with students' universities enhances the incentive salience of the brand for underage students. It, therefore, has implications for underage students' involvement with alcohol. Finally, in contrast to the Stautz et al. (2017) study, which found that exposure to alcohol advertisements did not affect the amount of alcohol consumed in a laboratory alcohol taste test, Kersbergen and Field's (2017) participants did drink more alcohol in a laboratory alcohol taste test when their attention was directed to the alcohol cues within alcohol advertisements.

As a final example of the impact of environmental factors on the attractiveness of drinking alcohol, the importance of the pricing of alcohol and taxation of it should be noted. In various countries, it has been shown that increasing the price of alcohol—whether through taxation or otherwise—has led to a reduction in alcohol consumption, including harmful patterns of drinking (Kumar, 2017; Mosher, Adler, Pamukcu, & Treffers, 2017; Ramirez & Jernigan, 2017; Staras et al., 2017; Xuan et al., 2015). A reduction in the price of alcohol, whether through a reduction in taxation or otherwise, has, conversely, resulted in increased consumption and drinking-related negative consequences (Zatoński, Sulkowska, Zatoński, Herbeć, & Muszyńska, 2015). In some locations (Canada, certain states in the United States, Russia, Moldova, Ukraine, and Uzbekistan), the price of alcohol is controlled through governmental minimum unit pricing (MUP), which Scotland also introduced in 2018 (Institute of Alcohol Studies, 2018). Although arguments for and against MUP have been advanced, evidence has been reported that MUP reduces alcohol consumption and the negative consequences of heavy drinking, especially among people with lower income (Fergie, Leifeld, Hawkins, & Hilton, 2019; Zhao & Stockwell, 2017). In the terms of the motivational model, price increases (and MUP) reduce the incentive value of drinking alcohol and make it more likely that drinkers will curb their drinking; a reduction in the price of alcohol *increases* the incentive value of drinking.

Measuring motives for drinking: drinking motives questionnaire—revised (Cooper, 1994)

Cox and Klinger's motivational model proposes four kinds of motives for drinking. Each of them is derived from the factorial combination of (a) the valence of the expected affective change from drinking alcohol (positive or negative) and (b) the source of the affective change (the direct, pharmacological effects of the alcohol or the indirect, instrumental effects of drinking on other positive or negative incentives in the person's life). The resulting four categories of drinking motives are (a) an increase in positive affect from the pharmacological effects of drinking, (b) an increase in positive affect from the instrumental effects of drinking, (c) a decrease in negative affect from the pharmacological effects of drinking, and (d) a decrease in negative affect from the instrumental effects of drinking. Regardless of the source of the affective change that the person expects, if the net change in affect is more positive than from other incentives, the decision will be to drink; if the net change is less positive than from other incentives, the decision will be not to drink.

Testing the validity of the assumptions of the motivational model, Cooper (1994) developed the Drinking Motives Questionnaire—Revised (DMQ—R), which measures four kinds of drinking motives that she identified among adolescent drinkers: Social, coping, enhancement, and conformity, which correspond approximately to the four kinds of affective change from drinking that Cox and Klinger proposed. Subsequent to the development of the DMQ—R, it has been used in numerous research studies to evaluate people's motives for drinking alcohol and as a model for other substance use. The results have been highly consistent in confirming in diverse samples across multiple countries the validity of the four categories of drinking motives that Cooper originally identified (see Cooper et al., 2016). This research also indicates that more people endorse appetitive motives for drinking (i.e., social and enhancement motives) than either of the avoidance motives (coping or conformity). Additionally, coping motives for drinking predispose drinkers to problematic drinking; enhancement motives predispose them to heavy use of alcohol.

Implications for treatment

Many problematic heavy drinkers of alcohol manage to adjust their rate of consumption to moderate levels or abstinence without professional assistance (Klingemann, Sobell, & Sobell, 2010), perhaps even a majority. The actual number varies greatly according to definitions of problematic drinking and recovery as well as the attributes of the sample investigated, but return to relatively adaptive living through self-change (*spontaneous recovery*) appears to be frequent.

An investigation that obtained qualitative data regarding what led to users' reduced use reported that "respondents' descriptions suggested that their perceptions of the costs and benefits of using and of not using substances reached a point where the scale no longer tipped in favor of excessive alcohol or drug use" (Sobell et al., 2001, p. 1482). The most common semantic attributes of the descriptions fit the categories of *cognitive evaluations* and *affect-related statements*. The few examples of the descriptions suggest consistency with our motivational model as described in the previous sections of this chapter. They also exemplify the kinds of changes sought through Systematic Motivational Counseling, which is briefly described below.

That nevertheless leaves many heavy drinkers who need help to recover. Based on premises of the motivational model, two kinds of interventions have been developed for helping drinkers to reduce their excessive use of alcohol. One of the interventions started with the observation that heavy drinkers selectively attend to alcohol-related stimuli in their environment. The attentional bias promotes craving, and it feeds into drinkers' motivation to imbibe (e.g., Cox et al., 2006; Field & Cox, 2008). Alcohol abusers' attentional distraction for alcohol-related stimuli can be even greater than their distraction for other goal-related stimuli (Cox, Blount, & Rozak, 2000; Fadardi, Ziaee, & Shamloo, 2009), suggesting that these drinkers are unable to obtain emotional satisfaction through the pursuit of other kinds of goals.

To help excessive drinkers to overcome their attention bias for alcohol-related stimuli, Fadardi and Cox (2009) developed the Attention-Control Training Program (ACTP). Across multiple studies evaluating ACTP, results have been promising for helping drinkers, other substance abusers, and overweight individuals to overcome their distraction for substance-related or food-related stimuli and thereby reduce their use of addictive substances or achieve their dieting goals (Bazzaz, Fadardi, & Parkinson, 2017; Cox, Fadardi, Hosier, & Pothos, 2015; Fadardi & Cox, 2009; Wiers et al., 2015; Ziaee, Fadardi, Cox, & Yazdi, 2016). Other researchers have developed different versions of attentional training (e.g., Field & Eastwood, 2005) or another kind of intervention for cognitive bias modification (CBM, e.g., approach-avoidance training; Rinck, Wiers, Becker, & Lindenmeyer, 2018).

Cristea, Kok, and Cuijpers (2016) conducted a meta-analysis of CBM interventions and concluded that the results cast doubt on the utility of CBM. Wiers, Boffo, and Field (2018), however, questioned the validity of Cristea et al.'s conclusions because the analysis inappropriately combined: (a) experimental laboratory studies with students who were not motivated to change with (b) randomized clinical trials with patients who were motivated to change. When Wiers et al. (2018) distinguished between these two types of studies, they concluded that (a) CBM has small effects on students' drinking but only if their cognitive bias has been successfully changed and (b) the very limited results on the use of CBM with patients is encouraging and should not be dismissed on the grounds of Cristea et al.'s (2016) analysis. Further to determine whether CBM can effectively reduce cognitive bias and addictive behaviors, Boffo et al. (2019) conducted a Bayesian meta-analysis of 14 studies of CBM with patients with an alcohol-use disorder or a tobacco-use disorder. Similar to Wiers et al. (2018), they concluded that there is insufficient evidence for concluding whether CBM is an effective intervention for alcohol-use and tobacco-use disorders. Boffo et al. (2019) recommended that research on CBM should continue until unequivocal conclusions can be reached.

Systematic Motivational Counseling (SMC) is the second intervention that is based on the motivational model. It is designed to modify drinkers' motivational structure (their goals and their ways of relating to them) by changing their maladaptive motivational patterns into adaptive ones. The overarching aim of SMC is to maximize the emotional satisfaction that drinkers derive from healthy, adaptive goal pursuits, thereby reducing their need to regulate their affect by drinking alcohol. In order to identify the motivational patterns to be targeted during the multicomponent counseling procedure, SMC starts by assessing drinkers' motivational structure, using the

Personal Concerns Inventory or a related instrument (Cox & Klinger, 2011b; Klinger & Cox, 2011b).

SMC has been adapted for use in various settings and with various client groups. For instance, clinically SMC has been successfully used to reduce substance use among patients with a traumatic brain injury (Cox et al., 2003) and in a group setting with a variety of other kinds of psychological disorders (Fuhrmann, Schroer, & Jong-Meyer, 2011) and with offenders (McMurran, Sellen, & Campbell, 2011). A self-help version has been used to help people in general with their personal goal attainments (de Jong-Meyer, 2011).

A brief, four-session version of SMC has also been developed. It is called Life Enhancement and Advancement Program (LEAP; Fadardi, Cox, Hosier, & Klinger, 2006) and was designed for use in a group setting. Using a 2 X 2 factorial design, Cox et al. (2015) evaluated the individual and combined effects of ACTP and of LEAP. The results indicated that the effects of the two interventions followed different time courses. At the three-month, post-intervention assessment, ACTP had reduced participants' alcohol consumption, but the reduction was no longer significant at the six-month follow-up. Contrariwise, the effects of LEAP on participants' alcohol consumption were significant at the six-month follow-up. This pattern of results suggests that ACTP can rapidly change the cognitive processes that are most proximal to drinking decisions, but that the changes do not endure. On the other hand, although the motivational patterns that LEAP targets are difficult to change, the changes that occur are more long-lasting.

There is, of course, depending on definitions of success, a tendency for the effects of treatments for addictions to weaken with the passage of time. As participants in treatment regimens return to their former lives, including their relationships with individuals with whom they shared consumption experiences, the relative influence of their relationships with treatment providers is likely to wane, leading to resumed consumption. For this reason, aftercare through regular post-treatment contacts with clients to shore up those relationships may be an important addition to treatment as usual. We have been unable to locate conclusive empirical support for the benefits of aftercare, but some relevant encouraging results are beginning to appear (Hutchison et al., 2019; Rubinsky et al., 2018).

Conclusions

Consistent with our motivational model, we infer from the body of evidence cited above and elsewhere (Cox & Klinger, 2011a; Klinger & Cox, 2011a) that deciding to drink alcohol is a choice that proceeds with the same systems and process entailed in all human choices. However, the process varies with individual differences, and under particular circumstances it becomes difficult to choose abstention. Choices among different courses of action depend on anticipated value of the consequences, in the form of anticipated resulting affect, as moderated by the length of delay before that outcome, and the degree of confidence that the result will occur. The person's degree of confidence may change significantly with changes in circumstances and in self-confidence regarding one's abilities to reach the respective goal. Individuals differ in how strongly they react emotionally to anticipations of both their goal attainments and possible failure, as well as differing in their neurochemical and systemic biochemical reactions to imbibed alcohol and their degrees of inhibitory control versus impulsiveness.

Because choices are always among courses of action, those individuals whose biochemistry disposes toward positive affective responses to alcohol will prefer drinking it over a wider range of alternative pursuits than would other individuals. As physical addictive processes develop with repeated consumption, the preference for drinking versus other pursuits increases. For this reason, and because frequently repeating some kinds of other goal attainments leads to diminishing degrees of positive affect upon each attainment, preference for alcohol may increase over time. In general, then, excessive drinking is likeliest to occur for favorably disposed individuals in the absence of sufficiently attractive alternative pursuits, such as valued personal relationships, parenthood, occupations, sports, etc.

Committing to goals renders individuals' perceptual and cognitive processes to prioritize goal-related cues and thoughts. Individuals who enjoy consuming alcohol are therefore quicker to attend to alcohol-related cues. Experiencing those cues, in turn, increases the likelihood of their desiring alcohol, thus boosting the likelihood of drinking over that of alternative pursuits.

These conclusions point to two kinds of treatment methods that have been shown to some degree effective. Training heavy drinkers to disattend to alcohol cues appears to reduce consumption over the relative short term of a few weeks or months. Systematic Motivational Counseling, whose objective is to eliminate commitment to insufficiently rewarding goals and to instate commitment to alternative, more rewarding goals, appears to reduce alcohol consumption over longer periods.

References

Acuff, S. F., Soltis, K. E., Luciano, M. T., Meshesha, L. Z., Pedrelli, P., Dennhardt, A. A., & Murphy, J. G. (2018). Depressive symptoms as predictors of alcohol problem domains and reinforcement among heavy drinking college students. *Psychology of Addictive Behaviors*, *32*(7), 792–799.

Aluja, A., Lucas, I., Blanch, A., & Blanco, E. (2019). Personality and disinhibitory psychopathology in alcohol consumption: A study from the biological-factorial personality models of Eysenck, Gray and Zuckerman. *Personality and Individual Differences*, *142*, 159–165.

Barry, A. E., Bates, A. M., Olusanya, O., Vinal, C. E., Martin, E., Peoples, J. E., ... Montano, J. R. (2016). Alcohol marketing on twitter and instagram: Evidence of directly advertising to youth/adolescents. *Alcohol and Alcoholism*, *51*(4), 487–492.

Bartholow, B. D., Loersch, C., Ito, T. A., Levsen, M. P., Volpert-Esmond, H., Fleming, K. A., ... Carter, B. K. (2018). University-affiliated alcohol marketing enhances the incentive salience of alcohol cues. *Psychological Science*, *29*(1), 83–94.

Bazzaz, M. M., Fadardi, J. S., & Parkinson, J. (2017). Efficacy of the attention control training program on reducing attentional bias in obese and overweight dieters. *Appetite*, *108*, 1–11.

Berridge, K. C. (2007). The debate over dopamine's role in reward: The case for incentive salience. *Psychopharmacology*, *191*, 391–431.

Bock, M., & Klinger, E. (1986). Interaction of emotion and cognition in word recall. *Psychological Research*, *48*, 99–106.

Boffo, M., Zerhouni, O., Gronau, Q. F., Beek, R. J. J., Nikolaou, K., Marsman, M., & Wiers, R. W. (2019). Cognitive bias modification for behavior change in alcohol and smoking addiction: Bayesian meta-analysis of individual participant data. *Neuropsychology Review*, *29*, 52–78.

Brandstätter, V., Herrmann, M., & Schüler, J. (2013). The struggle of giving up personal goals: Affective, physiological, and cognitive consequences of an action crisis. *Personality and Social Psychology Bulletin*, *39*(12), 1668–1682.

Bravo, A. J., Pilatti, A., Pearson, M. R., Mezquita, L., Ibáñez, M. I., & Ortet, G. (2018). Depressive symptoms, ruminative thinking, drinking motives, and alcohol outcomes: A multiple mediation model among college students in three countries. *Addictive Behaviors*, *76*, 319–327.

Brown, C. R. H., Duka, T., & Forster, S. (2018). Attentional capture by alcohol-related stimuli may be activated involuntarily by top-down search goals. *Psychopharmacology*, *235*(7), 2087–2099.

Brown, C. R. H., Forster, S., & Duka, T. (2018). Goal-driven attentional capture by appetitive and aversive smoking-related cues in nicotine-dependent smokers. *Drug and Alcohol Dependence*, *190*, 209–215.

Calafat, A., Blay, N. T., Hughes, K., Bellis, M., Juan, M., Duch, M., & Kokkevi, A. (2010). Nightlife young risk behaviours in Mediterranean versus other European cities: Are stereotypes true? *European Journal of Public Health*, *21*(3), 311–315.

Carr, S., O'Brien, K. S., Ferris, J., Room, R., Livingston, M., Vandenberg, B., ... Lynott, D. (2016). Child and adolescent exposure to alcohol advertising in Australia's major televised sports. *Drug and Alcohol Review*, *35*(4), 406–411.

Chinneck, A., Thompson, K., Dobson, K. S., Stuart, H., Teehan, M., & Stewart, S. H. (2018). Neurotic personality traits and risk for adverse alcohol outcomes: Chained mediation through emotional disorder symptoms and drinking to cope. *Substance Use & Misuse*, *53* (10), 1730–1741.

Choi, J., Park, E., Kim, J., & Park, S. (2017). Do causes of stress differ in their association with problem drinking by sex in Korean adolescents? *Addictive Behaviors*, *64*, 62–69.

Ciere, Y., Visser, A., Lebbink, J., Sanderman, R., & Fleer, J. (2016). Impaired mood in headache clinic patients: Associations with the perceived hindrance and attainability of personal goals. *Headache: The Journal of Head and Face Pain*, *56*(6), 1022–1032.

Cooper, M. L. (1994). Motivations for alcohol use among adolescents: Development and validation of a four-factor model. *Psychological Assessment*, *6*(2), 117–128.

Cooper, M. L., Kuntsche, E., Levitt, A., Barber, L. L., & Wolf, S. (2016). Motivational models of substance use: A review of theory and research on motives for using alcohol, marijuana, and tobacco. In K. J. Sher (Ed.), *Oxford handbook of substance use and substance use disorders* (Vol. 1, pp. 375–421). New York, NY: Oxford University Press.

Courtney, A. L., Rapuano, K. M., Sargent, J. D., Heatherton, T. F., & Kelley, W. M. (2018). Reward system activation in response to alcohol advertisements predicts college drinking. *Journal of Studies on Alcohol and Drugs*, *79*(1), 29–38.

Cox, W. M., Blount, J. P., & Rozak, A. M. (2000). Alcohol abusers' and nonabusers' distraction by alcohol and concern-related stimuli. *American Journal of Drug and Alcohol Abuse, 26*, 489–495.

Cox, W. M., Fadardi, J. S., Hosier, S. G., & Pothos, E. M. (2015). Differential effects and temporal course of attentional and motivational training on excessive drinking. *Experimental and Clinical Psychopharmacology, 23*(6), 445–454.

Cox, W. M., Fadardi, J. S., & Pothos, E. M. (2006). The addiction-Stroop test: Theoretical considerations and procedural recommendations. *Psychological Bulletin, 132*(3), 443–476.

Cox, W. M., Heinemann, A. W., Miranti, S. V., Schmidt, M., Klinger, E., & Blount, J. P. (2003). Outcomes of systematic motivational counseling for substance use following traumatic brain injury. *Journal of Addictive Diseases, 22*(1), 93–110.

Cox, W. M., & Klinger, E. (1988). A motivational model of alcohol use. *Journal of Abnormal Psychology, 97*(2), 168–180.

Cox, W. M., & Klinger, E. (1990). Incentive motivation, affective change, and alcohol use: A model. In W. M. Cox (Ed.), *Why people drink: Parameters of alcohol as a reinforcer* (pp. 291–314). New York: Amereon Press.

Cox, W. M., & Klinger, E. (2004). A motivational model of alcohol use: Determinants of use and change. In W. M. Cox, & E. Klinger (Eds.), *Handbook of motivational counseling: Concepts, approaches, and assessment* (pp. 121–138). Chichester, United Kingdom: Wiley.

Cox, W. M., & Klinger, E. (2011a). A motivational model of alcohol use: Determinants of use and change. In W. M. Cox, & E. Klinger (Eds.), *Handbook of motivational counseling: Goal-based approaches to assessment and intervention with addiction and other problems* (pp. 131–158). Chichester, United Kingdom: Wiley-Blackwell.

Cox, W. M., & Klinger, E. (2011b). Measuring motivation: The motivational structure questionnaire, personal concerns inventory, and their variants. In W. M. Cox, & E. Klinger (Eds.), *Handbook of motivational counseling: Goal-based approaches to assessment and intervention with addiction and other problems* (pp. 161–204). Chichester, United Kingdom: Wiley-Blackwell.

Cox, W. M., Klinger, E., & Fadardi, J. S. (2017a). Free will in addictive behaviors: A matter of definition. *Addictive Behaviors Reports, 5*, 94–103.

Cox, W. M., Klinger, E., & Fadardi, J. S. (2017b). Nonconscious motivational influences on cognitive processes in addictive behaviors. In N. Heather, & G. Segal (Eds.), *Addiction and choice* (pp. 259–285). Oxford, United Kingdom: Oxford University Press.

Cristea, I. A., Kok, R. N., & Cuijpers, P. (2016). The effectiveness of cognitive bias modification interventions for substance addictions: A meta-analysis. *PLoS One, 11*(9), 19.

de Jong-Meyer, R., Systematic motivational analysis as part of a self-help technique aimed at personal goal attainment. In W. M. Cox & E. Klinger (Eds.), *Handbook of motivational counseling: Goal-based approaches to assessment and intervention with addiction and other problems*, 2011, 349–372. Chichester, United Kingdom: Wiley-Blackwell.

de Looze, M. E., van Dorsselaer., Saskia, A. F. M., Monshouwer, K., & Vollebergh, W. A. M. (2017). Trends in adolescent alcohol use in the Netherlands, 1992–2015: Differences across sociodemographic groups and links with strict parental rule-setting. *International Journal of Drug Policy, 50*, 90–101.

Dickson P.A., James M.R., Heath A.C., Montgomery G.W., Martin N.G., Whitfield J.B., and Birley A.J. Effects of variation at the ALDH2 locus on alcohol metabolism, sensitivity, consumption, and dependence in Europeans, *Alcoholism: Clinical and Experimental Research* **30** (7), 2006, 1093–1100.

Dworkin, E. R., Cadigan, J., Hughes, T., Lee, C., & Kaysen, D. (2018). Sexual identity of drinking companions, drinking motives, and drinking behaviors among young sexual minority women: An analysis of daily data. *Psychology of Addictive Behaviors*, *32*(5), 540–551.

Eddington, K. M., Burgin, C. J., & Majestic, C. (2016). Individual differences in expectancies for change in depression: Associations with goal pursuit and daily experiences. *Journal of Social and Clinical Psychology*, *35*(8), 629–642.

Fadardi, J. S., & Cox, W. M. (2009). Reversing the sequence: Reducing alcohol consumption by overcoming alcohol attentional bias. *Drug and Alcohol Dependence*, *101*, 137–145.

Fadardi, J. S., Cox, W. M., Hosier, S. G., & Klinger, E. (2006). *Life enhancement and advancement programme (LEAP)*. Unpublished treatment manual, Bangor University.

Fadardi, J. S., Ziaee, S., & Shamloo, Z. S. (2009). Substance use and the paradox of good and bad attentional bias. *Experimental and Clinical Psychopharmacology*, *17*(6), 456–463.

Fergie, G., Leifeld, P., Hawkins, B., & Hilton, S. (2019). Mapping discourse coalitions in the minimum unit pricing for alcohol debate: A discourse network analysis of UK newspaper coverage. *Addiction*, *114*(4), 741–753.

Fernandes-Jesus, M., Beccaria, F., Demant, J., Fleig, L., Menezes, I., Scholz, U., . . . Cooke, R. (2016). Validation of the drinking motives questionnaire—Revised in six European countries. *Addictive Behaviors*, *62*, 91–98.

Field, M., & Cox, W. M. (2008). Attentional bias in addictive behaviors: A review of its development, causes, and consequences. *Drug and Alcohol Dependence*, *97*(1–2), 1–20.

Field, M., Duka, T., Eastwood, B., Child, R., Santarcangelo, M., & Gayton, M. (2007). Experimental manipulation of attentional biases in heavy drinkers: Do the effects generalise? *Psychopharmacology*, *192*(4), 593–608.

Field, M., & Eastwood, B. (2005). Experimental manipulation of attentional bias increases the motivation to drink alcohol. *Psychopharmacology*, *183*, 350–357.

Fleming, K. A., Bartholow, B. D., Hilgard, J., McCarthy, D. M., O'Neill, S. E., Juraeva, D., . . . Rietschel, M. (2015). XRCC5 as a risk gene for alcohol dependence: Evidence from a genome-wide gene-set-based analysis and follow-up studies in drosophila and humans. *Neuropsychopharmacology*, *40*(2), 361–371.

Fuhrmann, A., Schroer, B. M., & Jong-Meyer, R. (2011). Systematic motivational counseling in groups: Promoting therapeutic change through client interaction. In W. M. Cox, & E. Klinger (Eds.), *Handbook of motivational counseling: Goal-based approaches to assessment and intervention with addiction and other problems* (2nd ed., pp. 303–327). Wiley-Blackwell.

Gallopel-Morvan, K., Spilka, S., Mutatayi, C., Rigaud, A., Lecas, F., & Beck, F. (2017). France's Evin Law on the control of alcohol advertising: Content, effectiveness and limitations. *Addiction*, *112*, 86–93.

Ghassemi, M., Bernecker, K., Herrmann, M., & Brandstätter, V. (2017). The process of disengagement from personal goals: Reciprocal influences between the experience of action crisis and appraisals of goal desirability and attainability. *Personality and Social Psychology Bulletin*, *43*(4), 524–537.

Hamilton, H. R., & DeHart, T. (2017). Drinking to belong: The effect of a friendship threat and self-esteem on college student drinking. *Self and Identity*, *16*(1), 1–15.

Herrmann, M., Brandstätter, V., & Wrosch, C. (2019). Downgrading goal-relevant resources in action crises: The moderating role of goal reengagement capacities and effects on well-being. *Motivation and Emotion*. Available from https://doi.org/10.1007/s11031-019-09755-z, http://dx.doi.org.ezproxy.morris.umn.edu/.

Hutchison, S. L., Flanagan, J. V., Karpov, I., Elliott, L., Holsinger, B., Edwards, J., & Loveland, D. (2019). Care management intervention to decrease psychiatric and substance use disorder readmissions in medicaid-enrolled adults. *The Journal of Behavioral Health Services & Research*, *46*(3), 533–543.

Institute of Alcohol Studies (2018). *Minimum unit pricing*. <http://www.ias.org.uk/Alcohol-knowledge-centre/Price/Factsheets/Minimum-unit-pricing.aspx>.

Jang, O.-J., Park, S.-C., Kim, S. G., Lee, J.-S., & Kim, J.-H. (2019). How early life stress and insecure attachment affect decision-making style and motivation to use alcohol: A structural equation model. *Psychiatry and Clinical Psychopharmacology*, *29*, 178–181. Available from https://doi.org/10.1080/24750573.2019.1611019.

Juraeva, D., Treutlein, J., Scholz, H., Frank, J., Degenhardt, F., Cichon, S., ... Rietschel, M. (2015). XRCC5 as a risk gene for alcohol dependence: Evidence from a genome-wide gene-set-based analysis and follow-up studies in drosophila and humans. *Neuropsychopharmacology*, *40*(2), 361–371.

Keller, M. C., & Nesse, R. M. (2006). The evolutionary significance of depressive symptoms: Different adverse situations lead to different depressive symptom patterns. *Journal of Personality and Social Psychology*, *91*(2), 316–330.

Kersbergen, I., & Field, M. (2017). Visual attention to alcohol cues and responsible drinking statements within alcohol advertisements and public health campaigns: Relationships with drinking intentions and alcohol consumption in the laboratory. *Psychology of Addictive Behaviors*, *31*(4), 435–446.

Klingemann, H., Sobell, M. B., & Sobell, L. C. (2010). Continuities and changes in self-change research. *Addiction*, *105*(9), 1510–1518.

Klinger, E. (1975). Consequences of commitment to and disengagement from incentives. *Psychological Review*, *82*, 1–25.

Klinger, E. (1977). *Meaning and void: Inner experience and the incentives in people's lives*. Minneapolis: University of Minnesota Press.

Klinger, E. (1996). Emotional influences on cognitive processing, with implications for theories of both. In P. Gollwitzer, & J. A. Bargh (Eds.), *The psychology of action: Linking cognition and motivation to behavior* (pp. 168–189). New York: Guilford.

Klinger, E. (2013). Goal commitments and the content of thoughts and dreams: Basic principles. *Frontiers in Psychology*, *4*. Available from https://doi.org/10.3389/fpsyg.2013.00415.

Klinger, E., & Cox, W. M. (2011a). Motivation and the goal theory of current concerns. In W. M. Cox, & E. Klinger (Eds.), *Handbook of motivational counseling* (2nd ed., pp. 3–47). Chichester, UK: Wiley.

Klinger, E., & Cox, W. M. (2011b). The motivational structure questionnaire, personal concerns inventory, and their variants: Psychometric properties. In W. M. Cox, & E. Klinger (Eds.), *Handbook of motivational counseling: Goal-based approaches to assessment and intervention with addiction and other problems* (pp. 204–232). Chichester, United Kingdom: Wiley-Blackwell.

Koppe, K., & Rothermund, K. (2017). Let it go: Depression facilitates disengagement from unattainable goals. *Journal of Behavior Therapy and Experimental Psychiatry*, *54*, 278–284.

Kotter-Grühn, D., Scheibe, S., Blanchard-Fields, F., & Baltes, P. B. (2009). Developmental emergence and functionality of sehnsucht (life longings): The sample case of involuntary childlessness in middle-aged women. *Psychology and Aging*, *24*(3), 634–644.

Kumar, S. (2017). Price elasticity of alcohol demand in India. *Alcohol and Alcoholism*, *52*(3), 390–395.

Laghi, F., Bianchi, D., Pompili, S., Lonigro, A., & Baiocco, R. (2019). Cognitive and affective empathy in binge drinking adolescents: Does empathy moderate the effect of self-efficacy in resisting peer pressure to drink? *Addictive Behaviors*, *89*, 229–235.

Lindgren, K. P., Baldwin, S. A., Olin, C. C., Wiers, R. W., Teachman, B. A., Norris, J., ... Neighbors, C. (2018). Evaluating within-person change in implicit measures of alcohol associations: Increases in alcohol associations predict increases in drinking risk and vice versa. *Alcohol and Alcoholism*, *53*(4), 386–393.

Loxton, N. J., Bunker, R. J., Dingle, G. A., & Wong, V. (2015). Drinking not thinking: A prospective study of personality traits and drinking motives on alcohol consumption across the first year of university. *Personality and Individual Differences*, *79*, 134–139.

Mackinnon, S. P., Kehayes, I. L., Clark, R., Sherry, S. B., & Stewart, S. H. (2014). Testing the four-factor model of personality vulnerability to alcohol misuse: A three-wave, one-year longitudinal study. *Psychology of Addictive Behaviors*, *28*(4), 1000–1012.

Marks, I. M., & Nesse, R. M. (1994). Fear and fitness: An evolutionary analysis of anxiety disorders. *Ethology & Sociobiology*, *15*(5–6), 247–261.

McMurran, M., Sellen, J., & Campbell, J. (2011). Offenders' motivation: Measurement, structure, and content. In W. M. Cox, & E. Klinger (Eds.), *Handbook of motivational counseling: Goal-based approaches to assessment and intervention with addiction and other problems* (2nd ed., pp. 253–272). Wiley-Blackwell.

Mikheeva, O. V., & Tragesser, S. L. (2016). Personality features, disordered eating, and alcohol use among college students: A latent profile analysis. *Personality and Individual Differences*, *94*, 360–365.

Montes, K. S., Olin, C. C., Teachman, B. A., Baldwin, S. A., & Lindgren, K. P. (2018). Hazardous drinking has unique relationships with implicit and explicit drinking identity. *Addictive Behaviors*, *87*, 155–161.

Morgenstern, M., Li, Z., Li, Z., & Sargent, J. D. (2017). The party effect: Prediction of future alcohol use based on exposure to specific alcohol advertising content. *Addiction*, *112*(1), 63–70.

Mosher, J. F., Adler, S. S., Pamukcu, A. M., & Treffers, R. D. (2017). Review of state laws restricting local authority to impose alcohol taxes in the United States. *Journal of Studies on Alcohol and Drugs*, *78*(2), 241–248.

Nesse, R. M. (2000). Is depression an adaptation? *Archives of General Psychiatry*, *57*, 14–20.

Nesse, R. M. (2001). "Is depression an adaptation?": Reply. *Archives of General Psychiatry*, *58*, 1085–1086.

Nesse, R. M. (2019). *Good reasons for bad feelings*. Dutton/Penguin.

Nesse, R. M., & Ellsworth, P. C. (2009). Evolution, emotions, and emotional disorders. *American Psychologist*, *64*(2), 129–139.

Newlin, D. B., & Thomson, J. B. (1990). Alcohol challenge with sons of alcoholics: A critical review and analysis. *Psychological Bulletin*, *108*(3), 383–402.

Nicolai, J., Moshagen, M., & Demmel, R. (2018). A test of expectancy-value theory in predicting alcohol consumption. *Addiction Research & Theory*, *26*(2), 133–142.

Nikula, R., Klinger, E., & Larson-Gutman, M. K. (1993). Current concerns and electrodermal reactivity: Responses to words and thoughts. *Journal of Personality*, *61*, 63–84.

Noel, J. K., Babor, T. F., Robaina, K., Feulner, M., Vendrame, A., & Monteiro, M. (2017). Alcohol marketing in the Americas and Spain during the 2014 FIFA world cup tournament. *Addiction*, *112*, 64–73.

Office of National Statistics (2017). *Adult drinking habits in Great Britain: 2017*. <https://www.ons.gov.uk/releases/adultdrinkinghabitsingreatbritain2017>.

Ong, H., Khor, F., Balasupramaniam, K., & Say, Y. (2018). Genetic polymorphisms of alcohol-metabolizing enzymes and their association with alcoholism risk, personality and anthropometric traits among Malaysian university students. *Psychology, Health & Medicine*, *23*(2), 160–170.

Orford, J. (1984). The prevention and management of alcohol problems in the family setting: A review of work carried out in English-speaking countries. *Alcohol and Alcoholism*, *19*(2), 109–122.

Ostafin, B. D., & Palfai, T. P. (2006). Compelled to consume: The implicit association test and automatic alcohol motivation. *Psychology of Addictive Behaviors*, *20*(3), 322–327.

Owens, M. M., Syan, S. K., Amlung, M., Beach, S. R. H., Sweet, L. H., & MacKillop, J. (2019). Functional and structural neuroimaging studies of delayed reward discounting in addiction: A systematic review. *Psychological Bulletin*, *145*(2), 141–164.

Pisinger, V. S. C., Holst, C. A., Bendtsen, P., Becker, U., & Tolstrup, J. S. (2017). Perceived parental alcohol problems and drinking patterns in youth: A cross-sectional study of 69,030 secondary education students in Denmark. *Preventive Medicine: An International Journal Devoted to Practice and Theory*, *105*, 389–396.

Pool, E., Brosch, T., Delplanque, S., & Sander, D. (2016). Attentional bias for positive emotional stimuli: A meta-analytic investigation. *Psychological Bulletin*, *142*(1), 79–106.

Portero-Tresserra, M., Gracia-Rubio, I., Cantacorps, L., Pozo, O. J., Gomez-Gomez, A., Pastor, A., et al. (2018). Maternal separation increases alcohol-drinking behaviour and reduces endocannabinoid levels in the mouse striatum and prefrontal cortex. *European Journal of Neuropsychopharmacology*, *28*, 499–512.

Ramirez, R. L., & Jernigan, D. H. (2017). Increasing alcohol taxes: Analysis of case studies from Illinois, Maryland, and Massachusetts. *Journal of Studies on Alcohol and Drugs*, *78*(5), 763–770.

Rehm, J., Gmel, G. E., Sr., Gmel, G., Hasan, O. S. M., Imtiaz, S., Popova, S., ... Shuper, P. A. (2017). The relationship between different dimensions of alcohol use and the burden of disease—An update. *Addiction*, *112*(6), 968–1001.

Rettie, H. C., Hogan, L. M., & Cox, W. M. (2018). Negative attentional bias for positive recovery-related words as a predictor of treatment success among individuals with an alcohol use disorder. *Addictive Behaviors*, *84*, 86–91.

Rinck, M., Wiers, R. W., Becker, E. S., & Lindenmeyer, J. (2018). Relapse prevention in abstinent alcoholics by cognitive bias modification: Clinical effects of combining approach bias modification and attention bias modification. *Journal of Consulting and Clinical Psychology*, *86*(12), 1005–1016.

Room, R. (2013). Sociocultural aspects of alcohol consumption. In P. Boyle, P. Boffetta, A. B. Lowenfels, H. Burns, O. Brawley, W. Zatonski, & J. Rehm (Eds.), *Alcohol: Science, policy, and public health* (pp. 38–45). New York, NY: Oxford University Press.

Roos, C. R., Mann, K., & Witkiewitz, K. (2017). Reward and relief dimensions of temptation to drink: Construct validity and role in predicting differential benefit from acamprosate and naltrexone. *Addiction Biology*, *22*(6), 1528–1539.

Rubinsky, A., Ellerbe, L. S., Gupta, S., Phelps, T. E., Bowe, T., Burden, J. L., & Harris, A. (2018). Outpatient continuing care after residential substance use disorder treatment in the US veterans health administration: Facilitators and challenges. *Substance Abuse*, *39*(3), 322–330. Available from https://doi.org/10.1080/08897077.2017.1391923, http://dx.doi.org.ezproxy.morris.umn.edu/.

Rung, J. M., & Madden, G. J. (2018). Experimental reductions of delay discounting and impulsive choice: A systematic review and meta-analysis. *Journal of Experimental Psychology: General*, *147*(9), 1349–1381.

Schuckit, M. A. (2018). A critical review of methods and results in the search for genetic contributors to alcohol sensitivity. *Alcoholism: Clinical and Experimental Research*, *42*(5), 822–835.

Shield, K. D., Rehm, J., Gmel, G., Rehm, M. X., & Allamani, A. (2013). Alcohol consumption, alcohol dependence, and related mortality in Italy in 2004: Effects of treatment-based interventions on alcohol dependence. *Substance Abuse Treatment, Prevention, and Policy*, *8*, 10.

Shin, J., Lee, Y., Park, S., & Seo, E. (2018). Young individuals' consideration of goal-self alignment and its relations to goal commitment and social concern: Age differences and similarities. *Self and Identity*. Available from https://doi.org/10.1080/15298868.2018.1510850, http://dx.doi.org.ezproxy.morris.umn.edu/.

Siegel, M., Ross, C. S., Albers, A. B., DeJong, W., King, C., III, Naimi, T., & Jernigan, D. H. (2016). The relationship between exposure to brand-specific alcohol advertising and brand-specific consumption among underage drinkers - United States, 2011–2012. *Early Childhood Research Quarterly*, *42*(1), 4.

Sobell, L. C., Klingemann, H. K., Toneatto, T., Sobell, M. B., Agrawal, S., & Leo, G. I. (2001). Alcohol and drug abusers' perceived reasons for self-change in Canada and Switzerland: Computer-assisted content analysis. *Substance Use & Misuse*, *36*(11), 1467–1500.

Staras, S. A. S., Livingston, M. D., Christou, A. M., Jernigan, D. H., Stautz, K., Frings, D., … Marteau, T. M. (2017). Impact of alcohol-promoting and alcohol-warning advertisements on alcohol consumption, affect, and implicit cognition in heavy-drinking young adults: A laboratory-based randomized controlled trial. *British Journal of Health Psychology*, *22*(1), 128–150.

Stautz, K., Frings, D., Albery, I. P., Moss, A. C., & Marteau, T. M. (2017). Impact of alcohol-promoting and alcohol-warning advertisements on alcohol consumption, affect, and implicit cognition in heavy-drinking young adults: A laboratory-based randomized controlled trial. *British Journal of Health Psychology*, *22*(1), 128–150.

Stussi, Y., Ferrero, A., Pourtois, G., & Sander, D. (2019). Achievement motivation modulates Pavlovian aversive conditioning to goal-relevant stimuli. *Nature NPG Science of Learning*, *4*(4). Available from https://doi.org/10.1038/s41539-019-0043-3, 2019.

Tabakoff, B., & Hoffman, P. L. (2013). The neurobiology of alcohol consumption and alcoholism: An integrative history. *Pharmacology, Biochemistry and Behavior*, *113*, 20–37.

Terry-McElrath, Y., Stern, S. A., & Patrick, M. E. (2017). Do alcohol use reasons and contexts differentiate adolescent high-intensity drinking? data from U.S. high school seniors, 2005–2016. *Psychology of Addictive Behaviors*, *31*(7), 775–785.

Van Hemel-Ruiter, M. E., de Jong, P. J., Ostafin, B. D., & Wiers, R. W. (2015). Reward sensitivity, attentional bias, and executive control in early adolescent alcohol use. *Addictive Behaviors*, *40*, 84–90.

Van Hemel-Ruiter, M. E., Wiers, R. W., Brook, F. G., & de Jong, P. J. (2016). Attentional bias and executive control in treatment-seeking substance-dependent adolescents: A cross-sectional and follow-up study. *Drug and Alcohol Dependence*, *159*, 133–141.

Verhulst, B., Neale, M. C., & Kendler, K. S. (2015). The heritability of alcohol use disorders: A meta-analysis of twin and adoption studies. *Psychological Medicine*, *45*(5), 1061–1072.

Waleewong, O., Laslett, A., Chenhall, R., & Room, R. (2018). Seeking help for harm from others' drinking in five Asian countries: Variation between societies, by type of harm and by source of help. *Alcohol and Alcoholism*, *53*(6), 667–673.

Walters, H. & Kosten, T. A. Early life stress and the propensity to develop addictive behaviors. *International Journal of Developmental Neuroscience*. **78** (1), 2019, 156–169. https://doi.org/10.1016/j.ijdevneu.2019.06.004.

Weaver, E. R. N., Wright, C. J. C., Dietze, P. M., & Lim, M. S. C. (2016). 'A drink that makes you feel happier, relaxed and loving': Young people's perceptions of alcohol advertising on Facebook. *Alcohol and Alcoholism, 51*(4), 481–486.

White, V., Azar, D., Faulkner, A., Coomber, K., Durkin, S., Livingston, M., ... Wakefield, M. (2017). Adolescents' exposure to paid alcohol advertising on television and their alcohol use: Exploring associations during a 13-year period. *Addiction, 112*(10), 1742–1751.

Wiers, R. W., Boffo, M., & Field, M. (2018). What's in a trial? On the importance of distinguishing between experimental lab studies and randomized controlled trials: The case of cognitive bias modification and alcohol use disorders. *Journal of Studies on Alcohol and Drugs, 79*(3), 333–343.

Wiers, R. W., Houben, K., Fadardi, J. S., van Beek, P., Rhemtulla, M., & Cox, W. M. (2015). Alcohol cognitive bias modification training for problem drinkers over the web. *Addictive Behaviors, 40*, 21–26.

Wrosch, C., & Miller, G. E. (2009). Depressive symptoms can be useful: Self-regulatory and emotional benefits of dysphoric mood in adolescence. *Journal of Personality and Social Psychology, 96*(6), 1181–1190.

Wrosch, C., Miller, G. E., Scheier, M. F., Schulz, R., & Carver, C. S. (2007). Giving up on unattainable goals: Benefits for health? *Personality and Social Psychology Bulletin, 33*, 251–265.

Wrosch, C., Scheier, M. F., Miller, G. E., Schulz, R., & Carver, C. S. (2003). Adaptive self-regulation of unattainable goals: Goal disengagement, goal reengagement, and subjective well-being. *Personality and Social Psychology Bulletin, 29*, 1494–1508.

Xuan, Z., Chaloupka, F. J., Blanchette, J. G., Nguyen, T. H., Heeren, T. C., Nelson, T. F., & Naimi, T. S. (2015). The relationship between alcohol taxes and binge drinking: Evaluating new tax measures incorporating multiple tax and beverage types. *Addiction, 110*(3), 441–450.

Yan, J., Aliev, F., Webb, B. T., Kendler, K. S., Williamson, V. S., Edenberg, H. J., ... Dick, D. M. (2014). Using genetic information from candidate gene and genome-wide association studies in risk prediction for alcohol dependence. *Addiction Biology, 19*(4), 708–721.

Ystrom, E., Kendler, K. S., & Reichborn-Kjennerud, T. (2014). Early age of alcohol initiation is not the cause of alcohol use disorders in adulthood, but is a major indicator of genetic risk. A population-based twin study. *Addiction, 109*(11), 1824–1832.

Zatoński, W. A., Sulkowska, U., Zatoński, M. Z., Herbeć, A. A., & Muszyńska, M. M. (2015). Alcohol taxation and premature mortality in Europe. *The Lancet, 385*(9974), 1181.

Zhao, J., & Stockwell, T. (2017). The impacts of minimum alcohol pricing on alcohol attributable morbidity in regions of British Colombia, Canada with low, medium and high mean family income. *Addiction, 112*(11), 1942–1951.

Ziaee, S. S., Fadardi, J. S., Cox, W. M., & Yazdi, S. A. A. (2016). Effects of attention control training program on drug abusers' attentional bias and treatment outcomes. *Journal of Consulting and Clinical Psychology, 84*, 861–873.

Chapter 12

Alcohol consumption in context: The effect of psych-socio-environmental drivers

Rebecca Monk[1,2] and Derek Heim[1,2]
[1]*Department of Psychology, Edge Hill University, Ormskirk, West Lancashire, United Kingdom,*
[2]*Liverpool Centre for Alcohol Research, Liverpool Health Partners, Liverpool Science Park, Liverpool, United Kingdom*

Even a cursory quick Google Scholar search of the words 'alcohol' and 'theory' reveals that many of the top 'research hits' have tended to utilize social cognitive approaches such as Alcohol Expectancy Theory, Drinking Motives and the Theory of Planned Behavior. These social cognitive theories of alcohol consumption that have tended to dominate the research landscape in the field tend to explain consumption in terms of an interplay between people's beliefs (or 'cognitions') and, what are broadly described as, 'normative influences' (i.e., what significant others think about the behavior). According to these models, people's beliefs about (the effects of) alcohol interact with these wider influences to determine the likelihood that people have positive or negative attitudes towards alcohol consumption and, ultimately, the probability of engaging in the behavior. Other theories such as the Health Belief Model or Protection Motivation Theory, broadly speaking, consider humans as risk/benefit 'calculators' who are seen to semi-objectively weigh up in a rational fashion the pros and cons of drinking alcohol in a process that may be shaped by wider influences (e.g., media) and cues to action (e.g., public health campaigns; Champion & Skinner, 2008; Floyd et al., 2000).

Notwithstanding some successes at informing the development of intervention approaches such as those seeking to challenge normative belies surrounding peer prevalence of alcohol consumption (e.g., Moreira, Smith, & Foxcroft, 2009; Perkins, 2002) and their continued popularity for framing alcohol research, over the years several concerns with these approaches have been noted. Some of the limitations of social cognitive models have been methodological in nature. Indeed, despite the advantages of utilizing

The Handbook of Alcohol Use - Understandings from Synapse to Society.
DOI: https://doi.org/10.1016/B978-0-12-816720-5.00012-8

self-report questionnaires in research (Del Boca & Noll, 2000; Glovannucci et al., 1991; e.g., inexpensive, ask standardized and comparable questions, easily quantifiable), it has long been documented (and equally long ignored, perhaps) that self-report measures may not always be as reliable as the research community might hope. First, there have been questions raised regarding the practical application of self-report assessments. As has been highlighted in the wider academic literature, responses can be impacted by demand characteristics which cue participants about what is expected (Orne, 1962), by the expectations of researchers (Rosenthal et al., 1991; although see Cahalan, 2019 for a recent critical re-evaluation of some of the claims of the famous 'sane in insane places' study) and by the interaction between these beliefs and expectations.

To wit, reports about one's substance use have been shown to be shaped by a number of personal biases and appear to vary depending on the perceived demands of the task (Davies & Baker, 1987; Davies, & Best, 1996; Newham & Davies, 2007). This is illustrated by evidence suggesting that questionnaire responses may differ as a function of the context in which they are elicited. In the early 1970s a study of school children's alcohol consumption in Glasgow (Davies & Stacey, 1972) unexpectedly found that children's self-report of alcohol consumption appeared to be elevated when questionnaires were completed in school settings in the presence of peers as opposed to at home and, quite possibly, under the watchful eye of parents. This was an early indication of how self-reports of alcohol consumption may serve as a 'reputation management' resource in which individuals may exaggerate their consumption in some contexts (e.g., to look 'tough' in front of peers) or downplay it in others. Questionnaires also tend to present participants pre-defined responses which may constrain responses patterns. For example, established assessments of drinking motives arguably 'force' respondents into making associations between alcohol consumption and emotions (e.g., happy or sad) when these may not, in fact, reflect a person's views (Cook et al., 2020; Kunstche & Kuntsche, 2017). Even seemingly inconsequential factors such as the layout of questionnaires appear to impact responses (Budd, 1987). This is also evidenced in the alcohol literature which shows, for instance, that the use of multiple target questionnaire items (Melson et al., 2011) combined with socially desirable responding (Melson et al., 2016) may, at least in part, account for apparent misperceptions regarding what normative consumption behaviour is.

Overall, it appears that the notion of eliciting 'truthful cognitions' about substance use behaviors through self-report questionnaires can be problematic, as answers to questions may to an extent be conceptualized as acts of cognitive construction (Davies, 1992). The formative work by Davies (1992, 1997), in this way, illustrates that response to questions about substance use can serve functions for individuals and may reveal thought processes and motives and intentions underpinning these, as opposed to be statements of some 'objective truth'. This body of work suggests that is entirely possible for individuals to explain their substance use in terms of being 'helplessly addicted' in one context and in volitional terms of 'being in control' in another (Coggans & Davies, 1988; Davies & Baker, 1987).

An additional layer of complexity to establishing "truth" from self-report may come from memory distortions that can be exaggerated by the pharmacological effects of substances. While limitations of autobiographical memory mean that the task of recalling accurately past behaviors can be challenging in optimal circumstances (e.g., Skowronski, Walker, & Betz, 2003), memory impairments associated with alcohol consumption (Walker & Hunter, 1978; Weissenborn & Duka, 2003) and in absence of environmental stimuli which are known to aid recall (as Godden & Baddley's, 1975 seminal work attests) can exacerbate issues with recall. Empirical work illustrates this by pointing to discrepancies in alcohol consumption reports between real-time and retrospective accounts (Dulin, Alvarado, Fitterling, & Gonzalez, 2017; Merrill, Fan, Wray, & Miranda, 2020; Monk, Heim, Qureshi, & Price, 2015; Poulton, Pan, Bruns, Sinnott, & Hester, 2018). While this interesting research points to differences between real time and retrospective recall in alcohol behaviors, more work is required to understand the extent to which (situational) drivers may systematically distort self-reports of alcohol behaviors. The identification of contextually-shaped response patterns could have significant implications for refining both our understanding of real-world alcohol consumption and also the development of interventions.

Connected to this, the assessment of alcohol consumption and related beliefs in non-alcohol-related environments (e.g., laboratories or neutral environments often in isolation) may also explain why social cognitive models can sometimes struggle to account for how cognitive representations interact with situational demands to shape alcohol behaviors. In other words, these models tend to emphasize the extent to which people are shaped behaviorally by cognitive representations rather than being driven by what is occurring in the world around them. These models might, for example, find it difficult to account for how an individual may respond if, on a Saturday night, their friend returns from the bar with a drink they have purchased for them and places it on the table in front of the person. Normative belief theories may posit that one might appraise how acceptable their peers may view the acceptance (or indeed refusal) of this apparent offer. Risk/reward and expectancy models, on the other hand, may suggest that a person's decision to accept or refuse the drink may be the product of the perceived likelihood of positive and negative outcomes. However, none of these models outline (or account for) how things that are happening at that moment in time my influence these processes. Additionally, they do not take past behavior (see Conner & Armitage, 1998) into account - your friends might well know that you always say that you don't want a drink but always end up drinking it ('reluctantly') when it gets placed in front of you!

Situated cognition theorists suggest that knowing is inseparable from doing, as all knowledge is situated within activities that are bound to social, cultural and physical contexts (Brown, Collins, & Duguid, 1989). When considering activities that are socially, culturally and physically bound, alcohol consumption is a prominent example. Alcohol is a ubiquitous component of event where people celebrate (e.g., birthdays) and commiserate (e.g., funerals), it is an integral part of many types of social gathering (e.g., sporting events), it occurs at specific (socially-agreed) times and places and has culturally-defined knowledge structures which allows for shared expectations. (ask anyone in the UK and we'd wager that they would know what the archetypal "British pub" looks like, when and with whom people go, what one can expect to find there and how one would expect to behave) And yet, as highlighted, over the years research seeking to deepen our understanding of alcohol consumption has tended to downplay, or ignore, the significant impact of the actual social and environmental contexts in which people consume alcohol (Heim & Monk, 2017). Accordingly, researchers have increasingly moved to address this issue by focusing more closely on the social and contextual influences on alcohol behaviors and by employing more ecologically aware research methodologies. Indeed, there is an increasing awareness that drinking events are complex phenomena that are shaped by psychopharmacological effects of intoxication, interactions between individuals and groups, and are situated within multifaced environments (Clapp et al., 2018). As such, researchers have begun to model the complexity of drinking events to represent the interacting Micro (biological e.g., BAC, and psychological e.g., planned intoxication), Mezzo (social e.g., group intoxication) and macro (physical e.g., environmental promotion) drivers of consumption. This perspective sits rather analogously with the tenants of situated cognition.

Groups, beliefs and consumption

Proponents of situated cognition have long called for greater focus on how beliefs - structures of information - are (re)produced by the interactions people have with each other and with the "material and representational structures in their environments" (Greeno, 1997; p. 15). When applied to the field of alcohol consumption, this notion is supported by a growing body of research which suggests that beliefs about consumption promoting drinking are not static, but fluid, and constructed differentially in varying social and environmental contexts.

Before discussing this more recent literature in a bit more depth, it is worth noting that the view of interactionally situated cognition (Wortham, 2001) is not entirely novel within our field. For example, Skog's (1985) seminal contribution posits that (changes in) alcohol consumption are fundamentally and dialectically shaped by multiplicatively combining factors as well as the habits of interconnected others behaving as a collective. In another classic contribution, Macandrew and Edgerton (1969) coined the term 'drunken comportment' to refer to how people behave may when under the influence of alcohol. Drunken behavior, according to them, can differ as a function of cultural contexts and may be partly governed by socially agreed standards regarding what constitutes (un)acceptable alcohol/intoxicated behavior which may encompass 'freedoms' granted to intoxicated people. As such, they way in which we engage in alcohol consumption and the manifold ways we view that act, can be conceptualized as being profoundly socially and contextually shaped.

The alcohol myopia model (Steele & Josephs, 1990) also highlights the importance of considering social and cognitive factors in the study of alcohol consumption. As an influential theoretical explanation of alcohol-related individual risk-taking, the model posits that intoxication narrows attention, with focus being drawn away from the periphery and towards the most salient and readily processed cues, impairing ability to systematically process information. This theory has also been applied to the understanding of changes in normative beliefs in certain contexts. For example, intoxication may shift attentional resources towards group-level cues which may result in groups who are under the influence of alcohol being less cooperative than both intoxicated individuals and sober groups (Hopthrow, Abrams, Frings, & Hulbert, 2007). Likewise, alcohol intoxication has been found to amplify in-group biases to the detriment of out-groups (Zhou, Heim, Monk, Levy, & Pollard, 2018). Such studies begin to illustrate that the pharmacological effects of intoxication may shape social identity processes in group contexts. They also help explain the extent to which the perceived beliefs of others are intertwined with, and can shape, behaviors – including those related to alcohol consumption.

The reason why others' beliefs should be a key driver of one's own drinking is elucidated in by Festinger's (1954) classic work. His theory of social comparison asserts that it is a fundamental human drive to draw comparisons between ourselves and others, partly to help us ascertain what constitutes appropriate (social normative) behavior in given contexts. This can entail making decision about common beliefs (injunctive norms) and behaviors (descriptive norms) in order to determine how to act (Borsari & Carey, 2003). If one's behavior (e.g., consumption) is perceived as normative, no behavioral adjustment is required. However, oftentimes people incorrectly perceive their own attitudes/behaviors to be different to those of others, known as pluralistic ignorance (Berkowitz, 2004). In the study of alcohol consumption, this is referred to as a norm misperception - where a sense of cognitive dissonance results from believing one's own consumption to be different from typical consumption (Perkins, 2007) and behavior adjusted to redress this imbalance (Berkowitz, 2004). Notwithstanding earlier noted concerns related to an over-reliance on questionnaire measures which is also a concern in this domain, there is consistent evidence that people misjudge the level of alcohol others consume (e.g., Berkowitz, 2004; Borsari & Carey, 2001; Broadwater, Curtin, Martz, & Zrull, 2006; Carey, Borsari, Carey, & Maisto,

2006; Miley & Frank, 2006: Perkins, 2002, 2007; Perkins & Berkowitz, 1986; Perkins, Haines, & Rice, 2005; Perkins, Meilman, Leichliter, Cashin, & Presley, 1999; Wechsler & Kuo, 2000), including overestimation of drinks per week, frequency of consumption and consumption in a typical session are prevalent findings (Lewis & Neighbors, 2004; Thombs, Wolcott, & Farkash, 1997), and that such normative beliefs reliably predict consumption (e.g., Clapp & McDonnell, 2000; Larimer, Turner, Mallett, & Geisner, 2004; McAlaney & McMahon, 2007a, 2007b; Neighbors, Lee, Lewis, Fossos, & Larimer, 2007).

However, one limitation of this area of work is that a substantial portion of it examines normative beliefs in research environment's which are far removed from the typical contexts of consumption (See Monk & Heim, 2014a, 2014b for systematic review). This is problematic as alcohol-related contexts such as bars and pubs may, according to Lo Monaco, Piermattéo, Guimelli, and Ernst-Vintila (2011), act as 'normative frameworks' whereby the (in)appropriateness of behavior is partly be determined by people's current location or environment which may distort alcohol-related perceptions (McAlaney, Bewick, & Bauerle, 2010). Normative beliefs and resultant drinking may therefore be contextually shaped, and mirror apparent increases in consumption amongst specific groups or during particular events (see for example, Clapp & Shillington, 2001; 2001b; Clapp et al., 2003; Demers et al., 2002; Thombs et al., 1997). Indeed, observations from a staged wine tasting event (Kuendig & Kuntsche, 2012) support this notion. Here, drinking was found to be lower in the solitary condition than in the subsequent group tasting condition – a fact attributed to the participants' belief that it would not be appropriate, or normative, to drink large quantities when alone (versus in a group). Whilst normative beliefs can only be inferred from this study, the assertion that there may be contextual shifts is further supported by a small but important body of work (e.g., Cooke & French, 2011; Monk & Heim, 2013a, 2013b, 2013c; Pedersen, Labrie, & Lac, 2008). For example, research by Monk and Heim (2013a, 2013b, 2013c) identified elevated normative beliefs regarding the frequency of one's own and others' consumption when assessed during exposure to alcohol-related, as opposed to, neutral immersive cues. This growing body of work serves as a reminder of the need for alcohol researchers to more routinely capture contextual variability (such as with the use of simulated bar laboratories e.g., Frings et al., 2017) with a view to embracing more fully the situated cognition notion that the environments in which knowledge is constructed are a key to the production and understanding of knowledge.

In addition to normative beliefs that drive consumption, individuals' views about the likely positive and negative outcomes of consumption (termed outcome expectancies; Leigh & Stacy, 1993) have been found to be associated with self-reported consumption (e.g., Aas, Leigh, Anderssen, & Jakobsen, 1998; Anderson, Grunwald, Bekman, Brown, & Grant, 2011; Brown, Goldman, Inn, & Anderson, 1980; Carey, 1995; D'Alessio, Baiocco, & Laghi, 2006) as well as drinking measured in semi naturalistic bar environments (Bot, Engels, &

Knibbe, 2005; Hopthrow, Randsley de Moura, Meleady, Abrams, & Swift, 2014; Larsen, Engels, Wiers, Granic, & Spijkerman, 2012; Roehrich & Goldman, 1995). Similarly, motivational models of alcohol consumption suggest that people drink in order to achieve valued outcomes and, as such, useful for understanding consumption (Kuntsche et al., 2012). However, while earlier research conceptualized these cognitions as static, a growing body of literature suggests that these vary in different locations and across varying social environments (Monk & Heim, 2013a, 2013b; Wall, Hinson, McKee, & Goldstein, 2001; Wall, Mckee, & Hinson, 2000). Ecologically momentary assessment techniques have also begun to provide a more detailed picture of the changing nature of alcohol-related beliefs and cognitions. For example, Monk and Heim (2014a, 2014b) found that participants who were situated in a pub, bar or club and in a social group of friends reported heightened outcome expectancies in comparison to participants in other settings (e.g., being home and/or alone). In a similar vein, drinking motives - the reasons why people decide to drink (e.g., Cox & Klinger, 1988) - also appear to vary as a function of people's setting (e.g., Kuntsche & Labhart, 2012; Labhart et al., 2020; Smit, Groefsema, Luijten, Engels, & Kuntsche, 2015). This growing body of more ecologically aware work is therefore beginning to yield insights into the extent to which alcohol cognitions are *situated.*

Affect, beliefs and consumption

Having made the case for researchers in the field to embrace situated cognition as a means of better accounting for the extent to which consumption is mutable by the social environments in which people think and act with regards to alcohol, we now turn to argue for a greater consideration of possible internal influences on alcohol cognitions. In doing so, we suggest that there is also a need for social cognitive models of alcohol to better account for the impact affective states have on people's decisions to drink or to exercise restraint. One's own mood, and that of others, we outline, appear to represent significant influences on how individuals construct alcohol-related beliefs and on how they drink alcohol.

The ability of alcohol to induce positive, and ameliorate negative, affect was famously recognized in a brilliantly equivocal speech on prohibition by the Mississippi state representative Noah S. "Soggy" Sweat, Jr. (1922–96) in which he recounted alcohol's capacity to enable "a man to magnify his joy, and his happiness, and to forget, if only for a little while, life's great tragedies, and heartaches, and sorrows" (Noah Sweet, 1952 Mississippi State Legislature, cited in Atkinson, 2005, pg 102). As in politics, the ability of alcohol to affect the moods of others is also professed throughout mythology, the alcohol research literature and, sometimes, even both! Illustrating this point, the apparent inextricable link between alcohol and emotions is beautifully captured in Babor et al.'s (1983) memorably written introduction beginning with a French adaptation of a fable which we briefly retell here. In this tale, the revered Saint Martin brings a grape vine from Italy back to Gaul by transporting it inside the bone of a bird. During the journey, as it grows, it needs to be replanted into the bones of a lion and then into those of a donkey. On arriving in Gaul, it is then planted near an Abbey and, after some time, yields enough fruit to produce three pitchers of wine, which are consumed by the local monks. Legend says that after the first pitcher, the monks sang like birds and after the second they showed the courage of lions. After consuming the third pitcher, however, they made asses of themselves!

The large body of work which has examined motives and outcome expectancies in relation to alcohol behaviors (as highlighted above) provides ample support for the influence that alcohol exerts on mood. Indeed, the literature suggests that being motivated by the desire to achieve, or expectation of, experiencing positive affect, or reducing negative states, is associated with increased drinking quantities and frequencies (e.g., Kuntsche et al., 2014; Laghi, Bianchi, Pompili, Lonigro, & Baiocco, 2019). Motivational models of alcohol use therefore suggest that enhancement and coping motives exert an important influence on alcohol consumption (e.g., Armeli, Carney, Tennen, Affleck, & O'Neil, 2000). Consumption may consequently be viewed (at least partly) as a deliberative act undertaken in order to regulate one's mood (Tice, Bratslavsky, & Baumeister, 2001). Similarly, in line with the tension reduction (see Cappell & Herman, 1972) and self-medication hypotheses (see Khantzian, 1997), substance use may partly be a result of individuals' attempts to alter undesired states of minds, or affective states (Sayette, 2017). This, in turn, may make people consume alcohol in order to obtain these desired effects and highlight the extent to which consumption can be 'strategic' so as to alleviate negative mood (Koob, 2013). Accordingly, it has been suggested that low (negative) mood predict elevated levels of alcohol craving and consumption (e.g., Cleveland & Harris, 2010; Jones, Tiplady, Houben, Nederkoorn, & Field, 2018), as users seek to ameliorate negative affect by consuming the substance (Baker, Piper, McCarthy, Majeskie, & Fiore, 2004). However, bodies of work in this domain often consist of post hoc examinations of the beliefs that are likely to be triggered at the time of consumption, informing decision to drink or exercise restraint. On the other hand, a separate yet inter-related body of research also seeks to assess and/or manipulate mood and offers further support for the notion that alcohol improves mood (e.g., Rousseau, Irons, & Correia, 2011).

Enriching this body of knowledge, laboratory-based mood induction and priming techniques, have therefore increasingly featured in research (e.g., Rousseau et al., 2011; VanderVenn et al., 2016) with results indicating that negative affect can elevate approach tendencies (e.g., Cousijn et al., 2014), alcohol-related attentional biases (e.g., Field & Quigley, 2009; Hepworth, Mogg, Brignell, & Bradley, 2010) and the perceived value of alcohol (e.g., Amlung & MacKillop, 2014). Employing a taste test procedure, it has also been found that beer consumption may be elevated by priming individuals with negative affect words and that this may be moderated by severity of alcohol problems (Zack, Poulos, Fragopoulos, Woodford, & MacLeod, 2006). In this area too, research has capitalized on technological advances and utilized ecological momentary assessment techniques to document the extent to which people's moods are prone to change (e.g., Ebner-Priemer & Trull, 2009; Hektner, Schmidt, & Csikszentmihalyi, 2007; Johnson et al., 2008; Walz, Nauta, & aan het Rot, 2014). Alcohol research using these technologies, in a similar vein, indicates that consumptive practices can be related to positive affect (e.g., Kuntsche & Bruno, 2015; Peacock et al., 2015). In line with the self-medication hypothesis, a non-EMG study in which respondents were required to document their mood three times a day and alcohol consumption once per day found that affect variation may pose a risk factor for elevate consumption levels (Gottfredson & Hussong, 2013; see also Mohr, Arpin, & McCabe, 2015). Further evidence has accrued with respect to alcohol consumption influencing negative mood (e.g., De Wit, Söderpalm, Nikolayev, & Young, 2003), nervousness (Swendsen et al., 2000) and higher day-to-day positive affect (Peacock et al., 2015).

Notwithstanding some noteworthy findings (e.g., Zack et al, 2006) and a possible need for replication efforts (see Heirene, 2020), and despite the strong theoretical grounds for investigating the link between affective states and alcohol consumption, empirical findings have, however, been considerably more varied than might be expected. A review by Sayette (2017), for example, documents usefully how over the past decades, researchers interested in alcohol and mood have applied different perspectives to the question. These perspectives encompassed pharmacological-derived hypotheses, social learning approaches and, more recently, biobehavioral accounts that seek to understand more precisely the interplay between social, (anticipatory) cognitive and affective forces. The author outlines further that methodological differences (including the use of electric shocks to induce anxiety!) may play a role in shaping study outcomes. With these issues in mind, Sayette convincingly makes the case that researchers need to turn their attention towards more fully considering how environmental contexts are implicated in shaping the link between ofttimes fluctuating (see also Neumann & Strack, 2000; Parkinson & Simons, 2009; Swendsen et al., 2000) affect and consumption. Adding weight to this assertion, a recent study by our team (Monk et al., 2020) identified both mood and social context as distinct influences on alcohol behaviors. Specifically, using an EMA paradigm, we found that feeling unhappy prior to consumption was associated with increased in drinking. Once a drinking occasion had started, however, feeling happy appeared to be significantly associated with drinking larger quantities. Findings further suggest that alcohol consumption elevates mood and that being with friends was also associated with increased alcohol consumption.

Another potentially fruitful avenue for alcohol researchers interested in exploring the interplay between alcohol consumption and affective states concerns the possibility that, in addition to contexts shaping this association, is may also differ as a function of variable psychopharmacological effects of alcohol. A small body of research, in this way, suggests that mood may be impacted differently as a function of whether individuals' BAC levels are ascending or descending. Studies thus indicate that on the ascending limb of the BAC curve, people tend to be more likely to experience positive affect while on the descending limb people tend to experience more negative impacts (Earleywine & Martin, 1993; Sutker, Tabakoff, Goist, & Randall, 1983). However, in other research male respondents reported lower mood on the descending limb of the BAC curve in one study but not in a second where no differences between the ascending and descending curve were found (Söderlund, Parker, Schwartz, & Tulving, 2005). Merrill, Wardell, and Read (2009), on the other hand, found that higher tension reduction expectancies were positively related to lower mood following consumption among participants with low levels of BAC on the ascending curve.

Moving forward? Objective measures in alcohol research

It is worth considering that other areas of research have attempted to use what are described as more 'objective' measures of affect and consumption. Facial electromyography (EMG), for example, has been suggested as a means of assess objectively activation of facial muscles such as the corrugator supercilli and the zygomaticus major, which are suggested to be associated with facial expression of experiences of happiness (i.e., smiling) or sadness (i.e., frowning), for instance. For example, it has been found that heavy drinkers (versus light drinkers, based on self-report) show stronger responses to negatively valanced stimuli using this method (Glautier, O'Brien, & Dixon, 2001). Furthermore, more recent research using facial has used EMG alongside alcohol administration techniques to harness more systematically the mechanisms that may underlie the relationship between alcohol consumption and emotion. For example, our own work suggests that alcohol may intensify emotional responses to social stimuli and that objective (facial EMG) measures may be more sensitive to this process than self-report (Monk et al., Under Review).

There is also some emerging evidence to suggest that cortisol levels may hold promise for assessing more objectively the extent to which emotional and cognitive stress responses shape appetitive behaviors. Emotional eating, in this way, was found to be associated with a blunted cortisol stress response in a study by van Strien and Colleagues (2013) and other work lends support to the notion that individuals display of particularly marked emotional and cognitive stress reactions may be associated with particular cortisol responses (Schlotz, Hammerfald, Ehlert, & Gaab, 2011). Notwithstanding emerging criticism of the extent to which the Implicit Association Task (IAT) represents a measure of responses that are beyond the control of individual and a need for further clarification about what this methodology gauges (Yamaguchi & Beattie, 2020), other research has begun to use the IAT as an indirect measure of mood among lightly intoxicated individuals (see Ito, Matsuzaki, & Kawahara, 2018; Lindgren et al., 2018). Ito et al. (2018) found that IAT scores of mildly intoxicated participants were in a more cheerful mood following alcohol consumption compared to baseline assessment. Continued efforts to harness objective measures of emotive responses may therefore be fruitful avenues to pursue for researchers as they continue to unpick the dynamic relation between emotions and consumptions. One caveat to note, however, is that in seeking to increase the objectivity of data, this new line of enquiry has hitherto been dominated by laboratory techniques. Whilst this is likely due to the nature of the apparatus required for this research, alcohol researchers should continue to be mindful of situated cognition perspectives, taking care not to entirely remove alcohol consumption behaviors from the contexts in which they more naturally occur.

Another emerging method which may, to an extent, address concerns about laboratory-based work when studying psychosocial drivers of alcohol consumption is Secure Continuous Remote Alcohol Monitoring (SCRAM). This equipment provides 24/7 measures of alcohol consumption by taking continuous readings through the skin, typically via monitors fitted to the ankle. It is was originally marketed as tools to monitor compliance with abstinence; these devices are deployed increasingly as means to aid individuals in attempts to reduce consumption (e.g., Barnett et al., 2017; Neville, Williams, Goodall, Murer, & Donnelly, 2013), ensure abstinence (e.g., in cases where offenders are released on license with the condition of sobriety; Pepper et al., 2015), and to reduce rates of recidivism (Flango & Cheesman, 2009) as well as drink-driving (Voas, DuPont, Talpins, & Shea, 2011). Research also suggests that SCRAMs may provide wearers with a useful social tool to "excuse" them from drinking in situations where they may perceive social pressure to do so (Neville et al., 2013). Furthermore, there is growing interest in examining their utility in research projects which seek to identify more objective means of measuring consumption, away for self-reports (e.g., Caluzzi et al., 2019). However, concerns have been raised about the comfort, appearance, and susceptibility to tampering (Alessi, Barnett, & Petry, 2017; Caluzzi et al., 2019; McKnight, Fell, & Auld-Owens, 2012) of these devices. It has also been suggested that transdermal alcohol levels can lag breath alcohol levels (Leffingwell et al., 2013) and, while they may reliably detect two drinks or more (Sakai et al., 2006), they may be less accurate at detecting lower levels of consumption (Roache et al., 2015).

Similar technology has also been transferred into in smartwatches designed to track intoxication (e.g., Bactrack Skyn). These may address some concerns about the appearance of SCRAMs and convey research benefits (Gutierrez, Fast, Ngu, & Gao, 2015). However, this technology is in its infancy and more research concerning the efficacy/validity of this technological innovation seems prudent. A further potential avenue for exploration may be the use of alcohol biomarkers as a means of better understanding social and contextual drivers of consumption. Biomarkers are defined as "a characteristic that is objectively measured and evaluated as an indicator of normal biological processes, pathogenic processes or pharmacologic responses to a therapeutic intervention" (p. 91, Biomarkers Definitions Working Group, 2001). In addition to testing for drug use, they can be obtained from a variety of human tissues (e.g., blood, urine, hair) and used to assess objectively a person's current or past alcohol consumption (Freeman & Vrana, 2010). This is done by measuring the metabolites of alcohol (termed direct markers, e.g., Ethyl glucuronide (EtG), ethyl sulfate (EtS)) or changes in molecules/cells/tissues that result from chronic or acute alcohol exposure (termed indirect markers; e.g., mean corpuscular volume (MCV), gamma-glutamyltransferase (GGT), carbohydrate-deficient transferrin (CDT)). By allowing for the accurate measurement of alcohol intake and drinking patterns, these biomarkers may represent a significant advance in clinical care as well as valuable research tool (Freeman & Vrana, 2010). However, there are limitations to these biomarkers; their accuracy may be impacted by age, gender, other ingested substances, non-alcohol-associated diseases (e.g., hypertension, kidney and/or liver diseases) and incidental ethanol exposures (e.g., mouthwash; Jastrzębska et al., 2016). For this reason, new biomarkers continue to be identified and researched, to refine their use for more objectively measuring consumption of alcohol (Freeman & Vrana, 2010)).

In this way, Phosphatidylethanol (PEth) is a promising biomarker that may be less affected by the aforementioned limitations and which could possibly usefully complement the existing spectrum of tests (Jastrzębska et al., 2016). Indeed, research suggests that this method has high specificity and sensitivity, capable of measuring both prolonged as well as binge alcohol consumption (ibid) and that it may be the only marker that can detect moderate intake, while distinguishing this form of consumption from abstinence (Kechagias et al., 2015). There is diminutive yet growing research as to the relationship between PEth and alcohol consumption (e.g., Aradottir, Asanovska, Gjerss, Hansson, & Alling, 2006; Hahn et al., 2012; Helander et al., 2012; Isaksson, Walther, Hansson, Andersson, & Alling, 2011; Stewart, Law, Randall, & Newman, 2010). However, as with much of the research on biomarkers (Freeman & Vrana, 2010), there has been a reliance on testing amongst clinical populations (see also research by Schröck, Redondo, Fabritius, König, & Weinmann, 2016 who found a relationship between PEth levels of BAC levels in people convicted of driving under the influence). In other words, while research suggests that PEth levels are associated with self-reported consumption amongst those who abuse alcohol, how these may manifest in social drinkers has received considerably less attention (for notable exceptions see Stewart et al., 2010 for research with women on reproductive age and Comasco et al., 2009 for research with adolescents). There is therefore a need for further research to develop a clearer picture of the relationship between varying PEth levels and different drinking patterns, and to do so in non-clinical samples.

In summary, as technology and science become increasingly more advanced and widely available, researchers may be able to tap into the affordance of these advances to help answer increasingly nuanced questions about the psychosocial drivers of consumption and how they interact with psychopharmacological influences of the drug in question. However, while it is incumbent upon social scientists to embrace these methods, it is also important that they ensure the field does not become over medicalized – just as, in the same way, an over reliance on neurological research arguably resulted in a narrow vision of addiction as, for example, a brain disease as opposed to the product of a diverse interplay of psychological and social factors (Heim, Blomqvist, Edman, Room, & Storbjörk, 2014). Indeed, in the past, biomedical and psychosocial approaches have tended to develop somewhat disparately, partly driven methodological barriers. Going forward, researchers from different epistemological traditions may do well to collaborate to a greater degree to better account for the multifaceted nature of alcohol consumption and its varied drivers. New easy to use advanced techniques such as those which can now – quite literally – be tied to people's wrists may represent a valuable step towards this aim if used appropriately.

Concluding thoughts

In this chapter we have argued for the need of alcohol researchers interested in examining psychosocial drivers of alcohol consumption to move beyond the relative comfort of relying on research methods that seek to use questionnaires as a means of eliciting some form of 'objective truth'. Akin to Schrödinger's cat in physics, we need to embrace the fact that the way in which we ask questions will always, to a greater or lesser extent, shape the types of answers we get. Social scientists need to abandon the overly simplistic notion of cognitions being solely the outcome of brain processes in people's heads, embrace situated cognition perspectives, and treat people's beliefs and behaviors as a dialectically shaped outcome between individuals and society (as the somewhat out of fashion social interactionist literature suggested many years ago) as well as pharmacological properties of substances. Zinberg's (1984) notion of 'drug set and setting' appears as relevant to the field as ever and we now have the tools to better understand how the different influences impact the behavior in question.

References

Aas, N. H., Leigh, B. C., Anderssen, N., & Jakobsen, R. (1998). Two year longitudinal study of alcohol expectancies and drinking among Norwegian adolescents. *Addiction*, *93*, 373–384.

Alessi, S. M., Barnett, N. P., & Petry, N. M. (2017). Experiences with SCRAMx alcohol monitoring technology in 100 alcohol treatment outpatients. *Drug and Alcohol Dependence*, *178*, 417–424.

Amlung, M., & MacKillop, J. (2014). Understanding the effects of stress and alcohol cues on motivation for alcohol via behavioral economics. *Alcoholism: Clinical and Experimental Research, 38*(6), 1780–1789.

Anderson, K. G., Grunwald, I., Bekman, N., Brown, S. A., & Grant, A. (2011). To drink or not to drink: Motives and expectancies for use and non use in adolescence. *Addictive Behaviors, 36*, 972–979.

Aradottir, S., Asanovska, G., Gjerss, S., Hansson, P., & Alling, C. (2006). Phosphatidylethanol (PEth) concentrations in blood are correlated to reported alcohol intake in alcohol-dependent patients. *Alcohol and Alcoholism, 41*(4), 431–437.

Armeli, S., Carney, M. A., Tennen, H., Affleck, G., & O'Neil, T. P. (2000). Stress and alcohol use: A daily process examination of the stressor vulnerability model. *Journal of Personality and Social Psychology, 98*, 979–994.

Atkinson, J. M. (2005). Lend me your ears: All you need to know about making speeches and presentations. Oxford University Press on Demand.

Babor, T. F., Berglas, S., Mendelson, J. H., Ellingboe, J., & Miller, K. (1983). Alcohol, affect, and the disinhibition of verbal behavior. *Psychopharmacology, 80*(1), 53–60.

Baker, T. B., Piper, M. E., McCarthy, D. E., Majeskie, M. R., & Fiore, M. C. (2004). Addiction motivation reformulated: An affective processing model of negative reinforcement. *Psychological Review, 111*(1), 33–51.

Barnett, N. P., Celio, M. A., Tidey, J. W., Murphy, J. G., Colby, S. M., & Swift, R. M. (2017). A preliminary randomized controlled trial of contingency management for alcohol use reduction using a transdermal alcohol sensor. *Addiction, 112*(6), 1025–1035.

Berkowitz, A. D. (2004). An overview of the social norms approach. In L. Lederman, L. Stewart, F. Goodhart, & L. Laitman (Eds.), *Changing the culture of college drinking: A socially situated prevention campaign* (pp. 187–208). Cresskill, NJ: Hampton Press.

Biomarkers Definitions Working Group. (2001). Biomarkers and surrogate endpoints: preferred definitions and conceptual framework. *Clin. Pharmacology Ther., 69*, 89–95.

Borsari, B., & Carey, K. B. (2001). Peer influences on college drinking: A review of the research. *Journal of Substance Abuse, 13*(4), 391–424.

Borsari, B., & Carey, K. B. (2003). Descriptive and injunctive norms in college drinking: A meta-analytic integration. *Journal of Studies on Alcohol, 64*(3), 331–341.

Bot, S. M., Engels, R. C., & Knibbe, R. A. (2005). The effects of alcohol expectancies on drinking behaviour in peer groups: Observations in a naturalistic setting. *Addiction, 100*(9), 1270–1279.

Broadwater, K., Curtin, L., Martz, D. M., & Zrull, M. C. (2006). College student drinking: Perception of the norm and behavioral intentions. *Addictive Behaviors, 31*(4), 632–640.

Brown, J. S., Collins, A., & Duguid, P. (1989). Situated cognition and the culture of learning. *Educational Researcher, 18*(1), 32–42.

Brown, S. A., Goldman, M. S., Inn, A., & Anderson, L. R. (1980). Expectations of reinforcement from alcohol: Their domain and relation to drinking patterns. *Journal of Consulting and Clinical Psychology, 48*, 419–426.

Budd, R. J. (1987). Response bias and the theory of reasoned action. *Soc. Cognition, 5*(2), 95–107.

Cahalan, S. (2019). *The great pretender: The undercover mission that changed our understanding of madness*. Scotland, UK: Canongate books.

Caluzzi, G., Pennay, A., Cook, M., Wright, C., Norman, T., & Kuntsche, E. (2019). Transdermal monitors to assess alcohol consumption in real-time and real-life—a qualitative study on user-experience. *Addiction Res. & Theory, 27*(4), 354–361.

Cappell, H., & Herman, C. P. (1972). Alcohol and tension reduction: A review. *Quarterly Journal of Studies on Alcohol*, *33*, 33–64.

Carey, K. B. (1995). Alcohol-related expectancies predict quantity and frequency of heavy drinking among college students. *Psychology of Addictive Behaviours*, *9*, 236–241.

Carey, K. B., Borsari, B., Carey, M. P., & Maisto, S. A. (2006). Patterns and importance of self-other differences in college drinking norms. *Psychology of Addictive Behaviors*, *20*(4), 385.

Champion, V. L., & Skinner, C. S. (2008). The health belief model. *Health behavior and health education: Theory, research, and practice*, *4*, 45–65.

Clapp, J. D., Lange, J., Wong Min, J., Shillington, A., Johnson, M., & Voas, R. (2003). Two studies examining environmental predictors of heavy drinking by college students. *Prevention Science*, *4*, 99–108.

Clapp, J. D., Madden, D. R., Gonzalez Villasanti, H., Giraldo, L. F., Passino, K. M., Reed, M. B., & Fernandez Puentes, I. (2018). A system dynamic model of drinking events: Multi-level ecological approach. *Systems Research and Behavioral Science*, *35*(3), 265–281.

Clapp, J. D., & McDonnell, A. L. (2000). The relationship of perceptions of alcohol promotion and peer drinking norms to alcohol problems reported by college students. *Journal of College Student Development*.

Clapp, J. D., & Shillington, A. M. (2001). Environmental predictors of heavy episodic drinking. *American Journal of Drug and Alcohol Abuse*, *27*, 301–313.

Cleveland, H. H., & Harris, K. S. (2010). The role of coping in moderating within-day associations between negative triggers and substance use cravings: A daily diary investigation. *Addictive Behaviors*, *35*(1), 60–63.

Coggans, N., & Davies, J. B. (1988). Explanations for heroin use. *Journal of Drug Issues*, *18*(3), 457–465.

Comasco, E., Nordquist, N., Leppert, J., Oreland, L., Kronstrand, R., Alling, C., et al. (2009). Adolescent alcohol consumption: biomarkers PEth and FAEE in relation to interview and questionnaire data. *J. Stud. alcohol. drugs*, *70*(5), 797–804.

Conner, M., & Armitage, C. J. (1998). Extending the theory of planned behavior: A review and avenues for further research. *Journal of Applied Social Psychology*, *28*(15), 1429–1464.

Cooke, R., & French, D. P. (2011). The role of context and timeframe in moderating relationships within the theory of planned behaviour. *Psychology & Health*, *26*, 1225–1240.

Cook, M., Kuntsche, S., Labhart, F., & Kuntsche, E. (2020). Do different drinks make you feel different emotions? Examination of young adolescents– beverage-specific alcohol expectancies using the Alcohol Expectancy Task. *Addictive Behav.*, 106375.

Cox, W. M., & Klinger, E. (1988). A motivational model of alcohol use. *Journal of Abnormal Psychology*, *97*, 168–180. Available from https://doi.org/10.1037/0021-843X.97.2.168.

Cousijn, J., Luijten, M., & Wiers, R. W. (2014). Mechanisms underlying alcohol-approach action tendencies: the role of emotional primes and drinking motives. *Front. psychiatry*, *5*, 44.

D'Alessio, M., Baiocco, R., & Laghi, F. (2006). The problem of binge drinking among Italian university students: A preliminary investigation. *Addictive Behaviors*, *31*, 2328–2333.

Davies, J. B., & Best, D. W. (1996). Demand characteristics and research into drug use. *Psychol. Health*, *11*(2), 291–299.

Davies, J. B. (1997). *The myth of addiction* (2nd ed.). Amsterdam: Harwood Academic Publishers.

Davies, J. B., & Baker, R. (1987). The impact of self-presentation and interviewer bias effects on self-reported heroin use. *British Journal of Addiction*, *82*(8), 907–912.

Davies, J. & Stacey, B. (1972). Teenagers and alcohol. A developmental study in Glasgow. Vol. II.

Davies, J. B. (1992). *The Myth of Addiction: An Application of the Psychological Theory of Attribution to Illicit Drug Use*. Amsterdam: Harwood Academic Publishers.

De Wit, H., Söderpalm, A. H. V., Nikolayev, L., & Young, E. (2003). Effects of acute social stress on alcohol consumption in healthy subjects. *Alcoholism Clinical and Experimental Research*, *27*, 1270–1277.

Del Boca, F. K., & Noll, J. A. (2000). Truth or consequences: The validity of in health services research on addictions. *Addiction*, *95*, 347–360.

Demers, A., Kairouz, S., Adlaf, E. M., Gliksman, L. M., Newton-Taylor, B., & Marchand, A. (2002). Multilevel analysis of situational drinking among Canadian undergraduates. *Social Science & Medicine*, *55*, 415–424.

Dulin, P. L., Alvarado, C. E., Fitterling, J. M., & Gonzalez, V. M. (2017). Comparisons of alcohol consumption by timeline follow back vs. smartphone-based daily interviews. *Addiction Research & Theory*, *25*(3), 195–200.

Earleywine, M., & Martin, C. S. (1993). Anticipated stimulant and sedative effects of alcohol vary with dosage and limb of the blood alcohol curve. *Alcoholism: Clinical and Experimental Research*, *17*(1), 135–139.

Ebner-Priemer, U. W., & Trull, T. J. (2009). Ecological momentary assessment of mood disorders and mood dysregulation. *Psychological Assessment*, *21*(4), 463.

Festinger, L. (1954). A theory of social comparison processes. *Human Relations*, *7*(2), 117–140.

Field, M., & Quigley, M. (2009). Mild stress increases attentional bias in social drinkers who drink to cope: A replication and extension. *Experimental and Clinical Psychopharmacology*, *17*(5), 312.

Flango, V. E., & Cheesman, F. L. (2009). Effectiveness of the SCRAM alcohol monitoring device: A preliminary test. *Drug Court Review*, *6*(2), 109–134. Available from: http://www.ndci.org/sites/default/files/ndci/DCRVolume6_Issue2.pdf#page = 119.

Floyd, D. L., Prentice-Dunn, S., & Rogers, R. W. (2000). A meta-analysis of research on protection motivation theory. *Journal of Applied Social Psychology*, *30*(2), 407–429.

Freeman, W. M., & Vrana, K. E. (2010). Future prospects for biomarkers of alcohol consumption and alcohol-induced disorders. *Alcoholism: Clin. Exp. Res.*, *34*(6), 946–954.

Frings, D., Moss, A. C., Albery, I. P., Eskisan, G., Wilcockson, T. D. W., & Marchant, A. (2017). Environmental context influences visual attention to responsible drinking messages. *Alcohol and Alcoholism*, *53*(1), 46–51.

Glautier, S., O'Brien, J., & Dixon, J. (2001). Facial electromyographic (EMG) responses to emotionally significant visual images: Differences between light and heavy drinkers. *Drug and Alcohol Dependence*, *64*(3), 337–345.

Glovannucci, E., Colditz, G., Stampfer, M. J., Rimm, E. B., Litin., Sampson, L., & Willet, W. C. (1991). The assessment of alcohol consumption by a simple self-administered questionnaire. *American Journal of Epidemiology*, *133*, 810–817.

Godden, D. R., & Baddeley, A. D. (1975). Context-dependent memory in two natural environments: On land and underwater. *British Journal of Psychology*, *66 (3)*, 325–331.

Gottfredson, N. C., & Hussong, A. M. (2013). Drinking to dampen affect variability: Findings from a college student sample. *Journal of Studies on Alcohol Drugs*, *74*, 576–583.

Greeno, J. (1997). On claims that answer the wrong questions. *Educational Researcher*, *26*, 5–17.

Gutierrez, M. A., Fast, M. L., Ngu, A. H., & Gao, B. J. (2015). *Real-time prediction of blood alcohol content using smartwatch sensor data. ICSH* (pp. 175–186). Cham: Springer.

Hahn, J. A., Dobkin, L. M., Mayanja, B., Emenyonu, N. I., Kigozi, I. M., Shiboski, S., et al. (2012). Phosphatidylethanol (PEth) as a biomarker of alcohol consumption in HIV-positive patients in sub-Saharan. *Africa. Alcoholism: Clin. Exp. Res.*, *36*(5), 854–862.

Heim, D., Blomqvist, J., Edman, J., Room, R., Storbjörk, J., et al. (2014). Addiction: Not just brain malfunction. *Nature*, *507*, 40-40.

Heim, D., & Monk, R. L. (2017). Commentary on Thrul et al. (2017): A welcome step towards a more context-aware addiction science. *Addiction*, *112*, 440–441.

Heirene, R. M. (2020). A call for replications of addiction research: Which studies should we replicate and what constitutes a 'successful' replication? *Addiction Research & Theory*, 1–9.

Hektner, J. M., Schmidt, J. A., & Csikszentmihalyi, M. (2007). *Experience sampling method: Measuring the quality of everyday life*. Sage.

Helander, A., Péter, O., & Zheng, Y. (2012). Monitoring of the alcohol biomarkers PEth, CDT and EtG/EtS in an outpatient treatment setting. *Alcohol. Alcohol.*, *47*(5), 552–557.

Hepworth, R., Mogg, K., Brignell, C., & Bradley, B. P. (2010). Negative mood increases selective attention to food cues and subjective appetite. *Appetite*, *54*, 134–142.

Hopthrow, T., Abrams, D., Frings, D., & Hulbert, L. G. (2007). Groupdrink: The effects of alcohol on intergroup competitiveness. *Psychology of Addictive Behaviors*, *21*(2), 272.

Hopthrow, T., Randsley de Moura, G., Meleady, R., Abrams, D., & Swift, H. J. (2014). Drinking in social groups. Does 'groupdrink' provide safety in numbers when deciding about risk? *Addiction*, *109*(6), 913–921.

Isaksson, A., Walther, L., Hansson, T., Andersson, A., & Alling, C. (2011). Phosphatidylethanol in blood (B-PEth): A marker for alcohol use and abuse. *Drug Testing and Analysis*, *3*(4), 195–200.

Ito, M., Matsuzaki, N., & Kawahara, J. (2018). Measurement of mood states following light alcohol consumption: Evidence from the implicit association test. *Behavioral Sciences*, *8*, 79.

Jastrzębska, I., Zwolak, A., Szczyrek, M., Wawryniuk, A., Skrzydło-Radomańska, B., & Daniluk, J. (2016). Biomarkers of alcohol misuse: Recent advances and future prospects. *Przeglad Gastroenterologiczny*, *11*(2), 78.

Johnson, E. I., Husky, M., Grondin, O., Mazure, C. M., Doron, J., & Swendsen, J. (2008). Mood trajectories following daily life events. *Motivation and Emotion*, *32*(4), 251–259.

Jones, A., Tiplady, B., Houben, K., Nederkoorn, C., & Field, M. (2018). Do daily fluctuations in inhibitory control predict alcohol consumption? An ecological momentary assessment study. *Psychopharmacology*, *235*(5), 1487–1496.

Khantzian, E. J. (1997). The self-medication hypothesis of substance use disorders: A reconsideration and recent applications. *Harvard Review of Psychiatry*, *4*(5), 231–244.

Koob, G. F. (2013). Negative reinforcement in drug addiction: The darkness within. *Current Opinion in Neurobiology*, *23*, 559–563.

Kuendig, H., & Kuntsche, E. (2012). Solitary versus social drinking: An experimental study on effects of social exposures on in situ alcohol consumption. *Alcoholism: Clinical and Experimental Research*, *36*, 732–738. Available from https://doi.org/10.1111/j.1530-0277.2011.01663.x.

Kuntsche, E., & Bruno, R. (2015). Moody booze: Introducing the special section on affect regulation and substance use. *Drug and Alcohol Review*, *34*, 569–570.

Kuntsche, E., Gabhainn, S. N., Roberts, C., Windlin, B., Vieno, A., Bendtsen, P., ... Aasvee, K. (2014). Drinking motives and links to alcohol use in 13 European countries. *Journal of Studies on Alcohol And Drugs*, *75*(3), 428–437.

Kuntsche, E., & Kuendig, H. (2012). Beyond self-reports: drinking motives predict grams of consumed alcohol in wine-tasting sessions. *Exp. Clin. Psychopharmacol.*, *20*(4), 318.

Kuntsche, E., & Kuntsche, S. (2017). Development and initial validation of the alcohol expectancy task. *Alcoholism: Clin. Exp. Res.*, *41*(8), 1461–1470.

Kuntsche, E., & Labhart, F. (2012). Investigating the drinking patterns of young people over the course of the evening at weekends. *Drug and Alcohol Dependence*, *12*(3), 319–324.

Labhart, F., Tarsetti, F., Bornet, O., Santani, D., Truong, J., Landolt, S., ... Kuntsche, E. (2020). Capturing drinking and nightlife behaviours and their social and physical context with a smartphone application–investigation of users' experience and reactivity. *Addiction Research & Theory*, *28*(1), 62–75.

Laghi, F., Bianchi, D., Pompili, S., Lonigro, A., & Baiocco, R. (2019). Cognitive and affective empathy in binge drinking adolescents: Does empathy moderate the effect of self-efficacy in resisting peer pressure to drink? *Addictive Behaviors*, *89*, 229–235.

Larimer, M. E., Turner, A. P., Mallett, K. A., & Geisner, I. M. (2004). Predicting drinking behavior and alcohol-related problems among fraternity and sorority members: Examining the role of descriptive and injunctive norms. *Psychology of Addictive Behaviors*, *18*(3), 203.

Larsen, H., Engels, R. C., Wiers, R. W., Granic, I., & Spijkerman, R. (2012). Implicit and explicit alcohol cognitions and observed alcohol consumption: Three studies in (semi) naturalistic drinking settings. *Addiction*, *107*(8), 1420–1428.

Leffingwell, T. R., Cooney, N. J., Murphy, J. G., Luczak, S., Rosen, G., Dougherty, D. M., & Barnett, N. P. (2013). Continuous objective monitoring of alcohol use: twenty-first century measurement using transdermal sensors. *Alcoholism: Clinical and Experimental Research*, *37*(1), 16–22.

Leigh, B. C., & Stacy. (1993). Alcohol outcome expectancies: Scale construction and predictive utility in higher order confirmatory models. *Psychological Assessment*, *5*, 216–229.

Lewis, M. A., & Neighbors, C. (2004). Gender-specific misperceptions of college student drinking norms. *Psychology of Addictive Behaviors*, *18*(4), 334, *American College Health*, *49*(2), 57–64.

Lindgren, K. P., Ramirez, J. J., Wiers, R. W., Teachman, B. A., Norris, J., Olin, C. C., ... Neighbors, C. (2018). Mood selectively moderates the implicit alcohol association–drinking relation in college student heavy episodic drinkers. *Psychology of Addictive Behaviors*, *32*(3), 338.

Lo Monaco, G., Piermattéo, A., Guimelli, C., & Ernst-Vintila, A. (2011). Using the Black Sheep Effect to reveal normative stakes: The example of alcohol drinking contexts. *European Journal of Social Psychology*, *41*, 1–5.

MacAndrew, C., & Edgerton, R. B. (1969). *Drunken Comportment: A Social Explanation*. Chicago: Aldine.

McAlaney, J., Bewick, B. M., & Bauerle, J. (2010). *Social norms guidebook: A guide to implementing the social norms approach in the UK*. West Yorkshire, UK: University of Bradford, University of Leeds, Department of Health.

McAlaney, J., & McMahon, J. (2007a). Diagnosing and dealing with the 'new British disease'. *The Psychologist*, *20*, 738–741.

McAlaney, J., & McMahon, J. (2007b). Normative beliefs, misperceptions, and heavy episodic drinking in a British student sample. *Journal of Studies on Alcohol and Drugs*, *68*, 385–392.

McKnight, A. S., Fell, J. C., & Auld-Owens, A. (2012). *Transdermal alcohol monitoring: Case studies* (No. DOT HS 811 603). Available from http://www.nhtsa.gov/staticfiles/nti/pdf/811603.pdf.

Melson, A. J., Davies, J. B., & Martinus, T. (2011). Overestimation of peer drinking: error of judgement or methodological artefact? *Addiction*, *106*(6), 1078–1084.

Melson, A. J., Monk, R. L., & Heim, D. (2016). Self-other differences in student drinking norms research: The role of impression management, self–deception, and measurement methodology. *Alcoholism: Clin. Exp. Res.*, *40*(12), 2639–2647.

Merrill, J. E., Fan, P., Wray, T. B., & Miranda, R., Jr (2020). Assessment of alcohol use and consequences: Comparison of data collected via timeline followback interview and daily reports. *Journal of Studies on Alcohol and Drugs*, *81*(2), 212–219.

Merrill, J. E., Wardell, J. D., & Read, J. P. (2009). Is expectancy reality? Associations between tension reduction beliefs and mood following alcohol consumption. *Experimental and Clinical Psychopharmacology*, *17*(6), 434.

Miley, W. M., & Frank, M. (2006). Binge and non-binge college students' perceptions of other students' drinking habits. *College Student Journal*, *40*(2), 259–263.

Mohr, C. D., Arpin, S., & McCabe, C. T. (2015). Daily affect variability and context-specific alcohol consumption. *Drug and Alcohol Review*, *34*, 581–587.

Monk, R. L., & Heim, D. (2013a). Environmental context effects on alcohol-related outcome expectancies, efficacy and norms: A field study. *Psychology of Addictive Behaviors*, *27*, 814–818.

Monk, R. L., & Heim, D. (2013b). A critical systematic review of alcohol-related outcome expectancies. *Substance Use and Misuse*, *48*, 539–557.

Monk, R. L., Qureshi, A., & Heim, D. (2020). An examination of the extent to which mood and context are associated with real-time alcohol consumption. *Drug. alcohol. dependence*, *208*, 107880.

Monk, R. L., & Heim, D. (2013c). Panoramic projection: Affording a wider view on contextual influences on alcohol-related cognitions. *Experimental and Clinical Psychopharmacology*, *21*, 1–7.

Monk, R. L., & Heim, D. (2014a). A real-time examination of context effects on alcohol cognitions. *Alcoholism: Clinical and Experimental Research*, *38*, 2452–2459.

Monk, R. L., & Heim, D. (2014b). A systematic review of the alcohol norms literature: A focus on context. *Drugs: Education, Prevention & Policy*, *21*, 263–282.

Monk, R. L., Heim, D., Qureshi, A., & Price, A. (2015). "I have no clue what I drunk last night" using smartphone technology to compare in-vivo and retrospective self-reports of alcohol consumption. *PLoS One*, *10*, e0126209.

Monk, R. L., Qureshi, A., McLaughlin, O., Priest, M., Butler, J., & Heim, D. Drink and be merry: Exploring the effect of alcohol and social cues on emotional responses. Under Review.

Moreira, M. T., Smith, L. A., & Foxcroft, D. (2009). Social norms interventions to reduce alcohol misuse in university or college students. *Cochrane Database of Systematic Reviews*.

Neighbors, C., Lee, C. M., Lewis, M. A., Fossos, N., & Larimer, M. E. (2007). Are social norms the best predictor of outcomes among heavy-drinking college students? *Journal of Studies on Alcohol and Drugs*, *68*(4), 556–565.

Neumann, R., & Strack, F. (2000). "Mood contagion": The automatic transfer of mood between persons. *Journal of Personality and Social Psychology*, *79*, 211–223.

Neville, F. G., Williams, D. J., Goodall, C. A., Murer, J. S., & Donnelly, P. D. (2013). An experimental trial exploring the impact of continuous transdermal alcohol monitoring upon alcohol consumption in a cohort of male students. *PLoS One*, *8*(6), e67386.

Newham, R., & Davies, J. B. (2007). Attributions given by drug users from three different settings. *Addiction Res. & Theory*, *15*(3), 299–308.

Orne, M. T. (1962). On the social psychology of the psychological experiment: With particular reference to demand characteristics and their implications. *Am. psychologist*, *17*(11), 776.

Parkinson, B., & Simons, G. (2009). Affecting others: Social appraisal and emotion contagion in everyday decision making. *Journal of Personality and Social Psychology Bulletin*, *35*, 1071–1084.

Peacock, A., Cash, C., Bruno, R., & Ferguson, S. G. (2015). Day-by-day variation in affect, arousal and alcohol consumption in young adults. *Drug. Alcohol. Rev.*, *34*(6), 588–594.

Pedersen, E. R., Labrie, J. W., & Lac, A. (2008). Assessment of perceived and actual alcohol norms in varying contexts: Exploring social impact theory among college students. *Addictive Behaviors*, *33*, 552–564.

Perkins, H. W. (2002). Social norms and the prevention of alcohol misuse in collegiate contexts. *Journal of Studies on Alcohol, supplement*, *14*, 164–172.

Pepper, M., Dawson, P., & Unit, I. (2015). Alcohol Abstinence Monitoring Requirement. Available From: https://core.ac.uk/download/pdf/79455699.pdf

Perkins, H. W. (2007). Misperceptions of peer drinking norms in Canada: Another look at the "reign of error" and its consequences among college students. *Addictive Behaviors*, *32*(11), 2645–2656.

Perkins, H. W., & Berkowitz, A. D. (1986). Perceiving the community norms of alcohol use among students: Some research implications for campus alcohol education programming. *International Journal of the Addictions*, *21*(9–10), 961–976.

Perkins, H. W., Haines, M. P., & Rice, R. (2005). Misperceiving the college drinking norm and related problems: A nationwide study of exposure to prevention information, perceived norms and student alcohol misuse. *Journal of Studies on Alcohol*, *66*(4), 470–478.

Perkins, H. W., Meilman, P. W., Leichliter, J. S., Cashin, J. R., & Presley, C. A. (1999). Misperceptions of the norms for the frequency of alcohol and other drug use on college campuses. *Journal of American College Health*, *47*(6), 253–258.

Poulton, A., Pan, J., Bruns, L. R., Jr., Sinnott, R. O., & Hester, R. (2018). Assessment of alcohol intake: Retrospective measures versus a smartphone application. *Addictive Behaviors*, *83*, 35–41.

Roache, J. D., Karns, T. E., Hill-Kapturczak, N., Mullen, J., Liang, Y., Lamb, R. J., et al. (2015). Using transdermal alcohol monitoring to detect low-level drinking. *Alcoholism: Clin. Exp. Res.*, *39*(7), 1120–1127.

Roehrich, L., & Goldman, M. S. (1995). Implicit priming of alcohol expectancy memory processes and subsequent drinking behavior. *Experimental and Clinical Psychopharmacology*, *3*(4), 402.

Rosenthal, R., Kohn, P., Greenfield, P. M., & Carota, N. (1966). Data desirability, experimenter expectancy, and the results of psychological research. *J. Personality Soc. Psychol.*, *3*(1), 20.

Rousseau, G. S., Irons, J. G., & Correia, C. J. (2011). The reinforcing value of alcohol in a drinking to cope paradigm. *Drug and Alcohol Dependence*, *118*(1), 1–4.

Sakai, J. T., Mikulich-Gilbertson, S. K., Long, R. J., & Crowley, T. J. (2006). Validity of transdermal alcohol monitoring: fixed and self-regulated dosing. *Alcoholism: Clin. Exp. Res.*, *30*(1), 26–33.

Sayette, M. A. (2017). The effects of alcohol on emotion in social drinkers. *Behaviour Research and Theory*, *88*, 76–89.

Schlotz, W., Hammerfald, K., Ehlert, U., & Gaab, J. (2011). Individual differences in the cortisol response to stress in young healthy men: Testing the roles of perceived stress reactivity and threat appraisal using multiphase latent growth curve modeling. *Biological Psychology*, *87* (2), 257–264.

Schröck, A., Redondo, A. H., Fabritius, M. M., König, S., & Weinmann, W. (2016). Phosphatidylethanol (PEth) in blood samples from "driving under the influence" cases as indicator for prolonged excessive alcohol consumption. *International Journal of Legal Medicine*, *130*(2), 393–400.

Skowronski, J., Walker, W. R., & Betz, A. (2003). Ordering our world: An examination of time in autobiographical memory. *Memory*, *11*(3), 247–260.

Smit, K., Groefsema, M., Luijten, M., Engels, R., & Kuntsche, E. (2015). Drinking motives moderate the effect of the social environment on alcohol use: An event-level study among young adults. *Journal of Studies on Alcohol and Drugs*, *76*, 971–980. Available from https://doi.org/10.15288/jsad.2015.76.971.

Skog, O. J. (1985). The collectivity of drinking cultures: a theory of the distribution of alcohol consumption. *Br. J. addiction*, *80*(1), 83–99.

Söderlund, H., Parker, E. S., Schwartz, B. L., & Tulving, E. (2005). Memory encoding and retrieval on the ascending and descending limbs of the blood alcohol concentration curve. *Psychopharmacology*, *182*(2), 305–317.

Stewart, S. H., Law, T. L., Randall, P. K., & Newman, R. (2010). Phosphatidylethanol and alcohol consumption in reproductive age women. *Alcoholism: Clinical and Experimental Research*, *34*(3), 488–492.

Steele, C. M., & Josephs, R. A. (1990). Alcohol myopia: Its prized and dangerous effects. *American Psychologist*, *45*(8), 921.

Sutker, P. B., Tabakoff, B., Goist, K. C., Jr., & Randall, C. L. (1983). Acute alcohol intoxication, mood states and alcohol metabolism in women and men. *Pharmacology Biochemistry and Behavior*, *18*, 349–354.

Swendsen, J. D., Tennen, H., Carney, M. A., Affleck, G., Willard, A., & Hromi, A. (2000). Mood and alcohol consumption: An experience sampling test of the self-medication hypothesis. *Journal of Abnormal Psychology*, *109*, 198–204.

Thombs, D. L., Wolcott, B. J., & Farkash, L. G. (1997). Social context, perceived norms and drinking behavior in young people. *Journal of Substance Abuse*, *9*, 257–267.

Tice, D. M., Bratslavsky, E., & Baumeister, R. F. (2001). Emotional distress regulation takes precedence over impulse control: If you feel bad, do it!. *Journal of Personality and Social Psychology*, *80*(1), 53.

van Strien, T., Roelofs, K., & de Weerth, C. (2013). Cortisol reactivity and distress-induced emotional eating. *Psychoneuroendocrinology*, *38*(5), 677–684.

VanderVeen, J. D., Plawecki, M. H., Millward, J. B., Hays, J., Kareken, D. A., O'Connor, S., & Cyders, M. A. (2016). Negative urgency, mood induction, and alcohol seeking behaviors. *Drug and Alcohol Dependence*, *165*, 151–158.

Voas, R. B., DuPont, R. L., Talpins, S. K., & Shea, C. L. (2011). Towards a national model for managing impaired driving offenders. *Addiction*, *106*(7), 1221–1227.

Walker, D. W., & Hunter, B. E. (1978). Short-term memory impairment following chronic alcohol consumption in rats. *Neuropsychologia*, *16*, 545–553.

Wall, A. M., Hinson, R. E., McKee, S. A., & Goldstein, A. (2001). Examining alcohol outcome expectancies in laboratory and naturalistic bar settings: A within-subjects experimental analysis. *Psychology of Addictive Behaviors*, *15*, 219–226.

Wall, A. M., Mckee, S. A., & Hinson, R. E. (2000). Assessing variation in alcohol outcome expectancies across environmental context: An examination of the situational-specificity hypothesis. *Psychology of Addictive Behaviors*, *14*, 367–375.

Walz, L. C., Nauta, M. H., & aan het Rot, M. (2014). Experience sampling and ecological momentary assessment for studying the daily lives of patients with anxiety disorders: A systematic review. *Journal of Anxiety Disorders*, *28*(8), 925–937.

Wechsler, H., & Kuo, M. (2000). College students define binge drinking and estimate its prevalence: Results of a national survey. *Journal of American College Health*, *49*(2), 57–64.

Weissenborn, R., & Duka, T. (2003). Acute alcohol effects on cognitive function in social drinkers: Their relationship to drinking habits. *Psychopharmacology*, *165*, 306–312.

Wortham, S. (2001). Interactionally situated cognition: A classroom example. *Cognitive Science, 25*(1), 37–66.

Yamaguchi, M., & Beattie, G. (2020). The role of explicit categorization in the Implicit Association Test. *Journal of Experimental Psychology: General, 149*(5), 809–827.

Zack, M., Poulos, C. X., Fragopoulos, F., Woodford, T. M., & MacLeod, C. M. (2006). Negative affect words prime beer consumption in young drinkers. *Addictive Behaviors, 31*, 169–173.

Zhou, J., Heim, D., Monk, R., Levy, A., & Pollard, P. (2018). Allocating under the influence: Effects of alcohol intoxication and social identification on in-group favoritism. *Experimental and Clinical Psychopharmacology, 26*(3), 268.

Zinberg, N. E. (1984). Drug, set, and setting: The basis for controlled intoxicant use. New Haven, Connecticut: Yale University Press.

Section 4

The group

Chapter 13

I can keep up with the best: The role of social norms in alcohol consumption and their use in interventions

Sandra Kuntsche[1], Robin Room[1,2] and Emmanuel Kuntsche[1,3]
[1]Centre for Alcohol Policy Research, La Trobe University, Australia, [2]Centre for Social Research on Alcohol and Drugs, Department of Public Health Sciences, Stockholm University, Stockholm, Sweden, [3]Institute of Psychology, Eötvös Loránd University, Budapest, Hungary

Introduction

Alcohol consumption is a longstanding companion to mankind. It goes way back to at least Neolithic times (between 5000 to 10,000 years BCE), and some argue that human settlement was possibly caused by the fact that growing grains and staying at the same place facilitated alcohol production – and, as a consequence, alcohol consumption (Hanson, 1995). Nowadays, alcohol consumption is part and parcel of everyday life in most Western societies and its spread in other cultures is increasing (Bennett et al., 2018; WHO, 2019). Alcohol consumption is also deeply rooted in celebrations and social activities. Most people toast with a glass of champagne at a birthday party or to greet the New Year, sit down with a glass of beer while watching sports with friends and have white wine with fish. Such normative behavior most of us know and many follow because these traditions or norms facilitate social interactions. On the other hand, social expectations about behavior in a situation also impose limits on our drinking, i.e. most people would find it inappropriate to drink while driving a motor vehicle, attending a religious service, or being at a court hearing, etc. Interestingly, in the same setting, e.g. while being at work, defending a PhD thesis, or at a funeral, it is usually very inappropriate to drink alcohol (and there is formal and informal pressure not to drink), whereas after work, after the PhD defence, or after the funeral, it is often highly appropriate or even expected to consume alcohol. These social expectations, commonly described as norms - the expectations

The Handbook of Alcohol Use - Understandings from Synapse to Society.
DOI: https://doi.org/10.1016/B978-0-12-816720-5.00024-4

to drink (often a specific amount) or to abstain, and if drinking to drink more or to drink less - have been defined as "socially negotiated and contextually dependent modes of conduct" (Rimal & Lapinski, 2015). Such social norms help us to navigate in social interactions and to manage even unfamiliar situations by providing general behavioral guidance and an outline of what is expected and what is not. In an experimental study, Kuendig and Kuntsche (2012) were able to demonstrate that, depending on the circumstances, being in social company can both instigate and limit the amounts consumed compared to drinking alone. In other words, depending on the context, social company can either facilitate or limit alcohol consumption.

What are social norms and how do they work?

Saying "Please" and "Thank you", offering our seat to older people, chewing with your mouth closed and wearing the appropriate attire for an occasion are all fulfilling expectations most of us grew up with and follow. These shared conventions are called social norms, and they provide an overarching framework for all social interaction. However, the terminology of norms is not only a representation of collective agreements but is also used to describe personal perceptions of what behavior members of a group or society find to be acceptable or required (Aarts & Dijksterhuis, 2003). In contrast to laws or written agreements (Sunstein, 1996), social norms refer to a more informal understanding of what is right and wrong, appropriate or inappropriate, expected, acceptable or disallowed, and are commonly informally enforced, whether by a raised eyebrow or a snub or by some more stringent action.

When discussing social norms, it is important to keep in mind that as social beings we belong to more than one group. We are not only students or members of the same football club but family members, friends, we belong to certain ethnic or religious groups, or simply differ in age and gender. With each of the roles we have in our life come social norms, which often differ between roles. Conflict in norms regarding alcohol use can also arise from clashing roles (Kuntsche et al., 2006; Kuntsche, Knibbe, & Gmel, 2012; Kuntsche, Knibbe, Kuntsche, & Gmel, 2011), like having to supervise young kids while having a beer with friends, or from clashing drinking norms between different groups attending the same setting.

Before having a closer look on how social norms influence alcohol use, it is useful to get a broader understanding of what social norms are and how they influence our behavior in general. There have been different, although somewhat interconnected, concepts of social norms in different social science traditions.

Injunctive vs. descriptive norms

What are termed "social norms" in the sociological and anthropological literature are termed "injunctive norms" by psychologists, reflecting that the psychological literature uses "norms" also to refer to what a person believes are right based on one's own beliefs, moral and others' views on appropriate behavior, depending on the context and the group they are currently with; such beliefs are termed "perceived norms", and distributions of such beliefs in a population are called "descriptive norms" (for details see Lapinski & Rimal, 2005). For example, I can personally make sure that I bring my empty batteries to recycling stations because I think it is a good thing to do (injunctive norm) and behave correspondingly. However, I may be convinced that my co-citizens think differently and that they only recycle the bare minimum (descriptive norm). From a psychological point of view, the perspective of others concerning a norm is a factor in the individual's behavior, whether or not the perception matches the actual views. As social norms are often not formalised or explicitly stated, they rather describe a set of manners emerging from the shared interaction within the group. However, the individual members of the group may differ in their interpretation and individual perception of these general norms, as an individual's perception is influenced also by other factors, including previous experiences, beliefs, knowledge, and what they think other people in the same situation would do or think.

In research, by asking an individual about the norms and expectations within a given entity (society, culture, group), we are measuring the individual's perception of these group norms. Collective norms can be measured directly by observing behavior and interactions within the collectivity. They can also be inferred from aggregating the responses of individual members of the social entity concerning the entity's norms, but psychologists' differentiation of "descriptive norms" warns us that this measurement may differ from the actual application of the norms. The individual's perception of existing norms is not identical to the injunctive norm.

Social norms and alcohol use

As already noted, alcohol use is part and parcel of Western societies and often deeply embedded in their culture. Most alcohol consumption is social in nature, and indeed drinking together is often a medium of sociability. Much drinking occurs in a context of shared interests, and often of continuing relationships. But drinking also comes with rules. Collective drinking norms (Room, 1975; pp. 359–360) are defined as "a cultural rule or understanding affecting behaviour, ...enforced by sanctions ... not being the property of an individual or private understanding between people, ... but a relatively permanent rule share by a class of individuals who may not know each other." This definition invites an immediate question of what constitutes such a "class of people". The answer to this can be widely varied. A traditional answer would be in terms of a nation, society, tribal group or other well-defined and bounded sociocultural group. But cultural entities within which norms are shared can also be identified at many other levels.

Concerning drinking norms, in particular, a cultural entity in which drinking norms are shared is often termed a "drinking culture" (Savic, Room, Mugavin, Pennay, & Livingston, 2016), and this can exist also in a subgroup of a whole society, in what are variously identified by sociologists as subcultures, social worlds or social scenes – for instance, in social worlds defined by a common occupation, hobby or interest, or by a common worldview or social status (Room et al., in press). On the other hand, a drinking norm can be shared by populations beyond societal or cultural boundaries. For instance, the normative framework described variously as buying rounds, treating or shouting – the expectation that a group socialising together in a drinking place will each in turn buy a round of drinks for the whole group – exists among regular drinkers in a number of societies but not in others. Thus, an Irish woman who moved to Sweden noted that "Some things are just so ingrained that they are very hard to shake off.... I still feel compelled to offer to buy a round of drinks if out with a group, even though the culture here is that everyone pays for themselves" (Pihl, 2017).

In whatever cultural entity they are shared, drinking norms are often specified in terms of the social situation. The social situation also holds very different implications for drinking norms, for instance between a weekend party in someone's backyard and an appointment at the bank or doctor's office.

Whether it is considered appropriate to drink alcohol or not, and if considered appropriate, what amount is socially acceptable to be consumed varies not only between situations but also by characteristics of people in that situation, like their age, gender, and social responsibilities. Norms are likely to be different concerning drinking by a child or by an adult, for instance, and may also vary by other social differentiations. Thus, alcohol use comes with an extensive set of rules and norms, and the decision on which ones will come into play is defined by situational, individual and societal factors. Despite the wide differentiations between cultural groupings which can be found concerning drinking norms, comparisons of situational drinking norms across different social groups have found some commonalities. These comparisons have often been based on population survey questions on whether drinking at all, and to different levels, is acceptable in particular situations. While these answers have been interpreted as measuring injunctive norms, it should be recognized that the answers also include the dimension psychologists would term as descriptive norms. Looking across 12 societies on six continents, "dry" situations like having a drink before driving or when at lunch with work colleagues are consistently considered less appropriate for alcohol use than "wetter" situations like being in a bar with friends or attending a party (Room et al., 2019). While the acceptability of drinking varied between societies, as well as by the respondent's own drinking behavior, e.g. being abstinent or drinking heavily, there was considerable agreement on the relative *ranking* of situations in terms of the normativity of not drinking at all, both between societies and between fairly heavy drinkers and abstainers in the same society, and some agreement also on the relative ranking of situations on the acceptability of drinking enough "to feel the effects". However, if a norm is defined as something on which there is general agreement, it was clear from the results that while there are norms held at the societal level about situations in which it is not appropriate to drink at all, for situational norms in favor of drinking enough the feel the effects, one must look at smaller cultural groups, i.e. heavy drinking subcultures, than the society as a whole (Room et al., 2019). Each such social world of normative heavy drinking coexists with the larger society and is "tolerated so long as it conducts itself only within certain boundaries" (Room, 1975; p. 360).

There is one area, namely the college or university setting, where social norms, in particular descriptive norms (e.g., Arterberry, Smith, Martens, Cadigan, & Murphy, 2014; Massengale, Ma, Rulison, Milroy, & Wyrick, 2017; Reid & Carey, 2015) but also injunctive norms (Krieger et al., 2016), have been studied extensively. Research in this area is based on the assumption that those entering college or university often have wrong perceptions about the expectations and norms around alcohol use in these settings. So descriptive norms in these settings – beliefs about how many students drink heavily or to intoxication – may vary quite tremendously from the actual injunctive norms, reflecting that college freshmen or first year university students are entering a social world with which they have no lived experiences, often basing their assumptions on hearsay or depiction in movies and media or stories of friends and peers. But this does not necessarily mean that changing an individual's perceived descriptive norms will have an effect on the actual injunctive norms which operate when the individual is a student in a situation potentially involving drinking. Thus a review of studies which examined the role of descriptive norms in lowering the student's perception of how much students drank as mediating factor in the change of students' behavior found that results were mixed; "to what extent changing this construct drives subsequent behavior change remains unclear" (Reid & Carey, 2015, p. 217). A Cochrane review of 70 studies found a mean reduction from 13.7 to 12.8 drinks per week, and of peak blood alcohol level from 0.144% to 0.135%, after an intervention to change perception of norms, and concluded that the effects were "too small to be of relevance for policy or practice" (Foxcroft, Moreira, Almeida Santimano, & Smith, 2015). In the light of such findings, the U.S. government alcohol agency has put forward a research-based advice tool on reducing college drinking which, alongside individual-level persuasive measures such as changing perceived norms, includes measures operating at collective or environmental levels such as staff training, campus alcohol policies and guidelines, and restrictions on location of alcohol outlets (Cronce et al., 2018). Examples can be found in the wider world where injunctive norms concerning drinking in a social group clearly changed (Room et al., in press), but factors at collective and environmental levels were clearly involved in the change.

Interim summary

Social norms vary not only depending on with a specific culture but also with age, gender, social roles and situations that people find themselves in or engage with. We distinguish injunctive norms, i.e. a person' viewpoint on what is right based on one's own beliefs, moral and others' views on appropriate behavior, depending on the context and the group they are currently with and descriptive norms, i.e. distributions of such beliefs in a population. The latter are usually the focus of social norms interventions, which will be discussed later in this chapter.

Origins of social norms: children's perceptions of adult drinking

For an adult entering a new social world, for instance an occupational social world where people in the same industry or profession get together socially outside the workplace, we may presume that the main way of learning the customs of the new social world, including its drinking norms, is through amateur ethnography – observation and asking questions – and perhaps also from banter or direct reproof if the novice transgresses a norm (e.g. Roberts et al., 2019). Children, however, are in a different position. The majority of children in many societies are observers in a world where one or more of the adults important to them drinks alcohol, usually along with others, but in which abstinence is the norm for a child. They thus observe adult drinking norms, but from an outsider's perspective. There is a growing literature on children's perceptions of adult drinking norms, since it seems that these childhood perceptions influence the development of children's drinking practices as they mature.

Already relatively young children have an idea about drinking norms of adults

There is ample evidence on the distal and proximal factors that determine the full spectrum of alcohol use - from alcohol initiation to risky drinking - in adolescence and beyond (Kuntsche & Gmel, 2013). However, an increasing number of longitudinal studies have demonstrated that proximal cognitive factors related to alcohol use are rooted much earlier, that is, in childhood (Schulenberg & Maggs, 2008).

Already 24 years ago, a literature review was conducted on children's cognitions about alcohol and alcohol-specific norms (Lang & Stritzke, 1993). This review noted that children are not 'innocents' with respect to alcohol. Already at age three, children have alcohol-related knowledge, as they can recognize and identify alcoholic beverages. In addition, from age five on, children are aware of age-related alcohol norms (e.g., only adults consume alcohol), hold gender-specific alcohol norms (e.g., males like alcohol-related activities more than females), and know socially acceptable amounts of alcohol use (e.g., small versus large alcohol dose). Moreover, as early as six years of age, children have certain alcohol expectancies that seem to shift from primarily negative to primarily positive by the age of ten. Thus, insight into the influence of parental alcohol use in the acquisition of children's alcohol-related cognitions is crucial, as alcohol-related knowledge and alcohol-related norms are supposed to form the basis for alcohol expectancies (e.g., 'I expect that alcohol makes me sociable') and the transition to drinking motives (e.g., 'I drank [for the first time] to enjoy a party'). According to the Motivational Model of alcohol use (Cox & Klinger, 1988; Cox & Klinger, 1990), the latter are thought to constitute the final pathway towards alcohol initiation (Kuntsche & Müller, 2012) and subsequent drinking patterns, e.g., binge drinking (Andrews, Hampson, & Peterson, 2011; Donovan et al., 2004; Windle et al., 2008).

A recently conducted review (Voogt et al., 2017) revealed that children's knowledge about alcohol-related norms in the adult culture increased with age (Jahoda, Davies, & Tagg, 1980; Kuntsche, Le Mével, & Zucker, 2016; Spiegler, 1983; Zucker, Kincaid, Fitzgerald, & Bingham, 1995). Between three and six years old, children possess some knowledge of situation-specific alcohol-related norms, for example expecting alcohol consumption more often to occur when adults having a party than when engaging in outdoor activities such as having a picnic (Kuntsche et al., 2016). From the age of five onwards, children have been shown to be aware of age-related and sex-specific alcohol norms, for example that adults are more likely to consume alcohol than younger people, and that males are more likely to consume alcohol than females (Kuntsche et al., 2016; Zucker et al., 1995), and males were more often perceived as liking alcohol-related activities (Spiegler, 1983) than females and children. Children (aged 2.6–7 years) also reported that alcoholic beverages (e.g., beer, wine, whiskey) are used by adults only (Noll, Zucker, & Greenberg, 1990), and that adults prefer alcoholic beverages and children non-alcoholic beverages (Jahoda et al., 1980). Besides having knowledge of the culturally approved users of alcoholic beverages, children (aged 3–6 years) can indicate that adults drink in specific situations. For example, they more often attributed alcoholic beverages to adults in a party scene than when playing outdoors (Kuntsche et al., 2016). Moreover, children have some knowledge of socially acceptable amounts of alcohol use (Voogt et al., 2017; Voogt, Larsen, Poelen, Kleinjan, & Engels, 2013).

Parental and other role models for learning about alcohol-related norms in childhood

Socialization is the fundamental process by which children learn about their culture and the expected behaviors of their society; it occurs through a range of socialization agents (Velleman, 2009). The core principles defined by Social Learning Theory underlie primary socialization theory which suggests four primary social contexts (family, school, media and peer clusters) through which norms and behaviors are learned (Kobus, 2003). In childhood, parents act as the principal socialization agents (Steinberg, 2002). This theory emphasizes the relational bonds between social contexts that act as channels through which information is shared (Kobus, 2003).

Evidence indicates that it is not parental drinking per se which has a direct impact on the alcohol knowledge, norms and expectancies of children and alcohol use among adolescents, but rather the young people's exposure to this consumption, when the parents or other adults drink alcoholic beverages in the presence of the children and show the consequences of their drinking (Smit et al., 2018). This exposure to parental alcohol use and its consequences is associated with alcohol-related cognitions of the offspring rather than parental drinking per se. For example, recent Dutch studies have provided evidence that this exposure mediates the link between parental drinking and adolescents' alcohol expectancies both cross-sectionally (Smit, Voogt, Otten, Kleinjan, & Kuntsche, 2019) and over time (Smit, Voogt, Otten, Kleinjan, & Kuntsche, 2020). This effect is in line with the Cognitive Model of Intergeneration Transference (Campbell & Oei, 2010), suggesting that the observation of parental drinking habits contributes to what a child knows about alcohol (knowledge), its use in adult culture (norms), and what happens when alcohol is consumed (expectancies) (Campbell & Oei, 2010; Voogt et al., 2017). Like Social Learning Theory, this model suggests that children will not immediately adopt the behaviors they see, but that children's cognitions mediate the behavioral outcome. There may be a relatively long period of time between observation and modeling of the behavior (e.g. alcohol consumption); a time during which children process what they have seen (potentially in relation to other observed behavior) and create their own internal working models (Mares, Stone, Lichtwarck-Aschoff, & Engels, 2015), which subsequently are a condition for involvement in drinking behavior.

Among three to six-year olds, alcohol-related norms were found to be higher when parents drank frequently, at a higher quantity or during meals (Kuntsche & Kuntsche, 2019). As parents are the principal socialization agents in childhood (Steinberg, 2002), they are also the primary source of their children's alcohol-related knowledge (Zucker, Donovan, Masten, Mattson, & Moss, 2008; Zucker et al., 1995). The Cognitive Model of Intergenerational Transference (Campbell & Oei, 2010) assumes that parents' verbal affirmations of the perceived benefits of alcohol and children's observation of the effects of parental alcohol use are responsible for the intergenerational transference of alcohol-related cognitions, that is, what children (a) know about alcohol (i.e., alcohol-related knowledge); (b) know about alcohol use in the adult culture (i.e., alcohol-related norms), and

(c) believe about what occurs to others or themselves when drinking alcohol (i.e., alcohol expectancies).

However, parents are not the only source of children's alcohol-related knowledge about norms. Authors have argued that children acquire such knowledge when being exposed to alcohol advertisements or seeing actors drinking on television or in movies (Dalton et al., 2005; Hahn et al., 2000; Lang & Stritzke, 1993). In Switzerland, Kuntsche and Kuntsche (2019) found higher alcohol-related knowledge among those three to six-year olds who had frequent contact with adults outside the immediate family, such as frequent visits from relatives or frequent attendance at fairs and neighborhood parties.

Interim summary

To summarize, by observing parents and others engaging in alcohol use, ideas around the normativity of alcohol use, where it is appropriate to drink, who drinks what and why are formed from a very early age onward. Basically, as soon as a child can talk, he or she has an idea about adults' alcohol use. This knowledge grows with age and forms the cornerstone of one's own expectations and motivations to engage with alcohol later in life. Thus, a good understanding on how alcohol-related social norms are formed in early years provides the opportunity to inform parents about the crucial role they play in their children's knowledge about drinking and assist them in making alcohol a less ordinary commodity for future generations.

Social norms and interventions

Social norms, their misperception and the resulting influence on the individual's alcohol use have been in the focus of intervention efforts for decades. Based on a study from Perkins and Berkowitz (1986) the authors found that university students tend to overestimate their peer's alcohol use; a phenomena confirmed in later studies (for an overview see Dempsey, McAlaney, & Bewick, 2018). The evidence of the perceived misconception of other students' drinking has led to the development of the Social Norms Approach (Berkowitz, 2005), the by far most often applied method when it comes to addressing problematic alcohol consumption. Interventions using the Social Norms Approach use data on actual drinking behavior, usually based on a survey from a relevant reference group, such as all students in a college or all freshman of a given year, and provide this information to all incoming freshmen, often paired with normative feedback on their relevant position within the sample (e.g. above or under the mean). The feedback is intended to encourage reductions in alcohol use in those who drink above the norm.

Another more recent (and when thought through, not so different) approach, aiming at the change in Collective Social Norms, focuses on high risk consumption groups within a society. It aims to change the group's social norms related to alcohol use so that all members of the group will consequently change their drinking behavior in adaptation to the new norm. So instead of an individualistic approach where individuals are asked to adjust their drinking to the overall norm, this approach targets the drinking norm of the entire group to shift it towards more restrictive drinking. However, these cultural change approaches are rather new and less well studied than the Social Norms Approach. The following paragraphs will outline the current knowledge on the efficacy of both approaches.

Social norms approach

As mentioned above, the Social Norms approach aims to address the misperception on how much people drink and how many do so in a given situation. Interventions using the approach address these misperceptions based on two main assumptions: (A) the misperception of drinking norms drives the individual to engage in risky drinking behavior, i.e. a student drinks heavily because they perceive heavy drinking to be the norm and they want to fit in; and (B) by challenging the underlying misperception this behavior can be changed, i.e. the same student will drink less once they know that heavy drinking was the exception, not the norm. So, by providing the individual with information on the actual normative behavior, i.e. data on the actual drinking behavior of students in their year level (descriptive norm), and feedback about their own drinking relative to the group (normative feedback) these interventions try to adjust the individual's behavior closer to the norm, and thus to less drinking.

When explaining why these misperceptions occur in the first place three mechanisms have been proposed (see Dempsey et al., 2018):

A. the fundamental attribution error (Gilbert & Malone, 1995), i.e. misunderstanding the behavior of others by failing to acknowledge possible external causes of their actions; e.g. seeing a noisy group of people drinking at lunchtime, without knowing they are celebrating a major achievement they have been working on for weeks.

B. false consensus (Ross, Greene, & House, 1977), i.e. erroneously assuming others behave and think in the same way the individual does; e.g. by assuming finishing the day with a glass of wine or a beer is a common denominator to change from work to leisure.

C. pluralistic ignorance (Schroeder & Prentice, 1998), i.e. assuming the individual's behavior is atypical when in fact it is the norm, e.g. not drinking to intoxication at a college party.

However, these are only the major mechanisms and there might be more mechanisms, including methodological artefacts, such as recall bias, Hawthorne effect (i.e. adjustments in individual's behavior because they are under observation) or social desirability. Currently, a testable theory is lacking that clearly explains the mechanisms behind misperception of social norms, its impact on behavior change, and its utility as a target for interventions (Dempsey et al., 2018).

The growing popularity of these approaches is a reaction to the fact that educating people about the risks associated with a behavior is "stunningly ineffective" (Miller & Prentice, 2016; p. 353). Even worse, a series of experimental studies on the impact of responsible drinking messages depicted on posters in a laboratory bar setting found they had the opposite effects of the intended among undergraduate drinkers (Moss et al., 2015). The Social Norms Approach uses either *social marketing techniques* (for more details see Miller & Prentice, 2016) by using a kind of scattershot method. Via events, newspapers, flyers, posters and emails the message that peers' alcohol use is often overestimated is sent to all or as many people of a target group as possible. Messages are kept simple, e.g. 75% of all students don't drink more than 4 drinks on a single occasion – without further explanation. Regarding the prevention of alcohol use, these target groups often are college freshman or students in general (Dempsey et al., 2018). Sometimes the social marketing is replaced by or complemented with a *more personalized approach including normative feedback*, usually aiming at the individual and how their behavior fits within the behavior of their peer group (e.g. Lewis & Neighbors, 2006; Miller et al., 2013). However, this latter approach is less simplistic and the individual feedback makes its implementation more complicated because (1) the intervention needs to identify a peer group relevant to the individual to allow accurate and salient feedback, and (2) the information provided must have the potential to alter the individual's perception of the group norm. The latter is particularly relevant when normative feedback is used in the context of *brief interventions* (Prince & Carey, 2010). The perception of the norm will also be impacted by the individual's standing in the group and the significance this behavior has within the group (and for the individual). Approaches including normative feedback are therefore more labor-intensive but usually also more effective (Miller & Prentice, 2016). A third option is *focus group discussions* on misperceptions and their consequences. But this option is rarely used as it relies on well-trained facilitators so that participants will open up on their true attitudes and behaviors and is therefore very labor- and cost-intensive.

Another aspect to consider when it comes to changes in social norms and the efficacy of these interventions is the perceived intention of the provider of normative feedback, especially if messages are contradicting the individual's own experiences within the group. It seems that the credibility information is given is higher if it is based on personalized experience-based feedback or data from focus groups, as this provides more insider and detailed descriptions, potentially explaining why the misperception occurred in the first place (Miller & Prentice, 2016).

When examining the efficacy of the approach, the large majority of studies were found to have focused on colleges and University, addressing harmful drinking of students mainly in the US (Foxcroft et al., 2015; Dempsey et al., 2018). A recent Cochrane Review focusing on this particular setting found some significant longer term effects (more than 4 months) but concluded that the effect sizes, usually around −0.1 and −0.2 were too small be of relevance for policy or practice (Foxcroft et al., 2015). A lack of generalizability across samples in the different trials and the low to moderate quality of the studies may have contributed to this result. However, when interpreting these findings, it is important to keep in mind that these interventions use a far more minimalistic approach than other more labor and cost intense methods, e.g. brief motivational interviewing that require trained facilitators and often face-to-face interaction.

Another problem with the Social Norms Approach comes with the underlying assumption that the individual consumes alcohol mainly because they assume that this is what people in their group do. In other words, the approach does not challenge alcohol use per se; it challenges the amount and appropriateness of alcohol use, while assuming that we all have an exaggerated estimate of what others around us drink and that this in the end will make us drink more. This theory of false perception is not unchallenged (e.g. Pape, 2012), as it may also be the case that the individual's perception is not that false after all. This may occur for different reasons, such as having defined the reference group for the intervention not precisely enough, or not having considered age or gender differences in alcohol use. In this case, the individual may contest the norm we try to "market", as it does not match his or her own experiences or knowledge. Thus, the intervention designed to reduce alcohol use will not be effective, as the norms it tries to promote are not those shared by the individual. For example, Lewis and Neighbors (2006) concluded, in their review on the effectiveness of personalized normative feedback, that considering factors such as age, gender, other central group characteristics of the identified peer group are important in providing the feedback. However, considering only close friends' feedback was ineffective in their study, as participants know their friends and their drinking behavior well, leaving no room for misperceptions of drinking norms in this group. Reid and Carey (2015) found that descriptive norms were an important mediator between an intervention and behavioral change, but this effect varied by sample type. In higher risk samples, like mandated student samples, the evidence for descriptive norms being a moderator was less strong than in broader samples.

Overall, the Social Norm Approach in alcohol prevention and intervention seems to be best suited for those with high alcohol consumption - those exceeding the norm - and less effective for those who drink low amounts or around the group norm. These groups will not question or change their alcohol use as they still fit the norm. Even among those exceeding the group norm, changes in alcohol use may be limited as they will only decrease their alcohol use if they drank more than they wanted, feeling social pressure to do so, because they assumed it to be within the norm. All those for whom this is not the case may need more support than just providing them with the information that their alcohol use exceeds that of others and is thus beyond normative. They may even consider themselves a subgroup within their group where higher alcohol use is considered more normative than for the rest and then drink to conform to this excessive drinking norm. Heavy drinkers may also select or affiliate with groups that are more aligned with their own drinking. These are major limitation of the Social Norm Approach, and thus Miller and Prentice (2016, p. 348) conclude regarding its effectiveness: "The verdict on the empirical effects of norm-based interventions designed to change risky behaviors is still pending. Despite the popularity of these interventions, only a small subset includes the requisite controls to permit rigorous evaluation. ... However, systematic reviews of the actual effectiveness of these interventions have reached inconsistent conclusions. Tempering enthusiasm further, most of the supportive evidence rests on self-report data (for exceptions, see Johnson, 2012; Neighbors et al., 2011)".

Changing collective social norms

This second approach aims to shift collective social norms on alcohol use towards less risky and harmful drinking (Anderson, Jane-Llopis, Hasan, & Rehm, 2018); it is centered around environmental efforts first and foremost and has a strong focus on the common good. These interventions are largely framed around the availability of alcohol (Robaina & Babor, 2017), conceptualized as the physical availability (access and convenience), the economic availability (affordability) and the social availability (collective norms around alcohol use). Collective norms around alcohol use are not only shaped by the members of a culture or society but also marketing strategies of the alcohol industry (e.g. Petticrew et al., 2017).

At present there are only few interventions aiming to change the drinking culture (Anderson et al., 2018), accompanied by an evidence base including two reviews. Of these, one is a systematic review on community-based interventions to reduce underage drinking (Jones, 2014). Interventions included in this review aimed to change social norms and attitudes around underage alcohol use within communities. Studies included either targeted the whole community, only underage drinker or aimed to reduce the access to alcohol by minors. The approach to change collective social norms was most pronounced in the community-centered interventions whereas the other two either clearly targeted youth or enforcement of alcohol sale. The author concluded that those interventions who targeted the whole community had the potential to "not only change behaviour but also to change social norms" (Jones, 2014; p. 266).

The second review focused on policies to change existing drinking cultures (Savic et al., 2016). Savic and colleagues widen the understanding of drinking culture as being more than just the way we drink to include what makes us drink the way we do. The authors argue that by understanding "the meaning and use-values" as well as the places and societal regulations (norms) around drinking we should be able to shift alcohol-related norms and attitudes towards a social group being less permissive towards alcohol use. Savic and colleagues (2016) do not provide evidence for purposeful change, but they give pathways for how this can be done in future studies: by understanding how the micro- and macro-level of drinking cultures relate, how circumstances, setting and groups impact alcohol use and why these influences vary in magnitude depending on the other. In a later paper (Room et al., in press), some examples are given from historical and ethnographic studies of downward changes in drinking norms and practices in social groups where heavy drinking had been widely accepted. In 2019–20, in the Australian state of Victoria, the quasigovernmental public health agency is leading a program of community projects seeking to intervene to assist social worlds of heavy drinking to change their drinking norms and reduce heavy drinking (VicHealth, 2019).

Interim summary

Shifting alcohol-related norms towards less risky and harmful drinking is a more than two-decade old approach in the intervention and prevention of heavy alcohol use. Two concepts merit particular attention, the Social Norms approach, predominantly used in the context of college and University students, and the more recent approach on changing collective norms via community interventions. Whereas meta-analyses of studies in the former tradition found small but often short-term effects, studies in the latter are considered promising, but the number of studies is still too small to come to firm conclusions.

Conclusion

Social norms are a powerful mechanism defining an individual's behavior in their everyday life, and this holds true for alcohol-related norms. These norms and expectations are acquired at a very early age and are likely to shape the behavior in later years. Teaching parents, as the central agents of knowledge acquisition in early childhood about the impact of adult alcohol use on children's cognitions and their later approach to alcohol may be a useful tool in preventing the intergenerational transmission of alcohol use.

At present, interventions using the Social Norms Approach, in particular studied in college settings, have some potential to shift risky alcohol use to more moderate consumption. More recent approaches aim at shifting social norms among subgroups or in specific drinking cultures, rather than focusing on individual attitudes and expectations. Examples show that such interventions have some potential, albeit small, to prevent harmful alcohol use. The small effects may be caused by the large variability in measures and samples across the different trials together with the low to moderate quality of these studies. However, it is important to keep in mind that these interventions are quite simple in their approach to change risky drinking behavior by just making people reflect about how they behave compared to others.

References

Aarts, H., & Dijksterhuis, A. (2003). The silence of the library: Environment, situational norm, and social behavior. *Journal of Personality and Social Psychology*, *84*(1), 18–28.

Anderson, P., Jane-Llopis, E., Hasan, O. S. M., & Rehm, J. (2018). Changing collective social norms in favour of reduced harmful use of alcohol: A review of reviews. *Alcohol and Alcoholism*, *53*(3), 326–332.

Andrews, J. A., Hampson, S., & Peterson, M. (2011). Early adolescent cognitions as predictors of heavy alcohol use in high school. *Addictive Behaviors*, *36*(5), 448–455.

Arterberry, B. J., Smith, A. E., Martens, M. P., Cadigan, J. M., & Murphy, J. G. (2014). Protective behavioral strategies, social norms, and alcohol-related outcomes. *Addiction Research & Theory*, *22*(4), 279–285.

Bennett, J., Stevens, G., Mathers, C., Bonita, R., Rehm, J., Kruk, M., ... Ezzati, M. (2018). NCD Countdown 2030: Worldwide trends in non-communicable disease mortality and progress towards Sustainable Development Goal target 3.4. *Lancet*, *392*(10152), 1072–1088.

Berkowitz, A. D. (2005). *An overview of the social norms approach, . Changing the culture of college drinking: A socially situated health communication campaign* (1, pp. 193–214). Hampton Press.

Campbell, J. M., & Oei, T. P. S. (2010). A cognitive model for the intergenerational transference of alcohol use behavior. *Addictive Behaviors*, *35*(2), 73–83.

Cox, W. M., & Klinger, E. (1988). A motivational model of alcohol use. *Journal of Abnormal Psychology*, *97*(2), 168–180.

Cox, W. M., & Klinger, E. (1990). Incentive motivation, affective change, and alcohol use: A model. In W. M. Cox (Ed.), *Why people drink - Parameters of alcohol as a reinforcer* (pp. 291–314). New York, NY: Gardner Press, Inc.

Cronce, J. M., Toomey, T. L., Lenk, K., Nelson, T. F., Kilmer, J. R., & Larimer, M. E. (2018). NIAAA's College alcohol intervention matrix: CollegeAIM. *Alcohol Research: Current Reviews*, *39*(1), 43.

Dalton, M. A., Bernhardt, A. M., Gibson, J. J., Sargent, J. D., Beach, M. L., Adachi-Mejia, A. M., ... Heatherton, T. F. (2005). Use of cigarettes and alcohol by preschoolers while role-playing as adults: "Honey, have some smokes". *Archives of Pediatrics and Adolescent Medicine*, *159*(9), 854–859.

Dempsey, R. C., McAlaney, J., & Bewick, B. M. (2018). A critical appraisal of the social norms approach as an interventional strategy for health-related behavior and attitude change. *Frontiers in Psychology*, *9*, 2180.

Donovan, J. E., Leech, S. L., Zucker, R. A., Loveland-Cherry, C. J., Jester, J. M., Fitzgerald, H. E., ... Looman, W. S. (2004). Really underage drinkers: Alcohol use among elementary students. *Alcoholism: Clinical and Experimental Research*, *28*(2), 341–349.

Foxcroft, D. R., Moreira, M. T., Almeida Santimano, N. M. L., & Smith, L. A. (2015). Social norms information for alcohol misuse in university and college students. *Cochrane Database of Systematic Reviews* (12).

Gilbert, D. T., & Malone, P. S. (1995). The correspondence bias. *Psychological Bulletin, 117*(1), 21.

Hahn, E. J., Hall, L. A., Rayens, M. K., Burt, A. V., Corley, D., & Sheffel, K. L. (2000). Kindergarten children's knowledge and perceptions of alcohol, tobacco, and other drugs. *Journal of School Health, 70*(2), 51–55.

Hanson, D. J. (1995). *Preventing alcohol abuse: Alcohol, culture, and control.* Greenwood Publishing Group.

Jahoda, G., Davies, J. B., & Tagg, S. (1980). Parents' alcohol consumption and children's knowledge of drinks and usage patterns. *British Journal of Addiction, 75*(3), 297–303.

Johnson, M. B. (2012). Experimental test of social norms theory in a real-world drinking environment. *Journal of Studies on Alcohol and Drugs, 73*(5), 851–859.

Jones, S. C. (2014). Using social marketing to create communities for our children and adolescents that do not model and encourage drinking. *Health & Place, 30*, 260–269.

Kobus, K. (2003). Peers and adolescent smoking. *Addiction, 98*, 37–55.

Krieger, H., Neighbors, C., Lewis, M. A., LaBrie, J. W., Foster, D. W., & Larimer, M. E. (2016). Injunctive norms and alcohol consumption: A revised conceptualization. *Alcoholism: Clinical and Experimental Research, 40*(5), 1083–1092.

Kuendig, H., & Kuntsche, E. (2012). Solitary versus social drinking: An experimental study on effects of social exposures on in situ alcohol consumption. *Alcoholism: Clinical and Experimental Research, 36*(4), 732–738.

Kuntsche, E., & Gmel, G. (2013). Alcohol consumption in late adolescence and early adulthood-where is the problem? *Swiss Medical Weekly, 143*.

Kuntsche, S., Gmel, G., Knibbe, R. A., Kuendig, H., Bloomfield, K., Kramer, S., & Grittner, U. (2006). Gender and cultural differences in the association between family roles, social stratification, and alcohol use: A European cross-cultural analysis. *Alcohol and Alcoholism, 41* (Suppl_1), i37–i46.

Kuntsche, S., Knibbe, R. A., & Gmel, G. (2012). Parents' alcohol use: Gender differences in the impact of household and family chores. *European Journal of Public Health, 22*(6), 894–899.

Kuntsche, S., Knibbe, R. A., Kuntsche, E., & Gmel, G. (2011). Housewife or working mum—each to her own? The relevance of societal factors in the association between social roles and alcohol use among mothers in 16 industrialized countries. *Addiction, 106*(11), 1925–1932.

Kuntsche, E., & Kuntsche, S. (2019). Parental drinking and characteristics of family life as predictors of preschoolers' alcohol-related knowledge and norms. *Addictive Behaviors, 88*, 92–98.

Kuntsche, E., Le Mével, L., & Zucker, R. A. (2016). What do preschoolers know about alcohol? Evidence from the electronic Appropriate Beverage Task (eABT). *Addictive Behaviors, 61*, 47–52.

Kuntsche, E. N., & Müller, S. (2012). Why do young people start drinking? Motives for first-time alcohol consumption and links to risky drinking in early adolescence. *European Addiction Research, 18*(1), 34–39.

Lang, A. R., & Stritzke, W. G. (1993). Children and alcohol. *Recent Developments in Alcoholism, 11*, 73–85.

Lapinski, M. K., & Rimal, R. N. (2005). An explication of social norms. *Communication Theory*, *15*(2), 127–147.

Lewis, M. A., & Neighbors, C. (2006). Social norms approaches using descriptive drinking norms education: A review of the research on personalized normative feedback. *Journal of American College Health*, *54*(4), 213–218.

Mares, S. H., Stone, L. L., Lichtwarck-Aschoff, A., & Engels, R. C. (2015). Alcohol expectancies in young children and how this relates to parental alcohol use. *Addictive Behaviors*, *45*, 93–98.

Massengale, K. E. M., Ma, A., Rulison, K. L., Milroy, J. J., & Wyrick, D. L. (2017). Perceived norms and alcohol use among first-year college student-athletes' different types of friends. *Journal of American College Health*, *65*(1), 32–40.

Miller, M. B., Leffingwell, T., Claborn, K., Meier, E., Walters, S., & Neighbors, C. (2013). Personalized feedback interventions for college alcohol misuse: An update of Walters & Neighbors (2005). *Psychology of Addictive Behaviors*, *27*(4), 909.

Miller, D. T., & Prentice, D. A. (2016). Changing norms to change behavior. *Annual Review of Psychology*, *67*(1), 339–361.

Moss, A. C., Albery, I. P., Dyer, K. R., Frings, D., Humphreys, K., Inkelaar, T., ... Speller, A. (2015). The effects of responsible drinking messages on attentional allocation and drinking behaviour. *Addictive Behaviors*, *44*, 94–101.

Neighbors, C., Jensen, M., Tidwell, J., Walter, T., Fossos, N., & Lewis, M. A. (2011). Social-norms interventions for light and nondrinking students. *Group Processes & Intergroup Relations*, *14*(5), 651–669.

Noll, R. B., Zucker, R. A., & Greenberg, G. S. (1990). Identification of alcohol by smell among preschoolers: Evidence for early socialization about drugs occurring in the home. *Child Development*, *61*(5), 1520–1527.

Pape, H. (2012). Young people's overestimation of peer substance use: An exaggerated phenomenon? *Addiction*, *107*(5), 878–884.

Perkins, H. W., & Berkowitz, A. D. (1986). Perceiving the community norms of alcohol use among students: Some research implications for campus alcohol education programming. *International Journal of the Addictions*, *21*(9–10), 961–976.

Petticrew, M., Shemilt, I., Lorenc, T., Marteau, T. M., Melendez-Torres, G. J., O'Mara-Eves, A., ... Thomas, J. (2017). Alcohol advertising and public health: Systems perspectives versus narrow perspectives. *Journal of Epidemiology and Community Health*, *71*(3), 308–312.

Pihl, A. (2017). Ten things I've learned from two decades living in Sweden. *Irish Times*.

Prince, M. A., & Carey, K. B. (2010). The malleability of injunctive norms among college students. *Addictive Behaviors*, *35*(11), 940–947.

Reid, A. E., & Carey, K. B. (2015). Interventions to reduce college student drinking: State of the evidence for mechanisms of behavior change. *Clinical Psychology Review*, *40*, 213–224.

Rimal, R. N., & Lapinski, M. K. (2015). A re-explication of social norms, ten years later. *Communication Theory*, *25*(4), 393–409.

Robaina, K., & Babor, T. F. (2017). Alcohol industry marketing strategies in Latin America and the Caribbean: The way forward for policy research. *Addiction*, *112*, 122–124.

Roberts, S., Ralph, B., Elliott, K., Robards, B., Savic, M., Lindsay, J., ... Lubman, D. I. (2019). *Exploring men's risky drinking cultures*. Melbourne: Victorian Health Promotion Foundation.

Room, R. (1975). Normative perspectives on alcohol use and problems. *Journal of Drug Issues*, *5*(4), 358–368.

Room, R., MacLean, S., Pennay, A., Dwyer, R., Turner, K., & Saleeba, E. Changing risky drinking practices in different types of social worlds: Concepts and experiences. Drugs: Education, Prevention and Policy, in press.

Room, R., Kuntsche, S., Dietze, P., Munné, M., Monteiro, M., & Greenfield, T. K. (2019). Testing consensus about situational norms on drinking: A cross-national comparison. *Journal of Studies on Alcohol and Drugs*, *80*(6), 651–658.

Ross, L., Greene, D., & House, P. (1977). The false consensus phenomenon: An attributional bias in self-perception and social perception processes. *Journal of Experimental Social Psychology*, *13*(3), 279–301.

Savic, M., Room, R., Mugavin, J., Pennay, A., & Livingston, M. (2016). Defining "drinking culture": A critical review of its meaning and connotation in social research on alcohol problems. *Drugs: Education, Prevention and Policy*, *23*(4), 270–282.

Schroeder, C. M., & Prentice, D. A. (1998). Exposing pluralistic ignorance to reduce alcohol use among college students. *Journal of Applied Social Psychology*, *28*(23), 2150–2180.

Schulenberg, J. E., & Maggs, J. L. (2008). Destiny matters: Distal developmental influences on adult alcohol use and abuse. *Addiction*, *103*(1), 1–6.

Smit, K., Otten, R., Voogt, C., Kleinjan, M., Engels, R., & Kuntsche, E. (2018). Exposure to drinking mediates the association between parental alcohol use and preteen alcohol use. *Addictive Behaviors*, *87*, 244–250.

Smit, K., Voogt, C., Otten, R., Kleinjan, M., & Kuntsche, E. (2019). Exposure to parental alcohol use rather than parental drinking shapes offspring's alcohol expectancies. *Alcoholism: Clinical and Experimental Research*, *43*(9), 1967–1977.

Smit, K., Voogt, C., Otten, R., Kleinjan, M., & Kuntsche, E. (2020). Alcohol expectancies change in early to middle adolescence as a function of the exposure to parental alcohol use. *Drug and Alcohol Dependence*, 107938.

Spiegler, D. L. (1983). Children's attitudes toward alcohol. *Journal of Studies on Alcohol*, *44*(3), 545–552.

Steinberg, L. (2002). *Adolescence*. New York, NY, USA: McGraw-Hill.

Sunstein, C. R. (1996). Social norms and social roles. *Columbia Law Review*, *96*(4), 903–968.

Velleman, R. (2009). How do children and young people learn about alcohol: A major review of the literature for the Joseph Rowntree Foundation.

VicHealth. (2019). *Alcohol cultures framework*. Carlton South: VicHealth.

Voogt, C., Beusink, M., Kleinjan, M., Otten, R., Engels, R., Smit, K., & Kuntsche, E. (2017). Alcohol-related cognitions in children (aged 2–10) and how they are shaped by parental alcohol use: A systematic review. *Drug and Alcohol Dependence*, *177*, 277–290.

Voogt, C. V., Larsen, H., Poelen, E. A., Kleinjan, M., & Engels, R. C. (2013). Longitudinal associations between descriptive and injunctive norms of youngsters and heavy drinking and problem drinking in late adolescence. *Journal of Substance Use*, *18*(4), 275–287.

WHO. (2019). *Global status report on alcohol and health 2018*. World Health Organization.

Windle, M., Spear, L. P., Fuligni, A. J., Angold, A., Brown, J. D., Pine, D., ... Dahl, R. E. (2008). Transitions into underage and problem drinking: Developmental processes and mechanisms between 10 and 15 years of age. *Pediatrics*, *121*(Suppl. 4), S273–S289.

Zucker, R. A., Donovan, J. E., Masten, A. S., Mattson, M. E., & Moss, H. B. (2008). Early developmental processes and the continuity of risk for underage drinking and problem drinking. *Pediatrics*, *121*(Suppl 4), S252–S272.

Zucker, R. A., Kincaid, S. B., Fitzgerald, H. E., & Bingham, C. R. (1995). Alcohol schema acquisition in preschoolers: Differences between children of alcoholics and children of nonalcoholics. *Alcoholism: Clinical and Experimental Research*, *19*(4), 1011–1017.

Chapter 14

Alcohol consumption and group decision making

Hirotaka Imada, Tim Hopthrow and Dominic Abrams
Centre for the Study of Group Processes, School of Psychology, University of Kent, United Kingdom

In 2017, it was estimated that over 29 million people in the UK drank alcohol (Office for National Statistics, 2019). Although the number of drinkers has slightly decreased for the past decade, alcohol consumption is still commonplace. Moreover, the number of alcohol-related incidents (e.g., hospital admissions and deaths) has changed little. The National Health Service reported more than 300,000 hospital admissions and 5000 deaths due to alcohol consumption (NHS, 2018). Thus, alcohol consumption continues to pose substantial risks to individuals' health and society

Social and health psychologists have endeavored to address the issues around drinking, and our specific interest is in social drinking. Drinking in groups is ubiquitous, but national data collection exercises have not provided a clear quantification of factors such as group size or frequency, and nor is there clear evidence about whether social processes themselves are altered when people drink in groups, other than the prevalence of heavy episodic drinking that is assumed in many cases to be in groups.

Psychological research on alcohol intoxication was given particular impetus by the seminal work by Steele and Josephs (1988, 1990), who proposed the alcohol myopia model. This model holds that the influence of alcohol consumption on behavior results in part from the narrowed focus of information processing that follows alcohol intoxication, i.e., the alcohol myopia. Specifically, they argued that intoxication rendered individuals less attentive to cues that normally act as inhibitory controls on behavior (Monahan & Lannutti, 2000; Steele & Josephs, 1990). The alcohol myopia model was further supported and elaborated by Fromme, Katz, and D'Amico (1997) demonstrating that intoxicated individuals tended to base their judgement on an automatic expectation of positive outcomes, ignoring potential negative consequences. The theory has subsequently gained empirical support from a

The Handbook of Alcohol Use - Understandings from Synapse to Society.
DOI: https://doi.org/10.1016/B978-0-12-816720-5.00009-8

number of studies (Bayless & Harvey, 2017; Fromme et al., 1997; Giancola, Duke, & Ritz, 2011; Giancola, Josephs, Parrott, & Duke, 2010). Overall, the model established a cognitive mechanism arising from the pharmacological effects of alcohol consumption.

Risk taking behavior has been one of the most studied effects of alcohol intoxication. Previous studies looked at numerous forms of risk taking such as drunk-driving (Burian, Hensberry, & Liguori, 2003; Burian, Liguori, & Robinson, 2002; Guppy, 1994; Harrison & Fillmore, 2011; McMillen & Wells-Parker, 1987; Taylor et al., 2010; Van Dyke & Fillmore, 2015, 2017), violence and aggression (Permanen, 1991), sexual risk taking[1] (Davis, 2010; Rehm, Shield, Joharchi, & Shuper, 2012; Scott-Sheldon, Carey, Cunningham, Johnson, & Carey, 2016; Stall, McKusick, Wiley, Coates, & Ostrow, 1986), and gambling[2] (Bidwell et al., 2013; Lane & Cherek, 2000). Overall, these studies have consistently demonstrated that alcohol consumption increases various forms of risk-taking behavior.

Alcohol consumption and group decision making

Past research on alcohol predominantly focused on individual decision making following sole drinking and has consistently demonstrated that intoxicated individuals make significantly different decisions in various domains from those who are sober. However, people often consume alcohol during various social occasions (Ally, Lovatt, Meier, Brennan, & Holmes, 2016). Previous studies, in fact, have documented that alcohol consumption has been a social activity (Aitken, 1985; Gordon, Heim, & MacAskill, 2012) as well as a part of rituals (Dietler, 2006). Indeed, despite the negative impacts of alcohol intoxication on various behaviors, it has a positive role in building interpersonal relationships (Brown, Goldman, Inn, & Anderson, 1980; de Visser, Wheeler, Abraham, & Smith, 2013; Fairbairn et al., 2015; Freed, 1978; Gordon et al., 2012; Hull, 1981; Monahan & Lannutti, 2000), which is reflected by the prevalence of alcoholic beverages at diverse social events. Furthermore, it was also suggested that individuals tended to drink more in the presence of others (Eisenberg, Golberstein, & Whitlock, 2014; Thombs, Wolcott, & Farkash, 1997), implying drinking behavior itself would be different between sole and social drinking. This prior evidence all suggests that

1. Supporting the alcohol myopia model, when cues highlighting potential risks were present, individuals were less susceptible to the risk-enhancing effect of alcohol intoxication (MacDonald et al., 2000).

2. We would like to note that while laboratory experiments consistently demonstrated that alcohol consumption was associated with an increased risk-taking gambling, a field experiment revealed the positive effect of intoxication on risk-seeking behavior among male and young participants (Proestakis et al., 2013). However, it remains unclear whether this should be attributed to the low ecological validity of lab experiments or the fact that intoxicated individuals in the field experiment simply did not fully understand the nature of gambling they engaged with.

research should address both the incidence and the effects of social and group drinking.

In fact, social psychological work has robustly demonstrated that such group decision making, wherein a group of individuals together make a sole decision, involves several group processes that can potentially alter the way alcohol affects individual decision making. Therefore, it is important to ponder whether alcohol affects individual decision making in the same manner as it would group decision making. In addition, understanding how alcohol shapes group decision making also helps us to understand and tackle societal issues caused by alcohol consumption.

Sayette, Kirchner, Moreland, Levine, and Travis (2004) first shed light on how alcohol could affect risk taking behavior of a group of people in a laboratory.[3] They formed groups of four unacquainted individuals who consumed either alcoholic beverages (100-proof vodka: cranberry juice = 1: 3.5) or placebo drinks (flattened tonic water instead of vodka). Participants were asked to consume these in three doses 0.82 g/kg dose of alcohol, each over a 10 minute period, with the second and third doses starting at 10 and 20 minutes, respectively. They then engaged in an ice-breaker activity during a 20-min alcohol absorption time. Finally, they were presented with two options as to and additional questionnaires they would be asked to complete. As a group, they could decide to complete a further 30-min survey or they could toss a coin to determine that they would either have to complete a 60-min survey or no survey. Participants were given 150 seconds to make this decision, which was used as a measure of their risk taking behavior.

Consistent with previous studies on individual decision making, intoxicated groups were more likely to make the risk taking decision than placebo groups. However, it must be noted that there was no comparison condition in which participants made these decisions as separate individuals.

Sayette and colleagues' findings seemed to suggest that the alcohol myopia process that affects individuals would also apply to group decision making. However, without direct comparison to individual decision making, this conclusion was premature, and also there was no alternative mechanism proposed to account for the effect of alcohol consumption on group decision making. To address this, drawing upon social psychological work (Abrams et al., 1997), Abrams, Hopthrow, Hulbert, and Frings (2006) proposed that three different psychological mechanisms could affect the way that alcohol intoxication would affect group decision making, particularly in the risky

3. Prior research such as Connors and Sobell (1986), attempted to investigate the role of alcohol in group contexts, by controlling the presence of others. However, Connors and Sobell (1986) had one research confederate as an observing other, and it is unsure whether the mere presence of a person whose behavior was strictly scripted would have nay implications for the relationship between alcohol intoxication and group processes.

behavior domain: (1) group polarization, (2) deindividuation, and (3) group monitoring.

Group polarization

First, group polarization is defined as a phenomenon where deliberation tends to move groups towards a more extreme point in the direction indicated by their own pre-deliberation judgements (Kerr, Davis, Meek, & Rissman, 1975; Sunstein, 2002; Zuber, Crott, & Werner, 1992). This tendency has been consistently documented in various types of decision making, including risk taking behavior (Zuber et al., 1992). Steele and Josephs' (1990) alcohol myopia model posited that intoxicated individuals had increased attraction towards the risk compared to sober ones. Fromme et al. (1997) also suggested those who had consumed alcohol tended to focus on a restricted range of positive outcomes, ignoring potential negative events. Combined with group polarization, these findings implied that risk attraction might emerge more strongly in group decision making than individual decision making, as the inclination towards risk would tend to be more extreme in groups. Consequently, according to the group polarization account, it was expected that group decision making after the consumption of alcohol should be riskier than individual decision making.

Deindividuation

Second, deindividuation refers to a state where people lose self-consciousness, and this occurs especially when members of a group do not feel their behavior could be singled out by others (Festinger, Pepitone, & Newcomb, 1952). Previous studies found that under deindividuation, people tended to act in a less inhibited manner, resulting in increased non-normative behaviors (Diener, Lusk, DeFour, & Flax, 1980; Mullen, 1986). In addition, meta-analytic evidence also supported the reduction in self-attention and regulation in a group (Mullen, 1986). Drawing upon this past research, Abrams and colleagues reasonably assumed that deindividuation and alcohol might together affect group decision making in a way that additively increases risk taking tendencies. In other words, this perspective predicted that group decision making would yield risker behavior than individual decision making, given the tendency for alcohol consumption generally to disinhibit risk taking behavior. Unlike the group polarization perspective, deindividuation predicts that the risk-enhancing effect of alcohol intoxication would hold both among individuals and groups, regardless of the initial tendency of the group. Sayette et al.'s (2004) study revealed that groups were more likely to make risky decisions when intoxicated, consistent with the possibility that deindividuation processes occurred. However, as the study did not have individual decision making conditions, there is no way to know whether being in the groups *per se* resulted in any disinhibition and so it is not feasible to imply whether deindividuation was actually occurring.

Group monitoring

The third process proposed by Abrams et al. (2006) is group monitoring. The idea of group monitoring stems from seminal work on motivational accounts for individual performance in a group: social loafing and facilitation (for a review, see Karau & Williams, 1993). Studies on social loafing and social facilitation suggest that the presence of co-actors, particularly when behavior is visible and hence accountable, may motivate greater effort and better performance. When these factors are absent, in contrast, social loafing can take place, meaning that individuals are less likely to invest themselves in tasks. Thus, these theories suggest that face-to-face small group discussion would generally have a positive effect in performance of the group. More directly, moreover, Abrams et al. (2006) postulated that the process of making a group decision exposed each group members' thinking and reasoning, thereby enabling members to observe and monitor one another's inputs, and making it more likely that flawed or faulty reasoning would be rejected. Thus, although individuals may find it harder to self-regulate because they feel disinhibited, their attention to external cues that are focal in the situation (other group members) may compensate for effects such as alcohol myopia. These three theories provided different routes (i.e., motivational influences on individual performance in a group) that could explain how and why groups would make decisions differently from individuals when intoxicated. However, the group monitoring hypothesis was the only one that allowed for the possibility that groups might be less rather than more susceptible to the effects of alcohol myopia than individuals.

The group monitoring perspective built on research in the group decision making literature identifying that groups allow members to exchange intellectual resources and that this can result in improved decisions compared to those made by lone individuals (Abrams et al., 2006). Hopthrow and Hulbert (2005), for instance, demonstrated that groups could reach an optimal solution in social dilemmas through discussion. Several studies have provided support for the positive effect of group processes (Meleady, Hopthrow, & Crisp, 2013a; Meleady, Hopthrow, & Crisp, 2013b). Based upon these findings, Abrams et al. (2006) argued that unless tasks were extremely complex, group monitoring would allow members to confer and avoid making a non-optimal (i.e., risky) decision. Therefore, they hypothesized that group decision making process would mitigate the risk-enhancing influence of alcohol consumption.

Given the three possible mechanisms by which alcohol consumption could affect risk taking behavior of groups, Abrams et al. (2006) conducted a comprehensive study in order to further understand risk taking behavior among intoxicated groups and individuals. They, thus, directly examined how alcohol intoxication affected risk attraction among individuals and groups of four persons. They recruited 120 undergraduate students mostly by means of a staffed desk soliciting volunteers. They were randomly assigned to group decision or individual decision making conditions, and groups of four unacquainted individuals were formed for the former. Participants were told that they might consume a moderate amount of alcohol during the testing. In addition, they were asked to drink no alcoholic beverages for 18 hours eat no food for 3 hours prior to the study. Furthermore, before experimental sessions, participants were screened out by a revised version of the Alcohol Use Disorders Identification Test (AUDIT; Saunders, Aasland, Babor, De la Fuente, & Grant, 1993) such that only those who usually drank low to moderate amount of alcohol were eligible. Because of the potentially risky nature of the research, they carefully explained the format of the experiment and participants signed a medical consent form on a voluntary basis. Although they were free to discontinue their participation at any time during the testing, they were explicitly instructed that they could not leave the lab and their time in the laboratory was monitored in order to ensure their safety.

Regardless of the experimental condition, participants received a very strong tasting lozenge to disguise the taste of drink prior to drink administration. In the alcohol condition, they were asked to drink a mixture of vodka (1.13 g/kg) orange juice, and tonic water within 6 min. In the placebo condition, participants were given a mixture of orange juice and tonic water with 2 mL of vodka floating on the surface, to disguise the smell. (This amount was not sufficient to register in a BAC test device they used). It was followed by a 40-min alcohol absorption phase, where they watched a comedy show. This alcohol administration procedure resulted in participants in the alcohol condition being intoxicated at the 0.074% BAC (breath alcohol concentration) on average. Importantly, unlike Sayette et al. (2004), those who were in the individual condition and group condition completed the whole procedure, from alcohol induction, with nobody (in the individual condition) or with three other group members (in the group condition), respectively. In other words, individual decision making followed sole drinking and group decision making followed group drinking.

The risk attraction task employed 16 duplex bets (Slovic & Lichtenstein, 1968), which was more elaborate than the task used in Sayette et al. (2004). These bets varied in the amount of money they could win or lose as well as the probability of winning and losing. They were presented in the same manner to participants in both conditions, but those in the group condition could confer with group members to reach consensus and make group decisions. For each bet, they were asked to rate their commitment to gamble using a 10-point scale. To make sure that they believed that the decisions involved real monetary incentives, they were instructed that a random set of bets rated most favorably would be played with their own money. However, in actuality, no money was gambled.

The findings clearly supported the group monitoring hypothesis. There was a significant interaction between alcohol consumption and decision making such that the risk-enhancing effect of alcohol consumption was present among individuals but absent among groups. In other words, it was revealed that group decisions were less susceptible to the deleterious effect of intoxication. Abrams et al. (2006) also recorded decision making time and found that intoxicated groups took significantly longer to complete the risk attraction task, but this pattern was not observed among individuals. This suggested that group members were more-self-attentive and spent time conferring with other members the finding also supported the group monitoring hypothesis. Overall, Abrams et al. (2006) offered the first experimental evidence on the influence of moderate levels of alcohol on group decision making in comparison to individual decision making and showed a risk-suppressing effect of group contexts arguably through group monitoring.

Frings and colleagues provided further support for the group monitoring hypothesis with different behavior and contexts; Frings, Hopthrow, Abrams, Hulbert, and Gutierrez (2008), for example, found that while intoxicated individuals performed significantly worse at a vigilance task (i.e., a task requiring sustained attention) than sober individuals, intoxicated groups did not show such reduced performance. Moreover, they used mathematical modeling to further test the group monitoring hypothesis, based on Davis' Social Judgement Scheme (SJS: Davis, 1996). The SJS model assumed that group members would seek the highest degree of consensus in the group such that individual decisions that were close to the consensus were given more weight than outliers in the model. The model represented the process supposed to operate in the group monitoring hypothesis which assumes that group members would attend to cues in order to reach an accurate group consensus, rather than being distracted by extreme or erroneous individual recommendations from group members. Frings et al. (2008) established that the SJS model predicted group consensus well and better than other mathematical models predicting the group decision simply with central tendencies of the group e.g., Mean or Median, suggesting that group members discarded erroneous outliers and trusted the areas of consensus when making group decisions. Therefore, consistent with Abrams et al. (2006), Frings et al. (2008) showed evidence that group monitoring ameliorated the negative effect of alcohol consumption on vigilance typically observed among individuals in previous studies (e.g., Clifasefi, Takarangi, & Bergman, 2006; Koelega, 1995, 1998; Mongrain & Standing, 1989; Moskowitz & Depry, 1968; Rohrbaugh et al., 1988; Schulte, Müller-Oehring, Strasburger, Warzel, & Sabel, 2001). Specifically, they were able to show through mathematical modeling that groups were able to reduce the influence of members who made extreme judgments and thus ameliorate the potentially deleterious effects of alcohol consumption on the group's decision making.

Further support for the group monitoring hypothesis comes from the literature on fatigue. Fatigue is a physical and/or mental state that often leads to impaired decision quality (Gander, Millar, Webster, & Merry, 2008; Landrigan et al., 2004) and, therefore, can provide a domain that enables further testing of the group monitoring effects. In a sample of military personnel, Frings (2011) found that group monitoring could also alleviate the negative effect of fatigue on cognitive performance. Drawing on the preceding studies on group monitoring, they tested whether group decision making would also help individuals overcome fatigue-related impairment in decision quality. In line with the hypothesis, they demonstrated that while fatigued individuals performed worse in cognitive tasks than alert individuals, teams of fatigued individuals did not exhibit such impaired performance due to fatigue. Thus, overall, the group monitoring hypothesis has earned empirical support from several studies.

In a stark contrast to the findings in favor of the group monitoring hypothesis, Sayette, Dimoff, Levine, Moreland, and Votruba-Drzal (2012) conducted further research that found no support for group monitoring in risky behavior in groups. Specifically, as well as the individual and group decision conditions employed by Abrams et al. (2006), Sayette et al. (2012) added a non-alcohol condition in which participants knew they were drinking a non-alcoholic beverage. This allowed them to account for potential differences between pharmacological effects and dosage-set effect (i.e., the influence of the belief that they were drinking alcohol). Nonetheless, other methodological differences were present. Unlike Abrams et al. (2006), all participants consumed their drinks as a group, and then those in the individual decision making condition were taken away to make their decision privately. Thus, individual decision making followed group drinking. Using the coin toss decision from Sayette et al. (2004) as a measurement of risky behavior it emerged that the intoxicated and placebo groups were both more likely to choose the risky option compared to groups in the non-alcohol condition (47%, 44%, and 20%, respectively). By contrast, individual decision making was not affected by the drinking conditions at all (27%, 27%, 30%, respectively). Sayette et al.'s (2012) results suggested that alcohol intoxication did not have a risk-enhancing effect on individuals but that groups were rather susceptible to the effect of alcohol. Parenthetically, Sayette et al. (2012) also examined the effect of the gender composition of groups because it has been found that gender composition significantly affects group decisions (Dufwenberg & Muren, 2006; Hannagan & Larimer, 2010; Lamiraud & Vranceanu, 2018). However, they did not find a significant influence of gender.

Following the counterevidence from Sayette et al. (2012), Hopthrow, Randsley de Moura, Meleady, Abrams, and Swift (2014) conducted a further test of the group monitoring hypothesis. They were aware that results from lab experiments did not always correspond to those from field experiments (Mitchell, 2012), and they aimed to test the external validity of group monitoring effect using naturalistic drinking contexts. They recruited groups and individuals who had consumed or not consumed alcohol from bars and music events. This allowed them not only to potentially generalize the group monitoring hypothesis but also to have participants with a relatively high dosage of alcohol. Participants consuming alcohol, on average, had a mean BAC of 0.29, which is above the drink-drive limit in different countries (e.g., limits for private motorists: 0.08% in England, 0.05% in Scotland).

Hopthrow et al. (2014) asked all participants, regardless of whether they were groups or individuals, to individually answer two questions measuring individual risk behavior that were created based on the Choice Dilemma Questionnaire (Kogan & Wallach, 1964). For those who had consumed alcohol as a group, they first privately made individual decisions and then discussed the dilemma as a group to reach a group decision. Each question consisted of a short vignette where a protagonist was about to drink and drive, and participants were asked to indicate the lowest probability of having an accident resulting from drinking and driving. For example, one of them read, "You have been drinking in the pub with friends for the afternoon. You receive a phone call from your girlfriend/boyfriend who is at the airport having returned from holiday. S/he is not feeling well and doesn't have money for the taxi home. You are very excited about seeing your girlfriend/boyfriend again, but you are at the legal limit for drinking and driving. The chances that you would have an accident are increased by your alcohol consumption. However, to catch the train to the airport would cost a lot more money and would mean that your girlfriend/boyfriend would have to wait at the airport for twice as long." Participants were then presented a six-point scale to indicate the lowest probability of having an accident they would accept to pick up their partner. The item was scaled in the following manner: 1 = five in 10 chances, 2 = three in 10 chances, 3 = one in 10 chances, 4 = 0.5 in 10 chances, 5 = 0.1 in 10 chances, and 6 = should not drive.

Using multi-level analyzes, Hopthrow et al. (2014) accounted for the multiple risk decisions participants made and the fact that individuals are members of a group. They first revealed that decisions were riskier when made by individuals than by groups. Moreover, participants who had consumed more alcohol were more likely to make risker decisions. In addition to these main effects of decision making setting and alcohol consumption, there was a significant interaction such that intoxication levels affected individual but not group decisions. Moreover, individual and group decision making did not differ under lower BAC levels, but individuals indicated more attraction towards risk taking behavior under higher intoxication levels. These findings supported the group monitoring hypothesis that groups should be less susceptible to the risk-enhancing effect of alcohol consumption (see Fig. 14.1). Their findings provided a pivotal extension to the literature, replicating the group monitoring effect in naturally-occurring drinking contexts with a high dosage of alcohol.

The literature on alcohol and group decision making has generated mixed results, specifically as to whether groups could mitigate the negative effect of alcohol consumption. On the one hand, Abrams, Hopthrow, Frings, and colleagues have demonstrated in a number of experiments that while individuals tended to be easily influenced by alcohol, group monitoring reduced the extent to which their decision was affected by intoxication. On the other hand, Sayette and colleagues demonstrated that groups were, in general, more susceptible to the disinhibitory effect of alcohol. Overall, there remain some key questions to be addressed empirically. Why has past research yielded conflicting results? When are groups more vulnerable to the negative influence of alcohol consumption? What happens during group monitoring – how is it manifested during group interactions?

Task type

Previous studies employed various measurements for risk behavior: tossing a coin to avoid a time-consuming task (Sayette et al., 2004, 2012), a duplex bet task (Abrams et al., 2006), and questions, and risk-taking scenario measurement based on the CDQ (Hopthrow et al., 2014). However, no attempts

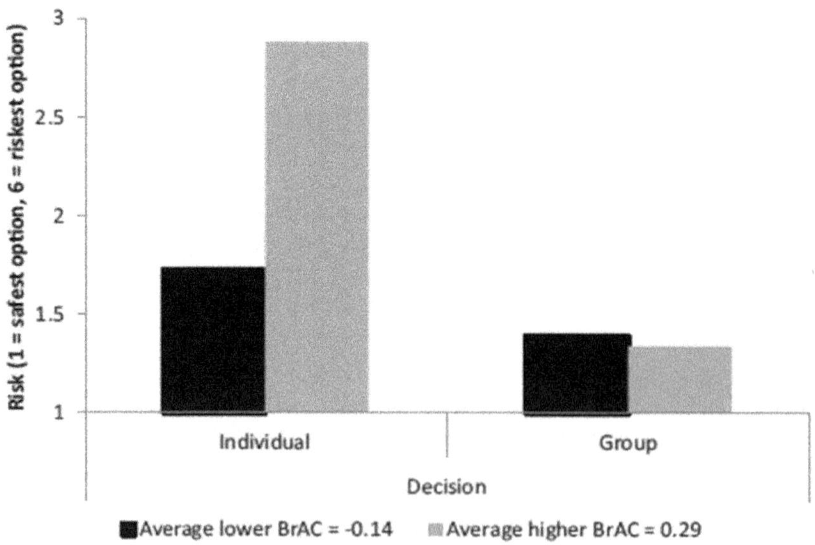

FIGURE 14.1 *From Hopthrow, T., Randsley de Moura, G., Meleady, R., Abrams, D., & Swift, H. J. (2014). Drinking in social groups. Does "groupdrink" provide safety in numbers when deciding about risk?* Addiction, *109(6), 913–921. https://doi.org/10.1111/add.12496.*

have been made so far to comprehensively examine the potential influence of task type on results. We shall discuss how different measurements might have contributed to generating conflicting findings.

One possibility is that the coin toss task used by Sayette et al. (2008, 2012) failed to capture risk seeking tendency. Given that people are motivated to affiliate, it seems reasonable to suppose that, once a group has formed, the prospect of spending more time together (i.e., in this case taking a longer survey with members) might be normative, attractive and even rewarding (Bernabé, Lisbona, Palací, & Martín-Aragón, 2016; Haslam et al., 2006; Stevens et al., 2020). Bernabé et al. (2016), for example, showed that identification with the group significantly increased the willingness to engage in group activities. Therefore, it is ambiguous whether participants viewed the coin-toss task as a prospective opportunity or as a risk. Other types of risk-taking measurements, such as the duplex bets used by Abrams et al. (2006), seem to present a clearer index of risk attraction. These considerations suggest that the interaction between alcohol consumption and decision making setting may depend on the type and contingencies of risk-taking. It is therefore plausible that group monitoring effects might work differently depending on which aspects of the task people are attending to (e.g., social versus material outcomes). At this point, we can simply note that the previous studies supporting the hypothesis suggest that group monitoring successfully suppress risk-seeking behavior inflated by alcohol consumption when risk-taking behavior involves financial and physical risks (Abrams et al., 2006; Hopthrow et al., 2014).

Another feature of the coin task is that it is less complex than those used in studies that supported the group monitoring hypothesis. Group monitoring improves the quality of group decisions by allowing members to exchange resources, but it should only make a difference if group members have insufficient capacity to process the information fully on their own. Thus, when a task is so simple that it does not leave much room for discussion or that a simple vote could be taken, group monitoring is unlikely to be as effective as when that the task is more complex and requires reasoning and discussion. Consistent with this account, Frings et al. (2008) demonstrated that group monitoring buffered against the influence of alcohol on performance on tasks requiring sustained attention, suggesting that the group monitoring exerted its positive influence on cognitively tough tasks. Thus, it seems that task complexity may be another important factor to consider in future studies.

In general, past research on alcohol consumption, regardless of whether the focus was on individual or group decision making, has not yet endeavored to systematize the effect of different risk measurements. Therefore, further research around the issue will help us elucidate boundary conditions for group monitoring to work as well as when alcohol intoxication increases individual risk-pursuit.

Social drinking vs. sole drinking

Alcohol administration methods might be another factor that has affected the results of the previous studies. In Abrams et al. (2006) and Hopthrow et al. (2014), participants who would make an individual risk decision consumed alcoholic (or placebo) beverage alone. By contrast, Sayette et al. (2012) had their participants drink as a group, regardless of whether they were in the group or individual decision making conditions. In other words, individual decision making followed social drinking. We argue this group setting might have primed the presence of others and subsequently influenced individual decision making by increasing self-monitoring. It may be this that resulted in the atypical finding that individual decision making was unaffected by alcohol intoxication. In fact, a recent study investigated how social drinking influences subsequent individual and group decision making and revealed that social drinking did not enhance the tendency for individuals to make risky decisions (Erskine-Shaw, Monk, Qureshi, & Heim, 2017). The finding suggests that the previously documented risk-enhancing effect of intoxication might be limited to when individuals solely consumed alcohol. In other words, sole and group drinking posed significantly different influences on following individual risk taking behavior. This suggests that it is important to consider the relationship between drinking conditions and the effect of alcohol. However, to our knowledge, there has not been any research directly addressing how sole and social drinking affect subsequent individual decision making. Therefore, future research should explore a potential interaction between drinking and decision making situations, which may clarify some of the inconsistencies in the literature.

This would have practical implications for dealing with alcohol-related issues in society. In the UK, for instance, pre-loading (drinking before attending nightlife) is commonplace (Hadfield & Newton, 2010). In such a circumstance, it is likely that when people gather to drink together, some of them have already consumed alcohol from sole drinking. Hughes, Anderson, Morleo, and Bellis (2008) found that such pre-loaders were more likely to be involved in drink-related incidents, and it would be of great importance to understand the potential interaction between drinking style (sole vs. group) and decision making condition (individual or group).

Dosage-set vs. pharmacological effect

It is important to distinguish pharmacological effects from dosage-set effects. Previous studies on alcohol consumption have predominantly relied on a placebo condition as a comparison with an intoxicated group. In Abrams et al. (2006), participants in the placebo condition had significantly lower expectancy as to how much they had consumed alcohol compared to those in the alcohol condition. Therefore, the risk-enhancing effect of alcohol on individual decision making was due to both alcohol intake and the higher level of expectation about intoxication. Accordingly, it remains unclear whether the group monitoring effect worked against pharmacological and/or expectancy effects.

Sayette et al. (2012) showed that groups in the placebo and alcohol conditions did not vary in risky behavior, but found that they made risker decisions compared to groups who knew they were drinking a non-alcoholic beverage, i.e., those without any expectation that they had consumed alcohol. This suggested that group monitoring might not reduce the effect of expectancy in decision making, but it was effective in reducing the pharmacological effect of intoxication. To date, the group monitoring hypothesis earned supports from studies comparing the placebo to the alcohol group. However, as past research on individual decision making revealed the importance of distinguishing expectancy from pharmacological effect (Burian et al., 2003; Proestakis et al., 2013), future studies should incorporate it into group decision studies. This would be an interesting direction to address the range of influence of group contexts in buffering against the risk-enhancing effect of alcohol.

Time pressure

Finally, there is another methodological issue concerning the debate: time pressure. Sayette and colleagues explicitly instructed groups to make a decision in 150 seconds (Sayette et al., 2004, 2012), while studies in favor of the group monitoring hypothesis did not impose any time limit on participants. Given that in Abrams et al. (2006), groups in the placebo and alcohol condition took, on average, 312 and 516 seconds to complete 16 decisions, the time pressure does not seem restricting. However, time pressure, rather than time constraint, has been found to substantially affect both individual and group decision making (Ibanez et al., 2008), and the mere presence of a time limit might have significantly affected decision making processes in previous studies.

According to the alcohol myopia model (Fromme et al., 1997; Steele & Josephs, 1988, 1990), intoxicated individuals can only attend to the most salient cue. In line with this, Hopthrow, Abrams, Frings, and Hulbert (2007) demonstrated that intoxicated groups were less likely to act cooperatively than sober groups, reasoning that the group context became the most salient context which resulted in intoxicated groups failing to reach an optimal (i.e., cooperative) decision. Based on these findings, it can be reasonably assumed that the time pressure might be the most salient cue in the situation, and groups in Sayette et al. (2012) failed to successfully engage in the group monitoring process. Furthermore, it can be speculated that time pressure prevented groups from initiating monitoring processes, consistent with past research showing that groups spent significantly more time in making decisions than individuals (Abrams et al., 2006). As no empirical evidence is available to support or refute these assumptions, it remains an open question whether time pressure may play an influential role in intoxicated decision making processes in groups.

Summary

Overall, Abrams, Hopthrow, and colleagues have found that group decision making is less susceptible to the risk-enhancing effect of alcohol intoxication (Abrams et al., 2006; Frings et al., 2008; Hopthrow et al., 2014), while Sayette and colleagues have argued that intoxicated groups are more likely to pursue risks (Sayette et al., 2004, 2012). However, due to several significant differences in methods, these different views are not necessarily contradictory and they point to various directions to test the group monitoring hypothesis. Future studies should systematically address how we should interpret previous findings, reflecting the methodological differences. It will be important tor identifying how and when group monitoring can prevent intoxicated groups from engaging in risky behavior, as this has direct implications for dealing with societal issues and accidents resulting from alcohol consumption.

Future directions

We reviewed the previous studies on the role of alcohol intoxication in group decision making and discussed the group monitoring hypothesis. We identified possible directions for future studies that will help to disentangle the contrasting findings. We now explore directions for future work that will be needed to provide a fuller account of behaviors in typical social drinking situations.

Alcohol x group decision making in different domains

Firstly, although an ample number of studies have addressed how alcohol intoxication affects individual behavior in various domains (e.g., risk-seeking behavior and aggression), only a few types of intoxicated group behavior have been studied. To date, the main body of the research has predominantly focused on risk-seeking behavior, with the exception of Hopthrow et al. (2007). They investigated cooperative behavior and found that alcohol consumption promoted intergroup competition among groups, although it did not change individual preference for intergroup cooperation. More research is needed to understand how this fits with the robust finding that drinking exacerbates discriminatory behavior and prejudice (Hunt & Laidler, 2001; Levine, Lowe, Best, & Heim, 2012; Loersch, Bartholow, Manning, Calanchini, & Sherman, 2015; Mitchell et al., 2015; Zhou, Heim, Monk,

Levy, & Pollard, 2018), but the reason they did not observe the competitive tendency among intoxicated individuals could be simply because Hopthrow et al. (2007) did not explicitly frame other groups as out-groups, suggesting that intergroup contexts were only mildly induced, or it may be the moderate amounts of alcohol that participants consumed. Regardless, they provided valuable additional evidence on intoxicated group behavior. Given that whether individual and group decision making are affected by alcohol consumption in the same manner depends on particular tasks or behaviors, future research should address how alcohol intoxication impacts other forms of group behavior.

Environmental factors

Secondly, as noted in Hopthrow et al. (2014), participants in previous studies took risk-taking assessment in quiet labs, which is not similar to naturally occurring situations where intoxicated groups have to make decisions, e.g., clubs, pubs, and parties. These contexts are relatively crowded, and noise levels tend to be high, which is likely to trigger the deindividuation process where individuals lose self-consciousness. Therefore, the group monitoring hypothesis may be supported in some contexts, but deindividuation in others. Contrary to group monitoring, deindividuation should increase the negative effects of alcohol intoxication (e.g., further enhanced risk-seeking tendency) among groups. Furthermore, Monk and Heim (2014) demonstrated that individuals' expectation about consequences of drinking significantly depended on drinking contexts (e.g., where and who they consumed alcohol). Although they did not elaborate on factors underpinning to the influence of such contexts, their finding alluded to the importance of considering the influence of environmental factors. Thus, the potential influence of actual decision making situations will surely be a relevant area for future research.

Social factors

Another factor in real drinking contexts is the constitution of the groups. Members of a group at a drinking occasion may vary in intoxication levels, so that some individuals may be completely sober. Previous studies looked at homogenous groups where all members had consumed the same amount of alcohol with a small variation in measured intoxication levels mostly resulted from differences in weight. Previous findings and theoretical backgrounds do not provide any predictions as to whether group monitoring occurs, for instance, in groups composed of both drunk and sober individuals.

It is also important to consider other social factors such as asymmetry in power and status among group members. Past research has consistently shown that individuals often base various types of judgment and behavior on these factors (Sturm & Antonakis, 2015), and power plays a relatively strong role in directing others towards a consensus (Hays & Goldstein, 2015). Given that social drinking is sometimes introduced to formal occasions (e.g., business meetings and academic conferences) where status and power tend to be salient, research accounting for processes in heterogeneous groups will further provide practical implications for the interaction between drinking and group decision making in real life.

Another interesting question is whether the closeness of relationships among social drinkers (e.g., friends, a partner, and family members) matters for subsequent risk-taking tendencies. With notable exceptions of Hopthrow et al. (2014) and Frings (2011), previous empirical work predominantly focused on groups of strangers (Abrams et al., 2006; Sayette et al., 2004, 2012), where groups norms specific to drinking had not formed yet. The former recruited groups of friends and the latter had army officer cadets working in the same branch. Together with other studies that used groups of random strangers, the group monitoring hypotheses apparently holds in different types of groups, but it remains unclear whether the effect would be moderated by the nature of groups or the closeness of the relationships, per se.

Group monitoring and the night time economy

Sociologists, criminologists, and psychologists have in recent years studied the night time economy, a concept that describes the transformation of towns and cities into places of drinking and other related past times once the traditional shops and businesses have closed after day time trading (Hadfield & Newton, 2010; Hayward & Hobbs, 2007; Liempt et al., n.d.; Roberts, 2005). Past research has shed light on the role of night time economy on aggressive behavior and related social issues (Chatterton, 2002; Copes, Hochstetler, & Forsyth, 2013; Taylor, Twigg, & Mohan, 2015; Townsley & Grimshaw, 2013; Wilkinson, Livingston, & Room, 2016).

Increasingly since the UK 2003 Licensing Act, town center drinking establishments have been remodeled to provide more space and excitement for large groups of drinkers (Hayward & Hobbs, 2007) that may lead to increasing issues of problematic behavior and further separation between groups of people that are looking to drink heavily and those that are not or are family groups. This separation could lead to a divergence of social norms that enforce responsible behavior and place more pressure on public and private agencies.

There is evidence to suggest that norms of responsible behavior can be reinforced. For example, since the recession in 2008, there have been increasing numbers of empty retail spaces in town centers. Hubbard (2019) highlights a new phenomenon, namely small pop-up craft beer establishments. These focus on high value and often high strength beer, but also on community-mindedness and meaningful social relationships between landlord and customers. This approach to social drinking is likely to result in more socially responsible behavior and may in a mixed night time economy help set more socially responsible behavioral norms reinforced by group monitoring.

One key problem, though, is the limited appeal of these outlets to diverse groups in the night time economy. The principle of being able to encourage socially responsible behavioral norms in a social drinking environment is important. Indeed, our research on the group monitoring effect would suggest that groups are capable of using self-monitoring processes to moderate their behavior and this capability should be mobilized where possible.

Further research should look at the ability to harness group monitoring in the night time economy to facilitate the co-location of different groups and the reinforcing of socially responsible norms.

Summary

On the whole, previous studies have relied upon laboratory experiments, and may not have captured potentially influential elements of social drinking. Although they have produced insights into the safe management of alcohol consumption, it seems that their practical implications might be limited, leaving multiple pathways through which future researchers would extend the understanding of the effect of intoxication in group decision making. We acknowledge that it is a challenge that investigation goes beyond lab experiments to account for factors in natural settings, but it is particularly important for this field to ensure findings are ecologically valid. Thus, we hope that researchers will expand and develop this key area of research.

Conclusion

Social and health psychologists have long investigated how alcohol intoxication influences various domains of behavior, since the proposition of the alcohol myopia model (Steele & Josephs, 1988, 1990). They have collated a number of studies on the role of alcohol consumption in shaping risk taking behavior, as major alcohol-related issues in society (e.g., drink driving and acute alcoholism) are relevant to risk taking tendencies. Past research consistently demonstrated that alcohol intoxication makes individuals attracted to risky choices and, thus, take risky actions.

Despite that alcohol consumption often takes place in social occasions (e.g., bar, festival, etc.), it was only until the early 2000s that researchers embarked on the empirical investigation of the potential role of group contexts. Abrams et al. (2006) was the first to provide evidence that the alcohol intoxication poses different effects on individual and group decision making; namely, they found support for the group monitoring hypothesis that group decision making is less susceptible to the risk-enhancing effect of alcohol compared to individual decision making. Several subsequent research further replicated and extended the finding (Frings, 2011; Frings et al., 2008; Hopthrow et al., 2014).

However, there are studies showing that group contexts do not suppress the negative effect of alcohol intoxication on risk taking behavior (Sayette et al., 2004, 2012). Interestingly, they also found that intoxicated individuals did not display risk seeking behavior, contrary to past research on individual decision making and alcohol consumption.

Overall, the previous literature on the role of alcohol intoxication on group decision making has obtained mixed results, as to whether groups can be a buffer against the risk-enhancing effect of alcohol. As we have reviewed, preceding studies employed different research design and measurements of risk taking behavior, and it would be premature to draw any conclusions. However, they consistently suggested that alcohol consumption exerts different influences on individuals and groups, and, more importantly, the effects are very sensitive to various factors (e.g., methodology and contextual factors). Therefore, we hope that future research will systematically account for potential moderators and ecological factors and better elucidate the relationship between alcohol consumption and decision making processes, which in turn aid us ways to protect individuals and society from the harmful effect of alcohol intoxication.

References

Abrams, D., Hopthrow, T., Hulbert, L., & Frings, D. (2006). "Groupdrink"? The effect of alcohol on risk attraction among groups versus individuals. *Journal of Studies on Alcohol*, *67*(4), 628–636. Available from https://doi.org/10.15288/jsa.2006.67.628.

Abrams, D., Hulbert, L.G., and Albery, I. 1997. Investigation of the relationship between alcohol use and group performance, Canterbury, United Kingdom: University of Kent, unpublished report.

Aitken, P. P. (1985). An observational study of young adults' drinking groups—II. Drink purchasing procedures, group pressures and alcohol consumption by companions as predictors of alcohol consumption. *Alcohol and Alcoholism*, *20*(4), 445–457. Available from http://www.ncbi.nlm.nih.gov/pubmed/4084375.

Ally, A. K., Lovatt, M., Meier, P. S., Brennan, A., & Holmes, J. (2016). Developing a social practice-based typology of British drinking culture in 2009-2011: Implications for alcohol policy analysis. *Addiction*, *111*(9), 1568–1579. Available from https://doi.org/10.1111/add.13397.

Bayless, S. J., & Harvey, A. J. (2017). Testing alcohol myopia theory: Examining the effects of alcohol intoxication on simultaneous central and peripheral attention. *Perception*, *46*(1), 90–99. Available from https://doi.org/10.1177/0301006616672221.

Bernabé, M., Lisbona, A., Palací, F. J., & Martín-Aragón, M. (2016). Social identity and engagement: An exploratory study at university. *Revista de Psicologia Del Trabajo y de Las Organizaciones*, *32*(2), 103–107. Available from https://doi.org/10.1016/j.rpto.2016.02.003.

Bidwell, L. C., MacKillop, J., Murphy, J. G., Grenga, A., Swift, R. M., & McGeary, J. E. (2013). Biphasic effects of alcohol on delay and probability discounting. *Experimental and Clinical Psychopharmacology, 21*(3), 214–221. Available from https://doi.org/10.1037/a0032284.

Brown, S. A., Goldman, M. S., Inn, A., & Anderson, L. R. (1980). Expectations of reinforcement from alcohol: Their domain and relation to drinking patterns. *Journal of Consulting and Clinical Psychology, 48*(4), 419–426. Available from https://doi.org/10.1037/0022-006X.48.4.419.

Burian, S. E., Hensberry, R., & Liguori, A. (2003). Differential effects of alcohol and alcohol expectancy on risk-taking during simulated driving. *Human Psychopharmacology, 18*(3), 175–184. Available from https://doi.org/10.1002/hup.473.

Burian, S. E., Liguori, A., & Robinson, J. H. (2002). Effects of alcohol on risk-taking during simulated driving. *Human Psychopharmacology, 17*(3), 141–150. Available from https://doi.org/10.1002/hup.384.

Chatterton, P. (2002). *"Squatting is still legal, necessary and free": A brief intervention in the corporate city, . Antipode* (Vol. 34, pp. 1–7). Blackwell Publishing Inc Issue 1. Available from https://doi.org/10.1111/1467-8330.00223.

Clifasefi, S. L., Takarangi, M. K. T., & Bergman, J. S. (2006). Blind drunk: The effects of alcohol on inattentional blindness. *Applied Cognitive Psychology, 20*(5), 697–704. Available from https://doi.org/10.1002/acp.1222.

Connors, G. J., & Sobell, M. B. (1986). Alcohol and drinking environment: Effects on affect and sensations, person perception, and perceived intoxication. *Cognitive Therapy and Research, 10*(4), 389–402. Available from https://doi.org/10.1007/BF01173293.

Copes, H., Hochstetler, A., & Forsyth, C. J. (2013). Peaceful warriors: Codes for violence among adult male bar fighters. *Criminology, 51*(3), 761–794. Available from https://doi.org/10.1111/1745-9125.12019.

Davis, J. H. (1996). *Group decision making and quantitative judgments: A consensus model. Understanding group behavior, Vol. 1: Consensual action by small groups* (pp. 35–59). Lawrence Erlbaum Associates, Inc.

Davis, K. C. (2010). The influence of alcohol expectancies and intoxication on men's aggressive unprotected sexual intentions. *Experimental and Clinical Psychopharmacology, 18*(5), 418–428. Available from https://doi.org/10.1037/a0020510.

de Visser, R. O., Wheeler, Z., Abraham, C., & Smith, J. A. (2013). "Drinking is our modern way of bonding": Young people's beliefs about interventions to encourage moderate drinking. *Psychology and Health, 28*(12), 1460–1480. Available from https://doi.org/10.1080/08870446.2013.828293.

Diener, E., Lusk, R., DeFour, D., & Flax, R. (1980). Deindividuation: Effects of group size, density, number of observers, and group member similarity on self-consciousness and disinhibited behavior. *Journal of Personality and Social Psychology, 39*(3), 449–459. Available from https://doi.org/10.1037/0022-3514.39.3.449.

Dietler, M. (2006). Alcohol: Anthropological/archaeological perspectives. *Annual Review of Anthropology, 35*(1), 229–249. Available from https://doi.org/10.1146/annurev.anthro.35.081705.123120.

Dufwenberg, M., & Muren, A. (2006). Gender composition in teams. *Journal of Economic Behavior and Organization, 61*(1), 50–54. Available from https://doi.org/10.1016/j.jebo.2005.01.002.

Eisenberg, D., Golberstein, E., & Whitlock, J. L. (2014). Peer effects on risky behaviors: New evidence from college roommate assignments. *Journal of Health Economics*, *33*(1), 126–138. Available from https://doi.org/10.1016/j.jhealeco.2013.11.006.

Erskine-Shaw, M., Monk, R. L., Qureshi, A. W., & Heim, D. (2017). The influence of groups and alcohol consumption on individual risk-taking. *Drug and Alcohol Dependence*, *179*, 341–346. Available from https://doi.org/10.1016/j.drugalcdep.2017.07.032.

Fairbairn, C. E., Sayette, M. A., Wright, A. G. C., Levine, J. M., Cohn, J. F., & Creswell, K. G. (2015). Extraversion and the rewarding effects of alcohol in a social context. *Journal of Abnormal Psychology*, *124*(3), 660–673. Available from https://doi.org/10.1037/abn0000024.

Festinger, L., Pepitone, A., & Newcomb, T. (1952). Some consequences of de-individuation in a group. *The Journal of Abnormal and Social Psychology*, *47*(2, Suppl.), 382–389. Available from https://doi.org/10.1037/h0057906.

Freed, E. X. (1978). Alcohol and mood: An updated review. *Substance Use and Misuse*, *13*(2), 173–200. Available from https://doi.org/10.3109/10826087809039273.

Frings, D. (2011). The effects of group monitoring on fatigue-related einstellung during mathematical problem solving. *Journal of Experimental Psychology: Applied*, *17*(4), 371–381. Available from https://doi.org/10.1037/a0025131.

Frings, D., Hopthrow, T., Abrams, D., Hulbert, L., & Gutierrez, R. (2008). Groupdrink: The effects of alcohol and group process on vigilance errors. *Group Dynamics*, *12*(3), 179–190. Available from https://doi.org/10.1037/1089-2699.12.3.179.

Fromme, K., Katz, E., & D'Amico, E. (1997). Effects of alcohol intoxication on the perceived consequences of risk taking. *Experimental and Clinical Psychopharmacology*, *5*(1), 14–23. Available from https://doi.org/10.1037/1064-1297.5.1.14.

Gander, P., Millar, M., Webster, C., & Merry, A. (2008). Sleep loss and performance of anaesthesia trainees and specialists. *Chronobiology International*, *25*(6), 1077–1091. Available from https://doi.org/10.1080/07420520802551428.

Giancola, P. R., Duke, A. A., & Ritz, K. Z. (2011). Alcohol, violence, and the alcohol myopia model: Preliminary findings and implications for prevention. *Addictive Behaviors*, *36*(10), 1019–1022. Available from https://doi.org/10.1016/j.addbeh.2011.05.006.

Giancola, P. R., Josephs, R. A., Parrott, D. J., & Duke, A. A. (2010). Alcohol myopia revisited: Clarifying aggression and other acts of disinhibition through a distorted lens. *Perspectives on Psychological Science*, *5*(3), 265–278. Available from https://doi.org/10.1177/1745691610369467.

Gordon, R., Heim, D., & MacAskill, S. (2012). Rethinking drinking cultures: A review of drinking cultures and a reconstructed dimensional approach. *Public Health*, *126*(1), 3–11. Available from https://doi.org/10.1016/j.puhe.2011.09.014.

Guppy, A. (1994). At what blood alcohol concentration should drink-driving be illegal? *BMJ*, *308*(6936), 1055. Available from https://doi.org/10.1136/bmj.308.6936.1055.

Hadfield, P., & Newton, A. D. (2010). *Factsheet: Alcohol, crime and disorder in the night-time economy*. Alcohol concern. <http://eprints.hud.ac.uk/id/eprint/9494/>.

Hannagan, R. J., & Larimer, C. W. (2010). *Does gender composition affect group decision outcomes? Evidence from a laboratory experiment, . Political behavior* (Vol. 32, pp. 51–67). Springer. Available from https://doi.org/10.2307/40587307.

Harrison, E. L. R., & Fillmore, M. T. (2011). Alcohol and distraction interact to impair driving performance. *Drug and Alcohol Dependence*, *117*(1), 31–37. Available from https://doi.org/10.1016/j.drugalcdep.2011.01.002.

Haslam, S. A., Ryan, M. K., Postmes, T., Spears, R., Jetten, J., & Webley, P. (2006). Sticking to our guns: social identity as a basis for the maintenance of commitment to faltering organizational projects. *Journal of Organizational Behavior*, *27*(5), 607–628. Available from https://doi.org/10.1002/job.370.

Hays, N. A., & Goldstein, N. J. (2015). Power and legitimacy influence conformity. *Journal of Experimental Social Psychology*, *60*, 17–26. Available from https://doi.org/10.1016/j.jesp.2015.04.010.

Hayward, K., & Hobbs, D. (2007). Beyond the binge in "booze Britain": Market-led liminalization and the spectacle of binge drinking. *British Journal of Sociology*, *58*(3), 437–456. Available from https://doi.org/10.1111/j.1468-4446.2007.00159.x.

Hopthrow, T., Randsley de Moura, G., Meleady, R., Abrams, D., & Swift, H. J. (2014). Drinking in social groups. Does "groupdrink" provide safety in numbers when deciding about risk? *Addiction*, *109*(6), 913–921. Available from https://doi.org/10.1111/add.12496.

Hopthrow, T., Abrams, D., Frings, D., & Hulbert, L. G. (2007). Groupdrink: The effects of alcohol on intergroup competitiveness. *Psychology of Addictive Behaviors*, *21*(2), 272–276. Available from https://doi.org/10.1037/0893-164X.21.2.272.

Hopthrow, T., & Hulbert, L. G. (2005). The effect of group decision making on cooperation in social dilemmas. *Group Processes and Intergroup Relations*, *8*(1), 89–100. Available from https://doi.org/10.1177/1368430205049253.

Hubbard, P. (2019). Enthusiasm, craft and authenticity on the High Street: micropubs as 'community fixers'. *Social and Cultural Geography*, *20*(6), 763–784. Available from https://doi.org/10.1080/14649365.2017.1380221.

Hughes, K., Anderson, Z., Morleo, M., & Bellis, M. A. (2008). Alcohol, nightlife and violence: The relative contributions of drinking before and during nights out to negative health and criminal justice outcomes. *Addiction*, *103*(1), 60–65. Available from https://doi.org/10.1111/j.1360-0443.2007.02030.x.

Hull, J. G. (1981). A self-awareness model of the causes and effects of alcohol consumption. *Journal of Abnormal Psychology*, *90*(6), 586–600. Available from https://doi.org/10.1037/0021-843X.90.6.586.

Hunt, G. P., & Laidler, K. J. (2001). Alcohol and violence in the lives of gang members. *Alcohol Research & Health: The Journal of the National Institute on Alcohol Abuse and Alcoholism*, *25*(1), 66–71. Available from http://www.ncbi.nlm.nih.gov/pubmed/11496969.

Ibanez, M., Czermak, S., & Sutter, M. (2008). Searching for a better deal - On the influence of group decision making, time pressure and gender in a search experiment. *Journal of Economic Psychology*, *30*(1), 1–10. https://doi.org/10.1016/j.joep.2008.10.003.

Karau, S. J., & Williams, K. D. (1993). Social loafing: A meta-analytic review and theoretical integration. *Journal of Personality and Social Psychology*, *65*(4), 681–706. Available from https://doi.org/10.1037/0022-3514.65.4.681.

Kerr, N. L., Davis, J. H., Meek, D., & Rissman, A. K. (1975). Group position as a function of member attitudes: Choice shift effects from the perspective of social decision scheme theory. *Journal of Personality and Social Psychology*, *31*(3), 574–593. Available from https://doi.org/10.1037/h0076483.

Koelega, H. S. (1995). Alcohol and vigilance performance: A review. *Psychopharmacology*, *118*(3), 233–249. Available from https://doi.org/10.1007/BF02245951.

Koelega, H. S. (1998). *Effects of caffeine, nicotine and alcohol on vigilance performance. Nicotine, caffeine and social drinking: Behaviour and brain function* (pp. 363–373). Harwood Academic Publishers.

Kogan, N., & Wallach, M. A. (1964). *Risk taking: A study in cognition and personality. Risk taking: A study in cognition and personality*. Holt, Rinehart & Winston.

Lamiraud, K., & Vranceanu, R. (2018). Group gender composition and economic decision-making: Evidence from the Kallystée business game. *Journal of Economic Behavior and Organization*, *145*, 294–305. Available from https://doi.org/10.1016/j.jebo.2017.09.020.

Landrigan, C. P., Rothschild, J. M., Cronin, J. W., Kaushal, R., Burdick, E., Katz, J. T., ... Czeisler, C. A. (2004). Effect of reducing interns' work hours on serious medical errors in intensive care units. *New England Journal of Medicine*, *351*(18), 1838–1848. Available from https://doi.org/10.1056/NEJMoa041406.

Lane, S. D., & Cherek, D. R. (2000). Analysis of risk taking in adults with a history of high risk behavior. *Drug and Alcohol Dependence*, *60*(2), 179–187. Available from https://doi.org/10.1016/S0376-8716(99)00155-6.

Levine, M., Lowe, R., Best, R., & Heim, D. (2012). 'We police it ourselves': Group processes in the escalation and regulation of violence in the night-time economy. *European Journal of Social Psychology*, *42*(7), 924–932. Available from https://doi.org/10.1002/ejsp.1905.

Liempt, I. van Aalst, I., & Schwanen, T. (n.d.). Introduction: Geographies of the urban night. In *Urban Studies* (Vol. 52, pp. 407–421). Sage Publications, Ltd. <https://doi.org/10.2307/26145983>.

Loersch, C., Bartholow, B. D., Manning, M., Calanchini, J., & Sherman, J. W. (2015). Intoxicated prejudice: The impact of alcohol consumption on implicitly and explicitly measured racial attitudes. *Group Processes and Intergroup Relations*, *18*(2), 256–268. Available from https://doi.org/10.1177/1368430214561693.

MacDonald, T. K., Fong, G. T., Zanna, M. P., abd Martineau, A. 2000. M.m Alcohol myopia and condom use: Can alcohol intoxication be associated with more prudent behavior? Journal of Personality and Social Psychology, *78*(4), 605–619. https://doi.org/10.1037/0022-3514.78.4.605.

McMillen, D. L., & Wells-Parker, E. (1987). The effect of alcohol consumption on risk-taking while driving. *Addictive Behaviors*, *12*(3), 241–247. Available from https://doi.org/10.1016/0306-4603(87)90034-7.

Meleady, R., Hopthrow, T., & Crisp, R. J. (2013a). Simulating social dilemmas: Promoting cooperative behavior through imagined group discussion. *Journal of Personality and Social Psychology*, *104*(5), 839–853. Available from https://doi.org/10.1037/a0031233.

Meleady, R., Hopthrow, T., & Crisp, R. J. (2013b). The group discussion effect: Integrative processes and suggestions for implementation. *Personality and Social Psychology Review*, *17*(1), 56–71. Available from https://doi.org/10.1177/1088868312456744.

Mitchell, G. (2012). Revisiting truth or triviality: The external validity of research in the psychological laboratory. *Perspectives on Psychological Science*, *7*(2), 109–117. Available from https://doi.org/10.1177/1745691611432343.

Mitchell, I. J., Gillespie, S. M., Leverton, M., Llewellyn, V., Neale, E., & Stevenson, I. (2015). Acute alcohol consumption and secondary psychopathic traits increase ratings of the attractiveness and health of ethnic ingroup faces but not outgroup faces. *Frontiers in Psychiatry*, *6*(FEB). Available from https://doi.org/10.3389/fpsyt.2015.00025.

Monahan, J. L., & Lannutti, P. J. (2000). Alcohol as social lubricant: Alcohol myopia theory, social self-esteem, and social interaction. *Human Communication Research*, *26*(2), 175–202. Available from https://doi.org/10.1093/HCR.

Mongrain, S., & Standing, L. (1989). Impairment of cognition, risk-taking, and self-perception by alcohol. *Perceptual and Motor Skills*, *69*(1), 199–210. Available from https://doi.org/10.2466/pms.1989.69.1.199.

Monk, R. L., & Heim, D. (2014). A real-time examination of context effects on alcohol cognitions. *Alcoholism: Clinical and Experimental Research, 38*(9), 2454–2459. Available from https://doi.org/10.1111/acer.12504.

Moskowitz, H., & Depry, D. (1968). Differential effect of alcohol on auditory vigilance and divided-attention tasks. *Quarterly Journal of Studies on Alcohol, 29*(1-A), 54–63.

Mullen, B. (1986). Atrocity as a function of lynch mob composition. *Personality and Social Psychology Bulletin, 12*(2), 187–197. Available from https://doi.org/10.1177/0146167286122005.

NHS. (2018). *Statistics on alcohol, England.* <https://digital.nhs.uk/data-and-information/publications/statistical/statistics-on-alcohol/2018>.

Office for National Statistics. (2019). *Alcohol-specific deaths in the UK.* <https://www.ons.gov.uk/peoplepopulationandcommunity/healthandsocialcare/causesofdeath/bulletins/alcoholrelateddeathsintheunitedkingdom/2018>.

Permanen, K. Alcohol in human violence, New York: Guilford Press, 1991.

Proestakis, A., Espín, A. M., Exadaktylos, F., Aguilar, A. C., Oyediran, O. A., & Palacio, L. A. (2013). The separate effects of self-estimated and actual alcohol intoxication on risk taking: A field experiment. *Journal of Neuroscience, Psychology, and Economics, 6*(2), 115–135. Available from https://doi.org/10.1037/npe0000004.

Rehm, J., Shield, K. D., Joharchi, N., & Shuper, P. A. (2012). Alcohol consumption and the intention to engage in unprotected sex: Systematic review and meta-analysis of experimental studies. *Addiction, 107*(1), 51–59. Available from https://doi.org/10.1111/j.1360-0443.2011.03621.x.

Roberts, M. (2005). Transformations in the night-time economy in English town centres: Challenges to management. *WIT Transactions on Ecology and the Environment*, 84. Available from https://doi.org/10.2495/SPD051532.

Rohrbaugh, J. W., Stapleton, J. M., Parasuraman, R., Frowein, H. W., Adinoff, B., Varner, J. L., ... Linnoila, M. (1988). Alcohol intoxication reduces visual sustained attention. *Psychopharmacology, 96*(4), 442–446. Available from https://doi.org/10.1007/BF02180021.

Saunders, J. B., Aasland, O. G., Babor, T. F., De la Fuente, J. R., & Grant, M. (1993). Development of the Alcohol Use Disorders Identification Test (AUDIT): WHO collaborative project on early detection of persons with harmful alcohol consumption-II. *Addiction, 88*(6), 791–804. Available from https://doi.org/10.1111/j.1360-0443.1993.tb02093.x.

Sayette, M. A., Dimoff, J. D., Levine, J. M., Moreland, R. L., & Votruba-Drzal, E. (2012). The effects of alcohol and dosage-set on risk-seeking behavior in groups and individuals. *Psychology of Addictive Behaviors, 26*(2), 194–200. Available from https://doi.org/10.1037/a0023903.

Sayette, M. A., Kirchner, T. R., Moreland, R. L., Levine, J. M., & Travis, T. (2004). Effects of alcohol on risk-seeking behavior: A group-level analysis. *Psychology of Addictive Behaviors, 18*(2), 190–193. Available from https://doi.org/10.1037/0893-164X.18.2.190.

Schulte, T., Müller-Oehring, E. M., Strasburger, H., Warzel, H., & Sabel, B. A. (2001). Acute effects of alcohol on divided and covert attention in men. *Psychopharmacology, 154*(1), 61–69. Available from https://doi.org/10.1007/s002130000603.

Scott-Sheldon, L. A. J., Carey, K. B., Cunningham, K., Johnson, B. T., & Carey, M. P. (2016). Alcohol use predicts sexual decision-making: A systematic review and meta-analysis of the experimental literature. *AIDS and Behavior, 20*, 19–39. Available from https://doi.org/10.1007/s10461-015-1108-9.

Slovic, P., & Lichtenstein, S. (1968). Importance of variance preferences in gambling decisions. *Journal of Experimental Psychology*, *78*(4 PART 1), 646–654. Available from https://doi.org/10.1037/h0026647.

Stall, R., McKusick, L., Wiley, J., Coates, T. J., & Ostrow, D. G. (1986). Alcohol and drug use during sexual activity and compliance with safe sex guidelines for AIDS: The AIDS Behavioral Research Project. *Health Education & Behavior*, *13*(4), 359–371. Available from https://doi.org/10.1177/109019818601300407.

Steele, C. M., & Josephs, R. A. (1988). Drinking your troubles away II: An attention-allocation model of alcohol's effect on psychological stress. *Journal of Abnormal Psychology*, *97*(2), 196–205. Available from https://doi.org/10.1037/0021-843X.97.2.196.

Steele, C. M., & Josephs, R. A. (1990). Alcohol myopia: Its prized and dangerous effects. *American Psychologist*, *45*(8), 921–933. Available from https://doi.org/10.1037/0003-066X.45.8.921.

Stevens, M., Rees, T., Coffee, P., Steffens, N. K., Alexander Haslam, S., & Polman, R. (2020). Leading us to be active: A two-wave test of relationships between identity leadership, group identification, and attendance. *Sport, Exercise, and Performance Psychology*, *9*(1), 128–142. Available from https://doi.org/10.1037/spy0000164.

Sturm, R. E., & Antonakis, J. (2015). Interpersonal power: A review, critique, and research agenda . *Journal of Management*, *41*(1), 136–163. Available from https://doi.org/10.1177/0149206314555769.

Sunstein, C. R. (2002). The law of group polarization. *Journal of Political Philosophy*, *10*(2), 175–195. Available from https://doi.org/10.1111/1467-9760.00148.

Taylor, B., Irving, H. M., Kanteres, F., Room, R., Borges, G., Cherpitel, C., … Rehm, J. (2010). The more you drink, the harder you fall: A systematic review and meta-analysis of how acute alcohol consumption and injury or collision risk increase together. *Drug and Alcohol Dependence*, *110*(1–2), 108–116. Available from https://doi.org/10.1016/j.drugalcdep.2010.02.011.

Taylor, J., Twigg, L., & Mohan, J. (2015). Understanding neighbourhood perceptions of alcohol-related anti-social behaviour. *Urban Studies*, *52*(12), 2186–2202. Available from https://doi.org/10.1177/0042098014543031.

Thombs, D. L., Wolcott, B. J., & Farkash, L. G. E. (1997). Social context, perceived norms and drinking behavior in young people. *Journal of Substance Abuse*, *9*(1), 257–267. Available from https://doi.org/10.1016/S0899-3289(97)90020-1.

Townsley, M., & Grimshaw, R. (2013). The consequences of queueing: Crowding, situational features and aggression in entertainment precincts. *Crime Prevention and Community Safety*, *15*(1), 23–47. Available from https://doi.org/10.1057/cpcs.2012.12.

Van Dyke, N. A., & Fillmore, M. T. (2015). Distraction produces over-additive increases in the degree to which alcohol impairs driving performance. *Psychopharmacology*, *232*(23), 4277–4284. Available from https://doi.org/10.1007/s00213-015-4055-2.

Van Dyke, N. A., & Fillmore, M. T. (2017). Laboratory analysis of risky driving at 0.05% and 0.08% blood alcohol concentration. *Drug and Alcohol Dependence*, *175*, 127–132. Available from https://doi.org/10.1016/j.drugalcdep.2017.02.005.

Wilkinson, C., Livingston, M., & Room, R. (2016). *Impacts of changes to trading hours of liquor licences on alcohol-related harm: A systematic review 2005-2015*, . *Public Health Research and Practice* (Vol. 26). Sax Institute Issue 4. Available from https://doi.org/10.17061/phrp2641644.

Zhou, J., Heim, D., Monk, R., Levy, A., & Pollard, P. (2018). Allocating under the influence: Effects of alcohol intoxication and social identification on in-group favoritism. *Experimental and Clinical Psychopharmacology*, *26*(3), 268–277. Available from https://doi.org/10.1037/pha0000186.

Zuber, J. A., Crott, H. W., & Werner, J. (1992). Choice shift and group polarization: An analysis of the status of arguments and social decision schemes. *Journal of Personality and Social Psychology*, *62*(1), 50–61. Available from https://doi.org/10.1037/0022-3514.62.1.50.

Further reading

Frings, D., Albery, I. P., Rolph, K., Leczfalvy, A., Smaczny, S., & Moss, A. C. (2017). Dyads experience over confidence in hand-eye coordination skills after placebo alcohol. *Journal of Applied Social Psychology*, *47*(3), 148–157. Available from https://doi.org/10.1111/jasp.12418.

Chapter 15

An identity-based explanatory framework for alcohol use and misuse

Daniel Frings and Ian P. Albery
Centre for Addictive Behaviours Research, School of Applied Sciences, London South Bank University, London, United Kingdom

Recent figures from the Substance Abuse and Mental Health Services Administration suggest that 14.5 million people in the US (aged over 12 years old) can be classified as having an alcohol use disorder (AUD) (Substance Abuse & Mental Health Services Administration, 2018). Problematic alcohol use is in turn ranked as one of the US's top five causes of premature death and disability (Centers for Disease Control & Prevention, 2020). The relative scale and cost of AUD is similar in other countries: Alcohol related harms cost the UK £21.5 billion a year associated with the burden on health-care, welfare and addiction related crime (Public Health England, 2018). In Australia, the direct cost of alcohol-related problems to society in 2010 was conservatively estimated at $14.35 billion (Manning, Smith, & Mazerolle, 2013). These costs do not count the emotional distress, family breakdown and co-morbid illnesses (both physical and psychological) that affect both those with AUD and those around them. Successful treatment for substance misuse, including AUD, has significant economic and social implications. For instance, in PricewaterhouseCoopers estimated the successful recovery of a substance using 21-year-old saves the UK around £730,000 (US$942,532) (PricewaterhouseCoopers, 2008). Each successful recovery also represents an enormous reduction in human suffering.

Given the above, there is a clear imperative to understand those psychosocial factors which lead people into alcohol misuse, can trigger attempts to change, and also increase the chances of a sustained change in drinking behavior. The current chapter explores these three stages from a theoretical perspective through the lens of the *social identity* perspective.

The Handbook of Alcohol Use - Understandings from Synapse to Society.
DOI: https://doi.org/10.1016/B978-0-12-816720-5.00013-X

What is a 'social identity'?

Social identity can be understood as the social categories which form part of the self, for instance 'us English' or 'us AA members' (Tajfel & Turner, 1979; Turner, Hogg, Oakes, Reicher, & Wetherell, 1987). The social identities that we have can change the way we understand the world, view people and situations and guide behavioral responses (see Brown, 2000). Having positive social identities, especially multiple ones, has been shown to be a buffer against various stressful events and a positive predictor of health outcomes in domains as varied as intrusive surgery, depression and dementia (Bule & Frings, 2016; Gleibs, Haslam, Haslam, & Jones, 2011; Jones & Jetten, 2011). They also help guide people's understanding of both their capabilities and how stressful a given situation is (Haslam & O'Brien, 2005). Related to this, having meaningful social connections with other people has been shown to be a key factor in positive mental and physical health (see Haslam, Jetten, Cruwys, Dingle, & Haslam, 2018; Jetten et al., 2017). Each individual holds multiple social identities which may be activated at different times according to how well they fit the situation relative to other identities (e.g. Turner et al., 1987).

Evidence, such as that highlighted above, suggests that social identities and social connections can have effects upon us and that we are likely to be aware of those effects. In other words, we are able to reflect upon ourselves as being a member of a social category. However, our identities are also likely to be more inaccessible to conscious inspection and awareness, and may impact attitudes and behavior more implicitly (Frings, Melichar, & Albery, 2016; Lindgren, Neighbors, Gasser, Ramirez, & Cvencek, 2017).

In the context of addiction, in particular alcohol consumption, identities may include those revolving around being a drinker, being addicted or becoming alcoholic, or being in recovery/teetotal. These identities, which can at times conflict with one another, exist against a backdrop of other social identities which may be psychologically important to an individual—such as those related to ethnicity, gender, professional identities, etc. As these social identities often form an integral part of the way that we understand the world, they are also likely to be an important factor in how people engage in alcohol-related behaviors (both problematically and non-problematically), may trigger help seeking for those drinking problematically, and help sustain positive outcomes for those in recovery. We now turn our discussion to how social identities can specifically relate to the development of alcohol misuse problems, as a trigger to treatment seeking and a support of positive recovery outcomes.

Identity/social connections as entry into alcohol misuse

A number of social identity and related processes have been linked with entry into a range of substance use disorders, including alcohol misuse.

Specific processes which have been identified as being potential risk factors include loneliness and risky social connections.

Social isolation, loneliness and alcohol misuse

Humans appear to have an innate need to belong, and feeling lonely or socially isolated has been linked to a variety of negative physical and mental health conditions and outcomes (Leigh-Hunt et al., 2017; Newman & Zainal, 2020; Shankar, Mcmunn, Banks, & Steptoe, 2011). One such outcome is alcohol use and misuse. As early as the 1950s both practitioners and researchers have theorised and observed links between a sense of loneliness and alcohol misuse (Bell, 1956). Early reviews of the literature around loneliness and alcohol misuse found (i) only mixed effects of links between feeling lonely and (ii) mixed evidence of increased loneliness amongst those suffering from alcohol addiction (Hornquist & Akerlind, 1987). Hornquist's review also revealed that, in some cases, no links between feeling lonely and later risk of our alcoholism were observed, nor were individuals battling alcohol addiction observed as being systematically more lonely than the general population. In contrast, other research indicates loneliness can be a precursor to alcohol misuse (Åkerlind & Hörnquist, 1992).

More recent research has focused on specific populations. For instance, a 12 month longitudinal study showed that adolescent alcohol misuse was predicted by loneliness, particularly amongst females (McKay, Konowalczyk, Andretta, & Cole, 2017). Amongst middle age and older adult drinkers, feeling lonely has been linked with an increased frequency of alcohol consumption, but not with an increased tendency towards binge drinking or at risk drinking (Canham, Mauro, Kaufmann, & Sixsmith, 2016). A relatively recent large-scale study of the correlates of amongst 18,000 people living in former Soviet Union regions also showed a strong link between loneliness and alcohol consumption—including hazardous drinking (Stickley et al., 2013).

Related to being lonely or socially isolated, difficulties fitting into society also seem to be a predictor of alcohol misuse. A recent study in Iran showed that people who undergo an *identity crisis*—a sense of not fitting into societies expectations—have also been shown to be more likely to misuse a variety of substances (Jamshidi & Asgharnejad-Farid, 2019). Similarly, internationally traveling students who experience acculturative stress (difficulty fitting into the host culture one is in, see Berry, 1997) have been shown to have a stronger link between alcohol use and related negative consequences (e.g. Ertl, Dillon, Martin, Babino, & De La Rosa, 2018). More generally, some evidence suggests that difficulty forming close social bonds (i.e. having insecure attachment styles) is linked with greater alcohol use (Anderson, Connor, Voisey, Young, & Gullo, 2019).

Through which processes may social isolation and loneliness increase the risk of problematic alcohol misuse and associated outcomes? A feeling of loneliness and/or social isolation may lead to alcohol use and misuse as a form of self-medication (i.e. utilizing the pharmacological effects of alcohol to reduce negative affective states (Khantzian, 1997; Levy, 2019)). Unfortunately, this can lead to a cycle where people become increasingly lonely as alcohol use becomes more problematic (see Hornquist & Akerlind, 1987). This chain of action has been observed in the literature, but the direction of causation remains unclear (see Haighton, 2017). However, studies in animal models (i.e. rats) suggested ethanol intake decreases the quality of social interaction amongst rats subjected to prior social isolation (see Marcolin, Baumbach, Hodges, & McCormick, 2020). A second mechanism may be that the need for social isolation is addressed by making connections with people or groups who encourage risky drinking.

Risky social connections and identities

One response to loneliness (and of course other factors) is to develop social connections. Whilst many social connections are positive (indeed, may even be required for optimal health) some can be problematic. Peer influence is recognized to be one of the strongest predictors of substance use and misuse (Ary, Duncan, Duncan, & Hops, 1999; Graupensperger, Benson, & Evans, 2018; Newcomb & Bentler, 1989; Villarosa, Kison, Madson, & Zeigler-Hill, 2016). Alcohol drinking norms also seem to be important. For instance, high identification with university sports teams in the UK (which, excluding 'elite' teams, often involve risky drinking during social events) has also been shown to be linked with greater alcohol consumption for team based sports (Zhou, Heim, & O'Brien, 2015). Other work has shown that a stronger identities with other in-group members is likely to lead to greater conformity with their in-group peers, the result of which maybe more willingness/intention to engage in normative risky behaviors (e.g. Graupensperger et al., 2018). Overestimating how much peers drink may also relate to problematic drinking (Davies, Martin, & Foxcroft, 2016). It has been argued that individuals will be less concerned about personal consumption practices if they (a) overestimate levels in their peers and (b) overestimate how much these peers approve of their behavior (Brett, Leavens, Miller, Lombardi, & Leffingwell, 2016; de Visser, Wheeler, Abraham, & Smith, 2013; Perkins, 2002).

Peer effects have also been demonstrated experimentally. For instance, priming people with a risky drinking identity (being a student) in contrast to identities with different drinking norms (being Spanish) led to lower quantity drinking expectations (Tarrant & Butler, 2011). People in recovery also identify social connections as a key factor in their addiction. A recent qualitative study suggests that making connections with a 'bad crowd' was retrospectively understood by a group of people in substance use recovery as a pathway into addiction (Dingle, Stark, Cruwys, & Best, 2015). The roles of social norms in drinking behaviors is more thoroughly explored in elsewhere in this volume by Fairbain and colleagues. A second related factor to social norms and group memberships is the stigma that can be attached to them, particularly to groups and identities linked with being 'addicted'.

Addiction, stereotypes and stigma

While social identities can be a powerful force for positive health and change, they can often be problematic when they are *stigmatised* or spoiled (Goffman, 1963 republished, 2014). Stigmatization refers to the process by which a person is socially devalued (in comparison with others) resulting in the reduction of an individual into to a single, negative trait or understanding (e.g. reducing the complexity of the person to being only an "alcoholic") (Schnyder, Panczak, Groth, & Schultze-Lutter, 2017). Others have suggested that stigma is the result of processes associated with labeling, attitudinal stereotyping, ignorance of others, status loss and discrimination (Link & Phelan, 2001; Thornicroft, Rose, Kassam, & Sartorius, 2007). One way in which stigmas are operationalised in interpersonal behavior is via stereotypes.

Stereotypes refer to the assumption of a number of traits and dispositions are assumed to be held by an individual based on the observation that they are a member of a particular group (Fiske, 2015). The stereotype content model (SCM: Fiske, Cuddy, Glick, & Xu, 2002) argues that the stereotypes we have about particular groups are dictated by the extent we see them as being warm (versus cold) and competent (versus incompetent). Different combinations of warmth and competent are theorised to have different emotional and behavioral outcomes. For instance, de Paula Couto and Koller (2012) report that groups such as the elderly are often perceived as being more warm than competent—eliciting feelings such as pity and helping behaviors. In contrast, people with addiction problems are often seen as being cold and incompetent (Fiske, 2018; Schomerus et al., 2011). Emotional responses associated with such people include disgust, and behavioral responses typically revolve around avoidance (Schomerus et al., 2011). Thus, from an identity perspective, holding a stigmatised identity as an alcoholic, or even the child of an alcoholic, is likely to lead to others viewing individual in a simplistic and negative way. As these negative expectations guides their interaction with this stereotype target (who may respond in kind in a negative manner), such stereotypes can become self-fulfilling (Burk & Sher, 1990; Schomerus et al., 2011).

Specific traits are also linked with 'being an alcoholic'. In a review of 17 population studies, Schomerus et al. (2011) observed that people suffering from alcohol dependency were (relative to those with non-substance -related issues) less likely perceived as being mentally ill, were perceived as responsible for the condition to a greater extent, were more likely to be socially rejected, discriminated against and generate negative emotional states.

Women with alcohol dependency can also face specific assumptions about sexual promiscuity and negative moral evaluation (Blumer, 1986; Carter, 1997).

Alcohol-related stereotypes can affect individuals both before, during and after treatment. For instance, Schomerus and colleagues present evidence to suggest that when stigma is internalized (i.e. people stigmatize themselves), people who are alcohol dependent have a lower drink refusal efficacy than those who do not self-stigmatize (Schomerus et al., 2011). DeJong, van den Brink, and Jansen (1993) observed that even alcohol therapists hold stereotypes towards those suffering alcohol problems, and their behaviors were influenced by these stereotypical beliefs (particularly when clients were men, where staff members could be more confronting and critical). Stigma can also be experienced people who are in long-term treatment—for example, those in methadone replacement therapy—from sources such as employees, healthcare workers, the general public and other sources (Earnshaw, Smith, & Copenhaver, 2013).

Alcoholism related stereotypes are also 'contagious', in that they influence evaluations about people around the dependent individual. For instance, various studies have shown that being a 'child of an alcoholic' leads to a set of secondary stereotypes—often leading to behaviors being interpreted as more pathological (see e.g. Burk & Sher, 1990 and also Harter (2000) for a review of risk factors empirically linked to being an adult child of an alcoholic).

Before we bring the discussion to stereotypes and alcohol use and misuse to a close, it is worth noting that having stigmatised identity does not always lead to soley negative outcomes. For instance, Crocker and Major's (1989) self-esteem buffering work indicates that, at times, people can use negative stereotypes held against them to offset the negative impacts of criticism. They also note that members of many stigmatised communities have a range of self-efficacy varying from very low to very high. It is also interesting to note that a desire to develop meaningful identities, even within stigmatised groups, has been identified as a pathway into addiction, including alcohol misuse (Dingle, Cruwys, & Frings, 2015). Finally, people do not always wish to leave alcohol-related stigmatised identities behind even when they are able to; as we will discuss later, one of the key predictors of relapses is the presence of alcohol problematic alcohol using networks.

Identity as a role for treatment initiation

How can identity spur people into seeking treatment for alcohol misuse? Many factors encourage people to move from addictive alcohol misuse to controlled or non drinking—either through spontaneous remission or via treatment—and no clear theoretical approach captures these entirely (see Cunningham, Sobell, Sobell, & Gaskin, 1994). However, an enduring narrative about the experience of a period of intense difficulty prompting change is present in many psychological therapeutic and spiritual approaches, both within and beyond the field of alcohol and addiction studies. In alcohol treatment, this process is often known as 'hitting rock bottom' (see (Kirouac & Witkiewitz, 2017; Kirouac, Frohe, & Witkiewitz, 2015)).

Hitting rock bottom in alcohol treatment discourse usually refers to a crisis associated with various aspects of one's life. Amongst individuals with alcohol problems, Kircouac and colleagues suggest these can be broken down into factors associated with health problems, existential issues, situational and environmental problems, context and, pertinently to the current chapter, social networks and social connections (Kirouac et al., 2015). In line with this, Dingle, Cruwys, and Frings (2015), on the basis of thematic analysis of interviews with residents of an Australian recovery community, argue that identity losses associated with addictive behaviors can be a trigger to change behavior via help seeking. This suggests that the realization of the loss of identity or recognition of acute social isolation can be an integral part of hitting rock bottom.

Whilst 'rock bottom' can be the result of the effects of experiencing dramatic occurrences, such as major illness, serious interpersonal conflict, legal problems and/or the loss of employment, it is not somewhere that is always arrived at suddenly, nor is it a prerequisite for change. The concept of the 'functioning' or even 'high functioning' alcoholic—someone who manages alcohol misuse and sustaining everyday life and relationships and alters drinking behavior *before* a crisis hits, exemplifies this. For such individuals, noticing a significant decrease in such functioning, can lead to the realization that one's drinking behavior is out of control and requires change before one life unravels—this is sometimes referred to as 'high bottom' recovery (Kirouac & Witkiewitz, 2017; Kirouac et al., 2015). Related literature suggest that such 'high bottoms' also have identity-based facets—for instance, people sometimes (but not always) discuss the loss of being a 'good' group member—such as being a good parent or an effective business person (Couvrette, Brochu, & Plourde, 2016).

Identity as a mechanism for sustained for change

Despite the significant potential impacts of successful treatment of AUD, there are a number of key barriers to their realization. Outcomes for people with AUD are generally good whilst they are in treatment (e.g. in residential treatment or attending outpatient services). For instance, number of days drinking typically declines (i.e. Frings, Hogan et al., 2018) and alcohol-related deaths are significantly lower for people who are currently attending treatment (Pavarin et al., 2017; Peeraphatdit et al., 2020). However, relapse rates and mortality risk increase significantly once treatment is completed (Ledda et al., 2019; Vaillant et al., 1983; Weisner, Thomas Ray, Mertens,

Satre, & Moore, 2003). The most common causes of relapse include social pressure, negative emotional states, and interpersonal conflict (Hodgins, el-Guebaly, & Armstrong, 1995) and exposure to these circumstances often increases when people return to their home environment after treatment. For these reasons, it is common for people with AUD to require several cycles of treatment before a stable recovery is achieved, and not all individuals persist in future recovery attempts.

When considering the role of identity is also important to think about if it is the identity *per se* which is generating effects, or rather the activities related to the general identity. To put this another way, is it the '*being*' and/or the '*doing*' which comprise the "active ingredient" of identity processes? If one generates a recovery based social identity by hanging out with one's friends, is it the activities you do with those people which causes a positive change, or something special about the shared identity you create? There are a number of reasons to suspect that identity is as important, if not more so, than the activities associated with building those identities. First, identities guide beliefs about what is normal and not, and influences behavior in a variety of situations (Brown, 2000). Second, as we will see below, identities seem to have effects on social cognitive functions that may operate outside of one's awareness (i.e. implicitly) and while these identities may include aspects associated with behavior, there are also likely to be cognitively distinct (see below for more in-depth discussion of this point, and also Frings & Albery, 2015; Frings, Moss, et al., 2018; Lindgren et al., 2018). Thirdly, in contexts where people are offered (or even mandated) to engage in the same behaviors (such as formal treatment settings) variance is observed in levels of identity—which typically predicts positive outcomes e.g. (Buckingham, Frings, & Albery, 2013). Perhaps most directly, recent research has shown that when both levels of engagement and also levels of identification are measured, it appears that identity accounts for the majority of variance in positive treatment outcomes (Taylor, McNamara, & Frings, 2019). If we can conceptually and evidentially argue that there is something 'special' about identity, the logical next question is understanding the processes through which identity acts upon recovery-related outcomes. One model which has attempted to do this is the social identity model of cessation maintenance (SIMCM; Frings & Albery, 2015, 2017). We review this model and associated research below.

The social identity model of cessation maintenance

The social identity model of cessation maintenance (SIMCM) provides a theoretical framework for understanding psychological and social cognitive processes which may underpin the link between identity and changes in habitual behaviors. As can be seen in Fig. 15.1, the model argues that the link between identity and positive outcomes, such as higher treatment retention

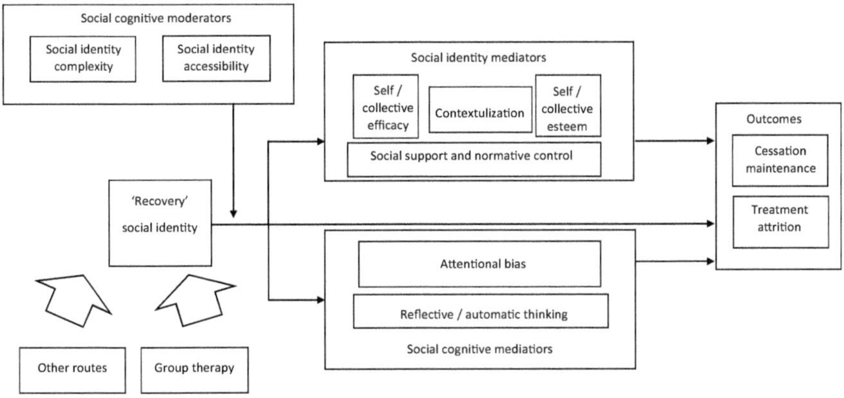

FIGURE 15.1 The social identity model of cessation maintenance.

(for those in treatment) and also maintenance of a change in behavior (which can range from abstinence to harm reduction), is moderated by the extent to which identities are cognitively accessible and utilized in context. When identities are activated, it is argued that they have an effect on outcomes through consciously available reflective processes, but also at a social cognitive level which may be unavailable for conscious inspection and *more* automated in nature. We discuss these two modes of operation below.

Reflective processes

One of the earliest reflective processes to be examined in the context of SIMCM was self efficacy—the sense that one has agency in achieving one's goals (Bandura, 1982). Buckingham, Frings, and Albery (2013) examined how people with varying addictive behaviors (including alcohol) identified with being a person who uses that substance, but also people who are in recovery. The extent to which people differentiated between these two identities was a predictor of how efficacious they felt about maintaining a behavioral change in the future. High levels of efficacy were also linked to incidences of past relapses. Similar work conducted by Dingle, Stark, Cruwys, and Best, (2015), showed that differentiating between using and non-using identities prospectively led to a change in emphasis towards non-using identities as well as decreased drinking, increased abstinence and increased life-satisfaction.

SIMCM also argues the social identities help contextualize our semantic understanding of events. For instance, one can understand returning to alcohol by having 'one drink' as a 'slip'—a warning sign that behavior may be changing negatively which suggests that one needs to be more mindful. In contrast, it can also be contextualized as a total 'relapse'—in which the majority of gains and progress one has made is either threatened or lost, and suggesting that one may have to start from scratch in one's recovery. Research suggests that people that who have a higher level of identity associated with being a member of a Fellowship also tend to see relapses as more costly than those who have a lower level of identity (Frings, Collins, Long, Pinto, & Albery, 2016). Contextualization can also affect the way we understand other people's stories and draw lessons from them. In many group-based treatment settings relating life narratives to others is a common feature. Often the expectation is that people learn from other's mistakes, sharing other's triumphs and gaining insight into their own patterns of behavior. In one study, Frings, Wood, Lionetti, and Albery (2019) measured levels of identity in one hundred and seventy people attending AA meetings. These participants were then asked to read an archetypal life narrative about a person who is in recovery from alcohol misuse, subsequently began drinking and hit rock bottom again before having a second—hopefully stronger—recovery attempt. High levels of identification with being an AA member were linked to an increased sense that the story was personally relevant and also that it would help in one's own recovery.

As with all groups, if one is regularly interacting with other people who share a group identity, interactions generate behavioral and attitudinal norms (ways in which group members expect other group members to behave). Groups tend to support individuals who behave normatively and also engage in remedial, sometimes punitive action, with people who deviate from group norms. Members of fellowships and SMART recovery participants in the Frings, Collins, et al. (2016) study highlighted normative behaviors as those which would line up with the group's goals (i.e. staying abstinence), and non-normative behaviors as those which disrupted the group's ability to meet those goals (such as attending meetings intoxicated, not maintaining confidentiality or sexually predatory behavior). Typically, participants expected that when group members broke the rules they would receive an inclusive—generally educational—response to help them become normative again. However, in some cases norm violations (particularly when perceived as potentially harmful to the group as a whole) could lead to social exclusion. Other research (focusing on gambling addiction) suggests that the act of offering help and social support is in itself protective to an equal or possibly even greater extent than is receiving help for some people (Hutchinson, Cox, & Frings, 2018).

In sum, one mechanism through which identities appear to support recovery is through the generation of social norms and the subsequent social support and normative control associated with them. However, it is important to note contraindicatory evidence to this idea. For example, interventions aimed at changing social influences and normative beliefs around drinking has only a relatively minor effect—as shown in metanalysis of 17.5k participants (Prestwich et al., 2016). Such interventions seem most efficacious when individuals see themselves as prototypical of the group whose norms are being discussed (Goode, Balzarini, & Smith, 2014). Such prototypically could be seen as a proxy for identity (indeed, it is theorised to be a key aspect of multi component models identity (Leach et al., 2008)).

Automatic processes

Alongside those more reflective thinking processes identified above, SIMCM argues that social identities also operate in a manner which is not open to conscious inspection by the individual; the process which an individual will have limited (if any) awareness of (Frings & Albery, 2015, 2017). That such dual processes, and specifically the interplay between reflective and intuitive systems, operate for the self-regulation of behavioral enactment has been the subject of contemporary work in the addictive behaviors field (see Friese & Hofmann, 2009; Moss & Albery, 2009; Wiers & Stacy, 2006).

These accounts allow for predictions to follow for how and when identity-based systems, such as social identity and self-concept, occur. The vast majority of work examining how implicit drinker identity predicts various measures of alcohol use and misuse has been concerned with personal (self) identities or those which concern how we think of ourselves in relation to others (see Lindgren, Ramirez, Namaky, Olin, and Teachman, (2016) for a review). Whilst evidence has accumulated specifically examining how one's explicit social identity, or that comprised of one's awareness of how similar one is to other in-group members and how different one sees oneself in relation to out-group members (see previous section), less evidence has been generated to examine the effects of implicit social-identities on alcohol-related outcomes. However, such work is beginning to emerge.

At the heart of the extant literature in this area are findings to suggest that measures of drinking behaviors (e.g. hazardous drinking, social drinking levels and *in-situ* drinking behaviors) *all* show differential independent relationships with implicit and explicit identities (which themselves are related but to lesser degree) both in cross-sectional studies and prospectively over time (Frings, Melichar, et al., 2016; Lindgren et al., 2013; Lindgren, Baldwin, Peterson, Wiers, & Teachman, 2020; Montes, Olin, Teachman, Baldwin, & Lindgren, 2018). Other studies have shown that such identities account for unique variance in drinking-related outcomes, over and above other predictors. These include alcohol expectancies, perceived drinking norms and, perhaps less significantly, drinking motives, prospectively (Lindgren et al., 2016). In addition, both self-reported and implicit drinker identity have been shown to covary with one's ability to refuse an alcoholic beverage; for example, in those with decreased drink-refusal self-efficacy and decreased public self-consciousness, high implicit identity was related to increased self-reported drinking (Foster, Neighbors, & Young, 2014) Moreover, in a currently unpublished study (Zimony, Albery, Lindgren, & Frings, n.d.) we used a taste preference test to measure actual drinking behavior (see Albery, Collins, Moss, Frings, and Spada, 2015). In this study, whilst implicit and explicit identities were not significantly related, explicit identity *only* was related to alcohol expectancies and correlated with the amount of alcohol poured to drink ratio (intention). Conversely, implicit identity was associated *only* with the amount of alcohol consumed of that poured (behavioral enactment). This pattern of responding was interpreted as showing a dissociation between implicit and explicit aspects of identity, not only for thoughts that may represent more reflective aspects of reasoning (alcohol-related expectancies), but also both in-the-moment behavioral intentions (how much a person pours for themselves to drink) and in-the-moment behavioral enactment (how much one consumes of that drink). In other work that has examined how much a person consumes *in-situ* as a function of implicit and explicit associations (i.e. alcohol-related including self-identity), this pattern of dissociation was not found when measures of self-control, cognitive capacity and incentivisation to refrain from drinking were also included (Lindgren et al., 2019). In addition, in testing the core concepts from the theory of planned behavior (attitude, subjective norms, perceived behavioral control [PBC]) alongside measures of intrinsic/extrinsic motivations and implicit drinking identity, Caudwell, Keech, Hamilton, Mullan, and Hagger (2019) showed *future* pre-drinking (the consumption of alcohol prior to a "night out") was associated with past behavior (past pre-drinking), PBC and implicit identity and not behavioral intentions. Finally, research has shown that the relationship between individual differences in reward sensitivity and self-reported drinking behavior is only mediated by explicit drinker identity and not implicit identity (Tatnell, Loxton, Modecki, & Hamilton, 2019). These findings highlight the idea that implicit identities are likely to operate independently of deliberative processes (such as intention formation) and as part of an *impulsive* response to activate previously learned associations (i.e. between identity and pre-drinking).

Are identities themselves 'addictive'?

Although identities have been shown to be an important predictor of positive outcomes in a variety of studies, it is worth noting that they are not a panacea. For instance, people with particular styles of relating to other people, specifically people who adopt a highly avoidant attachment style, are much more likely to stay in group based therapy and less likely to relapse (Marshall, Albery, & Frings, 2018). As discussed above, there are particular situations where social groups can exclude group members, even in organizations such as AA fellowships which are perceived as being highly inclusive. The psychological impact of such exclusion, particularly for people who may feel stigmatised and excluded from other groups is potentially severe. Moreover, for some, remaining actively engaged with peer support seems to be a prerequisite for sustaining recovery. For example, in Frings, Wood,

Lionetti, and Albery (2019), we observed participants who had been actively identifying as AA members for over 500 months, and asserted that there were abstinent for the majority of this time. From some treatment perspectives, maintaining a strong sense of identity is a positive outcome. However, it could also be viewed from other perspectives as exchanging one life-defining habit for another.

A related issues is that the suite of identities we hold are not static. To the extent that people in recovery may or may not transition between related identities, and that at different "life points" they are more or less likely to be identifying according to an established representation of a one group (relative to others), it is also likely that our behavior and experience will be subject to influence from different identities at different times. Importantly, this is not to say that one's active identity is the only identity ready to be accessed by an individual but that, within context and at a given time, one identity may be more available for processing and use and as such appears more salient. If we think of our identities functioning in this way it also becomes clear that they may never fully 'disappear'. A more useful way to think of the operation of our identities maybe that they rather wax and wane in their influence over the lifespan as a function of experience. In addition, just because identities lie dormant and are cognitively stored more remotely (e.g. in long term memory) does not mean that they are not accessible and cannot become re-activated and re-established quickly – this is especially the case with respect to those accessed implicitly. Work is required to examine the pattern of relationship between *active* and *inactive* social identities as a function of identity transitions, and importantly whether the nature of the relationship between these identities at different levels of processing is one of excitation/facilitation or inhibition. These are open areas of interest for future research.

Implications for practice

There is now a growing literature supporting the notion that both social identities and social connections can be pivotal in the success of failure of an individual's addiction recovery journey. While there are nascent interventions which explicitly use identity and connections as their foundation (see for example work by Dingle and colleagues focusing on Groups 4 Belonging elsewhere this volume) we would argue that practitioners can also draw a number of more generalized lessons when approaching service design and delivery.

Identity is an important treatment target in and of itself

As discussed above, social identities and social connections can be an important trigger for people to seek treatment and important predictors of later recovery outcomes. Both cross-sectional (i.e. Buckingham et al., 2013) and longitudinal (Dingle, Stark, et al., 2015; Wolff, von Hippel, Brener, & von Hippel, 2015) studies suggest that having a high (or relatively higher) identity as in recovery, and/or differentiating between recovery and addiction related identities are all positively related to better outcomes. Thus, it's reasonable to assume that providing therapeutic space for people to work on their identities—either in terms of differentiating between past and present selves, developing aspirational future selves, or constructing protective identities around recovery are likely to be beneficial. Similarly, in line with evidence for social connection-based interventions on a variety of mental health issues, and noting the recent evidence surrounding Group 4 Health and Groups 4 Belonging, training packages which aim to facilitate people in recovery's ability to generate positive social connections (and manage or reduce the emphasis on potentially harmful ones) should continue to be a treatment priority. Adding these elements to existing treatment packages is likely to leverage the value of the latter to the extent that identities can potentially increase treatment engagement, reduce attrition and strengthen recovery prospects in the vulnerable post treatment phase.

Identity can be used to generate attitudinal change

As well as being considered a potential therapeutic / intervention target in and of itself, social identities can also be seen as a way of helping people reach other treatment targets. For instance, if clients have a social identity which contains an understanding that having a single drink is a risky proposition, they can be encouraged to think about these identities when they are in potentially risky situations, and potentially reinforcing drink refusal efficacy (see Oei & Morawska, 2004). If individuals need to feel more positive self-worth, they could be encouraged to think about how they are similar to other positively evaluated group members, who may have faced the same challenges and setbacks successfully. Identities may also be used to help shape an understanding of the cost of relapse to the self and others (although, as we noted above, this approach is not without risks).

Clients must be aware of, and prepared to deal with, stereotypes they may encounter

As discussed above, negative stereotypes associated with having a history of alcohol addiction are widespread, global and enduring. While for some clients a history of addiction may be a 'hidden' stigmatising trait, for others it will be highly visible. Training to help clients understand the form and nature of stereotypes, their likely effects on interactions, and the risk of acting defensively (creating self-filling prophecies) can help those in recovery have realistic expectations about others responses to them when they learn of their previous addiction, and can also help clients prepare appropriate, positive response strategies. Care needs to be taken that information at this is provided to clients at an appropriate stage—arguably when recovery is well established and people are able to think about the challenges of the future rather than focusing on immediate well-being. Care also must be taken not to overemphasize the challenge stereotypes present and thus generate a demotivating force in someone's recovery.

Peer mentors/helpers may be able to effectively help shape contextualization

Another important implication of research suggesting that social identities lead one to feel more interchangeable with other group papers is that people who are seen to be part of one's ingroup may have a greater impact on the self than those that are not. It may be that peer helpers (people with lived experience of addiction issues who are helping others on their own recovery journeys, including but not limited to Fellowship sponsors, therapeutic community house leaders, 'buddies' and peer mentors) may have a particular role to play in helping people develop new identities, or in conveying the meanings values and norms that a given recover identity encapsulates. Alongside the socialization process, a range of evidence (from non-addiction domains) suggest that ingroup members are more able to criticize aspects of the ingroup than are outgroup members (e.g. Hornsey, Oppes, & Svensson, 2002). Peer helpers may thus be uniquely position within a recovery journey to be critical of aspects of being an active addict (or equivalent) that a client may feel positive about and/or be unwilling or unable to relinquish (for instance, perceptions of camaraderie, pleasure, or substance use as a coping mechanism).

Identities need to be internalized cognitively to be effective

As we have seen above, SIMCM argues that identity has both explicit and implicit components, and these may at times be disassociated. Complimentary to this, research by variety of research groups suggests that implicitly held identities are an important predictor of behavior, especially when such disassociation is present (e.g. see Lindgren et al., 2017). An important treatment implication here is that while identities are important, they cannot be forced. The conscious development and enactment of a particular set of identities, reflections about social norms, and experiences of social connection and support are all likely to be effective in the short term, and when they are repeatedly made salient. However, in the longer term—when immediate reinforcement and reminders are perhaps absent, or when pre-existing identities (such as being a drinker) are activating in competition to new identities—it is the extent to which recovery identities are been internalized (i.e. are consistently accessible in a broad range of contexts) that dictate their impact on behavior. This may explain why the period immediately after recovery, for around six months, seems to be one of intense vulnerability to relapse: during this phase it is possible that while identities are being reflectively held and engaged with, the social cognitive architecture which is underpinning them is not sufficiently well established to "out compete" pre-existing identities associated with more harmful behavior patterns. This reinforces the need for strong follow-up services to allow new protective identities to bed in. For example, one recent study has explored the effect of one particular type of thinking, 'growth mindsets', in relation to problem drinking over time (Lindgren, Burnette, Hoyt, Peterson, & Neighbors, 2020). Among a group of heavy drinkers those with pronounced explicit drinking identity, and who also had stronger growth mindsets, were shown to self-report a decrease in consumption over time. There was no effect for implicit identity.

Identity work is not risk-free

As indicated above, people are often reluctant to give up valued identities (even if they're objectively harmful) and efforts to encourage people to do so prematurely may lead to therapeutic disruption, resistance through reaffirmation of behaviors (i.e. relapsing), or withdrawal from treatment programs. For those who actively endorse new recovery related identities, failing to live up to the expectations of a new identity (such as remaining sober in abstinence-based programs) may incur a greater cost to the self if it's reduces one's ability to realistically identify with a valued new ingroup membership. Thus, those working with people in recovery need to take care to make sure that identity processes are appropriately managed such that people are able to change their relationship with old identities, but also be secure in new positive ones. This is particularly case in therapeutic modes which involve a lot of group work (both in formal treatment programs and those which are peer led such as AA or SMART). In such contexts, particular care must be taken to ensure that people are not excluded, and normative infractions are righted inclusively where possible.

As the above indicates, social identity and social connections may well be applicable to the treatment of alcohol use and misuse in a variety of ways. The challenge facing both researchers and practitioners is the development and testing of specific methods and approaches, and their robust evaluation. To achieve this, researchers and practitioners must work collaboratively to develop implement and test new approaches. The authors of this chapter (and no doubt authors of other chapters in this volume) are keen to work with colleagues in all different areas of the field to help realize this goal.

Conclusion

This chapter has adopted a social-identity based perspective to explore potential mechanisms through which one's categorization of oneself as a group member relative to membership of other possible groups furthers our understanding of how people begin their drinking careers, how this may (or may not) develop to a pattern of misuse, and also how identity transitions may predict change in drinking behavior. Factors including aspects of social isolation and loneliness, the need to form interpersonal social connections and to dissociate oneself from *others* in alternative groups, as well as the role in stigmatization, were all argued to facilitate social identity function and drinking behavior. In addition, social identity processes were reconceptualised cognitively to encompass evidence to suggest that one's social identity as, for instance, a drinker, is better informed by understanding thoughts and feelings which we are either aware of or unaware of. Finally, we explored how social identities may be of benefit in the development of interventions in alcohol use and misuse.

References

Åkerlind, I., & Hörnquist, J. O. (1992). Loneliness and alcohol abuse: A review of evidences of an interplay. *Social Science and Medicine*, *34*, 405–414. Available from https://doi.org/10.1016/0277-9536(92)90300-F.

Albery, I. P., Collins, I., Moss, A. C., Frings, D., & Spada, M. M. (2015). Habit predicts in-the-moment alcohol consumption. *Addictive Behaviors*, *41*, 78–80. Available from https://doi.org/10.1016/J.ADDBEH.2014.09.025.

Anderson, L. E., Connor, J. P., Voisey, J., Young, R. M. D., & Gullo, M. J. (2019). The unique role of attachment dimensions and peer drinking in adolescent alcohol use. *Personality and Individual Differences*, *149*, 118–122. Available from https://doi.org/10.1016/j.paid.2019.05.048.

Ary, D. V., Duncan, T. E., Duncan, S. C., & Hops, H. (1999). Adolescent problem behavior: The influence of parents and peers. *Behaviour Research and Therapy*, *37*, 217–230. Available from https://doi.org/10.1016/S0005-7967(98)00133-8.

Bandura, A. (1982). Self-efficacy mechanism in human agency. *American Psychologist*, *37*, 122–147. Available from https://doi.org/10.1037/0003-066X.37.2.122.

Bell, R. (1956). Alcohol and loneliness. *Journal of Social Therapy*, *2*, 171–181.

Berry, J. (1997). Immigration, acculturation, and adaptation. *Applied Psychology*, *46*, 5–34. Available from https://doi.org/10.1111/j.1464-0597.1997.tb01087.x.

Blumer, H. (1986). Symbolic interactionism : Perspective and method. University of California Press.

Brett, E. I., Leavens, E. L., Miller, M. B., Lombardi, N., & Leffingwell, T. R. (2016). Normative perceptions of alcohol-related consequences among college students. *Addictive Behaviors*, *58*, 16–20. Available from https://doi.org/10.1016/j.addbeh.2016.02.008.

Brown, R. (2000). Social identity theory: Past achievements, current problems and future challenges. *European Journal of Social Psychology*, *30*, 745–778. Available from https://doi.org/10.1002/1099-0992(200011/12)30:6 < 745::AID-EJSP24 > 3.0.CO;2-O.

Buckingham, S. A., Frings, D., & Albery, I. P. (2013). Group membership and social identity in addiction recovery. *Psychology of Addictive Behaviors*, *27*, 1132–1140. Available from https://doi.org/10.1037/a0032480.

Bule, B., & Frings, D. (2016). The role of group membership continuity and multiple memberships on mental well-being amongst post-operative stoma patients. *Psycho-Oncology*, *25*, 726–728. Available from https://doi.org/10.1002/pon.4006.

Burk, J. P., & Sher, K. J. (1990). Labeling the child of an alcoholic: Negative stereotyping by mental health professionals and peers. *Journal of Studies on Alcohol*, *51*, 156–163. Available from https://doi.org/10.15288/jsa.1990.51.156.

Canham, S. L., Mauro, P. M., Kaufmann, C. N., & Sixsmith, A. (2016). Association of alcohol use and loneliness frequency among middle-aged and older adult drinkers. *Journal of Aging and Health*, *28*, 267–284. Available from https://doi.org/10.1177/0898264315589579.

Carter, C. S. (1997). Ladies don't: A historical perspective on attitudes toward alcoholic women. *Affilia - Journal of Women and Social Work*, *12*, 471–485. Available from https://doi.org/10.1177/088610999701200407.

Caudwell, K. M., Keech, J. J., Hamilton, K., Mullan, B. A., & Hagger, M. S. (2019). Reducing alcohol consumption during pre-drinking sessions: Testing an integrated behaviour-change model. *Psychology and Health*, *34*, 106–127. Available from https://doi.org/10.1080/08870446.2018.1518527.

Centers for Disease Control and Prevention. (2020). *Alcohol Related Disease Impact (ARDI) application*. Retrieved June 1, 2020, from <https://nccd.cdc.gov/DPH_ARDI/Default/Report.aspx?T = AAM&P = f6d7eda7-036e-4553-9968-9b17ffad620e&R = d7a9b303-48e9-4440-bf47-070a4827e1fd&M = 8E1C5233-5640-4EE8-9247-1ECA7DA325B9&F = &D>.

Couvrette, A., Brochu, S., & Plourde, C. (2016). The "deviant good mother": Motherhood experiences of substance-using and lawbreaking women. *Journal of Drug Issues*, *46*, 292–307. Available from https://doi.org/10.1177/0022042616649003.

Crocker, J., & Major, B. (1989). Social stigma and self-esteem: The self-protective properties of stigma. *Psychological Review*, *96*, 608–630. Available from https://doi.org/10.1037/0033-295X.96.4.608.

Cunningham, J. A., Sobell, L. C., Sobell, M. B., & Gaskin, J. (1994). Alcohol and drug abusers' reasons for seeking treatment. *Addictive Behaviors*, *19*, 691–696. Available from https://doi.org/10.1016/0306-4603(94)90023-X.

Davies, E. L., Martin, J., & Foxcroft, D. R. (2016). Age differences in alcohol prototype perceptions and willingness to drink in UK adolescents. *Psychology, Health & Medicine*, *21*, 317–329. Available from https://doi.org/10.1080/13548506.2015.1051556.

DeJong, C. A. J., van den Brink, W., & Jansen, J. A. M. (1993). Sex role stereotypes and clinical judgement: How therapists view their alcoholic patients. *Journal of Substance Abuse Treatment*, *10*, 383–389. Available from https://doi.org/10.1016/0740-5472(93)90023-U.

de Paula Couto, M. C. P., & Koller, S. H. (2012). Warmth and competence: Stereotypes of the elderly among young adults and older persons in Brazil. *International Perspectives in Psychology: Research, Practice, Consultation*, *1*, 52–62. Available from https://doi.org/10.1037/a0027118.

de Visser, R. O., Wheeler, Z., Abraham, C., & Smith, J. A. (2013). "Drinking is our modern way of bonding": Young people's beliefs about interventions to encourage moderate drinking. *Psychology and Health*, *28*, 1460–1480. Available from https://doi.org/10.1080/08870446.2013.828293.

Dingle, G. A., Stark, C., Cruwys, T., & Best, D. (2015). Breaking good: Breaking ties with social groups may be good for recovery from substance misuse. *British Journal of Social Psychology*, *54*, 236–254. Available from https://doi.org/10.1111/bjso.12081.

Dingle, G. A., Cruwys, T., & Frings, D. (2015). Social identities as pathways into and out of addiction. *Frontiers in Psychology*, *6*, 1795. Available from https://doi.org/10.3389/fpsyg.2015.01795.

Earnshaw, V., Smith, L., & Copenhaver, M. (2013). Drug addiction stigma in the context of methadone maintenance therapy: An investigation into understudied sources of stigma. *International Journal of Mental Health and Addiction*, *11*, 110–122. Available from https://doi.org/10.1007/s11469-012-9402-5.

Ertl, M. M., Dillon, F. R., Martin, J. L., Babino, R., & De La Rosa, M. (2018). Alcohol use exacerbates acculturative stress among recently immigrated, young adult Latinas. *Journal of Immigrant and Minority Health*, *20*, 594–602. Available from https://doi.org/10.1007/s10903-017-0586-4.

Fiske, S. T. (2015). Intergroup biases: A focus on stereotype content. *Current Opinion in Behavioral Sciences*, *3*, 45–50. Available from https://doi.org/10.1016/j.cobeha.2015.01.010.

Fiske, S. T. (2018). Stereotype content: Warmth and competence endure. *Current Directions in Psychological Science*, *27*, 67–73. Available from https://doi.org/10.1177/0963721417738825.

Fiske, S. T., Cuddy, A. J. C., Glick, P., & Xu, J. (2002). A model of (often mixed) stereotype content: Competence and warmth respectively follow from perceived status and competition. *Journal of Personality and Social Psychology*, *82*, 878–902.

Foster, D. W., Neighbors, C., & Young, C. M. (2014). Drink refusal self-efficacy and implicit drinking identity: An evaluation of moderators of the relationship between self-awareness and drinking behavior. *Addictive Behaviors*, *39*, 196–204. Available from https://doi.org/10.1016/j.addbeh.2013.09.024.

Friese, M., & Hofmann, W. (2009). Control me or I will control you: Impulses, trait self-control, and the guidance of behavior. *Journal of Research in Personality*, *43*, 795–805. Available from https://doi.org/10.1016/j.jrp.2009.07.004.

Frings, D., & Albery, I. P. (2015). The social identity model of cessation maintenance: Formulation and initial evidence. *Addictive Behaviors*, *44*, 35–42. Available from https://doi.org/10.1016/j.addbeh.2014.10.023.

Frings, D., & Albery, I. P. (2017). Developing the social identity model of cessation maintenance: Theory, evidence and implications. In S. Buckingham, & D. Best (Eds.), *Addiction, behavioural change and social identity. The pathway to resilience and recovery* (pp. 128–148). Oxon: Routledge.

Frings, D., Collins, M., Long, G., Pinto, IR., & Albery, I. P. (2016). A test of the Social Identity Model of Cessation Maintenance: The content and role of social control. *Addictive Behaviors Reports*, *3*, 77–85. Available from https://doi.org/10.1016/j.abrep.2016.02.003.

Frings, D., Hogan, C. J., Jn-Pierre, K. H., Wood, K. V., Holmes, M., & Albery, I. P. (2018). Online and face-to-face extended brief interventions for harmful alcohol use: Client characteristics, attendance and treatment outcomes. *Counselling Psychology Quarterly*, 1–12. Available from https://doi.org/10.1080/09515070.2018.1555516.

Frings, D., Melichar, L., & Albery, I. P. (2016). Implicit and explicit drinker identities interactively predict in-the-moment alcohol placebo consumption. *Addictive Behaviors Reports*, *3*, 86–91.

Frings, D., Moss, A. C., Albery, I. P., Eskisan, G., Wilcockson, T. D. W., & Marchant, A. P. (2018). Environmental context influences visual attention to responsible drinking messages. *Alcohol and Alcoholism*, *53*, 46–51. Available from https://doi.org/10.1093/alcalc/agx076.

Frings, D., Wood, K. V., Lionetti, N., & Albery, I. P. (2019). Tales of hope: Social identity and learning lessons from others in alcoholics anonymous: A test of the social identity model of cessation maintenance. *Addictive Behaviors, 93*, 204–211. Available from https://doi.org/10.1016/j.addbeh.2019.02.004.

Gleibs, I., Haslam, C., Haslam, S., & Jones, J. (2011). Water clubs in residential care: Is it the water or the club that enhances health and well-being? *Psychology & Health, 26*, 1361–1377.

Goffman E. Stigma and Social Identity. In T.L Anderson (Ed.), *Understanding deviance: Connecting classical and contemporary perspectives.* (pp. 256–266). 2014. Taylor and Francis, Oxford. (Reprinted from *Stigma: Notes on the management of spoiled identity.* by E. Goffman, 1963, Penguin, London).

Goode, C., Balzarini, R. H., & Smith, H. J. (2014). Positive peer pressure: Priming member prototypicality can decrease undergraduate drinking. *Journal of Applied Social Psychology, 44*, 567–578. Available from https://doi.org/10.1111/jasp.12248.

Graupensperger, S. A., Benson, A. J., & Evans, M. B. (2018). Everyone else is doing it: The association between social identity and susceptibility to peer influence in NCAA athletes. *Journal of Sport and Exercise Psychology, 40*, 117–127. Available from https://doi.org/10.1123/jsep.2017-0339.

Haighton, C. (2017). *Thinking behind alcohol consumption in old age: Psychological and sociological reasons for drinking in old age. Alcohol and Aging: Clinical and Public Health Perspectives* (pp. 3–16). Springer International Publishing. Available from https://doi.org/10.1007/978-3-319-47233-1_1.

Harter, S. L. (2000). Psychosocial adjustment of adult children of alcoholics: A review of the recent empirical literature. *Clinical Psychology Review, 20*, 311–337. Available from https://doi.org/10.1016/S0272-7358(98)00084-1.

Haslam, C., Jetten, J., Cruwys, T., Dingle, G., & Haslam, S. A. (2018). *The new psychology of health: Unlocking the social cure*. London: Routledge.

Haslam, S. A., & O'Brien, A. (2005). Taking the strain: Social identity, social support, and the experience of stress. *British Journal of Social Psychology, 44*, 355–370.

Hodgins, D. C., el-Guebaly, N., & Armstrong, S. (1995). Prospective and retrospective reports of mood states before relapse to substance use. *Journal of Consulting and Clinical Psychology, 63*, 400–407. Available from https://doi.org/10.1037//0022-006x.63.3.400.

Hornquist, J. O., & Akerlind, I. (1987). Loneliness correlates in advanced alcohol abusers II. Clinical and psychological factors. *Scandinavian Journal of Social Medicine, 15*, 225–232. Available from https://doi.org/10.1177/140349488701500404.

Hornsey, M. J., Oppes, T., & Svensson, A. (2002). "It's OK if we say it, but you can't": Responses to intergroup and intragroup criticism. *European Journal of Social Psychology, 32*, 293–307. Available from https://doi.org/10.1002/ejsp.90.

Hutchinson, P., Cox, S., & Frings, D. (2018). Helping you helps me: Giving and receiving social support in recovery groups for problem gamblers. *Group Dynamics: Theory, Research, and Practice, 22*, 187–199. Available from https://doi.org/10.1037/gdn0000090.

Jamshidi, H., & Asgharnejad-Farid, A. A. (2019). The role of identity crisis and emotional intelligence in predicting substance abuse among high-school students. *Chronic Diseases Journal, 7*, 16–21. Available from https://doi.org/10.22122/CDJ.V7I1.372.

Jetten, J., Haslam, S. A., Cruwys, T., Greenaway, K. H., Haslam, C., & Steffens, N. K. (2017). Advancing the social identity approach to health and well-being: Progressing the social cure research agenda. *European Journal of Social Psychology, 47*, 789–802. Available from https://doi.org/10.1002/ejsp.2333.

Jones, J. M., & Jetten, J. (2011). Recovering from strain and enduring pain: Multiple group memberships promote resilience in the face of physical challenges. *Social Psychological and Personality Science, 2*, 239–244. Available from https://doi.org/10.1177/1948550610386806.

Khantzian, E. J. (1997). *The self-medication hypothesis of substance use disorders: A reconsideration and recent applications. Harvard Review of Psychiatry*. Lippincott Williams and Wilkins. Available from https://doi.org/10.3109/10673229709030550.

Kirouac, M., Frohe, T., & Witkiewitz, K. (2015). Toward the operationalization and examination of "hitting bottom" for problematic alcohol use: A literature review. *Alcoholism Treatment Quarterly, 33*, 312–327. Available from https://doi.org/10.1080/07347324.2015.1050934.

Kirouac, M., & Witkiewitz, K. (2017). Identifying "hitting bottom" among individuals with alcohol problems: Development and evaluation of the Noteworthy Aspects of Drinking Important to Recovery (NADIR). *Substance Use and Misuse, 52*, 1602–1615. Available from https://doi.org/10.1080/10826084.2017.1293104.

Leach, C. W., van Zomeren, M., Zebel, S., Vliek, M. L. W., Pennekamp, S. F., Doosje, B., & Spears, R. (2008). Group-level self-definition and self-investment: A hierarchical (multicomponent) model of in-group identification. *Journal of Personality and Social Psychology, 95*, 144–165. Available from https://doi.org/10.1037/0022-3514.95.1.144.

Ledda, R., Battagliese, G., Attilia, F., Rotondo, C., Pisciotta, F., Gencarelli, S., & Attilia, M. L. (2019). Drop-out, relapse and abstinence in a cohort of alcoholic people under detoxification. *Physiology & Behavior, 198*, 67–75. Available from https://doi.org/10.1016/J.PHYSBEH.2018.10.009.

Leigh-Hunt, N., Bagguley, D., Bash, K., Turner, V., Turnbull, S., Valtorta, N., & Caan, W. (2017). An overview of systematic reviews on the public health consequences of social isolation and loneliness. *Public Health, 152*, 157–171. Available from https://doi.org/10.1016/j.puhe.2017.07.035.

Levy, M. (2019). The many faces (and potential dangers) of self-medication as an explanatory concept for substance use. *International Journal for the Advancement of Counselling, 41*, 15–24. Available from https://doi.org/10.1007/s10447-018-9341-3.

Lindgren, K. P., Baldwin, S. A., Olin, C. C., Wiers, R. W., Teachman, B. A., Norris, J., & Neighbors, C. (2018). Evaluating within-person change in implicit measures of alcohol associations: Increases in alcohol associations predict increases in drinking risk and vice versa. *Alcohol and Alcoholism, 53*, 386–393. Available from https://doi.org/10.1093/alcalc/agy012.

Lindgren, K. P., Baldwin, S. A., Peterson, K. P., Wiers, R. W., & Teachman, B. A. (2020). Change in implicit alcohol associations over time: Moderation by drinking history and gender. *Addictive Behaviors, 107*, 106413. Available from https://doi.org/10.1016/j.addbeh.2020.106413.

Lindgren, K. P., Baldwin, S. A., Ramirez, J. J., Olin, C. C., Peterson, K. P., Wiers, R. W., & Neighbors, C. (2019). Self-control, implicit alcohol associations, and the (lack of) prediction of consumption in an alcohol taste test with college student heavy episodic drinkers. *PLoS One, 14*, e0209940. Available from https://doi.org/10.1371/journal.pone.0209940.

Lindgren, K. P., Burnette, J. L., Hoyt, C. L., Peterson, K. P., & Neighbors, C. (2020). Growth mindsets of alcoholism buffer against deleterious effects of drinking identity on problem drinking over time. *Alcoholism: Clinical and Experimental Research, 44*, 233–243. Available from https://doi.org/10.1111/acer.14237.

Lindgren, K. P., Neighbors, C., Gasser, M. L., Ramirez, J. J., & Cvencek, D. (2017). A review of implicit and explicit substance self-concept as a predictor of alcohol and tobacco use and misuse. *The American Journal of Drug and Alcohol Abuse*, *43*, 237–246. Available from https://doi.org/10.1080/00952990.2016.1229324.

Lindgren, K. P., Neighbors, C., Teachman, B. A., Wiers, R. W., Westgate, E., & Greenwald, A. G. (2013). I drink therefore I am: Validating alcohol-related implicit association tests. *Psychology of Addictive Behaviors*, *27*, 1–13. Available from https://doi.org/10.1037/a0027640.

Lindgren, K. P., Ramirez, J. J., Namaky, N., Olin, C. C., & Teachman, B. A. (2016). Evaluating the relationship between explicit and implicit drinking identity centrality and hazardous drinking. *Addictive Behaviors Reports*, *4*, 87–96. Available from https://doi.org/10.1016/J.ABREP.2016.10.004.

Link, B. G., & Phelan, J. C. (2001). Conceptualizing stigma. *Annual Review of Sociology*, *27*, 363–385. Available from https://doi.org/10.1146/annurev.soc.27.1.363.

Manning, M., Smith, C., & Mazerolle, P. (2013). The societal costs of alcohol misuse in Australia. *Trends and Issues in Crime and Criminal Justice*, 1–6.

Marcolin, M. L., Baumbach, J. L., Hodges, T. E., & McCormick, C. M. (2020). The effects of social instability stress and subsequent ethanol consumption in adolescence on brain and behavioral development in male rats. *Alcohol*, *82*, 29–45. Available from https://doi.org/10.1016/j.alcohol.2019.08.003.

Marshall, S. W., Albery, I. P., & Frings, D. (2018). Who stays in addiction treatment groups? Anxiety and avoidant attachment styles predict treatment retention and relapse. *Clinical Psychology & Psychotherapy*, *25*, 525–531. Available from https://doi.org/10.1002/cpp.2187.

McKay, M. T., Konowalczyk, S., Andretta, J. R., & Cole, J. C. (2017). The direct and indirect effect of loneliness on the development of adolescent alcohol use in the United Kingdom. *Addictive Behaviors Reports*, *6*, 65–70. Available from https://doi.org/10.1016/j.abrep.2017.07.003.

Montes, K. S., Olin, C. C., Teachman, B. A., Baldwin, S. A., & Lindgren, K. P. (2018). Hazardous drinking has unique relationships with implicit and explicit drinking identity. *Addictive Behaviors*, *87*, 155–161. Available from https://doi.org/10.1016/j.addbeh.2018.07.011.

Moss, A. C., & Albery, I. P. (2009). A dual-process model of the alcohol-behavior link for social drinking. *Psychological Bulletin*, *135*, 516–530. Available from https://doi.org/10.1037/a0015991.

Newcomb, M. D., & Bentler, P. M. (1989). Substance use and abuse among children and teenagers. *American Psychologist*, *44*, 242–248. Available from https://doi.org/10.1037/0003-066X.44.2.242.

Newman, M. G., & Zainal, N. H. (2020). The value of maintaining social connections for mental health in older people. *The Lancet Public Health*, *5*, e12–e13. Available from https://doi.org/10.1016/S2468-2667(19)30253-1.

Oei, T. P. S., & Morawska, A. (2004). A cognitive model of binge drinking: The influence of alcohol expectancies and drinking refusal self-efficacy. *Addictive Behaviors*, *29*, 159–179. Available from https://doi.org/10.1016/S0306-4603(03)00076-5.

Pavarin, R. M., Caputo, F., Zoli, G., Domenicali, M., Bernardi, M., & Gambini, D. (2017). Mortality risk in a cohort of Italian alcoholic individuals treated for alcohol dependence. *Drug and Alcohol Review*, *36*, 186–191. Available from https://doi.org/10.1111/dar.12366.

Peeraphatdit (Bee), T., Kamath, P. S., Karpyak, V. M., Davis, B., Desai, V., Liangpunsakul, S., & Simonetto, D. A. (2020). Alcohol rehabilitation within 30 days of hospital discharge is associated with reduced readmission, relapse, and death in patients with alcoholic hepatitis.

Clinical Gastroenterology and Hepatology, *18*(477–485), e5. Available from https://doi.org/10.1016/j.cgh.2019.04.048.

Perkins, H. W. (2002). Social norms and the prevention of alcohol misuse in collegiate contexts. *Journal of Studies on Alcohol*, *63*, 164–172. Available from https://doi.org/10.15288/jsas.2002.s14.164.

Prestwich, A., Kellar, I., Conner, M., Lawton, R., Gardner, P., & Turgut, L. (2016). Does changing social influence engender changes in alcohol intake? A meta-analysis. *Journal of Consulting and Clinical Psychology*, *84*, 845–860. Available from https://doi.org/10.1037/ccp0000112.

PricewaterhouseCoopers. (2008). *Review of prison-based drug treatment funding*. Retrieved from <http://drugslibrary.wordpress.stir.ac.uk/files/2017/05/prison-drug-treatment-funding.pdf>.

Public Health England. (2018). *Alcohol and drug prevention, treatment and recovery: Why invest*? Retrieved from <https://www.gov.uk/government/publications/alcohol-and-drug-prevention-treatment-and-recovery-why-invest/alcohol-and-drug-prevention-treatment-and-recovery-why-invest>.

Schomerus, G., Corrigan, P. W., Klauer, T., Kuwert, P., Freyberger, H. J., & Lucht, M. (2011). Self-stigma in alcohol dependence: Consequences for drinking-refusal self-efficacy. *Drug and Alcohol Dependence*, *114*, 12–17. Available from https://doi.org/10.1016/j.drugalcdep.2010.08.013.

Schnyder, N., Panczak, R., Groth, N., & Schultze-Lutter, F. (2017). Association between mental health-related stigma and active help-seeking: systematic review and meta-analysis. *The British Journal of Psychiatry*, *210*(4), 261–268.

Shankar, A., Mcmunn, A., Banks, J., & Steptoe, A. (2011). Loneliness, social isolation, and behavioral and biological health indicators in older adults. *Health Psychology*, *30*, 377–385. Available from https://doi.org/10.1037/a0022826.

Stickley, A., Koyanagi, A., Roberts, B., Richardson, E., Abbott, P., Tumanov, S., & McKee, M. (2013). Loneliness: Its correlates and association with health behaviours and outcomes in nine countries of the former Soviet Union. *PLoS One*, *8*, e67978. Available from https://doi.org/10.1371/journal.pone.0067978.

Substance Abuse and Mental Health Services Administration. (2018). *Key substance use and mental health indicators in the United States: Results from the 2017 National Survey on Drug Use and Health*. Retrieved March 25, 2019, from <https://www.samhsa.gov/data/report/2017-nsduh-annual-national-report>.

Tajfel, H., & Turner, J. (1979). An integrative theory of intergroup conflict. In W. G. Austin, & S. Worchel (Eds.), *The social psychology of intergroup relations* (pp. 33–47). Monterey, CA: Brooks/Cole.

Tarrant, M., & Butler, K. (2011). Effects of self-categorization on orientation towards health. *British Journal of Social Psychology*, *50*, 121–139. Available from https://doi.org/10.1348/014466610X511645.

Tatnell, D. G., Loxton, N. J., Modecki, K. L., & Hamilton, K. (2019). Testing a model of reward sensitivity, implicit and explicit drinker identity and hazardous drinking. *Psychology & Health*, *34*, 1407–1420. Available from https://doi.org/10.1080/08870446.2019.1606221.

Taylor, I., McNamara, N., & Frings, D. (2019). The 'doing' or the 'being'? Understanding the roles of involvement and social identity in peer-led addiction support groups. *Journal of Applied Social Psychology*, *50*, 3–9. Available from https://doi.org/10.1111/jasp.12635.

Thornicroft, G., Rose, D., Kassam, A., & Sartorius, N. (2007). *Stigma: Ignorance, prejudice or discrimination? British Journal of Psychiatry*. Cambridge University Press. Available from https://doi.org/10.1192/bjp.bp.106.025791.

Turner, J. C., Hogg, M. A., Oakes, P. J., Reicher, S. D., & Wetherell, M. S. (1987). *Rediscovering the social group: A self-categorization theory*. Basil Blackwell.

Vaillant, G. E., Clark, W., Cyrus, C., Milofsky, E. S., Kopp, J., Wulsin, V. W., & Mogielnicki, N. P. (1983). Prospective study of alcoholism treatment: Eight-year follow-up. *The American Journal of Medicine*, *75*, 455–463. Available from https://doi.org/10.1016/0002-9343(83)90349-2.

Villarosa, M., Kison, S., Madson, M., & Zeigler-Hill, V. (2016). Everyone else is doing it: Examining the role of peer influence on the relationship between social anxiety and alcohol use behaviours. *Addiction Research & Theory*, *24*, 124–134. Available from https://doi.org/10.3109/16066359.2015.1086758.

Weisner, C., Thomas Ray, G., Mertens, J. R., Satre, D. D., & Moore, C. (2003). Short-term alcohol and drug treatment outcomes predict long-term outcome. *Drug and Alcohol Dependence*, *71*, 281–294. Available from https://doi.org/10.1016/S0376-8716(03)00167-4.

Wiers, R. W., & Stacy, A. W. (2006). Implicit cognition and addiction. *Current Directions in Psychological Science*, *15*, 292–296. Available from https://doi.org/10.1111/j.1467-8721.2006.00455.x.

Wolff, N., von Hippel, C., Brener, L., & von Hippel, W. (2015). Implicit identification with drug and alcohol use predicts retention in residential rehabilitation programs. *Psychology of Addictive Behaviors*, *29*, 136–141. Available from https://doi.org/10.1037/adb0000004.

Zhou, J., Heim, D., & O'Brien, K. (2015). Alcohol consumption, athlete identity, and happiness among student sportspeople as a function of sport-type. *Alcohol and Alcoholism*, *50*, 617–623. Available from https://doi.org/10.1093/alcalc/agv030.

Zimony A., Albery I., Lindgren K.P., & Frings D. (n.d.). Dissociation effects of implicit and explicit drinker identity of intention formation and behavioural enactment. Paper in preperation.

Section 5

Cultural questions

Chapter 16

Alcohol consumption and cultural systems: Global similarities and differences

Miyuki Fukushima Tedor
Department of Criminology, Anthropology, and Sociology, Cleveland State University, Cleveland, OH, United States

Introduction

> *Alcohol has influenced virtually every civilization. Alcohol production, trade, consumption, and regulation have helped shape the cultural, social, political, and economic spheres in societies around the world.*
>
> Hames (2012, p. 1)

As one of the few legal psychoactive substances in most parts of the world and one that is also consumed for socialization and cultural and religious rituals, alcohol has historically been the most popular psychoactive substance in the world, consumed by almost half of the global population. Alcohol consumption is so common that in many languages the verb "to drink" implies drinking alcohol (Heath, 1986). For instance, most Japanese would understand *nomini iku* (translated as "going out to drink") to mean going out to drink alcohol. There are, however, considerable within country and between countries variations in the consumption of alcohol that are explained by sociocultural factors like gender and age, the law and religion, economic wealth of individuals and society, and the culture surrounding alcohol consumption.

National variations in alcohol consumption

In 2015, United Nations member states adopted Sustainable Development Goals (SDGs), which include the achievement of "good health and well-being" that covers the reduction of harmful effects of alcohol use. Alcohol consumption has been linked to an increased risk for disease, injury, and

The Handbook of Alcohol Use - Understandings from Synapse to Society.
DOI: https://doi.org/10.1016/B978-0-12-816720-5.00011-6

violence, and these alcohol-related risks are found to be substantially more detrimental to the vulnerable members of society, especially in poor countries, than to those with economic wealth. The World Health Organization (WHO), therefore, holds that the production and consumption of alcohol could significantly undermine other SDGs, including "ending poverty," "reducing inequalities between and within countries," and "achieving gender equality" (Global Status Report on Alcohol and Health, 2018, p. 3).

The Global Health Observatory is the WHO's data source for more than 1000 health-related data points collected from its member states to monitor the progress toward SDGs. Included in the Observatory is the Global Information System on Alcohol and Health (GISAH), a repository for the health data of each member state related to alcohol consumption, harm related to alcohol consumption, and policy responses to reduce the negative effects of alcohol consumption. The alcohol consumption data for this chapter mainly come from the WHO's GISAH, more specifically from the most recent publication of *Global Status Report on Alcohol and Health*[1] based on survey data collected in 2016, which included 173 WHO member states and covered 98.3% of the world population (Global Status Report on Alcohol and Health, 2018).

The WHO reports that alcohol consumption, measured in terms of its levels and patterns, varies considerably across regions[2] of the world (see Fig. 16.1). Overall, higher-income countries in the Europe, the Americas, and the Western Pacific regions had the greatest alcohol consumption, while Muslim-majority countries of the East Mediterranean region had the least alcohol consumption, and lower- to middle-income countries in the South-East Asian and the African regions had moderate alcohol consumption (Global Status Report on Alcohol and Health, 2018).

Levels of alcohol consumption

Prevalence of current drinkers

Alcohol consumption is so common worldwide that, according to the WHO, more than half of the world population over 15 years of age were current (43.0%) or former (12.5%) consumers[3] of alcohol in 2016. The prevalence

---

[1]The WHO conducted the *WHO Global Survey on Alcohol and Health* and published a series of reports in 1999, 2001, 2004, 2011, 2014, and 2018. The data summarized in this chapter are from the WHO's 2018 *Global Status Report on Alcohol and Health* based on the 2016 data.

[2]The WHO divides the world into six regions: the *Africa region* includes 47 member states, the *Americas region* includes 35 member states, the *South-East Asia region* includes 11 member states, the *Europe region* includes 53 member states, the *Eastern Mediterranean region* includes 21 member states and Palestine, and the *Western Pacific region* includes 27 member states. For more information, see Appendix IV of Global Status Report on Alcohol and Health (2018).

[3]Current drinkers are those who have consumed alcohol within the past 12 months, and former drinkers are those who used to drink but did not consume any alcohol within the past 12 months.

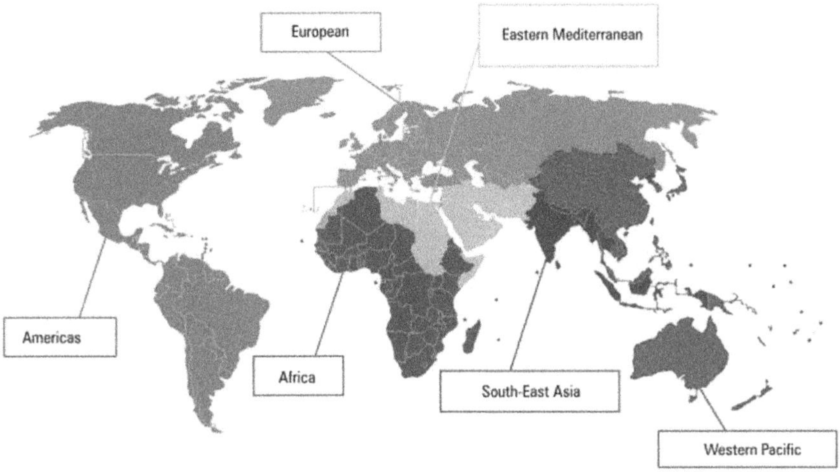

FIGURE 16.1. Six world regions used in the WHO's global status report on alcohol and health.

of alcohol consumption, however, varied by region. The Europe region (59.9%) had the highest prevalence of current drinkers, while the Eastern Mediterranean region (2.9%) had the lowest prevalence of current drinkers. Like the Europe region, the majority of the population 15 years and older in the Americas (54.1%) and the Western Pacific (53.8%) regions were current drinkers, while the South-East Asia (33.1%) and the Africa (32.2%) regions fell in the middle for the prevalence of current drinkers (Global Status Report on Alcohol and Health, 2018).

Amount of alcohol consumed

The WHO reports that the average amount of alcohol consumed worldwide measured in alcohol per capita (APC) among the population older than 15 years of age was 6.4 L per year of pure alcohol. The APC also varies across regions (see Fig. 16.2), but the pattern is similar to that for the prevalence of current drinkers with the Europe region (9.8 L) having the highest and the Eastern Mediterranean region (0.6 L) having the lowest APC consumption. The Americas (8.0 litters), Western Pacific (7.3 L), Africa (6.3 L), and South-East Asia (4.5 L) regions fell in the middle in terms of APC consumption. The highest level of APC consumption (7.5 L or higher) were observed in high-income countries in the Europe, the Americas, and the Western Pacific regions (Global Status Report on Alcohol and Health, 2018).

Prevalence of lifetime abstainers

The majority of people over 15 years of age in the world (57%) did not drink alcohol in the past 12 months in 2016, according to the WHO. Of those who

Total alcohol per capita (15+ years) consumption, in litres of pure alcohol, 2010

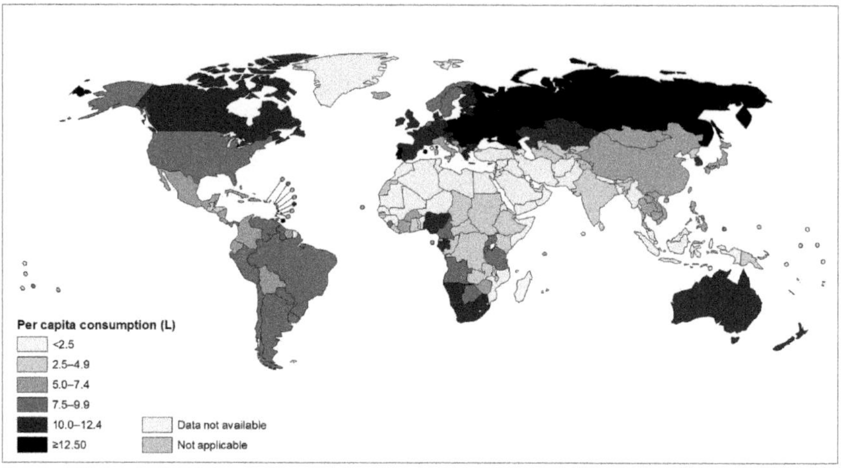

The boundaries and names shown and the designations used on this map do not imply the expression of any opinion whatsoever on the part of the World Health Organization concerning the legal status of any country, territory, city or area or of its authorities, or concerning the delimitation of its frontiers or boundaries. Dotted and dashed lines on maps represent approximate border lines for which there may not yet be full agreement.

Data Source: World Health Organization
Map Production: Health Statistics and Information Systems (HSI)
World Health Organization

World Health Organization

FIGURE 16.2. Total alcohol per capita (APC) consumption by country, 2010.

did not drink, almost an equal percentage of the population of the world over 15 years of age were lifetime abstainers of alcohol (44.5%) as were current drinkers (43.0%). The prevalence of lifetime abstainers also varied across regions with the highest prevalence of lifetime abstainers found in the Eastern Mediterranean (94.9%), corresponding to their low prevalence of current drinkers, while the Americas (16.9%) region had the lowest prevalence of lifetime abstainers. Over half of the populations over 15 years old of the South-East Asia (56.6%) and the African (57.5%) regions were lifetime abstainers, while the Europe (23.5%) and the Western Pacific (38.2%) regions fell in the middle in terms of the prevalence of lifetime abstainers (Global Status Report on Alcohol and Health, 2018).

Patterns of alcohol consumption

Type of alcohol consumed

Alcoholic beverages consist of three major types that vary in the content of alcohol with *spirits* having the highest alcoholic content followed by *wine* and then *beer* having the lowest alcoholic content. The WHO reports that worldwide, spirits (44.8%) were the most common type of alcoholic beverage, followed by beer (34.3%), then wine (11.7%). The commonly consumed type of alcohol also varied by region. The Americas region had the highest prevalence of beer consumption (53.8%), while the Europe region had the highest prevalence of wine consumption (29.8%), though beer was more

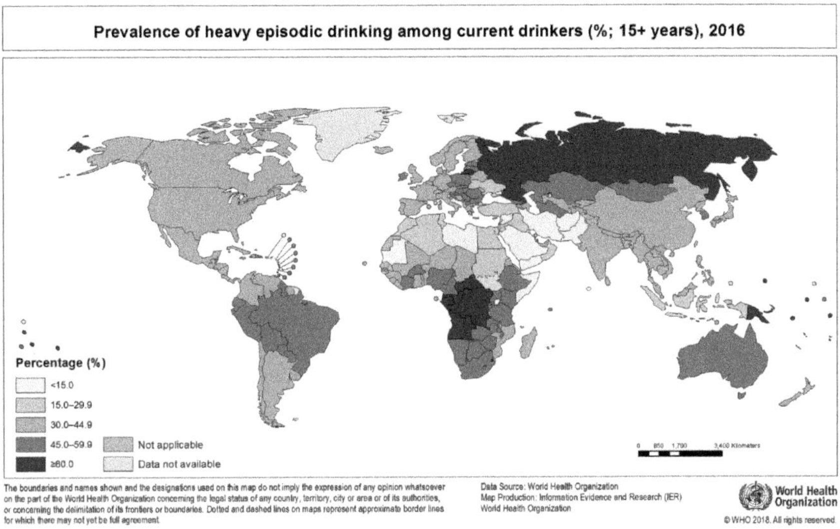

FIGURE 16.3. Percentage of heavy episodic drinking (HED) among people age 15 and older by country, 2010.

popularly consumed (40.0%) than wine in the Europe region. Spirits were the most popularly consumed type of alcoholic beverage in the Eastern Mediterranean (48.3%), the South-East Asia (87.9%), and the Western Pacific (58.8%) regions. Finally, other-type of alcohol[4] was the most popularly consumed alcoholic beverage in the Africa region (65.1%) (Global Status Report on Alcohol and Health, 2018).

The WHO also collects information on the consumption of unregulated alcohol, such as homemade, smuggled, or surrogate alcohol that are not meant for consumption, like mouthwash, and found that 25.5% of all alcohol consumed worldwide in 2016 was unregulated alcohol. Unregulated alcohol consumption was the highest among alcohol-banned and low-income countries where the access to regulated alcohol is limited and made up almost half of all alcohol consumed in the Eastern Mediterranean and the South-East Asia regions (Global Status Report on Alcohol and Health, 2018).

Prevalence of heavy episodic drinking

Problematic drinking behavior, such as heavy episodic drinking (HED),[5] also varies by region (see Figs. 16.3 and 16.4). According to the WHO,

[4]Other type of alcohol includes "fortified wines, rice wine, palm wine or other fermented beverages made of banana, sorghum, millet or maize" (Global Status Report on Alcohol and Health, 2018, p. 47).

[5]HED is defined as "60 or more grams of pure alcohol on at least one single occasion at least once per month" (Global Status Report on Alcohol and Health, 2018, p. 47).

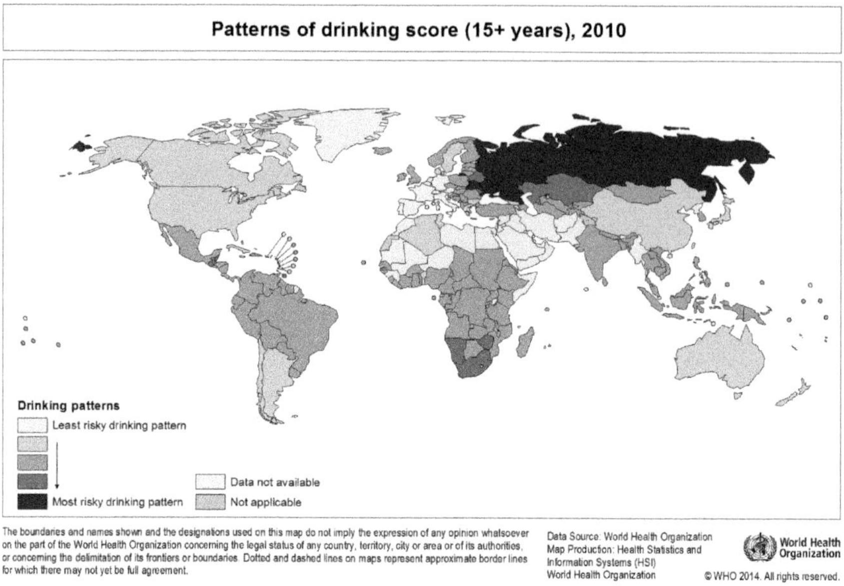

FIGURE 16.4. Patterns of drinking from least risky to most risky by country, 2010.

the prevalence of HED among all drinkers was the highest in the Europe region (26.4%), especially in the Russian Federation where more than 60% of current drinkers engaged in HED, while the lowest among the Eastern Mediterranean region (0.5%), consistent with the overall patterns found with prevalence of current drinkers and abstainers. The Western Pacific (21.9%), the Americas (21.3%), and the Africa (21.3%) regions had a similar prevalence of HED, while the South-East Asia region (13.9%) fell in between the Europe and the East Mediterranean regions, though some sub-Saharan African countries (e.g., Angola, Democratic Republic of Congo), some South American countries (e.g., Bolivia, Brazil, Paraguay, and Peru), and Australia had a high prevalence of HED (Global Status Report on Alcohol and Health, 2018).

Prevalence of alcohol use disorders

According to the WHO, 5.1% of people older than 15 years of age globally suffered from alcohol use disorder (AUD)[6] in 2016. The prevalence of AUD varied by region, where the Europe region had the highest prevalence of AUD (8.8%) followed closely by the Americas region (8.2%), while the Eastern Mediterranean region had the lowest prevalence of AUD (0.8%). The other regions were similar in the prevalence of AUD: 4.7% in the

---

[6]Alcohol use disorder (AUD) defined by the *Diagnostic and Statistical Manual of Mental Disorders-5* (DSM-5).

Western Pacific, 3.9% in Southeast Asia, and 3.7% in Africa regions of each respective population 15 years or older suffered from AUD in 2016. The pattern observed with the prevalence of both HED and AUD reflect closely to the pattern found with the overall prevalence of alcohol consumption, such that the countries with a higher alcohol consumption experienced a higher prevalence of problems with alcohol consumption (Global Status Report on Alcohol and Health, 2018).

Cross-cultural research examines within country and between countries similarities and differences in behaviors. Comparing alcohol consumption across countries is not easy, however, because a myriad of social and individual factors affect alcohol consumption, such as culture, history, and law surrounding alcohol consumption (social factors), and gender, age, religion, and social class (individual factors). In addition, most countries are not homogenous and consist of multiple groups with different but shared patterns of beliefs and behaviors concerning alcohol consumption. As a commodity in the free market economy in many countries, moreover, alcohol consumption is influenced greatly by its availability and advertisement, perhaps more so than the cultural tradition of alcohol consumption in some countries. Finally, globalization and the commercialization of alcohol have increasingly blurred the national/regional boundaries.

It should, therefore, be noted that there are considerable variations within each of the WHO's six regions in not only alcohol consumption but also history, politics, economy, laws, and policies surrounding alcohol production, regulation, and consumption, minority relationships, and culture surrounding alcohol consumption. For instance, the Western Pacific region includes Anglo-Saxon countries like Australia and New Zealand and Asian countries like Japan, China, and South Korea. In addition, there are a number of studies that examined and found considerable differences in the consumption of alcohol patterns across Europe (Anderson & Baumberg, 2006).

Sociocultural correlates of alcohol consumption

Alcohol consumption is a social act, and thus solitary engagement of this behavior is rare (Heath, 1995), and alcohol consumption is an integral part of everyday life in many societies. As such, many sociocultural factors have considerable influence on this behavior, and some of the regional variations found in the WHO data are significantly related to sociocultural factors like age and gender, the law and religion, economic wealth of society, and culture surrounding alcohol consumption. Each of these factors are examined in this chapter, while referring to other cross-cultural studies that supplement the WHO data. The patterns of regional variations seen in these factors overall resemble the patterns of regional variations found in the prevalence of alcohol consumption, such that the prevalence of alcohol consumption among youth and females are the highest in higher-income countries in the

Europe region followed by the Americas and the Western Pacific regions and the lowest in the Eastern Mediterranean region, while the lower- and middle-income countries in the Southeast Asia and the Africa regions fall somewhere in the middle.

Age and law

Alcohol consumption among youth

The attitude toward drinking among youth (usually defined as younger than 18 years of age) varies by society. Drinking is central to the rites of passage in many countries (Hames, 2012), symbolizing the passage to adulthood. Many societies consider drinking among youth as a part of youthful rebellion during the period of time when youth often test the boundaries of their restricted autonomy and status within society (Heath, 1995). Some countries in Europe are known to introduce children at young age to wine during meals or for cerebration (Järvinen & Room, 2007). Though most countries instituted a national minimum age for purchasing alcohol, the minimum drinking age and other laws surrounding drinking among youth vary greatly by country.

According to the WHO, more than a quarter of youth between the ages of 15 and 19 years old worldwide were current drinkers (26.5%) in 2016. The regional difference in alcohol consumption among youth in this age group reflects the regional difference in the alcohol consumption of its entire population, though youth in this age group in all regions were less likely than their respective total population to be current drinkers or to engage in HED. Like the prevalence of current drinkers for the total population, the prevalence of current drinkers among youth in this age group was the highest in the Europe region (43.8%) and the lowest in the Eastern Mediterranean region (1.2%), while the Americas (38.2%) and the Western Pacific (37.9%) regions had almost twice the prevalence of the Africa (21.4%) and the South-East Asia (21.1%) regions (Global Status Report on Alcohol and Health, 2018).

Similar to the prevalence of current drinking among youth, the WHO also reports that the HED among youth between the ages 15–19 years old (see Fig. 16.5) was the highest in the Europe (24.1%) and the lowest in the Eastern Mediterranean (0.2%) regions, while the Western Pacific (18.8%) and the Americas (18.5%) regions had a higher prevalence of HED among youth than that of the Africa (12.7%) and the South-East Asia (10.2%) regions. Like the total population, the HED among youth was more common in high-income countries, such as Australia, Canada, New Zealand, and the United States. Among the population between the ages of 15–24 years old, overall engagement in HED was more common than any other age groups in most regions and the prevalence of HED among this age group was higher

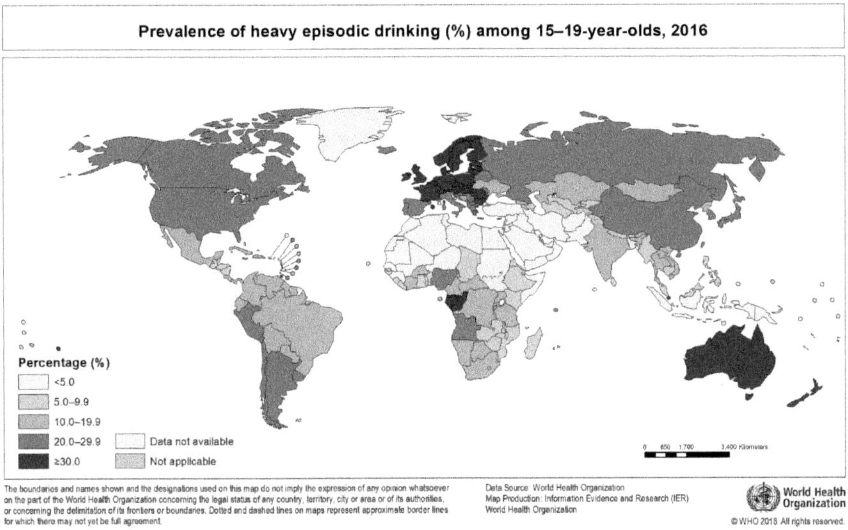

FIGURE 16.5. Percentage of heavy episodic drinking (HED) among youth by country, 2016.

than that of the total population in all regions, except in the Eastern Mediterranean region (Global Status Report on Alcohol and Health, 2018).

The early consumption of alcohol is one of the best predictors of experience with problems with drinking later in life (e.g., DeWit, Adlaf, Offord, & Ogborne, 2000; Warner & White, 2003). The 2014 National Survey on Drug Use and Health conducted in the United States, for instance, found that the prevalence of alcohol dependence or abuse[7] was almost four times higher for those who began drinking at age 14 or younger (15.4%) than those who began drinking at age 18 or older (3.8%) (Center for Behavioral Health Statistics and Quality, 2015). This association is found in other countries and found irrespective of preexisting psychological and other health problems (Liang & Chikritzhs, 2012, 2014). This is problematic as the WHO study found that many youth who were current drinkers began drinking before age 15 years old (Global Status Report on Alcohol and Health, 2018).

Legal minimum age for purchasing alcohol

Because of the strong connection between the early onset of drinking and later development of problem drinking, delaying the consumption of alcohol is advocated as an effective way to prevent the development of AUD (Bonomo, Bowes, Coffey, Carlin, & Patton, 2004). Raising the minimum age for purchasing alcohol could reduce alcohol consumption and alcohol-related problem behaviors among youth (Wagenaar & Toomey, 2002).

[7]Alcohol dependence and abuse are renamed as alcohol use disorder (AUD) in DSM-5.

According to the WHO, more than 90% of member states in 2016 had a national (or subnational) minimal legal age for purchasing alcohol, while eleven of mostly low-income member states located in the African region had no minimum legal age for purchasing alcohol. The minimum legal age for purchasing alcohol ranged worldwide from 13 years old in Burkina Faso to 25 years old in Eritrea, and the most popular minimum legal drinking age worldwide was 18 years old (over 100 WHO member states). The national legal drinking age for the aforementioned high-income countries with a high HED among youth was 18 years old in 2016, except in the United States where the national minimum drinking age is 21 years old (Global Health Observatory Data Repository, 2019).

According to the WHO, most countries in the Europe region with the high prevalence of alcohol consumption and HED among youth had the national legal drinking age at 18 years old. Only three countries (out of 53 countries) in the Europe region had a minimum legal drinking age above 18 years old (20 years old in Finland and Iceland and 21 years old in Kazakhstan). Though the European Union's repeated, but unsuccessful, attempt to set the minimum drinking age at 18 years old, seven countries in the Europe region had the minimum drinking age younger than 18 years old in 2016 (16 years old in Belgium, Germany, Luxemburg, San Marino, and Switzerland; and 17 years old in Cyprus and Malta). Of 21 member states in the Eastern Mediterranean region, only seven had a national minimum drinking age (others totally banned alcohol, had no national minimum drinking age, or did not report the information to the WHO), which included16 years old in Morocco; 18 years old in Jordan, Lebanon, and Syria; and 21 years old in Egypt, Iraq, and Oman (Global Health Data Observatory Repository, 2019).

Gender

Alcohol consumption among women

In all six WHO regions of the world in 2016, females compared to males were less likely to be current drinkers, were more likely to be former drinkers and lifetime abstainers, consumed a lower amount of APC, and were less likely to engage in HED. The WHO reports that the prevalence of current drinking among males was 53.7% and that for females was 32.4% worldwide in 2016. The regional difference in the male-to-female ratio of the prevalence of current drinkers matched the overall regional difference in alcohol consumption, such that while the Europe region had the smallest gender difference in the prevalence of current drinking (the male/female ratio of 1.3), followed closely by the Americas and the Western Pacific regions (both had the male/female ratio of 1.6), the Eastern Mediterranean region had the largest gender difference in the prevalence of current drinking (the male/female ratio = 3.8). Once again, the Africa and the South-East

Asia regions fell in the middle in terms of the gender difference in the prevalence of current drinking (both had the male/female ratio = 2.1). The total APC consumption worldwide in 2016 among males was 19.4 L per year, while females drank less than half of the amount that males drank (7.0 L per year). The male-to-female ratio of the APC did not differ much across the six regions and ranged from 2.7 to 2.8 (Global Status Report on Alcohol and Health, 2018).

Males and females differ in both rates and patterns of most behaviors that are considered deviant; males overall engage in deviance at higher rates than females, and the more serious and strongly condemned the behavior by society, the wider the gender difference (Daly, 1998; Hirtenlehner et al., 2014; Steffensmeier & Allan, 1996; Steffensmeier, Allen, & Streifel, 1989). Because alcohol consumption is not considered a serious nor strongly condemned behavior in most countries, compared to some other deviant behaviors (e.g., drug use), the gender difference in its prevalence is relatively small. For strongly condemned drinking behaviors such as problematic drinking, however, the gender difference tends to be greater. Confirming this, the WHO reports that the gender difference in the prevalence of the experience with HED (50.2% for males and 19.9% for females) was greater than that for current drinking (53.7% for males and 32.4% for females) in 2016. The male-to-female ratio for HED did not vary much across regions (ranged from 2.1 to 2.7), except in the Eastern Mediterranean region where the gender difference was twice in size (male/female ratio was 4.2) (Global Status Report on Alcohol and Health, 2018).

Reflecting the higher prevalence of deviance in general among youth, whether males or females, peaking around late teens to early twenties, the gender difference in substance use, including alcohol use, tends to be smaller among youth compared to older populations. Among 15-year-old boys and girls, for instance, the WHO's school survey project found that the past 30 days alcohol use shows very little gender difference in many countries (Global Status Report on Alcohol and Health, 2018). Furthermore, the gender difference in alcohol use among youth has possibly decreased over time in many countries because of the increase in gender equality around the world (more about this in the next section). The Monitoring the Future Survey conducted in the United States, for instance, reports that there was a 23%-point difference in the prevalence of "having five or more drinks in a row" among 12th grade boys and girls in 1975, which shrunk to a five percentage-point gender difference in 2014 (Johnston, O'Malley, Miech, Backman, & Schulenberg, 2015).

Gender norms and alcohol consumption

Gender norms that shape our beliefs concerning what behaviors are accepted in any given situation, including those associated with drinking alcohol, could explain the gender difference in alcohol consumption found in the WHO data. Alcohol use has historically been more strongly condemned among females compared to males, and gender norms are in general more restrictive of female behaviors and social interactions compared to those of males (Blume, 1997; Eagly & Wood, 1991; Eron & Huesmann, 1989; Kunkel & Nielsen, 1998; Tibbetts & Herz, 1996). Heath (1995, p. 337) notes that "[i]n many groups, drinking together is an important way men act out their stereotypes of masculinity with boisterous behavior, frequent expressions of aggression, boasting about their capacities for drink and sex, and otherwise underscoring exaggerated caricatures." Men in the United Kingdom and Australia, for instance, have been known to engage in a custom of buying rounds of drinks among friends and coworkers, which could perpetuate the male-dominated alcohol culture in these countries (Hall & Hunter, 1995; Plant, 1995).

Empirical research indicates that gender norms concerning all aspects of behaviors and social interactions, including alcohol consumption, are more strongly prescribed in countries characterized by greater gender inequality (Kashima et al., 1995; Nayak, Byrne, Martin, & Abraham, 2003), thus creating greater differences in behaviors of males and females in countries with greater gender inequality than countries that are more egalitarian. Likewise, cross-cultural research indicates a greater gender difference in alcohol use found in societies that adhere to more traditional gender roles compared to egalitarian societies (Gefou-Madianou, 1992; Tedor, Quinn, Wilsnack, Wilsnack, & Greenfield, 2018; Wilsnack, Vogeltanz, Wilsnack, & Harris, 2000; Wilsnack, Wilsnack, Kristjanson, Vogeltanz-Holm, & Gmel, 2009).

The data from the WHO on the gender difference in alcohol consumption with the data from the World Economic Forum's Global Gender Gap Report (2018)[8] that ranks countries on the index of gender equality[9] are combined to examine the relationship between the gender difference in alcohol consumption and gender equality. The zero-order correlation analysis indicates that the gender differences in prevalence of lifetime abstainers ($r = -0.69$, $P < .001$, $n = 149$), non-current drinkers ($r = -0.67$ $P < .001$, $n = 149$), HED ($r = -0.51$, $P < .001$, $n = 149$), and AUD ($r = -0.33$, $P < .001$, $n = 144$) were all significantly and negatively related to the index of gender equality.[10] Confirming previous studies, these negative relationships indicate that the greater the gender equality, the smaller the gender difference in

[8]Of the 194 countries, 45 countries did not have the index score on gender equality.

[9]The index was calculated based on "economic participation and opportunity," "educational attainment," "health and survival," and "political empowerment" (Global Gender Gap Report, 2018, p. 4).

[10]The total number of cases indicated by n varies because not all information was reported by countries examined in the report.

alcohol consumption measured in terms of the prevalence of current drinking, lifetime abstinence, and the experience with HED and AUD.

Religion and law

Religion often plays an important role in guiding and controlling behaviors that are morally uncertain, such as ascetic behaviors involving drinking, eating, and sex, especially when secular controls are weak or unclear on these behaviors (Burkett & White, 1974; Cochran, 1988; Grasmick, Bursik, & Cochran, 1991; Middleton & Putney, 1962; Tittle & Welch, 1983). Though many religions have incorporated alcohol into its religious rituals, others outright prohibit or discourage alcohol consumption (e.g., Islam and some Protestant denominations). The attitude toward alcohol, however, often varies significantly within the same religion (Tuck, Robinson, Agic, Ialomiteanu, & Mann, 2017), across countries of the same religion, and within the same country when different religious groups are examined (Engs, Hanson, Gliksman, & Smythe, 1990). When examined at the individual level, religiosity has a strong preventive effect on alcohol consumption, moreover, no matter the religion (Cochran, Beeghly, & Bock, 1988). It is, therefore, important to consider not just the religion or religious denomination but also the level of religiosity (measured, for instance, as the frequency of religious service attendance) in explaining alcohol use at the individual level.

In 2016, 99 countries that reported to the WHO had some kind of national alcohol policy in place; higher-income countries (67%) were more likely than lower-income countries (15%) to have in place a national alcohol policy, while the majority of countries in the Americas and African regions did not have a national alcohol policy in 2016 (Global Status Report on Alcohol and Health, 2018).

Of the countries that had a national alcohol policy, the WHO reports that eleven countries instituted a total ban on alcohol. These countries were in the Africa (Mauritania), the Eastern Mediterranean (Afghanistan, Iran, Libya, Pakistan, Saudi Arabia, Somalia, Sudan, United Arab Emirates, Yemen) and the South-East Asia (Maldives) regions (Global Status Report on Alcohol and Health, 2018). All eleven of these dry countries were Muslim-majority countries, but not all Muslim-majority countries (e.g., Algeria, Azerbaijan, Bangladesh, Egypt, Gambia, Guinea, Indonesia, Jordan, Kosovo, Morocco, Niger, Senegal, Somalia, among others) banned alcohol in 2016. Islam has a long history of prohibition of alcohol consumption and other intoxicants. Many Muslims are even against taking medicines that contain alcohol (Powell, 2004). Many Muslim-majority countries, however, do not necessarily have a clearly developed national policy on alcohol consumption (Al-Ansari, Thow, Day, & Conigrave, 2016).

The attitude toward alcohol in Christianity changed over time and varies across denominations and countries. In Medieval Europe, wine was consumed as a part of daily life, theology was often done while drinking alcohol, and many churches made their own beers (Robertson, 2004). Protestant Christianity overall has adopted a more prohibitive attitude toward alcohol consumption today and advocates abstinence, while considering drinking as a sinful behavior. When the United States experimented on the national ban on alcohol between 1920 and 1933, the temperance movement was led by Protestant church members, and total or partial bans on alcohol consumption at the local level still remain in place to this day mainly in the south (Robertson, 2004).

Like other religious writings, the Hebrew Bible offers mixed messages on alcohol consumption, considering its overindulgence as a sin but also considering wine as a gift from God. Like most religions, however, Judaism overall discourages the heavy consumption and encourages moderate consumption of alcohol (Hames, 2012; Neumark, Rahav, Teichman, & Hasin, 2001). Alcohol consumption is found to be significantly lower among Jews compared to Protestants (Yeung & Greenwald, 1992) and that Jews overall have less favorable attitude toward alcohol than Protestants (Loewenthal, Macleod, Cook, Lee, & Goldblatt, 2003).

Practiced by more than 500 million people worldwide, mostly in Asia, Buddhism consists of many different denominations/schools. Though the view on drinking and intoxication might vary by denomination, alcohol has played an important part of religious ceremonies in the Buddhist tradition. Buddhism, however, teaches against excessive alcohol consumption and encourages moderate use like most religions that do not prohibit drinking (Newman, Shell, Li, & Innadda, 2006). Studies that compare the alcohol consumption across different religions, however, often find that those who identify as Buddhists engage in a higher level of problem drinking, often equally as high as atheists, compared to those who identify as Baptist, Christian, Hindu, Jewish, or Muslim (Tuck et al., 2017), and Buddhists often have a much more favorable attitude toward alcohol, almost as favorable as non-religious individuals, compared to Christians and Muslims (Najjar, Young, Leasure, Henderson, & Neighbors, 2016). Some studies also find that Buddhists were least religious when it was measured in terms of the frequency of religious service attendance (Tuck et al., 2017 in the case of Canadian population).

Since the Vedic Period in 1500–700 BCE, alcohol has been part of everyday lives in India where Hinduism was born and mainly practiced. During the Vedic Period, an intoxicating drink, *soma*, was considered sacred, and *sura*, a kind of beer, was popularly consumed among the general public. Alcoholic beverages were, however, prohibited among Brahmins. During the Islamic rule in 1100–1800 CE, alcohol consumption in the form of wine remained in India, though Islam strongly prohibited the consumption of any intoxicants. Under the British rule in 1800–1847, the consumption of alcohol gradually increased, and the first brewery was established in India in 1805 by British colonists who craved beers. The Indian Pale Ale refers to the brew of beer that became popular in India. After independence in 1970s, some states in India attempted to prohibit alcohol consumption, and today one big and three small Indian states have legal prohibition of the sales of alcohol, but alcohol consumption remains an important part of everyday life for many Indians (Sharma, Tripathi, & Pelto, 2010), where 38.3% of the population of India over 15 years of age are current drinkers (Global Status Report on Alcohol and Health, 2018).

Economic wealth

Alcohol consumption is often related to status and economic wealth because drinking requires monetary resources. Individuals with greater economic wealth are, therefore, more likely than those who are poor in any society to consume alcohol and are less likely to be abstainers (Bloomfield, Grittner, Kramer, & Gmel, 2006). Alcohol consumption is also related to status as those with a higher status often have greater access to alcohol because of their wealth than those with a lower status in the society, especially in poorer countries (Global Status Report on Alcohol and Health, 2018). In any given society, however, for the same amount of alcohol, those who are poor and their family members experience much greater harm from alcohol consumption (e.g., chronic and infectious diseases and alcohol-related injuries) than those with greater economic wealth and their family members who have the means to offset the harms (Schmidt & Room, 2012), and such health inequality is more pronounced in countries without universal healthcare like the United States (Global Status Report on Alcohol and Health, 2018).

As an important source of tax in many countries, alcohol is also significantly intertwined with economy, the law, and the politics. Some states in India, for instance, abandoned the idea of instituting full prohibition because of the money from taxation that alcohol can generate and an increase in alcohol black market during prohibition (Sharma et al., 2010). Countries that have higher levels of alcohol consumption are overall those with greater economic wealth in the Europe, the Americas, and the Western Pacific regions. Indeed, as discussed in the previous section, the WHO indicates overall these countries tend to have a higher prevalence of current drinkers, a lower prevalence of lifetime abstainers, and tend to drink more alcohol than countries with a less economic wealth.

The economic progress of society often accompanies an increase in alcohol consumption and a decrease in abstinence, except in Muslim-majority countries (Probst, Manthey, & Rehm, 2017). Moreover, economic progress of society also accompanies an increase in alcohol-related harm because of the increase in its overall consumption that results from the commercialization of alcohol and an increase in availability of alcohol in the society (Rorabaugh, 1979). Because of the globalization and commercialization of alcohol more quickly spreading around the globe today, middle- and lower-income countries have experienced much faster spread of alcohol than they could put in place ways to counter the harms associated with alcohol consumption. For instance, Eastern Europe after the collapse of the Soviet Union experienced the spread of commercialized alcohol and unprecedented increase in alcohol consumption and harms resulting from alcohol consumption (Neufeld & Rehm, 2018), resulting in Russian Federation having the highest prevalence of HED worldwide, as discussed earlier.

According to the WHO, the prevalence of HED and consumption of unregulated APC was much higher in middle- and lower-income counties (almost 40% of all alcohol consumed) than in high-income countries (11.4% of all alcohol consumed), likely explaining the much more detrimental negative health effects of alcohol consumption experienced by those who are poor compared to those with wealth, especially in poor countries. Though the richer countries such as those in Europe had the highest consumption of alcohol, the poorer countries such as those in Africa tend to suffer the greatest amount of harmful effects of alcohol consumption while unfortunately having the lowest government commitment to implementing interventions for reducing the harms associated with alcohol consumption (Global Status Report on Alcohol and Health, 2018).

Culture surrounding alcohol consumption

> *Alcohol is a cultural artifact; the form and meanings of drinking alcoholic beverages are culturally defined, as are the uses of any other major artifact. The form is usually quite explicitly stipulated, including the kind of drink that can be used, the amount and rate of intake, the time and place of drinking, the accompanying ritual, the sex and age of the drinker, the roles involved in drinking, and the role behavior proper to drinking. The meanings of drinking, its relation to other aspects of the culture and society, are usually more implicit. Thus drinking in a particular society may be either a sacred or a profane act, depending on the context, and the people may not be aware of the basic principles and meaning that are actually involved.*
>
> Marshall (1979, p. 15)

There have been almost as many definitions of culture offered as there are people who study culture. Cross-cultural psychologists, Matsumoto and Juang (2004, p. 12), consider culture as "a sociopsychological construct, a sharing across people of psychological phenomena such as values, attitudes, beliefs, and behaviors." Culture encompasses everything, including material objects (e.g., the drinkware used for a specific alcoholic beverage), symbols (e.g., languages used to describe "inebriation"), practices (e.g., rituals for drinking), norms (e.g., accepted behaviors while intoxicated), beliefs (e.g., expectations of psychoactive effects of alcohol), and values (e.g., the importance of alcohol in a religion). Cultural systems refer to the interconnections among these different elements of culture that govern our behaviors and interactions with others and keep some order in society.

Scholars have long examined similarities and differences between societies' cultures surrounding alcohol consumption in order to explain the variations in problem drinking across societies. This section summarizes some of the popular typologies of culture on alcohol consumption, each of which focuses on different aspects of culture (see for a summary, Heath, 1995; Room & Mäkelä, 2000; Savic, Room, Mugavin, Pennay, & Livingston, 2016; Wilson, 2005).

Wine, beer, and spirits cultures

When examining country variations in alcohol consumption, scholars popularly group countries based on the type of alcoholic beverages predominantly consumed and to attempt to subscribe unique drinking behaviors and attitudes toward drinking, such that Germany and Australia are seen as "beer culture," France, Chile, Greece, and Italy are seen as "wine culture" or "Mediterranean culture," Poland and Russia are seen as "spirits culture." Wine cultures tend to drink alcohol in moderate amounts with meals, while beer cultures tend to drink alcohol at bars (Sulkunen, 1976, 1983).

Heath (1995), however, argues that this typology poses several problems. First, there are considerable geographic variations within any given society in the type of alcoholic beverages popularly consumed (e.g., there are regions in France where beers are more predominantly consumed than wine). Second, popular alcoholic beverage often varies by different segments of society (e.g., there are often gender, ethnic, and class differences in the preferred type of alcoholic beverage). Third, many societies have adopted alcoholic beverages that are not indigenous through importation or colonialization and economic exploitation and have favored different types of alcoholic beverage at different times periods (e.g., wine was not the predominant alcoholic beverage in Spain and Italy only until a century ago). It is, therefore, difficult to assume that a unique culture has developed and is shared by the people based on a type of alcoholic beverage that is predominately preferred today in any given society.

Four cultural patterns of drinking

Pittman (1964) created a typology of cultural patterns of alcohol consumption based on the difference in the attitude toward alcohol consumption: *abstinence cultures* strongly condemn the consumption of alcoholic beverages in any form (e.g., Muslims and some Protestants), *ambivalent cultures* hold both negative and positive attitudes toward alcohol consumption (e.g., English-speaking and Scandinavian nations), *permissive cultures* condemn excessive consumption but tolerate moderate consumption of alcohol (e.g., Jews and Italians), *overly permissive cultures* tolerate alcohol consumption and even the state of inebriation or "drunkenness" under some circumstances (e.g., French and Japanese). Some countries might fit in more than one of these cultural patterns. For instance, unlike other societies, Mohan and Sharma (1995) argue that India never accepted alcohol as a part of everyday discourse nor a part of religious ritual, thus there are no shared normative patterns of alcohol consumption or attitude toward alcohol. India would, thus, fit both abstinence and permissive cultural patterns.

Temperance culture

According to Heath (1995), Protestant English-speaking countries such as the United States and Scandinavian countries like Sweden are considered temperance cultures because of their long history of the temperance movement and the deep-seated perception of alcohol as a serious social problem by some segments of society. This might explain why solitary drinking, as a shameful behavior that needs to be engaged in secret, rather than social drinking that describes alcohol consumption in most societies, is more common in the United States compared to other countries (Heath, 1995; Keough, O'Connor, & Stewart, 2018). Studies of alcohol and research institutions (e.g., National Institute of Health), dominated by researchers in the U.S., therefore, tend to take the "alcohol as a social problem" and "alcohol as a disease" approach (Savic & Room, 2014). Studies find that countries that are characterized by temperance culture tend to have lower prevalence of overall alcohol consumption but exhibit unhealthy relationships with alcohol with high prevalence of problem drinking (e.g., binge drinking) and, thus, the experience with greater negative health consequences of alcohol consumption (Peele, 2010).

Wet culture vs. dry culture

Countries that are considered "wet culture" are those with fewer restrictions placed on the regulation of alcohol consumption, production, and sales (such as Denmark, France, Spain, and Italy), while countries that are considered "dry culture" or "temperance culture" (see above) are those with greater restriction on alcohol regulation (such as Egypt, the United States, and Sweden). Wet cultures tend to have a more favorable attitude toward alcohol consumption, have a high level of alcohol consumption, and experience greater alcohol-related health problems but less drinking to get drunk or drunkenness. Dry cultures, on the other hand, tend to have less frequent drinking but more heavy drinking, drunkenness, and other alcohol-related social problems such as violence (Room & Mitchell, 1972; Savic et al., 2016). Room (1976) attributes the high occurrence of alcohol-related social problems in dry cultures to their long history of temperance and their deep-seated perception of alcohol as a serious social problem, as discussed above. This typology is one of the first to consider the difference in the system of social control (i.e., alcohol regulation) in explaining alcohol consumption and related problems (Savic et al., 2016).

Cultural norms of alcohol consumption

Room and Mäkelä (2000) offered a comprehensive typology that includes seven dimensions of culture of alcohol consumption. The first dimension is concerned with the *regularity* in which alcohol is consumed, such as whether or not drinking is incorporated as a part of daily routine (e.g., drinking with meals in wine-drinking countries) or done only for special circumstances (e.g., religious ritual or cerebration). The second dimension is concerned with the *extent of drunkenness*, which takes into account the country difference in the definition of "drunkenness" and the purpose of such intoxication (e.g., some religious practices incorporate the state of intoxication). The other five dimensions are concerned with the *purpose* of drinking (e.g., for nutrition, intoxication, socializing), *social control* of drinking (e.g., alcohol regulation), the *context* of the drinking (e.g., the cultural position of the drinker), *drinking-related problems* and their controls, and *expectations* of behaviors while intoxicated.

Like gender norms, cultural norms surrounding drinking affect how people drink and the beliefs concerning behaviors associated with drinking that are considered acceptable or problematic, such as inebriation, excessive drinking, public display of intoxication, and alcohol-related violence (Greenfield & Room, 1997; Room & Mäkelä, 2000). Mizruchi and Perrucci (1970) classified countries broadly into three types based on the difference in the cultural norms surrounding alcohol consumption but not specific behaviors associated with drinking. According to them, proscriptive cultures strongly condemn alcohol consumption (e.g., Muslims, Mormons, Methodists) and lack prescriptive norms or specific drinking norms (e.g., how much alcohol is appropriate, who should drink, and how to drink, and so on) that guide prescriptive cultures that condemn drunkenness but consider drinking as an expected behavior (e.g., Jews, Italians). Mizruchi and Perrucci (1970) argue that individuals from prospective cultures who begin drinking with individuals from prescriptive cultures, therefore, are more likely to develop drinking problems because they lack norms surrounding drinking. According to Mizruchi and Perrucci (1970), permissive cultures, like proscriptive cultures, have no specified norms surrounding alcohol consumption (e.g., North American, Finnish), therefore, those who drink in permissive cultures are also more likely to experience drinking problems.

Savic et al. (2016) offer two major critiques and suggestions for the study of alcohol culture. First, most typologies of drinking culture focus solely on alcohol consumption and problems of alcohol consumption, thereby isolating "alcohol consumption and problems from the network of other possible interactional and cultural factors involved" (Savic et al., 2016, p. 279). Alcohol consumption, like any other social behaviors, is not done in a vacuum. The exclusive focus on the behavior to explain its culture, therefore, ignores how the social structure and culture interact. For instance, none of the typology considers how economic inequality between countries might explain country variations or how economic inequality within a country might explain individual variations in the ways this behavior is engaged or problems of this behavior are experienced. Second, while most typologies only focused on the culture of drinking at the macro or country level, it is also important to consider the interactions among all different levels (e.g., individual, group, and country). None of the typology, for instance, considers how drinking culture might affect drinking behaviors differently for men and women or racial ethnic minorities.

Conclusion

The WHO's *Global Survey on Alcohol and Health* report highlighted differences in the level and pattern of alcohol consumption across regions of the world and some sociocultural correlates of alcohol consumption such as age, gender, the law, religion, and economy. The report also underlined the way alcohol consumption perpetuates economic inequality within and between societies because of its detrimental health, social, and economic effects on the vulnerable members in any society, especially in lower-income counties. WHO, therefore, states that the production and consumption of alcohol, especially in absence of societal intervention, could significantly undermine the United Nations' goals of "ending poverty," "reducing inequalities between and within countries," and "achieving gender equality" (Global Status Report on Alcohol & Health, 2018, p. 3). Any cross-cultural study of alcohol and typology of culture on alcohol consumption, therefore, should take into account the existing economic inequality, health disparity, gender inequality, the political disparity or the lack of government commitment for prevention and the detrimental effect of globalization and increasing commercialization of alcohol in lower-income countries.

References

Al-Ansari, B., Thow, A. M., Day, C. A., & Conigrave, K. M. (2016). Extent of alcohol prohibition in civil policy in Muslim majority countries: The impact of globalization. *Addiction*, *10*, 1703.

Anderson, P., & Baumberg, B. (2006). *Alcohol in Europe: A public health perspective*. UK: Institute of Alcohol Studies.

Bloomfield, K., Grittner, U., Kramer, S., & Gmel, G. (2006). Social inequalities in alcohol consumption and alcohol-related problems in the study countries of the EU concerted action 'gender, culture and alcohol problems: A multi-national study'. *Alcohol and Alcoholism, 41*(1), 26–36.

Blume, S. B. (1997). Women and alcohol: Issues in social policy. In R. W. Wilsnack, & R. D. Wilsnack (Eds.), *Gender and alcohol: Individual and social perspectives* (pp. 462–489). New Brunswick, NJ: Rutgers Center of Alcohol Studies.

Bonomo, Y. A., Bowes, G., Coffey, C., Carlin, J. B., & Patton, G. C. (2004). Teenage drinking and the onset of alcohol dependence: A cohort study over seven years. *Addiction, 99*(12), 1520–1528.

Burkett, S. R., & White, M. (1974). Hellfire and delinquency: Another look. *Journal for the Scientific Study of Religion, 13*(4), 455–462.

Center for Behavioral Health Statistics and Quality. (2015). *Behavioral health trends in the United States: Results from the 2014 National Survey on Drug Use and Health* (HHS Publication No. SMA 15-4927, NSDUH Series H-50). <http://www.samhsa.gov/data/>.

Cochran, J. K. (1988). The effect of religiosity on secular and ascetic deviance. *Sociological Focus, 21*(4), 293–306.

Cochran, J. K., Beeghly, L., & Bock, E. W. (1988). Religiosity and alcohol behavior: An exploration of reference group theory. *Sociological Forum, 3*, 256–276.

Daly, K. (1998). Gender, crime, and criminology. In M. H. Tonry (Ed.), *The handbook of crime and punishment* (pp. 85–108). New York: Oxford University Press.

DeWit, D. J., Adlaf, E. M., Offord, D. R., & Ogborne, A. C. (2000). Age at first alcohol use: A risk factor for the development of alcohol disorders. *American Journal of Psychiatry, 157*(5), 745–750.

Eagly, A. H., & Wood, W. (1991). Explaining sex differences in social behavior: A meta-analytic perspective. *Personality and Social Psychology Bulletin, 17*(3), 306–315.

Engs, R. C., Hanson, D. J., Gliksman, L., & Smythe, C. (1990). Influence of religion and culture on drinking behaviours: A test of hypotheses between Canada and the USA. *British Journal of Addiction, 85*, 1475–1482.

Eron, L. D., & Huesmann, L. R. (1989). The genesis of gender differences in aggression. In M. Luzzcz, & T. Niemela (Eds.), *Psychological development: Perspective across the life-span* (pp. 55–67). New York: Elsevier Science.

Gefou-Madianou, D. (Ed.), (1992). *Alcohol, gender and culture*. New York: Routledge.

Global Health Observatory Data Repository. 2019. <http://apps.who.int/gho/data/node.home> Accessed 28.03.19.

Global Status Report on Alcohol and Health (2018). Geneva, Switzerland: World Health Organization; 2018. Licence: CC BY-NC-SA 3.0 IGO.

Grasmick, H. G., Bursik, R. J., Jr., & Cochran, J. K. (1991). "Render unto Caesar what is Caesar's": Religiosity and taxpayers' inclination to cheat. *Sociological Quarterly, 32*(2), 251–266.

Greenfield, T. K., & Room, R. (1997). Situational norms for drinking and drunkenness: Trends in the U.S. adult population, 1979–1990. *Addiction, 92*(1), 33–47.

Hall, W., & Hunter, E. (1995). Australia. In D. B. Heath (Ed.), *International handbook on alcohol and culture* (pp. 7–19). Westport, CT: Greenwood.

Hames, G. (2012). *Alcohol in world history*. New York: Routledge.

Heath, D. B. (1986). Cultural definitions of drinking: Notes toward a semantic approach. *The Drinking and Drug Practices Surveyor, 21*, 17–22.

Heath, D. B. (Ed.), (1995). *International handbook on alcohol and culture*. Westport, CT: Greenwood Press.

Hirtenlehner H., Blackwell B., Leitgoeb H., and Bacher J. (2014). Explaining the gender gap in juvenile shoplifting: a power-control theoretical analysis. *Deviant Behavior. 35*(1), 41–65.

Järvinen, M., & Room, R. (Eds.), (2007). *Youth drinking cultures: European experiences*. Burlington, VT: Ashgate Publishing Company.

Johnston, L. D., O'Malley, P. M., Miech, R. A., Backman, J. G., & Schulenberg, J. E. (2015). *Monitoring the future national survey results on drug use, 1975–2014: Volume 2, college students and adults ages 19–55*. Ann Arbor, MI: The University of Michigan, Institute for Social Research.

Kashima, Y., Yamaguchi, S., Kim, U., Choi, S., Gelfand, M. J., & Yuki, M. (1995). Culture, gender, and self: A perspective from individualism-collectivism research. *Journal of Personality and Social Psychology, 69*(5), 925–937.

Keough, M. T., O'Connor, R. M., & Stewart, S. H. (2018). Solitary drinking is associated with specific alcohol problems in emerging adults. *Addictive Behaviors, 76*, 285–290.

Kunkel, C., & Nielsen, J. M. (1998). Gender, residual deviance, and social control. *Deviant Behavior, 19*(4), 339–360.

Liang, W., & Chikritzhs, T. (2012). The association between age at first use of alcohol and alcohol consumption levels among adult general drinking population. *Journal of Public Health, 20*, 615–620.

Liang, W., & Chikritzhs, T. (2014). Age at first use of alcohol predicts the risk of heavy alcohol use in early adulthood: A longitudinal study in the United States. *International Journal of Drug Policy, 26*(2), 131–134.

Loewenthal, K. M., Macleod, A. K., Cook, S., Lee, M., & Goldblatt, V. (2003). Beliefs about alcohol among UK Jews and Protestants: Do they fit the alcohol-depression hypothesis? *Social Psychiatry and Psychiatric Epidemiology (Print), 3*, 122.

Marshall, M. (Ed.), (1979). *Beliefs, behaviors, & alcoholic beverages: A cross-cultural survey*. Ann Arbor, MI: The University of Michigan Press.

Matsumoto, D., & Juang, L. (2004). *Culture and psychology* (3rd ed.). Belmont, CA: Thomson, Wadsworth.

Middleton, R., & Putney, S. (1962). Religion, normative standards, and behavior. *Sociometry, 25*, 145–152.

Mizruchi, E. H., & Perrucci, R. (1970). *Prescription, proscription and permissiveness: Aspects of norms and deviant drinking behavior*. New Haven, CT: College and University Press.

Mohan, D., & Sharma, H. K. (1995). India. In D. B. Heath (Ed.), *International handbook on alcohol and culture* (pp. 128–141). Westport, CT: Greenwood.

Najjar, L. Z., Young, C. M., Leasure, L., Henderson, C. E., & Neighbors, C. (2016). Religious perceptions of alcohol consumption and drinking behaviours among religious and non-religious groups. *Mental Health, Religion & Culture, 19*(9), 1028–1041.

Nayak, M. B., Byrne, C. A., Martin, M. K., & Abraham, A. G. (2003). Attitudes toward violence against women: A cross-national study. *Sex Roles, 49*(7/8), 333–342.

Neufeld, M., & Rehm, J. (2018). Effectiveness of policy changes to reduce harm from unrecorded alcohol in Russia between 2005 and now. *International Journal of Drug Policy, 51*, 1–9.

Neumark, Y. D., Rahav, G., Teichman, M., & Hasin, D. (2001). Alcohol drinking patterns among Jewish and Arab men and women in Israel. *Journal of Studies on Alcohol, 62*, 443–447.

Newman, I. M., Shell, D. F., Li, T., & Innadda, S. (2006). Buddhism and adolescent alcohol use in Thailand. *Substance Use & Misuse, 41*(13), 1789–1800.

Peele, S. (2010). Alcohol as evil – Temperance and policy. *Addiction Research & Theory, 18*(4), 374–382.
Pittman, D. J. (1964). *Social and cultural factors in drinking patterns, pathological and non-pathological, . Selected papers presented at the 27th international congress on alcohol and alcoholism* (Vol. 1, pp. 1–13). Lausanne: International Council on Alcohol and Alcoholism.
Plant, M. A. (1995). The United Kingdom. In D. B. Heath (Ed.), *International handbook on alcohol and culture* (pp. 289–299). Westport, CT: Greenwood.
Powell, A. J. (2004). Only in paradise: Alcohol and Islam. In C. K. Robertson (Ed.), *Religion and alcohol: Sobering thoughts* (pp. 95–110). New York: Peter Lang Publishing, Inc.
Probst, C., Manthey, J., & Rehm, J. (2017). Understanding the prevalence of lifetime abstinence from alcohol: An ecological study. *Drug and Alcohol Dependence, 178*(1), 126–129.
Robertson, C. K. (2004). Mixed drinks or mixed messages? An introduction. In C. K. Robertson (Ed.), *Religion and alcohol: Sobering thoughts* (pp. 1–10). New York: Peter Lang Publishing, Inc.
Room, R. (1976). Ambivalence as a sociological explanation: The case of cultural explanations of alcohol problems. *American Sociological Review, 41*(6), 1047.
Room, R., & Mäkelä, K. (2000). Typologies of the cultural position of drinking. *Journal of Studies on Alcohol, 61*(3), 475–483.
Room, R., & Mitchell, A. (1972). Notes on cross-national and cross- cultural studies. *Drinking and Drug Practices Surveyor, 5*, 16–20.
Rorabaugh, W. J. (1979). *The alcoholic republic: An American tradition*. New York: Oxford University Press.
Savic, M., & Room, R. (2014). Differences in alcohol-related research publication output between countries: A manifestation of societal concern? *European Addiction Research, 20* (6), 319.
Savic, M., Room, R., Mugavin, J., Pennay, A., & Livingston, M. (2016). Editor's choice: Defining 'drinking culture': A critical review of its meaning and connotation in social research on alcohol problems. *Drugs: Education, Prevention & Policy, 23*(4), 270–282.
Schmidt, L., & Room, R. (2012). Alcohol and the process of economic development: Contributions from ethnographic research. *International Journal of Alcohol and Drug Research, 1*, 1–15.
Sharma, H. K., Tripathi, B. M., & Pelto, P. J. (2010). The evolution of alcohol use in India. *AIDS & Behavior, 14*, 8–17.
Steffensmeier, D., & Allen, E. (1996). Gender and crime: Toward a gendered theory of female offending. *Annual Review of Sociology, 22*, 459–487.
Steffensmeier, D., Allan, E., & Streifel, C. (1989). Development and female crime: A cross-national test of alternative explanations. *Social Forces, 68*, 262–283.
Sulkunen, P. (1976). Drinking patterns and the level of alcohol consumption: An international overview. In R. Gibbins, Y. Israel, H. Kalant, R. E. Popham, W. Schmidt, & R. G. Smart (Eds.), *Research advances in alcohol and drug problems* (Vol. 3). New York: Wiley.
Sulkunen, P. (1983). Alcohol consumption and the transformation of living conditions. In R. G. Smart, F. B. laser, Y. Israel, H. Kalant, R. E. Popham, & W. Schmidt (Eds.), *Research advances in alcohol and drug problems* (Vol. 7, pp. 247–298). New York: Plenum Press.
Tedor, M. F., Quinn, L. M., Wilsnack, L. C., Wilsnack, R. W., & Greenfield, T. K. (2018). Gender and country differences in alcohol-aggression expectancy and alcohol-related intimate partner violence. *Deviant Behavior, 39*(5), 554–575.
The Global Gender Gap Report. (2018). Geneva, Switzerland: World Economic Forum.
Tibbetts, S. G., & Herz, D. C. (1996). Gender differences in factors of social control and rational choice. *Deviant Behavior, 17*(2), 183–208.

Tittle, C. R., & Welch, M. R. (1983). Religiosity and deviance: Toward a contingency theory of constraining effects. *Social Forces*, *61*(3), 653–682.

Tuck, A., Robinson, M., Agic, B., Ialomiteanu, A., & Mann, R. (2017). Religion, alcohol use and risk drinking among Canadian adults living in Ontario. *Journal of Religion & Health*, *56*(6), 2023.

Warner, L. A., & White, H. R. (2003). Longitudinal effects of age at onset and first drinking situations on problem drinking. *Substance use and misuse*, *38*(14), 1983–2016.

Wagenaar, A. C., & Toomey, T. L. (2002). Effects of minimum drinking age laws: Review and analyses of the literature from 1960 to 2000. *Journal of Studies on Alcohol*, *14*, 206–225.

Wilsnack, R. W., Vogeltanz, N. D., Wilsnack, S. C., & Harris, T. R. (2000). Gender differences in alcohol consumption and adverse drinking consequences: Cross-cultural patterns. *Addiction*, *95*(2), 251–265.

Wilsnack, R. W., Wilsnack, S. C., Kristjanson, A. F., Vogeltanz-Holm, N. D., & Gmel, G. (2009). Gender and alcohol consumption: Patterns from the multinational GENACIS project. *Addiction*, *104*(9), 1487–1500.

Wilson, T. M. (Ed.), (2005). *Drinking cultures: Alcohol and identity*. New York: Berg.

Yeung, P. P., & Greenwald, S. (1992). Jewish Americans and Mental Health – Results of the NIMH catchment area study. *Osical Psychiatry and Psychiatric Epidemiology*, *27*, 292–297.

Chapter 17

Alcohol and the legal system: Effects of alcohol on eyewitness testimony

Julie Gawrylowicz[1] and Georgina Bartlett[2]
[1]*Division of Psychology and Forensic Science, School of Applied Sciences, Abertay University, Dundee, United Kingdom,* [2]*Centre for Addictive Behaviours Research, Division of Psychology, School of Applied Sciences, London South Bank University, London, United Kingdom*

Prevalence and extent of the intoxicated witness problem

There is a strong association between alcohol consumption and crime. The Office for National Statistics (ONS) reported that in England and Wales in the year ending 2017 more alcohol-related offenses were reported to the police than non-alcohol related offenses (Office for National Statistics, 2018). Furthermore, crime often occurs in and around places where alcohol is sold and consumed. Leonard, Quigley, and Collins (2002) found that bars were the most common location to experience aggression and threats. In England and Wales, 25% of incidents of stranger violence took place in pubs and clubs (ONS, 2017). Alcohol seems to be a triggering factor for antisocial behavior. In Scotland, 46% of violent crimes involved offenders under the influence (Scottish Crime and Justice Survey, 2019). In Norway, 53% of assault victims being treated at an emergency department reported that their attacker was under the influence (Steen & Hunskaar, 2004). A similar picture emerges for victims to crime. Scottish victims reported to have consumed alcohol prior to violent incidents in 25% of the cases (Scottish Crime and Justice Survey, 2019). In the Netherlands between 1970 and 1998, 36% of victims attending a Trauma Center for violence-related injuries had consumed alcohol (Kingma, 2000). In addition to victims and perpetrators, a considerable number of eyewitnesses are under the influence of alcohol. A survey of US police officers found that 53% of investigators reported that contact with intoxicated witnesses is common and a further 20% that it is very common (Evans, Schreiber Compo, & Russano, 2009). A more recent survey with English Police Officers found that in 44% of interviews

The Handbook of Alcohol Use - Understandings from Synapse to Society.
DOI: https://doi.org/10.1016/B978-0-12-816720-5.00016-5

witnesses were drunk at the time of the crime (Crossland, Kneller, & Wilcock, 2018). Palmer, Flowe, Takarangi, and Humphries (2013) studied cases involving sober and intoxicated witnesses in felony criminal cases that were sampled from a US Attorney's case archive. Thirteen percent of the witnesses and 29% of the suspects across all cases were reportedly under the influence of alcohol. Intriguingly, intoxicated witnesses were significantly more likely than sober ones to have been given the opportunity to describe the perpetrator to the police and they were equally likely to take part in an identification parade. From both surveys and the archival analysis (Crossland et al., 2018; Evans et al., 2009; Palmer et al., 2013) it transpired that witnesses and victims are not routinely breathalyzed at the scene and that officers use their own judgment, often involving monitoring behavioral and physical cues (e.g. blood shot eyes and/or slurred speech), to determine intoxication. The surveys (Crossland et al., 2018; Evans et al., 2009) also revealed that standardized guidelines or procedures for police officers regarding when and how to best interview intoxicated witnesses and victims were often lacking and that many officers were unsure about the effectiveness of the procedures employed by their department.

To summarize, violence often takes place in environments where alcohol is sold and consumed. A considerable number of perpetrators, victims and eyewitnesses are under the influence of alcohol. Standardised procedure regarding how and when to best interview intoxicated individuals are often lacking and police officers regularly use their own judgement to determine intoxication in witnesses.

Attitudes and perceptions of intoxicated witnesses and victims

The Criminal Justice System in the United Kingdom utilizes a trial by jury of one's peers and as such, it becomes increasingly important to understand how potential jury members perceive intoxicated witnesses. CPS guidelines state that a person is able to give evidence as long as they are capable of understanding the questions put to them, and can give responses that are understandable (Crown Prosecution Service, 2018). There is no legislation in place denying a witness who was intoxicated at the time of the crime the right to give evidence. Nonetheless, there have been cases dismissed or defendants acquitted on the grounds of the witness being intoxicated at the time of the offense. In 2016, the mugging of victim Phoebe Greenwood never reached trial due to her intoxication at the time of the attack (Greenwood, 2016). Similarly in 2018, Mathew McKay was acquitted from a shooting in 2015 due to the intoxication of key witnesses in the case (CBC, 2019). Such examples clearly demonstrate that how intoxicated witnesses and victims are perceived does matter for the outcome of criminal trials.

Research by Evans et al. (2019) examined mock jurors' perceptions of both witnesses and victims under varying levels of intoxication. Participants rated the intoxicated witnesses as less credible than the sober ones. Interestingly, there was no significant difference in credibility ratings between mildly and extremely intoxicated witnesses. The rating of credibility did not differ according to witness type i.e. bystander or victim or by crime type i.e. sexual assault or battery. Similarly, Lynch, Wasarhaley, Golding, and Simcic (2013) found that mock jurors rated the credibility of a rape victim as much lower and were less likely to settle on a guilty verdict when the victim was intoxicated. Unfortunately, intoxicated victims of sexual assault are often judged as more responsible for the event (Abbey, 2002). In a study by Sims, Noel, and Maisto (2007) college students were more likely to blame a victim for an assault if she had consumed alcohol compared to a soft drink.

Negative attitudes towards intoxicated witnesses and victims are not limited to the general public. Schuller and Stewart (2000) studied police officers' attitudes and found that as victim intoxication increased the perceived credibility and blame for the perpetrator decreased. Likewise, Stewart and Maddren (1997) found that police officers were more likely to blame drunk victims in an intimate partner violence scenario compared to sober ones. Kassin, Tubb, Hosch, and Memon (2001) surveyed legal psychologists and found that 90% agreed that alcohol impairs an eyewitness' later recall ability. A similar study with judges established that the majority agreed that alcohol intoxication reduces the reliability of witnesses (Houston, Hope, Memon, & Read, 2010).

To summarize, studies of juror decision making demonstrate that intoxicated witnesses are often considered less credible and reliable, whilst intoxicated victims are often seen as more responsible for their own victimisation. This suggests that an intoxicated victim's access to a fair trial might be comprised at multiple stages during the process of Criminal Justice. Given the prevalence of intoxicated individuals coming into contact with the Criminal Justice System and the often negative beliefs held against them, it is surprising to see that research has just recently seen a burst in studies examining how alcohol intoxication impacts memory performance in real-life settings.

The impact of alcohol on eyewitness memory performance

Interview format

Most empirical studies in the lab or the field have used free recall, cued recall, or recognition tests to study eyewitness memory performance (see Fisher & Schreiber Compo, 2017, for an overview). During free recall, participants are usually instructed to report all the details they can recall from the event, with no additional cues or questions to jog their memory. Conversely, cued recall measures often include more specific questions about the incident; such as "Where was the safe located in the office?" or "What color was the perpetrator's shirt?". In a recognition test, participants are usually presented with one or multiple stimuli and asked whether they have seen them before. Previous research with sober witnesses has generally shown that free recall procedures usually elicit more accurate accounts than other question formats (Memon, Meissner, & Fraser, 2010).

Schreiber Compo et al. (2017) asked placebo, control and alcohol participants to recall a filmed theft. Memory was tested with a free recall and subsequently a cued recall test immediately and after a delay. At the immediate recall attempt, no significant group differences were observed in the percentage of accurate and inaccurate details reported during free and cued recall. However, one-week later, intoxicated participants recalled fewer accurate details compared to sober participants during free and cued recall and more inaccurate details than the placebo group during cued recall. Altman, Schreiber Compo, McQuiston, Hagsand, and Cervera (2018) and van Oorsouw and Merckelbach (2012) have tested intoxicated bar patrons' memory for a simulated crime under elevated levels of alcohol (BAC > 0.08%). Altman et al. (2018) found that as BAC levels increased the amount of accurate information decreased in both free and cued recall format. Only during cued recall did an increase in BAC levels lead to an increase in inaccurate details. Similarly, van Oorsouw and Merckelbach (2012) found a decrease in completeness and accurate details when BACs increased for both free and cued recalls, but only in the cued recall did inaccurate details increase with increased BACs. Hagsand, Roos-af-Hjelmsäter, Granhag, Fahlke, and Gordh (2017) directly compared free and cued recall data and found that intoxicated witnesses recalled fewer details during free recall compared to sober ones, but there were no group differences during cued recall. Both groups were more accurate during free than cued recall. Flowe, Takarangi, Humphries, and Wright (2016) tested women's memory for a hypothetical assault scenario with a recognition test and found that alcohol had a negative impact on the amount of information provided but did not impact memory report accuracy (accuracy calculated after excluding "don't know" responses). However, they did not include a free or cued recall format making it impossible to make direct comparisons.

Overall, research suggests that open-ended free recall formats are the best way to interview sober and intoxicated witnesses alike. Whereas free recall may lead to less complete accounts by intoxicated witnesses, accounts are probably more accurate and contain fewer errors compared to those elicited with cued recall formats.

Interview timing

Recent research discovered that English law enforcement officers often take initial details from intoxicated witnesses directly after the incident has occurred, but a thorough evidential interview will only be conducted later when the witness is sober again (Crossland et al., 2018). We know from a large body of research that as the delay between memory encoding and retrieval increases the quality and quantity of the subsequent memory report decreases (Read & Connoly, 2007). Only little is known about how alcohol and delay interact and whether it should be recommended to police officers to wait for witnesses to sober up or to interview them as soon as possible in a still intoxicated state.

Findings from lab studies that have examined the effect of moderate doses of alcohol on immediate memory recall suggest that alcohol intoxication may not be necessarily detrimental to memory accuracy (e.g. La Rooy, Nicol, & Terry, 2013; Schreiber Compo et al., 2011). Only few studies so far have actually included a delayed interview in their experimental design. Yuille and Tollestrup (1990) interviewed some sober and some mildly intoxicated mock-witnesses directly after the event and all after a delay. Delayed recall attempts were overall more complete but slightly less accurate regardless of intoxication condition. An immediate recall attempt resulted in an increase in details during the delayed interview in both sober and intoxicated individuals (27.87% and 24.99%, respectively). Similarly, Hagsand et al. (2017) found that all mock-witness were more detailed and accurate during the immediate compared to the delayed interview. The early recall attempt led to 30% new and accurate details during the delayed interview. La Rooy et al. (2013) found that across beverage conditions, a second retrieval attempt resulted in additional new and correct information. In fact, 18% of recalled information in the repeated interview was new and accurate, whereas only 1% was inconsistent.

Taken together, research suggests that an immediate recall attempt in addition to a subsequent delayed interview is preferable regardless of the intoxication state of the witness, as it might lead to additional accurate information, which could lead to an important breakthrough in a criminal investigation.

Alcohol dosage

The majority of lab-based applied memory studies have tested mildly to moderately intoxicated mock-witnesses, whose intoxication levels were around the UK drink and drive limit (BAC 0.05–0.08%). Not dosing higher than 0.08% is often done due to ethical reasons and to ensure appropriate health and safety procedures can be followed. Most studies examining mildly to moderately intoxicated witnesses have found no alcohol related differences in memory performance (La Rooy et al. 2013; Schreiber Compo et al., 2012) or less complete but not necessarily less accurate reports (Flowe et al. 2016; Hagsand, Roos-af-Hjelmsäter, Anders Granhag, Fahlke, & Söderpalm-Gordh, 2013; Hildebrand Karlén, Roos, Fahlke, Granhag, & Gordh, 2017). A common criticism is that these intoxication levels are unrepresentative of those encountered by officers in the real world. Studies that were able to achieve higher BACs are those that were conducted in the field. Field studies usually recruit participants from local bars or pubs, where participants consume alcohol at their own discretion and therefore often reach higher BAC levels. Altman et al. (2018) tested bar patrons with intoxication levels higher than 0.08%. They found that with increasing BACs the amount and accuracy of the recalled information decreased. Most alcohol memory studies focus on witnessed events, however, in the real world witnesses are often not passive bystanders but might be actively involved as victims, perpetrators, or rescuers. To overcome this limitation, van Oorsouw, Merckelbach, and Smeets (2015) asked bar patrons to enact a mock-theft and subsequently tested their memory about it. Their severely intoxicated group had a mean BAC of 0.16%. During free recall conditions sober participants recalled more correct details than intoxicated ones. During cued recall, the severely intoxicated participants recalled fewer correct details and made more errors than sober ones. An earlier field study by Van Oorsouw and Merckelbach (2012) found a similar dose-dependent effect of alcohol on recall accuracy. Sober, moderately (mean BAC 0.06%) and severely intoxicated (mean BAC 0.17%) bar patrons were tested. While BACs increased recall completeness and accuracy decreased. Crossland, Kneller, and Wilcock (2016) also approached participants in bar settings and asked them to watch a mock-crime. Participants in the high intoxication conditions reached a mean BAC of 0.14%. Memory was tested 3–5 days later. Contrary to other studies, alcohol did not impact recall completeness or accuracy when tested with a free recall or a recognition test. A subsequent study revealed less complete memory reports during free recall and a higher number of 'don't know responses' during the recognition test.

In general, research suggests that at low to moderate levels of intoxication, eyewitness memory may be less complete, but not necessarily less accurate than that of a sober witness. However, when considering elevated intoxication levels in more realistic settings it appears that alcohol can negatively affect recall completeness as well as accuracy. This seems to be especially the case when memory is tested with cued recall formats. Unfortunately, field studies are still rare in the alcohol and eyewitness memory domain, probably due to practical (e.g. gaining access) and ethical (e.g. obtaining consent from already intoxicated individuals) obstacles involved when testing already intoxicated individuals.

The impact of alcohol on suggestibility

Suggestibility refers to an individual's inclination to take on information from another source often encountered during a social interaction (Ridley, 2012). Much of what we know about suggestibility in an eyewitness context nowadays comes from research using the misinformation paradigm (Loftus, Miller, & Burns, 1978). During the typical misinformation paradigm, participants watch a stimuli (e.g. a video or a slide show) and are then presented with contradictory information before subsequently engaging in a memory test. The post-event misinformation might be included in a written narrative (Vallano & Compo, 2011) or in leading questions (Lee, 2004). Research has shown that a substantial number of participants take on misinformation and incorporate it in their subsequent memory reports, this phenomenon is called the misinformation effect (Frenda, Nichols, & Loftus, 2011). Research regarding the impact of alcohol on the misinformation effect is still in its infancy and studies have revealed mixed findings. Schreiber Compo et al. (2012) provided participants with an alcoholic beverage, a placebo or a beverage containing no alcohol. Thereafter, participants watched a staged crime during which a confederate stole a laptop. The misinformation was provided during a telephone call from the experimenter to the University Technology Services 'to report' the mock-crime. Shortly thereafter, participants were questioned about the crime during a face-to-face interview. The typical misinformation effect was found, that is participants reported more false information for those items they had previously received misinformation about. No significant differences between intoxication groups were found. Flowe et al. (2019) employed a fully-balanced design during which participants either received alcohol and expected alcohol, received alcohol but did not expect alcohol, received no alcohol but expected alcohol or received no alcohol and did not expect alcohol. After beverage administration, participants engaged in an interactive sexual assault scenario. Seven days later participants were all sober and received misinformation in the form of a written narrative. Subsequently, participants were interviewed about the incident and completed a multiple-choice recognition test. Similarly to the findings by Schreiber Compo et al. (2012), Flowe et al. (2019) did not find that the consumption of alcohol nor participant's expectancies about what kind of beverage they consumed were associated with reporting misinformation. On the contrary, three field studies by van Oorsouw, Broers, and Sauerland (2019) and van Oorsouw et al. (2015) found that severely intoxicated individuals were more prone to accept misinformation compared to sober ones. Memory completeness mediated the misinformation effect, thus less complete memory recall was associated with higher suggestibility. Severely intoxicated individuals might have found it harder to detect discrepancies between one's own recollection of an event and the presented misinformation due to alcohol-related poor memory for the original event (van Oorsouw et al., 2019).

Two studies have examined how alcohol affects suggestibility if consumed after the to-be-remembered event is encoded but before the memory for the event is tested (Gawrylowicz, Ridley, Albery, Barnoth, & Young, 2017; Santtila, Ekholm, & Niemi, 1999). Santtila et al. (1999) used the

Gudjonsson Suggestibility Scale 2 (GSS2), which measures an individual's proneness to go along with yielding questions and to shift answers in light of negative feedback. Participants read the GSS2 story and then consumed alcohol or a soft drink. Fifty minutes later the GSS2 was administered. Intriguingly, they found that intoxicated individuals were less likely to accept misinformation presented in the form of leading questions, however, they were not less likely to change their answers when confronted with negative feedback. Likewise, Gawrylowicz et al. (2017) showed that mock-witnesses were less suggestible to misinformation encountered via a written narrative when they consumed alcohol after having seen a staged distractor crime but before their memory for the event was tested. This counterintuitive beneficial effect of alcohol on suggestibility might be due to reduced retrograde interference (Mueller, Lisman, & Spear, 1983). Alcohol might prevent the formation of new memories, thereby protecting already existing memories by reducing potential interference.

Taken together, it is too early to draw any ultimate conclusions from the limited research available on the impact of alcohol on eyewitness suggestibility. The three studies that did find evidence for increased suggestibility in the intoxicated were field studies. It could be argued that lab studies employed intoxication levels that were too low to generate any reliable misinformation effects.

Recall of intimate partner violence

A multi-country study on women's health and domestic violence by the World Health Organization found that on all sites the odds of intimate partner violence (IPV) were higher in relationships where one or both partners had alcohol problems (Abramsky et al., 2011). From an applied perspective, it is therefore important to study specifically how alcohol impacts women's and men's perceptions and recollections of IPV. Hildebrand Karlén, Hjelmsäter, Fahlke, Granhag, and Söderpalm-Gordh (2015) investigated the ability of intoxicated male and female participants to recall footage of an IPV incident. Intoxicated females, but not males, recalled significantly fewer details compared to their sober counterparts. Intoxication had no significant effect on the accuracy of recalled information for either males or females. Their findings seem to echo previous studies on the effect of alcohol intoxication on eyewitness memory in general. Mild to moderate intoxication may reduce the number of details reported, but accuracy is not affected. Whilst the findings allude to a gender difference in recall, this might be explained by significantly higher BACs reached by female participants. In a similar study conducted by the same research team half of the intoxicated and sober participants were asked to recall the IPV scenario immediately and all recalled it after a one-week delay (Hildebrand Karlén, Roos Af Hjelmsäter, Fahlke, Granhag, & Söderpalm-Gordh, 2017). The intoxicated group was less complete but as accurate as the sober one. Immediate recall had a positive impact on recall completeness during the delayed interview.

Hildebrand Karlén, Roos, and Gudjonsson (2019) further investigated how intoxicated and sober individuals recall different emotional context of an escalating IPV scenario. The IPV film was divided into three stages: neutral (emotional neutral discussion), verbally aggressive (verbal argument), and physical aggressive (physical violence). Again, intoxicated individuals reported fewer details than sober ones. All participants reported most details from the verbally aggressive stage, fewer details from the neutral stage and least details from the physically aggressive stage. Both groups reported more details during the immediate than the delayed interview.

Thus, research focusing on IPV scenarios replicate the findings from studies including more general eyewitness scenarios (e.g. thefts). That is, intoxicated witness accounts might be less complete but not less accurate. Furthermore, the research highlights the importance of interviewing witnesses immediately regardless of their intoxication state.

Potential mechanisms underlying alcohol-related effects on eyewitness memory

Alcohol myopia theory (AMT)

Steele and Josephs (1990) proposed that alcohol limits the number of internal and external cues we can perceive and process in any given situation. Intoxicated individuals become more short-sighted and immediate and salient experiences become more influential on decision making and behavior. This state is called *alcohol myopia*. Many researchers in the eyewitness memory domain have used AMT to predict and explain alcohol-related memory deficits. According to AMT intoxicated witnesses should have better memory recall for central details compared to peripheral details. Central details pertain to the appearance and action of key figures (e.g. perpetrators and victims), whereas peripheral details refer to information in the surroundings (e.g. furniture). One of the first mock-witness studies testing this hypothesis was conducted by Schreiber Compo et al. (2011). In line with AMT, intoxicated participants recalled fewer accurate peripheral details compared to sober ones, however, no differences between groups in the number of recalled accurate central details were found. In contrast, van Oorsouw and Merckelbach (2012) found reduced recall of accurate central details in severely and moderately intoxicated participants compared to sober ones under free recall conditions. With regards to peripheral details, only severe intoxication reduced correct recall compared to sober controls. Under cued recall conditions, no interactions between intoxication level and type of detail recalled were observed. Flowe et al. (2016) examined how alcohol influences women's memory for a hypothetical sexual assault after a 24 hour and 4 month delay. They too did not find that alcohol consumption significantly impacted the type of detail mock-witnesses recalled. In general, individuals' memory was better for central details than for peripheral ones regardless of intoxication level. Harvey, Kneller, and Campbell (2013) used eye tracking to explore visual fixations during encoding of pictorial stimuli under the influence of alcohol. In line with AMT, intoxicated participants made more fixations to the central region of the pictures compared to their sober counterparts. However, no alcohol-related differences in the number of recalled central versus peripheral details were found.

From the mixed research findings obtained so far it remains questionable whether AMT is a suitable framework to explain alcohol-related differences in eyewitness event recall. Whereas some studies (Harvey et al., 2013; Schreiber Compo et al., 2011) found support for AMT others were not able to back it up (Flowe et al., 2016; van Oorsouw & Merckelbach, 2012).

Hypervigilance hypothesis

Individuals' beliefs and expectations about the impact of alcohol intoxication can influence their behaviors and cognitions. Specifically, individuals who believe that they have consumed alcohol might become hypervigilant to compensate for any detrimental effects of alcohol consumption on performance. Testa et al. (2006) showed that women who believed that they were drinking alcohol exhibited more careful behaviors when confronted with a sexual assault scenario. They argued that woman in the placebo group must have recognized their heightened vulnerability and therefore responded to the scenario with increased vigilance.

Some eyewitness memory studies have found evidence for hypervigilance too. Evans et al. (2019) assigned participants to an alcohol, placebo and control condition and asked them to encode a video of a mock-crime and to either recall it immediately or after a week's delay. At the delayed testing session, participants were again randomly assigned to the alcohol, placebo or control condition. Placebo and control participants performed similarly during both the immediate and delayed recall session, and better than the alcohol group during the delayed session. In line, with the hypervigilance hypothesis, Evan's et al. (2019) argued that placebo participants might have paid extra attention during encoding and were more careful when responding at retrieval, which ultimately led to performance that was as accurate as the control group. Schreiber Compo et al. (2011) found that placebo participants more often expressed uncertainty in their responses compared to sober and intoxicated participants. They argued that hypervigilance led placebo participants to be more sensitive to the fallibility of their own memories. Gawrylowicz et al. (2019) used a fully-balanced placebo design to examine the impact of alcohol and expectancies on mock-witness event recall and don't know responding. In addition to the placebo, alcohol and control group, they included a reverse placebo group. Participants in the reverse placebo group did receive alcohol but did not expect any. The reverse placebo group performed consistently poorer (made more errors and gave fewer correct answers) during cued-recall compared to all other groups. In line with hypervigilance it could be speculated that unknowingly consuming alcohol led to reduced vigilance and hence poorer memory performance. Compared to the alcohol and the placebo groups, the reverse placebo group did not expect any detrimental effects of alcohol and therefore did not attempt to compensate for them. A similar 2×2 factorial design was used by Flowe et al. (2019). Women who expected alcohol provided less complete accounts and they showed better discriminability between correct and erroneous responding compared to those who did not expect alcohol. The findings could be interpreted in favor of the hypervigilance account, that is, women who expected alcohol might have applied a more stringent report criterion at retrieval to compensate for any negative effects of alcohol on memory recall, subsequently leading to less complete reports. At the same time, the expectancy manipulation might have led to increased attention at encoding leading to enhanced discrimination accuracy during the recognition test.

Thus, individuals' expectations about the outcomes of alcohol consumption might lead to hypervigilance, which might subsequently lead to improved performance. From a memory perspective, this can happen at encoding (paying more attention to the stimuli presented), retrieval (engaging in more thorough metacognitive control and monitoring processes), or both. Research seems to support the hypervigilance hypothesis, however, more research is needed employing more complex designs implementing adequate placebo controls.

Disinhibition

Several laboratory studies have shown that intoxication can impair performance on measures of behavioral response inhibition, such as the Stop-Signal Task (SST) and the Go/No-Go Task (Weafer & Fillmore, 2008). From a cognitive perspective, alcohol-related disinhibition might lead to the application of more liberal response criteria on measures of memory performance, that is individuals' are less likely to opt out of responding and more likely to provide an erroneous response (Janssen & Anne, 2019). In line with disinhibition, Gawrylowicz et al. (2019) found that intoxicated witnesses were less likely to use 'don't know' responses to opt out of responding. Yet others did not find increased 'don't know' responding in the intoxicated (Schreiber Compo et al., 2012). While some even found increased 'don't know' responding with increasing BAC levels (Altman et al., 2018; Crossland et al., 2016; Flowe et al., 2016).

If alcohol leads to reduced inhibition, then intoxicated suspects should be more likely to disclose criminal actions. Mindthoff, Hagsand, Schreiber

Compo, and Evans (2019) examined the reporting of transgressions carried out by themselves or others in intoxicated and sober participants. Overall, participants were more likely to disclose a personal transgression than someone else's' transgression. Alcohol did not lead to increased disclosure of criminal actions. Suchotzki, Crombez, Debey, Van Oorsouw, and Verschuere (2014) studied whether alcohol consumption would make it more difficult for participants to lie. Sober and intoxicated individuals completed the Sheffield Lie Test, during which they were instructed to answer general knowledge questions, such as "Is Amsterdam in the Netherlands?", truthfully or deceptively. In addition, they completed a SST to assess behavioral response inhibition. Although, alcohol intake was associated with impaired response inhibition on the SST, no evidence was found that intoxication hampers lying.

Thus, although alcohol intoxication seems to lead to poorer performance on behavioral measures of response inhibition, it does not seem to shift individuals response criterion on cognitive measures, such as episodic memory tasks and tasks involving the disclosure of transgressions, or lying. However, given the wide variety of paradigms used, and the sparse number of studies available so far, it is too early to rule out disinhibition completely to explain alcohol-related memory deficits.

Methodological challenges and future research directions

One methodological issue present in alcohol administration studies is the timing and rate of alcohol absorption. An examination into the variability in alcohol absorption during a drinking session found that the average peak BAC was 0.073 with a range of 0.047–1.00 g/dL (Winek, Wahba, & Dowdell, 1996). The average peak time, i.e. when the BAC reached its highest was 17.4 minutes, ranging from 0 to 74 minutes. Other factors such as the timing and nature of one's last meal and participants' gender can further impact upon absorption rate and target BAC, as seen in Hildebrand Karlén et al. (2015) where female participants reached significantly higher BACs than males.

To complicate things even further, research has shown that memory encoding and retrieval might be affected differently depending on the specific limb of the BAC curve. Söderlund, Parker, Schwartz, and Tulving (2005) showed that alcohol impaired encoding in cued and free recall and recognition of completed word fragments regardless of limb, but word recognition was only impaired during the ascending BAC. Thus, how alcohol affects our memory not only depends on the memory task utilized, but also on the specific timing of when the memory was tested, that is on the ascending or the descending limb of the BAC curve. Future studies should therefore examine the effects of alcohol on eyewitness memory performance on different limbs on the BAC curve to shed more light on when exactly episodic memory might be impaired.

Whilst there are methodological difficulties associated with the timing of the alcohol administration and absorption, there are also challenges associated with assigning appropriate control groups. Studies typically use a control group, in which participants are knowingly not consuming alcohol, and/or a placebo group, in which participants are under the impression that they are consuming alcohol but do actually not receive any. The placebo condition is useful in measuring the behavioral and cognitive effects of expecting alcohol in the absence of pharmacological effects. Eyewitness memory studies have now begun to use fully-balanced placebo designs to control for alcohol expectancies (see Flowe et al., 2019; Gawrylowicz et al., 2019). In addition, to the usual alcohol, placebo and sober control group, a fourth group is included: the reverse placebo group (individuals do not believe that they received alcohol when they actually did). Gawrylowicz et al. (2019) found that their reverse placebo group performed consistently poorer on a cued recall task, they gave fewer correct responses and made more errors compared to the alcohol, control and placebo group. Flowe et al. (2019) found a significant expectancy effect for recall completeness when participants were interviewed with the Self-administered Interview. There was no significant effect of actual alcohol consumption. These findings suggest that pharmacological effects of alcohol might not be solely responsible for differences in memory performance, but that alcohol-related expectancies play a crucial role too.

Including placebo groups can be challenging, as it requires convincing people that they did or did not receive alcohol when in fact they did or did not. In Flowe et al.'s (2019) study 27% of participants who had been told that they received tonic water thought that they drank alcohol, whereas 22% believed they had alcohol when in fact they consumed tonic. Similarly, Schreiber Compo et al. (2017) reported that 16% of placebo participants believed that they had not consumed alcohol. Even if the placebo manipulation is successful, placebo participants often report feeling less intoxicated than their intoxicated counterparts (Kneller & Harvey, 2016).

To summarize, the administration of alcohol in laboratory settings comes with a myriad of methodological challenges. These challenges range from variations in peak BACs to ensuring timing of administration is appropriate and equal. What's more is that the inclusion of viable placebo groups is often not possible, as the drink deception is often difficult to execute, especially in the reverse placebo condition.

Conclusion and applied implications

Archival and survey studies demonstrate that intoxicated witnesses are overrepresented in the Criminal Justice System (Crossland et al., 2018; Evans et al., 2009; Palmer et al., 2013), so a highly relevant applied question is whether they can provide complete and accurate testimony. Many lay people and professionals alike hold negative attitudes towards intoxicated witnesses' ability to provide reliable memory accounts (e.g. Evans & Compo, 2010; Kassin et al., 2001). Existing studies have reported diverging results, which might be somewhat due to the diverse methodologies used. The most consistent result so far across studies suggests that there is a negative relationship between BAC and recall completeness (see Jores, Colloff, Kloft, Smailes, & Flowe, 2019 for a recent meta-analysis). That is intoxicated mock-witnesses often recall fewer details than sober individuals. Accuracy was often not affected in studies using low to moderate intoxication levels (e.g. Flowe et al., 2016; Hagsand et al., 2017; Schreiber Compo et al., 2012). However, studies employing higher intoxication levels (BACs > 0.08), as often encountered in the real world, have found an increase in the number of errors with increasing BAC (e.g. Altman et al., 2018; van Oorsouw et al., 2012; 2015). A crucial question for police officers is when and how to best interview intoxicated witnesses. Is it better to interview an intoxicated witness directly, or to delay the interview until the witness is sober? Based on the reviewed literature (e.g. Hagsand et al., 2017; Schreiber Compo et al., 2017; Yuille & Tollestrup, 1990), it should be recommended to minimize any time delays between the witnessed incident and the subsequent police interview, as the detrimental impact of time seems to be larger than that of alcohol on eyewitness memory reports. Ideally, a repeated interview would then follow when the witness is sober again, as this might result in additional forensically relevant information (LaRooy et al., 2013). When interviewing intoxicated and sober witnesses alike, a free-recall format should be ideally used, including open-ended questions and non-leading prompts. Given that some research found that alcohol, especially at higher levels, might increase suggestibility (van Oorsouw et al., 2015, 2019), it is of utmost importance to use appropriate interviewing techniques with this special witness population.

What mechanisms underlie alcohol-related differences in episodic memory performance? Most research reviewed here seems to support hypervigilance. Expectancies and beliefs about the negative effects of alcohol on one's memory performance can make individuals more vigilant and cautious and lead to compensatory behaviors to counteract the deteriorating effects of alcohol. Mixed support was provided for AMT and disinhibition. It is probably most likely that all three mechanisms simultaneously affect memory performance to some degree or the other. Future research should further try to disentangle physiological and metacognitive effects of alcohol to better understand the magnitude of the impact each of them has on memory performance.

So are intoxicated witnesses better than their reputation? Under ideal conditions, that is when individuals have an unobstructed view, the delay between the incident and the later interview is kept minimal, the level of intoxication is low to moderate, appropriate interview formats are utilized and other influencing factors, like trauma, divided attention, and the presence of weapons, are missing, intoxicated witnesses can provide accounts which albeit less detailed are not less accurate than those by sober individuals. The "blanket" assumption that a drunk witness is unreliable does not seem to hold true and more research is needed to examine how we can best support intoxicated witnesses.

References

Abbey, A. (2002). Alcohol-related sexual assault: A common problem among college students. *Journal of Studies on Alcohol Supplement*, *14*, 118–128. Available from https://doi.org/10.1037/0021-843X.88.2.153.

Abramsky, T., Watts, C. H., Garcia-Moreno, C., Devries, K., Kiss, L., Ellsberg, M., & Heise, L. (2011). What factors are associated with recent intimate partner violence? Findings from the WHO multi-country study on women's health and domestic violence. *BMC Public Health*, *11*, 109. Available from https://doi.org/10.1186/1471-2458-11-109.

Altman, C. M., Schreiber Compo, N., McQuiston, D., Hagsand, A. V., & Cervera, J. (2018). Witnesses' memory for events and faces under elevated levels of intoxication. *Memory*, *26* (7), 946–959. Available from https://doi.org/10.1080/09658211.2018.1445758.

CBC News. (2019). *Victim, father handcuffed in court kerfuffle after man acquitted in shooting involving stolen RCMP gun*. Retrieved 29 July 2019, from <https://www.cbc.ca/news/canada/manitoba/matthew-mckay-acquitted-1.4493008>.

Crossland, D., Kneller, W., & Wilcock, R. (2016). Intoxicated witnesses: Testing the validity of the alcohol myopia theory. *Applied Cognitive Psychology*, *30*, 270–281. Available from https://doi.org/10.1002/acp.3209.

Crossland, D., Kneller, W., & Wilcock, R. (2018). Intoxicated eyewitnesses: Prevalence and procedures according to England's police officers. *Psychology, Crime & Law*, *24*(10), 979–997. Available from https://doi.org/10.1080/1068316X.2018.1474216.

Evans, J. R., & Compo, N. S. (2010). Mock jurors' perceptions of identifications made by intoxicated eyewitnesses. *Psychology, Crime and Law*, *16*(3), 191–210. Available from https://doi.org/10.1080/10683160802612890.

Evans, J. R., Schreiber Compo, N., Carol, R. N., Nichols-Lopez, K., Holness, H., & Furton, K. G. (2019). The impact of alcohol intoxication on witness suggestibility immediately and after a delay. *Applied Cognitive Psychology*, *33*(3), 358–369. Available from https://doi.org/10.1002/acp.3502.

Evans, J. R., Schreiber Compo, N., & Russano, M. B. (2009). Intoxicated witnesses and suspects: Procedures and prevalence according to law enforcement. *Psychology, Public Policy, and Law*, *15*(3), 194–221. Available from https://doi.org/10.1037/a0016837.

Fisher, R. P., & Schreiber, N. (2017). Interview protocols to improve eyewitness memory. In M. P. Toglia, J. D. Read, D. F. Ross, & R. C. L. Lindsay (Eds.), *The Handbook of Eyewitness Psychology* (Volume I, pp. 53–80). Abington, MA: Taylor and Francis Group.

Flowe, H. D., Takarangi, M. K., Humphries, J. E., & Wright, D. S. (2016). Alcohol and remembering a hypothetical sexual assault: Can people who were under the influence of alcohol during the event provide accurate testimony? *Memory*, *24*(8), 1042–1061. Available from https://doi.org/10.1080/09658211.2015.1064536.

Flowe, H. D., Humphries, J. E., Takarangi, M. K., Zelek, K., Karoğlu, N., Gabbert, F., & Hope, L. (2019). An experimental examination of the effects of alcohol consumption and exposure to misleading postevent information on remembering a hypothetical rape scenario. *Applied Cognitive Psychology*, 1–21. Available from https://doi.org/10.1002/acp.3531.

Frenda, S. J., Nichols, R. M., & Loftus, E. F. (2011). Current issues and advances in misinformation research. *Current Directions in Psychological Science*, *20*(1), 20–23. Available from https://doi.org/10.1177/0963721410396620.

Gawrylowicz, J., Ridley, A. M., Albery, I. P., Barnoth, E., & Young, J. (2017). Alcohol-induced retrograde facilitation renders witnesses of crime less suggestible to misinformation. *Psychopharmacology*, *234*, 1267–1275. Available from https://doi.org/10.1007/s00213-017-4564-2.

Gawrylowicz, J., Scoboria, J., Teodorini, R., & Albery, I. P. (2019). Intoxicated eyewitnesses: The effect of a fully balanced placebo design on event memory and metacognitive control. *Applied Cognitive Psychology*, *33*(3), 344–357. Available from https://doi.org/10.1002/acp.3504.

Greenwood, P. (2016). I was violently attacked but my case was dropped because I had been drinking. Retrieved 8 August 2019, from <https://www.theguardian.com/lifeandstyle/2016/jan/18/i-was-violently-attacked-but-my-case-was-dropped-been-drinking>.

Hagsand, A., Roos-af-Hjelmsäter, E., Anders Granhag, P., Fahlke, C., & Söderpalm-Gordh, A. (2013). Do sober eyewitnesses outperform alcohol intoxicated eyewitnesses in a lineup? *The European Journal of Psychology Applied to Legal Context*, *5*(1), 23–47.

Hagsand, A. V., Roos-af-Hjelmsäter, E., Granhag, P. A., Fahlke, C., & Gordh, A. S. (2017). Witnesses stumbling down memory lane: The effects of alcohol intoxication, retention interval, and repeated interviewing. *Memory*, *25*(4), 531–543. Available from https://doi.org/10.1080/09658211.2016.1191652.

Harvey, A. J., Kneller, W., & Campbell, A. C. (2013). The elusive effects of alcohol intoxication on visual attention and eyewitness memory. *Applied Cognitive Psychology*. Available from https://doi.org/10.1002/acp.2940.

Hildebrand Karlén, M., Roos Af Hjelmsäter, E., Fahlke, C., Granhag, P. A., & Söderpalm-Gordh, A. (2017). To wait or not to wait? Improving results when interviewing intoxicated witnesses to violence. *Scandinavian Journal of Psychology*, *58*(1), 15–22. Available from https://doi.org/10.1111/sjop.12345.

Hildebrand Karlén, M., Roos, E., Fahlke, C., Granhag, P. A., & Gordh, A. S. (2017). Alcohol intoxicated witnesses: Perception of aggression and guilt in intimate partner violence. *Journal of Interpersonal Violence*, *32*(22), 3448–3474. Available from https://doi.org/10.1177/0886260515599656.

Hildebrand Karlén, M., Roos af Hjelmsäter, E., Fahlke, C., Granhag, P. A., & Söderpalm Gordh, A. (2015). Alcohol intoxicated eyewitnesses' memory of intimate partner violence. *Psychology, Crime & Law*, *21*(2), 156–171. Available from https://doi.org/10.1080/1068316X.2014.951644.

Hildebrand Karlén, M., Roos, E., & Gudjonsson, G. H. (2019). The devil is not only in the details: Gist and detail elaboration in intoxicated witnesses' reports of interpersonal violence. *Psychology, Crime and Law*, *25*(4), 319–344. Available from https://doi.org/10.1080/1068316X.2018.1526936.

Houston, K., Hope, L., Memon, A., & Read, J. D. (2010). Expert testimony on eyewitness evidence: In search of common sense. *Behavioral Sciences & The Law*, *28*(2), 211–223. Available from https://doi.org/10.1002/bsl.

Janssen, S. M., & Anne, M. (2019). And one more for the road: Commentary on the Special Issue on alcohol and eyewitness memory. *Applied Cognitive Psychology*, *33*(3), 456–462. Available from https://doi.org/10.1002/acp.3562.

Jores, T., Colloff, M. F., Kloft, L., Smailes, H., & Flowe, H. D. (2019). A meta-analysis of the effects of acute alcohol intoxication on witness recall. *Applied Cognitive Psychology*. Available from https://doi.org/10.1002/acp.3533.

Kassin, S. M., Tubb, V. A., Hosch, H. M., & Memon, A. (2001). On the "general acceptance" of eyewitness testimony research: A new survey of the experts. *American Psychologist*, *56*(5), 405–416. Available from https://doi.org/10.1037/0003-066X.56.5.405.

Kingma, J. (2000). Alcohol consumption in victims of violence: A trend study for the period 1970-1998. *Psychological Reports*, *87*(3), 803–811. Available from https://doi.org/10.2466/pr0.2000.87.3.803.

Kneller, W., & Harvey, A. J. (2016). The European Journal of Psychology Applied to Legal Context confidence ratings, and response time. *The European Journal of Psychology Applied to Legal Context*, *8*(1), 11–18. Available from https://doi.org/10.1016/j.ejpal.2015.09.001.

La Rooy, D., Nicol, A., & Terry, P. (2013). Intoxicated eyewitnesses: The effects of alcohol on eyewitness recall across repeated interviews. *Open Journal of Medical Psychology*, *2*, 107–114. Available from https://doi.org/10.4236/ojmp.2013.23017.

Leonard, K. E., Quigley, B. M., & Collins, R. L. (2002). Physical aggression in the lives of young adults. *Journal of Interpersonal Violence*, *17*(5), 533–550. Available from https://doi.org/10.1177/0886260502017005004.

Lee, K. (2004). Age, neuropsychological, and social cognitive measures as predictors of individual differences in susceptibility to the misinformation effect. *Applied Cognitive Psychology*, *18*(8), 997–1019. Available from https://doi.org/10.1002/acp.1075.

Loftus, E. F., Miller, D. G., & Burns, H. J. (1978). Semantic integration of verbal information into a visual memory. *Journal of Experimental Psychology: Human Learning and Memory*, *4*(1), 19–31. Available from https://doi.org/10.1037/0278-7393.4.1.19.

Lynch, K. R., Wasarhaley, N. E., Golding, J. M., & Simcic, T. (2013). Who bought the drinks? Juror perceptions of intoxication in a rape trial. *Journal of Interpersonal Violence*, *28*(16), 3205–3222. Available from https://doi.org/10.1177/0886260513496900.

Memon, A., Meissner, C. A., & Fraser, J. (2010). The Cognitive Interview: A meta-analytic review and study space analysis of the past 25 years. *Psychology, Public Policy, and Law*, *16*(4), 340.

Mindthoff, A., Hagsand, A. V., Schreiber Compo, N., & Evans, J. R. (2019). Does alcohol loosen the tongue? Intoxicated individuals' willingness to report transgressions or criminal behavior carried out by themselves or others. *Applied cognitive psychology*, *33*(3), 414–425. Available from https://doi.org/10.1002/acp.3480.

Mueller, C. W., Lisman, S. A., & Spear, N. E. (1983). Alcohol enhancement of human memory: Tests of consolidation and interference hypotheses. *Psychopharmacology*, *80*(3), 226–230. Available from https://doi.org/10.1007/BF00436158.

Office of National Statistics. (2017). *Crime and justice: Focus on violent crime and sexual offences, year ending March 2015*. <https://www.ons.gov.uk/peoplepopulationandcommunity/crimeandjustice/compendium/focusonviolentcrimeandsexualoffences/yearendingmarch 2016>.

Office for National Statistics. (2018). *Data on alcohol related incidents, years ending March 2011 to March 2017, Crime Survey for England and Wales*. <https://www.ons.gov.uk/

peoplepopulationandcommunity/crimeandjustice/adhocs/009372dataonalcoholrelatedincidentsyearsendingmarch 2011tomarch 2017crimesurveyforenglandandwales>.

Palmer, F. T., Flowe, H. D., Takarangi, M. K. T., & Humphries, J. E. (2013). Intoxicated witnesses and suspects: An archival analysis of their involvement in criminal case processing. *Law and Human Behavior*, *37*(1), 54–59. Available from https://doi.org/10.1037/lhb0000010.

Read, J. D., & Connolly, D. A. (2007). The effects of delay on long-term memory for witnessed events. In M. P. Toglia, J. D. Read, D. F. Ross, & R. C. L. Lindsay (Eds.), *The handbook of eyewitness psychology* (Vol. 1, pp. 117–155). Mahwah, NJ: Lawrence Erlbaum Associates Publishers, Memory for events.

Ridley, A. M. (2012). *Suggestibility. Suggestibility in legal contexts* (pp. 1–19). John Wiley & Sons, Ltd. Retrieved from <https://onlinelibrary.wiley.com/doi/abs/10.1002/9781118432907.ch1>.

Santtila, P., Ekholm, M., & Niemi, P. (1999). The effects of alcohol on interrogative suggestibility: The role of state-anxiety and mood states as mediating factors. *Legal and Criminological Psychology*, *4*(1), 1–13. Available from https://doi.org/10.1348/135532599167707.

Schreiber Compo, N., Evans, J. R., Carol, R. N., Kemp, D., Villalba, D., Ham, L. S., & Rose, S. (2011). Alcohol intoxication and memory for events: A snapshot of alcohol myopia in a real-world drinking scenario. *Memory*, *19*(2), 202–210. Available from https://doi.org/10.1080/09658211.2010.546802.

Schreiber Compo, N., Evans, J. R., Carol, R. N., Villalba, D., Ham, L. S., Garcia, T., & Rose, S. (2012). Intoxicated eyewitnesses: Better than their reputation? *Law and Human Behavior*, *36*(2), 77–86. Available from https://doi.org/10.1037/h0093951.

Schreiber Compo, N., Carol, R. N., Evans, J. R., Pimentel, P., Holness, H., Nichols-Lopez, K., Rose, S., & Furton, K. G. (2017). Witness memory and alcohol: The effects of state- dependent recall. *Law and Human Behavior*, *41*(2), 202–215. Available from https://doi.org/10.1037/lhb0000224.

Schuller, R. A., & Stewart, A. (2000). Police responses to sexual assault complaints: The role of perpetrator/complainant intoxication. *Law and Human Behavior*, *24*(5), 535–551. Available from https://doi.org/10.1023/A:1005519028528.

Sims, C. M., Noel, N. E., & Maisto, S. A. (2007). Rape blame as a function of alcohol presence and resistance type. *Addictive Behaviors*, *32*, 2766–2775. Available from https://doi.org/10.1016/j.addbeh.2007.04.013.

Söderlund, H., Parker, E. S., Schwartz, B. L., & Tulving, E. (2005). Memory encoding and retrieval on the ascending and descending limbs of the blood alcohol concentration curve. *Psychopharmacology*, *182*(2), 305–317. Available from https://doi.org/10.1007/s00213-005-0096-2.

Steele, C. M., & Josephs, R. A. (1990). Alcohol myopia: Its prized and dangerous effects. *American Psychologist*, *45*(8), 921–933. Available from https://doi.org/10.1037/0003-066X.45.8.921.

Steen, K., & Hunskaar, S. (2004). Violence in an urban community from the perspective of an accident and emergency department: A two-year prospective study. *Medical Science Monitor*, *10*(2), CR79, Retrieved from https://www.medscimonit.com/abstract/index/idArt/11573.

Stewart, A., & Maddren, K. (1997). Police officers' judgements of blame in family violence: The impact of gender and alcohol. *Sex Roles*, *37*(11–12), 921. Available from https://doi.org/10.1007/BF02936347.

Suchotzki, K., Crombez, G., Debey, E., Van Oorsouw, K., & Verschuere, B. (2014). In vino veritas? Alcohol, response inhibition and lying. *Alcohol and Alcoholism, 50*(1), 74–81. Available from https://doi.org/10.1093/alcalc/agu079.

Testa, M., Fillmore, M. T., Norris, J., Abbey, A., Curtin, J. J., Leonard, K. E., & Hayman, L. W. (2006). Understanding alcohol expectancy effects: Revisiting the placebo condition. *Alcoholism: Clinical and Experimental Research, 30*(2), 339–348. Available from https://doi.org/10.1111/j.1530-0277.2006.00039.x.

Vallano, J. P., & Compo, N. S. (2011). A comfortable witness is a good witness: Rapport-building and susceptibility to misinformation in an investigative mock-crime interview. *Applied Cognitive Psychology, 25*(6), 960–970. Available from https://doi.org/10.1002/acp.1789.

van Oorsouw, K., & Merckelbach, H. (2012). The effects of alcohol on crime-related memories: A field study. *Applied Cognitive Psychology, 26*(1), 82–90. Available from https://doi.org/10.1002/acp.1799.

van Oorsouw, K., Merckelbach, H., & Smeets, T. (2015). Alcohol intoxication impairs memory and increases suggestibility for a mock crime: A field study. *Applied Cognitive Psychology, 29*(4), 493–501. Available from https://doi.org/10.1002/acp.3129.

van Oorsouw, K., Broers, N. J., & Sauerland, M. (2019). Alcohol intoxication impairs eyewitness memory and increases suggestibility: Two field studies. *Applied Cognitive Psychology, 33*(3), 439–455. Available from https://doi.org/10.1002/acp.3561.

Victims & witnesses | The Crown Prosecution Service. (2018). Retrieved 29 July 2019, from <https://www.cps.gov.uk/victims-witnesses>.

Weafer, J., & Fillmore, M. T. (2008). Individual differences in acute alcohol impairment of inhibitory control predict ad libitum alcohol consumption. *Psychopharmacology, 201*(3), 315–324. Available from https://doi.org/10.1007/s00213-008-1284-7.

Winek, C. L., Wahba, W. W., & Dowdell, J. L. (1996). Determination of absorption time of ethanol in social drinkers. *Forensic Science International, 77*(3), 169–177. Available from https://doi.org/10.1016/0379-0738(95)01859-X.

Yuille, J. C., & Tollestrup, P. A. (1990). Some effects of alcohol on eyewitness memory. *Journal of Applied Psychology, 75*(3), 268–273. Available from https://doi.org/10.1037/0021-9010.75.3.268.

Further reading

Babor, T., et al. (2010). *Alcohol: No ordinary commodity: Research and public policy* (Second edition). Oxford: Oxford University Press.

Colloff, M. F., & Flowe, H. D. (2016). The effects of acute alcohol intoxication on the cognitive mechanisms underlying false facial recognition. *Psychopharmacology*, 2139–2149, https://doi.org/10.1007/s00213-016-4263-4.

Cutler, B. L., Penrod, S. D., & Dexter, H. R. (1990). *Juror sensitivity to eyewitness identification evidence. Law and human behavior*. Germany: Springer. Available from https://doi.org/10.1007/BF01062972.

Fillmore, M. T., & Blackburn, J. (2002). Compensating for alcohol-induced impairment: Alcohol expectancies and behavioral disinhibition. *Journal of Studies on Alcohol, 63*, 237–246. Available from https://doi.org/10.15288/jsa.2002.63.237.

Flowe, H. D., Colloff, M. F., Karoğlu, N., Zelek, K., Ryder, H., Humphries, J. E., & Takarangi, M. K. T. (2017). The effects of alcohol intoxication on accuracy and the confidence–accuracy relationship in photographic simultaneous line-ups. *Applied Cognitive Psychology*. Available from https://doi.org/10.1002/acp.3332.

Scottish Government. (2019). *Scottish crime and justice survey 2017/2018: Main findings.* Edinburgh: Scottish Government. Available from https://www.gov.scot/publications/scottish-crime-justice-survey-2017-18-main-findings/.

Victims & witnesses | The Crown Prosecution Service. (2018). Retrieved 29 July 2019, from <https://www.cps.gov.uk/victims-witnesses>.

Zeichner, A., & Pihl, R. O. (1979). Effects of alcohol and behavior contingencies on human aggression. *Journal of Abnormal Psychology, 88*(2), 153–160. Available from https://doi.org/10.1037/0021-843X.88.2.153.

Chapter 18

Spiritual and religious influences

Paramabandhu Groves
Camden and Islington NHS Foundation Trust, London, United Kingdom

Introduction

Alcohol has a long and intimate history with religion and spirituality. Symbolic of blood, it is used as a sacrament as in the Christian Eucharist and in rituals from other traditions. For example, alcohol is used in the blood bowl ritual of Chinese religions, which is performed to enable a deceased mother pass from hell to be fully transformed into an ancestor (Cann, 2016). Alcohol may be used as a libation to spirits, whether ancestors or gods. Taken to intoxication, alcohol may be used to induce a state that facilitates access to the spiritual world (Room, 2013; Washburne, 1968).

What is spirituality?

Spirituality has a broad range of meanings that can be hard to define clearly. A working definition from the European SPES Institute (2017) states: "Spirituality is people's multiform search for a transcendent meaning of life that connects them to all living beings and brings them in touch with God or 'Ultimate Reality'". Reviewing the addiction literature, Cook (2004) found 13 aspects to spirituality, which are listed in Table 18.1. Most of the studies were from Christian or 12-Step spirituality. The concepts that were found most frequently were '*transcendence*' and '*relatedness*', which were found respectively in over 40% and 30% of the papers studied. The next commonest were '*core/force/soul*' and '*meaning/purpose*', which were found in over 10% of the papers.

Walker, Godlaski, and Staton-Tindall (2013) noted ten ideas about spirituality that were not found in Cook's study. In particular they commented on the absence of awe and of compassion. Awe or radical amazement, especially of the transcendent, is associated with a sense of vastness and immeasurability. It might be expected to be included since it gives a larger perspective on life and by expanding the sense of personal time available, for oneself and others, promotes positive moral behavior. Compassion is

The Handbook of Alcohol Use - Understandings from Synapse to Society.
DOI: https://doi.org/10.1016/B978-0-12-816720-5.00008-6

TABLE 18.1 Components of spirituality (Cook, 2004).

Component	Meaning in brief
1. Relatedness	Interpersonal relationships
2. Transcendence	Recognition of a transcendent dimension to life
3. Humanity	The distinctiveness of humanity
4. Core/force/soul	The inner 'core', 'force' or 'soul' of a person
5. Meaning/purpose	Meaning and purpose in life
6. Authenticity/truth	Authenticity and truth
7. Values	Values, importance and worth
8. Non-materiality	Opposition of the spiritual to the material
9. (Non) religiousness	Opposition of spirituality to, or identity with, religion
10. Wholeness	Holistic wellness, wholeness or health
11. Self-knowledge	Self-knowledge and self-actualization
12. Creativity	Creativity of the human agent
13. Consciousness	Consciousness and awareness

common to many spiritual traditions and might be expected in response to suffering, notably those suffering from problems related to addiction.

Miller (1998) considers spirituality to have three elements. Firstly behavior, such as spiritual practices like prayer or meditation. Secondly belief, which could include belief in a deity, inter-relatedness of beings or spirit, and life beyond physical death. Thirdly experiences, for example feelings of peace, oneness or other experiences that foster one's conviction in spirituality.

Whereas spirituality is personal and subjective, religion may be understood as the activity of institutions within which individuals may practice, and so tends to be social rather than individual. Many people access spirituality through organized religion, but others experience or practice spirituality without involvement in formal religion. Although spirituality and religion are not identical there is clearly a large overlap, and for that reason this chapter explores the literature relating to both spirituality and religion.

Spiritual and religious understandings of alcohol misuse

Although as noted above, alcohol plays a part in many religious contexts, religions may view the misuse of alcohol as a spiritual problem. In Christianity addiction typically is associated with sin or rebellion against God (Cook, 2009). Although within this there appear to be different understandings. For example, addiction to alcohol may be seen as a moral failing, or more broadly that addiction is part of the human condition of being sinful. In contrast, Cook (2009, p. 146) has argued that rather than sin, grace is central to a Christian theological understanding of addiction. Grace is the unmerited favor freely bestowed on humans by God, which finds an important place in Christian spirituality in the context of the experience of powerlessness against alcohol addiction. The choice in addiction is seen to be between self-will and God's will, with surrendering to God's will as the way to overcome addiction (Mercadante, 2015). The Latter-day Saints similarly emphasize the importance of choice. Addiction is seen as the result of ignoring God's will and falling prey to Satan, although once someone is dependent on alcohol they are viewed as unable to make a wise choice (Holt, 2015). Moreover, according to Latter-day Saint teaching, in continuing with addictive behavior one is forfeiting eternal relationships (with loved ones and with God) for temporary and ultimately futile relationships with alcohol. Given that addiction is regarded as going against God's commandments, someone may be reluctant to admit to problematic alcohol use and be ashamed to seek help.

Initially Islam recognized benefits from alcohol use, as well as adverse effects, although the latter were considered greater. Gradually the Qur'an came to prohibit alcohol use, regarding it as the "Handiwork of Satan", owing to the negative effects of drinking, such as being unable to recite the Qur'an correctly and precipitating fighting (Ali, 2014). When someone forgets that they have a sacred side, as well as a profane side, they may neglect their true purpose, which is to worship God and come under the influence of Satan leading to problematic alcohol use. In addition, any sinful activity is thought to produce spiritual agitation, which may be covered over by alcohol use.

Buddhism advocates abstention from or minimal use of alcohol to avoid intoxication. The Buddha recognized and commented on the possible adverse consequences of alcohol use such as loss of wealth, increased quarreling, losing a good reputation, and weakening of intellect (Dīgha Nikāya, 1995, p. 462). Although Buddhist scriptures do not give a theory on alcohol addiction, a central concern of Buddhism is craving as a chief cause of suffering, which provides a starting point for a Buddhist understanding of addiction (Groves & Farmer, 1994). Behaviors resulting from craving, such as alcohol misuse, are regarded as unskillful, that is unwise, simply because they produce undesirable effects. The choice to act with craving is seen as stemming from spiritual ignorance, by which is meant a clouding of the mind due to not seeing the true nature of reality. Alcohol as an intoxicant only exacerbates this clouding of the mind.

In a letter to Bill W, the co-founder of Alcoholics Anonymous (AA), Carl Jung described addiction to alcohol as a spiritual problem. He used the phrase *spiritus contra spiritum*, meaning literally, 'spirit against spirit'

(Sacred Connections, 2016). That is, the drive for the use of alcohol was seen as a thwarted spiritual search. Jung suggested that craving for alcohol was the search on a lower level for the spiritual thirst for wholeness or union with God. Leonard (1990), a Jungian analyst, has expanded on this idea describing archetypes that reflect the ambiguity between addiction and spirituality. For example, she refers to the Romantic archetype – one who rejects established norms and conventions and feels rejected by society – operating in the early phase of addiction, as the seduction, especially by altered mental states and escape from difficult quotidian realities. Properly understood the Romantic archetype could be seen as a yearning for unification with the divine, but short-circuited through alcohol or drugs, it leads to problematic use. Leonard observes that the word addict, from the Latin *addictus*, meaning one who has given one's assent to, originally had a positive connotation of surrendering, especially one's voice, to the gods. Later it came to mean being enslaved, in particular a slave to debt or theft.

Spirituality and religion as preventative forces

A large body of literature suggests that involvement with spirituality or religion may be associated with lower incidence of alcohol misuse (Witkiewitz, McCallion, & Kirouac, 2016). Alcohol consumption varies between different religions as well as according to whether individuals are actively involved with spirituality or religion.

Bakke (2015) notes that about half of the world's population does not drink alcohol. Quoting World Health Organization (WHO) statistics, he observes that the highest prevalence of non-drinking is in Eastern Mediterranean Region that includes the Muslim countries of the Middle East and North Africa, with 89.8% non-drinkers. This is followed by the WHO South East Asian Region, with 76.6% lifetime abstainers, then the African region with 57.4%. Islam has a strong and explicit ban on alcohol, although exceptions, albeit controversially, have sometimes been made (Sheikh & Islam, 2018). In studies of countries with people from both religions, Muslims are generally less likely to drink than Christians (Amit, Hasking, & Manderson, 2013; Badr, Taha, & Dee, 2014; Ghandour, Karam, & Maalouf, 2009) and than Jews (Sznitman et al., 2015). However, among Christians rates of abstinence vary between different affiliations, with those from American evangelical churches appearing to have particularly high rates of abstinence. A United States National Survey revealed that the Latter-day Saints had the highest abstinence with 82.1% being teetotal, followed by the Church of God (79.1%) and the Assemblies of God (71.4%) (Michalak, Trocki, & Bond, 2006). 54.8% of Baptists were abstainers, 39.7% of Methodists, 28.7% of Catholics and 19.9% of Lutherans. By comparison, the same survey showed that 78.0% of Muslims were abstinent, 30.8% of Jewish and 25.1% of those with no religion. Those declaring no religion were a miscellaneous group including those who identified as spiritual, but without a religion.

The findings that religion is protective has been replicated among a wide range of different groups. For example, students in Brazil (Gomes, Andrade, Izbicki, Moreira-Almeida, & Oliviera, 2013), the Lebanon (Ghandour et al., 2009), South Africa (Amoateng, Setlalentoa, & Udomboso, 2017), Thailand (Newman, Shell, Li, & Innadda, 2006), the United Kingdom (El Ansari, Sebena, & Stock, 2014) and the United States (Wells, 2010), who have religious involvement, are less likely to use alcohol or use alcohol heavily. Similarly, religious attendance is protective among Canadian aboriginals (Rawana & Ames, 2012) and Latinos in Texas (Garcia, Ellison, Sunil, & Hill, 2013). Native specific practices are protective for homeless American Indians and Alaska Natives (Wendt et al., 2017).

How might religion and spirituality prevent alcohol misuse?

Prohibition by a religion, as in Islam, appears to lead to high rates of abstinence from alcohol, although if the prohibition is broken, greater levels of misuse may ensue. Thus, Arab Muslim men in Israel who do drink have higher levels of misuse than Israeli Arab Christians who drink (Baron-Epel et al., 2015). The same pattern has been observed comparing Arab students and Jewish students in Israel (Sznitman et al., 2015). Those who perceive their religious tradition to be more proscriptive appear to have lower levels of alcohol use (Kathol & Sgoutas-Emch, 2016). Scharer (2017) found that among undergraduate students from a wide range of religious traditions, fundamentalism reduced the impact of descriptive drinking norms on alcohol consumption, but not on alcohol-related problems. Breaking a moral code may result in shame, which is a global negative evaluation of oneself. Shame may be distinguished from guilt, which relates to the negative evaluation of a behavior, and which may be positive. Shame appears to be associated with higher levels of hazardous drinking (Prosek et al., 2017). For those whose religion prohibits alcohol, drinking may lead to shame, and this dysphoric affect may provoke further drinking, creating a negative cycle.

The high rates of abstinence among Christian Evangelical denominations may be due to the teaching on Christian perfection (Warner, 2009). The early Protestants eschewed asceticism, with celibacy before marriage being the only form of abstinence that Luther and Calvin advocated. Wesley, the founder of Methodism, also did not recommend teetotalism, although he did ban distilled spirits. However, he did popularize the idea that with sufficient striving one could achieve perfection, also called sanctification. This was taken up by New School Calvinists who started the American Temperance Society in 1826. In the pursuit of Christian perfection, the abstinence from alcohol was added to, through banning or discouraging other substances such as tobacco, coffee, tea and meat. The churches that take an especially strict interpretation of the doctrine of Christian perfection, as indicated through including various other taboos, are those denominations above that have the highest rates of abstinence from alcohol.

Religious participation may be more effective than just holding religious beliefs (Carmack & Lewis, 2016; Witkiewitz et al., 2016) and spirituality without religious affiliation may not be protective against alcohol misuse (King et al., 2013). For Christian adolescents, church attendance may be sufficient to prevent staring drinking, but for young adults greater Christian commitment appears to become more important as protective against drinking (Hope & Cook, 2001). Kathol and Sgoutas-Emch (2016) found that religious singing or chanting and reading of sacred texts was associated with lower alcohol use. Among Jewish young men in Israel, the orthodox were found to consume less alcohol than the secular (Nakash, Nagar, Barker, & Lotan, 2016). For the orthodox, religion appeared to provide a sense of meaning that protected against alcohol use. In addition, religious practices provided a lifestyle, such as low exposure to mass media, that contributed to less alcohol use. The perception of close friends' alcohol use may also mediate the positive effects of religiosity on alcohol consumption (Brechting & Carlson, 2015). The protective effect of religiousness may also be partly mediated by less positive alcohol expectancies among those with stronger religious affiliation (Sauer-Zavala, Burris, & Carson, 2014).

Several studies have looked at what sorts of relationship with God or the transcendent affects alcohol use and misuse. Hernandez, Salerno, and Bottoms (2010) examined the type of relationship with God held by undergraduates. Those who had a secure attachment appeared to misuse alcohol less than those with an avoidant or anxious-ambivalent style of attachment to God. The former tended to use trust- and faith-based spiritual coping styles, whereas the latter used more self-directing coping styles, which may be associated with feelings of abandonment by God. Hernandez and colleagues suggested this coping style may be key to mediating alcohol use, with alcohol being used as an alternative to manage negative affect in the face of feelings of being abandoned by God. A secure attachment may also allow doubt to be seen as positive and enable an individual to confront existential questions. This questing style of religiosity together with an intrinsic motivation, that is, feeling free to engage in religious practice, may be factors that mediate protection against hazardous alcohol use (Jankowski et al., 2015).

The type of relationship one has with God may affect drinking outcomes. For instance, Klassen and Grekin (2017) found that positive religious coping, such as feeling connected with God or with something transcendent like nature, was related to less frequent future episodes of heavy drinking among students. However, negative religious coping, for example perceiving stressful events in one's life as a punishment from God, was unrelated to heavy episodic drinking. Moore (2014) showed that belief that God has influence over drinking behavior, referred to as God locus of control, was associated with not drinking alcohol among college students.

Exploring the stages of drinking behavior, religion and spirituality may affect not just whether an individual starts drinking, but also protect against developing at-risk drinking. However, once someone has commenced at-risk drinking, other factors, such as genetic influences, may affect the speed of development of alcohol dependency, regardless of religion and spirituality (Haber et al., 2013). Childhood religiosity, while generally protective against early drinking, may be insufficient to offset the negative effects of childhood adversity on early patterns of heavy drinking (Porche, Fortuna, Wachholtz, & Stone, 2015).

Religion and spirituality in the recovery from alcohol misuse

As well as protecting individuals from developing problematic alcohol use, religion and spirituality may enhance recovery from alcohol misuse in both treatment-seeking and non-treatment-seeking populations (Al-Omari, Hamed, & Tariah, 2015; Rodríguez et al., 2018; Witkiewitz et al., 2016). Spiritual and religious experiences may prompt some people to seek treatment for problematic alcohol use (Witkiewitz et al., 2016). A review by Castaldelli-Maia and Bhugra (2014) suggests that religion and spirituality may help maintain abstinence, although a strong local drinking culture may still make individuals highly vulnerable to relapse. Possible means whereby spirituality and religion may promote recovery include the use of religious coping (Martin, Ellingsen, Tzilos, & Rohsenow, 2015), through giving greater meaning in life (Kleftaras & Katsogianni, 2012), and by improving mental health through the enhancement of forgiveness (Webb, Robinson, & Brower, 2011). The emphasis on aspects of spirituality such as forgiveness and gratitude may be especially helpful for women seeking treatment for alcohol misuse (Charzyńska, 2015). On a macro-level, religious and spiritual movements may provoke a collective 'sobering-up' in response to widespread drunkenness, as for example the temperance movement in the US and Europe in the 19th and early 20th centuries (Room, 2013). Untoward acts of nature, such as an earthquake, may be interpreted as punishment by God for drunkenness, leading to a widespread change in drinking behavior. Butler (as cited in Room, 2013) describes dramatic changes in drinking behavior following an earthquake in Ecuador in 1987. Ritual festivals that previously had been drunken fiestas became more sober, and public sobriety was viewed as important for resolving both social and spiritual problems.

Support for recovery may also be found through a return to a traditional culture with its links to spiritual or religious concepts and practices or through a spiritually oriented treatment. Such treatments may be addressed to all people with alcohol problems or have been created for adherents of particular religious denominations. They may be a stand-alone treatment or as an adjunct to conventional treatment. Of all the spiritual approaches to treatment, the most widespread is AA.

Alcoholics anonymous

The starting point for AA may be traced to a profound spiritual experience that led Bill W, at that time a struggling alcoholic, to give up drinking. He described crying out to God in despair and then experiencing "an illumination of enormous impact and dimension" (Sacred Connections, 2016). Bill W was also influenced by the Oxford Group, which was an independent evangelical Christian organization that was popular in the 1930s. The Oxford Group regarded anything that led to alienation from God as a sin, of which the principal sin was selfishness. Addictive behavior was seen as such a sin and a symptom of alienation from God. The solution proposed by the Oxford Group was God Control, that is, allowing God to control one's actions. The founders of AA were involved in the Oxford Group and took up some of its key principles. This led to the foundation of AA with a Christian-based spirituality at the heart with alcoholism viewed as a spiritual illness (Mercadante, 2015).

AA was founded in 1935. From the 1940s it expanded rapidly to become a worldwide organization, having over two million active members by the end of the century (Alcoholics Anonymous, 2019). In 1939 a book was published, generally referred to as the "Big Book", to describe how to recover from alcoholism. The core of the therapeutic process is based upon Twelve Steps (Alcoholics Anonymous Great Britain, 2019) (see Table 18.2).

The first three steps bring to the fore the centrality of powerlessness in relation to alcohol and the need for surrendering to a spiritual solution – God *as we understood Him*. The qualifier, as we understood Him, has enabled AA to be adopted by a wide range of people with different religious and spiritual backgrounds, and those with none. Nevertheless, the frequent usage of the term God, has put off some people who consider AA to be too religious. Possibly in order to minimize this problem, from the 1960s, AA has described itself as "spiritual, but not religious" (Kurtz & White, 2015). How the "Higher Power" is interpreted varies between nations, probably depending on how strongly secular or not the local culture is. The International Collaborative Study of Alcoholics Anonymous found that the proportion of people who viewed the Higher Power as a Christian God ranged from only 13% in Sweden, to between a third and a half in Iceland, Poland, Mexico and Switzerland (Mäkelä et al., 1996). Thus, even in the most strongly Christian countries studied, a half or more did not conceive of the Higher Power in terms of a Christian God.

Having accepted the philosophical or spiritual underpinnings as laid out in the first three steps, the preponderance of the steps, that is steps four to ten, deal with ethical behavior. The emphasis is on recognizing ethical shortcomings and, with the assistance of God, making amends, wherever possible

TABLE 18.2 The twelve steps of alcoholics anonymous.

Step		Key themes
One	We admitted we were powerless over alcohol - that our lives had become unmanageable.	Recognition of powerless in relation to alcohol and need for a relationship with a transcendent Power
Two	Came to believe that a Power greater than ourselves could restore us to sanity.	
Three	Made a decision to turn our will and our lives over to the care of God as we understood Him.	
Four	Made a searching and fearless moral inventory of ourselves.	Ethical behavior
Five	Admitted to God, to ourselves and to another human being the exact nature of our wrongs.	
Six	Were entirely ready to have God remove all these defects of character.	
Seven	Humbly asked Him to remove our shortcomings.	
Eight	Made a list of all persons we had harmed, and became willing to make amends to them all.	
Nine	Made direct amends to such people wherever possible, except when to do so would injure them or others.	
Ten	Continued to take personal inventory and when we were wrong promptly admitted it.	
Eleven	Sought through prayer and meditation to improve our conscious contact with God as we understood Him, praying only for knowledge of His will for us and the power to carry that out.	On-going spiritual practice
Twelve	Having had a spiritual awakening as the result of these steps, we tried to carry this message to alcoholics and to practice these principles in all our affairs.	Helping others

directly to the people involved. Step ten emphasizes that the attention to moral failings should continue as an on-going practice. The need for on-going work is also brought out in the final two steps. Step eleven involves seeking for help through spiritual practice by means of prayer and meditation. Finally, step twelve has an altruistic dimension, by exhorting sharing what has been learnt with other alcoholics. In particular, someone who has reached this stage may become a sponsor, to support others work through the steps.

In 1950 the Twelve Traditions were adopted internationally to describe the basis for the operation of the fellowship (Alcoholics Anonymous Great Britain, 2019). Each AA group operates autonomously and aims to be fully self-supporting. As the name of the fellowship implies, there is an emphasis on anonymity and on helping people to stop drinking as the principal aim. The orientation towards God and away from personal prestige or power is drawn out in the second tradition: "For our group purpose there is but one ultimate authority - a loving God as He may express Himself in our group conscience. Our leaders are but trusted servants; they do not govern".

The informal autonomous nature of groups within the fellowship has lent itself to some variations in approach, enabling for example the creation of gender-specific groups, such as Women for Sobriety. The ambiguity of the Higher Power while allowing potential appeal to people from a wide range of backgrounds, has also led to tension within the organization between those who wish to stress the Christian nature of AA and those who do not. Thus, on the one hand, the "Big Book Fundamentalists" draw inspiration from the Christian roots of AA, declaring Christian conversion to be key to sobriety. On the other, the "Modern Secularisers" aim to respond to those with no religious affiliation. Other secular alternatives have been set up along the lines of AA, such as Rational Recovery and SMART recovery (Kurtz & White, 2015).

Although AA is peer-led, its popularity has led health professionals to use its principles in treatment, as for example the Minnesota Model. This was created in Minnesota state in the 1950s, as an intensive 28-day in-patient program delivered by professional and trained recovering peers, combined with participation in AA during and after the treatment (Anderson, McGovern, & DuPont, 1999). Twelve Step Facilitation (TSF) was developed as one of three treatment modalities in Project MATCH, a large research trial to study treating dependent drinkers. Consisting of up to 12 sessions, the aim of TSF was to acquaint patients with the principles of AA and encourage attending AA meetings (Project MATCH Research Group, 1993).

Studies consistently show that people participating in AA have favorable outcomes (Cook, 2009; Kelly, 2017). In the rigorous Project MATCH trial, TSF was found to be as effective as other treatments and that its effects were mediated through AA attendance and active AA involvement. Kelly (2017) has questioned how far AA's successful outcomes are mediated by religious or spiritual mechanisms. His review of the literature suggests that for those with more severe addiction problems, changes in spirituality may indeed be important, although alongside other factors such as learning to manage negative affects without drinking. For those with less severe drinking problems, benefits appear to be mainly mediated by social mechanisms, such as dropping drinkers from one's social circle. The expansion of AA to include a much broader range of severity of alcohol problems, might account for a wider set of recovery pathways as AA has developed. However, how spiritual the mediating mechanisms are may depend to some extent on how broad a conception of spirituality one has, and whether this includes human qualities prominent in AA such as gratitude, hope and forgiveness. Jung's "protective wall of human community" although typically viewed as purely secular, could be seen as spiritual, since it contributes to going beyond self-centeredness (Kurtz, 2017). Pragmatically, the spiritual storyline, Kelly suggests, may act as a means of cohering the set of twelve step therapeutic approaches.

Exploring what spiritual and religious factors might be important for outcomes, Dermis and Galanter (2016) reviewed studies conducted on twelve step members, and concluded that predictors of a positive outcome included feeling God's presence daily, believing in the universality of a Higher Power, and serving as an AA sponsor. They suggested that the first of these may fulfill a need for a daily sense of spiritual renewal and foster a sense of gratitude for the gift of sobriety. The universality of a Higher Power may provide a connection to wider humanity, and acting as a sponsor give a greater sense of purpose to life.

Given that reducing or stopping drinking alone might lead to changes in spirituality, Krentzman, Strobbe, Harris, Jester, and Robinson (2017), attempted to disentangle changes due to AA independently of changes due to reduced drinking. They found that less drinking was associated with higher levels of purpose in life and self-forgiveness. AA involvement was associated with increased positive religious coping, daily spiritual experiences, and forgiveness of others. Both reduced drinking and AA involvement were independently associated with spiritual or religious practices.

Kurtz and White (2015) consider the two principal dimensions of spirituality in AA to be "beyond", that is, transcendence, through surrender to God or a Higher Power, and "between", which is connection and mutuality, through association with others in meetings and by sponsorship. They also identified six facets of recovery spirituality: release, gratitude, humility, tolerance, forgiveness and being-at-home. The release is from the bondage of addiction, which is likely also to promote gratitude. In turn, gratitude is further encouraged through writing a list of things one feels grateful for. Humility refers to eschewing notions of being perfect or of no value. Tolerance counteracts righteous indignation and forgiveness works against resentment. Finding a community that one can be accepted in, despite one's flaws, can produce a sense of being-at-home.

Mindfulness

Following the introduction of mindfulness to help with chronic pain and stress in the late 1970s by Kabat-Zinn (1990), there has been a burgeoning interest in the application of mindfulness to a range of mental health disorders. Mindfulness appears to lend itself in particular to preventing relapse into addictive behavior, although it may also be viewed as useful to provide spiritual support and promotion of well-being in the overall recovery journey (Groves, 2014).

In a therapeutic context, mindfulness may be considered to be the deliberate paying of attention to present experience with an attitude of curiosity and kindness. Mindfulness is cultivated through formal practices, such as the body scan or meditation following the breath, and through informal practices, by which is meant cultivating mindful attention in daily life for example when walking to the bus stop or taking a shower, or through a mini-meditation called a breathing space. Usually mindfulness is taught in a group format. A course of mindfulness-based relapse prevention (MBRP) or mindfulness-based addiction recovery (MBAR) typically lasts 6–8 weeks. Emphasis is placed on becoming aware of high-risk situations, and managing negative affects and substance-related cognitions. Problematic thoughts and emotions are responded to by holding in mindful awareness and changing the relationship to them, rather than by trying to change the content of the experience. Through this, mindfulness may help to prevent relapse by enabling individuals to become more aware of the overall relapse process, especially the automatic processes that can drive relapse, as well as by desensitising to relapse triggers (Curtis, Zack, & McMain, 2002).

There have been several reviews of studies of the efficacy of mindfulness in addictions (Sancho et al., 2018; Wilson et al., 2017). Overall there is some support for the use of mindfulness in helping to reduce drinking, although with mixed findings and limitations in the research that has been conducted to date. The strongest evidence appears to be in reducing craving and improving mood-state and emotional dysregulation, which is consistent with how mindfulness is thought to work. Given this, at present mindfulness is probably best used as an adjunct to standard treatment.

Religious-affiliated treatments

Practitioners from a number of religions have drawn on their own tradition to respond to problematic alcohol use among members of their faith group. The commonest response has been to adapt the twelve steps of AA to their own tradition. The Millati Islami is an example of the twelve steps adapted for Muslims (Ali, 2014). Particular Islamic practices are included such as *Salaat* (prayer service) and *Iqraa* (reading and studying), which replace prayer and meditation in the usual eleventh step. Addiction is seen as a test from Allah, and since God in Islam is seen as ineffable, the qualifier "as we understood Him" is omitted. From the moral section of the steps, admitting wrongs to another is also left out, since Islam discourages making sins public. Similarly, the Latter-day Saints have adapted the twelve steps in line with their own theology (Holt, 2015). Belief in the atonement of Jesus Christ is seen as central to overcoming addiction. Coming into relationship with Christ by recognizing the impact of sin, individuals are able to be released from the suffering caused by sin, including addiction.

The twelve steps are generally considered to be consistent with Jewish (Loewenthal, 2014) and Quaker spirituality (Chambers, 2015). In the case of Quakers, prayer and meditation may be particularly important elements in supporting recovery. Some treatment programs have been created that include Jewish spiritual teachings, sometimes Kabbalistic, to provide culturally sensitive treatment that provides a sense of meaning to people's lives in recovery.

Native Americans have made use of the twelve steps, again with changes to reflect their own belief system (Owen, 2014). For example, the eleventh step has been altered to (italics to indicate the change): "Seek through prayer and meditation to improve our conscious contact with *the Equality and Brotherhood of all Mother Earth's children and the Great Balancing Harmony of the Total Universe*". The changes draw out important values for Native Americans, such as respect for nature and the concept of balance. Also included are traditional practices, including elements of the medicine wheel, purification through sweat lodges and the sacred pipe.

Re-affirming Aboriginal spirituality has been seen as way forward to help respond to alcohol problems among indigenous people in Australia, which the twelve steps may support (d'Abbs & Chenhall 2013). Spirituality is seen as connecting Aboriginal people to each other, to the earth and to a higher being. The concept of powerlessness in AA has been applied to the experience of indigenous people in post-colonial Australia with a loss of spirituality.

Buddhists have found overlap between the twelve steps and the ethical and meditative aspects of Buddhist practice (Groves, 2014). In particular, the inclusion of meditation in the eleventh step, has stimulated Buddhist or Buddhist-inspired twelve step groups that emphasize meditation. Details of such groups, sometimes called Eleventh Step Groups, are given by the Buddhist Recovery Network (2019). Perhaps owing to the popularity of mindfulness and the centrality of meditation in Buddhism, there has been a burgeoning of these groups, which increased in the US from 94 in 2014 to 155 in 2016 (Groves, 2019, p. 235).

Some practitioners have wanted to find ways of creating a more fully Buddhist approach to recovery. Levine (2014) has developed a treatment program called Refuge Recovery that is based on the Buddhist teaching of the Four Noble Truths. The emphasis is on recognizing suffering caused by

TABLE 18.3 Eight step recovery.

One	Accepting that our human life will bring suffering
Two	Seeing how we create extra suffering in our lives
Three	Recognizing impermanence shows us that our suffering can end
Four	Being willing to step onto the path of recovery, and discover freedom
Five	Transforming our speech, actions, and livelihood
Six	Placing positive values at the center of our lives
Seven	Making every effort to stay on the path of recovery
Eight	Helping others to share the benefits I have gained

addiction and that recovery is possible, especially through practising ethics, meditation and wisdom. Mason-John and Groves (2018) developed Eight Step Recovery, which integrates elements of some standard psycho-social treatments, such as Motivational Enhancement Therapy, with traditional Buddhist ideas and practices (see Table 18.3). Both Eight Step and Refuge Recovery encourage the formation of Sangha, that is, the creation of friendship and support among people practicing in these communities.

Naikan was developed by a Yoshimoto Ishin in Japan in the 1940s, from Jodu Shinshu Buddhism (Ozawa-de Silva, 2007). The emphasis is on eschewing self-centeredness by cultivating gratitude through intensive reflection on what one has been given. From the 1960s it has been used to treat people with alcohol problems (Suwaki, 1980). A follow-up study of 129 patients found an abstinent rate of 49% at one year (Takemoto, Usukine, & Otsu, 1979).

Conclusions

Given that alcohol is one of humanity's most widely used substances, it is not surprising that it should intersect with such important areas of life as religion and spirituality. Religion, especially, and spirituality both appear to be protective against alcohol misuse. Spiritual and religious approaches to treatment have been developed that appear to be helpful. The most widespread is AA, which as well as being popular in its own right has inspired programs that are influenced by other religious and spiritual traditions.

Some concern has been expressed at the possible degrading or distorting of a religious tradition through its involvement with treating alcohol misuse. For example, some Native Americans fear that employing for wages traditional healers will compromise them (Owen, 2014). There has also been discussion as to whether mindfulness taken out of its Buddhist context is a helpful adaptation or merely distorts and trivialises (Vélez de Cea, 2016). Perhaps a greater block to the use of spiritual and religious approaches is the skepticism of professionals (Kelly, 2017). However, to not make use of assistance from spiritual and religious traditions is to forgo a rich source of help and support that may have the advantage of providing benefit not just in the early phases of seeking treatment, but also on the long journey of recovery.

References

Alcoholics Anonymous. (2019). Retrieved from <https://www.aa.org/assets/en_US/smf-132_en.pdf> Accessed 21.05.19.

Alcoholics Anonymous Great Britain. (2019). Retrieved from <https://www.alcoholics-anonymous.org.uk/About-AA> Accessed 22.05.19.

Ali, M. (2014). Perspectives on drug addiction in Islamic history and theology. *Religions*, *5*, 912–928. Available from https://doi.org/10.3390/rel5030912.

Al-Omari, H., Hamed, R., & Tariah, H. A. (2015). The role of religion in the recovery from alcohol and substance abuse among Jordanian adults. *Journal of Religion & Health*, *54*, 1268–1277. Available from https://doi.org/10.1007/s10943-014-9868-5.

Amit, N., Hasking, P., & Manderson, L. (2013). Demographic factors associated with alcohol use among young men in rural areas of Sarawak. *Addiction Research & Theory*, *21*(5), 391–401. Available from https://doi.org/10.3109/16066359.2012.731114.

Amoateng, Y. A., Setlalentoa, B. M. P., & Udomboso, C. (2017). Does religion affect alcohol and tobacco use among students at North-West University, South Africa? *African Population Studies*, *31*(1), 3212–3224.

Anderson, D. J., McGovern, J. P., & DuPont, R. L. (1999). The origins of the Minnesota model of addiction treatment – A first person account. *Journal of Addictive Diseases*, *18*(1), 107–114. Available from https://doi.org/10.1300/J069v18n01_10.

Badr, L. K., Taha, A., & Dee, V. (2014). Substance abuse in middle eastern adolescents living in two different countries: Spiritual, cultural, family and personal factors. *Journal of Religion & Health*, *53*, 1060–1074. Available from https://doi.org/10.1007/s10943-013-9694-1.

Bakke, Ø. (2015). Are nondrinkers missing from the picture? *Substance Use & Misuse*, *50*, 512–516. Available from https://doi.org/10.3109/10826084.2015.987184.

Baron-Epel, O., Bord, S., Elias, W., Zarecki, C., Shiftan, Y., & Gesser-Edelsburg, A. (2015). Alcohol consumption among Arabs in Israel: A qualitative study. *Substance Use & Misuse*, *50*, 268–273. Available from https://doi.org/10.3109/10826084.2014.962051.

Brechting, E. H., & Carlson, C. R. (2015). Religiousness and alcohol use in college students: Examining descriptive drinking norms as mediators. *Journal of Child & Adolescent Substance Abuse*, *24*, 1–11. Available from https://doi.org/10.1080/1067828X.2014.958000.

Buddhist Recovery Network. (2019). Retrieved from <http://buddhistrecovery.org> Accessed 24.05.19.

Cann, C. K. (2016). Mothers and spirits: Religious identity, alcohol, and death. *Religions*, *7*, 94. Available from https://doi.org/10.3109/10826084.2015.978623.

Carmack, C. C., & Lewis, R. K. (2016). Assessing whether religious behaviors and positive and negative affect are associated with alcohol use and abuse among a sample of college students living in the Midwest. *Journal of Religion & Health*, *55*, 1107–1119. Available from https://doi.org/10.1007/s10943-016-0214-y.

Castaldelli-Maia, J. M., & Bhugra, D. (2014). Investigating the interlinkages of alcohol use and misuse, spirituality and culture – Insights from a systematic review. *International Review of Psychiatry*, *26*(3), 352–367. Available from https://doi.org/10.3109/09540261.2014.899999.

Chambers, H. (2015). Spirituality and Quaker approaches to substance use and addiction. *Religions*, *6*, 385–403. Available from https://doi.org/10.3390/rel6020385.

Charzyńska, E. (2015). Sex differences in spiritual coping, forgiveness, and gratitude before and after a basic alcohol addiction treatment program. *Journal of Religion & Health*, *54*, 1931–1949. Available from https://doi.org/10.1007/s10943-015-0002-0.

Cook, C. C. H. (2004). Addiction and spirituality. *Addiction*, *99*, 539–551. Available from https://doi.org/10.1111/j.1360-0443.00715.x.

Cook, C. C. H. (2009). Substance misuse. In C. C. H. Cook, A. Powell, & A. Sims (Eds.), *Spirituality and psychiatry* (pp. 139–168). London: Royal College of Psychiatrists.

Curtis, B. F., Zack, M., & McMain, S. (2002). An information-processing analysis of mindfulness: Implications for relapse prevention in the treatment of substance abuse. *Clinical Psychology: Science and Practice*, *9*, 275–299. Available from https://doi.org/10.1093/clipsy.9.3.275.

d'Abbs, P., & Chenhall, R. (2013). Spirituality and religion in response to substance misuse among indigenous Australians. *Substance Use & Misuse*, *48*, 1114–1129. Available from https://doi.org/10.3109/10826084.2013.800746.

Dermis, H., & Galanter, M. (2016). The role of twelve-step-related spirituality in addiction recovery. *Journal of Religion & Health*, *55*, 510–521. Available from https://doi.org/10.1007/s10943-015-0019-4.

Dīgha Nikāya. (1995). *The long discourses of the Buddha.* Translated by M. Walshe. Boston, MA: Wisdom

El Ansari, W., Sebena, R., & Stock, C. (2014). Do importance of religious faith and healthy lifestyle modify the relationship between depressive symptoms and four indicators of alcohol consumption? A survey of students across seven universities in England, Wales, and Northern Ireland. *Substance Use & Misuse*, *49*, 211–220. Available from https://doi.org/10.3109/10826084.2013.824476.

European SPES Institute. (2017). *Spiritual-based humanism.* Retrieved from <http://eurospes.org/content/our-mission-spiritual-based-humanism> Accessed 07.05.19.

Garcia, G., Ellison, C. G., Sunil, T. S., & Hill, T. D. (2013). Religion and selected health behaviors among Latinos in Texas. *Journal of Religion & Health*, *52*, 18–31. Available from https://doi.org/10.1007/s10943.012.9640-7.

Ghandour, L. A., Karam, E. G., & Maalouf, W. E. (2009). Lifetime alcohol use, abuse and dependence among university students in Lebanon: Exploring the role of religiosity in different religious faiths. *Addiction*, *104*, 940–948. Available from https://doi.org/10.1111/j.1360-0443.2009.02575x.

Gomes, F. C., Andrade, A. G., Izbicki, R., Moreira-Almeida, A., & Oliviera, L. G. (2013). Religion as a protective factor against drug use among Brazilian university students: A national survey. *Revista Brasiliera de Psiquiatria*, *35*, 29–37. Available from https://doi.org/10.1016/j.2012.05.010.

Groves, P. (2014). Buddhist approaches to addiction recovery. *Religions*, *5*, 985–1000. Available from https://doi.org/10.3390/rel50x000x.

Groves, P. (2019). Spirituality and addiction. In L. Zsolnai, & B. Flanagan (Eds.), *The Routledge international handbook of spirituality in society and the professions* (pp. 231–238). Abingdon: Routledge.

Groves, P., & Farmer, R. (1994). Buddhism and addictions. *Addiction Research*, *2*, 183–194.

Haber, J. R., Grant, J. D., Sartor, C. E., Koenig, L. B., Heath, A., & Jacob, T. (2013). Religion/spirituality, risk, and the development of alcohol dependence in female twins. *Psychology of Addictive Behaviors*, *27*(3), 562–572. Available from https://doi.org/10.1037/a0031915.

Hernandez, G., Salerno, J. M., & Bottoms, B. L. (2010). Attachment to God, spiritual coping, and alcohol use. *The International Journal for the Psychology of Religion*, *20*, 97–108. Available from https://doi.org/10.1080/10508611003607983.

Holt, J. (2015). A latter-day saint approach to addiction: Aetiology, consequences and treatment in a theological context. *Religions*, *6*, 1–13. Available from https://doi.org/10.3390/rel6010001.

Hope, L. C., & Cook, C. C. H. (2001). The role of Christian commitment in predicting drug use amongst church affiliated young people. *Mental Health, Religion & Culture*, *4*(2), 109–117. Available from https://doi.org/10.1080/13674670110048336.

Jankowski, P. J., Hardy, S. A., Zamboanga, B. L., Ham, L. S., Schwartz, S. J., Kim, S. Y., ... Cano, M. A. (2015). Religiousness and levels of hazardous alcohol use: A latent profile analysis. *Journal of Youth & Adolescence*, *44*, 1968–1983. Available from https://doi.org/10.1007/s10964-015-0302-4.

Kabat-Zinn, J. (1990). *Full catastrophe living: Using the wisdom of your body and mind to face stress, pain and illness*. New York: Dell Publishing.

Kathol, N., & Sgoutas-Emch, S. (2016). Alcohol use in college: The relationship between religion, spirituality, and proscriptive attitudes toward alcohol. *Journal of Religion & Health*, *56*, 437–449. Available from https://doi.org/10.1007/s10943-016-0210-2.

Kelly, J. (2017). Is alcoholics anonymous religious, spiritual, neither? Findings from 25 years of mechanisms of behaviour change research. *Addiction*, *112*, 929–936. Available from https://doi.org/10.1111/add.13590.

King, M., Marston, S., McManus, S., Brugha, T., Meltzer, H., & Bebbington, P. (2013). Religion, spirituality and mental health: Results from a national study of English households. *British Journal of Psychiatry*, *202*, 68–73. Available from https://doi.org/10.1192/bjp.bp.112.112003.

Klassen, B. J., & Grekin, E. R. (2017). Different forms of spirituality and heavy episodic drinking among college students. *Journal of American College Health*, *65*(2), 131–138. Available from https://doi.org/10.1080/07448481.2016.1262866.

Kleftaras, G., & Katsogianni, I. (2012). Spirituality, meaning in life, and depressive symptomatology in individuals with alcohol dependence. *Journal of Spirituality in Mental Health*, *14*, 268–288. Available from https://doi.org/10.1080/19349637.2012.730469.

Krentzman, A. R., Strobbe, S., Harris, J. I., Jester, J. M., & Robinson, E. A. R. (2017). Decreased drinking and alcoholics anonymous are associated with different dimensions of spirituality. *Psychology of Religion & Spirituality*, *9*(Supplement 1), S40–S48. Available from https://doi.org/10.1037/rel10000121.

Kurtz, L. F. (2017). The recovery community as a location for secular spirituality. *Addiction*, *112*, 939–940.

Kurtz, E., & White, W. L. (2015). Recovery spirituality. *Religions*, *6*, 58–81. Available from https://doi.org/10.3390/rel6010058.

Leonard, S. L. (1990). *Witness to the fire. Creativity and the veil of addiction*. Boston, MA: Shambhala.

Levine, N. (2014). *Refuge recovery: A Buddhist path to recovering from addiction*. New York: HarperCollins.

Loewenthal, K. M. (2014). Addiction: Alcohol and substance abuse in Judaism. *Religions*, *5*, 972–984. Available from https://doi.org/10.3390/rel15040972.

Mäkelä, K., Arminen, I., Bloomfield, K., Eisenbach-Stangl, I., Bergmark, K. H., Kurube, N., et al. (1996). *Alcoholics anonymous as a mutual help movement: A study in eight societies*. Madison, WI: University of Wisconsin Press.

Martin, R. A., Ellingsen, V. J., Tzilos, G. K., & Rohsenow, D. J. (2015). General and religious coping predict drinking outcomes for alcohol dependent adults in treatment. *The American Journal on Addiction, 24*, 240–245. Available from https://doi.org/10.1111/ajad.12181.

Mason-John, V., & Groves, P. (2018). *Eight step recovery: Using the Buddha's teachings to overcome addiction*. Cambridge: Windhorse Publications.

Mercadante, L. (2015). Sin and addiction: Conceptual enemies or fellow travellers? *Religions, 6*, 614–625. Available from https://doi.org/10.3390/rel6020614.

Michalak, L., Trocki, K., & Bond, J. (2006). Religion and alcohol in the U.S. national alcohol survey: How important is religion for abstention and drinking? *Drug & Alcohol Dependence, 87*, 268–280. Available from https://doi.org/10.1016/j.drugalcdep.2006.07.013.

Miller, W. (1998). Researching the spiritual dimensions of alcohol and other drug problems. *Addiction, 93*, 979–999.

Moore, E. (2014). Assessing God locus of control as a factor in college students' alcohol use and sexual behavior. *Journal of American College Health, 62*(8), 578–587.

Nakash, O., Nagar, M., Barker, Y., & Lotan, D. (2016). The association between religiosity and alcohol use: The mediating role of meaning in life and media exposure. *Mental Health, Religion & Culture, 19*(6), 574–586. Available from https://doi.org/10.1080/13674676.2016.1217515.

Newman, I. M., Shell, D. F., Li, T., & Innadda, S. (2006). Buddhism and adolescent alcohol use in Thailand. *Substance Use & Misuse, 41*, 1789–1800. Available from https://doi.org/10.1080/10826080601006490.

Owen, S. (2014). Walking in balance: Native American recovery programmes. *Religions, 5*, 1037–1049. Available from https://doi.org/10.3390/rel5041037.

Ozawa-de Silva, C. (2007). Demystifying Japanese therapy: An analysis of Naikan and the Ajase complex through Buddhist thought. *Ethos, 35*, 411–446.

Porche, M. V., Fortuna, L. R., Wachholtz, A., & Stone, R. T. (2015). Distal and proximal religiosity as protective factors for adolescent and emerging adult alcohol use. *Religions, 6*, 365–384. Available from https://doi.org/10.3390/rel6020365.

Project MATCH Research Group. (1993). Project MATCH: Rationale and methods for a multisite clinical trial matching patients to alcoholism treatment. *Alcoholism: Clinical and Experimental Research, 17*, 1130–1145.

Prosek, E. A., Giordano, A. L., Holm, J. M., Bevly, C. M., Sender, K. M., Ramsey, Z. B., & Abernathy, M. R. (2017). Experiencing shame: Collegiate alcohol abuse, religiosity and spirituality. *Journal of College Counselling, 20*, 126–138. Available from https://doi.org/10.1002/jocc.12065.

Rawana, J. S., & Ames, M. E. (2012). Protective predictors of alcohol use trajectories among Canadian Aboriginal youth. *Journal of Youth and Adolescence, 41*, 229–243. Available from https://doi.org/10.1007/s10964-011-9716-9.

Rodríguez, L. A., Villa, F., Hernández, E. K., Castillo, R. A., Gómez, D. A., & Navarro, E. I. P. (2018). Factors associated to not drinking alcoholic beverages in dependent individuals on recovery. *Investigación y Educación en Enfermería, 36*(3), e07. Available from https://doi.org/10.17533/udea.iee.v36n3e07.

Room, R. (2013). Spirituality, intoxication and addiction: Six forms of relationship. *Substance Use & Misuse, 48*, 1109–1113. Available from https://doi.org/10.3109/10826084.2013.803879.

Sacred Connections. (2016). *The history of alcoholics anonymous C. G. Jung / Bill W. Letters - Spiritus contra Spiritum*. Retrieved from <http://12wisdomsteps.com/related_topics/history/carl_jung.html> Accessed 06.05.19.

Sancho, M., de Gracia, M., Rodríguez, R. C., Mallorquí-Bagué, N., Sánchez-González, J., Trujols, J., ... Menchón, J. M. (2018). Mindfulness-based interventions for the treatment of substance and behavioural addictions: A systematic review. *Frontiers in Psychiatry*, *9*. Available from https://doi.org/10.3389/fpsyt.2018.00095, article 95.

Sauer-Zavala, S., Burris, J. L., & Carson, C. R. (2014). Understanding the relationship between religiousness, spirituality, and underage drinking: The role of positive alcohol expectancies. *Journal of Religion & Health*, *53*, 68–78. Available from https://doi.org/10.1007/s10943-012-9598-5.

Scharer, J. L. (2017). The role of religious fundamentalism in college students' perceived drinking norms, alcohol consumption, and alcohol-related problems. *Mental Health, Religion & Culture*, *20*(2), 188–201. Available from https://doi.org/10.1080/13674676.2017.133404.

Sheikh, M., & Islam, T. (2018). Islam, alcohol and identity: Towards a critical Muslim studies approach. *ReOrient*, *3*(2), 185–211.

Suwaki, H. (1980). Japan: Culturally based treatment of alcoholism. In G. Edwards, & A. Arif (Eds.), *Drug Problems in the sociocultural context: A basis for policies and programme planning* (pp. 139–143). Geneva: World Health Organization.

Sznitman, S. R., Bord, S., Elias, W., Gesser-Edelsburg, A., Shiftan, Y., & Baron-Epel, O. (2015). Examining differences in drinking patterns among Jewish and Arab university students in Israel. *Ethnicity & Health*, *20*(6), 594–610. Available from https://doi.org/10.1080/13557858.2014.961411.

Takemoto, T., Usukine, K., & Otsu, M. (1979). A follow-up study of alcoholic patients treated by naikan therapy. Paper presented at the Second Annual Meeting on Naikan. Kyoto, Japan.

Vélez de Cea, J. A. (2016). *Mindfulness for secular purposes: Distortion or adaptation of the Buddha's teachings?* Retrieved from <http://www.icdv.net/2014paper/ws5_08_en__Mindfulness_for_secular_purposes_400086783.pdf> Accessed 24.05.19.

Walker, R., Godlaski, T. M., & Staton-Tindall, M. (2013). Spirituality, drugs, and alcohol: A philosophical perspective. *Substance Use & Misuse*, *48*, 1233–1245. Available from https://doi.org/10.3109/10826084.2013.799020.

Warner, J. (2009). Temperance, alcohol, and the American evangelical: A reassessment. *Addiction*, *104*, 1075–1084. Available from https://doi.org/10.1111/j.1360-0443.2009.0261.x.

Washburne, C. (1968). Primitive religion and alcohol. *International Journal of Comparative Sociology*, *9*(1), 97–105.

Webb, J. R., Robinson, E. A. R., & Brower, K. J. (2011). Mental health, not social support, mediates the forgiveness-alcohol outcome relationship. *Psychology of Addictive Behaviors*, *25* (3), 462–473. Available from https://doi.org/10.1037/a0022502.

Wells, G. M. (2010). The effect of religiosity and campus alcohol culture on collegiate alcohol consumpsion. *Journal of American College Health*, *58*(4), 295–304.

Wendt, D. C., Collins, S. E., Nelson, L. A., Serafini, K., Clifasefi, S. L., & Donovan, D. M. (2017). Religious and spiritual practices among homeless urban American Indians and Alaska Natives with severe alcohol problems. *American Indian & Alaska Native Mental Health Research*, *24*(3), 39–62.

Wilson, A. D., Roos, C. R., Robinson, C. S., Stein, E. R., Manuel, J. A., Enkema, M. C., ... Witkiewitz, K. (2017). Mindfulness-based interventions for addictive behaviors: Implementation issues on the road ahead. *Psychology of Addictive Behaviors*, *31*(8). Available from https://doi.org/10.1037/adb0000319.

Witkiewitz, K., McCallion, E., & Kirouac, M. (2016). Religious affiliation and spiritual practices: An examination of the role of spirituality in alcohol use and alcohol use disorder. *Alcohol Research: Current Reviews*, *38*(1), 55–58.

Chapter 19

Alcohol use in adolescence across U.S. race/ethnicity: Considering cultural factors in prevention and interventions

Leah M. Bouchard[1], Sunny H. Shin[1,2] and Karen G. Chartier[1,2]
[1]*School of Social Work, Virginia Commonwealth University, Richmond, VA, United States,*
[2]*Department of Psychiatry, School of Medicine, Virginia Commonwealth University, Richmond, VA, United States*

Introduction

The purpose of this chapter is to describe drinking behaviors that are typical during adolescence and the ways that race/ethnicity are associated with alcohol consumption during this development stage. For the purposes of this chapter, adolescence is defined based on years of age. We define individuals ages 13–18 as adolescents, and we are considering adolescence as separate from young or emerging adulthood, which typically includes individuals between the ages of 18 and 25. Race/ethnicity will include the major U.S. census groups of Hispanic/Latino and non-Hispanic Black/African American, Asian, Native American/American Indian, and White. These population groups are broad and encompass a lot of diversity within them, including by gender, nationality, generational status, and rural and urban residence. When possible, we describe within racial/ethnic group differences that are important for understanding alcohol consumption during adolescence. We start below by providing an overview of adolescence as a developmental stage by considering the biological, psychological, and social changes that are occurring for most adolescents. We do this to set the stage for talking about the consequences and definitions of high-risk drinking during adolescence and how the typical course of alcohol consumption, from age of onset to any alcohol consumption and binge drinking and risk for alcohol use disorders can be different across racial/ethnic groups. We then describe intervention approaches that have been shown to be effective with adolescents, with a

The Handbook of Alcohol Use - Understandings from Synapse to Society.
DOI: https://doi.org/10.1016/B978-0-12-816720-5.00017-7

focus on empirically supported mechanisms for reducing alcohol consumption. At the end of the chapter, we discuss the importance of tailoring evidence-based interventions for diverse racial/ethnic populations, and we describe risk and protective factors that are differentially associated with adolescent drinking behaviors by race/ethnicity. We suggest that these differences should be considered when adapting interventions to the needs of a specific group. Further, considerations should be made for international application as race/ethnicity vary along with the importance of other sociodemographic features and cultural differences cross-nationally.

Adolescence as a developmental stage

Adolescence is a time of transition between childhood and adulthood characterized by numerous biological, psychological, and social changes that make this age group more susceptible to initiating and using alcohol. The Surgeon General emphasized in the first Call to Action on the prevention and reduction of underage drinking that in order to decrease the incidents and occurrences of adolescent alcohol use, it must be understood in its developmental contexts (U.S. Department of Health and Human Services, 2007).

Biological changes

Adolescence is characterized by unique and fundamental restructuring of the brain. Behaviorally, these brain changes manifest themselves in a number of ways (Bava & Tapert, 2010). For example, during adolescence, neurotransmitters in the prefrontal cortex responsible for transmitting behavioral responses to emotional stimuli have not yet reached full maturation. This ongoing maturation of the prefrontal cortex can leave adolescents receptive to heightened levels of sensitivity to reward pleasures and a decreased capability to inhibit responses, therefore resulting in a higher likelihood of participating in risk-seeking behaviors such as experimentation with alcohol (Whitesell, Bachand, Peel, & Brown, 2013). These neurobiological developments, combined with exposure to psychological and social risk factors, such as those described below, could leave adolescents more susceptible to participating in alcohol use (Patrick & Shulenberg, 2014).

Psychological changes

Psychological changes adolescents often experience at this age include the development of operational thought processes, organized communication, increased self-awareness and focus on independence, and identity formation (Berk, 2007). During this age, the actual and psychological perceived importance of what happens 'present-day' outweighs the concept of future thought processes. Youth have difficulty relating to events and experiences outside of their own existences (Ogden & Hagen, 2014). They become more sensitive to immediate social reward stimuli during this developmental period (Bava & Tapert, 2010; Ogden & Hagen, 2014). This puts them at increased risk for engaging in dangerous behaviors with immediate gratification, such as drug and/or alcohol use or sensation-seeking activities.

During adolescence, behavioral self-regulation plays a vital role in determining whether or not adolescents participate in substance using behaviors. For some, the transition into adolescence associates itself with a right to operate independently of others, especially adults, despite the paucity and comprehension of independence and self-identity. Therefore, the processes involved when an individual thinks, does, says, and feels, play important roles in making decisions, especially with a younger population. Some of these important decision-making risk factors include the decreased inhibition control and low levels of harm avoidance, combined with high levels of reward-seeking tendencies noted above (Monahan, King, Shulman, Cauffman, & Chassin, 2015).

Further, coping strategies begin to develop and mature during adolescence as individuals are faced with growing stressful circumstances in combination with seeking independence and autonomy from their parents or caregivers. Some adolescents develop positive coping strategies; however, others may cope with substances such as alcohol (Cooper, Wood, Orcutt, & Albino, 2003). For example, research showed alcohol use is related to anxiety (Borges, Lejuez, & Felton, 2018), suggesting it may be a coping strategy for adolescents experiencing social anxiety or other forms of anxiety. More frequent use and greater quantities of alcohol were also related with higher levels of depression (Cairns, Yap, Pilkington, & Jorm, 2014) and with victimization experiences (Topper, Castellanos-Ryan, Mackie, & Conrod, 2011). See Zimmer-Gembeck and Skinner (2011) and Compas, Connor-Smith, Saltzman, Thomsen, and Wadsworth (2001) for an expanded discussion of this topic, i.e., coping styles during adolescence.

Social changes

Adolescence is often characterized by reduced social/parental control and greater freedom to choose behaviors and lifestyles. Young people also become more closely bonded to their peers (Ogden & Hagen, 2014). They tend to pay more attention to advice and feedback of peers and express fewer interests in parents' activities. They may distance themselves from parents or caregivers at this time as they seek independence. Moving from dependence to independence is coupled with critical identity formation, which drives adolescents to seek out people they can look up to or places and groups in which they can belong (Ogden & Hagen, 2014).

Belongingness becomes essential and may take the form of adolescents quickly and uncritically ascribing to beliefs or positions if it brings them closer to people they admire. This combination of seeking to belong and drawing closer to peers may lead to stronger peer influence, particularly as it pertains to use of substances such as alcohol. Middle adolescence (ages 14–17) is specifically vulnerable to the initiation of substance using behaviors based on different risk factors, namely low levels of impulse control and enhanced reward-seeking tendencies. Perceived norms, the presence of peers, and inexperience in self-regulatory intuitiveness leaves adolescents particularly sensitive to these risk factors and thus increases the likelihood of engaging in substance use (Chassin, Fora, & King, 2004).

Consequences of alcohol use for adolescents

There are numerous consequences related to adolescent alcohol use, including for neurodevelopment, risky behaviors, and physical and mental health. Several large U.S. cohort studies have sought to clarify the relationship between adolescent brain development and alcohol use, including the National Consortium on Alcohol and NeuroDevelopment (NCANDA) (Pfefferbaum et al., 2016, 2018) and the Adolescent Brain Cognitive Development (ABCD) study (Lisdahl et al., 2018). Alcohol use can have a long-term impact on the brain, especially if consumed in large quantities or high frequency during adolescence when the brain is undergoing critical structural and functional maturation. Control over inhibitions also become more refined during adolescence; however, research shows use of substances such as alcohol during the adolescent years can hinder this refinement (Steinberg, 2008 as cited in López-Caneda, Rodríguez Holguín, Cadaveira, Corral, & Doallo, 2014). Consequences of this hindrance may include resulting psychiatric diagnoses such as conduct disorder (Zoccolillo, 1993 as cited in López-Caneda et al., 2014).

Related to adolescent brain functioning, alcohol increases impulsivity in adolescents who are already experiencing higher rates of impulsivity when compared to other age groups (Skala & Walter, 2013). Impulsivity increases the likelihood of risky behavior such as committing crimes, getting into fights, risky sexual behaviors (e.g., unprotected sex), and being injured. Similar consequences are linked to the effects of alcohol use (Boden & Fergusson, 2011). The alcohol myopia model (Giancola, Josephs, Parrott, & Duke, 2010; Steele & Josephs, 1990) points to the narrowing effect of alcohol intoxication on attention to prominent provocative cues, rather than less prominent inhibiting cues to explain the relationship between alcohol and disinhibited behaviors. Engaging in risk-taking can lead to alcohol-related accidents like falls or motor vehicle accidents that may result in both acute injuries and loss of life or long-term injuries. Engaging in risky sexual behavior can lead to chronic sexually transmitted diseases or unexpected pregnancy.

Risk-taking with alcohol use also puts adolescents at an increased risk for other negative health effects attributed to binge drinking, such as alcohol poisoning (Hingson & Kenkel, 2004). Binge drinking, which is defined in more detail later in the chapter, is characterized by a high intake of alcohol in a short period of time. This drinking pattern can have a profound impact on the adolescent brain as it is in a critical state of development by overall reduction in brain capacity, impairment of long-term memory capacity, impairment of long-term functioning of the frontal lobe (responsible for emotion regulation), increased reactivity, and impairment of the brain's ability to learn (Jones, Lueras, & Nagel, 2018). Binge drinking has also been linked to increased likelihood for alcohol use and misuse issues in adulthood, with binge drinking in later adulthood being linked to more chronic health conditions. Further, alcohol use has been linked to being overweight and obese (Boden & Fergusson, 2011). These issues have long-term impacts on an individual's physical health which may put adolescents who drink in large quantities at increased risk for early onset health problems.

Aside from the physical consequences, these issues also come with mental health implications. Alcohol use can have short- and long-term effects on the adolescent and their mental health. Alcohol use is associated with increased suicidality in adolescents experiencing depression between 13 and 15 years of age (Bossarte & Swahn, 2011). For females, depression and substance use are bidirectionally associated—suggesting alcohol use in adolescence may increase the risk of depression and vice versa (Danzo, Connell, & Stormshak, 2017). These studies suggest alcohol use may both be a result of and contributor to mental health concerns. Further, alcohol use in adolescence contributes to alcohol use in adulthood, which can result in long-term effects of early drinking that impact individuals into their adult lives (Zucker, 2008). However, a more typical alcohol use trajectory for binge drinking is that, after increasing during late adolescence and peaking in the early 20 s, levels decline as individuals enter their mid-20s and experience developmental changes like taking on more adult roles and responsibilities (Lee & Sher, 2018).

Defining patterns of alcohol consumption

Alcohol is prevalently used amongst adolescents despite the increased risk associated with their developmental life stage (Skala & Walter, 2013). In fact, adolescents use alcohol more than any other substance due to a combination of factors including accessibility and legality above a certain age marker. In the U.S., the drinking age is 21 years old. However, adolescents are likely to have siblings or other affiliates of legal age, which increases access (Wechsler & Nelson, 2010). There are different ways to characterize alcohol consumption that are based on the quantity and frequency of drinks and the time span across which they are consumed. These drinking patterns are used diagnostically by clinicians, including by administering the Alcohol Use Disorders Identification Test (AUDIT) to detect early stage high-risk drinking, and have implications for the varying alcohol-related consequences reviewed above (U.S. Department of Health and Human Services, 2018a).

One way to describe alcohol consumption is by different levels of drinking: from lower- to moderate- and high-risk drinking, with excessive drinking patterns including binge drinking and heavy drinking. These drinking levels are defined differently depending on the age of the individual, in that the cut points for each level are different for adults, older adolescents (16–18), and younger adolescents (ages 12–15). First, here are the cut points for adults to help illustrate how they are different for younger individuals. In adults, low-risk drinkers are considered to be at low risk for developing an alcohol use disorder. According to the current National Institute on Alcohol Abuse and Alcoholism (U.S. Department of Health and Human Services, 2018a) standard, female adult drinkers are low-risk if they consume no more three alcoholic beverages in a day and no more than seven in a week. Male adult drinkers are low-risk if they consume no more than four alcoholic beverages in a day and no more than fourteen in a week. Consequently, high-risk adult drinkers are those who are drinking over these daily and weekly guidelines. Moderate drinking for adults is defined by the U.S. Department of Health and Human Services (2015) as one drink in a single day for female drinkers and two drinks in a single day for male drinkers.

The Practitioner's Guide for Alcohol Use Screening and Brief Intervention is one resource for understanding these low-, moderate-, and high-risk cut points for levels of drinking during adolescence (U.S. Department of Health and Human Services, 2018a). They are based on the number of drinking days per year and month, rather than drinks per day and week as with adults. Further, because the U.S. legal drinking age is 21 years old, there are no set recommendations for low-risk drinking for adolescents (Department of Health, 2015). In fact, any drinking or drinking on one day per year for younger adolescents (12–15) is considered to be at least a moderate risk. Moderate-risk drinking for older adolescents ranges from consuming alcohol about every other month or 6 days per year for those ages 16–17 and about monthly or 12 days per year for 18-year-olds. High-risk adolescent drinking is stratified by even smaller age groups with sequential increases in drinking per year for each group. The cut points include 1 day of drinking for youth ages 11 and under; drinking about every month or 6 days for ages 12–15; drinking about monthly or 12 days at age 16; drinking about twice monthly or 24 days at age 17; and drinking about weekly or 52 days at age 18.

While the above definitions are designed to be easily applied in clinical practice and prevention work, other definitions of alcohol consumption are used by epidemiological studies that survey levels of drinking and problems with drinking in the population. In the next section, prevalence rates and descriptive information for various drinking behaviors in U.S. adolescents are presented. The definitions used by the NIAAA and the Substance Abuse and Mental Health Services Administration (SAMHSA) for two excessive drinking behaviors (binge and heavy drinking) are given here to provide background for information that is reported later. First, the NIAAA defines binge drinking as alcohol consumption that results in a blood alcohol concentration (BAC) level of 0.08 g/dL (U.S. Department of Health and Human Services, 2015). According to the definition, this level of intoxication occurs when drinking four (female) to five (male) alcoholic beverages within a two-hour time period. SAMHSA defines binge drinking by applying the same cutoffs of 4 + or 5 + alcoholic beverages for females and males, respectively, but uses the less specific timeframe of 'within a single period of time'. To qualify as someone who binges, according to the SAMHSA definition, this pattern of drinking must occur at least one day within the most recent month. Heavy alcohol use is defined by SAMHSA as multiple incidents of binge drinking (5 + in the past 30 days). As was the case with adult lower-, moderate-, and high-risk drinking levels, these definitions of binge and heavy drinking developed for adults do not convert well to younger age groups (Chung, Creswell, Bachrach, Clark, & Martin, 2018). Because of their smaller body sizes, adolescents are likely to reach BACs over 0.08 g/dL within two hours at lower levels of consumption. Chung et al. (2018), therefore, warn that national surveys using adult-based definitions may underestimate rates of binge drinking in adolescent samples.

Adolescence and drinking behaviors

Drinking patterns vary across early-, middle-, and late-adolescence, which can be observed when comparing data on age of alcohol use onset, any alcohol use and binge drinking by maturation. Early onset is often defined as initiating alcohol prior to the age of 15 years old. The U.S. Department of Health and Human Services (2017b) reports that a third of adolescents have had at least one alcoholic beverage by the age of 15, which increases to nearly two-thirds (60%) of adolescents by the age of 18. Earlier, we briefly described how rates of binge drinking in the population decline at the end of young adulthood, after increasing during later adolescence. The 2017 Monitoring the Future Survey, which assesses students in grades 8th through 12th (approximately ages 13–18), further shows variation in drinking behaviors when comparing late adolescence with younger age groups. Alcohol use is more prevalent in late-adolescence when compared to early-adolescence, with a third (33%) of 12th graders reporting any alcohol use in the past 30 days compared to 8% of 8th graders (Centers for Disease Control and U.S. Department of Health and Human Services, 2016a). Regarding binge drinking, 19% of 12th graders report this behavior during the past 30 days compared to only 2% of 8th graders.

Patterns of alcohol consumption also vary across race and ethnicity, putting some population groups at heightened risk for short- and long-term alcohol-related consequences. Continuing with age of onset example, studies consistently show that the onset of alcohol use is earlier for White adolescents whereas minority population adolescents typically use alcohol and other drugs in lower quantities and begin use much later in adolescence (Park, McCoy, Erausquin, & Bartlett, 2018). Assessing differences and similarities for different drinking behaviors may help identify higher and lower risk groups, which can inform more targeted prevention and intervention efforts. Below, we describe alcohol use behaviors for adolescents in the US general population before considering racial/ethnic group differences in these behaviors using both data from the most recently available National Survey on Drug Use and Health (NSDUH) and other published studies. We also describe concurrent alcohol and other drug use for adolescents including racial/ethnic group differences at the end of this section.

Prevalence rates in the past 30 days

A number of surveys have attempted to gauge drinking patterns of adolescents in the general population with some differing findings likely due to differences in survey methodology. We report past 30-day data from two different surveys here. The Youth Risk Behavior Surveillance System (YRBSS) is maintained by the Centers for Disease Control and Prevention (CDC) and includes a national school-based survey, while the NSDUH is directed by SAMHSA and involves a random sample of households. In the 2017 Youth Risk Behavior Survey, it was reported that 30% of high schoolers drank some alcohol, 14% of high schoolers binge drank, 6% of high schoolers drove a car after consuming, and 17% of high schoolers were passengers in a car driven by someone who had been drinking alcohol (U.S. Department of Health and Human Services, 2018b). This data further reiterates the consequences of underage alcohol consumption with the affiliated risk behavior of drinking and driving or being party to drinking and driving. The 2016 NSDUH assessed alcohol use of youth aged 12–20 and found 19% reported drinking alcohol and 12% reported binge drinking (Centers for Disease Control and U.S. Department of Health and Human Services, 2016a). The small variation between alcohol consumption rates and binge drinking rates in the NSDUH sample supports findings that much of adolescent alcohol consumption is in the form of binge drinking. Adolescents have fewer occurrences of drinking when compared to adults; however, they drink substantially more when they do engage in the behavior (U.S. Department of Health and Human Services, 2017b). U.S. Department of Health and Human Services (2017b) reports 11% of all alcohol consumption in the United States can be attributed to adolescents and young adults aged 12–20, which can be explained by binge drinking. For adolescents, 90% of their alcohol consumption is in the form of binge drinking (U.S. Department of Health and Human Services, 2017b).

Differences across race/ethnicity

These patterns of alcohol consumption vary slightly across race/ethnicity. Table 19.1 presents prevalence rates for alcohol consumption of adolescents at three different time intervals (lifetime, past year, and past 30 days) from the 2017 NSDUH. Participants who identified as White reported the highest prevalence of lifetime alcohol use (45%), followed by those identifying as "two or more races" (43.5%), Hispanic or Latino (39.7%), American Indian or Alaska Native (37%), Black or African American (32.6%), and Asian (30.7%). These trends identifying which race/ethnicity is most affected by alcohol use largely persist across past year and past month alcohol use, with a slight reduction in prevalence across all races and ethnicities. The prevalence of binge alcohol use in the past month was highest amongst participants who identified as White (14.9%), followed by the two or more races group (10.7%), American Indian or Alaska Native (9.5%), Asian (7.1%), and Black or African-American (7.0%). Prevalence rates drop importantly across all races/ethnicities for heavy alcohol use in the past month (five or more

TABLE 19.1 Percentages of alcohol prevalence across race and ethnicity.

	Lifetime alcohol use	Past year alcohol use	Past month alcohol use	Past month binge drinking	Past month heavy drinking
White	45.0	39.5	23.5	14.9	3.5
Black or African American	32.6	25.3	12.8	7.0	0.8
American Indian or Alaska Native	37.0	29.2	13.2	9.5	0.4
Asian	30.7	26.8	15.1	7.1	0.8
Two or more races	43.5	37.4	20.9	10.7	1.9
Hispanic or Latino[a]	39.7	32.1	16.5	9.6	1.7

[a]*Estimates are from the 2017 National Survey on Drug Use and Health; Participants were between the ages of 12–20 years old.*

instances of binge drinking in the past month), but trends regarding which race/ethnicity is most affected by alcohol use persist. White adolescents reported the highest frequency of heavy drinking (3.5%).

Across alcohol use behaviors in the 2017 NSDUH, Black or African American adolescents have the lowest prevalence and White adolescents have the highest prevalence. These trends are supported further in peer-reviewed literature. In a study of heavy episodic drinking in the U.S., based on data from NSDUH, Keyes and Miech (2013) found White adolescents aged 15–19 had higher odds of drinking than the average odds of drinking for adolescents of this age group. Black adolescents in this age group had lower odds than the average and Hispanic/Latino adolescents had odds equal to the average. White adolescents, those who traditionally benefit from more privileged social statuses, drink with greater prevalence when compared to all other racial and ethnic groups (Orcutt & Schwabe, 2011). Consistently, Black or African American adolescents drink at rates below the national average (U.S. Department of Health and Human Services, 2017a). Though American Indians and Alaska Native adults experience high rates of alcohol problems, adolescent drinking is still below the national average for this age group (21.9% and 22.8%, respectively). American Indian and Alaska Native adolescents do experience high rates of past-month binge drinking when compared to the national average based on national data (14.3% and 13.8%, respectively), which raises concern considering the historical trauma and substance use impact on this group. Asian Americans have traditionally been considered to be a low-risk drinking group, but there is evidence that problematic drinking rates are increasing for younger Asian Americans (Iwamoto, Kaya, Grivel, & Clinton, 2016). Kane et al. (2017) identified differences in use and binge drinking among Asian subgroups and show that Korean, Japanese and Filipino American adolescents drink at higher rates than other Asian American groups. This study in Asian American adolescents (Kane et al., 2017) and others in Hispanic/Latino adolescents (Bacio, Mays, & Lau, 2013) show the importance of disaggregating larger racial/ethnic groups by nationality and generational status in the U.S. (i.e., nativity) to reveal subgroups of youth who are drinking at riskier levels. Few studies have compared alcohol use outcomes for African American and Black Caribbean youth (Epstein, Williams, & Botvin, 2002); therefore, this remains an area for additional study.

Concurrent alcohol and other drug use

Alcohol is the most prevalently used drug across the board; however, adolescents often use more than one substance (Banks, Rowe, Mpofu, & Zapolski, 2017; U.S. Department of Health and Human Services, 2017b). Despite this, few studies have examined concurrent alcohol and drug use across racial and ethnic groups during the development period of adolescence. Comorbidity of alcohol and other drug use in adolescence puts youth at increased risk for negative alcohol-related consequences such as increased likelihood of illicit drug use, poorer overall physical health, and higher rates of juvenile justice-involvement which have been found to persist into adult justice system-involvement (Banks et al., 2017). Banks et al. (2017), using 2011–2014 NSDUH data, found concurrent substance use to account for 42% of substance use within the past month. Further, this study found that White adolescents were more likely to use cigarettes only and to concurrently use alcohol and cigarettes or alcohol, cigarettes, and marijuana when compared to any other racial/ethnic group. Prevalence estimates of alcohol-only use remain low amongst Hispanic or Latino, Black or African American, and Native American or American Indian groups; however, these racial/ethnic groups were more likely to be marijuana-only users and African American youth were at high risk for concurrent alcohol and marijuana use. Conversely, Asian Americans were the most likely to be alcohol-only users.

Prevention and intervention efforts

The Institute of Medicine (Institute of Medicine, 1994) uses the following classifications to categorize prevention intervention programs: (1) universal, (2) selective, and (3) indicated programs (see Table 19.2, below). After introducing this classification system, one example for each classification is described, followed by an example of a multilevel intervention. We provide a general overview of each program and identify the risk and protective factors that it targets. The example programs selected are a very small portion of those available; additional resources can be found through SAMHSA's

TABLE 19.2 Institute of Medicine classifications for prevention intervention programs.

Universal	Programs designed to address the general population rather than a specific group. Universal programs can be viewed as a broad prevention approach to delay the onset of behaviors or actions, such as alcohol use in middle schools. Everyone in the targeted population can benefit from the program.
Selective	Programs designed to adhere more to a selected subgroup of the population as opposed to general. Selective interventions specifically target subgroups that would be considered more at risk than the general population from which it is derived, such as children of alcoholic parents.
Indicated	Programs designed to target individuals already engaged in high-risk behaviors or actions. Indicated programs aim to help prevent an individual's behavior from transitioning to a diagnosis or addiction, such as an adolescent who experimented with alcohol or participated in regular alcohol use but not diagnosed as dependent yet.

Evidence-based Practices Resource Center and publications like the Surgeon General's Report on Alcohol, Drugs, and Health (Substance Abuse and Mental Health Services Administration, 2019; U.S. Department of Health and Human Services, 2016b).

We use the programs described to highlight well-established mechanisms for reducing risky drinking behaviors in adolescents (Chartier, Hesselbrock, & Hesselbrock, 2010): (1) substance use refusal skills and normative education to buffer peer influences and perceived social drinking norms; (2) family management and attachment to strengthen parental monitoring and reduce family conflict and the effects of substance use by family members; (3) emotional management and positive academic skills to dampen emotional distress and strengthen school achievement and bonding; and (4) community organization and restrictions on sales to underage drinkers to reduce the availability of alcohol. The IOM's program classification is contingent upon the population with which the program is targeting and the associated risk level of that population. Each classification provides a different level of involvement, which are discernable below.

Universal level

LifeSkills training. Life Skills Training (LST) is example of a valid, evidence-based, universal prevention program with more than two decades worth of trials and testing, including positive outcomes with White, Black or African American, and Hispanic or Latino adolescents (U.S. Department of Health and Human Services, 2016b). Primarily, this program focuses on students in middle school with booster sessions that extend into early high school and addresses a great deal of risk and protective factors related to substance use refusal skills, self-management skills, and general social skills (Botvin, Griffin, Paul, & Macaulay, 2003). This three-year program teaches the students about personal and social skills, particularly in relation to substance use refusal and normative education. Repetition and constant exposure of LST over a three year period, including 15 sessions during the first year, 10 during the second and, 5 during the third have resulted in a 37% reduction in the prevalence of tobacco, alcohol, and illicit drug use with rates subsequently decreasing years after exposure to the program well into high school (Botvin, Baker, Dusenbury, Botvin, & Diaz, 1995; Botvin et al., 2003; Scheier & Botvin, 1995). LST is generalizable to various racial/ethnic groups.

Selective level

Strengthening families program. The Strengthening Families Program (SFP) is an example of an empirically-supported selective prevention intervention for youth in pre-teen years and early adolescence. The SFP targets the family etiology of youth substance use and delinquency including in the high-risk subgroup of children of substance using parents (Kumpfer, 1998; Kumpfer & Alvarado, 1998). The SFP is a family skills training designed to affect parent, child, and family factors through parent training, children's social skills training, and family role-playing. In order to increase protective family factors, (Kumpfer, 1998) emphasizes three critical components of family interaction: (1) family attachment, bonding, and affective relationships; (2) guidance in making good friends through supervision and support; and (3) the transmission of norms and skills through discussion and role modeling. The SFP was modified and shown to be effective for families of different racial and ethnic groups, in rural and urban settings, and in countries outside the U.S., such as Canada, Costa Rica, France, Russia, Thailand, and South Africa (Kumpfer, Pinyuchon, Teixeira de Melo, & Whiteside, 2008).

Indicated level

Reconnecting youth program. Finally, a modern example of a successful, evidence-based, indicated-level classification intervention program is the Reconnecting Youth Program (RY) (Eggert, Thompson, Herting, & Randell, 2001). RY specifically targets and screens students in high school who have the potential to drop out due to poor school achievement, or a multitude of other emotional or cognitive behaviors. Participation in RY, which specifically targets key elements of self-esteem, personal control, communication, depression and anger management, and drug use monitoring, unveiled that students in the program increased school performance, gained control over mood and emotions, and decreased substance using behaviors. This daily, semester-long course has helped develop and strengthen cognitive and emotional skills in students and has fostered positive academic skill sets, leaving participants less prone to dropping out of school.

Multi-level prevention interventions

Prevention approaches that are context-specific and take into account many risk and protective factors are needed. Some successful models of multilevel, multiyear interventions exist (e.g., Project Northland; Perry et al., 1996), including for African American and Hispanic/Latino youth living in urban settings (Komro et al., 2008) and American Indian communities (Moore et al., 2018). These interventions focused on youth in early- and mid-adolescence and implemented both individual- and community-level strategies. Examples of individual-level strategies were classroom curricula and brief motivational interviewing for youth and educational activities and activities that increase involvement for parents. Community-level activities included peer-planned alcohol-free activities, community mobilization and outreach to raise awareness of alcohol-related problems, the passage of more restrictive alcohol-related ordinances, and beverage service training and compliance checks to reduce sales to underage youth and intoxicated patrons. Given the mechanisms that contribute to alcohol use in adolescents are many, more work in this area is warranted.

Culturally adapted evidence-based interventions

Proven mainstream prevention interventions may not generalize when they are insufficiently sensitive to the needs and preferences of local community members. To start, when selecting an intervention, special attention to the target population will help ensure its acceptance within the community (Gilder et al., 2011). Blume (2016), for example, points out how prevention interventions that align with core community beliefs and values like the central role of family (e.g., family-oriented approaches) have been successful. Culturally-relevant adaptations may also be needed to reduce the incongruence between a specific intervention and the beliefs and values of the local community. The cultural adaptation of interventions has been defined as "systematic modification of an EBT [evidence-based treatment] or intervention protocol to consider language, culture, and context in such a way that it is compatible with the client's cultural patterns, meaning, and values" (Bernal, Jimenez Chafey, & domenech Rodriguez, 2009, p. 362). This is a balancing process and involves maintaining fidelity to an intervention while tailoring it to be more sensitive to cultural and social differences amongst racial and ethnic groups (Burlew, Copeland, Ahuama-Jonas, & Calsyn, 2013). Substance use literature has found that evidence-based interventions (EBIs) that are culturally adapted improve overall outcomes for specific racial and ethnic groups (Burlew et al., 2013). Behavior and attitudes about substance use behaviors are influenced by racial and ethnic cultural and social traditions, which makes culturally adapted EBIs critical in addressing alcohol use. Representative studies have shown substance use EBIs are more effective with some racial/ethnic groups than others and universal approaches are less effective overall when implemented generically with racial/ethnic minorities.

Motivational interventions are an example of an EBI that has been successfully implemented with diverse racial/ethnic populations. Motivational interviewing (MI) is associated with reductions in risky alcohol use and other health behaviors in African American and Hispanic/Latino adolescents (Ewing, Wray, Mead, & Adams, 2012), and has been adapted utilizing a community-based participatory research (CBPR) approach and integrated with traditional practices for use with American Indian youth (Dickerson, Brown, Johnson, Schweigman, & D'Amico, 2016). Motivational interviewing (MI) is a therapy technique based on the premise that an individual's change is most sustainable when their motivation for change is enhanced in the therapeutic process compared to being instructed how to change their behavior in the therapeutic process (Carroll et al., 2006). MI is a short-term technique that maintains low costs for providers while also garnering impressive empirical support in clinical trials for its effectiveness with individuals who use substances. Motivational enhancement therapy (MET) is rooted in the tenets of MI and has been proven effective in substance use client retention and the reduction of alcohol use (Ball et al., 2007), though not specifically with adolescents. MET was culturally adapted by Longshore and Grills (2000) by creating racial/ethnic familiarity in treatment. This culturally adapted version of MET was found to be more effective than generic MET when implemented with racially/ethnically diverse groups.

Social and cultural factors and adolescent alcohol use

When considering racially/ethnically diverse adolescents, additional risk and protective factors may have important influences on drinking behaviors and certain factors may be more relevant for some adolescent subgroups than others. In this final section of the chapter we review risk and protective factors that go beyond those highlighted in our above description of example prevention intervention programs. In selecting these factors, we considered how some racial/ethnic groups are more impacted by recent immigration experiences or exposure to stressors like adverse childhood events or discrimination. We considered how religion, socioeconomic status, and where a person lives - in this case we focus on rural communities and U.S. regions - may intersect with race/ethnicity to influence alcohol use during adolescence.

Acculturation/accumulative stress

Acculturation and accumulative stress, or stress involved in adjusting to a new dominant culture and feeling pressure to adopt the new dominant culture especially regarding the dominant culture's drinking norms, impacts alcohol use in minority racial/ethnic groups (Park, Anastas, Shibusawa, & Nguyen, 2014). An often-used proxy of acculturation is nativity with those who are born in the U.S. considered to be more acculturated than those born in their country of origin. For both Asian American and Hispanic/Latino adolescents, individuals who are more acculturated are at greater risk for alcohol use, with mediational mechanisms for Hispanic/Latino adolescents being reductions of family closeness and an increased association with substance-using peers (Bacio et al., 2013; Iwamoto et al., 2016). Similarly, Martinez (2006) and Unger, Ritt-Olson, Wagner, Soto, and Baezconde-Garbanati (2009) showed that parent-child acculturation discrepancies, e.g., greater acculturation among adolescents than their parents, are associated with adolescent alcohol use through higher family stress and lower family cohesion. This social context is often coupled with acculturative stress. In a study of different Asian immigrant subgroups, Park et al. (2014) found acculturation and the associated stress to predict alcohol use, though not in adolescents. Alamilla et al. (2019) found acculturative stress and the associated instances of marginalization, alienation, and rejection increased the risk of alcohol use for U.S.-born racial and ethnic minority groups born into immigrant families. In a small study of recently immigrated Hispanic adolescents in late adolescence (14–17 years old), Meca et al. (2019) found bicultural stress, the pressure of adopting a new culture while maintaining your old culture, predicted onset of alcohol use. This suggests acculturation and acculturative stress are racially and ethnically-related risk factors that can increase the risk of alcohol use in minority adolescents.

Immigration status

Adolescents may be impacted by their immigration status, especially those belonging to racial and ethnic groups with recent immigration experiences (e.g., Hispanic/Latino, Asian). Immigration status itself may create stress that contributes to substance use. Roblyer, Grzywacz, Cervantes, and Merten (2016) studied adolescents in families with undocumented immigrants, pointing to the stress of undocumented immigration and its impact on substance use. Adolescents in this situation were more likely to engage in other forms of substance use (i.e., cigarette, marijuana); however, cultural practices normalizing alcohol consumption at family events and gatherings and denormalizing binge drinking or generally consuming alcohol in moderation due to modeled responsible drinking from adults may protect against the effect of immigration status on riskier drinking behaviors. This merits further study; yet is in line with earlier studies suggesting that living in a neighborhood with a higher density of Hispanics/Latinos may be a protective factor for alcohol use problems (Molina, Alegria, & Chen, 2012). In a study of Hispanic/Latino adolescents, Pena et al. (2008) found immigrant status to be a significant predictor for problematic alcohol consumption. This suggests that while there are protective effects from living in a Hispanic/Latino community against alcohol consumption, stress and risk affiliated with immigration is not fully mitigated and can still affect alcohol use in adolescence.

Exposure to adverse childhood experiences

A "double jeopardy" hypothesis posits that experiencing multiple social stressors may be particularly detrimental (Hatch, 2005), leading adolescents to engage in problem behaviors and substance use as a way of coping (Lloyd & Turner, 2008). Adverse childhood experiences (ACEs) often reflect periods of turmoil in a child's life. These incidents can include experiencing childhood abuse and neglect, having imprisoned family members, exposure to household mental illness and substance misuse, and household violence.

The CDC discovered more than half (59.4%) of its adult sample ($n = 26,229$) from five states reported exposure to at least one ACE prior to age 18, while 8.7% reported experiencing five or more ACEs (Bynum et al., 2010). Two subsequent studies in separate American Indian communities reported prevalence estimates of 78% and 83% for exposure to at least one ACE prior to age 18, with one study reporting 20% of its American Indian sample with six or more ACEs (Brockie, Dana-Sacco, Wallen, Wilcox, & Campbell, 2015; Warne et al., 2017). Despite race/ethnic differences in the number and types of ACEs experienced, including a study showing higher rates for most ACEs for Blacks and Hispanics/Latinos compared to Whites (Lee & Chen, 2017), the positive effects for ACEs with heavier drinking are similar when compared across racial/ethnic groups (Lee & Chen, 2017; Warne et al., 2017). Past research posits that ACEs exposure increases risk for adolescent alcohol use. For example, using a sample of 8417 adult health maintenance organization (HMO) members, Dube et al. (2006) examined the relationship between multiple ACEs and alcohol use, including age of adolescent initiation. They found that those who had experienced ACEs were two to three times more likely to initiate alcohol use by age 14. Further, the ACE score (total number of ACEs) had a graded relationship with alcohol use initiation in adolescence. That is, as the total number of ACEs increases, so does the likelihood of early onset of alcohol use. Furthermore, Shin, Miller, and Teicher (2013) examined the relationship between ACEs and heavy episodic drinking (HED) in adolescence. In a population-based sample of 8503 adolescents, the authors identified two notable findings: (1) history of ACEs was associated with steeper increases in HED rates, and (2) greater frequency of ACEs was associated with both steeper increases in HED rates and persistently elevated HED over time.

Discrimination experiences

Discrimination is a risk factor for the development of substance use in adolescents. Discrimination literature demonstrates the relationship between onset of alcohol use and timing of discrimination experiences (e.g. Austin, 2004). Further, the literature suggests discrimination plays a critical role in consequences related to alcohol use despite minority youth using alcohol in lower frequencies when compared to White youth (Banks, Winningham, Wu, & Zapolski, 2019). Numerous studies have linked perceived discrimination as a stressor to increased alcohol use and earlier onset of use, particularly in African-American, Indigenous, and Hispanic/Latino youth (e.g. Armenta, Sittner, & Whitbeck, 2016; Cheadle & Whitbeck, 2011; Madkour et al., 2015). Discrimination has also been linked to adverse mental health outcomes outside of alcohol use (Goto, Couto, & Bastos, 2013), which is associated with alcohol use in adolescence and adulthood (e.g. Danzo et al., 2017), putting these populations at increased risk.

Cultural identity

Ethnic identity has been found to protect youth from alcohol use. Strong ethnic identity is associated with reduced alcohol use in minority youth (Banks et al., 2019). When Black youth reported their race to be a central part of their identity, they engaged in lower frequencies of alcohol use (Caldwell, Sellers, Bernat, & Zimmerman, 2004). This is congruent in the Hispanic/Latino community with Perreira et al. (2019) finding strong ethnic identity to be associated with lower susceptibility to alcohol- and smoking-related behaviors. However, identifying with an ethnic subculture in the Hispanic/Latino community, such as Cholo, is associated with increased risk of substance use (Unger, Thing, Soto, & Baezconde-Garbanati, 2014). It is important to understand the resilience of ethnic identity and its protective effects against alcohol use when working with minority racial/ethnic groups.

Religion

Some religious affiliations view any alcohol use or excessive alcohol use as directly in contrast to their belief systems, which may protect adolescent members of these religious groups from developing problematic drinking due to dogma and social norms. Religion's relationship with alcohol use has been studied across various countries (e.g., Spain, Canada, U.S.), all finding religiosity to impact the perception and use of alcohol for adolescents. For example, a representative study conducted in the U.S., using data from the 2007 NSDUH, found religiosity to protect against drinking alongside non-permissive parenting strategies (Gryczynski & Ward, 2012). Some racial and ethnic groups are culturally inclined to religious involvement or to affiliation with denominations with more restrictive drinking rules. African Americans are more likely to believe in God when compared to other racial/ethnic groups, as presented in Table 19.3, and have stronger religious affiliation (Pew Research Center, 2014b); therefore, religious protection against alcohol use may in part explain low rates of alcohol consumption amongst adolescents in this racial group. African American adolescents are also more likely to be influenced by parents than peers, which may enhance the protection of religion if valued by their family (Dickens, Jackman, Stanley, Swaim, & Chavez, 2018). The religion of Islam prohibits alcohol consumption (Sheikh & Islam, 2018), and is practiced by individuals from several different racial/ethnic groups. Young people (ages 18–29) who identify as Muslim have a greater prevalence of religious group membership when compared to other religions (Pew Research Center, 2014a). This may protect Muslim adolescents from problematic drinking in their youth if they adhere to Islam's

TABLE 19.3 Belief in God by race/ethnicity.

	Absolutely certain (%)	Fairly certain (%)	Not too/ not at all certain (%)	Don't know (%)	Do not believe in God (%)	Other (%)[a]	*N*
White	61	20	5	1	11	3	24,900
Black	83	11	2	1	2	1	3394
Asian	44	23	12	1	19	2	937
Latino	59	26	6	1	6	1	3814
Other/multi-racial	66	18	5	1	8	3	1504

[a]*Other category includes those that don't know if they believe in God.*

prescriptions and proscriptions on alcohol, although few studies are available to confirm these relationships (Arfken, Arnetz, Fakhouri, Ventimiglia, & Jamil, 2011; Arfken, Broadbridge, Jamil, & Arnetz, 2014).

Socioeconomic status

Poverty disproportionately impacts minority racial and ethnic groups in the U.S. (i.e., Black and Hispanic). Based on 2017 data from the NSDUH, which is shown in Table 19.4, alcohol consumption rates for adolescent are relatively consistent across poverty levels; however, consequences of alcohol consumption may differentially impact those in poverty. Kendler et al. (2014) found socioeconomic status to be an indicator of alcohol consumption in 16- and 18-year-olds. High SES was found to be associated with greater frequency of alcohol use; however, low SES was found to be associated with greater prevalence and alcohol-related behavioral problems. This means that White adolescents, who experience less poverty comparatively, drink more frequently; however, Black and Hispanic adolescents, who experience more poverty, are more likely to have alcohol-related behavior problems even though they consume importantly less alcohol when compared to their White counterparts. Collins (2016) explored the relationship between alcohol-related outcomes and socioeconomic status, specifically education, employment, income, and housing, through a meta-analysis. Findings showed

TABLE 19.4 Estimates of alcohol use by U.S. poverty level.

	Lifetime alcohol use	Past year alcohol use	Past month alcohol use	Binge drinking	Heavy drinking
Less than 100% of the poverty level	40.2	32.3	18.5	10.9	2.5
100–199% of the poverty level	39.8	32.3	17.5	10.8	1.7
200% or more of the poverty level	40.9	35.8	20.0	12.0	2.4

Note: The federal poverty level guidelines are assumed annually based on household income and family size (U.S. Centers for Medicare & Medicaid Services, 2018).
Estimates are from the 2017 National Survey on Drug Use and Health; and Participants were ages of 12–20 (U.S. Department of Health and Human Services., 2017a).

individuals (not specific to adolescents) with higher socioeconomic status consume more alcohol than individuals with lower socioeconomic status. Even still, individuals with lower socioeconomic status experience more severe alcohol-related consequences creating greater disparity. Regarding adolescents, Poonawalla, Kendzor, Owen, and Caughy (2014) found downward socioeconomic mobility (e.g., adolescent's family moves from middle income to low income) to be associated with any use of alcohol in the past-year. This raises concern for adolescents who experience these trajectories in socioeconomic status, which may be related to race/ethnicity considering previously noted research.

Geographic location

Geographic location impacts adolescents and their alcohol use due to issues of cultural and/or community norms, access alcohol, and issues of supervision. We here use geographic location to refer to rural or urban environments and different regions of the U.S. Alcohol use patterns vary by geographic location (Dixon & Chartier, 2016). Table 19.5 shows prevalence estimates

TABLE 19.5 Percentages of alcohol use by county type and geographic region.

	Past month alcohol use	Binge drinking	Heavy drinking
County type			
Large metro	19.4	11.2	2.0
Small metro	21.0	13.6	3.5
Nonmetro, Urbanized	20.1	13.1	2.7
Nonmetro, Less urbanized	16.2	9.8	1.5
Nonmetro, Completely rural	18.8	13.6	3.4
Geographic region			
Northeast	23.8	15.9	4.1
Midwest	21.3	13.3	3.1
South	17.6	10.6	1.8
West	18.7	10.6	1.8

Note: Estimates are from the 2017 National Survey on Drug Use and Health; Participants were between the ages of 12 and 20 (U.S. Department of Health and Human Services., 2017a).

for any alcohol use and binge and heavy drinking by county type as well as U.S. geographic region (U.S. Department of Health and Human Services, 2017a). Data indicate complete rurality is associated with higher rates of binge and heavy drinking, second only to adolescents living in small metro areas. Regionally, adolescents in the Northeast and Midwest of the U.S. drink at higher rates across the board. Studies looking at degrees of rurality and substance use found high school-aged adolescents who lived on farms had greater prevalence of alcohol consumption when compared to high school-aged adolescents who lived within town limits (Rhew, Hawkins, & Oesterle, 2011), confirming trends in data that show rurality to be associated with increased alcohol use.

Race and ethnicity intersect with geographic location in several ways that inform the understanding the alcohol use by adolescents. Fig. 19.1 shows the geographic dispersion for where people reside across the United States by race/ethnicity. Sparsely populated communities remain largely White, which may help explain the increased alcohol use and alcohol-related issues in rural areas (Cable, 2013). Some sparsely populated communities appear to have a notable proportion of Hispanic individuals as well (Cable, 2013). For African-American youth, being rural may be a protective factor with them experiencing fewer stressors in their immediate environment (Gibbons et al., 2007). This will be important when considering the intersection of culture with prevention and intervention for adolescent alcohol use. The U.S. regions with higher drinking rates are also disproportionately comprised of White adolescents, whereas the South and West experience greater diversity of racial and ethnic groups (Cable, 2013). This aligns with data that asserts White adolescents consume alcohol in greater quantity and frequency when compared to other racial and ethnic groups

FIGURE 19.1 Geographic dispersion of race/ethnicity in the U.S. *Image Copyright, 2013, Weldon Cooper Center for Public Service, Rector and Visitors of the University of Virginia (Dustin A. Cable, creator).*

International perspective

Studies and data reviewed in the sections above mainly focus on the U.S. adolescent samples. Therefore, it is important to recognize that adolescent alcohol use patterns vary across world regions and countries, and to consider the factors that contribute to such differences. The World Health Organization (2018) global status report on alcohol and health presents prevalence rates of current drinking for 15–19 years old by WHO region. These rates were higher in the European (43.8%), Americas (38.2%), and Western Pacific (37.9%) Regions and lower in the African (21.4%), South-East Asian (21.1%), and Eastern Mediterranean (1.2%) Regions. Prevalence rates for HED in adolescents followed a similar pattern, i.e., 24.1–18.5% in Europe, Americas, and Western Pacific Regions and 12.7–0.5% in African, South-East Asian, and Eastern Mediterranean Regions. One study further distinguished European countries based on whether adolescents residing there were mainly non-alcohol users ($n = 8$), mild but frequent alcohol users ($n = 6$), or whether there was a high proportion of adolescents who were heavy episodic drinkers ($n = 11$) (Braker & Soellner, 2016), showing additional within-region variability in adolescent drinking behaviors.

Legal practices, social drinking norms, and culture differences (along with other factors) shift the usage and perception of alcohol by adolescents in international contexts (World Health Organization, 2018). Below we describe some examples.

Legal practices

Whereas the U.S. legal drinking age is 21 years old, it is much lower (typically 16 or 18 years of age) in most other countries (World Health Organization, 2018). This changes the availability of alcohol for adolescents engaging in alcohol use (Carpenter, Merage, & Dobkin, 2011). Laws regulating driving practices also vary internationally and shift the risk-taking behaviors associated with drinking. In some countries (World Health Organization, 2018), the legal driving age is much older than the U.S. legal driving age of 16-years-old. If adolescents do not have the legal ability to drive, the risk associated with drinking and driving importantly decreases (Wechsler & Nelson, 2010).

Social drinking norms

The normalization of drinking in some countries around the world may protect adolescents from engaging in binge drinking or other high-risk drinking behaviors. In cultures where moderate drinking habits are modeled in the home and adolescents are exposed to alcohol in a controlled environment, such as with their parents, they are less likely to develop problematic drinking behaviors (Molina et al., 2012). This is important to consider, particularly in those European cultures where drinking is normalized early on in the home with moderate but regular alcohol use (Room & Makela, 2000).

Other cultural factors

Other differences in norms and attitudes toward alcohol are observed within countries, including based on an adolescent's cultural background and religious affiliation. For example, in Sweden, drinking status was lowest for adolescent migrants from non-European countries, attributed to low alcohol use for females in such countries of origin as Iran, Iraq, Lebanon, and Thailand and to migrants born in countries where Islam was the most common religion (Curtis, Thompson, & Fairbrother, 2018). In Australia, rates of alcohol use were higher for Australian- and other-Western-country-born adolescents, while rates were lower for immigrant adolescents from Asia and Africa partially explained by greater parental monitoring and disapproval of alcohol use by parents (Chan et al., 2016).

These examples are not intended to be exhaustive, but are meant to show how differences in laws and policies, drinking norms, and other cultural factors may influence adolescent alcohol use internationally. The relevance of social constructs such as race/ethnicity also depend on the country and vary internationally, and other socio-demographic features (gender, age, religious affiliation, socioeconomic status, etc.) may provide more relevant social groups when examining adolescent alcohol use in other countries. The lessons learned in adapting EBP for racial/ethnic groups in the U.S. then extend to international contexts, by emphasizing the modification of interventions to the local context (Blume, 2016; Burlew et al., 2013; Gilder et al., 2011). Kumpfer et al. (2008) described this process as time-consuming and "requiring careful assessment of local political, religious, and economic context as well as cultural norms and family practices of country and internal ethnic groups" (p. 229).

Conclusion

This chapter has outlined the role race/ethnicity plays in adolescent alcohol use. Adolescence is a vulnerable time biologically, psychologically, and socially which makes the brain particularly susceptible to the short- and long-term effects of alcohol. These development changes also make adolescence a time when youth are more likely to initiate drinking. Different environments and racial/ethnic groups are more susceptible to initiating alcohol use at younger ages and drinking greater quantities. This is the case for White youth, particularly those who live in rural communities and at higher socioeconomic status. Further, different racial/ethnic groups are at greater risk for consequences of alcohol use in adolescence regardless of the

frequency with which that group consumes alcohol. Black and Hispanic/Latino adolescents of lower socioeconomic status are at greater risk for alcohol-related problems. Generally, there is also concern about drinking behaviors for American Indian/Alaska Native youth and low concern for Asian American youth. American Indian/Alaska Natives drink at lower rates than other racial/ethnic groups, but tend to binge drink when they do consume alcohol. There is evidence that drinking rates for Asian American youth
are rising in those who are U.S. born, making them a group to watch. While well-supported risk and protective factors influence drinking for all adolescents and the mechanisms targeted by evidence-based prevention and interventions programs, it is imperative that interventions use culturally-informed practices to best serve racial/ethnic minority youth, which also applies to the cultural adaptation of interventions in international contexts. Certain racial/ethnic groups are more susceptible to experiences like racial/ethnic discrimination and acculturative stress and may have protective factors such as a strong cultural identity and religious affiliations that are relevant to the prevention of alcohol use and related problems in adolescents. Practitioners, policy-makers, and researchers must understand the implications of failing to consider racial/ethnic differences when developing prevention and intervention programming or policy for diverse groups of adolescents.

References

Alamilla, S. G., Barney, B. J., Small, R., Wang, S. C., Schwartz, S. J., Donovan, R. A., & Lewis, C. (2019). Explaining the immigrant paradox: The influence of acculturation, enculturation, and acculturative stress on problematic alcohol consumption. *Behavioral Medicine (Washington, D.C.)*, 1–13. Available from https://doi.org/10.1080/08964289.2018.1539945.

Arfken, C. L., Arnetz, B. B., Fakhouri, M., Ventimiglia, M. J., & Jamil, H. (2011). Alcohol use among Arab Americans: What is the prevalence? *Journal of Immigrant and Minority Health/Center for Minority Public Health*, *13*(4), 713–718. Available from https://doi.org/10.1007/s10903-011-9447-8.

Arfken, C. L., Broadbridge, C. L., Jamil, H., & Arnetz, B. B. (2014). Immigrant Arab Americans and alcohol use: Longitudinal study. *Journal of Immigrant and Minority Health/Center for Minority Public Health*, *16*(6), 1303–1306. Available from https://doi.org/10.1007/s10903-013-9960-z.

Armenta, B. E., Sittner, K. J., & Whitbeck, L. B. (2016). Predicting the onset of alcohol use and the development of alcohol use disorder among indigenous adolescents. *Child Development*, *87*(3), 870–882. Available from https://doi.org/10.1111/cdev.12506.

Austin, A. A. (2004). Alcohol, tobacco, other drug use, and violent behavior among Native Hawaiians: Ethnic pride and resilience. *Substance Use & Misuse*, *39*(5), 721–746.

Bacio, G. A., Mays, V. M., & Lau, A. S. (2013). Drinking initiation and problematic drinking among Latino adolescents: Explanations of the immigrant paradox. *Psychology of Addictive Behaviors: Journal of the Society of Psychologists in Addictive Behaviors*, *27*(1), 14–22. Available from https://doi.org/10.1037/a0029996.

Ball, S. A., Martino, S., Nich, C., Frankforter, T. L., Van Horn, D., Crits-Christoph, P., ... National Institute on Drug Abuse Clinical Trials, N. (2007). Site matters: Multisite randomized trial of motivational enhancement therapy in community drug abuse clinics. *Journal of Consulting and Clinical Psychology*, *75*(4), 556–567. Available from https://doi.org/10.1037/0022-006X.75.4.556.

Banks, D. E., Rowe, A. T., Mpofu, P., & Zapolski, T. C. B. (2017). Trends in typologies of concurrent alcohol, marijuana, and cigarette use among US adolescents: An ecological examination by sex and race/ethnicity. *Drug and Alcohol Dependence*, *179*, 71–77. Available from https://doi.org/10.1016/j.drugalcdep.2017.06.026.

Banks, D. E., Winningham, R. D., Wu, W., & Zapolski, T. C. B. (2019). Examination of the indirect effect of alcohol expectancies on ethnic identity and adolescent drinking outcomes. *The American Journal of Orthopsychiatry*, *89*(5), 600–608. Available from https://doi.org/10.1037/ort0000390.

Bava, S., & Tapert, S. F. (2010). Adolescent brain development and the risk for alcohol and other drug problems. *Neuropsychology Review*, *20*(4), 398–413. Available from https://doi.org/10.1007/s11065-010-9146-6.

Berk, L. E. (2007). *Development through the lifespan*. Boston, MA: Allyn and Bacon.

Bernal, G., Jimenez Chafey, M. I., & domenech Rodriguez, M. M. (2009). Cultural adaptations of treatments: A resource for considering culture in evidence-based practice. *Professional Psychology, Research and Practice*, *40*(4), 361–368. Available from https://doi.org/10.1037/a0016401.

Blume, A. W. (2016). Advances in substance abuse prevention and treatment interventions among racial, ethnic, and sexual minority populations. *Alcohol Research: Current Reviews*, *38*(1), 47–54.

Boden, J. M., & Fergusson, D. M. (2011). Alcohol and depression. *Addiction (Abingdon, England)*, *106*(5), 906–914. Available from https://doi.org/10.1111/j.1360-0443.2010.03351.x.

Borges, A. M., Lejuez, C. W., & Felton, J. W. (2018). Positive alcohol use expectancies moderate the association between anxiety sensitivity and alcohol use across adolescence. *Drug and Alcohol Dependence*, *187*, 179–184. Available from https://doi.org/10.1016/j.drugalcdep.2018.02.029.

Bossarte, R. M., & Swahn, M. H. (2011). The associations between early alcohol use and suicide attempts among adolescents with a history of major depression. *Addictive Behaviors*, *36*(5), 532–535. Available from https://doi.org/10.1016/j.addbeh.2010.12.031.

Botvin, G. J., Baker, E., Dusenbury, L., Botvin, E. M., & Diaz, T. (1995). Long-term follow-up results of a randomized drug abuse prevention trial in a white middle-class population. *JAMA: the Journal of the American Medical Association*, *273*(14), 1106–1112.

Botvin, G. J., Griffin, K. W., Paul, E., & Macaulay, A. P. (2003). Preventing tobacco and alcohol use among elementary school students through life skills training. *Journal of Child & Adolescent Substance Abuse*, *12*(4), 1–17. Available from https://doi.org/10.1300/J029v12n04_01.

Braker, A. B., & Soellner, R. (2016). Alcohol drinking cultures of European adolescents. *European Journal of Public Health*, *26*(4), 581–586. Available from https://doi.org/10.1093/eurpub/ckw033.

Brockie, T. N., Dana-Sacco, G., Wallen, G. R., Wilcox, H. C., & Campbell, J. C. (2015). The relationship of adverse childhood experiences to PTSD, depression, poly-drug use and suicide attempt in reservation-based native American adolescents and young adults. *American Journal of Community Psychology*, *55*(3–4), 411–421. Available from https://doi.org/10.1007/s10464-015-9721-3.

Burlew, A. K., Copeland, V. C., Ahuama-Jonas, C., & Calsyn, D. A. (2013). Does cultural adaptation have a role in substance abuse treatment? *Social Work in Public Health*, *28*(3–4), 440–460. Available from https://doi.org/10.1080/19371918.2013.774811.

Bynum, L., Griffin, T., Ridings, D. L., Wynkoop, K. S., Anda, R. F., Edwards, V., ... Croft, J. B. (2010). Adverse childhood experiences reported by adults—Five states, 2009. *Morbidity and Mortality Weekly Report*, *59*, 1609–1613.

Cable, D. A. (2013). *The racial dot map* GitHub. University of Virginia: Weldon Cooper Center for Public Service.

Cairns, K. E., Yap, M. B., Pilkington, P. D., & Jorm, A. F. (2014). Risk and protective factors for depression that adolescents can modify: A systematic review and meta-analysis of longitudinal studies. *Journal of Affective Disorders*, *169*, 61–75. Available from https://doi.org/10.1016/j.jad.2014.08.006.

Caldwell, C. H., Sellers, R. M., Bernat, D. H., & Zimmerman, M. A. (2004). Racial identity, parental support, and alcohol use in a sample of academically at-risk African American high school students. *American Journal of Community Psychology*, *34*(1–2), 71–82.

Carpenter, C., Merage, P., & Dobkin, C. (2011). The minimum legal drinking age and public health. *The Journal of Economic Perspectives: A Journal of the American Economic Association*, *25*(2), 133–156.

Carroll, K. M., Ball, S. A., Nich, C., Martino, S., Frankforter, T. L., Farentinos, C., ... National Institute on Drug Abuse Clinical Trials, N. (2006). Motivational interviewing to improve treatment engagement and outcome in individuals seeking treatment for substance abuse: A multisite effectiveness study. *Drug and Alcohol Dependence*, *81*(3), 301–312. Available from https://doi.org/10.1016/j.drugalcdep.2005.08.002.

Chan, G. C., Kelly, A. B., Connor, J. P., Hall, W. D., Young, R. M., & Williams, J. W. (2016). Does parental monitoring and disapproval explain variations in alcohol use among adolescents from different countries of birth? *Drug and Alcohol Review*, *35*(6), 741–749. Available from https://doi.org/10.1111/dar.12413.

Chartier, K. G., Hesselbrock, M. N., & Hesselbrock, V. M. (2010). Development and vulnerability factors in adolescent alcohol use. *Child and Adolescent Psychiatric Clinics of North America*, *19*(3), 493–504. Available from https://doi.org/10.1016/j.chc.2010.03.004.

Chassin, L., Fora, D. B., & King, K. M. (2004). Trajectories of alcohol and drug use and dependence from adolescence to adulthood: The effects of familial alcoholism and personality. *Journal of Abnormal Psychology*, *113*(4), 483–498. Available from https://doi.org/10.1037/0021-843X.113.4.483.

Cheadle, J. E., & Whitbeck, L. B. (2011). Alcohol use trajectories and problem drinking over the course of adolescence: A study of north American indigenous youth and their caretakers. *Journal of Health and Social Behavior*, *52*(2), 228–245. Available from https://doi.org/10.1177/0022146510393973.

Chung, T., Creswell, K. G., Bachrach, R., Clark, D. B., & Martin, C. S. (2018). Adolescent binge drinking. *Alcohol Research: Current Reviews*, *39*(1), 5–15.

Collins, S. E. (2016). Associations between socioeconomic factors and alcohol outcomes. *Alcohol Research: Current Reviews*, *38*(1), 83–94.

Compas, B. E., Connor-Smith, J. K., Saltzman, H., Thomsen, A. H., & Wadsworth, M. E. (2001). Coping with stress during childhood and adolescence: Problems, progress, and potential in theory and research. *Psychological Bulletin*, *127*(1), 87–127.

Cooper, M. L., Wood, P. K., Orcutt, H. K., & Albino, A. (2003). Personality and the predisposition to engage in risky or problem behaviors during adolescence. *Journal of Personality and Social Psychology*, *84*(2), 390–410. Available from https://doi.org/10.1037/0022-3514.84.2.390.

Curtis, P., Thompson, J., & Fairbrother, H. (2018). Migrant children within Europe: A systematic review of children's perspectives on their health experiences. *Public Health*, *158*, 71–85. Available from https://doi.org/10.1016/j.puhe.2018.01.038.

Danzo, S., Connell, A. M., & Stormshak, E. A. (2017). Associations between alcohol-use and depression symptoms in adolescence: Examining gender differences and pathways over time. *Journal of Adolescence*, *56*, 64–74. Available from https://doi.org/10.1016/j.adolescence.2017.01.007.

Department of Health. (2015). Key recommendations: Components of healthy eating patterns. In *U.S. Department of Health*. Retrieved from https://health.gov/our-work/food-nutrition/2015-2020-dietary-guidelines/guidelines/chapter-1/key-recommendations/.

Dickens, D. D., Jackman, D. M., Stanley, L. R., Swaim, R. C., & Chavez, E. L. (2018). Alcohol consumption among rural African American and White adolescents: The role of religion, parents, and peers. *Journal of Ethnicity in Substance Abuse*, *17*(3), 273–290. Available from https://doi.org/10.1080/15332640.2016.1179155.

Dickerson, D. L., Brown, R. A., Johnson, C. L., Schweigman, K., & D'Amico, E. J. (2016). Integrating motivational interviewing and traditional practices to address alcohol and drug use among urban American Indian/Alaska native youth. *Journal of Substance Abuse Treatment*, *65*, 26–35. Available from https://doi.org/10.1016/j.jsat.2015.06.023.

Dixon, M. A., & Chartier, K. G. (2016). Alcohol use patterns among urban and rural residents: Demographic and social influences. *Alcohol Research: Current Reviews*, *38*(1), 69–77.

Dube, S. R., Miller, J. W., Brown, D. W., Giles, W. H., Felitti, V. J., Dong, M., & Anda, R. F. (2006). Adverse childhood experiences and the association with ever using alcohol and initiating alcohol use during adolescence. *The Journal of Adolescent Health: Official Publication of the Society for Adolescent Medicine*, *38*(4), 444. Available from https://doi.org/10.1016/j.jadohealth.2005.06.006, e441-410.

Eggert, L. L., Thompson, E. A., Herting, J. R., & Randell, B. P. (2001). *Reconnecting youth to prevent drug abuse, school dropout and suicidal behaviors among high-risk youth innovations in adolescent substance abuse intervention* (pp. 51–84). Oxford: Elsevier Science.

Epstein, J. A., Williams, C., & Botvin, G. J. (2002). How universal are social influences to drink and problem behaviors for alcohol use? A test comparing urban African-American and Caribbean-American adolescents. *Addictive Behaviors*, *27*(1), 75–86. Available from https://doi.org/10.1016/s0306-4603(00)00165-9.

Ewing, S. W. F., Wray, A. M., Mead, H. K., & Adams, S. K. (2012). Two approaches to tailoring treatment for cultural minority adolescents. *Journal of Substance Abuse Treatment*, *43* (2), 190–203. Available from https://doi.org/10.1016/j.jsat.2011.12.005.

Giancola, P. R., Josephs, R. A., Parrott, D. J., & Duke, A. A. (2010). Alcohol myopia revisited: Clarifying aggression and other acts of disinhibition through a distorted lens. *Perspectives on Psychological Science: A Journal of the Association for Psychological Science*, *5*(3), 265–278. Available from https://doi.org/10.1177/1745691610369467.

Gibbons, F. X., Reimer, R. A., Gerrard, M., Yeh, H. C., Houlihan, A. E., Cutrona, C., ... Brody, G. (2007). Rural-urban differences in substance use among African-American adolescents. *The Journal of Rural Health: Official Journal of the American Rural Health Association and the National Rural Health Care Association*, *23*(Suppl.), 22–28. Available from https://doi.org/10.1111/j.1748-0361.2007.00120.x.

Gilder, D. A., Luna, J. A., Calac, D., Moore, R. S., Monti, P. M., & Ehlers, C. L. (2011). Acceptability of the use of motivational interviewing to reduce underage drinking in a Native American community. *Substance Use & Misuse*, *46*(6), 836–842. Available from https://doi.org/10.3109/10826084.2010.541963.

Goto, J. B., Couto, P. F., & Bastos, J. L. (2013). [Systematic review of epidemiological studies on interpersonal discrimination and mental health]. *Cadernos de Saude Publica / Ministerio da Saude, Fundacao Oswaldo Cruz, Escola Nacional de Saude Publica*, *29*(3), 445–459. Available from https://doi.org/10.1590/s0102-311x2013000300004.

Gryczynski, J., & Ward, B. W. (2012). Religiosity, heavy alcohol use, and vicarious learning networks among adolescents in the United States. *Health Education & Behavior: the Official Publication of the Society for Public Health Education*, *39*(3), 341–351. Available from https://doi.org/10.1177/1090198111417623.

Hatch, S. L. (2005). Conceptualizing and identifying cumulative adversity and protective resources: Implications for understanding health inequalities. *The Journal of Gerontology: Series B Psychological Sciences and Social Sciences*, *60*(Spec 2), 130–134. Available from https://doi.org/10.1093/geronb/60.Special_Issue_2.S130.

Hingson, R., & Kenkel, D. (2004). Social, health, and economic consequences of underage drinking. In R. J. Bonnie, & M. E. O'Connell (Eds.), *Reducing underage drinking: A collective responsibility*. Washington, DC: National Academies Press (US).

Institute of Medicine. (1994). Reducing risks for mental disorders: Frontiers for preventive intervention research. In P. J. Mrazek, & R. J. Haggerty (Eds.), *Committee on prevention of mental disorders, division of biobehavioral sciences and mental disorders*. Washington, DC: National Academy Press.

Iwamoto, D. K., Kaya, A., Grivel, M., & Clinton, L. (2016). Under-researched demographics: Heavy episodic drinking and alcohol-related problems among Asian Americans. *Alcohol Research: Current Reviews*, *38*(1), 17–25.

Jones, S. A., Lueras, J. M., & Nagel, B. J. (2018). Effects of binge drinking on the developing brain. *Alcohol Research: Current Reviews*, *39*(1), 87–96.

Kane, J. C., Damian, A. J., Fairman, B., Bass, J. K., Iwamoto, D. K., & Johnson, R. M. (2017). Differences in alcohol use patterns between adolescent Asian American ethnic groups: Representative estimates from the National Survey on Drug Use and Health 2002–2013. *Addictive Behaviors*, *64*, 154–158. Available from https://doi.org/10.1016/j.addbeh.2016.08.045.

Kendler, K. S., Gardner, C. O., Hickman, M., Heron, J., Macleod, J., Lewis, G., & Dick, D. M. (2014). Socioeconomic status and alcohol-related behaviors in mid- to late adolescence in the Avon longitudinal study of parents and children. *Journal of Studies on Alcohol and Drugs*, *75*(4), 541–545. Available from https://doi.org/10.15288/jsad.2014.75.541.

Keyes, K. M., & Miech, R. (2013). Age, period, and cohort effects in heavy episodic drinking in the US from 1985 to 2009. *Drug and Alcohol Dependence*, *132*(1–2), 140–148. Available from https://doi.org/10.1016/j.drugalcdep.2013.01.019.

Komro, K. A., Perry, C. L., Veblen-Mortenson, S., Farbakhsh, K., Toomey, T. L., Stigler, M. H., ... Williams, C. L. (2008). Outcomes from a randomized controlled trial of a multi-component alcohol use preventive intervention for urban youth: Project northland Chicago. *Addiction (Abingdon, England)*, *103*(4), 606–618. Available from https://doi.org/10.1111/j.1360-0443.2007.02110.x.

Kumpfer, K. L. (1998). The strengthening families program. In R. S. Ashery, E. B. Robertson, & K. L. Kumpfer (Eds.), *Drug abuse prevention through family interventions*. Rockville, MD: National Institute on Drug Abuse.

Kumpfer, K. L., & Alvarado, R. (1998). *Effective family strengthening interventions*. Juvenile Justice Bulletin. Family Strengthening Series. (NCJ-171121). Washington, DC.

Kumpfer, K. L., Pinyuchon, M., Teixeira de Melo, A., & Whiteside, H. O. (2008). Cultural adaptation process for international dissemination of the strengthening families program. *Evaluation & the Health Professions*, *31*(2), 226–239. Available from https://doi.org/10.1177/0163278708315926.

Lee, M. R., & Sher, K. J. (2018). "Maturing out" of binge and problem drinking. *Alcohol Research: Current Reviews*, *39*(1), 31–42.

Lee, R. D., & Chen, J. (2017). Adverse childhood experiences, mental health, and excessive alcohol use: Examination of race/ethnicity and sex differences. *Child Abuse & Neglect*, *69*, 40–48. Available from https://doi.org/10.1016/j.chiabu.2017.04.004.

Lisdahl, K. M., Sher, K. J., Conway, K. P., Gonzalez, R., Feldstein Ewing, S. W., Nixon, S. J., ... Heitzeg, M. (2018). Adolescent brain cognitive development (ABCD) study: Overview of substance use assessment methods. *Developmental Cognitive Neuroscience*, *32*, 80–96. Available from https://doi.org/10.1016/j.dcn.2018.02.007.

Lloyd, D. A., & Turner, R. J. (2008). Cumulative lifetime adversities and alcohol dependence in adolescence and young adulthood. *Drug and Alcohol Dependence*, *93*(3), 217–226. Available from https://doi.org/10.1016/j.drugalcdep.2007.09.012.

Longshore, D., & Grills, C. (2000). Motivating illegal drug use recovery: Evidence for a culturally congruent intervention. *Journal of Black Psychology*, *26*(3), 288–301.

López-Caneda, E., Rodríguez Holguín, S., Cadaveira, F., Corral, M., & Doallo, S. (2014). Impact of alcohol use on inhibitory control (and vice versa) during adolescence and young adulthood: A review. *Alcohol and Alcoholism*, *49*(2), 173–181. Available from https://doi.org/10.1093/alcalc/agt168.

Madkour, A. S., Jackson, K., Wang, H., Miles, T. T., Mather, F., & Shankar, A. (2015). Perceived discrimination and heavy episodic drinking among African-American youth: Differences by age and reason for discrimination. *The Journal of Adolescent Health: Official Publication of the Society for Adolescent Medicine*, *57*(5), 530–536. Available from https://doi.org/10.1016/j.jadohealth.2015.07.016.

Martinez, C. R. (2006). Effects of differential family acculturation on latino adolescent substance use. *Family Relations*, *55*(3), 306–317. Available from https://doi.org/10.1111/j.1741-3729.2006.00404.x.

Meca, A., Zamboanga, B. L., Lui, P. P., Schwartz, S. J., Lorenzo-Blanco, E. I., Gonzales-Backen, M. A., ... Lizzi, K. M. (2019). Alcohol initiation among recently immigrated Hispanic adolescents: Roles of acculturation and sociocultural stress. *The American Journal of Orthopsychiatry*, *89*(5), 569–578. Available from https://doi.org/10.1037/ort0000352.

Molina, K. M., Alegria, M., & Chen, C. N. (2012). Neighborhood context and substance use disorders: A comparative analysis of racial and ethnic groups in the United States. *Drug and Alcohol Dependence*, *125*(Suppl. 1), S35–S43. Available from https://doi.org/10.1016/j.drugalcdep.2012.05.027.

Monahan, K. C., King, K. M., Shulman, E. P., Cauffman, E., & Chassin, L. (2015). The effects of violence exposure on the development of impulse control and future orientation across adolescence and early adulthood: Time-specific and generalized effects in a sample of juvenile offenders. *Development and Psychopathology*, *27*(4pt1), 1267–1283. Available from https://doi.org/10.1017/S0954579414001394.

Moore, R. S., Gilder, D. A., Grube, J. W., Lee, J. P., Geisler, J. A., Friese, B., ... Ehlers, C. L. (2018). Prevention of underage drinking on California Indian reservations using individual- and community-level approaches. *American Journal of Public Health*, *108*(8), 1035–1041. Available from https://doi.org/10.2105/AJPH.2018.304447.

Ogden, T., & Hagen, K. A. (2014). *Adolescent mental health: Prevention and intervention*. New York, NY: Routledge.

Orcutt, J. D., & Schwabe, A. M. (2011). Gender, race/ethnicity, and deviant drinking: A longitudinal application of social structure and social learning theory. *Sociological Spectrum*, *32*(1), 20–36. Available from https://doi.org/10.1080/02732173.2012.628553.

Park, E., McCoy, T. P., Erausquin, J. T., & Bartlett, R. (2018). Trajectories of risk behaviors across adolescence and young adulthood: The role of race and ethnicity. *Addictive Behaviors*, *76*, 1–7. Available from https://doi.org/10.1016/j.addbeh.2017.07.014.

Park, S. Y., Anastas, J., Shibusawa, T., & Nguyen, D. (2014). The impact of acculturation and acculturative stress on alcohol use across Asian immigrant subgroups. *Substance Use & Misuse*, *49*(8), 922–931. Available from https://doi.org/10.3109/10826084.2013.855232.

Patrick, M. E., & Shulenberg, J. E. (2014). Prevalence and predictors of adolescent alcohol use and binge drinking in the United States. *Alcohol Research: Current Reviews*, *35*(2), 193–200.

Pena, J. B., Wyman, P. A., Brown, C. H., Matthieu, M. M., Olivares, T. E., Hartel, D., & Zayas, L. H. (2008). Immigration generation status and its association with suicide attempts, substance use, and depressive symptoms among latino adolescents in the USA. *Prevention Science: the Official Journal of the Society for Prevention Research*, *9*(4), 299–310. Available from https://doi.org/10.1007/s11121-008-0105-x.

Perreira, K. M., Marchante, A. N., Schwartz, S. J., Isasi, C. R., Carnethon, M. R., Corliss, H. L., ... Delamater, A. M. (2019). Stress and resilience: Key correlates of mental health and substance use in the Hispanic community health study of Latino youth. *Journal of Immigrant and Minority Health / Center for Minority Public Health*, *21*(1), 4–13. Available from https://doi.org/10.1007/s10903-018-0724-7.

Perry, C. L., Williams, C. L., Veblen-Mortenson, S., Toomey, T. L., Komro, K. A., Anstine, P. S., ... Wolfson, M. (1996). Project Northland: Outcomes of a communitywide alcohol use prevention program during early adolescence. *American Journal of Public Health*, *86* (7), 956–965. Available from https://doi.org/10.2105/ajph.86.7.956.

Pew Research Center. (2014a). *2014 Religious Landscape study. Age distribution by religious group*. Washington, DC. Retrieved from <https://www.pewforum.org/religious-landscape-study/age-distribution/>.

Pew Research Center. (2014b). *2014 Religious Landscape study. Belief in God by race/ethnicity*. Washington, DC. Retrieved from <https://www.pewforum.org/religious-landscape-study/compare/belief-in-god/by/racial-and-ethnic-composition/>.

Pfefferbaum, A., Kwon, D., Brumback, T., Thompson, W. K., Cummins, K., Tapert, S. F., ... Sullivan, E. V. (2018). Altered brain developmental trajectories in adolescents after initiating drinking. *The American Journal of Psychiatry*, *175*(4), 370–380. Available from https://doi.org/10.1176/appi.ajp.2017.17040469.

Pfefferbaum, A., Rohlfing, T., Pohl, K. M., Lane, B., Chu, W., Kwon, D., ... Sullivan, E. V. (2016). Adolescent development of cortical and white matter structure in the NCANDA sample: Role of sex, ethnicity, puberty, and alcohol drinking. *Cerebral Cortex*, *26*(10), 4101–4121. Available from https://doi.org/10.1093/cercor/bhv205.

Poonawalla, I. B., Kendzor, D. E., Owen, M. T., & Caughy, M. O. (2014). Family income trajectory during childhood is associated with adolescent cigarette smoking and alcohol use. *Addictive Behaviors*, *39*(10), 1383–1388. Available from https://doi.org/10.1016/j.addbeh.2014.05.005.

Rhew, I. C., Hawkins, J. D., & Oesterle, S. (2011). Drug use and risk among youth in different rural contexts. *Health & Place*, *17*(3), 775–783. Available from https://doi.org/10.1016/j.healthplace.2011.02.003.

Roblyer, Z. M. I., Grzywacz, J. G., Cervantes, R. C., & Merten, M. J. (2016). Stress and alcohol, cigarette, and marijuana use among Latino adolescents in families with undocumented immigrants. *Journal of Child and Family Studies*, *25*(2), 475–487. Available from https://doi.org/10.1007/s10826-015-0249-9.

Room, R., & Makela, K. (2000). Typologies of the cultural position of drinking. *Journal of Studies on Alcohol*, *61*(3), 475–483. Available from https://doi.org/10.15288/jsa.2000.61.475.

Scheier, L. M., & Botvin, G. J. (1995). Effects of early adolescent drug use on cognitive efficacy in early-late adolescence: A developmental structural model. *Journal of Substance Abuse*, *7* (4), 379–404. Available from https://doi.org/10.1016/0899-3289(95)90011-X.

Sheikh, M., & Islam, T. (2018). Islam, alcohol, and identity: Towards a critical Muslim studies approach. *ReOrient*, *3*(2), 185–211. Available from https://doi.org/10.13169/reorient.3.2.0185.

Shin, S. H., Miller, D. P., & Teicher, M. H. (2013). Exposure to childhood neglect and physical abuse and developmental trajectories of heavy episodic drinking from early adolescence into young adulthood. *Drug and Alcohol Dependence*, *127*(1–3), 31–38. Available from https://doi.org/10.1016/j.drugalcdep.2012.06.005.

Skala, K., & Walter, H. (2013). Adolescence and ulcohol: A review of the literature. *Neuropsychiatrie: Klinik, Diagnostik, Therapie und Rehabilitation: Organ der Gesellschaft Osterreichischer Nervenarzte und Psychiater*, *27*(4), 202–211. Available from https://doi.org/10.1007/s40211-013-0066-6.

Steele, C. M., & Josephs, R. A. (1990). Alcohol myopia. Its prized and dangerous effects. *The American Psychologist*, *45*(8), 921–933. Available from https://doi.org/10.1037//0003-066x.45.8.921.

Steinberg L. (2008). A social neuroscience perspective on adolescent risk-taking. *Developmental Review*, 28, 78–106.

Substance Abuse and Mental Health Services Administration. (2019, 04/14/19). *Evidence-based practices resource center*. Retrieved from <https://www.samhsa.gov/ebp-resource-center>.

Topper, L. R., Castellanos-Ryan, N., Mackie, C., & Conrod, P. J. (2011). Adolescent bullying victimisation and alcohol-related problem behaviour mediated by coping drinking motives over a 12 month period. *Addictive Behaviors*, *36*(1–2), 6–13. Available from https://doi.org/10.1016/j.addbeh.2010.08.016.

U.S. Department of Health and Human Services. (2007). *The surgeon general's call to action to prevent and reduce underage drinking*. Rockville, MD.

U.S. Department of Health and Human Services. (2015). *Dietary guidelines 2015-2020: Alcohol*. Rockville, MD. Retrieved from <https://health.gov/dietaryguidelines/2015/guidelines/appendix-9/>.

U.S. Department of Health and Human Services. (2016a). *Fact sheets: Underage drinking*. Atlanta, GA. Retrieved from <https://www.cdc.gov/alcohol/fact-sheets/underage-drinking.htm>.

U.S. Department of Health and Human Services. (2016b). *Surgeon General's Report on Alcohol, Drugs, and Health*. Washington, DC. Retrieved from <https://addiction.surgeongeneral.gov/index.php/table-of-contents>.

U.S. Department of Health and Human Services. (2017a). *2017 National Survey on Drug Use and Health (NSDUH). Table 2.50B - Alcohol Use in Lifetime, past year, and past month and binge and heavy alcohol use in past month among person aged 12 to 20, by demographic characteristics: Percentages, 2016 and 2017*. Rockville, MD. Retrieved from <https://www.samhsa.gov/data/sites/default/files/cbhsq-reports/NSDUHDetailedTabs2017/NSDUHDetailedTabs2017.htm#tab2-50B>.

U.S. Department of Health and Human Services. (2017b). *Underage drinking*. Rockville, MD. Retrieved from <https://pubs.niaaa.nih.gov/publications/UnderageDrinking/UnderageFact.htm>.

U.S. Department of Health and Human Services. (2018a). *Alcohol screening and brief intervention for youth: A practitioner's guide*. Rockville, MD. Retrieved from <https://www.niaaa.nih.gov/sites/default/files/publications/YouthGuide.pdf>.

U.S. Department of Health and Human Services. (2018b). *Youth risk behavior surveillance—United States, 2017*. Rockville, MD. Retrieved from <https://www.cdc.gov/healthyyouth/data/yrbs/pdf/2017/ss6708.pdf>.

Unger, J. B., Ritt-Olson, A., Wagner, K. D., Soto, D. W., & Baezconde-Garbanati, L. (2009). Parent–child acculturation patterns and substance use among hispanic adolescents: A longitudinal analysis. *The Journal of Primary Prevention*, *30*(3–4), 293–313. Available from https://doi.org/10.1007/s10935-009-0178-8.

U.S. Centers for Medicare & Medicaid Services. (2018). Federal Poverty Level (FPL). Retrieved from https://www.healthcare.gov/glossary/federal-poverty-level-FPL/.

Unger, J. B., Thing, J., Soto, D. W., & Baezconde-Garbanati, L. (2014). Associations between ethnic labels and substance use among Hispanic/Latino adolescents in Los Angeles. *Substance Use & Misuse*, *49*(8), 1007–1016. Available from https://doi.org/10.3109/10826084.2013.795172.

Warne, D., Dulacki, K., Spurlock, M., Meath, T., Davis, M. M., Wright, B., & McConnell, K. J. (2017). Adverse childhood experiences (ACE) among American Indians in South Dakota and associations with mental health conditions, alcohol use, and smoking. *Journal of Health Care for the Poor and Underserved*, *28*(4), 1559–1577. Available from https://doi.org/10.1353/hpu.2017.0133.

Wechsler, H., & Nelson, T. F. (2010). Will increasing alcohol availability by lowering the minimum legal drinking age decrease drinking and related consequences among youths? *American Journal of Public Health*, *100*(6), 986–992. Available from https://doi.org/10.2105/AJPH.2009.178004.

Whitesell, M., Bachand, A., Peel, J., & Brown, M. J. (2013). Familial, social, and individual factors contributing to risk for adolescent substance use. *Journal of Addiction*, 1–9. Available from https://doi.org/10.1155/2013/579310.

World Health Organization. (2018). *Global status report on alcohol and health 2018*. Geneva. Retrieved from <https://apps.who.int/iris/bitstream/handle/10665/274603/9789241565639-eng.pdf?ua = 1>.

Zimmer-Gembeck, M. J., & Skinner, E. A. (2011). The development of coping across childhood and adolescence: An integrative review and critique of research. *International Journal of Behavioral Development*, *35*(1), 1–17. Available from https://doi.org/10.1177/0165025410384923.

Zucker, R. A. (2008). Anticipating problem alcohol use developmentally from childhood into middle adulthood: What have we learned? *Addiction (Abingdon, England)*, *103*(Suppl. 1), 100–108. Available from https://doi.org/10.1111/j.1360-0443.2008.02179.x.

Zoccolillo M. Gender and the development of conduct disorder. *Development and Psychopathology*, 5, 1993, 65–78.

Chapter 20

Alcohol use and misuse: Perspectives from seldom heard voices

Tran H. Le, Anthony M. Foster, Phoenix R. Crane and Amelia E. Talley
Department of Psychological Sciences, Texas Tech University, Lubbock, TX, United States

The overrepresentation of marginalized populations in alcohol disparities research has gained increasing attention over the last decade. In light of this attention, burgeoning evidence suggests the risks of alcohol use and misuse, as well as associated problems and consequences, differ by race/ethnicity, gender identity, sexual orientation, age, and other factors. Herein, we use the term "vulnerable populations" to refer to various groups of people who may be at an increased risk for negative consequences from alcohol use as a result of their respective group identities. Although there are a number of marginalized communities deserving of attention, the current chapter focuses on recent research, published over the past 20 years, within five vulnerable populations: (1) racial/ethnic minorities, (2) women, (3) lesbian, gay, bisexual, and transgender (LGBT) individuals, (4) military veterans, and (5) older adults. The size of these populations allowed for a discussion of *shared* perspectives, but their constituents were also diverse enough to warrant consideration of sub-groups' *unique* experiences.

To better understand factors that may potentiate alcohol use and alcohol-related consequences in vulnerable populations, this chapter also sought to integrate the extant quantitative and qualitative literatures and provide a broad overview of the experiences of individuals from each community, using quotations to give voice to their perspectives. In doing so, we seek to breathe life into the statistics, while simultaneously providing an opportunity to listen to the seldom heard voices of those most vulnerable to alcohol-related harms. Given the relatively vast literature available for each vulnerable population, the current chapter is but a brief discussion of contemporary research trends and is by no means meant to be exhaustive. This area of research would greatly benefit from meta-analytic studies to determine the

The Handbook of Alcohol Use - Understandings from Synapse to Society.
DOI: https://doi.org/10.1016/B978-0-12-816720-5.00001-3

extent to which vulnerable populations, including intersecting sub-groups, are at risk for alcohol-related health disparities and under what conditions.

Main sections of this chapter address demographic features of each vulnerable group, disparities in prevalence of alcohol use and misuse, extant prevention strategies/interventions, and potential directions for future research, with relevant meta-analyses cited in-text for further reading. Although we will focus on each group, in turn, it should be noted that overlapping and interdependent systems of discrimination or disadvantage can, and do, impact the frequency of alcohol use and severity of alcohol misuse within each of these vulnerable populations. Thus, this chapter concludes with a brief discussion on the value of addressing alcohol-related outcomes using the *intersectionality* framework.

Racial/ethnic minorities

> *We would get beer and drive all over. I lost three good jobs from drinking. I was bumming money from my folks, sisters, friends. I would say I'd pay them back but I had no job. I would drink around, sit at Jimtown[1] with my husband until someone would offer us a drink. We were living on G.A.[2] once in a while. I hocked stuff, to buy drinks.*
>
> Prussing (2007, pp. 511–512)

Recent research has supported that alcohol use and misuse among racial/ethnic minority groups continues to pose a significant health problem (e.g., Delker, Brown, & Hasin, 2016; Mulia, Tam, Bond, Zemore, & Li, 2018). Given the rapidly increasing proportion of racial/ethnic minorities in the United States, we present research from a wide selection of published work, focusing primarily on the larger racial/ethnic sub-groups, including Hispanics/Latinxs, Blacks, Asians, and American Indians/Alaska Natives. Although approximately nine million people self-reported more than one race in the 2010 U.S. Census, the current section is limited to individuals who reported only one race/ethnicity (U.S. Census Bureau, 2010). By highlighting the experiences of members of the aforementioned communities, we hope to shed light on potential social and cultural risk factors that may account for varying estimates in patterns of alcohol use and treatment utilization.

Alcohol use and misuse disparities

Nationally representative surveys show that rates of early onset drinking (i.e., before age 15) vary greatly across racial/ethnic groups. Results from

---

1. Jimtown is a local bar near the reservation border where this field study was conducted (Prussing, 2007).
2. G.A., or General Assistance, is "a public assistance program administered by the Bureau of Indian Affairs" (Prussing, 2007, p. 512).

the National Epidemiologic Survey on Alcohol Related Conditions (NESARC-II), for example, found that the prevalence of early onset drinking was highest among Native Americans (16.4%), followed by Hispanics/Latinxs (7.93%), Whites (7.07%), Asians (6.03%), and Blacks (5.52%) (Chartier & Caetano, 2010). Additionally, typical alcohol consumption has been shown to vary by racial/ethnic identification. For example, among adults aged 18 and older, results from the 2017 National Survey on Drug Use and Health (NSDUH) suggest that lifetime alcohol use was lowest for Asians (68.5%), highest for Whites (90.8%) and American Indians/Alaska Natives (86.7%), and similar for Blacks (78.5%) and Hispanics/Latinxs (80.2%) (Center for Behavioral Health Statistics and Quality [CBHSQ], 2018).

With regard to binge, or heavy episodic, drinking (i.e., consuming four or more drinks for women and five or more drinks for men within a single day), the 2017 NSDUH showed that the prevalence of past-month binge drinking among adults was highest for American Indians/Alaska Natives (29.6%) and Hispanics/Latinxs (28.6%), followed by Whites (27.3%), Blacks (24.9%), and Asians (14.2%). Among the same age group (i.e., aged 18+), rates of past-month heavy alcohol use, defined as binge drinking on 5 or more days in the past month, were highest among Whites (7.7%), followed by American Indians/Alaska Natives (7.3%), Hispanics/Latinxs (5.5%), Blacks (4.8%), and Asians (2.1%).

Although the fifth edition of the *Diagnostic and Statistical Manual of Mental Disorders* (DSM-5) is currently used to diagnose alcohol use disorder (AUD) (American Psychiatric Association [APA], 2013), previous publications utilized DSM-IV criteria to determine the prevalence of AUD. According to the DSM-IV (APA, 1994), AUD described two distinct disorders: alcohol abuse and alcohol dependence. Whereas the diagnostic criteria for alcohol abuse required respondents to endorse one or more (out of four) "abuse" criteria in the past year (e.g., continued use of alcohol, despite problems with family or friends), the diagnostic criteria for alcohol dependence required respondents to endorse three or more (out of seven) "dependence" criteria in the past year (e.g., used alcohol in greater quantities or for a longer time than intended). In 2017, the overall estimated percentage of persons, aged 12 or older, who had been previously diagnosed with AUD was 5.3% (2.9% and 2.5% for alcohol dependence and alcohol abuse, respectively) (CBHSQ, 2018). Among adults aged 18 years or older, the percentage of American Indians/Alaska Natives who had been previously diagnosed with either type of AUD in the past year was 10.1%, followed by Whites (6.1%), Hispanics/Latinxs (5.3%), Blacks (4.9%), and Asians (3.2%). Thus, findings from the extant literature suggest that people from indigenous tribes of North America (i.e., American Indians; Alaska Natives) are at greatest risk of alcohol misuse, followed by those from Hispanic/Latinx communities.

A number of potential mediating and moderating factors associated with increased drinking among racial/ethnic minority sub-populations have been identified throughout the years. For example, findings suggest that immigrants may be at greater risk for alcohol use and misuse due to greater reliance on alcohol as a means of coping with acculturative stressors (e.g., cultural shock, language barriers, documentation status) (see Lui & Zamboanga, 2018a, 2018b for reviews). Additional factors recently examined in the extant literature include ethnic drinking cultures (e.g., Cook, Bond, Karriker-Jaffe, & Zemore, 2013; Cook & Caetano, 2014; Cook, Karriker-Jaffe, Bond, & Lui, 2015), racial prejudice/discrimination (e.g., Gilbert & Zemore, 2016; Mulia et al., 2008; Zemore et al., 2016), and racial residential segregation (e.g., Williams & Collins, 2001).

Prevention and interventions

Given the racially/ethnically-specific risk factors associated with alcohol consumption, there is a crucial need for tailored prevention, intervention, and treatment programs (Schmidt, Greenfield, & Mulia, 2006). Indeed, data by race/ethnicity from the 2017 NSDUH showed that 10.7% of American Indians/Alaska Natives aged 18 or older *needed* alcohol treatment in the past year alone, followed by Whites (6.3%), Hispanics/Latinxs (5.6%), Blacks (5.5%), and Asians (3.2%). Alarmingly, only 2.1%, 0.5%, 0.4%, 0.9%, and 0.1% of American Indians/Alaska Natives, Whites, Hispanics/Latinxs, Blacks, and Asians, respectively, reported actually *receiving* treatment at an alcohol-treatment specialty facility.

Accumulating evidence suggests that existing racial and ethnic alcohol-related disparities may result from barriers related to beliefs about stigma regarding alcoholism (e.g., Chartier, Miller, Harris, & Caetano, 2016), differences in insurance coverage (e.g., Chartier & Caetano, 2010; Weisner, Matzger, Tam, & Schmidt, 2002), and a relative lack of adequate service coverage (e.g., Vaeth, Wang-Schweig, & Caetano, 2017). Importantly, research suggests that even when racial/ethnic minorities are able to access services, they are more likely to report lower treatment satisfaction (Tonigan, 2003) and less likely to complete addiction treatment (Saloner & Cook, 2013), perhaps due, in part, to a lack of tailored content.

Preliminary evidence suggests that the implementation of racially appropriate and culturally sensitive intervention programs (e.g., racial/ethnic patient-provider matching) are a viable option for treating alcohol-related problems within American Indian or Alaskan Native communities (e.g., McDonell et al., 2016) as well as Hispanic/Latinx communities (e.g., Field & Caetano, 2010; Lee et al., 2011). Furthermore, qualitative work in this area has highlighted the need for intervention programs which provide multilingual treatment services for clients who identify English as a secondary language:

The problem is that if the psychologist does not understand the cultural aspects, well they're going to focus only on the education that they have received. Maybe a lot of the things they do will not help, although some things might... Sometimes language is a barrier, not everybody speaks perfect English. Most of these programs are in English.

Valdez, Garcia, Ruiz, Oren, and Carvajal (2018, p. 1952)

Future directions

Future research in this domain require careful consideration of various environmental, cultural, personal, and biological risk factors that may contribute to disparate alcohol-related outcomes (e.g., historical factors, cultural norms, immigration status, alcohol-metabolizing genes, etc.) (Chartier & Caetano, 2010; Vaeth et al., 2017; Zemore et al., 2018). Given the rapidly expanding diversification of the U.S. landscape, it is increasingly important for clinicians to enact prevention and treatment strategies tailored toward racial/ethnic minority persons. Much like racial/ethnic identification, gender identification also has a strong impact on risk of alcohol use and misuse.

Women

I did not want to marry this man. I was perfectly happy having a love affair with him, but he felt differently about it and forced the situation. So... both sets of parents were anxious for us to get married, and again, I kind of went along with what other people wanted us to do.

Paris and Bradley (2001, p. 657)

As the above quotation exemplifies, women face unique circumstances due to the various social norms associated with their gender identity, including, but not limited to, gender-based expectations to marry and conceive children. Although the term "women" can include cisgender and transgender women, within the context of our discussion, the term "women" will refer to cisgender women, unless otherwise stated, given that most extant research only includes cisgender women. We briefly touch upon alcohol use among individuals with diverse gender (and sexual minority) identities in the subsequent section on LGBT populations. Moreover, a distinction between the terms, "female" and "woman," must be noted. Whereas the term "female" typically refers to one's reproductive biology, the term "woman" refers to one's gender identity and expression (APA, 2015). Both aspects are necessary to consider to better understand differences in alcohol use as well as motivations to use and subsequently, misuse alcohol.

Alcohol use and misuse disparities

Even at comparable rates of alcohol consumption, females have more negative alcohol-related consequences than males (NIAAA, 1999). This is due, in part, to differences in body fat and water volume between the sexes, with females having greater body fat and lower water volume, on average, resulting in differences in alcohol solubility (Frezza et al., 1990). Consequently, females are more likely to become intoxicated faster and at higher levels than males who are drinking the same amount of alcohol at the same rate (Frezza et al., 1990). Although females, compared to males, typically consume less alcohol less frequently and are less likely to become hazardous drinkers (Buzzetti, Parikh, Gerussi, & Tsochatzis, 2017), they are more likely to report adverse alcohol-related health outcomes earlier and over a shorter period of time relative to males (Keyes, Martins, Blanco, & Hasin, 2010; Milic et al., 2018; NIAAA, 2006).

Fluctuations in sex-related hormone levels (i.e., due to menstrual cycle, contraceptive use, pregnancy) have also been shown to impact alcohol metabolism, and consequently, alcohol-related outcomes. Specifically, studies have shown that females experience faster alcohol absorption, higher blood-alcohol levels, and longer periods of intoxication during specific phases of the menstrual cycle (e.g., Erol, Ho, Winham, & Karpyak, 2019; Muti et al., 1998; Reichman et al., 1993). By contrast, in studies that have recruited females who did and did not use oral contraceptives, no significant differences in alcohol use were reported (e.g., Little, Moore, Guzinski, & Perez, 1980; Sutker, Tabakoff, Goist, & Randall, 1983). Older adulthood among females poses unique circumstances which can also impact alcohol consumption (see Buzzetti et al., 2017; Milic et al., 2018).

In addition to biological differences, the experience of identifying as a woman also contributes to disparities in alcohol use and misuse. Of the many unique experiences women share, being sexually objectified, or having one's humanity reduced to being an object of sexual desire, has been recently linked to food-restricted alcohol consumption among college-aged women (i.e., limiting food consumption prior to alcohol intake) (Eisenberg, Johnson, & Zucker, 2018). Among women in general, and including those with intersecting stigmatized identities (e.g., sexual assault survivors), alcohol may be used as a form of self-medication to ameliorate distress associated with experiencing those traumatic events, which may be more common in disadvantaged social groups:

> *When I was a teenager I tended to abuse alcohol and I realize now that I was trying to drown out the pain of growing up as a survivor of molestation by a family member... And my last sexual experience with a man was also a rape. And that is what made me realize that I'd rather be with women.*
>
> Drabble and Trocki (2014, p. 190)

Prevention and interventions

Historically, most alcohol prevention efforts have focused on pregnant women. The Center for Disease Control and Prevention in the U.S. declares there is no safe amount of alcohol use during pregnancy or while trying to get pregnant and that drinking alcohol can cause the fetus to develop abnormal facial features, growth and central nervous system problems, and abnormal brain development. Despite widespread distribution of this information, recent data among pregnant women between the ages of 15 and 44 showed that 9.3% reported using alcohol at least once in the past month (SAMHSA, 2017). Considering that women who use alcohol during pregnancy are also more likely to use other substances (e.g., opioids), targeted screening and intervention has been recommended as a prevention strategy, in addition to current prenatal care programs (Bakhireva et al., 2018).

At subsequent stages in life, late onset of AUD may occur in older women, especially among those who experience a traumatic life event, such as losing a loved one (Milic et al., 2018). In response, cognitive-behavioral therapy (CBT) has been recommended as one form of intervention for this vulnerable population (e.g., Hallgren, Epstein, & McCrady, 2019). For older women whose increased alcohol use may be intended to reduce symptoms resulting from sex-hormone fluctuations, hormone replacement therapy (e.g., estrogen pills) has been recommended to counteract the physical effects of menopause (Buzzetti et al., 2017; Milic et al., 2018).

Unfortunately, women may be less likely to receive treatment for AUD, especially when they perceive a relative lack of social support and economic resources related to childcare, experiences of trauma, and social stigma (e.g., McCaul et al., 2019). Moreover, due to issues related to pregnancy, childcare responsibilities, custody threats, transportation, and financial status, pregnant (vs. non-pregnant) women are less likely to seek alcohol treatment (Agabio, Pisanu, Luigi Gessa, & Franconi, 2017). In response to these gender-specific issues, women-only substance-related care centers (e.g., AUD treatment programs which provide childcare services) have been implemented to encourage treatment-seeking and program-retention among women who have been diagnosed with AUD. Current statistics point toward the effectiveness of these tailored programs on greater treatment-seeking and increased retention rates of those enrolled (e.g., Agabio et al., 2017; McCaul et al., 2019; Niv & Hser, 2007). Based on the literature, having women-only treatment programs and medical services that are sensitive to various lifespan considerations is necessary to remove barriers and improve access to care among women struggling with AUD.

Future directions

Women comprise a diverse group of individuals with varying biological systems, social identities, and lived experiences, resulting in different motivations and responses to the use and misuse of alcohol. As the proportion of women who drink in the general population increases, additional work should examine risk of alcohol misuse among those with female role models who are also heavy drinkers (e.g., Talley, Hughes, Wilsnack, & Hughes, 2018) or those who report heavy peer norms for alcohol use (e.g., Talley, Brown, Stevens, & Littlefield, 2014). With additional research, mental and physical health outcomes could be improved upon for women. For individuals who possess diverse sexual and/or gender minority identities (e.g., LGBT), we see a similar need.

LGBT populations

> *There's high levels of drinking...but it has to do with...isolation and access to socialization opportunities...There are like links to LGBT people and you know, poor health and...behaviors and things like that, but I wouldn't just brand LGBT people is effectively what I'm saying...*
>
> Emslie, Lennox, and Ireland (2015, p. 12)

The excerpt above is an example of the role alcohol-specific socialization plays in drinking behaviors among individuals with sexual and gender minority (SGM) identities, including lesbian, gay, bisexual, and transgender/transsexual (LGBT) individuals. Findings from a sizable body of research indicate that self-identified LGBT individuals are at increased risk for alcohol use and misuse compared to their heterosexual, cisgender counterparts (e.g., Hughes, 2005; Hughes & Eliason, 2002). The current discussion is limited to research concerning the LGBT sub-populations, specifically, to provide a broad overview of the most current research on a diverse group of individuals who share similar experiences with regard to issues surrounding sexuality, gender, and identity.

Alcohol use and misuse disparities

Previous research has shown that sexual minority youth report earlier onset drinking compared to their heterosexual peers (e.g., Fish, Watson, Porta, Russell, & Saewyc, 2017). Similarly, results from population-based studies suggest that sexual minority youth are more likely than heterosexual youth to report lifetime and past-month alcohol use, past-month binge drinking, and more frequent past-month drinking (Corliss, Rosario, Wypij, Fisher, & Austin, 2008; Talley, Hughes, Aranda, Birkett, & Marshal, 2014). Among transgender youth, Reisner and colleagues (2014) found that gender minority youth had increased odds of past-year alcohol use compared to cisgender youth.

With regard to LGBT adults (i.e., aged 18 or older), past research suggests that rates of drinking among SGM individuals are higher than those of the general public (Hughes, 2005; Hughes & Eliason, 2002). In a recent review, Hughes, Wilsnack, and Kantor (2016) reported results, synthesized from a wide body of research, that were congruent with many of the aforementioned findings on alcohol use among LGBT-identified individuals. Consistently, findings show that a non-heterosexual sexual orientation identity is generally associated with increased substance use behaviors (e.g., McCabe, Hughes, Bostwick, West, & Boyd, 2009; McCabe, West, Hughes, & Boyd, 2013). Among gender minorities, the extant literature suggests that transgender individuals have high rates of alcohol use compared to cisgender individuals (e.g., Coulter et al., 2015; Glynn & van den Berg, 2017).

The prevalence of binge drinking among LGBT individuals has gained much attention in recent years, prompting researchers to conclude that alcohol misuse is an important behavioral health concern in this population. Indeed, recent research suggests that sexual minority youth are at elevated risk for high-intensity binge drinking episodes, relative to their heterosexual peers (Fish, Schulenberg, & Russell, 2019; Talley et al., 2014). Notably, problem-drinking behaviors among LGBT individuals persist throughout adolescence and into adulthood (e.g., Hatzenbuehler, Corbin, & Fromme, 2008; Marshal et al., 2008; Marshal, Friedman, Stall, & Thompson, 2009). Results from multiple other studies have found a high prevalence of binge drinking among transgender populations in adulthood (Coulter et al., 2015; James et al., 2016; Keuroghlian, Reisner, White, & Weiss, 2015; Scheim, Bauer, & Shokoohi, 2016).

Consequently, there is growing consensus among researchers that sexual minority individuals experience disproportionate rates of AUDs compared to heterosexual individuals (Amadio, 2006; Hughes, 2005; McCabe et al., 2013; Schuler, Rice, Evans-Polce, & Collins, 2018). Moreover, some research has shown that lesbians and bisexual women tend to report higher prevalence of AUD, even compared to gay and bisexual men (e.g., Green & Feinstein, 2012). Transgender individuals tend to also report significantly elevated prevalence of disordered alcohol use compared to other LGBT sub-groups (Keuroghlian et al., 2015; Reback & Fletcher, 2014; Reisner et al., 2016; Santos et al., 2014).

Minority stress has long been theorized to be a primary factor contributing to LGBT individuals' increased likelihood for alcohol misuse (Meyer, 1995, 2003). More specifically, sexual orientation self-concept ambiguity (Talley & Stevens, 2017), structural stigma (Hatzenbuehler, Jun, Corliss, & Austin, 2015), rejection sensitivity (Pachankis, Hatzenbuehler, & Starks, 2014), sexual orientation-based discrimination (Slater, Godette, Huang, Ruan, & Kerridge, 2017), sexual and gender identity disclosure (Whitehead, Shaver, & Stephenson, 2016), and internalized homophobia (Dorn-Medeiros & Doyle, 2018) have been documented as potential risk factors impacting the prevalence and severity of alcohol use and misuse in LGBT sub-populations. It has also been suggested that tolerant drinking norms in LGBT-friendly spaces (e.g., gay bars/clubs) may contribute to LGBT individuals' heightened risk for AUD (Cochran, Grella, & Mays, 2012).

Prevention and interventions

Although the literature is somewhat equivocal, previous research suggests that some LGBT-identified individuals are much less likely to seek treatment for alcohol misuse, compared to heterosexual persons, due, in part, to concerns about being marginalized by treatment staff (e.g., Travers & Schneider, 1996). Perhaps even more alarming, Cochran, Peavy, and Robohm (2007) found that approximately 70% of the "LGBT" substance use treatment programs listed in the 2002 Substance Abuse and Mental Health Service Administration (SAMHSA) database were, in actuality, no different from generic substance-treatment services offered to the general population. Despite recent calls to action to address alcohol-related disparities among SGM populations, the need for empirically tested and effectively tailored treatment programs persists (e.g., Fish & Baams, 2018; Glynn & van den Berg, 2017; Stevens, 2012).

Previous research shows differential patterns of alcohol treatment initiation and utilization among LGBT-identified individuals (e.g., Allen & Mowbray, 2016). Whereas some studies have found no differences in treatment utilization for alcohol-related problems between men who have sex with men and men who do not, others report differences in treatment utilization between lesbian- and bisexual-identified women and their heterosexual counterparts (e.g., Cochran, Keenan, Schober, & Mays, 2000; Drabble, Midanik, & Trocki, 2005). Specifically, Cochran et al. (2000) found that lesbian and bisexual women may be *more* likely to receive treatment for alcohol-related problems compared to heterosexual women. Unfortunately, reasons for greater service utilization were not investigated. Among transgender individuals, those with more access to gender-affirming health care (e.g., cross-hormone and/or surgery utilization) reported higher odds of lifetime treatment for substance use disorder compared to others with relatively less access (e.g., Keuroghlian et al., 2015).

Although some LGBT sub-groups may be more likely to report treatment seeking, alcohol treatment programs may be underutilized by this population, in general, due to various systematic, socioeconomic, and socio-cultural barriers (e.g., anticipated maltreatment, homophobic/transphobic personnel) (Allen & Mowbray, 2016; Lombardi & van Servellen, 2000). Even addressing these treatment barriers, findings from qualitative work on the role of alcohol in identity construction among LGBT people suggests that many perceive drinking as central to identity development and the commercial gay scene:

> *It's a culture thing to go on the gay scene, get drunk, so maybe people don't realize they have an issue with alcohol.*
>
> Emslie et al. (2015, p. 10)

Future directions

To be more responsive to the treatment needs of SGM individuals, LGBT-affirmative treatment programs should strive to improve competency among medical staff to increase provider knowledge of LGBT health needs as they relate to alcohol use and misuse. Implementing culturally informed interventions that consider the central role of identity construction in LGBT drinking may also facilitate greater access to alcohol treatment among LGBT sub-groups at greater risk of misuse (e.g., Emslie et al., 2015; Nuttbrock, 2012). Although future work will be necessary to reduce hazardous drinking among SGM populations, an improved understanding of alcohol-related disparities from the perspective of these seldom heard voices will undoubtedly strengthen our ability to effectively meet the needs of this community. In addition to SGM populations, hazardous drinking has been a long-standing concern among veterans.

Veterans

Unheard certainly, but not unrecognized. War veterans are recognized and widely represented within research... although with good intentions, researchers would write on our behalf but with this came an absence of voice.

Bulmer and Jackson (2016, p. 28)

Veterans (i.e., military members that have finished their active service) constitute a diverse group of individuals with regard to sex, age, race/ethnicity, sexual orientation, gender identity, marital status, branch, military component, combat experience, and comorbid mental health concerns (e.g., Burnett-Zeiger et al., 2011). Given that veterans can identify with any number of minority and/or marginalized social groups, relations among trauma and alcohol misuse in this vulnerable population are impacted by a wide range of socio-cultural factors. For example, among women veterans, alcohol misuse is more prevalent among those who are younger, have been exposed to direct combat, have been victims of sexual assault during active service, and have been diagnosed with post-traumatic stress disorder (PTSD) (Hoggatt, Williams, Der-Martirosian, Yano, & Washington, 2015). Alarmingly, Hoggatt et al. (2015) suggest that more than one in three women in a nationally representative sample of women veterans were at risk for alcohol misuse. Among women veterans with diverse sexual identities, childhood trauma was found to interact with adulthood physical victimization (both as a civilian and during active duty), symptoms of depression, and symptoms of PTSD to exacerbate risk of alcohol misuse (Lehavot, Browne, & Simpson, 2014).

Alcohol use and misuse disparities

Among veterans, in general, disparities in alcohol use and misuse are long-standing. Similar to the other vulnerable populations, age is a key factor pertaining to the onset of alcohol-related disparities, particularly in conjunction with other demographic factors. For instance, male service members who are younger, White, unmarried, have more direct combat experience, and suffer from depression and/or PTSD are at greater risk for alcohol misuse (Burnett-Zeiger et al., 2011). By contrast, self-reported alcohol use was lower among older (vs. younger) LGBT veterans, suggesting that multiple marginalized identities may promote greater resilience, as in cases where older LGBT veterans were protected against excessive rates of alcohol misuse (Cortes, Fletcher, Latini, & Kauth, 2018).

Within this vulnerable population, PTSD symptom clusters (hyperarousal, re-experiencing, and avoidance/numbing) and depression, in particular, are key predictors of alcohol use and increase the likelihood of alcohol misuse. For example, age and combat exposure influence how likely veterans are to experience each of the aforementioned PTSD symptom clusters, and subsequently, alcohol consumption interacts with these clusters to potentiate aggression for some individuals (e.g., Taft et al., 2007). Specifically, levels of alcohol misuse were found to account for the positive relation between hyperarousal and self-reported aggression (e.g., threatening someone, being verbally abusive) (Taft et al., 2007). Although being unmarried is a risk factor for veteran alcohol use and misuse, among veterans who are married, alcohol use is related to incidence of marital aggression, both physical and psychological (e.g., Savarese, Suvak, King, & King, 2001). In particular, among veterans who report greater levels of hyperarousal, incidences of physical aggression between romantic partners also tend to be greater (Savarese et al., 2001).

In some circumstances, however, moderate alcohol use appears to have a therapeutic effect among some veterans, with regard to reducing self-reported PTSD symptoms (e.g., Jakupcak et al., 2010). Specifically, correlational research has linked an increase in PTSD emotional numbing symptoms with greater alcohol consumption, suggesting that alcohol use may serve as a coping mechanism to "facilitate detachment or blunting of negative emotions" (Jakupcak et al., 2010, p. 842). For a more complete review on the relation between exposure to trauma, PTSD, and alcohol misuse, see Stewart (1996). Given that perceived isolation and social disconnectedness during reintegration are known to be risk-factors for alcohol misuse among veterans, trends in the extant literature on veteran alcohol use, including self-medication expectancies and increased risk of intimate partner violence, warrant further examination (e.g., Pietrzak et al., 2010).

Prevention and interventions

Because alcohol use and misuse typically have the presumed self-medicating function of ameliorating the impact of trauma, the critical period of preventing disordered alcohol use may be during the time of reintegration. Although veterans experience many unique stressors during reintegration, such as a sense of alienation, previous research has shown that sharing combat-based narratives may be an effective form of treatment for this vulnerable population. Using this form of therapy, veterans are provided an opportunity to articulate a fully integrated personal narrative, whether it be in the context of social support and transition-support groups or military cultural competence training, to create a sense of community and connectedness (Demers, 2011). Based on current research examining veteran reintegration, it is crucial that veterans are given a chance to explore and garner meaning from their military experiences, not to just receive diagnosis, medication, and referral, in instances of PTSD and/or AUD diagnosis:

> *... a sense of war and its embodied effects cannot be defined within a single representation where there is little or no room for individual subjective narratives – it silences that embodied voice. To get a sense of who I am, and my experiences of living with war, you have to understand my journey.*
>
> Bulmer and Jackson (2016, p. 28)

Among women veterans, this is particularly important, given the accumulation of experiences due to both their veteran status as well as their gender identity. In addition to the high rates of homelessness among veterans in general, which comes with its own risk of alcohol misuse, women veterans are at an increased risk of homelessness due, in part, to their overrepresentation as victims of intimate partner violence (e.g., Dichter, Wagner, Borrero, Broyles, & Montgomery, 2017).

Although there are a variety of treatments tailored for veterans experiencing PTSD, interventions which facilitate meaning-making experiences appear to be particularly important (e.g., Mowatt & Bennett, 2011). An examination of one sample of veteran narratives indicated common themes for meaning-making: the necessity of camaraderie among other veterans, the compounded mental stress due to post-war regret, the complexity of retrospective recollection, and also the viability of nature and physical activity as an effective form of treatment, at least among White males (Mowatt & Bennett, 2011). Moreover, recreational therapy (e.g., therapeutic fly-fishing), may disrupt the potentially negative and lasting effects of trauma by fulfilling searches for social meaning through narrative development (Mowatt & Bennett, 2011).

Unfortunately, gaps in treatment seeking may be due to differences in general referrals for treatment, individual characteristics, and/or physical barriers to accessing treatment (e.g., transportation) (Burnett-Zeiger et al., 2011). Individual characteristics can include the fear of being stigmatized for seeking treatment and inadvertently, hurting one's military career, especially among individuals who are high-ranking (Burnett-Zeiger et al., 2011). In particular, service members are reluctant to receive mental health treatment even when referred because there is a shared concern about it appearing on their record, in addition to other potential social ramifications, such as fear of being treated differently by both peers and those in leadership positions (Burnett-Zeiger et al., 2011). Gaps in treatment are also influenced by race/ ethnicity, with some work suggesting that Native American (compared to White and Black) veterans are more likely to receive formal services for alcohol misuse (e.g., Ross, Fortney, Lancaster, & Booth, 1998). Nevertheless, it is uncertain how effective those treatments are and their attrition rates over time.

For veterans with diverse sexual and gender identities, impediments to effective treatment seeking are impacted by a variety of factors. In a sample of over six thousand women veterans, Kimerling et al. (2015) found that about half indicated a perceived need for mental health services, with about 84% of that subset of women actually receiving health care from the Department of Veteran Affairs (VA). Focusing on that subset, less than half reported satisfaction with the care they were receiving (Kimerling et al., 2015). Results also indicated that when treatment services tailored for women veterans were available (e.g., having a woman health provider and women-only treatment groups), it doubled the odds of women utilizing these services (Kimerling et al., 2015). Other research has pointed to the effectiveness of alcohol interventions that include personalized feedback, such as providing information to develop PTSD management skills (Luciano et al., 2019), conducting focus groups (Abraham, Wright, White, Booth, & Cucciare, 2017), and cognitive processing therapy (Kaysen et al., 2014). Among lesbian and bisexual women veterans, interventions that address the differential types and rates of victimization are necessary, though further research is required to gauge their effectiveness for reducing alcohol misuse (e.g., Lehavot et al., 2014).

Future directions

Given the extant research on veteran populations, a concerted effort should be made to give veterans the power to structure their own narratives about their experiences related to their service. Furthermore, the further development of tailored interventions for veterans with varying intersecting social identities could facilitate social connectedness and meaning-making by increasing contact between veterans during and after reintegration (Straus et al., 2019). Although being young is a risk-factor for veterans regarding alcohol misuse, older adults also have distinct stressors which may impact alcohol use and misuse.

Older adults

> *By putting the problem somewhere else, whether it's in the room or in the balcony or whatever, then you're separating yourself from the guilt. I'm not a bad person; I'm just a person with a problem.*
>
> Gardner and Poole (2009, p. 611)

A number of factors have been found to influence alcohol consumption among older adults (i.e., ages 55 years or older). In some instances, increased alcohol use is associated with retirement and widowhood, whereas decreased alcohol use is associated with hospitalization and the onset of chronic illnesses (e.g., Perreira & Sloan, 2001). In addition to being an older adult, other identity factors, such as possessing a marginalized sexual identity, can impose unique stressors (e.g., mistreatment and victimization (Teaster & Sokan, 2016); risk of social isolation due to changes in social care networks (Brennan-Ing, Seidel, Larson, & Karpiak, 2013)), which may influence alcohol use and risk of misuse, as has been shown among older LGB adults (Veldhuis, Talley, Hancock, Wilsnack, & Hughes, 2017).

With regard to alcohol use and misuse, statistics for older adults vary depending on demographics as well as means of data collection. For instance, in one sample ($N = 925$), 52% of older adults reported total abstinence from alcohol, with older women reporting higher levels of abstinence than men (Satre, Mertens, Arean, & Weisner, 2004). In another study with a sample of about 700 older adults, followed over the course of 20 years, the likelihood that both men and women would engage in excessive drinking declined as they entered their 70s and 80s, with 48.6% of men and 27.1% of women reporting that they consumed two or more alcoholic drinks a day (Moos, Schutte, Brennan, & Moos, 2009). Other studies have shown that, for a majority of older adults, alcohol use does not vary significantly over time (e.g., Perreira & Sloan, 2001).

Alcohol use and misuse disparities

In terms of consumption, alcohol use tends to be lower among older adults who adhere to their health care provider's advice and have no close family or friends who facilitate or encourage consumption (Satre et al., 2004). Research has suggested that *daily* alcohol use remains consistent in older adulthood, particularly among older men relative to older women (e.g., Christie, Bamber, Powell, Arrindell, & Pant, 2013). Under some circumstances, alcohol use may not be detrimental for mental and physical health among older adults. For instance, in a prospective observational study with over 6000 older adults, moderate alcohol consumption (vs. abstinence) was associated with higher cognitive functioning, based on word recall and numerical reasoning, and greater subjective well-being and lower depressive symptoms (Lang, Wallace, Huppert, & Melzer, 2007; see also Veldhuis et al., 2017).

Among older adults, generational cohort and genetic effects can account for some differences in alcohol-related outcomes. Regarding cohort effects, rates of alcohol misuse among older adults in the U.S. tend to be higher among those who are a part of the "baby boomers" generation (Alpert, 2014). Other factors, such as genetic differences, can result in differential health outcomes among older adults who use alcohol. In one nested, case-control study of over 300 matched-cases, the incidence of dementia was greater when alcohol use exceeded two drinks a day; however, when alcohol use was light-to-moderate (e.g., one to six drinks a week), the incidence of dementia was lower (Mukamal et al., 2003). Among older adults, a history of problematic alcohol use influenced the degree to which stressful life events, such as divorce and widowhood, resulted in decreased or increased alcohol use (e.g., Perreira & Sloan, 2001).

One prevalent concern in older adulthood is the interactive effects of consuming alcohol while taking medication. Specifically, there are a number of negative alcohol-medication interactions (AMI) that may contribute to increased blood alcohol levels and, subsequently, brain sensitivity toward alcohol (Moore, Whiteman, & Ward, 2007). In some instances, long-term heavy alcohol use among older adults results in increased drug metabolism, whereby higher doses of medication are needed to yield the desirable therapeutic effect; in other cases, reduced drug metabolism is shown, increasing the risk of an overdose (Moore et al., 2007). Consuming alcohol can also interfere with the effectiveness of various medications as well as yield a variety of aversive physical health concerns, such as gastrointestinal bleeding, impaired psychomotor function, and hypotension (e.g., Moore et al., 2007). Place of residence is another risk factor when AMI is considered, as older adults living in rural (vs. urban) areas experience the highest risk of aversive medication interactions due to alcohol consumption (Zanjani et al., 2016).

Prevention and interventions

Because the onset of alcohol use and misuse is brought upon partly in response to extenuating life circumstances, such as the loss of family members or close friends, some prevention strategies have focused on encouraging adaptive coping strategies among older adults. Similar to veteran populations, one way to facilitate positive coping is through narrative therapy. Based on the existing qualitative research, there is an expressed need for older adults to define themselves on their own terms if treatments are to be efficacious:

> *...we have different stories and they [sic] are positive aspects to draw on, and that we can retell our story... we are challenged by narrative therapy to, through awareness, to become aware of the story we're telling ourselves and make choices of what short story we want to tell ourselves, and that there's more than one story. There can be many stories.*
>
> Gardner and Poole (2009, pp. 611–612)

The need to have power over one's personal narrative is especially crucial among older adults with marginalized sexual identities. Focus groups are thus another method of risk prevention; in this therapeutic approach, inaccurate stereotypes are discussed at length to decrease the pressure to misuse alcohol among LGBT adults entering older adulthood (e.g., Emslie, Lennox, & Ireland, 2017).

For older adults who experience alcohol misuse or have been diagnosed with AUD, alternative interventions include marriage and family therapy (e.g., Morgan, Brosi, & Brosi, 2011), as well as interventions targeting risk reduction. With regard to community-level interventions, some programs have focused on reducing the risk of AMI by creating print education materials to increase awareness about AMI among older adults who consume alcohol regularly while taking medication (e.g., Zanjani, Allen, Schoenberg, Martin, & Clayton, 2018). Other promising methods of risk reduction include information dissemination and attitude change about AMI using "prevention BINGO" (see Benza, Calvert, & McQuown, 2010). Overall, compared to younger adults (ages 18–39), older adults tend to have more positive outcomes: older adults are less likely to report both alcohol and general drug-dependence following treatment (e.g., for 11 different substances) and were more likely to adhere to their addiction treatment plans (Satre et al., 2004).

Older adults continue to experience disparities in (effective) treatment-seeking due, in part, to health problems. Some older adults experience limited mobility and functional impairments, which can contribute to social and physical isolation. Consequently, older adults may be at increased risk for alcohol misuse, especially if they are unaware of the risks associated with their alcohol consumption or perceive barriers to seeking necessary treatment (Cooper, 2012). Among older adult women, existing large-scale alcohol intervention approaches may not prove effective, as they often fail to consider factors unique to the experiences of women (Epstein, Fischer-Elber, & Al-Otaiba, 2008).

Future directions

Although the preceding section considered a number of factors that impact the onset, prevalence, and severity of alcohol misuse among older adults, there is much to be known about the differential experiences and unique stressors of older adults who possess multiple diverse minority identities, such as those who identify as a SGM or who live with various types of disabilities. In order to better serve the needs of marginalized groups within older adult populations, future research should examine specific motivations to use alcohol, including when contraindicated by current medication regimes, to inform more efficacious interventions. Thus far, we have discussed five vulnerable populations individually, however, because social identities often overlap, a discussion of intersectionality is essential.

Discussion

Intersectionality

The theory of intersectionality was originally introduced by legal feminist scholar Kimberlé Crenshaw (1989) to describe the experiences of Black women, who live at the intersection of race and gender. Intersectional theory posits that individuals with multiple social categorizations have unique experiences that are not simply determined from the sum or average of their constituent categorizations but, rather, some interactive effect. Examples of such intermingling social categorizations include race/ethnicity, gender identity, sexual identity, and age, among others (e.g., Demant et al., 2018). Current theorizing suggests that marginalized individuals experience various types of prejudice and discrimination that contribute to risk of substance misuse (e.g., Gibbons et al., 2012; Meyer, 2003; Talley & Littlefield, 2014) as well as generally low well-being (e.g., Degenhardt & Hall, 2001; Merline, O'Malley, Schulenberg, Bachman, & Johnston, 2004).

Multiple marginalized social identities can interact to impact alcohol-related behavior, beginning in adolescence (e.g., Talley et al., 2014). Recent examinations of the Global Drug Survey, conducted in 2015, sought to better understand the protective and non-protective effects of intersecting social identities (i.e., ethnicity, sexual identity, gender identity) on lifetime and recent alcohol use, in addition to high-risk/harmful alcohol use in adulthood (e.g., Demant et al., 2018; Mereish & Bradford, 2014). Alcohol use was determined by asking about any lifetime and past-year consumption, whereas misuse was determined using the Alcohol Use Disorders Identification Test (AUDIT). Across both studies, findings suggested that individuals who reported both a minority ethnicity as well as a minority sexual orientation were *less* likely to report recent high-risk/harmful alcohol use than either sexual minority or ethnic minority participants alone (Demant et al., 2018; Mereish & Bradford, 2014). Both studies also showed participants who reported being sexual minority women were at *higher* risk of alcohol misuse, compared to those who reported being women or sexual minority alone. Findings from the Global Drug Survey are consistent with other work suggesting that women with intersecting, marginalized sexual minority identities may be at higher risk of alcohol use (e.g., Marshal et al., 2008), and persons with both a sexual and ethnic minority identity, in general, appear to be at lower risk of alcohol misuse (e.g., Blosnich, Lehavot, Glass, & Williams, 2017; Pollock et al., 2012).

Although these discrepant trends may seem counterintuitive, they are indicative of differences in the type and quantity of minority stressors that are associated with some intersectional identities, compared to others. That is, because various forms of social stratification necessarily constitute differences in people's day-to-day experiences with privilege and oppression, it is not necessarily the case that possessing multiple marginalized identities will *automatically* result in increased risk for alcohol misuse. On the one hand, recent findings suggest that, in some instances, multiple marginalized social identities may confer protective benefits with regard to alcohol behaviors perhaps due, in part, to relevant socio-cultural factors such as religiosity (e.g., Drabble, Trocki, & Klinger, 2016; Wallace, Brown, Bachman, & Laveist, 2003), nativity (i.e., foreign-born vs. U.S.-born) (e.g., Daniel-Ulloa et al., 2014), strong familial ties (e.g., Catalano et al., 1992), or norms that prohibit/promote alcohol use (e.g., Caetano, Clark, & Tam, 1998). In other instances, intersectional identities may exacerbate risk of alcohol misuse due to converging tributaries of minority stress (e.g., heterosexism, sexism, and racism) and group-based norms that condone alcohol use (e.g., Bowleg, Huang, Brooks, Black, & Burkholder, 2003; Collins, 2000; Greene, 2000; Newcomb, Heinz, & Mustanski, 2012). Taken together, theorizing (Bowleg, 2012) and empirical work (e.g., Mereish & Bradford, 2014) suggest that possessing intersecting marginalized identities, particularly a minority ethnic/racial identity, may proffer resilience in combatting risk of alcohol misuse, as some identities afford greater opportunities to develop coping resources and to access community support when encountering prejudice.

Emerging evidence also suggests that tailored alcohol interventions can be helpful in improving the outcomes of individuals with intersecting identities. As mentioned previously, there is support that racially appropriate and culturally sensitive intervention programs (e.g., racial/ethnic patient-provider matching), which are tailored for Hispanic/Latinx communities (Field & Caetano, 2010; Lee et al., 2011), can be effective in treating alcohol-related problems. By logical extension, tailored interventions for multiple marginalized individuals would also be expected to improve treatment outcomes. For example, women veterans appear to benefit from tailored, women-only alcohol treatment interventions (e.g., Kimerling et al., 2015). Moreover, tailored alcohol-intervention approaches have also shown promise among women (e.g., Agabio et al., 2017; McCaul et al., 2019; Niv & Hser, 2007), sexual minorities (e.g., Talley, 2013), and older adult populations (e.g., Zanjani et al., 2018). Such interventions are designed to address group-specific socio-cultural barriers to accessing treatment for alcohol problems and to improve retention rates in alcohol-treatment programs within marginalized groups.

From a public health perspective, there is a need for additional research into the health and well-being of individuals with multiple marginalized social identities, particularly with regard to understanding risk of alcohol use and misuse (Mereish & Bradford, 2014). For example, additional work is needed to understand why protective behavioral or coping strategies utilized by gay and bisexual ethnic minority men may not translate as well for reducing risk of alcohol misuse among sexual minority women. Understanding the role of community connectedness and intersecting identity-related *characteristics*, as opposed to mere social categorizations, in potentiating alcohol misuse and consequences can be useful for designing more effective intervention and prevention programs.

Conclusion

This chapter attempted to integrate quantitative and qualitative research to provide a broad overview of the unique experiences of individuals from a variety of vulnerable populations and to better understand group-based features that may increase the likelihood of alcohol use and alcohol-related outcomes. Recent evidence suggests that alcohol use and misuse is likely to differ based on individuals' race/ethnicity, gender identity, sexual orientation, age, and other factors. Although we focused on five major vulnerable populations, other marginalized communities experience disproportionate risks associated with alcohol-related harms (e.g., rural dwellers, people with disabilities, sexual assault survivors). Whereas those from a given vulnerable population likely share important social and cultural perspectives, it can easily be argued that these overarching *and* overlapping populations are diverse enough to compel the consideration of their *unique* individual difference characteristics and experiences. Taken together, evidence suggests that providing opportunities to amplify the seldom heard voices of marginalized individuals in our society will improve overall efforts to prevent and treat alcohol misuse in these communities.

References

Abraham, T. H., Wright, P., White, P., Booth, B. M., & Cucciare, M. A. (2017). Feasibility and acceptability of shared decision-making to promote alcohol behavior change among women veterans: Results from focus groups. *Journal of Addictive Diseases*, *36*, 252–263. Available from: https://doi.org/10.1080/10550887.2017.1373318.

Agabio, R., Pisanu, C., Luigi Gessa, G., & Franconi, F. (2017). Sex differences in alcohol use disorder. *Current Medicinal Chemistry*, *24*(24), 2661–2670.

Allen, J. L., & Mowbray, O. (2016). Sexual orientation, treatment utilization, and barriers for alcohol related problems: Findings from a nationally representative sample. *Drug and Alcohol Dependence*, *161*(1), 323–330.

Alpert, P. T. (2014). Alcohol abuse in older adults: An invisible population. *Home Health Care Management and Practice*, *26*, 269–272. Available from: https://doi.org/10.1177/1084822314527765.

Amadio, D. M. (2006). Internalized heterosexism, alcohol use, and alcohol-related problems among lesbians and gay men. *Addictive Behaviors*, *31*(7), 1153–1162.

American Psychiatric Association. (1994). *Diagnostic and statistical manual of mental disorders* (4th ed.). Washington, DC: Author.

American Psychiatric Association. (2013). *Diagnostic and statistical manual of mental disorders* (5th ed.). Arlington, VA: Author.

American Psychological Association. (2015). Definitions related to sexual orientation and gender diversity in APA documents [PDF file]. Retrieved from: <https://www.apa.org/pi/lgbt/resources/sexuality-definitions.pdf>.

Bakhireva, L. N., Shrestha, S., Garrison, L., Leeman, L., Rayburn, W. F., & Stephen, J. M. (2018). Prevalence of alcohol use in pregnant women with substance use disorder. *Drug and Alcohol Dependence*, *187*, 305–310. Available from: https://doi.org/10.1016/j.drugalcdep.2018.02.025.

Benza, A. T., Calvert, S., & McQuown, C. B. (2010). Prevention BINGO: Reducing medication and alcohol use risks for older adults. *Aging and Mental Health*, *14*, 1008–1014. Available from: https://doi.org/10.1080/13607863.2010.501067.

Blosnich, J. R., Lehavot, K., Glass, J. E., & Williams, E. C. (2017). Differences in alchol use and alcohol-related health care among transgender and nontransgender adults: Findings from the 2014 Behavioral Risk Factor Surveillance System. *Journal of the Studies on Alcohol and Drugs*, *78*(6), 861–866. Available from: https://doi.org/10.15288/jsad.2017.78.861.

Bowleg, L., Huang, J., Brooks, K., Black, A., & Burkholder, G. (2003). Triple jeopardy and beyond: Multiple minority stress and resilience among Black lesbians. *Journal of Lesbian Studies*, *7*, 87–108.

Bowleg, L. (2012). The problem with the phrase Women and Minorities: Intersectionality – an important theoretical framework for public health. *American Journal of Public Health*, *102*(7), 1267–1273. Available from: https://doi.org/10.2105/AJPH.2012.300750.

Brennan-Ing, M., Seidel, L., Larson, B., & Karpiak, S. E. (2013). Social care networks and older LGBT adults: Challenges for the future. *Journal of Homosexuality*, *61*(1), 21–52. Available from: https://doi.org/10.1080/00918369.2013.835235.

Bulmer, S., & Jackson, D. (2016). "You do not live in my skin": Embodiment, voice, and the veteran. *Critical Military Studies*, *2*, 25–40. Available from: https://doi.org/10.1080/23337486.2015.1118799.

Burnett-Zeiger, I., Ilgen, M., Valenstein, M., Zivin, K., Gorman, L., Blow, A., . . . Chermack, S. (2011). Prevalence and correlates of alcohol misuse among returning Afghanistan and Iraq Veterans. *Addictive Behaviors*, *36*, 801–806. Available from: https://doi.org/10.1016/j.addbeh.2010.12.032.

Buzzetti, E., Parikh, P. M., Gerussi, A., & Tsochatzis, E. (2017). Gender differences in liver disease and the drug-dose gender gap. *Pharmacological Research*, *120*, 97–108.

Caetano, R., Clark, C. L., & Tam, T. (1998). Alcohol consumption among- racial/ethnic minorities: Theory and research. *Alcohol Health and Research World*, *22*(4), 233242.

Catalano, R. F., Morrison, D. M., Wells, E. A., Gillmore, M. R., Iritani, B., & Hawkins, J. D. (1992). Ethnic differences in family factors related to early drug initiation. *Journal of Studies on Alcohol*, *53*(3), 208–217.

Center for Behavioral Health Statistics and Quality. (2018). *2017 National survey on drug use and health: Detailed tables*. Rockville, MD: Substance Abuse and Mental Health Services Administration.

Chartier, K. G., & Caetano, R. (2010). Ethnicity and health disparities in alcohol research. *Alcohol Research & Health*, *33*(1–2), 152.

Chartier, K. G., Miller, K., Harris, T. R., & Caetano, R. (2016). A 10-year study of factors associated with alcohol treatment use and non-use in a US population sample. *Drug and Alcohol Dependence*, *160*, 205–211.

Christie, M. M., Bamber, D., Powell, C., Arrindell, T., & Pant, A. (2013). Older adult problem drinkers: Who presents for alcohol treatment? *Aging And Mental Health*, *17*, 24–32. Available from: https://doi.org/10.1080/13607863.2012.696577.

Cochran, B. N., Peavy, K. M., & Robohm, J. S. (2007). Do specialized services exist for LGBT individuals seeking treatment for substance misuse? A study of available treatment programs. *Substance Use & Misuse*, *42*(1), 161–176.

Cochran, S. D., Grella, C. E., & Mays, V. M. (2012). Do substance use norms and perceived drug availability mediate sexual orientation differences in patterns of substance use? Results from the California Quality of Life Survey II. *Journal of Studies on Alcohol and Drugs*, *73*(4), 675–685.

Cochran, S. D., Keenan, C., Schober, C., & Mays, V. M. (2000). Estimates of alcohol use and clinical treatment needs among homosexually active men and women in the US population. *Journal of Consulting and Clinical Psychology*, *68*(6), 1062–1071.

Collins, P. H. (2000). *Black feminist thought: Knowledge, consciousness, and the politics of empowerment* (2nd ed.). New York: Routledge.

Cook, W. K., Bond, J., Karriker-Jaffe, K. J., & Zemore, S. (2013). Who's at risk? Ethnic drinking cultures, foreign nativity, and problem drinking among Asian American young adults. *Journal of Studies on Alcohol and Drugs*, *74*(4), 532–541.

Cook, W. K., & Caetano, R. (2014). Ethnic drinking cultures, gender, and socioeconomic status in Asian American and Latino drinking. *Alcoholism: Clinical and Experimental Research*, *38*(12), 3043–3051.

Cook, W. K., Karriker-Jaffe, K. J., Bond, J., & Lui, C. (2015). Asian American problem drinking trajectories during the transition to adulthood: Ethnic drinking cultures and neighborhood contexts. *American Journal of Public Health*, *105*(5), 1020–1027.

Cooper, L. (2012). Combined motivational interviewing and cognitive-behavioral therapy with older adult drug and alcohol abusers. *Health and Social Work*, *37*, 173–179. Available from: https://doi.org/10.1093/hsw/hls023.

Corliss, H. L., Rosario, M., Wypij, D., Fisher, L. B., & Austin, S. B. (2008). Sexual orientation disparities in longitudinal alcohol use patterns among adolescents: Findings from the Growing Up Today Study. *Archives of Pediatrics & Adolescent Medicine*, *162*(11), 1071–1078.

Cortes, J., Fletcher, T. L., Latini, D. M., & Kauth, M. R. (2018). Mental health differences between older and younger lesbian, gay, bisexual, and transgender veterans: Evidence of resilience. *Journal of Aging and Mental Health*, *42*, 162–171. Available from: https://doi.org/10.1080/07317115.2018.1523264.

Coulter, R. W., Blosnich, J. R., Bukowski, L. A., Herrick, A. L., Siconolfi, D. E., & Stall, R. D. (2015). Differences in alcohol use and alcohol-related problems between transgender-and nontransgender-identified young adults. *Drug and Alcohol Dependence*, *154*, 251–259.

Crenshaw, K. (1989). Demarginalizing the intersection of race and sex: A black feminist critique of antidiscrimination doctrine, feminist theory and antiracist politics. *University of Chicago Legal Forum*, 139–168.

Daniel-Ulloa, J., Reboussin, B. A., Gilbert, P. A., Mann, L., Alonzo, J., Downs, M., & Rhodes, S. D. (2014). Predictors of heavy episodic drinking and weekly drunkenness among immigrant Latinos in North Carolina. *American Journal of Men's Health*, *8*(4), 339–348.

Degenhardt, L., & Hall, W. (2001). The relationship between tobacco use, substance-use disorders and mental health: Results from the national survey of mental health and well-being. *Nicotine and Tobacco Research*, *3*, 225–234. Available from: https://doi.org/10.1080/14622200110050457.

Delker, E., Brown, Q., & Hasin, D. S. (2016). Alcohol consumption in demographic subpopulations: An epidemiologic overview. *Alcohol Research: Current Reviews*, *38*(1), 7–15.

Demant, D., Oviedo-Trespalacios, O., Carroll, J.-A., Ferris, J. A., Maier, L., Barratt, M. J., & Winstock, A. R. (2018). Do people with intersecting identities report more high-risk alcohol use and lifetime substance use? *International Journal of Public Health*, *63*, 621–630. Available from: https://doi.org/10.1007/s00038-018-1095-5.

Demers, A. (2011). When veterans return: The role of community in reintegration. *Journal of Loss and Trauma*, *16*, 160–179. Available from: https://doi.org/10.1080/15325024.2010.519281.

Dichter, M. E., Wagner, C., Borrero, S., Broyles, L., & Montgomery, A. E. (2017). Intimate partner violence, unhealthy alcohol use, and housing instability among women veterans in the Veterans Health Administration. *Psychological Services*, *14*, 246–249. Available from: https://doi.org/10.1037/ser0000132.

Dorn-Medeiros, C. M., & Doyle, C. (2018). Alcohol as coping: Internalized homophobia and heterosexism's role in alcohol use among lesbians. *Journal of LGBT Issues in Counseling*, *12*(3), 142–157.

Drabble, L., Midanik, L. T., & Trocki, K. (2005). Reports of alcohol consumption and alcohol-related problems among homosexual, bisexual and heterosexual respondents: Results from the 2000 National Alcohol Survey. *Journal of Studies on Alcohol*, *66*(1), 111–120.

Drabble, L., & Trocki, K. (2014). Alcohol in the life narratives of women: Commonalities and differences by sexual orientation. *Addiction Research and Theory*, *22*, 186–194. Available from: https://doi.org/10.3109/16066359.2013.806651.

Drabble, L., Trocki, K. F., & Klinger, J. L. (2016). Religiosity as a protective factor for hazardous drinking and drug use among sexual minority and heterosexual women: Findings from the National Alcohol Survey. *Drug and Alcohol Dependence*, *161*, 127–134.

Eisenberg, M. H., Johnson, C. C., & Zucker, A. N. (2018). Starving for a drink: Sexual objectification is associated with food-restricted alcohol consumption among college women, but not men. *Women and Health*, *58*, 175–187. Available from: https://doi.org/10.1080/03630242.2017.1292342.

Emslie, C., Lennox, J., & Ireland, L. (2017). The role of alcohol in identity construction among LGBT people: A qualitative study. *Sociology of Health & Illness*, *39*(8), 1465–1479.

Emslie, C., Lennox, J. C., & Ireland, L. (2015). *The social context of LGBT people's drinking in Scotland*. Glasgow: Glasgow Caledonian University/Scottish Health Action on Alcohol Problems.

Epstein, E. E., Fischer-Elber, K., & Al-Otaiba, Z. (2008). Women, aging, and alcohol use disorders. *Journal of Women and Aging*, *19*, 31–48. Available from: https://doi.org/10.1300/J074v19n01_03.

Erol, A., Ho, A. M. C., Winham, S. J., & Karpyak, V. M. (2019). Sex hormones in alcohol consumption: A systematic review of evidence. *Addiction Biology*, *24*(2), 157–169.

Field, C., & Caetano, R. (2010). The role of ethnic matching between patient and provider on the effectiveness of brief alcohol interventions with Hispanics. *Alcoholism: Clinical and Experimental Research*, *34*(2), 262–271.

Fish, J. N., & Baams, L. (2018). Trends in alcohol-related disparities between heterosexual and sexual minority youth from 2007 to 2015: Findings from the Youth Risk Behavior Survey. *LGBT Health*, *5*(6), 359–367.

Fish, J. N., Schulenberg, J. E., & Russell, S. T. (2019). Sexual minority youth report high-intensity binge drinking: The critical role of school victimization. *Journal of Adolescent Health*, *64*(2), 186–193.

Fish, J. N., Watson, R. J., Porta, C. M., Russell, S. T., & Saewyc, E. M. (2017). Are alcohol-related disparities between sexual minority and heterosexual youth decreasing? *Addiction*, *112*(11), 1931–1941.

Frezza, M., di Padova, C., Pozzato, G., Terpin, M., Baraona, E., & Lieber, C. S. (1990). High blood alcohol levels in women: The role of decreased gastric alcohol dehydrogenase activity and first-pass metabolism. *New England Journal of Medicine*, *322*(2), 95–99.

Gardner, P. J., & Poole, J. M. (2009). One story at a time: Narrative therapy, older adults, and addictions. *Journal of Applied Gerontology*, *28*, 600–620. Available from: https://doi.org/10.1177/0733464808330822.

Gibbons, F. X., O'Hara, R. E., Stock, M. L., Gerrard, M., Weng, C.-Y., & Wills, T. A. (2012). The erosive effects of racism: Reduced self-control mediates the relation between perceived racial discrimination and substance use in African American adolescents. *Journal of Personality and Social Psychology*, *102*, 1089–1104. Available from: https://doi.org/10.1037/a0027404.

Gilbert, P. A., & Zemore, S. E. (2016). Discrimination and drinking: A systematic review of the evidence. *Social Science & Medicine*, *161*, 178–194.

Glynn, T. R., & van den Berg, J. J. (2017). A systematic review of interventions to reduce problematic substance use among transgender individuals: A call to action. *Transgender Health*, *2*(1), 45–59.

Greene, B. (2000). African American lesbian and bisexual women. *Journal of Social Issues*, *56*, 239–249.

Green, K. E., & Feinstein, B. A. (2012). Substance use in lesbian, gay, and bisexual populations: An update on empirical research and implications for treatment. *Psychology of Addictive Behaviors*, *26*(2), 265–278.

Hallgren, K. A., Epstein, E. E., & McCrady, B. S. (2019). Changes in hypothesized mechanisms of changed before and after initiating abstinence in cognitive-behavioral therapy for women with alcohol use disorder. *Behavior Therapy*. Available from: https://doi.org/10.1016/j.beth.2019.01.009, in press.

Hatzenbuehler, M. L., Corbin, W. R., & Fromme, K. (2008). Trajectories and determinants of alcohol use among LGB young adults and their heterosexual peers: Results from a prospective study. *Developmental Psychology*, *44*(1), 81–90.

Hatzenbuehler, M. L., Jun, H. J., Corliss, H. L., & Austin, S. B. (2015). Structural stigma and sexual orientation disparities in adolescent drug use. *Addictive Behaviors*, *46*, 14–18.

Hoggatt, K. J., Williams, E. C., Der-Martirosian, C., Yano, E. M., & Washington, D. L. (2015). National prevalence and correlates of alcohol misuse in women veterans. *Journal of Substance Abuse Treatment*, *52*, 10–16. Available from: https://doi.org/10.1016/j.jsat.2014.12.003.

Hughes, T. L. (2005). Alcohol use and alcohol-related problems among lesbians and gay men. In J. Fitzpatrick, J. Stevenson, & L. Summers (Eds.), *Annual review of nursing research: Alcohol use, misuse, abuse and addiction* (Volume 23, pp. 283–325). Springer Publishing Company.

Hughes, T. L., & Eliason, M. (2002). Substance use and abuse in lesbian, gay, bisexual and transgender populations. *Journal of Primary Prevention*, *22*(3), 263–298.

Hughes, T. L., Wilsnack, S. C., & Kantor, L. W. (2016). The influence of gender and sexual orientation on alcohol use and alcohol-related problems: Toward a global perspective. *Alcohol Research: Current Reviews*, *38*(1), 121–132.

Jakupcak, M., Tull, M. T., McDermott, M. J., Kaysen, D., Hunt, S., & Simpson, T. (2010). PTSD symptom clusters in relationship to alcohol misuse among Iraq and Afghanistan war veterans seeking post-deployment VA health care. *Addictive Behaviors*, *35*, 840–843.

James, S. E., Herman, J. L., Rankin, S., Keisling, M., Mottet, L., & Anafi, M. (2016). *The report of the 2015 US transgender survey*. Washington, DC: National Center for Transgender Equality. https://www.transequality.org/sites/default/files/docs/USTS-Full-Report-FINAL.PDF. Accessed 5.03.18.

Kaysen, D., Schumm, J., Pedersen, E. R., Seim, R. W., Bedard-Gilligan, M., & Chard, K. (2014). Cognitive processing therapy for veterans with comorbid PTSD and alcohol use disorders. *Addictive Behaviors*, *39*, 420–427. Available from: https://doi.org/10.1016/j.addbeh.2013.08.016.

Keuroghlian, A. S., Reisner, S. L., White, J. M., & Weiss, R. D. (2015). Substance use and treatment of substance use disorders in a community sample of transgender adults. *Drug and Alcohol Dependence*, *152*, 139–146.

Keyes, K. M., Martins, S. S., Blanco, C., & Hasin, D. S. (2010). Telescoping and gender differences in alcohol dependence: New evidence from two national surveys. *American Journal of Psychiatry*, *167*(8), 969–976.

Kimerling, R., Pavao, J., Greene, L., Karpenko, J., Rodriguez, A., Saweikis, M., & Washington, D. L. (2015). Access to mental health care among women veterans: Is VA meeting women's needs? *Medical Care*, *53*, S97–S104. Available from: https://doi.org/10.1097/MLR.0000000000000272.

Lang, I., Wallace, R. B., Huppert, F. A., & Melzer, D. (2007). Moderate alcohol consumption in older adults is associated with better cognition and well-being than abstinence. *Age and Aging*, *36*, 256–261. Available from: https://doi.org/10.1093/ageing/afm001.

Lee, C. S., López, S. R., Hernández, L., Colby, S. M., Caetano, R., Borrelli, B., & Rohsenow, D. (2011). A cultural adaptation of motivational interviewing to address heavy drinking among Hispanics. *Cultural Diversity and Ethnic Minority Psychology*, *17*(3), 317–324.

Lehavot, K., Browne, K. C., & Simpson, T. L. (2014). Examining sexual orientation disparities in alcohol misuse among women veterans. *American Journal of Preventative Medicine*, *47*, 554–562. Available from: https://doi.org/10.1016/j.amepre.2014.07.002.

Little, R. E., Moore, D. E., Guzinski, G. M., & Perez, A. (1980). Absence of effect of exogenous estradiol on alcohol consumption in women. *Subst Alcohol Actions Misuse*, *1*, 551–556.

Lombardi, E. L., & van Servellen, G. (2000). Building culturally sensitive substance use prevention and treatment programs for transgendered populations. *Journal of Substance Abuse Treatment*, *19*(3), 291–296.

Luciano, M. T., McDevitt-Murphy, M. E., Acuff, S. F., Bellet, B. W., Tripp, J. C., & Murphy, J. G. (2019). Posttraumatic stress disorder symptoms improve after an integrated brief alcohol intervention for OEF/OIF/OND veterans. *Psychological Trauma: Theory, Research, Practice, and Policy*, *11*, 459–465. Available from: https://doi.org/10.1037/tra0000378.

Lui, P. P., & Zamboanga, B. L. (2018a). Acculturation and alcohol use among Asian Americans: A meta-analytic review. *Psychology of Addictive Behaviors*, *32*(2), 173–186.

Lui, P. P., & Zamboanga, B. L. (2018b). A critical review and meta-analysis of the associations between acculturation and alcohol use outcomes among Hispanic Americans. *Alcoholism: Clinical and Experimental Research*, *42*(10), 1841–1862.

Marshal, M. P., Friedman, M. S., Stall, R., King, K. M., Miles, J., Gold, M. A., ... Morse, J. Q. (2008). Sexual orientation and adolescent substance use: A meta-analysis and methodological review. *Addiction*, *103*(4), 546–556.

Marshal, M. P., Friedman, M. S., Stall, R., & Thompson, A. L. (2009). Individual trajectories of substance use in lesbian, gay and bisexual youth and heterosexual youth. *Addiction*, *104*(6), 974–981.

McCabe, S. E., Hughes, T. L., Bostwick, W. B., West, B. T., & Boyd, C. J. (2009). Sexual orientation, substance use behaviors and substance dependence in the United States. *Addiction*, *104*(8), 1333–1345.

McCabe, S. E., West, B. T., Hughes, T. L., & Boyd, C. J. (2013). Sexual orientation and substance abuse treatment utilization in the United States: Results from a national survey. *Journal of Substance Abuse Treatment*, *44*(1), 4–12.

McCaul, M. E., Roach, D., Hasin, D. S., Weisner, C., Chang, G., & Sinha, R. (2019). Alcohol and women: A brief overview. *Alcoholism: Clinical and Experimental Research*.

McDonell, M. G., Nepom, J. R., Leickly, E., Suchy-Dicey, A., Hirchak, K., Echo-Hawk, A., ... Buchwald, D. (2016). A culturally-tailored behavioral intervention trial for alcohol use disorders in three American Indian communities: Rationale, design, and methods. *Contemporary Clinical Trials*, *47*, 93–100. Available from: https://doi.org/10.1016/j.cct.2015.12.010.

Mereish, E. H., & Bradford, J. B. (2014). Intersecting identities and substance use problems: Sexual orientation, gender, race, and lifetime substance use problems. *Journal of Studies on Alcohol and Drugs*, *75*(1), 179–188.

Merline, A. C., O'Malley, P. M., Schulenberg, J. E., Bachman, J. G., & Johnston, L. D. (2004). Substance use among adults 35 years of age: Prevalence, adulthood predictors, and impact of adolescent substance use. *American Journal of Public Health*, *94*, 96–102. Available from: https://doi.org/10.2105/AJPH.94.1.96.

Meyer, I. H. (1995). Minority stress and mental health in gay men. *Journal of Health and Social Behavior*, *36*(1), 38–56.

Meyer, I. H. (2003). Prejudice, social stress, and mental health in lesbian, gay, and bisexual populations: Conceptual issues and research evidence. *Psychological Bulletin*, *129*(5), 674–697.

Milic, J., Glisic, M., Voortman, T., Borba, L. P., Asllanaj, E., Rojas, L. Z., … Franco, O. H. (2018). Menopause, ageing, and alcohol use disorders in women. *Mauritas*, *111*, 100–109. Available from: https://doi.org/10.1016/j.maturitas.2018.03.006.

Moore, A. A., Whiteman, E. J., & Ward, K. T. (2007). Risks of combined alcohol-medication use in older adults. *American Journal of Geriatric Pharmacotherapy*, *5*, 64–74.

Moos, R. H., Schutte, K. K., Brennan, P. L., & Moos, B. S. (2009). Older adults' alcohol consumption and late-life drinking problems: A 20-year perspective. *Society for the Study of Addiction*, *104*, 1293–1302. Available from: https://doi.org/10.1111/j.1360-0443.2009.02604.x.

Morgan, M. L., Brosi, W. A., & Brosi, M. W. (2011). Restorying older adults' narratives about self and substance abuse. *American Journal of Family Therapy*, *39*, 444–455. Available from: https://doi.org/10.1080/01926187.2011.560784.

Mowatt, R. A., & Bennett, J. (2011). War narratives: Veteran stories, PTSD effects, and therapeutic fly-fishing. *Therapeutic Recreation Journal*, *45*, 286–308.

Mukamal, K. J., Kuller, L. H., Fitzpatrick, A. L., Longstreth, W. T., Jr., Mittleman, M. A., & Siscovick, D. S. (2003). Prospective study of alcohol consumption and risk of dementia in older adults. *Journal of the American Medical Association*, *289*, 1405–1413.

Mulia, N., Tam, T. W., Bond, J., Zemore, S. E., & Li, L. (2018). Racial/ethnic differences in life-course heavy drinking from adolescence to midlife. *Journal of Ethnicity in Substance Abuse*, *17*(2), 167–186.

Mulia, N., Ye, Y., Zemore, S. E., & Greenfield, T. K. (2008). Social disadvantage, stress, and alcohol use among Black, Hispanic, and White Americans: Findings from the 2005 US National Alcohol Survey. *Journal of Studies on Alcohol and Drugs*, *69*(6), 824–833.

Muti, P., Trevisan, M., Micheli, A., Krogh, V., Bolelli, G., Sciajno, R., … Berrino, F. (1998). Alcohol consumption and total estradiol in premenopausal women. *Cancer Epidemiol Biomarkers Prevention*, *7*, 189–193.

National Institute on Alcohol Abuse and Alcoholism (NIAAA). (1999). *Are women more vulnerable to alcohol's effects?* (Vol. 46). Bethesda, MD: National Institutes of Health.

National Institute on Alcohol Abuse and Alcoholism (NIAAA). (2006). *Alcohol use and alcohol use disorders in the United States: Main findings from the 2001–2002 National Epidemiologic Survey on Alcohol and Related Conditions (NESARC)* (Vol. 8). Bethesda, MD: National Institutes of Health.

Newcomb, M. E., Heinz, A. J., & Mustanski, B. (2012). Examining risk and protective factors for alcohol use in lesbian, gay, bisexual, and transgender youth: A longitudinal multilevel analysis. *Journal of Studies on Alcohol and Drugs*, *73*(5), 783–793.

Niv, N., & Hser, Y. I. (2007). Women-only and mixed-gender drug abuse treatment programs: Service needs, utilization and outcomes. *Drug and Alcohol Dependence*, *87*(2–3), 194–201.

Nuttbrock, L. A. (2012). Culturally competent substance abuse treatment with transgender persons. *Journal of Addictive Diseases*, *31*(3), 236–241.

Pachankis, J. E., Hatzenbuehler, M. L., & Starks, T. J. (2014). The influence of structural stigma and rejection sensitivity on young sexual minority men's daily tobacco and alcohol use. *Social Science & Medicine*, *103*, 67–75.

Paris, R., & Bradley, C. L. (2001). The challenge of adversity: Three narratives of alcohol dependence, recovery, and adult development. *Qualitative Health Research*, *11*, 647–667. Available from: https://doi.org/10.1177/104973201129119352.

Perreira, K. M., & Sloan, F. A. (2001). Life events and alcohol consumption among mature adults: A longitudinal analysis. *Journal of Studies on Alcohol*, *64*, 501–508.

Pietrzak, R. H., Goldstein, M. B., Malley, J. C., Rivers, A. J., Johnson, D. C., & Southwick, S. M. (2010). Risk and protective factors associated with suicidal ideation in veterans of operations enduring freedom and Iraqi freedom. *Journal of Affective Disorders*, *123*, 102–107. Available from: https://doi.org/10.1016/j.jad.2009.08.001.

Pollock, J. A., Halkitis, P. N., Moeller, R. W., Solomon, T. M., Barton, S. C., Blachman-Forshay, J., ... Love, H. T. (2012). Alcohol use among young men who have sex with men. *Substance Use & Misuse*, *47*, 12–21. Available from: https://doi.org/10.3109/10826084.2011.618963.

Prussing, E. (2007). Reconfiguring the empty center: Drinking, sobriety, and identity in Native American women's narratives. *Culture, Medicine, and Psychiatry*, *31*, 499–526. Available from: https://doi.org/10.1007/s11013-007-9064-0.

Reback, C. J., & Fletcher, J. B. (2014). HIV prevalence, substance use, and sexual risk behaviors among transgender women recruited through outreach. *AIDS and Behavior*, *18*(7), 1359–1367.

Reichman, M. E., Judd, J. T., Longcope, C., Schatzkin, A., Clevidence, B. A., Nair, P. P., ... Taylor, P. R. (1993). Effects of alcohol consumption on plasma and urinary hormone concentrations in premenopausal women. *Journal of the National Cancer Institute*, *85*(9), 722–727. Available from: https://doi.org/10.1093/jnci/85.9.722.

Reisner, S. L., Biello, K. B., Hughto, J. M. W., Kuhns, L., Mayer, K. H., Garofalo, R., & Mimiaga, M. J. (2016). Psychiatric diagnoses and comorbidities in a diverse, multicity cohort of young transgender women: Baseline findings from project LifeSkills. *JAMA Pediatrics*, *170*(5), 481–486.

Ross, R., Fortney, J., Lancaster, B., & Booth, B. M. (1998). Age, ethnicity, and comorbidity in national sample of hospitalized alcohol-dependent women veterans. *Psychiatric Services*, *49*, 663–668. Available from: https://doi.org/10.1176/ps.49.5.663.

Saloner, B., & Cook, B. L. (2013). Blacks and Hispanics are less likely than whites to complete addiction treatment, largely due to socioeconomic factors. *Health Affairs*, *32*(1), 135–145.

Santos, G. M., Rapues, J., Wilson, E. C., Macias, O., Packer, T., Colfax, G., & Raymond, H. F. (2014). Alcohol and substance use among transgender women in San Francisco: Prevalence and association with human immunodeficiency virus infection. *Drug and Alcohol Review*, *33*(3), 287–295.

Satre, D. D., Mertens, J. R., Arean, P. A., & Weisner, C. (2004). Five-year alcohol and drug treatment outcomes of older adults versus middle-aged and younger adults in a managed care program. *Addiction*, *99*, 1286–1297. Available from: https://doi.org/10.1111/j.1360-0443.2004.00831.x.

Savarese, V. W., Suvak, M. K., King, L. A., & King, D. W. (2001). Relationships among alcohol use, hyperarousal, and marital abuse and violence in Vietnam veterans. *Journal of Traumatic Stress*, *14*, 717–732.

Scheim, A. I., Bauer, G. R., & Shokoohi, M. (2016). Heavy episodic drinking among transgender persons: Disparities and predictors. *Drug and Alcohol Dependence*, *167*, 156–162.

Schmidt, L., Greenfield, T., & Mulia, N. (2006). Unequal treatment: Racial and ethnic disparities in alcoholism treatment services. *Alcohol Research*, *29*(1), 49–54.

Schuler, M. S., Rice, C. E., Evans-Polce, R. J., & Collins, R. L. (2018). Disparities in substance use behaviors and disorders among adult sexual minorities by age, gender, and sexual identity. *Drug and Alcohol Dependence*, *189*, 139–146.

Slater, M. E., Godette, D., Huang, B., Ruan, W. J., & Kerridge, B. T. (2017). Sexual orientation-based discrimination, excessive alcohol use, and substance use disorders among sexual minority adults. *LGBT Health*, *4*(5), 337–344.

Stevens, S. (2012). Meeting the substance abuse treatment needs of lesbian, bisexual and transgender women: Implications from research to practice. *Substance Abuse and Rehabilitation*, *3*(Suppl. 1), 27–36.

Stewart, S. H. (1996). Alcohol abuse in individuals exposed to trauma: A critical review. *Psychological Bulletin*, *120*, 83–112. Available from: https://doi.org/10.1037/0033-2909.120.1.83.

Straus, E., Norman, S. B., Haller, M., Southwick, S. M., Hamblen, J. L., & Pietrzak, R. H. (2019). Differences in protective factors among U.S. veterans with posttraumatic stress disorder, alcohol use disorder, and their comorbidity: Results from the National Health and Resilience in Veterans Study. *Drug and Alcohol Dependence*, *194*, 6–12. Available from: https://doi.org/10.1016/j.drugalcdep.2018.09.011.

Substance Abuse and Mental Health Services Administration (SAMHSA). (2017). National Survey on Drug Use and Health (NSDUH).

Sutker, PB., Tabakoff, B., Goist, K. C., Jr, & Randall, C. L. (1983). Acute alcohol intoxication, mood states and alcohol metabolism in women and men. *Pharmacology Biochemistry and Behavior*, *18*, 349–354.

Taft, C. T., Kaloupek, D. G., Schuman, J. A., Marshall, A. D., Panuzio, J., King, D. W., & Keane, T. M. (2007). Posttraumatic stress disorder symptoms, physiological reactivity, alcohol problems, and aggression among military veterans. *Journal of Abnormal Psychology*, *116*, 498–507. Available from: https://doi.org/10.1037/0021-843X.116.3.498.

Talley, A. E. (2013). Recommendations for improving substance abuse treatment interventions for sexual minority substance abusers. *Drug and Alcohol Review*, *32*, 539–540.

Talley, A. E., Brown, J. L., Stevens, A. K., & Littlefield, A. K. (2014). Do peer norms moderate the relation between sexual self-concept ambiguity identity and alcohol involvement? *Journal of Studies on Alcohol and Drugs*, *75*, 1023–1031.

Talley, A. E., Hughes, T. L., Aranda, F., Birkett, M., & Marshal, M. P. (2014). Exploring alcohol-use behaviors among heterosexual and sexual minority adolescents: Intersections with sex, age, and race/ethnicity. *American Journal of Public Health*, *104*(2), 295–303.

Talley, A. E., Hughes, M. L., Wilsnack, S. C., & Hughes, T. L. (2018). Women's self-perceived similarity to their mother and associations with patterns of alcohol misuse over 20 years. *Alcohol and Alcoholism*, *53*, 707–715. Available from: https://doi.org/10.1093/alcalc/agy059.

Talley, A. E., & Littlefield, A. K. (2014). Pathways between concealable stigmatized identities and substance misuse. *Social and personality psychology compass*, *8*(10), 569–582. Available from: https://doi.org/10.1111/spc3.12117.

Talley, A. E., & Stevens, J. E. (2017). Sexual orientation self-concept ambiguity: Scale adaptation and validation. *Assessment*, *24*(5), 632–645. Available from: https://doi.org/10.1177/1073191115617016.

Teaster, P. B., & Sokan, A. E. (2016). Mistreatment and victimization of LGBT elders. In D. A. Harley, & P. B. Teaster (Eds.), *Handbook of LGBT elders: An interdiscplinary approach to principles, practices, and policies* (pp. 343–357). New York: Spring Science and Business Media.

Tonigan, J. S. (2003). Project match treatment participation and outcome by self-reported ethnicity. *Alcoholism: Clinical and Experimental Research, 27*(8), 1340–1344.

Travers, R., & Schneider, M. (1996). Barriers to accessibility for lesbian and gay youth needing addictions services. *Youth & Society, 27*(3), 356–378.

U.S. Census Bureau (2010). Overview of race and Hispanic origin: 2010. Retrieved from https://www.census.gov/prod/cen2010/briefs/c2010br-02.pdf.

Vaeth, P. A., Wang-Schweig, M., & Caetano, R. (2017). Drinking, alcohol use disorder, and treatment access and utilization among US racial/ethnic groups. *Alcoholism: Clinical and Experimental Research, 41*(1), 6–19.

Valdez, L. A., Garcia, D. O., Ruiz, J., Oren, E., & Carvajal, S. (2018). Exploring structural, sociocultural, and individual barriers to alcohol abuse treatment among hispanic men. *American Journal of Men's Health, 12*(6), 1948–1957.

Veldhuis, C. B., Talley, A. E., Hancock, D. W., Wilsnack, S. C., & Hughes, T. L. (2017). To your health? Alcohol use, age, and perceived mental and physical health in a community sample of lesbian and bisexual women. *LGBT Health, 4*, 419–426.

Wallace, J. M., Jr, Brown, T. N., Bachman, J. G., & Laveist, T. A. (2003). The influence of race and religion on abstinence from alcohol, cigarettes and marijuana among adolescents. *Journal of Studies on Alcohol, 64*(6), 843–848.

Weisner, C., Matzger, H., Tam, T., & Schmidt, L. (2002). Who goes to alcohol and drug treatment? Understanding utilization within the context of insurance. *Journal of Studies on Alcohol, 63*(6), 673–682.

Whitehead, J., Shaver, J., & Stephenson, R. (2016). Outness, stigma, and primary health care utilization among rural LGBT populations. *PLoS One, 11*(1), e0146139.

Williams, D. R., & Collins, C. (2001). Racial residential segregation: A fundamental cause of racial disparities in health. *Public Health Reports, 116*(5), 404–416.

Zanjani, F., Allen, H., Schoenberg, N., Martin, C., & Clayton, R. (2018). Acceptability of intervention materials to decrease risk for alcohol and medication interactions among older adults. *Evaluation and Program Planning, 67*, 160–166. Available from: https://doi.org/10.1016/j.evalprogplan.2017.12.010.

Zanjani, F., Smith, R., Slavova, S., Charnigo, R., Schoenberg, N., Martin, C., & Clayton, R. (2016). Concurrent alcohol and medication poisoning hospital admissions among older rural and urban residents. *American Journal of Drug and Alcohol Abuse, 42*, 422–430. Available from: https://doi.org/10.3109/00952990.2016.1154966.

Zemore, S. E., Karriker-Jaffe, K. J., Mulia, N., Kerr, W. C., Ehlers, C. L., Cook, W. K., ... Greenfield, T. K. (2018). The future of research on alcohol-related disparities across US racial/ethnic groups: A plan of attack. *Journal of Studies on Alcohol and Drugs, 79*(1), 7–21.

Zemore, S. E., Ye, Y., Mulia, N., Martinez, P., Jones-Webb, R., & Karriker-Jaffe, K. (2016). Poor, persecuted, young, and alone: Toward explaining the elevated risk of alcohol problems among Black and Latino men who drink. *Drug and Alcohol Dependence, 163*(1), 31–39.

Section 6

Taking it into practice

Chapter 21

Theory-driven interventions: How social cognition can help

Kristen P. Lindgren[1], Angelo M. DiBello[2], Kirsten P. Peterson[1] and Clayton Neighbors[3]

[1]*Department of Psychiatry and Behavioral Sciences, University of Washington, Seattle, WA, United States,* [2]*Department of Psychology, City University of New York, Brooklyn College, Brooklyn, NY, United States,* [3]*Department of Psychology, University of Houston, Houston, TX, United States*

Introduction

The global and local burden of problematic alcohol use is substantial. Globally, 5% of all deaths and 5% of diseases and injuries result from problematic alcohol use (World Health Organization, 2019). A similarly significant burden is found within the US, with problematic alcohol use ranked among the top five causes of premature death and disability (Office of the Surgeon General, 2016). In addition to the large public health costs associated with problematic alcohol use, there is also a vast treatment gap, with 78% (globally) and 90% (in the US) of individuals not receiving care (Kohn, Saxena, Levav, & Saraceno, 2004; Office of the Surgeon General, 2016). Collectively, these figures could lead to speculation that problematic alcohol use suffers from a lack of treatment options, but in actuality, numerous, efficacious interventions for problematic alcohol use have been developed. Key to the current chapter is the development of psychosocial interventions, generally, and of interventions that have been informed by theories of social cognition, specifically.

Theories of social cognition, broadly speaking, are concerned with how people think and feel about people, including themselves (Fiske & Taylor, 2017). In this chapter, we focus on how theories *are being*, and in select instances, *could be* applied to reduce problematic drinking. Consistent with our definition of social cognition, our review includes theories that focus on thoughts and feelings about one's self as well as those that focus on thoughts and feelings about others. We also focus on theories that consider social cognitive processes that are introspective and reflective (typically assessed directly via self-report measures) and that are impulsive and reflexive (typically assessed indirectly via

The Handbook of Alcohol Use - Understandings from Synapse to Society.
DOI: https://doi.org/10.1016/B978-0-12-816720-5.00006-2

implicit measures). Ultimately, we focus on (1) how one thinks and feels about one's *self*—both generally and in relation to alcohol—and (2) how one thinks and feels *about other people*—both generally and in relation to alcohol; and we consider how both, in turn, influence one's drinking.

Our goal is to provide a targeted review of long-standing and emergent applications of social cognitive theories to interventions for problematic drinking. We have organized our review of these theories as follows: we begin with a brief primer on the specific theory, then describe how that theory has been (or could be) applied to intervention, and if available, summarize empirical findings. Our summary of findings includes discussion of where along the problematic drinking continuum the intervention has been tested, the kinds of populations that the intervention has been tested on (age/developmental period, gender, race/ethnicity, cultural groups, countries), and how well the intervention works. Our review opens with long-standing, established applications of social cognitive theories to intervention and then moves to those that are more recent and emergent. We note the timing of the application of the theory to intervention does not necessarily correlate with the origin of the theory (i.e., more recent/emergent applications include a mix of both "old" and "new" social cognitive theories). Finally, we close with a summary of lessons learned across theories, and identify gaps and propose next steps.

Established applications of theories of social cognition to interventions for problematic drinking

Social cognitive theory

While the majority of theoretical frameworks reviewed in this chapter have been or could be described as social cognitive theories, references to Social Cognitive Theory (SCT) proper are reserved almost exclusively to the work of Albert Bandura. Bandura's work under the umbrella of SCT (Bandura, 1986, 1989, 2012) formerly called Social Learning Theory (Bandura, 1977b; Bandura & Walters, 1963) offers explanations for the initiation, escalation, reduction, and termination of problematic alcohol and other drug use. In a review of the literature on psychosocial approaches to addressing alcohol disorders from 1940 to 2012, Social Learning Theory was identified as a key theoretical foundation for cognitive-behavioral treatment approaches (McCrady, Owens, Borders, & Brovko, 2014), which became prominent in the 70s and continue to have a strong presence. Self-efficacy, a central construct in SCT, was incorporated as an important and focal element within Motivational Interviewing (Miller & Rollnick, 1991, 2013), a prominent approach for alcohol treatment and brief interventions since the 1990s.

SCT presents a relatively comprehensive theory of human motivation and behavior based on reciprocal influences of cognitive, behavioral, and environmental factors (Bandura, 1986, 1989, 2012). Individuals are proposed to regulate their actions based on anticipated outcomes of behavior, which are informed by prior personal experience and/or observations of others' outcomes following similar actions. Bandura's seminal work on observational learning demonstrated that behaviors and associated outcomes are often learned in the absence of personal reinforcement or enactment of the observed behavior (Bandura, Ross, & Ross, 1961; Bandura & Walters, 1963). Key studies demonstrated, for example, that children learned to behave aggressively simply by observing others being reinforced for behaving aggressively (Bandura et al., 1961; Bandura & Walters, 1963). The far reaching implications of this work echo in findings demonstrating the influence of parents, peers, and media on the initiation of drinking behavior (Anderson, de Bruijn, Angus, Gordon, & Hastings, 2009; Ary, Tildesley, Hops, & Andrews, 1993; Gibbons et al., 2010; Moreno & Whitehill, 2014). Further, exposure to drinking models appears to be cognitively mediated through expectancies, perceptions of friends' drinking, willingness to drink, and positive thoughts about the typical person who drinks (i.e., prototypes; (Dal Cin et al., 2009; Scheier & Botvin, 1997)). Overall, SCT and supporting research suggest that increasing exposure to positive, non- or moderate-drinking models and to negative, heavy-drinking models and reducing exposure to positive, heavy-drinking models and negative, non- or moderate-drinking models is likely to delay initiation and escalation of drinking.

SCT suggests that self-efficacy plays a fundamental role in efforts to change one's behavior (Bandura, 1977a, 1989, 2012). Self-efficacy refers to peoples' beliefs in their ability to affect change and is, according to SCT, a necessary prerequisite for intentional change. When self-efficacy is extremely low, individuals do not believe that they have the abilities to bring about successful change and consequently have little reason to try to affect change. Conversely, when self-efficacy is high, individuals are very confident that they can affect change and that they have the ability, resources, and/or determination to bring about success. Self-efficacy has, with some exceptions (e.g., Demmel, Nicolai, & Jenko, 2006), been relatively consistently associated with successful change efforts in alcohol and other substance use (Bandura, 1999; Kadden & Litt, 2011; Morgenstern et al., 2016). It has been adopted and incorporated within alcohol treatment approaches, including Relapse Prevention (Marlatt & Donovan, 2005) and Motivational Interviewing (Miller & Rollnick, 2013). For example, supporting self-efficacy is a key principle in the practice of Motivational Interviewing, whereby practitioners encourage elaboration of statements expressing self-efficacy to change harmful drinking patterns; place emphasis on previous successful efforts to change; and focus on strengths and abilities related to change.

As a model of health behavior change, SCT has much to offer. Among the concrete suggestions offered by this conceptualization is that self-efficacy, in combination with other SCT factors, may be a useful treatment matching factor (Sharma, 2005), with more structure and personal attention needed for individuals with lower self-efficacy. Further, it has been suggested that many constructs proposed in other models of health behavior change (e.g., Health Beliefs Model [Carpenter, 2010] and Theory of Planned Behavior [Ajzen, 1991; Armitage, Harris, & Arden, 2011]) can be more parsimoniously integrated within a SCT approach, where overarching constructs include self-efficacy; outcome expectations (i.e., social, physical, and self-evaluative); impediments and facilitators of change; and proximal and distal health goals (Bandura, 2004). In sum, SCT presents a useful overarching model of changes in drinking. Generation of novel interventions and treatment approaches based on SCT could be facilitated by more precise specifications of where constructs which have been extensively studied in the alcohol literature fit within this framework. For example, SCT proposes that outcome expectations theoretically precede goals (Bandura, 2004). Further, social norms are considered to fit under the broad category of goals. Alcohol expectancies and social norms have both been extensively studied outside of the framework of SCT (Jones, Corbin, & Fromme, 2001; Neighbors, Lee, Lewis, Fossos, & Larimer, 2007). How well findings from these independent literatures support their proposed placement within SCT has received little empirical examination or validation.

Theories of social norms

While there are many perspectives that focus on or incorporate social norms, there is no single or dominant perspective, which can be identified as Social Norms Theory. Perhaps the earliest systematic empirical study of social norms from a psychological perspective began with the work of Muzafer Sherif (1936). Sherif defined social norms as rules, values, or standards of behavior based on the prevailing attitudes and behaviors within a specific group of people. Sherif demonstrated that in the absence of clear objective standards, individuals revise their subjective evaluations toward the average other group members, which they believe to be more accurate. Subsequent work by Asch (1951) and Deutsch and Gerard (1955) revealed distinct motivations for conforming to group norms, including the desire to have the most accurate information and the desire to be accepted by others. These motivations roughly approximate the distinction between descriptive norms and injunctive norms, a central distinction in modern theories of social norms, beginning with the work of Robert Cialdini and colleagues. Their studies and theory (e.g., Focus Theory of Normative Conduct) solidified earlier work in social norms (Cialdini, Kallgren, & Reno, 1991; Reno, Cialdini, & Kallgren, 1993) and articulate the distinction between descriptive norms, which refer to objective behaviors (e.g., how much people drink), and injunctive norms, which refer to approval of a given behavior (e.g., the extent to which people approve or disapprove of drinking).

Seminal applications of social norms in the study of drinking among US college students compared perceived social norms (i.e., "how much do you think the average college student drinks") versus actual social norms (i.e., the actual amount that other college students drink). Importantly, findings indicate that individuals' estimates of others' drinking are almost always higher than actual norms and that those estimates (i.e., perceived descriptive norms) are positively associated with drinking behavior (Baer, Stacy, & Larimer, 1991; Perkins, 2002). Additional findings indicate that individuals also tend to overestimate injunctive norms related to drinking (Prentice & Miller, 1993); that discrepancies between perceived and actual norms are larger for more distal reference groups (e.g., other students) than more proximal reference groups (e.g., friends); and that perceived norms for more proximal groups tend to be more highly correlated with drinking relative to more distal reference groups (Baer et al., 1991; Borsari & Carey, 2001, 2003).

Social norms have been applied extensively in brief alcohol interventions and treatment approaches. Given that individuals tend to overestimate descriptive drinking norms and that perceived norms are associated with drinking, many interventions have attempted to correct norms misperceptions as a strategy to reduce drinking. Universal approaches have utilized social norms marketing, where posters, flyers, television ads, and other media provide accurate drinking norms. For example, in a statewide social norms marketing project, television ads communicated messages such as "Most Montana Young Adults [4 out of 5] don't drink and drive," accompanied by the source of data (Perkins, Linkenbach, Lewis, & Neighbors, 2010). Findings for norms marketing have been mixed as a strategy to reduce drinking, with some studies finding support (DeJong et al., 2006; Mattern & Neighbors, 2004; Turner, Perkins, & Bauerle, 2008) and others not (Clapp, Lange, Russell, Shillington, & Voas, 2003; DeJong et al., 2009; Russell, Clapp, & DeJong, 2005). Social norms marketing appears to work better in settings with relatively fewer contradictory messages (Scribner et al., 2011).

More consistent findings have been evident for personalized normative feedback using descriptive drinking norms. Personalized normative feedback assesses perceived norms and self-reported actual drinking and then provides personalized feedback comparing individuals' own drinking and their perceptions of typical drinking among their peers with the actual drinking norms of their peers. When administered to heavier drinkers, personalized normative feedback typically shows individuals that they think others drink much more than others actually drink and that the individuals drink much more than others actually drink (Lewis & Neighbors, 2006). Support for personalized normative feedback in reducing perceived norms and drinking has been relatively consistent (see reviews by Dotson, Dunn, & Bowers, 2015; Miller et al., 2013; Walters & Neighbors, 2005). Though personalized normative feedback can be administered via computer, it appears that is it more effective when a computer-based version is delivered in a lab-setting or study location (and thus, is in-person to a degree) versus delivered remotely (i.e., via a website; Rodriguez et al., 2015). While personalized normative feedback has been largely evaluated in college populations, it has also been found effective among risky drinkers in the general population; among US veterans (Cunningham, Wild, Bondy, & Lin, 2001; Pedersen, Parast, Marshall, Schell, & Neighbors, 2017); and as an active component of multi-component feedback among active duty military personnel (Rodriguez, Neighbors, Walker, & Walton, 2019).

Recent applications of theories of social cognition to interventions for problematic drinking

Theory of planned behavior

The theory of planned behavior (TPB), has been routinely used to examine health behaviors, including problematic alcohol use (Ajzen, 1991, 2012; Cooke, Dahdah, Norman, & French, 2016). This model suggests that the most important determinant of an individual's behavior is their intention to perform that behavior, with three cognitive variables—attitudes, subjective norms, and perceived behavioral control—said to be the direct determinants of intention. Attitudes are relatively stable evaluative judgments about aspects of a person's experience (e.g., an idea, a person, a behavior, etc.) that range from negative to positive and are influenced by situational factors, including observations of one's own behavior. Attitudes represent a key explanatory variable in many theories of health behavior; research has shown attitudes predict both intention and behavior (Bem, 1967; Glasman & Albarracín, 2006; Montano & Kasprzyk, 2008). Consistent with the information above, subjective norms include two different types, descriptive and injunctive. Finally, perceived behavioral control represents the extent to which a person feels they have control over performing a desired behavior when faced with internal and external barriers and is often operationalized as self-efficacy (Bandura, 1977a, 2012).

Generally, attitudes, norms, and perceived behavior control appear to account for a large proportion of variance with respect to one's behavioral intentions (44%) as well as in health behavior (19%) in prospective studies (McEachan, Conner, Taylor, & Lawton, 2011). With respect to the evaluation of alcohol use, a recent meta-analysis found that alcohol-related attitudes have the strongest associations with intentions (random effect size = 0.62), followed by subjective norms (random effect size = 0.47), and finally perceived behavioral control (random effect size = 0.31); intentions, in turn, predicted drinking behavior (random effect size = 0.54; Cooke et al., 2016). Thus, TPB constructs have strong predictive validity for alcohol use.

Recent research has aimed to leverage these constructs, as well as principles of cognitive dissonance, in the service of intervention. Briefly, cognitive dissonance theory suggests that individuals have an inner drive to hold their attitudes and beliefs in agreement with one another and to avoid inconsistency (Festinger, 1957; Harmon-Jones & Mills, 2019). The result of inconsistent cognitions (i.e., dissonance) has been described as an unpleasant state of arousal, negative affect, or psychological discomfort, a state that individuals are motivated to reduce or eliminate. This cognitive tension can result from discrepancies between cognitions about behaviors, perceptions, attitudes, beliefs, or feelings and may relate to the self, another person, a group, or environmental contexts (Cooper, 2007, 2012; Harmon-Jones & Mills, 2019).

Using principles of cognitive dissonance and key constructs from the TPB (attitudes & norms), an intervention was developed to reduce alcohol consumption in UK university students (Norman et al., 2018). Results indicated that participants who viewed messages targeting beliefs pertinent to TPB (attitudes and norms) that were inconsistent with their current behavior had significantly less favorable cognitions about binge drinking, consumed less alcohol, engaged in binge drinking less frequently, and had less harmful patterns of alcohol consumption during their first 6 months at university. Additional recent work aimed to target two of the key predictive variables in the TPB, attitudes and intentions, using principles of cognitive dissonance to reduce alcohol use (DiBello, Carey, & Cushing, 2018). This study, conducted with US college students, attempted to create attitude-behavior dissonance in order to make individuals feel hypocritical if they were to espouse reasons why heavy drinking is negative while engaging in the behavior themselves. A brief counter-attitudinal advocacy manipulation was adapted to the alcohol prevention context wherein individuals who reported engaging in problematic drinking responded to a writing prompt where they (a) discussed reasons why heavy drinking is harmful and (b) provided ways that students like them could avoid such alcohol related problems. This inconsistency, between their behavior and the writing activity, was used to create a feeling of cognitive dissonance in an effort to motivate behavior change. Pilot study findings indicated strong support for the feasibility and acceptability of the intervention and evidence of short-term effects in reducing drinking intentions and drinking behavior. Taken together, these findings represent an important step in the alcohol intervention field as they demonstrate the promise of the TPB as both an explanatory model of drinking behavior and provide direct targets for intervention. Consistent with the TPB, other theoretical frameworks, such as the Prototype Willingness Model, also utilize attitudes and norms as important predictors of drinking and other health related behaviors.

Prototype willingness

The Prototype Willingness Model (PWM; Gerrard, Gibbons, Houlihan, Stock, & Pomery, 2008), an extension of the TPB (Ajzen, 1991, 2012), proposes a dual process model aimed at improving the predictive validity of existing theories of health risk behaviors. There are two general pathways said to influence one's engagement in health risk behaviors, a reasoned path and a reactive path. The reasoned path, to a health risk behavior like alcohol use, is said to be affected by three components: one's attitudes about alcohol use, beliefs that alcohol use is normative, and believing access to alcohol is easy. The PWM also acknowledges a reactive path wherein alcohol use occurs in unplanned instances. This path models an individual's willingness to drink when given the opportunity; it is predicted by one's prototypes of drinkers. A prototype is the mental representation or image of the type of person who engages in a risk behavior, such as the representation of a "typical" drinker. The PWM has been broadly applied and has been found to explain unique variance in several health risks behaviors (e.g., alcohol use, smoking, risky sexual behavior) ranging from adolescence through adulthood (Gibbons, Houlihan, & Gerrard, 2009; Hukkelberg & Dykstra, 2009; Rivis, Sheeran, & Armitage, 2006). Importantly, the PWM has been found to predict alcohol use better than the TPB among adolescents, partly because willingness is a better predictor than intentions for adolescents, especially those who have not yet initiated drinking or who are unable to predict when and where alcohol might be available (Gibbons et al., 2016; Todd, Kothe, Mullan, & Monds, 2016). Interestingly, emergent work suggests that in addition to holding a prototype of a typical drinker, individuals also have prototypes of a person who abstains from engaging in health risk behaviors (Litt & Lewis, 2016). Further, those abstainer prototypes have been found to have the same predictive influence on a person's willingness to not use substances as user prototypes have been found to predict willingness to use (Rivis et al., 2006). Put another way, when measured, abstainer prototypes appear to evidence an inhibiting effect on alcohol use whereas use prototypes evidence a disinhibiting effect on alcohol use. Overall, these findings highlight the utility the PWM as well as the incorporation of dual-process models into research and prevention and intervention development. While the TPB and PWN models focus on reason and social-reaction based pathways for intervention, other social psychological theories, namely Self-Affirmation Theory, focus instead on the self and more individual based motivations.

Self- affirmation theory

According to Self-Affirmation Theory (Steele, 1999), people are motivated to maintain a sense of personal adequacy or integrity, which can be threatened psychologically by information from the environment (e.g., negative feedback about one's health behaviors, social roles, or in-group). Response to psychological threat often invokes maladaptive information processing that represents defensive responses to preserve the integrity of the self (Cohen & Sherman, 2014). This includes defensive avoidance (i.e., failure to attend to or engage with unpleasant or "threatening" information) and/or message derogation (i.e., dismissing the validity or value of the message). Such efforts at self-protection, often labeled "resistance," can be triggered by situations that narrows one's focus to a particular dimension of oneself (e.g., "heavy drinker") when information is provided that is perceived as threatening (e.g., your drinking behavior is causing negative consequences; Sherman & Cohen, 2006). However, ample research shows these maladaptive responses to threat can be reduced via a simple strategy of self-affirmation. Researchers have utilized a variety of methods to induce self-affirmation, including the completion of values scales, writing about a central value, and providing positive personality feedback (for reviews, see McQueen & Klein, 2006; Napper, Harris, & Epton, 2009). These activities all serve the same function, namely to expand an individual's focus and enable a more holistic view of one's self. Instead of just being a "drinker," individuals who self-affirm are given the opportunity to focus on many aspects of their personal identity that are important to them (e.g., their faith or role as a parent/sibling/student), thus reducing the threat associated with negative feedback given about a specific area (e.g., their [heavy] drinking). Self-affirmation does not work by merely boosting self-esteem (McQueen & Klein, 2006); crucially, it also counters the tendency to narrow attention to one part of the self that is threatened (Cohen & Sherman, 2014). By broadening their perspective, self-affirmed individuals see the new information as less threatening and have more mental energy to approach (instead of avoid) it.

Functionally, interventions involve engaging participants in an affirmation activity prior to providing health information that can be perceived as negative or threatening. In the context of alcohol use, individuals have been found to be more receptive of information about the health risks of alcohol use following completion of an affirmation and have evidenced short-term reductions in drinking (Armitage et al., 2011; Armitage, Rowe, Arden, & Harris, 2014; Ehret & Sherman, 2018; Fox, Harris, & Jessop, 2017). Two recent meta-analyses confirm that use of brief self-affirmation exercises prior to exposure to health risk information has a positive effect on a wide range of health behaviors including alcohol use ($ds = 0.26–0.32$, Epton, Harris, Kane, van Koningsbruggen, & Sheeran, 2015; Sweeney & Moyer, 2015). The results of these studies suggest that self-affirmation is equally efficacious across adolescents, college students, as well as community populations. Thus, this research suggests that self-affirmation, when applied to problematic alcohol use, resulted in reductions in alcohol use up to two months.

Emergent applications of theories of social cognition to interventions for problematic drinking

Social identity and self-categorization theories

A long-standing and influential social cognitive theory, Social Identity Theory (Tajfel & Turner, 1979) and its later extension, Self-categorization Theory (Turner, Hogg, Oakes, Reicher, & Wetherell, 1987), focus on the importance of groups and their relative status differences in social cognition. Specifically, they suggest that perceived memberships in groups (i.e., social identities) affect how we perceive and feel about ourselves and others and, ultimately, how we behave. Social Identity Theory focuses more on the motivational component of identities (i.e., identities as a way to maintain positive self-esteem) whereas Self-categorization Theory focuses more on the cognitive processing component of identities (i.e., which identity becomes activated in a given context and the [socially-shared] meaning of a given identity or identities). Social identities are also posited to maximize the differences between members of one's in-group and members of one's out-group and to minimize the differences between members of one's in-group, with individuals taking on the values and behaviors of their in-group and minimizing the values and behaviors of out-groups. According to Social Identity Theory, individuals will favor their in-group (s), and there is evidence that individuals preferentially reward in-groups over out-groups, that in-group favoritism can occur automatically, and that in-group favoritism increases as in-group identification increases (Fiske & Taylor, 2017).

Social Identity Theory and Self-categorization Theory have been extended to consider social identities related to using and recovery from alcohol and other drugs (Best et al., 2016; Frings & Albery, 2015). Though these extended models vary in their emphasis on the importance of systemic changes in social context (Best et al., 2016) versus on the importance of individual differences and cognitive processing (Frings & Albery, 2015), they converge on the importance of group membership and identity in substance use recovery.

These models also directly point to targets for intervention. For example, Best et al.'s (2016) social identity model of recovery conceptualizes recovery as an inherently social process in which the development of a positively-perceived recovery-oriented social group (whether a formal recovery group like Alcoholics Anonymous [AA] or an informal non-using group), along with a recovery-based social identity and activities/behavioral associated with that identity, is essential. Consistent with the model, studies with Australian adult samples found that the establishment of a recovery identity is associated with treatment retention, engagement, and other treatment outcomes (Beckwith, Best, Dingle, Perryman, & Lubman, 2015; Dingle, Stark, Cruwys, & Best, 2015; Haslam et al., 2019). Further, positive changes in one's social network and social identity (e.g., increased social connectedness, increased engagement with others in recovery, and more diversity of social groups) appear to be associated with improvement in quality of life in a study of Australian adults in recovery (Bathish et al., 2017). Frings and Albery's (2015) social identity model of cessation similarly focuses on the importance of developing an identity associated with a recovery group to increase esteem and efficacy for one's self and for the group. Social connectedness to the group is viewed as a crucial way to facilitate and maintain recovery. The social identity model of cessation also specifies key cognitive processes, such increasing the complexity and familiarity of the recovery identity, so that the new recovery identity can be activated easily and by a range of stimuli and thus become more accessible (in relation to pre-treatment/pre-recovery using identity).

Direct applications of social identity theories to interventions for problematic drinking are nascent. Though recovery fellowships such as AA clearly have a strong sense of group identity and emphasis on the power of the group/community, their principles and traditions do not stem from social identity theories but rather from the lived experiences of individuals seeking to stop drinking. A theory-driven, groups-based identity intervention, Groups 4 Health has been recently developed (Haslam, Cruwys, Haslam, Dingle, & Chang, 2016), but to our knowledge, it has only been implemented with young adults experiencing distress. While there is preliminary support for the intervention (which aims to provide education about social groups and their impact on health and help individuals identify and strengthen valued identities both in terms of specified mechanisms of action and outcomes), there is a need for direct application with problematic drinkers. Finally, while increasing a social identity's complexity and familiarity is a novel treatment target, to our knowledge, strategies to do so are not yet part of interventions.

Theories of implicit cognition

Formal theories of implicit cognition emerged in the late 1980s and early 1990s, with a key formulation advanced by Greenwald and Banaji (1995) that there are cognitive traces of past experience that affect current behavior, that are not available to self-report or introspection, and that may take the form of implicit attitudes, esteem, and stereotypes. This formulation then expanded to include traces about the self or implicit self-concept (Greenwald et al., 2002). With the development of measures posited to assess such traces (e.g., the Implicit Association Test; Greenwald, McGhee, & Schwartz, 1998), theories of implicit cognition have risen in prominence generally (Strack & Deutsch, 2004) and in the context of addiction and substance use (Stacy & Wiers, 2010; Wiers & Gladwin, 2017). Despite these theories roots in social and personality psychology and social cognition, early adaptations to problematic drinking overlooked the potential importance of cognitive traces related to the self or others and instead focused on cognitive traces related to alcohol itself (e.g., Wiers, van Woerden, Smulders, & de Jong, 2002).

Since 2011, numerous studies have sought to fill that gap. They have established that implicit self-concept related to drinking alcohol is a robust predictor of problematic alcohol use concurrently and longitudinally, including in US college student and more diverse US samples (for a review, see Lindgren, Neighbors, Gasser, Ramirez, & Cvencek, 2016). Two key findings are that measures of implicit self-concept related to drinking alcohol can predict prospective drinking even after controlling for explicit measure counterparts (Gray, LaPlante, Bannon, Ambady, & Shaffer, 2011; Lindgren, Neighbors, Teachman, et al., 2016) and that increases in implicit self-concept related to drinking alcohol are associated with subsequent increases in risk for hazardous drinking and vice-versa (Lindgren et al., 2018).

The above findings, coupled with the fact that implicit self-concept related to drinking alcohol is not specifically targeted in any existing intervention (Lindgren, Neighbors, Gasser, et al., 2016) suggest the possibility that this implicit self-concept could represent a novel intervention target. We know of one published set of studies that has sought to do so (Lindgren et al., 2015) via adapting a method developed to shift cognitive traces related to alcohol and approach (e.g., a cognitive bias modification task to retrain alcohol approach tendencies; Wiers, Eberl, Rinck, Becker, & Lindenmeyer, 2011; Wiers, Rinck, Kordts, Houben, & Strack, 2010). Those studies, with US college student drinkers, yielded null results. Shifting implicit self-concept related to alcohol may require the development of novel cognitive bias tasks and/or novel methods to reduce the impact of implicit self-concept on drinking. Finally, although untested to date, it is possible that interventions adapted from other theoretical perspectives (e.g., theories of possible selves) could also have an impact on implicit self-concept.

Possible selves theory

Possible selves are mental representations of one's self in the future, reflecting one's expectations, hopes, and fears (Markus & Nurius, 1986). They function as reference points for current self-evaluations and motivate behavior via self-regulatory processes, striving for consistency with the hoped-for or expected selves and prevention of feared selves. Perceived attainability of and desire for possible selves is shaped by social norms, standards, and interactions (Erikson, 2019). Studies exploring the relation between possible selves and alcohol use in adolescents and college students have found that higher levels of alcohol use or misuse at follow up were predicted by stronger expectations that their future selves would possess more negative attributes associated with binge drinkers (Quinlan, Jaccard, & Blanton, 2006) and by having fewer positive expected selves (Aloise-Young, Hennigan, & Leong, 2001). Individuals who listed their primary hoped-for (among drinkers) or feared (among abstainers) self as one related to academics reported lower levels of alcohol use at one-year follow-up in a sample of adolescents transitioning from middle to high school (Lee et al., 2015).

Possible selves have been successfully targeted in interventions to improve adolescents' academic performance or motivations (e.g., Oyserman, Terry, & Bybee, 2002) and select health behaviors, including increasing college students' negative attitudes toward smoking and intentions to quit (Song, Kim, Kwon, & Jung, 2013) and increasing exercise among adults (e.g., Murru & Ginis, 2010). The presence of a discrepancy between the current and possible self has been viewed as necessary to yield a behavior change (Oyserman, James, Markman, Klein, & Suhr, 2009). Possible selves are expected to have greater potential for change when they are imagined vividly, believed to be truly possible and within one's control, and linked to specific strategies for achieving desired selves and/or avoiding feared selves (Erikson, 2019).

It may be effective to target possible selves in alcohol misuse prevention and intervention efforts (see, Lee et al., 2015, for preliminary evidence with adolescents). One viable method might be to administer a writing exercise to prompt individuals to imagine a given discrepant alcohol-related possible self (e.g., abstainer, low-risk or moderate drinker, person in recovery) and describe this future self in detail. Given the importance of social support in the validation of possible selves, it has been recommended to prompt inclusion of *possible others*—other persons one's future self expects to interact with—in these descriptions (Erikson, 2019). Initial data from our laboratory indicates that this approach is feasible and acceptable to US college students with a history of problematic drinking. For example, participants ($N = 41$) reported being able to vividly imagine and easily write about their future self as a low-risk drinker, finding their descriptions highly plausible and relatable, and reported that doing so allowed them to see their life in a new way (Lindgren, unpublished data, 2019). Although it may be sufficient to exclusively target desired selves in interventions aimed at reducing current drinking (Lee et al., 2015) it may be appropriate to also prompt consideration of feared selves in preventative efforts for abstainers or light drinkers. The potential for applying theories of possible selves to interventions for problematic drinking appears promising.

Implicit theories

Implicit theories may also have the potential to inform or be integrated into interventions for problematic drinking. Implicit theories about human attributes consider whether individuals' view those attributes to be malleable, supporting a growth mindset, or incremental theory, or immutable, supporting a fixed mindset, or entity theory (Dweck & Leggett, 1988). Growth mindsets are considered to be more adaptive because they recognize one's potential for change, and they are generally found to be associated with positive outcomes (Dweck, 2000). Fixed mindsets are considered to be limiting because they reflect beliefs that people lack the ability to change and are generally found to be associated with negative outcomes (Dweck, 2000). People can hold implicit theories about various attributes/domains (e.g., intelligence, personality). For example, implicit theories about willpower consider self-control to be either a limited resource (fixed mindset) or non-limited resource (growth mindset; Job, Dweck, & Walton, 2010). Growth mindsets about willpower has been linked to better self-regulation, academic performance, personal goal striving, and subjective well-being, even when demands are high (Bernecker, Herrmann, Brandstätter, & Job, 2017; Job, Walton, Bernecker, & Dweck, 2015).

Problematic drinking and addiction are characterized by issues with impulse control and willpower to resist temptation (Bechara, 2005) and by beliefs about ability—or lack thereof—to control and take responsibility for drinking behavior (Bandura, 1977a, 1989, 1999; Kadden & Litt, 2011). Problematic drinkers who attribute their behavior to external factors out of their control (endorsing an external locus of control), as opposed to believing they have personal control over their behavior (endorsing an internal locus of control), are more likely to have greater alcohol dependency, lower treatment success rates, and higher rates of relapse (Yeh, 2008). Having an external locus of control appears similar to having a fixed mindset whereas having an internal locus of control appears similar to having a growth mindset. Further, stronger endorsement of a fixed mindset about in relation to drinking (i.e., that it is very difficult to change) has been shown to be positively associated with problematic drinking (Schroder, Dawood, Yalch, Donnellan, & Moser, 2016).

Interventions to promote growth mindsets—by training adolescents or college students on implicit theories, sharing scientific findings supporting the malleability of attributes, providing strategies oriented toward a growth mindset, and/or having students complete more engaging activities—have primarily been used to target implicit theories of intelligence. These interventions have generally been successful in their efforts to increase academic achievement (e.g., Burnette, Russell, Hoyt, Orvidas, & Widman, 2018). Promoting a growth mindset in the domains of willpower and drinking tendencies might similarly be helpful for problematic drinkers who have fixed mindsets about willpower and their ability to change drinking, but to our knowledge, this has not yet been tested to date.

Social cognitive deficits

A final emergent area with respect to how social cognition can inform interventions for problematic drinking concerns the potential for deficits in social cognition to be novel intervention targets. Findings from a recent meta-analysis (Bora & Zorlu, 2017) found support for two social cognitive deficits—namely, deficits in emotion recognition (especially disgust and anger) and in theory of mind (the ability to attribute intentions, feelings, and beliefs to others and to use this information to predict what others will do)—to be associated with alcohol use disorder. Specifically, when comparing performance on tasks of facial emotion recognition and on the ability to the decode other's mental states and reason about other's mental states, individuals with alcohol use disorder showed deficits compared to healthy controls (*d*s ranged from 0.46 to 0.72). These findings dovetail with suggestions that these deficits may contribute to the many interpersonal problems that problematic drinkers experience in their careers, families, and day-to-day social interactions (see, for example, Le Berre, Fama, & Sullivan, 2017). Further, findings indicated larger deficits as a function of longer interval duration of problematic drinking and more depressive symptoms. These findings, along with the larger literature about social cognitive deficits found across multiple clinical domains, ranging from psychiatric, neurological, and developmental clinical conditions (see Cotter et al., 2018), suggest that social cognitive deficits could represent potential transdiagnostic vulnerabilities. Further, there is some evidence from other clinical fields (e.g., schizophrenia) that these deficits are potentially modifiable via intervention. For example, the Social Cognition and Interaction Program (Penn, Roberts, Combs, & Sterne, 2007) is a 24-week intervention for individuals with schizophrenia that includes, among other topics, specific training in emotional recognition and navigating social situations (including how to differentiate personal and situational attributions and learn to make social "guesses"). Findings from a recent review suggest that such interventions can be effective, especially for improving emotional recognition and theory of mind (see Grant, Lawrence, Preti, Wykes, & Cella, 2017). Crucial, to our knowledge, unanswered questions concern how these kinds of interventions might be adapted for use with problematic drinkers and whether they will ultimately be found to be efficacious.

Lessons learned

Collectively, theories of social cognition have made substantial, novel contributions to interventions for problematic drinking, and recent applications suggest that they continue to have the potential to do so. A key thread throughout many of the theories and their application to problematic drinking is Bandura's enduring Social Cognitive Theory. His early emphasis on modeling has direct translation to the initiation and escalation of substance use and speaks to common threads in many interventions about limiting exposure to individuals who drink (or who drink heavily) and increasing exposure to individuals who do not drink (or who drink rarely/moderately; McCrady et al., 2014). One can also see links between modeling and social norms approaches, which emphasize the importance of understanding and correcting individuals' perceptions about how much others drink or approve of particular drinking behaviors. These approaches are among the most efficacious brief interventions for reducing risky drinking in young adults (Leeman, Perez, Nogueira, & DeMartini, 2015; Reid & Carey, 2015). Similarly, Bandura's emphasis on self-efficacy (Bandura, 1977a, 2012) has been directly applied to teaching individuals skills to refuse or limit their drinking, and it has links to the implicit theory literature, which emphasizes the importance of growth mindsets (i.e., beliefs that people and/or their drinking *can* change) to behavior change.

A second thread throughout many theories of social cognition and their application to is the importance of social identities and the self-concept. Social Identity Theory and Self-categorization theory have long emphasized the importance of groups and identification with groups. Applications to problematic drinking and addiction emphasize the importance of group membership to promote more adaptive drinking (i.e., moderation) or abstinence. While much of this work is, to date, focused on etiology and mechanism, the creation of a brief intervention focused on identifying and developing valued social identities (e.g., Haslam et al., 2016) is innovative and promising, and has potential transdiagnostic implications.

A second key application is the importance of the self-concept in relations to drinking, which spans Self-categorization Theory, theories of possible selves and implicit self-concept related to drinking alcohol. Though emergent with respect to application, these theories suggest the importance of developing a self-concept related to drinking that is adaptive (whether referring to abstaining or moderation), that is complex and familiar (to increase likelihood of being activated), and that is positive, with the likelihood that discrepancy between this self and one's current self will motivate behavior change. A key insight from self-affirmation theory is the importance of individuals feeling good about themselves prior to receiving feedback about their drinking (Epton et al., 2015). While there is preliminary evidence for the utility of affirmation exercises as a standalone intervention strategy, one could imagine that existing interventions that include the provision of feedback (e.g., personalized normative feedback approaches) or emergent interventions that ask individuals to consider a more adaptive possible self in relations to drinking might be enhanced by the addition of an affirmation exercise.

Finally, advances in understanding the social cognition processes indicate that there are specific components that could be leveraged in interventions. For example, recent work has identified key social cognitive deficits associated with problematic drinking (i.e., emotion recognition and theory of mind), and they may represent novel, malleable treatment targets. Similarly, identity-related theories suggest that increasing the familiarity and complexity of a more adaptive identity related to drinking could facilitate a reduction or cessation of drinking as well as maintain recovery.

Future directions

Though researchers have made strides in developing and evaluating cutting edge interventions based on the principles of various social cognitive theories, there is still much work to be done. First, there is a clear need for intervention research with broader groups of individuals, including those at different stages of alcohol use, from different countries, with different sexual orientations, and with different cultural values. As an example, much of the work done examining social norms efficacy (social norms campaigns, personalized normative feedback), self-affirmation theory, and the TPB has been conducted among younger adults (i.e., 18–25 year olds) from the US who meet criteria for heavy drinking (4+/5+ drinks for men and women respectively). Relatedly, emergent research suggests that US sexual minority youth endorse higher descriptive norms and more permissive injunctive norms about a variety of substance use behaviors, including alcohol, when compared to their heterosexual peers, and these norms partially account for disparities in multiple substance use behaviors (Mereish, Goldbach, Burgess, & DiBello, 2017). However, we know of no research to date that has incorporated this information into a personalized normative feedback adapted for sexual minority youth. Additional intervention research is also needed in a broader range of countries. We also note that the research available from interventions based on these theories was primarily conducted among Western, Educated, Industrialized, Rich, and Democratic (WEIRD) societies (see Fiske & Taylor, 2017). Consequently, there is little to no evidence about the efficacy of this work in countries that are not Western or democratic, nor is there evidence in countries where alcohol is illegal or more highly regulated. The above are just three examples of where research needs to advance the scope and scale of intervention efforts.

Finally, we note breadth and depth of extant theories of social cognition and the potential to create novel, standalone, developmentally appropriate (from the vantage of age and level of problematic drinking) interventions that rely fully on those theories. Bandura's social cognitive theory (Bandura, 1977b, 1999, 2012) provides one potential overarching model and approach. One could envision a series of interventions that include the components from the overarching model and integrates best practices from subsequent social cognitive theories (e.g., social norm theories and/or TPB) and their intervention approaches. In contrast to this top-down approach, one could also imagine a bottom-up approach that would include intervention components that seek to address cognitive processing deficits (i.e., theory of mind, emotional recognition); to build self-efficacy; to affirm the self and visualize alterative, adaptive future selves or identities; to reduce problematic perceptions about others and their drinking, and to identify and develop valued social identities that are adaptive with respect to reducing or abstaining from drinking. Such interventions have great promise and the potential to alleviate the tremendous burden of problematic drinking.

References

Ajzen, I. (1991). The theory of planned behavior. *Organizational Behavior and Human Decision Processes*, *50*(2), 179–211. Available from https://doi.org/10.1016/0749-5978(91)90020-T.

Ajzen, I. (2012). The theory of planned behavior. In P. A. M. V. Lange, A. W. Kruglanski, & E. T. Higgins (Eds.), *Handbook of theories of social psychology* (Vol. 1, pp. 438–459). Thousand Oaks, CA: Sage Publications Ltd.

Aloise-Young, P. A., Hennigan, K. M., & Leong, C. W. (2001). Possible selves and negative health behaviors during early adolescence. *The Journal of Early Adolescence*, *21*(2), 158–181. Available from https://doi.org/10.1177/0272431601021002002.

Anderson, P., de Bruijn, A., Angus, K., Gordon, R., & Hastings, G. (2009). Impact of alcohol advertising and media exposure on adolescent alcohol use: A systematic review of longitudinal studies. *Alcohol and Alcoholism*, *44*(3), 229–243. Available from https://doi.org/10.1093/alcalc/agn115.

Armitage, C. J., Harris, P. R., & Arden, M. A. (2011). Evidence that self-affirmation reduces alcohol consumption: Randomized exploratory trial with a new, brief means of self-affirming. *Health Psychology*, *30*(5), 633–641. Available from https://doi.org/10.1037/a0023738.

Armitage, C. J., Rowe, R., Arden, M. A., & Harris, P. R. (2014). A brief psychological intervention that reduces adolescent alcohol consumption. *Journal of Consulting and Clinical Psychology*, *82*(3), 546–550. Available from https://doi.org/10.1037/a0035802.

Ary, D. V., Tildesley, E., Hops, H., & Andrews, J. A. (1993). The influence of parent, sibling, and peer modeling and attitudes on adolescent use of alcohol. *International Journal of the Addictions*, *28*(9), 853–880. Available from https://doi.org/10.3109/10826089309039661.

Asch, S. E. (1951). Effects of group pressure upon the modification and distortion of judgments. In H. Guetzkow (Ed.), *Groups, leadership and men; research in human relations* (pp. 177–190). Oxford: Carnegie Press.

Baer, J. S., Stacy, A., & Larimer, M. (1991). Biases in the perception of drinking norms among college students. *Journal of Studies on Alcohol and Drugs*, *52*(6), 580.

Bandura, A. (1977a). Self-efficacy: Toward a unifying theory of behavioral change. *Psychological Review*, *84*(2), 191–215. Available from https://doi.org/10.1037/0033-295X.84.2.191.

Bandura, A. (1977b). *Social learning theory*. Englewood Cliffs, NJ: Prentice-Hall, Inc.

Bandura, A. (1986). *Social foundations of thought and action: A social cognitive theory*. Englewood Cliffs, NJ: Prentice-Hall, Inc.

Bandura, A. (1989). Human agency in social cognitive theory. *American Psychologist*, *44*(9), 1175–1184. Available from https://doi.org/10.1037/0003-066X.44.9.1175.

Bandura, A. (1999). A sociocognitive analysis of substance abuse: An agentic perspective. *Psychological Science*, *10*(3), 214–217. Available from https://doi.org/10.1111/1467-9280.00138.

Bandura, A. (2004). Health promotion by. *Social Cognitive Means. Health Education & Behavior*, *31*(2), 143–164. Available from https://doi.org/10.1177/1090198104263660.

Bandura, A. (2012). Social cognitive theory. In P. A. M. V. Lange, A. W. Kruglanski, & E. T. Higgins (Eds.), *Handbook of Theories of Social Psychology* (Vol. 1, pp. 349–373). Thousand Oaks, CA: Sage Publications Ltd.

Bandura, A., Ross, D., & Ross, S. A. (1961). Transmission of aggression through imitation of aggressive models. *The Journal of Abnormal and Social Psychology*, *63*(3), 575–582. Available from https://doi.org/10.1037/h0045925.

Bandura, A., & Walters, R. H. Social learning and personality development. 1963. Holt, Rinehart and Winston: New York.

Bathish, R., Best, D., Savic, M., Beckwith, M., Mackenzie, J., & Lubman, D. I. (2017). "Is it me or should my friends take the credit?" The role of social networks and social identity in recovery from addiction: Social networks and social identity in addiction recovery. *Journal of Applied Social Psychology*, *47*(1), 35–46. Available from https://doi.org/10.1111/jasp.12420.

Bechara, A. (2005). Decision making, impulse control and loss of willpower to resist drugs: A neurocognitive perspective. *Nature Neuroscience*, *8*(11), 1458–1463. Available from https://doi.org/10.1038/nn1584.

Beckwith, M., Best, D., Dingle, G., Perryman, C., & Lubman, D. (2015). Predictors of flexibility in social identity among people entering a therapeutic community for substance abuse. *Alcoholism Treatment Quarterly*, *33*(1), 93–104. Available from https://doi.org/10.1080/07347324.2015.982465.

Bem, D. J. (1967). Self-perception: An alternative interpretation of cognitive dissonance phenomena. *Psychological Review*, *74*(3), 183–200. Available from https://doi.org/10.1037/h0024835.

Bernecker, K., Herrmann, M., Brandstätter, V., & Job, V. (2017). Implicit theories about willpower predict subjective well-being: Willpower theories and well-being . *Journal of Personality*, *85*(2), 136–150. Available from https://doi.org/10.1111/jopy.12225.

Best, D., Beckwith, M., Haslam, C., Alexander Haslam, S., Jetten, J., Mawson, E., & Lubman, D. I. (2016). Overcoming alcohol and other drug addiction as a process of social identity transition: The social identity model of recovery (SIMOR). *Addiction Research & Theory*, *24*(2), 111–123. Available from https://doi.org/10.3109/16066359.2015.1075980.

Bora, E., & Zorlu, N. (2017). Social cognition in alcohol use disorder: A meta-analysis: Social cognition in AUD. *Addiction*, *112*(1), 40–48. Available from https://doi.org/10.1111/add.13486.

Borsari, B., & Carey, K. B. (2001). Peer influences on college drinking: A review of the research. *Journal of Substance Abuse*, *13*(4), 391–424. Available from https://doi.org/10.1016/S0899-3289(01)00098-0.

Borsari, B., & Carey, K. B. (2003). Descriptive and injunctive norms in college drinking: A meta-analytic integration. *Journal of Studies on Alcohol*, *64*(3), 331–341.

Burnette, J. L., Russell, M. V., Hoyt, C. L., Orvidas, K., & Widman, L. (2018). An online growth mindset intervention in a sample of rural adolescent girls. *British Journal of Educational Psychology*, *88*(3), 428–445. Available from https://doi.org/10.1111/bjep.12192.

Carpenter, C. J. (2010). A meta-analysis of the effectiveness of health belief model variables in predicting behavior. *Health Communication*, *25*(8), 661–669. Available from https://doi.org/10.1080/10410236.2010.521906.

Cialdini, R. B., Kallgren, C. A., & Reno, R. R. (1991). A focus theory of normative conduct: A theoretical refinement and reevaluation of the role of norms in human behavior. *Advances in Experimental Social Psychology*, *24*(20), 1–243.

Clapp, J. D., Lange, J. E., Russell, C., Shillington, A., & Voas, R. B. (2003). A failed norms social marketing campaign. *Journal of Studies on Alcohol*, *64*(3), 409–414. Available from https://doi.org/10.15288/jsa.2003.64.409.

Cohen, G. L., & Sherman, D. K. (2014). The psychology of change: Self-affirmation and social psychological intervention. *Annual Review of Psychology*, *65*(1), 333–371. Available from https://doi.org/10.1146/annurev-psych-010213-115137.

Cooke, R., Dahdah, M., Norman, P., & French, D. P. (2016). How well does the theory of planned behaviour predict alcohol consumption? A systematic review and meta-analysis. *Health Psychology Review*, *10*(2), 148–167. Available from https://doi.org/10.1080/17437199.2014.947547.

Cooper, J. (2007). *Cognitive dissonance: Fifty years of a classic theory*. Thousand Oaks, CA: Sage Publications Ltd.

Cooper, J. (2012). Cognitive dissonance theory. In P. A. M. V. Lange, A. W. Kruglanski, & E. T. Higgins (Eds.), *Handbook of theories of social psychology* (Vol. 1, pp. 377–397). Thousand Oaks, CA: Sage Publications Ltd.

Cotter, J., Granger, K., Backx, R., Hobbs, M., Looi, C. Y., & Barnett, J. H. (2018). Social cognitive dysfunction as a clinical marker: A systematic review of meta-analyses across 30 clinical conditions. *Neuroscience & Biobehavioral Reviews*, *84*, 92–99. Available from https://doi.org/10.1016/j.neubiorev.2017.11.014.

Cunningham, J. A., Wild, T. C., Bondy, S. J., & Lin, E. (2001). Impact of normative feedback on problem drinkers: A small-area population study. *Journal of Studies on Alcohol*, *62*(2), 228–233.

Dal Cin, S., Worth, K. A., Gerrard, M., Gibbons, F. X., Stoolmiller, M., Wills, T. A., & Sargent, J. D. (2009). Watching and drinking: Expectancies, prototypes, and friends' alcohol use mediate the effect of exposure to alcohol use in movies on adolescent drinking. *Health Psychology*, *28*(4), 473–483. Available from https://doi.org/10.1037/a0014777.

DeJong, W., Schneider, S. K., Towvim, L. G., Murphy, M. J., Doerr, E. E., & Simonsen, N. R. (2006). A multisite randomized trial of social norms marketing campaigns to reduce college student drinking. *Journal of Studies on Alcohol*, *67*(6), 868–879. Available from https://doi.org/10.15288/jsa.2006.67.868.

DeJong, W., Schneider, S. K., Towvim, L. G., Murphy, M. J., Doerr, E. E., & Simonsen, N. R. (2009). A multisite randomized trial of social norms marketing campaigns to reduce college student drinking: A replication failure. *Substance Abuse*, *30*(2), 127–140. Available from https://doi.org/10.1080/08897070902802059.

Demmel, R., Nicolai, J., & Jenko, D. M. (2006). Self-efficacy and alcohol relapse: Concurrent validity of confidence measures, self-other discrepancies, and prediction of treatment outcome. *Journal of Studies on Alcohol*, *67*(4), 637–641. Available from https://doi.org/10.15288/jsa.2006.67.637.

Deutsch, M., & Gerard, H. B. (1955). A study of normative and informational social influences upon individual judgment. *The Journal of Abnormal and Social Psychology*, *51*(3), 629.

DiBello, A. M., Carey, K. B., & Cushing, V. (2018). Using counterattitudinal advocacy to change drinking: A pilot study. *Psychology of Addictive Behaviors*, *32*(2), 244–248. Available from https://doi.org/10.1037/adb0000334.

Dingle, G. A., Stark, C., Cruwys, T., & Best, D. (2015). Breaking good: Breaking ties with social groups may be good for recovery from substance misuse. *British Journal of Social Psychology*, *54*(2), 236–254. Available from https://doi.org/10.1111/bjso.12081.

Dotson, K. B., Dunn, M. E., & Bowers, C. A. (2015). Stand-alone personalized normative feedback for college student drinkers: A meta-analytic review, 2004 to 2014. *PLoS One*, *10*(10), 0139518.

Dweck, C. S. (2000). *Self-theories: Their role in motivation, personality, and development*. Philadelphia, PA: Psychology Press.

Dweck, C. S., & Leggett, E. L. (1988). A social-cognitive approach to motivation and personality. *Psychological Review*, *95*(2), 256–273. Available from https://doi.org/10.1037/0033-295X.95.2.256.

Ehret, P. J., & Sherman, D. K. (2018). Integrating self-affirmation and implementation intentions: Effects on college student drinking. *Annals of Behavioral Medicine*, *52*(8), 633–644. Available from https://doi.org/10.1093/abm/kax032.

Epton, T., Harris, P. R., Kane, R., van Koningsbruggen, G. M., & Sheeran, P. (2015). The impact of self-affirmation on health-behavior change: A meta-analysis. *Health Psychology*, *34*(3), 187–196. Available from https://doi.org/10.1037/hea0000116.

Erikson, M. G. (2019). Potentials and challenges when using possible selves in studies of student motivation. In H. Henderson, J. Stevenson, & A. M. Bathmaker (Eds.), *Possible selves and higher education: New interdisciplinary insights* (pp. 13–19). New York: Routledge.

Festinger, L. (1957). *A theory of cognitive dissonance*. Stanford: Stanford University Press.

Fiske, S. T., & Taylor, S. E. (2017). *Social cognition: From brains to culture* (Third edition). Los Angeles, London, New Delhi, Singapore, Washington, DC, Melbourne: SAGE.

Fox, K. J., Harris, P. R., & Jessop, D. C. (2017). Experimentally manipulated self-affirmation promotes reduced alcohol consumption in response to narrative information. *Annals of Behavioral Medicine*, *51*(6), 931–935. Available from https://doi.org/10.1007/s12160-017-9912-2.

Frings, D., & Albery, I. P. (2015). The social identity model of cessation maintenance: Formulation and initial evidence. *Addictive Behaviors*, *44*, 35–42. Available from https://doi.org/10.1016/j.addbeh.2014.10.023.

Gerrard, M., Gibbons, F. X., Houlihan, A. E., Stock, M. L., & Pomery, E. A. (2008). A dual-process approach to health risk decision making: The prototype willingness model. *Developmental Review*, *28*(1), 29–61. Available from https://doi.org/10.1016/j.dr.2007.10.001.

Gibbons, F. X., Houlihan, A. E., & Gerrard, M. (2009). Reason and reaction: The utility of a dual-focus, dual-processing perspective on promotion and prevention of adolescent health risk behaviour. *British Journal of Health Psychology*, *14*(Pt 2), 231–248. Available from https://doi.org/10.1348/135910708 × 376640.

Gibbons, F. X., Kingsbury, J. H., Wills, T. A., Finneran, S. D., Dal Cin, S., & Gerrard, M. (2016). Impulsivity moderates the effects of movie alcohol portrayals on adolescents' willingness to drink. *Psychology of Addictive Behaviors*, *30*(3), 325–334. Available from https://doi.org/10.1037/adb0000178.

Gibbons, F. X., Pomery, E. A., Gerrard, M., Sargent, J. D., Weng, C.-Y., & Wills, T. A. (2010). Media as social influence: Racial differences in the effects of peers and media on adolescent alcohol cognitions and consumption. *Psychology of Addictive Behaviors*, *24*(4), 649–659. Available from https://doi.org/10.1037/a0020768.

Glasman, L. R., & Albarracín, D. (2006). Forming attitudes that predict future behavior: A meta-analysis of the attitude-behavior relation. *Psychological Bulletin*, *132*(5), 778–822. Available from https://doi.org/10.1037/0033-2909.132.5.778.

Grant, N., Lawrence, M., Preti, A., Wykes, T., & Cella, M. (2017). Social cognition interventions for people with schizophrenia: A systematic review focussing on methodological quality and intervention modality. *Clinical Psychology Review*, *56*, 55–64. Available from https://doi.org/10.1016/j.cpr.2017.06.001.

Gray, H. M., LaPlante, D. A., Bannon, B. L., Ambady, N., & Shaffer, H. J. (2011). Development and validation of the alcohol identity implicit associations test (AI-IAT). *Addictive Behaviors*, *36*(9), 919–926. Available from https://doi.org/10.1016/j.addbeh.2011.05.003.

Greenwald, A. G., & Banaji, M. R. (1995). Implicit social cognition: Attitudes, self-esteem, and stereotypes. *Psychological Review*, *102*(1), 4–27.

Greenwald, A. G., Banaji, M. R., Rudman, L. A., Farnham, S. D., Nosek, B. A., & Mellott, D. S. (2002). A unified theory of implicit attitudes, stereotypes, self-esteem, and self-concept. *Psychological Review*, *109*(1), 3–25. Available from https://doi.org/10.1037/0033-295X.109.1.3.

Greenwald, A. G., McGhee, D. E., & Schwartz, J. L. K. (1998). Measuring individual differences in implicit cognition: The implicit association test. *Journal of Personality and Social Psychology*, *74*(6), 1464–1480. Available from https://doi.org/10.1037/0022-3514.74.6.1464.

Harmon-Jones, E., & Mills, J. (2019). In E. Harmon-Jones (Ed.), *An introduction to cognitive dissonance theory and an overview of current perspectives on the theory*. Washington, DC: American Psychological Association.

Haslam, C., Best, D., Dingle, G. A., Staiger, P. K., Savic, M., Bathish, R., ... Lubman, D. I. (2019). Social group membership before treatment for substance dependence predicts early identification and engagement with treatment communities. *Addiction Research & Theory*, 1–10. Available from https://doi.org/10.1080/16066359.2018.1537393.

Haslam, C., Cruwys, T., Haslam, S. A., Dingle, G., & Chang, M. X.-L. (2016). Groups 4 health: Evidence that a social-identity intervention that builds and strengthens social group membership improves mental health. *Journal of Affective Disorders*, *194*, 188–195. Available from https://doi.org/10.1016/j.jad.2016.01.010.

Hukkelberg, S. S., & Dykstra, J. L. (2009). Using the prototype/willingness model to predict smoking behaviour among Norwegian adolescents. *Addictive Behaviors, 34*(3), 270–276. Available from https://doi.org/10.1016/j.addbeh.2008.10.024.

Job, V., Dweck, C. S., & Walton, G. M. (2010). Ego depletion—Is it all in your head? Implicit theories about willpower affect self-regulation. *Psychological Science*. Available from https://doi.org/10.1177/0956797610384745.

Job, V., Walton, G. M., Bernecker, K., & Dweck, C. S. (2015). Implicit theories about willpower predict self-regulation and grades in everyday life. *Journal of Personality and Social Psychology, 108*(4), 637–647. Available from https://doi.org/10.1037/pspp0000014.

Jones, B. T., Corbin, W., & Fromme, K. (2001). A review of expectancy theory and alcohol consumption. *Addiction, 96*(1), 57–72. Available from https://doi.org/10.1046/j.1360-0443.2001.961575.x.

Kadden, R. M., & Litt, M. D. (2011). The role of self-efficacy in the treatment of substance use disorders. *Addictive Behaviors, 36*(12), 1120–1126. Available from https://doi.org/10.1016/j.addbeh.2011.07.032.

Kohn, R., Saxena, S., Levav, I., & Saraceno, B. (2004). The treatment gap in mental health care. *Bulletin of the World Health Organization, 82*, 858–866.

Le Berre, A.-P., Fama, R., & Sullivan, E. V. (2017). Executive functions, memory, and social cognitive deficits and recovery in chronic alcoholism: A critical review to inform future research. *Alcoholism: Clinical and Experimental Research, 41*(8), 1432–1443. Available from https://doi.org/10.1111/acer.13431.

Lee, C.-K., Corte, C., Stein, K. F., Park, C. G., Finnegan, L., & McCreary, L. L. (2015). Prospective effects of possible selves on alcohol consumption in adolescents: Possible selves and adolescent alcohol use. *Research in Nursing & Health, 38*(1), 71–81. Available from https://doi.org/10.1002/nur.21641.

Leeman, R. F., Perez, E., Nogueira, C., & DeMartini, K. S. (2015). Very-brief, web-based interventions for reducing alcohol use and related problems among college students: A review. *Frontiers in Psychiatry, 6*, 129. Available from https://doi.org/10.3389/fpsyt.2015.00129.

Lewis, M. A., & Neighbors, C. (2006). Social norms approaches using descriptive drinking norms. Education: A review of the research on personalized normative feedback. *Journal of American College Health, 54*(4), 213–218.

Lindgren, K. P., Baldwin, S. A., Olin, C. C., Wiers, R. W., Teachman, B. A., Norris, J., ... Neighbors, C. (2018). Evaluating within-person change in implicit measures of alcohol associations: Increases in alcohol associations predict increases in drinking risk and vice versa. *Alcohol and Alcoholism*. Available from https://doi.org/10.1093/alcalc/agy012.

Lindgren, K. P., Neighbors, C., Gasser, M. L., Ramirez, J. J., & Cvencek, D. (2016). A review of implicit and explicit substance self-concept as a predictor of alcohol and tobacco use and misuse. *The American Journal of Drug and Alcohol Abuse*, 1–10. Available from https://doi.org/10.1080/00952990.2016.1229324.

Lindgren, K. P., Neighbors, C., Teachman, B. A., Baldwin, S. A., Norris, J., Kaysen, D., & Wiers, R. W. (2016). Implicit alcohol associations, especially drinking identity, predict drinking over time. *Health Psychology, 35*(8), 908–918. Available from https://doi.org/10.1037/hea0000396.

Lindgren, K. P., Wiers, R. W., Teachman, B. A., Gasser, M. L., Westgate, E. C., Cousijn, J., & Neighbors, C. (2015). Attempted training of alcohol approach and drinking identity associations in US undergraduate drinkers: Null results from two studies. *PLoS One, 10*(8), e0134642. Available from https://doi.org/10.1371/journal.pone.0134642.

Litt, D. M., & Lewis, M. A. (2016). Examining a social reaction model in the prediction of adolescent alcohol use. *Addictive Behaviors*, *60*, 160–164. Available from https://doi.org/10.1016/j.addbeh.2016.04.009.

Markus, H., & Nurius, P. (1986). Possible selves. *American Psychologist*, *41*(9), 954–969. Available from https://doi.org/10.1037/0003-066X.41.9.954.

Marlatt, G. A., & Donovan, D. M. (2005). *Relapse prevention: Maintenance strategies in the treatment of addictive behaviors*. New York: Guilford Press.

Mattern, J. L., & Neighbors, C. (2004). Social norms campaigns: Examining the relationship between changes in perceived norms and changes in drinking levels. *Journal of Studies on Alcohol*, *65*(4), 489–493. Available from https://doi.org/10.15288/jsa.2004.65.489.

McCrady, B. S., Owens, M. D., Borders, A. Z., & Brovko, J. M. (2014). Psychosocial approaches to alcohol use disorders since 1940: A review. *Journal of Studies on Alcohol and Drugs, Supplement* (s17), 68–78. Available from https://doi.org/10.15288/jsads.2014.s17.68.

McEachan, R. R. C., Conner, M., Taylor, N. J., & Lawton, R. J. (2011). Prospective prediction of health-related behaviours with the theory of planned behaviour: A meta-analysis. *Health Psychology Review*, *5*(2), 97–144. Available from https://doi.org/10.1080/17437199.2010.521684.

McQueen, A., & Klein, W. M. P. (2006). Experimental manipulations of self-affirmation: A systematic review. *Self and Identity*, *5*(4), 289–354. Available from https://doi.org/10.1080/15298860600805325.

Mereish, E. H., Goldbach, J. T., Burgess, C., & DiBello, A. M. (2017). Sexual orientation, minority stress, social norms, and substance use among racially diverse adolescents. *Drug and Alcohol Dependence*, *178*, 49–56. Available from https://doi.org/10.1016/j.drugalcdep.2017.04.013.

Miller, M. B., Leffingwell, T., Claborn, K., Meier, E., Walters, S., & Neighbors, C. (2013). Personalized feedback interventions for college alcohol misuse: An update of Walters & Neighbors (2005). *Psychology of Addictive Behaviors*, *27*(4), 909–920. Available from https://doi.org/10.1037/a0031174.

Miller, W. R., & Rollnick, S. (1991). *Motivational interviewing: Preparing people to change addictive behavior*. New York: Guilford Press.

Miller, W. R., & Rollnick, S. (2013). *Motivational interviewing: Helping people* (3rd ed.). New York: Guilford Press, change.

Montano, D. E., & Kasprzyk, D. (2008). In K. Glanz, B. K. Rimer, & K. Viswanath (Eds.), *Theory of reasoned action, theory of planned behavior, and the integrated behavioral model*. San Francisco, CA: Jossey-Bass.

Moreno, M. A., & Whitehill, J. M. (2014). Influence of social media on alcohol use in adolescents and young adults. *Alcohol Research: Current Reviews*, *36*(1), 91–100.

Morgenstern, J., Kuerbis, A., Houser, J., Muench, F. J., Shao, S. J., & Treloar, H. (2016). Within-person associations between daily motivation and self-efficacy and drinking among problem drinkers in treatment. *Psychology of Addictive Behaviors*, *30*(6), 630–638. Available from https://doi.org/10.1037/adb0000204.

Murru, E. C., & Ginis, K. A. M. (2010). Imagining the possibilities: The effects of a possible selves intervention on self-regulatory efficacy and exercise behavior. *Journal of Sport and Exercise Psychology*, *32*(4), 537–554. Available from https://doi.org/10.1123/jsep.32.4.537.

Napper, L., Harris, P. R., & Epton, T. (2009). Developing and testing a self-affirmation manipulation. *Self and Identity*, *8*(1), 45–62. Available from https://doi.org/10.1080/15298860802079786.

Neighbors, C., Lee, C. M., Lewis, M. A., Fossos, N., & Larimer, M. E. (2007). Are social norms the best predictor of outcomes among heavy-drinking college students. *Journal of Studies on Alcohol and Drugs*, *68*(4), 556–565.

Norman, P., Cameron, D., Epton, T., Webb, T. L., Harris, P. R., Millings, A., & Sheeran, P. (2018). A randomized controlled trial of a brief online intervention to reduce alcohol consumption in new university students: Combining self-affirmation, theory of planned behaviour messages, and implementation intentions. *British Journal of Health Psychology*, *23*(1), 108–127. Available from https://doi.org/10.1111/bjhp.12277.

Office of the Surgeon General. (2016). *Facing addiction in America: The Surgeon General's report on alcohol, drugs, and health*. Retrieved from U.S. Department of Health and Human Services (HHS) website: <https://addiction.surgeongeneral.gov/surgeon-generalsreport.pdf>.

Oyserman, D., & James, L. (2009). Possible selves: From content to process. In K. D. Markman, W. M. P. Klein, & J. Suhr (Eds.), *Handbook of imagination and mental stimulation* (pp. 337–394). New York: Psychology Press.

Oyserman, D., Terry, K., & Bybee, D. (2002). A possible selves intervention to enhance school involvement. *Journal of Adolescence*, *25*(3), 313–326. Available from https://doi.org/10.1006/jado.2002.0474.

Pedersen, E. R., Parast, L., Marshall, G. N., Schell, T. L., & Neighbors, C. (2017). A randomized controlled trial of a web-based, personalized normative feedback alcohol intervention for young-adult veterans. *Journal of Consulting and Clinical Psychology*, *85*(5), 459–470. Available from https://doi.org/10.1037/ccp0000187.

Penn, D. L., Roberts, D. L., Combs, D., & Sterne, A. (2007). Best practices: The development of the social cognition and interaction training program for schizophrenia spectrum disorders. *Psychiatric Services*, *58*(4), 449–451. Available from https://doi.org/10.1176/ps.2007.58.4.449.

Perkins, H. W. (2002). Social norms and the prevention of alcohol misuse in collegiate contexts. *Journal of Studies on Alcohol, Supplement* (s14), 164–172. Available from https://doi.org/10.15288/jsas.2002.s14.164.

Perkins, H. W., Linkenbach, J. W., Lewis, M. A., & Neighbors, C. (2010). Effectiveness of social norms media marketing in reducing drinking and driving: A statewide campaign. *Addictive Behaviors*, *35*(10), 866–874. Available from https://doi.org/10.1016/j.addbeh.2010.05.004.

Prentice, D. A., & Miller, D. T. (1993). Pluralistic ignorance and alcohol use on campus: Some consequences of misperceiving the social norm. *Journal of Personality and Social Psychology*, *64*(2), 243.

Quinlan, S. L., Jaccard, J., & Blanton, H. (2006). A decision theoretic and prototype conceptualization of possible selves: implications for the prediction of risk behavior. *Journal of Personality*, *74*(2), 599–630. Available from https://doi.org/10.1111/j.1467-6494.2006.00386.x.

Reid, A. E., & Carey, K. B. (2015). Interventions to reduce college student drinking: State of the evidence for mechanisms of behavior change. *Clinical Psychology Review*, *40*, 213–224. Available from https://doi.org/10.1016/j.cpr.2015.06.006.

Reno, R. R., Cialdini, R. B., & Kallgren, C. A. (1993). The transsituational influence of social norms. *Journal of Personality and Social Psychology*, *64*(1), 104.

Rivis, A., Sheeran, P., & Armitage, C. J. (2006). Augmenting the theory of planned behaviour with the prototype/willingness model: Predictive validity of actor versus abstainer prototypes for adolescents' health-protective and health-risk intentions. *British Journal of Health Psychology*, *11*(Pt 3), 483–500. Available from https://doi.org/10.1348/135910705 × 70327.

Rodriguez, L. M., Neighbors, C., Rinker, D. V., Lewis, M. A., Lazorwitz, B., Gonzales, R. G., & Larimer, M. E. (2015). Remote versus in-lab computer-delivered personalized normative feedback interventions for college student drinking. *Journal of Consulting and Clinical Psychology, 83*(3), 455–463. Available from https://doi.org/10.1037/a0039030.

Rodriguez, L. M., Neighbors, C., Walker, D., & Walton, T. (2019). Mechanisms of intervention efficacy for soldiers with untreated substance use disorder. *Manuscript in Review*.

Russell, C. A., Clapp, J. D., & DeJong, W. (2005). Done 4: Analysis of a failed social norms marketing campaign. *Health Communication, 17*(1), 57–65. Available from https://doi.org/10.1207/s15327027hc1701_4.

Scheier, L. M., & Botvin, G. J. (1997). Expectancies as mediators of the effects of social influences and alcohol knowledge on adolescent alcohol use: A prospective analysis. *Psychology of Addictive Behaviors, 11*(1), 48–64. Available from https://doi.org/10.1037/0893-164X.11.1.48.

Schroder, H. S., Dawood, S., Yalch, M. M., Donnellan, M. B., & Moser, J. S. (2016). Evaluating the domain specificity of mental health–related mind-sets. *Social Psychological and Personality Science, 7*(6), 508–520. Available from https://doi.org/10.1177/1948550616644657.

Scribner, R. A., Theall, K. P., Mason, K., Simonsen, N., Schneider, S. K., Towvim, L. G., & DeJong, W. (2011). Alcohol prevention on college campuses: The moderating effect of the alcohol environment on the effectiveness of social norms marketing campaigns. *Journal of Studies on Alcohol and Drugs, 72*(2), 232–239. Available from https://doi.org/10.15288/jsad.2011.72.232.

Sharma, M. (2005). Enhancing the effectiveness of alcohol and drug education programs through social cognitive theory. *Journal of Alcohol and Drug Education, 49*(3), 3–7.

Sherif, M. (1936). *The psychology of social norms*. Oxford: Harper.

Sherman, D. K., & Cohen, G. L. (2006). The psychology of self-defense: Self-affirmation theory. In M. P. Zanna (Ed.), *Advances in experimental social psychology* (Vol. 38, pp. 183–242). San Diego, CA: Elsevier Academic Press.

Song, H., Kim, J., Kwon, R. J., & Jung, Y. (2013). Anti-smoking educational game using avatars as visualized possible selves. *Computers in Human Behavior, 29*(5), 2029–2036. Available from https://doi.org/10.1016/j.chb.2013.04.008.

Stacy, A. W., & Wiers, R. W. (2010). Implicit cognition and addiction: A tool for explaining paradoxical behavior. *Annual Review of Clinical Psychology, 6*(1), 551–575. Available from https://doi.org/10.1146/annurev.clinpsy.121208.131444.

Steele, C. M. (1999). The psychology of self-affirmation: Sustaining the integrity of the self. In R. F. Baumeister (Ed.), *The self in social psychology* (pp. 372–390). New York: Psychology Press.

Strack, F., & Deutsch, R. (2004). Reflective and impulsive determinants of social behavior. *Personality and Social Psychology Review: An Official Journal of the Society for Personality and Social Psychology, Inc, 8*(3), 220–247. Available from https://doi.org/10.1207/s15327957pspr0803_1.

Sweeney, A. M., & Moyer, A. (2015). Self-affirmation and responses to health messages: A meta-analysis on intentions and behavior. *Health Psychology, 34*(2), 149–159. Available from https://doi.org/10.1037/hea0000110.

Tajfel, H., & Turner, J. C. (1979). An intergrative theory of intergroup conflict. In W. G. Austin, & S. Worchel (Eds.), *The social psychology of intergroup relations* (pp. 33–47). Monterey, CA: Brooks/Cole Publishing Co.

Todd, J., Kothe, E., Mullan, B., & Monds, L. (2016). Reasoned versus reactive prediction of behaviour: A meta-analysis of the prototype willingness model. *Health Psychology Review, 10*(1), 1–24. Available from https://doi.org/10.1080/17437199.2014.922895.

Turner, J. C., Hogg, M. A., Oakes, P. J., Reicher, S. D., & Wetherell, M. S. (1987). *Rediscovering the social group: A self-categorization theory*. Oxford: Blackwell.

Turner, J., Perkins, W., & Bauerle, J. (2008). Declining negative consequences related to alcohol misuse among students exposed to a social norms marketing intervention on a college campus. *Journal of American College Health*, *57*(1), 85–93. Available from https://doi.org/10.3200/JACH.57.1.85-94.

Walters, S. T., & Neighbors, C. (2005). Feedback interventions for college alcohol misuse: What, why and for whom. *Addictive Behaviors*, *30*(6), 1168–1182. Available from https://doi.org/10.1016/j.addbeh.2004.12.005.

Wiers, R., & Gladwin, T. E. (2017). *Reflective and impulsive processes in addiction and the role of motivation. Reflective and impulsive determinants of human behavior* (pp. 173–188). New York: Psychology Press.

Wiers, R. W., Eberl, C., Rinck, M., Becker, E. S., & Lindenmeyer, J. (2011). Retraining automatic action tendencies changes alcoholic patients' approach bias for alcohol and improves treatment outcome. *Psychological Science*, *22*(4), 490–497. Available from https://doi.org/10.1177/0956797611400615.

Wiers, R. W., Rinck, M., Kordts, R., Houben, K., & Strack, F. (2010). Retraining automatic action-tendencies to approach alcohol in hazardous drinkers. *Addiction (Abingdon, England)*, *105*(2), 279–287. Available from https://doi.org/10.1111/j.1360-0443.2009.02775.x.

Wiers, R. W., van Woerden, N., Smulders, F. T. Y., & de Jong, P. J. (2002). Implicit and explicit alcohol-related cognitions in heavy and light drinkers. *Journal of Abnormal Psychology*, *111*(4), 648–658.

World Health Organization. (2019). Alcohol. Retrieved from <https://www.who.int/news-room/fact-sheets/detail/alcohol>.

Yeh, M.-Y. (2008). Measuring readiness to change and locus of control belief among male alcohol-dependent patients in Taiwan: Comparison of the different degrees of alcohol dependence: Alcohol dependence. *Psychiatry and Clinical Neurosciences*, *62*(5), 533–539. Available from https://doi.org/10.1111/j.1440-1819.2008.01846.x.

Chapter 22

Taking social identity into practice

Genevieve A. Dingle[1], Isabella Ingram[2], Catherine Haslam[1] and Peter J. Kelly[2]
[1]*School of Psychology, The University of Queensland, Brisbane, Australia,* [2]*School of Psychology, The University of Wollongong, Wollongong, Australia*

In contrast to most other theories that emphasize how individual biological or psychological factors explain the onset and maintenance of alcohol use disorders, the social identity approach emphasizes social influence and the role of social group relationships on drinking behavior and problems. Social identity theorising (after Tajfel & Turner, 1979; Turner, Hogg, Oakes, Reicher, & Wetherell, 1987), recognizes that our sense of self is informed not only by attributes and traits that are unique to us as individuals (e.g., "I am artistic"), but also by the social groups to which we belong (e.g., "we single parents", or "we cyclists"). The groups that form part of our social identity can influence the way we think, feel and act in different situations. For example, membership in groups can affect our response to stress and challenge, to whom we turn for support, and to whom we give support (e.g., helping and volunteering) (Jetten, Haslam, Iyer, & Haslam, 2009). The social identity approach applied to issues of health and wellbeing has been dubbed the Social Cure approach (see Haslam, Jetten, Cruwys, Dingle, & Haslam, 2018; Jetten, Haslam, & Haslam, 2012; Jetten, Haslam, Haslam, Dingle, & Jones, 2014).

In this chapter, we explore how the social identity approach applies to addiction recovery. First, we will consider the social influence on drinking behavior and evidence suggesting that the need for belonging is a driving force for problematic drinking. Then we will describe research that demonstrates the importance of moving away from heavy drinking groups and reconnecting with or joining sober groups and communities as determinants of ongoing recovery. Finally, we describe Groups 4 Belonging – a new intervention that integrates the social identity approach to health with mindfulness based cognitive therapy strategies to help participants successfully engage with sober groups that will help to support and sustain their recovery.

The Handbook of Alcohol Use - Understandings from Synapse to Society.
DOI: https://doi.org/10.1016/B978-0-12-816720-5.00010-4

Social influences on drinking

When it comes to alcohol use, social influence is a potent force that takes a number of forms. Parents, siblings and friends commonly model drinking behavior, which can affect a young person's drinking behavior at that time and later on in development (e.g., Eisenberg, Toumbourou, Catalano, & Hemphill, 2014; Van Der Vorst, Engels, Meeus, Deković, & Van Leeuwe, 2005). Peer influence operates both face-to-face and online, with one study finding that exposure to their peers' alcohol-related social media posts predicted students' drinking behavior 6 months later; an effect that was particularly strong in males (Boyle, LaBrie, Froidevaux, & Witkovic, 2016). Wider media is also influential with research finding a positive association between exposure to alcohol advertising and drinking outcomes in young people (Morgenstern, Isensee, Sargent, & Hanewinkel, 2011). These behaviors and representations form the basis of group and societal norms that have the capacity to influence us in positive or negative ways (Haslam et al., 2018).

Social influence also affects recovery trajectories. People who relapse after treatment for alcohol use disorders commonly list social pressure as a reason (Hodgins, el-Guebaly, & Armstrong, 1995). Indeed, whole relapse prevention programs have been developed around understanding the (often social) contextual risks for relapse and developing skills such as drink refusal self-efficacy to avoid relapsing in these situations (e.g., Witkiewitz and Marlatt, 2004). People's need for belonging and connection does not diminish during treatment; we continue to connect with others even if they are heavy drinkers or substance users. Therefore, social influence needs to be carefully managed during and after treatment to ensure ongoing recovery.

Social identity and problematic drinking

Increasingly, evidence is showing that social group ties have a central role to play in the development and recovery from addiction, and that these trajectories might best be understood as processes of identity change that are driven by people's social group memberships. The onset of alcohol misuse involves a change from seeing oneself as a 'social drinker' to seeing oneself as a 'heavy drinker' or an 'alcoholic' that occurs in the context of increasing involvement and perceived importance of drinking groups (ingroups) relative to non-drinking groups (outgroups). Sometimes this process is self-identified, but in other cases, it is people close to the individual who identify them as 'an alcoholic' – see quote from a participant in Dingle, Cruwys, and Frings (2015, p. 6), below. Similarly, successful attempts at recovery typically involve distancing from heavy drinking groups and affiliating more strongly with either new or pre-existing non-heavy-drinking groups that support a new 'recovery' or 'non-drinker' identity. The latter transition becomes possible when people come to see that membership of heavy drinking groups need not define them and that by moving away from these groups - or limiting contact with these groups to times and places that are low risk for drinking - they can regain a positive identity.

In fact, two distinct social identity related pathways have been found among adults experiencing an addiction (Dingle et al., 2015; see Fig. 22.1). Interviews with adults residing in a drug and alcohol therapeutic community (a third of whom nominated alcohol as their primary drug of concern) revealed one pathway in which participants described a *loss of valued social groups and identities* due to the onset of addiction. As the following comment illustrates, these individuals described their identity as a substance user in negative and stigmatized terms, even in comparison to other substance users:

> *My mate who I lived with used to smoke pot and drink but he never used to drink as much. He told me that I was getting worse and worse, and eventually he said: "in my consensus I think you are an alcoholic now."*
>
> Male in treatment for alcohol use

Other participants described a second pathway into addiction, characterized by *social identity gain* enabled by becoming a member of a new valued group or network. This was especially true for individuals who had been socially isolated prior to addiction and who found that the onset of their addiction provided them with new group memberships that helped to meet their need for belonging. In the words of one participant:

> *All I cared about was fitting in with some people and I found that through bad kids and gangs, and sort of the crime, and all that kind of lifted. Obviously drinking, my older sister introduced me to drinking when I was 12, by the age of 13, I was pretty much binge drinking every day at school.*
>
> Male, in treatment for amphetamine use

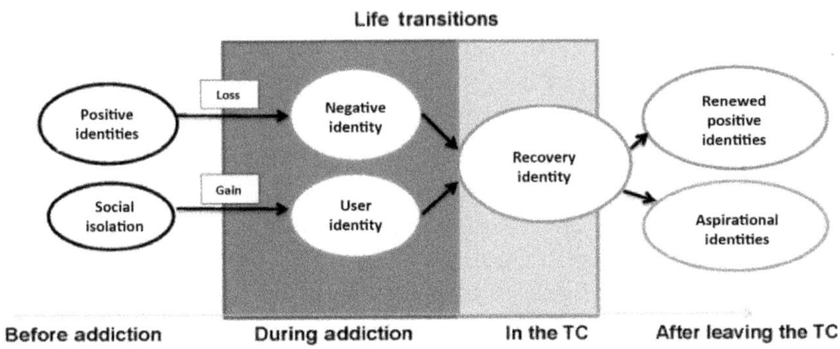

FIGURE 22.1 Thematic map derived from interviews with adults in a therapeutic community showing two distinct social identity related pathways into and out of addiction. *Reprinted from Dingle, G. A., Cruwys, T., & Frings, D. (2015). Social identities as pathways into and out of addiction.* Frontiers in Psychology, 6, *1795. doi: 10.3389/fpsyg.2015.01795, with permission of the authors.*

Beyond the therapeutic community context, social influences on problematic drinking have also been highlighted among participants of outpatient alcohol treatment and aftercare (e.g., Stout, Kelly, Magill, & Pagano, 2012). Irrespective of the treatment setting or the person's pathway in to problematic drinking, a driving force appears to be a need for belonging (Dingle, 2018), which has been described as a basic human need (Baumeister & Leary, 1995; Maslow, 1943). Somewhat counterintuitively, this need for belonging and reconnecting with others can also prompt people to do something about their problematic drinking and to enter treatment (Dingle et al., 2015).

Social factors at treatment entry

Entering a residential therapeutic community (TC) for abstinence-based treatment and rehabilitation requires the individual to move into the community for a period of several months, constantly surrounded by peers in shared accommodation and in therapeutic groups, and to learn how to live without substance use. Some people do not feel comfortable with this social environment. One study reported that 17% of people leave the TC within the first week (Darke, Campbell, & Popple, 2012). So what contributes to engagement and identification with others in a TC?

There is emerging evidence that people's group memberships *before* treatment entry and the extent to which they saw themselves as in recovery at the point of treatment entry contributed to their readiness to develop a TC identity (Haslam, Best, Dingle, et al., 2019). When individuals form a new social identity as a member of the TC, they report feeling a sense of acceptance and freedom from judgement and discrimination. As a participant in the study by Dingle et al. (2015) described:

> *Everyone was just so supportive; sometimes it felt like they are psychic because I would just be sitting somewhere having a cigarette and someone would ask "How you traveling in your head?" and I would think, "How did you know I was in that bad headspace right now?"*
>
> Female, 3 weeks in treatment for alcohol use

Therapeutic Communities promote recovery by providing the basis for a shared identity among their members. This shared identity is often centered around norms of abstinence and "right living" (e.g., embracing values such as honesty and respect for self and others, and adoption of a healthy lifestyle). The social identity approach suggests that it is this sense of connection to others in turn increases members' willingness to engage with treatment and to accept support within the TC (Haslam, O'Brien, Jetten, Vormedal, & Penna, 2005). It is also the case that the groups we identify with give us meaning and purpose, an opportunity to 'enact' our new identity through contributing to the group and supporting others. This is important because identity is connected to behavior in a sort of self-fulfilling prophecy. A series of experimental studies of behavioral confirmation have established that randomly manipulated expectations about an individual can lead others to treat that person accordingly in social interactions, and this treatment in turn elicits behavior from the individual that confirms the initially false expectation (see Vignoles, 2017). In a recovery context that supports an individuals' identity as a sober and responsible person, they are likely to enact this identity through their behavior. This is reflected in the following quote from another participant in the Dingle et al. (2015) study:

> *You have to work your way into these positions. You become a mentor – leading a new person into life at [the therapeutic community]. Took a while for me to get to be a mentor. I was stubborn. Everything was black and white. So it took a while for me to be settled in [the therapeutic community] in a way that I could mentor a new person. The next step is residential house manager. You are in control of 10–12 people in the house.*
>
> Male, 27 weeks in treatment for alcohol misuse

The importance of contributing to the group – realised through identity enactment—is also apparent among members of mutual support groups such as Alcoholics Anonymous (AA). Along these lines, a comprehensive analysis of mutual support groups by Moos (2008) found that bonding and support, obtaining an abstinence-focused role model, and doing service work within the group were all vital ingredients to successful outcomes. These features of enactment also emerged in a review of 24 studies that investigated the value of AA membership for people with alcohol dependence (Groh, Jason, & Keys, 2008). The common theme here is that people must feel a sense of belonging within their treatment group or community in order to stay engaged and to adopt attitudes and behaviors that are consistent with recovery and become embedded in their self-concept as a non-drinker.

Adjustment to social identity change: a theoretical framework

As the foregoing literature suggests, recovery from addiction is far from straightforward and there are a range of challenges that can undermine this process. However, researchers have also identified a number of mechanisms that can support well-being during life transitions to ease the process. According to the Social Identity Model of Identity Change (SIMIC, Fig. 22.2), wellbeing is protected to the extent that people (a) gain new positive group memberships and/or (b) maintain their connections with existing positive groups, provided (c) that these group memberships are compatible (Haslam, Holme, et al., 2008; Jetten, Haslam, Haslam, & Branscombe, 2009). This model has been validated in the context of a range of life transitions including commencement of university study, becoming a parent, becoming homeless, retirement from the workforce, and immigrating (see

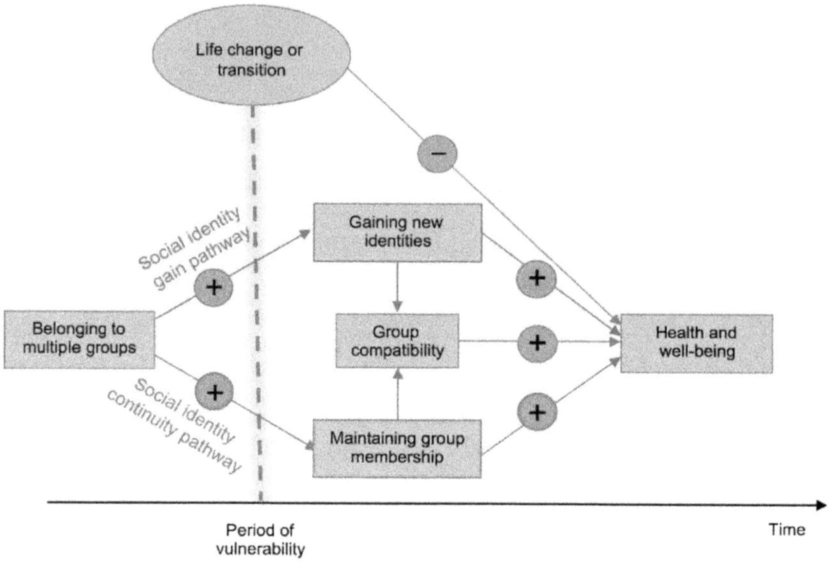

FIGURE 22.2 The social identity model of identity change (SIMIC) (see Haslam, Holme, et al., 2008; Jetten et al., 2009).

Haslam et al., 2018 for a review). Much of this research shows that maintaining group memberships and identities that existed before the transition as well as gaining new group memberships and identities after the transition are better for health and wellbeing. This is because the individual has more group based psychosocial resources to help them cope with the transition. However, in the case of addiction, there is clear evidence that moving away from former groups and identities (i.e., those associated with heavy drinking) is better for health and wellbeing (Dingle, Stark, Cruwys, & Best, 2015). Thus, joining and identifying with new sober groups and networks may therefore be the key to successful recovery.

Speaking to this is the Social Identity Model of Recovery (SIMOR; Best, Beckwith, & Haslam, 2015) that describes recovery as a socially negotiated process that involves changes in the proportion of a person's social group memberships that serve to support either substance use or abstinence. At the start of the recovery journey, a person's substance using groups will tend to be more salient and influential. Early recovery involves increased exposure to groups that support recovery and a commensurate shift in the salience and influence of these groups. Finally, as a person enters a phase of stable recovery, recovery-supportive groups gain greater meaning in a person's life. Here group norms and attitudes that support recovery exert a strong influence and abstinence becomes embedded as part of a person's self-concept. The SIMOR model recognizes that a person's recovery trajectory is not only contingent on their membership of structured addiction treatment groups (such as TC, AA, and other therapy groups connected with alcohol and other drug treatment services) but is also shaped by their membership of a wider array of groups that support (or do not support) abstinence and recovery. In these terms, recovery maintenance and relapse hinge on the relative influence of these counter-vailing social psychological forces.

Evidence that social groups and identities matter in recovery

Consistent with the SIMOR model, there is evidence of identity change involving a shift from self-categorizing as an 'addict' to a 'person in recovery' or a 'non-user' in the course of treatment (Buckingham, Frings, & Albery, 2013). This research identified two processes linked to higher abstinence self-efficacy and better health. The first process, *evaluative differentiation*, involves people in treatment coming to evaluate the addict identity increasingly negatively at the same time that they evaluate the recovery identity more positively. The second process, *identity preference*, occurs when a person identifies more strongly as a person in recovery at the same time that they identify less strongly as an addict; thereby gaining a more positive sense of self. Buckingham et al. (2013) found that greater evaluative differentiation was associated with higher self-efficacy and reduced relapse and substance use among members attending AA and NA in the UK. Furthermore, identity preference was related to higher self-efficacy and lower relapse among a sample of people quitting smoking.

Further evidence that socially mediated identity change is implicated in recovery comes from studies conducted in therapeutic communities. One study (Dingle et al., 2015) showed that early in TC treatment, most participants identified quite highly with their substance-using social groups. During the first month of treatment, however, 76% of the participants reported a decrease in their sense of identification with substance-using social groups, while their identification with other members of the TC increased steadily across fortnightly measurement intervals. The researchers conducted follow-up assessments with a representative subsample of 60 of participants around seven months after they had left the TC. Here the extent of identity change (measured by the difference between user identity and recovery identity ratings over the treatment period) accounted for 34% of the variance in drinking quantity, 41% of the variance in drinking frequency, 5% of the variance in other drug use frequency, and 49% of the variance in life satisfaction. Importantly too, these analyses controlled for initial substance dependence severity and social identity ratings at entry to the TC. This pattern of results was replicated in a larger sample of 307 adults entering five TCs (see Best et al., 2016 for study details). In this study, the extent to which participants endorsed a recovery identity over a substance user identity was related to their commitment to sobriety, mood, and wellbeing six months after entry to a TC, after accounting for substance related variables and identity scores at entry to treatment.

A qualitative analysis involving in-depth interviews with 8 adults who had remained abstinent 12 months after treatment in a private hospital alcohol treatment service further supports the importance of social identity and network change in recovery (Whitehead, 2010). In this study, there were six men and two women, aged from 28 to 57 years. From thematic analysis of interview transcripts, four themes emerged: factors that led problematic addiction/ drinking; strategies to ensure abstinence; processes of identity change; and integration of the 'addict' and the 'non-drinker' identities. In this clinical setting, patients described both social and emotional factors that led to becoming a problematic drinker in that they had relied on alcohol as a way of coping with other issues such as anxiety, sleep and health problems, and a sense of overwhelming responsibility.

My father died...and basically I was told that I am now the man of the family. I must be there to support my whole family. ...it put me with a focus to trying to do too much for everyone else, and basically run myself down and um... yeah take too much on.

Participant 3

Strategies to ensure abstinence in this sample included using alternatives to alcohol to manage anxiety and cravings, and consciously thinking of the negative consequences of drinking.

What you thought was helping you was probably making you much worse as you weren't dealing with it [anxiety].

Participant 1

What has your drinking cost you in your life? Have a look at the following. Bring up awareness and say well I've lost this.

Participant 8

Using social support networks was a prevalent strategy described as essential for successful recovery. These were in the form of family and friends, AA meetings, and aftercare groups at the hospital. Formal support groups allowed patients the opportunity for self-reflection, then sharing personal experiences with people who shared a social identity (Whitehead, 2010).

You see other people, I think that's where the groups are just magic, pure magic. Because you can see ... you know they, somebody else might have exactly the same problem as you and they go for it in a different way, and you think, 'oh I might try that.'

Participant 6

Participants also described how they managed their social contact to minimize the risk of drinking:

Stay away from old stomping grounds for a while. That's been really important.

Participant 8

What I do find now, when people try to say to you, 'Come on, even if you only have one or two', I say, 'It's not an issue, I don't want a drink'.

Participant 2

For these hospital patients, it appeared that the successful transition from 'problematic drinker' to 'non-drinker' involved some degree of acceptance and reconciling of the two identities:

Yeah. I can't have it [alcohol] - it's simple as that. So, I suppose I was an addict to alcohol, so I'll always be an addict to alcohol. If you look at it like that. I want to always be aware of it. That's where the complacency thing comes in. But it's not wake up in the morning and think "God I'm an addict, can't drink". No - what a way to live... oh that would be horrid. That would... you're putting too much value on it.

Participant 6

Trying not to make addiction a huge part of my life. Trying to be aware that it's there, as a much smaller part of my life, but filling the void.

Participant 5

These quotations suggest that for some people, recovery involves accepting that both drinking and non-drinking identities are part of your life. For others, it is about reducing the emphasis on their drinking identity so that it does not take over their whole self-concept. Thus, reconciliation of social group mediated identities is important to achieve in recovery. Helping people to recognize these identities in their wider social network is a first step towards working with them in treatment. A procedure called Social Identity Mapping was designed for this purpose.

Social identity mapping in recovery

Social identity mapping (SIM; Cruwys et al., 2016) provides a useful visual representation of a person's social group memberships that can capture current networks and also those around periods of transition (e.g., when entering into treatment, before becoming dependent). The mapping exercise can be completed paper-and-pencil style using sticky notes and colored pens (Cruwys, Steffens, et al., 2016; Haslam et al., 2018), or online using a web-based version (Bentley et al., 2019). In the former, participants write each of their meaningful social groups on a sticky note, representing the importance of each group by selecting a small, medium or large sized sticky note. They then affix the notes onto a large piece of backing paper, and add ratings (out of 10) to each group for variables of interest such as: how positive they feel about being a member of each group and how much support they get from the group. They draw lines between the groups to represent the extent to which pairs of groups are compatible. Finally, representing an extension to the addiction treatment context (where it is referred to as SIM:AR), participants add sticky dots to each group to represent the group norms in relation to alcohol use. Red dots indicating heavy use, yellow dots indicating social or occasional drinking, and green dots indicating non-drinking or people in recovery (Beckwith et al., 2019; Best et al., 2014; Haslam, Best, Dingle, et al., 2019).

Once completed, participants can choose to share their maps in a treatment group, and use their map as a basis for the development of social network change goals to support their recovery. These goals might include renewing ties with groups that are supportive of abstinence, decreasing or modifying the nature of activities with groups whose norms support heavy substance use, or developing new group memberships that represent important aspects of the individual's identity but which are not associated with substance use. Fig. 22.3 provides an example of how one member of a TC, "Matt", mapped the groups that were important to him.

To explore the therapeutic potential for social identity mapping, Best et al. (2014) used the SIM method in their work with six TC residents. In their maps, these residents reported an average of five meaningful groups that they felt connected to. The most common groups that they identified were family (26% of groups), followed by the TC group and mutual support groups (13% each). Less frequently depicted groups included extended family, friends, and other people who use substances, other services, religious

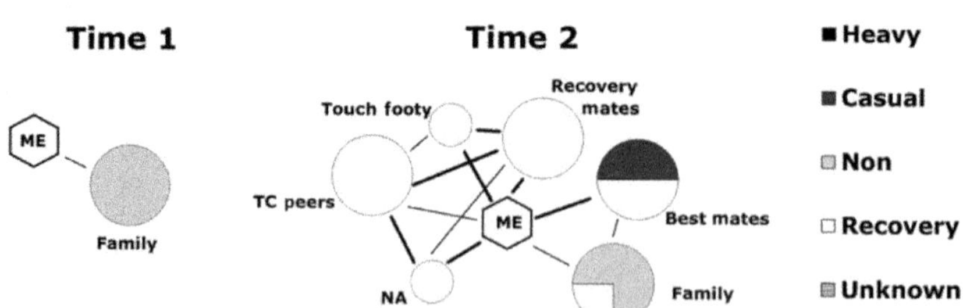

FIGURE 22.3 Social identity map for "Matt". *Adapted from Haslam, C., Dingle, G., Best, D., Mackenzie, J., & Beckwith, M. (2017). Social identity mapping: Measuring social identity change in recovery from addiction. In S.A. Buckingham & D. Best (Eds.),* Addiction, behavioural change and social identity: The path to resilience and recovery. *London: Routledge.*

groups, and leisure groups. Four of the six participants rated their identification with the TC as strong (mean of 6 out of 7) and identification with mutual support groups such as AA was also high (mean = 6), whereas identification with family and other groups was somewhat lower (means = 5.6 and 5.5 respectively). The maps also highlighted the extent of cohesion within participants' social networks. For example, one participant's map pointed to incompatibility between friendship groups, among whom substance use was high, and family groups who were infrequent substance users or non-users. When this participant planned for her departure from the TC, she used the mapping process to identify two key social goals that she wanted to pursue upon her return home. The first was to distance herself from a social network of substance users who would be a major risk for relapse; the second, was to develop social group activities that were not limited to her family alone.

This mapping exercise helps to highlight that in an addiction context where groups can be both helpful and harmful to health, it is important to assess people's social group networks and the behavioral norms that are associated with their various groups. The mapping process serves as a practical tool for bringing these networks to light. Importantly too, the process empowers participants by giving them insight into the possible sources of risk, but also protection, within their social networks so that they can self manage these more effectively. Nevertheless, working effectively with people's group-based networks requires care. A SIM might identify the presence of numerous groups that promote heavy substance use, which one might be tempted to recommend dropping to remove temptation. But doing so without attending to developing new groups or reconnecting with those that do not promote substance misuse, risks leaving a person feeling empty and socially disconnected – 'the void' in the words of the previous participant - and this has worse outcomes than maintaining using groups alone (Haslam, Dingle, Best, Mackenzie, & Beckwith, 2017).

It is also important to remember that identification with addiction treatment groups is not the only way of supporting recovery. Broader social groups and associated identities that are supportive of recovery, such as parent identity (Gunn & Samuels, 2019), peer group identity (Savolainen, Kaakinen, Sirola, & Oksanen, 2018), occupational identity (Best, 2016), arts groups (Williams, Dingle, Jetten, & Rowan, 2019), and sporting group identities (Hutton-Brown, 2017) – can also play a role. Of course, each of these can be problematic identities if they involve substance misuse. For instance, heavy drinking is normative in some sporting team contexts (Zhou, Heim, & O'Brien, 2015). In fact, recent research has found that a person's readiness for recovery is enhanced if they belonged to more social groups before entering treatment (Haslam, Best, et al., 2019). Therefore, social targets for treatment should emphasize both developing positive new identities (e.g., a recovery identity), but also reconnecting with social and family groups that support abstinence goals. This is more easily said than done, as people in recovery face a number of barriers to joining with others that include stigma, loneliness, fear of negative evaluation, and mistrust of others. Neglecting these in intervention results in suboptimal outcomes.

Challenges to building new (sober) group memberships

Several studies have found that people with substance use disorders are more highly stigmatised than people who experience other health conditions (Corrigan, 2005; Room, 2005). *Stigma* surrounding certain behaviors (e.g., substance use during pregnancy) and groups (e.g., people who inject drugs) are widely accepted, culturally endorsed, and enshrined in policy (e.g., criminal law). Stigma often leads to the marginalization and devaluation of substance-using groups and the creation of unhelpful 'us–them' divisions between those who need help and other members of society who might be able to provide it. This also means that, in addition to the many challenges that people with substance abuse problems confront when they go into treatment, they must also deal with the fact that they belong to a highly stigmatised social group. Stigma has numerous consequences including ill-treatment by others and loneliness (Hornquist & Akerlind, 1987; Itzick, Segal, & Possick, 2019).

Loneliness is an emotional experience of unwanted social isolation arising when the relationships that one currently has does not match with the quality or quantity of relationships that they desire (Peplau & Perlman, 1982) and it is often characterized by distress, despair, and emptiness (Weiss, 1973). It is widespread across addiction treatment samples (56%–79%) (Ingram, Kelly, Deane, Baker, & Raftery, 2018; Li, Zhong, Xu, Zhu, & Lu, 2017), and is related to a number of poor health, social and substance use outcomes (Ingram, Kelly, Deane, Baker, Goh, Raftery & Dingle, in preparation). Loneliness is particularly problematic for recovery, as it is a potential antecedent to substance use. It is also associated with hypervigilance for social threats and can lead a person to distance themselves from others (Layden, Cacioppo, & Cacioppo, 2019). This, in turn, perpetuates a cycle of mistrust of others that exacerbates difficulties accessing and engaging with health providers (Merrill, Rhodes, Deyo, Marlatt, & Bradley, 2002).

Mistrust, an abiding belief that others are likely to treat you badly or harm you in some way, is common amongst people with alcohol addiction. A study that compared scores on the Young Schema Questionnaire (which assesses 15 maladaptive schemas including mistrust/abuse) from 50 people with alcohol use disorders compared with 50 controls demonstrated this (Roper, Dickson, Tinwell, Booth, & McGuire, 2010). The study found that the mistrust/abuse schema was the most strongly endorsed maladaptive schema in the alcohol sample ($Mdn = 4.10/5$), and was markedly higher than in the controls ($Mdn = 1.9/5$). Participants endorsed the mistrust schema significantly less strongly ($Mdn = 3.0$) after a brief residential alcohol treatment involving group cognitive behavioral therapy but not schema focused therapy per se, indicating that supportive group contexts can help people to modify their mistrust schemas. Mistrust is particularly common among individuals with a history of interpersonal abuse or neglect, a substantial subgroup in any alcohol treatment service. For example in one study, participants in a therapeutic community were screened using the posttraumatic symptom checklist and more than half of the sample met criteria for a diagnosis of PTSD, most commonly due to interpersonal types of trauma (Perryman, Dingle, & Clark, 2016). Clearly, mistrust beliefs have the potential to act as a barrier against joining new groups and communities because people are vigilant to potential interpersonal threat and tend to avoid getting close to others and sharing their experiences for fear of being manipulated, betrayed or otherwise hurt in the process.

Social anxiety disorder is another disorder that commonly co-occurs with alcohol use disorders. A review of research in this field revealed that a *fear of negative evaluation* explains the link between the two disorders, as well as coping motives for disordered drinking (e.g., Morris, Stewart, & Ham, 2005). Fear of negative evaluation is a fear of making a mistake or appearing to be nervous, stupid or awkward in front of others, attracting scrutiny, and evaluating the consequences of such scrutiny as severe. This belief could prevent people from reconnecting with old groups who they have had conflict with in the past and potentially act a barrier to joining new groups because affected individuals are concerned that others will judge them negatively and reject them.

In summary, stigma, loneliness, mistrust, and fear of negative evaluation present clear challenges in supporting identity change in recovery. People in treatment for alcohol use will need to identify these potential barriers and to learn skills to overcome them in an intervention that focuses on managing their social group based social identities.

An intervention for social identity management in addiction: Groups 4 Belonging

What emerges from the above review are the numerous challenges that people face in the course of undergoing identity change to achieve recovery goals. This includes recognition of the social factors that influence the onset and development of addiction and the role that people's group memberships play in maintaining substance misuse and also in supporting recovery. Recognizing which groups are a source of protection or harm for health and well-being is key, but, in the addiction context, doing so without attending the barriers caused by stigma and mistrust is likely to lead to suboptimal outcomes. Addressing all these elements is a newly developed intervention program—Groups 4 Belonging—which we describe in the remainder of the chapter.

Groups 4 Belonging (Dingle, Ingram, Haslam, & Kelly, 2019a) is a 6x90 minute session group-based intervention that aims to give people the knowledge and strategies they need to increase their social group belonging and reduce feelings of loneliness whilst addressing risk factors particular to the addiction context (i.e., stigma, mistrust) when pursuing recovery. It draws primarily on the *Groups 4 Health* program, which is a social identity theory derived intervention that targets the building and maintenance of positive social group identifications, as a theoretical agent of change in enhancing health and well-being through reducing loneliness (Haslam, Cruwys, Haslam, Dingle, & Chang, 2016; Haslam et al., 2019). The intervention targets key SIMIC processes of multiple group membership, group identification, group maintenance, group gain, and group compatibility and does so through providing an in-vivo group experience where participants learn about tackling social disconnection with others who face similar challenges. By drawing on each other's knowledge and resources, the group's membership as a collective is as much a part of the intervention as the content of the program itself.

Two studies have examined the acceptability, feasibility and efficacy of the program and found that it has positive effects on loneliness, mood, and social anxiety (). In particular the more rigorous evaluation using randomised controlled trial methodology found that Group 4 Health produced a greater reduction in loneliness (d = -1.16) and social anxiety ($d = -0.53$) than treatment-as-usual (TAU, $ds = -0.36$, 0.03, respectively). Depression declined significantly in both Groups 4 Health ($d = -0.67$) and TAU ($d = -0.35$), but follow-up analyses showed this was greater in Groups 4 Health among those not receiving adjunct psychopharmacological treatment and whose symptoms were milder. Importantly too, analysis showed that for all outcomes evidence of reliable improvement was greater in response to Groups 4 Health (where reliable change was observed in 21–47% of participants) than to TAU (where reliable change was observed in 5–32% of TAU participants).

Groups 4 Belonging takes four of the five Groups 4 Health modules—*Schooling, Scoping, Sourcing and Scaffolding*—and extends on these to include components of mindfulness based cognitive behavior therapy to target particular barriers experienced in addiction contexts that might undermine their capacity to connect with others in ways that support their recovery. The first session includes psychoeducation and a card sorting activity about the relative importance of social factors for health and longevity alongside of other well-known health factors such as exercise, diet, smoking and weight. Facilitators then guide participants to create a SIM to visualize their own social networks.

Session two focuses on the meaning and consequences of loneliness, and participants learn how to identify and address thoughts and feelings associated with loneliness. They practice two mindfulness exercises as strategies for detaching from these unhelpful thoughts and sensations that are risks for drinking. In the third session, participants are taught to differentiate between the quantity and quality of their social connections. They complete an imagery exercise to help identify their values in relationships and explore how the groups identified in their SIM groups reflect important values that they hold.

The focus of session four is reconnecting with existing social groups. Participants consider how groups currently meet their needs how they anticipate these groups will meet their needs as they progress through the recovery pathway. They complete an exercise in how to manage knock-backs. They also discuss stigma and how it may be overcome in order to connect with others. Social goals are developed for reconnecting with known groups, which are further developed in session five that focuses on developing new group memberships. Here participants explore group-based activities in their community and ways to overcome any fears they have about facing negative evaluation from others. Participants continue working on their social goals between sessions.

The sixth (and final) session reviews participants' progress on their social goals, and focuses on overcoming barriers associated with mistrust. It also includes an exercise in which participants use music listening as an alternative to mindfulness practice for regulating negative emotions. Groups 4 Belonging differs from other psychotherapy programs (e.g., cognitive behavior therapy, motivational interviewing, 12-step facilitation) in a number of important ways:

- As in Groups 4 Health, it uses experiential learning from key activities in each session rather than relying heavily on textual information;
- It recognizes the importance of the in-vivo group experience component of the program which allows participants to learn with others who face similar challenges and have similar recovery goals;
- It is guided by well-established theories – drawing on social identity theory and cognitive theories, which together regard addictive behaviors as caused not by individual traits or skills deficits, but by wider social determinants and individuals' responses to their social circumstances.
- It focuses participants on social goals (such as reconnecting with former groups or building new group memberships that are supportive of recovery) that are likely to sustain their recovery after leaving treatment, rather than emphasizing primarily behavioral goals (such as decreasing or abstaining from substance use) which are vulnerable to relapse outside of treatment;
- It is accessible to and can be delivered by workers from a range of professional backgrounds (e.g., nursing, social work, psychology, counseling, etc) who can apply the theoretical and research foundations of the program presented in this facilitators' manual.

A feasibility trial of the Groups 4 Belonging program is in progress in several sites in Australia (Dingle, Ingram, Haslam, & Kelly, 2019b). Three of the sites are residential rehabilitation services and one is an after-care (outpatient) service for adults who have completed residential rehabilitation and are living in the community. Early feedback from participants indicates that the Groups 4 Belonging program aligns well with messages and therapeutic strategies learned in residential programs such as the need to develop a recovery support network, to take values based actions, and to consider the differences between loneliness, 'isolating' from others, and taking some time alone to reflect. The program has not yet been trialed in a harm-minimization context where controlled drinking (rather than abstinence) is the treatment goal. Recent U.S. research has found that reductions in World Health Organization drinking risk level aligns with patients' goals more strongly than abstinence, recognize more people as being successfully treated, and were maintained at 1-year follow up (Witkiewitz, et al., 2019). The implication of this finding is that low- to moderate-drinking social groups could be included in an individual's recovery network. Further development of the SIMOR model and evidence from the Group 4 Belonging intervention is required to confirm this possibility.

Conclusions

Theoretical and empirical research on the social identity approach to recovery from alcohol addiction indicates that social factors are important in the onset and development of problematic drinking, and when harnessed in treatment, they are predictive of positive longer-term outcomes. These social groups based identities and norms related to alcohol use can be visualized using Social Identity Mapping. Group and community based treatments where participants develop a sense of belonging and identification with a new sober group are helpful because they provide the individual with sources of in-group support, opportunities to enact their recovery identity through contributing to the group, and sober norms and attitudes that guide their own behavior. When people in treatment have few recovery-supportive groups in their network, they will benefit from assistance to reconnect with existing groups and/or to join new groups that are likely to support their ongoing recovery. In so doing, a number of barriers to connecting with others need to be taken into account and overcome, including stigma, loneliness, mistrust, and fear of negative evaluation. These social identity principles and empirical research drawn from samples of people in alcohol treatment underpin a new intervention program called Groups 4 Belonging. While still in the early stages of empirical testing, we think that Groups 4 Belonging provides clinicians and clients with a set of practical skills and exercises to understand the social factors driving alcohol use, and to harness these in the service of sustained health and wellbeing.

References

Baumeister, R. F., & Leary, M. R. (1995). The need to belong: Desire for interpersonal attachments as a fundamental human motivation. *Psychological Bulletin, 117*(3), 497–529. Available from https://doi.org/10.1037/0033-2909.117.3.497.

Beckwith, M., Best, D., Savic, M., Haslam, C., Bathish, R., Dingle, G., Mackenzie, J., Staiger, P. K., & Lubman, D. I. (2019). Social identity mapping in recovery (SIM-R): Development and application of a visual method. *Addiction Research & Treatment, 27*(6), 462–471. Available from https://doi.org/10.1080/16066359.2018.1544623.

Bentley, S. V., Greenaway, K., Haslam, S. A., Cruwys, T., Steffens, N. K., Haslam, C., & Cull, B. (2019). Online social identity mapping. *Journal of Personality and Social Psychology, 118*(2), 213–241. Available from https://doi.org/10.1037/pspa0000174.

Best, D. (2016). An unlikely hero? Challenging stigma through community engagement. *Drugs and Alcohol Today, 16*(1), 106–116. Available from https://doi.org/10.1108/DAT-09-2015-0054.

Best D., Beckwith M., Haslam C., Haslam S.A., Jetten J., Mawson E., and Lubman D. I. (2016). Overcoming alcohol and other drug addiction as a process of social identity transition: The social identity model of recovery (SIMOR). *Addiction Research & Theory, 24*, 111–123. Available from https://doi.org/10.3109/16066359.2015.1075980.

Best, D., Haslam, C., Staiger, P., Dingle, G., Savic, M., Bathish, R., Alexander, J., Beckwith, M., & Lubman, D. I. (2016). Social Networks and Recovery (SONAR): Characteristics of a longitudinal outcome study in five therapeutic communities in Australia. *Therapeutic Communities, 37*(3), 131–139. Available from https://doi.org/10.1108/TC-04-2016-0012.

Best, D., Lubman, D., Savic, M., Wilson, A., Dingle, G., Haslam, S. A., Haslam, C., & Jetten, J. (2014). Social and transitional identity: Exploring social networks and their significance in a therapeutic community setting. *Therapeutic Communities, 35*(1), 10–20. Available from https://doi.org/10.1108/TC-04-2013-0007.

Boyle, S. C., LaBrie, J. W., Froidevaux, N. M., & Witkovic, Y. D. (2016). Different digital paths to the keg? How exposure to peers' alcohol-related social media content influences drinking among male and female first-year college students. *Addictive Behaviours, 57*, 21–29. Available from https://doi.org/10.1016/j.addbeh.2016.01.011.

Buckingham, S. A., Frings, D., & Albery, I. P. (2013). Group membership and social identity in addiction recovery. *Psychology of Addictive Behaviors, 27*, 1132–1140. Available from https://doi.org/10.1037/a0032480.

Corrigan, P. W. (2005). *On the stigma of mental illness: Implications for research and social change*. Washington, DC: American Psychological Association.

Cruwys, T., Steffens, N. K., Haslam, C., Haslam, S. A., Jetten, J., & Dingle, G. A. (2016). Social Identity Mapping (SIM): The comprehensive visual assessment of subjective group memberships. *British Journal of Social Psychology, 55*, 613–642. Available from https://doi.org/10.1111/bjso.12155.

Darke, S., Campbell, G., & Popple, G. (2012). Retention, early dropout and treatment completion among therapeutic community admissions. *Drug and Alcohol Review, 31*, 64–71. Available from https://doi.org/10.1111/j.1465-3362.2011.00298.x.

Dingle, G. (2018). *Addiction and the importance of belonging*. The Psychologist, May 2018, British Psychological Society.

Dingle, G. A., Cruwys, T., & Frings, D. (2015). Social identities as pathways into and out of addiction. *Frontiers in Psychology, 6*, 1795. Available from https://doi.org/10.3389/fpsyg.2015.0179510.1111/asap.12089.

Dingle, G. A., Haslam, C., Best, D., Chan, G., Staiger, P. K., Savic, M., Beckwith, M., Mackenzie, J., Bathish, R., & Lubman, D. I. (2019). Social identity differentiation predicts commitment to sobriety and wellbeing in residents of therapeutic communities, Accepted In Press, *Social Science & Medicine*, *237*(2019), 112459.

Dingle, G. A., Ingram, I., Haslam, C., & Kelly, P. J. (2019a). *Groups 4 Belonging – How social connections can help with addiction recovery*. University of Queensland and University of Wollongong, Facilitators Manual.

Dingle, G. A., Ingram, I., Haslam, C., & Kelly, P. J. (2019b). Groups 4 Belonging – A group intervention for people with addiction that integrates social identity and cognitive behavioural approaches. *Poster presented at the 9 th World Congress of Behavioral and Cognitive Therapies*, 17–20 July 2019, Berlin, Germany.

Dingle, G. A., Stark, C., Cruwys, T., & Best, D. (2015). Breaking good: Breaking ties with social groups may be good for recovery from substance misuse. *British Journal of Social Psychology*, *54*, 236–254. Available from https://doi.org/10.1111/bjso.12081.

Eisenberg, M. E., Toumbourou, J. W., Catalano, R. F., & Hemphill, C. (2014). *Journal of Youth and Adolescence*, *43*(9), 1486–1497. Available from https://doi.org/10.1007/s10964-014-0111-1.

Groh, D. R., Jason, L. A., & Keys, C. B. (2008). Social network variables in alcoholics anonymous: A literature review. *Clinical Psychological Review*, *28*, 430–450. Available from https://doi.org/10.1016/j.cpr.2007.07.014.

Gunn, A., & Samuels, G. M. (2019). Promoting recovery identities among mothers with histories of addiction: Strategies of family engagement. *Family Process*. Available from https://doi.org/10.1111/famp.12413.

Haslam, C., Best, D. W., Dingle, G. A., Staiger, P. K., Savic, M., Bathish, R., Jock Mackenzie, J., Beckwith, M., Kelly, A. J., & Lubman, D. I. (2019). Social group membership before treatment for substance dependence predicts early identification and engagement with treatment communities. *Addiction Research and Theory*. Available from https://doi.org/10.1080/16066359.2018.1537393.

Haslam, C., Cruwys, T., Chang, M. X. L., Bentley, S. V., Haslam, S. A., Dingle, G. A., & Jetten, J. (2019). GROUPS 4 HEALTH reduces loneliness and social anxiety in adults with psychological distress: Findings from a randomised controlled trial. *Journal of Consulting and Clinical Psychology*, *87*(9), 787–801. Available from https://doi.org/10.1037/ccp0000427.

Haslam, C., Cruwys, T., Haslam, S. A., Dingle, G., & Chang, M. X.-L. (2016). GROUPS 4 HEALTH: Evidence that a social-identity intervention that builds and strengthens social group membership improves mental health. *Journal of Affective Disorders*, *194*, 188–195. Available from https://doi.org/10.1016/j.jad.2016.01.010.

Haslam, C., Dingle, G., Best, D., Mackenzie, J., & Beckwith, M. (2017). Social identity mapping: Measuring social identity change in recovery from addiction. In S. A. Buckingham, & D. Best (Eds.), *Addiction, behavioural change and social identity: The path to resilience and recovery*. London: Routledge.

Haslam, C., Holme, A., Haslam, S. A., Iyer, A., Jetten, J., & Williams, W. H. (2008). Maintaining group memberships: Social identity continuity predicts well-being after stroke. *Neuropsychological Rehabilitation*, *18*, 671–691. Available from https://doi.org/10.1080/09602010701643449.

Haslam, C., Jetten, J., Cruwys, T., Dingle, G. A., & Haslam, S. A. (2018). *The new psychology of health – Unlocking the social cure*. London: Routledge.

Haslam, S. A., O'Brien, A., Jetten, J., Vormedal, K., & Penna, S. (2005). Taking the strain: Social identity, social support, and the experience of stress. *British Journal of Social Psychology*, *44*(3), 355–370. Available from https://doi.org/10.1348/014466605X37468.

Hodgins, D. C., el-Guebaly, N., & Armstrong, S. (1995). Prospective and retrospective reports of mood states before relapse to substance use. *Journal of Consulting and Clinical Psychology*, *63*(3), 400–407. Available from https://doi.org/10.1037/0022-006X.63.3.400.

Hörnquist, J. O., & Akerlind, I. (1987). Loneliness correlates in advanced alcohol abusers. II. Clinical and psychological factors. *Scandinavian Journal of Social Medicine*, *15*(4), 225–232.

Hutton-Brown, T. (2017). Turn your life around. (Blog about how ParkRun helped the author to recovery from addiction). Retrieved from <https://blog.parkrun.com/uk/2017/03/30/turn-your-life-around/>.

Ingram, I., Kelly, P. J., Deane, F. P., Baker, A. L., & Raftery, D. K. (2018). Loneliness in treatment-seeking substance-dependent populations: Validation of the social and emotional loneliness scale for adults–short version. *Journal of Dual Diagnosis*, 1–9.

Ingram, I., Kelly, P. J., Deane, F. P., Baker, A. L., Goh, M. C. W., Raftery, D. K., Dingle, G. A. (2020). Loneliness in substance dependent populations: A narrative systematic review. *Drug and Alcohol Review*, *39*(5), 447–483. Available from https://doi.org/10.1111/dar.13064.

Itzick, M., Segal, J., & Possick, C. (2019). Relationships in the lives of Israeli women coping with drug addiction: An ecosystemic perspective. *Journal of Social & Personal Relationships*, *36*(3), 741–760.

Jetten, J., Haslam, C., & Haslam, S. A. (Eds.), (2012). *The social cure - Identity, health and well-being*. London: Routledge.

Jetten, J., Haslam, C., Haslam, S. A., Dingle, G. A., & Jones, J. (2014). How groups affect our health and wellbeing: The path from theory to policy. *Social Issues and Policy Review*, *8*(1), 102–128.

Jetten, J., Haslam, S. A., Haslam, C., & Branscombe, N. R. (2009). The social cure. *Scientific American Mind*, *20*(5), 26–33. Available from https://doi.org/10.1038/scientificamerican-mind0909-26.

Jetten, J., Haslam, S. A., Iyer, A., & Haslam, C. (2009). Turning to others in times of change: Social identity and coping with stress. In S. Stürmer, & M. Snyder (Eds.), *The psychology of prosocial behavior: Group processes, intergroup relations, and helping* (pp. 139–156). Oxford: Blackwell.

Layden, E. A., Cacioppo, J. T., & Cacioppo, S. (2019). Loneliness predicts a preference for larger interpersonal distance within intimate space. *PLoS One*, *13*(9), e0203491.

Li, H. J., Zhong, B. L., Xu, Y. M., Zhu, J. H., & Lu, J. (2017). Sleep in lonely heroin-dependent patients receiving methadone maintenance treatment: Longer sleep latency, shorter sleep duration, lower sleep efficiency, and poorer sleep quality. *Oncotarget*, *8*(51), 89278–89283.

Maslow, A. H. (1943). A theory of human motivation. *Psychological Review*, *50*(4), 370–396.

Merrill, J. O., Rhodes, L. A., Deyo, R. A., Marlatt, G. A., & Bradley, K. A. (2002). Mutual mistrust in the medical care of drug users: The keys to the "narc" cabinet. *Journal of General Internal Medicine*, *17*(5), 327–333. Available from https://doi.org/10.1046/j.1525-1497.2002.10625.x.

Moos, R. H. (2008). Active ingredients of substance use-focused self-help groups. *Addiction*, *103*, 387–396. Available from https://doi.org/10.1111/j.1360-0443.2007.02111.x.

Morgenstern, M., Isensee, B., Sargent, J. D., & Hanewinkel, R. (2011). Exposure to alcohol advertising and teen drinking. *Preventive Medicine*, *52*(2), 146–151. Available from https://doi.org/10.1016/j.ypmed.2010.11.020.

Morris, E. P., Stewart, S. H., & Ham, L. S. (2005). The relationship between social anxiety disorder and alcohol use disorders: A critical review. *Clinical Psychology Review*, *25*(6), 734–760. Available from https://doi.org/10.1016/j.cpr.2005.05.004.

Peplau, L. A., & Perlman, D. (1982). *Loneliness: A sourcebook of current theory, research, and therapy*. Wiley Interscience.

Perryman, C., Dingle, G., & Clark, D. (2016). Changes in posttraumatic stress disorders symptoms during and after therapeutic community drug and alcohol treatment. *Therapeutic Communities*, *37*(4), 170–183. Available from https://doi.org/10.1108/TC-06-2016-0013.

Room, R. (2005). Stigma, social inequality and alcohol and drug use. *Drug and Alcohol Review*, *24*(2), 143–155. Available from https://doi.org/10.1080/09595230500102434.

Roper, L., Dickson, J. M., Tinwell, C., Booth, P. G., & McGuire, J. (2010). Maladaptive cognitive schemas in alcohol dependence: Changes associated with a brief residential abstinence program. *Cognitive Therapy & Research*, *34*, 207–215. Available from https://doi.org/10.1007/s10608-009-9252-z.

Savolainen, I., Kaakinen, M., Sirola, A., & Oksanen, A. (2018). Addictive behaviors and psychological distress among adolescents and emerging adults: A mediating role of peer group identification. *Addictive Behaviours Reports*, *7*, 75–81. Available from https://doi.org/10.1016/j.abrep.2018.03.002.

Stout R. L., Kelly J. F., Magill M., & Pagano M. E. (2012). Association between social influences and drinking outcomes across three years. *Journal of Studies on Alcohol and Drugs*, *73*(3), 489–497. Available from http://doi.org/10.15288/jsad.2012.73.489.

Tajfel., & Turner. (1979). An integrative theory of intergroup conflict. In Austin, & Worehel (Eds.), *The social psychology of intergroup relations* (pp. 33–47). Monterey: Brooks/Cole.

Turner J. C., Hogg, M., Oakes, P. J., Reicher, S. and Wetherell, M. S. (1987). Rediscovering the Social Group: A Self-Categorization Theory. Oxford: Blackwell.

Van Der Vorst, H., Engels, R. C. M. E., Meeus, W., Deković, M., & Van Leeuwe, J. (2005). The role of alcohol-specific socialization in adolescents' drinking behaviour. *Addiction*, *100* (10), 1464–1476. Available from https://doi.org/10.1111/j.1360-0443.2005.01193.x.

Vignoles, V. L., (2017). Identity: Personal and social. Chapter in *Oxford Handbook of Personality and social psychology* (2nd ed.), edited by Kay Deaux and Mark Snyder.

Weiss, R. S. (1973). *Loneliness: The experience of emotional and social isolation*. Cambridge, MA: The MIT Press.

Whitehead, V. (2010). Identity transition and abstinence from alcohol: A thematic analysis of interviews with clients following treatment. Unpublished dissertation for a Masters in Clinical Psychology, The University of QLD.

Williams, E., Dingle, G. A., Jetten, J., & Rowan, C. (2019). Identification with arts-based groups improves mental wellbeing in adults with chronic mental health conditions. *Journal of Applied Social Psychology*, *49*(1), 15–26. Available from https://doi.org/10.1111/jasp.12561.

Witkiewitz, K., Falk, D. E., Litten, R., Hasin, D. S., Kranzler, H. R., Mann, K. F., O'Malley, S. S., & Anton, R. F. (2019). Maintenance of World Health Organization risk drinking level reductions and posttreatment functioning following a large alcohol use disorder clinical trial. *Alcoholism: Clinical and Experimental Research*, *43*(5), 979–998. Available from https://doi.org/10.1111/acer.14018.

Witkiewitz, K., & Marlatt, G. A. (2004). Relapse prevention for alcohol and drug problems: That was Zen, this is Tao. *American Psychologist*, *59*(4), 224–235. Available from https://doi.org/10.1037/0003-066X.59.4.22.

Zhou, J., Heim, D., & O'Brien, K. (2015). Alcohol consumption, athlete identity, and happiness among student sportspeople as a function of sport-type. *Alcohol and Alcoholism*, *50*(5), 617–623. Available from https://doi.org/10.1093/alcalc/agv030.

Chapter 23

Working together: Opportunities and barriers to evidence-based practice

Jan Larkin[1] and Daniel Donkor[2]
[1]School of Psychology, Turning Point, London, United Kingdom, [2]Lead Clinical Psychologist, Turning Point, London, United Kingdom

The term 'evidence-based' has become something of a buzz word in international treatment services as a way of determining the worth of that service. But what does 'evidence-based' really mean in the context of alcohol treatment and how does it manifest itself through the experiences that people have in commissioned services?

In order to address this question, we need to examine where the 'evidence' comes from and then look at how it relates to practice. We will do this through the lens of different perspectives including those people with alcohol problems and the people who work with them.

So, where does the evidence come from? The National Institute of Health and Care Excellence (NICE) became a legal entity in 1999 and is a non-departmental public body that provides national guidance and advice to improve health and social care in England. NICE guidelines 'make evidence-based recommendations on a wide range of topics, from preventing and managing specific conditions, improving health, and managing medicines in different settings, to providing social care and support to adults and children, and planning broader services and interventions to improve the health of communities. NICE guideline recommendations are based on the best available evidence. We use a wide range of different types of evidence and other information – from scientific research using a variety of methods, to testimony from practitioners and people using services' (NICE, 2018a).

However, there have been a number of criticisms levelled at the process of NICE guidance development. One such criticism is that 'the language and research approach used in formulating the most recent guidelines... is firmly embedded within the model of biological medicine (or biomedical model)

The Handbook of Alcohol Use - Understandings from Synapse to Society.
DOI: https://doi.org/10.1016/B978-0-12-816720-5.00019-0

which underpins the rest of NICE's work for the NHS. This model assumes that patient experiences (symptoms) are indicative of underlying conditions which need to be diagnosed in order for an appropriate treatment to be prescribed' (Guy, Thomas, Stephenson, & Loewenthal, 2011). Alcohol use is not necessarily driven by an underlying condition, nor by solely biological factors, but mediated by a host of social, psychological, economic and spiritual influences. Another critique is that treatments approved by NICE have to reach such a high standard of rigorous academic evaluation, that other treatments may in fact be effective but not researched enough through Randomized Controlled Trials to meet the NICE recommendation threshold.

A seminal paper by Professor Jim Orford challenges existing treatment research methods by suggesting that we may not be asking the right questions in the right way (Orford, 2008). This paper describes a number of ways in which existing research methodology is insufficient: 'failing to account for the outcome equivalence paradox; neglecting relationships in favor of techniques; failing to integrate treatment research and research on unaided change; imposing an inappropriate time-scale on the change process; failing to take a systems or social network view; ignoring therapists' tacit theories; not including the patient's view; and displaying an ignorance of modern developments in the philosophy of science'. The 'outcome equivalence paradox' mentioned first in this list is also known as the 'Dodo Bird Verdict' (from the Dodo bird in Alice in Wonderland: '*everybody* has won and *all* shall have prizes' in the race). It seems that this may be somewhat the case in treatment for alcohol misuse: A number of studies have shown that a range of different treatments for alcohol problems are equally effective and suggest that the therapeutic relationship is in fact the essential element for behavior change (Cook, Heather, McCambridge, & United Kingdom Alcohol Treatment Trial Research Team, 2015).

An alternative to 'evidence-based practice' is 'practice-based evidence'. Here, there is a recognition that with human behavior there is rarely an identifiable ' cause and effect', that real life is messier than a Randomised Controlled Trial. In practice-based evidence, people are grouped by shared factors rather than inclusion and exclusion criteria. Here, clinicians 'have systematically collected real world data and synthesized them into guidelines for practice' (Swisher, 2010, p. 4).

This chapter will discuss challenges to translating the evidence base into practice and some examples of good practice in this area. This issue will be addressed from different perspectives: the individual with alcohol difficulties; their family members or concerned others; treatment providers; those who commission services and academics involved in the generation of evidence. Some of these perspectives were gained for the purposes of this chapter by interviewing a range of people related in some way to alcohol services. Other perspectives are offered from a review of key national documents and the research literature. As Clinical Psychologists in this field, we also draw on our own experiences of supporting people with alcohol problems, their family members and staff within a commissioned environment. Some conclusions and recommendations will then be drawn from these perspectives.

The premise of evidence based practice is to improve safer service delivery and create better outcomes for service users (NICE, 2018b). In 2011, the Oxford Centre for Evidence-based Medicine (OCEBM) revised practice guidelines grading levels of evidence. Randomised Control trials are categorised as the pinnacle for gathering evidence (OCEBM, 2011). Mechanism-based reasoning, for instance, a claim that an intervention works, has lowest ranking. Ironically, client opinion is not explicitly acknowledged within the grading classification. With a bias for randomised control trials there is a danger that client informed research and a focus on client centered outcomes are lost (Greenhalgh, Snow, Ryan, Rees, & Sailsbury, 2015). Perhaps unsurprisingly then, clients are not always aware of the term 'evidence based practice'. However, examples of evidence-based practice can be observed in this description of the treatment journey of Otis, a peer mentor in a substance use treatment service, who had previously experienced his own problems with alcohol use. A peer mentor is a positive role model, drawing upon their own experiences of addiction, treatment and recovery to support and inspire the recovery of others. Otis is a pseudonym name to preserve anonymity.

A client perspective of alcohol treatment: Otis

Otis said that he had always drunk socially, but over a three-year period the drinking gradually increased to where he was drinking a litre of vodka daily. He described a 'trio of events' which caused the drinking to escalate. Otis lost his job when the company he worked for went into administration. Not long after that, his marriage of five years ended. Otis described being left with nothing and having to move home to live with his parents. The final event was when Otis' father lost his fight with cancer. Otis described overwhelming feelings of guilt because of what he felt he had put his family through; his drinking increased.

Otis said that he got a part-time job working in a pub. He was coming in to work intoxicated. One Friday after a particular bad night, Otis arrived at work; the landlord looked at him and immediately took him to see his GP. The doctor gave Otis the number for the local drug and alcohol service and advised that he should stop drinking. Otis took his doctor literally, stopped drinking immediately and called the substance misuse service in the evening. Evidence-based practice would advise that if a person is drinking dependently, they seek professional support and to taper alcohol consumption to minimize symptoms of alcohol withdrawal rather than stopping suddenly. Otis went in to alcohol withdrawals. The substance misuse service was closed for the weekend, however it had an out of hours service. Over the weekend, Otis received telephone support from the person on duty out of hours, until he could be assessed the next day.

Otis remained abstinent and was encouraged to attend a mindfulness based relapse prevention group (Bowen, Chawla, & Marlatt, 2011). There is a growing movement for services to provide group work interventions but with only mixed findings for their effectiveness (Orchowski & Johnson, 2012; Wendt & Gone, 2017). Otis described how his anxiety levels were massive when he attended the group for the first time; he did not believe he could do it. Otis experienced a panic attack and had to leave. His key-worker encouraged him to return the following week. Otis did go back and at first, he didn't want to change and said that he was just 'going through the motions', but slowly change crept up on him. With support from his key-worker, Otis secured housing and moved from the family home, but this presented the problem of isolation, being in a new place, on his own and not knowing anyone.

Otis said that outwardly, all was well and he got a job working as a cashier. Inwardly, the guilt surrounding his Dad dying was still there. On the anniversary of his father's death Otis relapsed. The drinking increased to one litre of vodka a day and he stopped eating and sleeping. Otis tried to hide the drinking and said he thought he was being clever and getting away with it. Otis described how after a heavy night, he went in to work drunk. He was behind the till and collapsed. The only thing that he remembers was the tannoy, "we have a problem with Otis". He was taken to hospital by ambulance, saw a nurse specialist and went through an unplanned alcohol detoxification over a period of six days. Otis said that he came out of hospital and relapsed immediately, resulting in a readmission to hospital.

During this period in hospital, Otis said that he was visited by a peer mentor (a volunteer with lived experience of alcohol problems). These visits helped him to re-establish the connection with the drug and alcohol service. A plan was made for Otis to return to treatment and to receive counseling. Otis said that counseling was the best thing for him. He was able to talk about his Dad, about his own guilt and feel supported in his grief. It was important that he felt able to draw his own conclusions.

Otis completed his treatment with the service and has remained abstinent for two years. He talks of how his confidence has grown through becoming a peer mentor himself: "Looking after people is what makes me happy and if I can help anyone who is in the same state that I was in, that is a good thing. I needed people to really listen. The key-workers don't really have the time they would like to spend with clients as they have so many. If I had that, it would have been so beneficial to think things through in conversation".

The emotional pain of loss, guilt, and shame is particularly evident in Otis's experiences of living with alcohol. His account conveys how it is human connection, particularly with his manager, key-worker, peer mentor and counselor which he found helpful in recovery; being given the time to be able to talk and be heard. With the evidence base favouring RCTs and quantitative over qualitative methodologies, it is perhaps harder for these nuances of treatment to be captured. Motivational Interviewing (MI) with its emphasis on 'MI Spirit' (Collaboration, Acceptance, Evocation and Compassion) as a fundamental component for helping people resolve ambivalence (Miller & Rollnick, 2013), has been widely researched and found to support recovery in alcohol addiction. It is encouraging to see that such a body of research has sought to address which elements of our interaction furthers human connection and promotes recovery with others. We will continue this theme by discussing next the social and relational environment around the person with alcohol problems.

A family member perspective

Looking through the lens of alcohol treatment from a family member perspective, we draw upon a number of years of research literature to shed light on what is often a neglected view point. There are a number of challenges for family members (or concerned others) in understanding which treatments for alcohol misuse are effective and in helping loved ones to access those treatments. In addition, access to support for family members in their own right can be compromised for a number of reasons. These include: patchy geographical delivery of support services for family members; lack of knowledge about services which do exist; attitudes towards asking for support and location of support services.

For family members of people using alcohol problematically, sources of information on how to access evidence-based treatment for their loved ones can be confusing and varied. These sources can include social and traditional media, where advertising can portray alcohol use as normal, desirable and enhancing of attributes such as hedonism, extroversion and sophistication (Critchlow, MacKintosh, Hooper, Thomas, & Vohra, 2019). The other end of the spectrum is the portrayal of those who are dependent on alcohol as suffering from a disease, with the only effective treatment option being withdrawal from their social network and a period of residential rehabilitation (UK-Rehab, n.d). There can be a bewildering array of treatment options for alcohol misuse, including mutual aid, drop in provision, structured individual and group approaches, medications and recovery focussed social initiatives such as recovery cafes and activities. In addition to all the stress and strain brought about by living with someone affected by alcohol misuse, family members can face either a lack of alcohol-specific treatment options in their area or a wide range of provision, based on a number of different therapeutic models, none of which are easy for most people to understand or navigate. Where there are services specifically aimed at those who misuse alcohol, these services may be co-located with drug treatment services traditionally known as focussed on opiate users. Family members may not perceive their loved one as being able to benefit from a service associated with drugs other than alcohol (PHE, 2018b).

Even when family members know where and how to access treatment with their loved one, there are a number of other barriers which operate, based sometimes on previous negative experiences with treatment services. Family members may be worried about being 'blamed' for the alcohol misuse of their loved one and being closely associated with an alcohol dependent person carries its own stigma (Adfam, 2012).These worries could further alienate family members from supporting their loved ones to seek help and contribute to the social isolation experienced by many family members living with problems that could be misunderstood by their colleagues and friends (Orford, 2013).

Some practical considerations can also be challenging for family members in helping the person misusing alcohol to seek support. Treatment services can be located some distance away and require a number of visits, particularly for dependent alcohol users, before accessing a medically-assisted detoxification (PHE, 2018b). Lack of finances for transport, poor transport networks in rural areas and work commitments can make it very difficult for family members to support their loved ones in seeking treatment.

The picture is not, however, entirely bleak. Many treatment services are now becoming much more inclusive of the needs of family members, providing information on evidence-based interventions without compromising the confidentiality of the person misusing alcohol. For example, some charitable organizations are forging links with local universities to carry out research in this area. Provision of clear information on service websites can be very helpful, such as a single number to contact where family members can find out about local services and have contact with an empathic and knowledgeable person. Provision of more information and options on national websites specifically for family members affected by substance use can help family members to understand treatment provision and dispel some of the myths about alcohol use (for example websites by Adfam and Alcohol Change UK, n.d.).

Thus far our focus has been on how family members might access information and support for their loved ones to seek treatment. However, family members often need support for themselves in their own right. Living with someone misusing alcohol is usually stressful and affects the physical and psychological health of family members (Orford, Copello, Velleman, & Templeton, 2010). Even if the person misusing alcohol is not ready to make any changes, years of research evidence confirm that offering evidence-based interventions for family members themselves can have significant effects on their own health and well-being (Copello, Templeton, Orford, & Velleman, 2010). There are also a number of mutual aid organizations offering support for family members in their own right, such as Al Anon and

SMART Family & Friends, offering a range of therapeutic models (Al-Anon Family Groups, n.d.; SMART Family & Friends, n.d.).

Whilst there is a robust evidence base for structured interventions with family members in their own right, (Orford et al., 2010) in reality provision and support for family members can be inconsistent across geographical areas (Adfam, 2013). Whereas substance misuse treatment services are often commissioned to provide separate support for family members, evaluation by commissioners of service performance usually only refers to alcohol users themselves rather than support for their families. In a world of shrinking budgets, support for family members is often seen as an aspiration rather than a necessity. Where support is provided for family members, it may not reflect advances in the evidence base and may be unstructured and open ended. Some family members benefit from drop in type support groups but often there is little choice of the type of support for family members within an area. Whilst treatment services acknowledge that different service users benefit from different types of treatment, this acknowledgment often does not extend to family members who may be offered a 'one size fits all' service — if any. Adfam in its 'Making it Happen' report and advice to commissioners offers a helpful insight into the range of interventions and support that can be commissioned for family members in their own right (Adfam, 2017).

As with obstacles to accessing support for their loved ones, family members may also be reluctant to access support for themselves. There may be little readily available local information to suggest that even when their loved ones are not ready to make changes, understanding and support for themselves can alleviate some of the stresses and strains inherent in living with someone who uses alcohol problematically.

Again, there are areas of good practice within an organization and across localities, where there is a range of types of support for family members, ranging from brief telephone support to open ended unstructured groups to structured individual and group interventions specifically focussing on living with someone's alcohol misuse (for example those provided by Scottish Families Affected by Alcohol & Drugs). Another example of valuable support for family members is Grandparents Plus, a national organization which provides social and practical support for kinship carers (those often caring for grandchildren where their own children have substance misuse problems) (Grandparents Plus, n.d.).

Another fundamental need is that of evidence based interventions with young people affected by parental substance misuse. The evidence for efficacy of these interventions is in its infancy, yet the scale of the problem is becoming increasingly apparent (Velleman & Templeton, 2018). A number of challenges exist which make it difficult for young people to get support for living with parental alcohol misuse. One is that this type of support often falls through a commissioning gap – not being commissioned by adult treatment services or by those for young people as the latter generally focus on those who are themselves using substances. Another challenge is that more systemic interventions, where a whole family approach is taken, can require more resources in terms of practitioner skill level, training and supervision. However, the prevalence of evidence-based approaches that seek to support young people affected by parental alcohol misuse is slowly becoming more widespread. An example of a government initiative to fund projects of this type is the Innovation Fund where Public Health England encouraged commissioners to bid for funding for new innovations in this area from partnerships of providers (PHE, 2018c). It is to be hoped that initiatives of this type herald the recognition of a need for embedding this provision within mainstream substance misuse services.

This ring-fenced funding may in itself help to add to the evidence base of which interventions are effective with young people in helping them to cope with often devastating and painful effects of living with a parent with an alcohol problem.

Drawing together perspectives on barriers and opportunities relating to family members, it is clear that there are a number of ways in which treatment services can bridge the gap between research and practice. There are also some existing areas of good practice that can be built on. So what stops many treatment services from carrying out evidence-based practice whether for family members or for people with alcohol problems?

A treatment service staff perspective

In order to understand more about this issue, we turn to the experiences of some staff working within the field of alcohol treatment – a service manager and a Recovery Worker, working with two different service providers. They outline the challenges they perceive in working with alcohol clients in an evidence-based way within the current climate.

When we think about a staff member's perspective of evidence-based practice, it is important to recognize that the term 'staff' is a broad one, incorporating those in a number of different roles. Some roles, such as that of a clinical psychologist, may well align themselves more closely with the concept and understanding of evidence-based practice. People in other roles may perceive themselves to be more detached from the evidence base.

Conversations with a manager and Recovery Worker indicate differences in levels of understanding of what the term 'evidence-based practice' means and what the evidence base recommends. They raise the question of whether it is important to understand the concept of evidence-based practice in order to support people with alcohol problems effectively. If staff are doing their job without fully understanding the underpinnings of what they are doing, does it mean that they do any less of a good job? It could be argued that musicians like Jimi Hendrix couldn't read musical notation and still produced ground-breaking music.

In our interviews, some skepticism was expressed about the evidence base, the manager describing it as a 'corporate buzz word' and a 'fad', indicating a transient way of 'dressing up' something that is already being done. Substance misuse services were seen as having changed greatly within the last 10 years - staff spoke of seeing colleagues leave and not be replaced because of reduced budgets, thereby increasing caseloads. There was a perception of people entering services with increasingly more complex needs, and greater pressure on staff to support people through their recovery in order to produce outcomes and meet targets set by commissioners. For staff, the equation of larger caseloads with more complex people and reduced resources, does not add up. Under such pressure, staff may revert to familiar ways of working and be less receptive to changes driven by the current evidence base.

From this perspective, the evidence base can be seen as a faceless entity, which stops them working in a way that they would like and may even feel like a hindrance. A manager spoke of how long the research process can take and how slowly it filters through to treatment. In the fast pace of modern services, the research process may take too long to be helpful when current change is necessary. A pressure for implementing change partly comes from short commissioning cycles where services need to change to meet new commissioning priorities. Also, providers differ in their own treatment philosophies and approaches. Service delivery and the shape of interventions inevitably does change due to staff moving on, the emergence of new interventions and shifting commissioning priorities, all in the climate of austerity. Such changes are often made under the guise of a change in the evidence base practice, which can therefore be perceived as being transient in nature, even though in reality NICE guidance does not change frequently. Specific guidance notes are updated only a few times in a decade. Staff can struggle with change (Dubois, Bentein, Mansour, Gilber, & Bédard, 2014) and if not managed well, it may be that it is the 'evidence base' which is blamed as the driver of service level changes and thus perceived as unreliable, inconsistent and unsupportive of service delivery.

Finally, our interviews revealed that because national guidance is based on randomised controlled trials (RCTs), staff can perceive it as too prescriptive and 'one size fits all'. This can be dissonant with the person-centered approach favored by staff.

A commissioner perspective

Moving now from a service provider to a commissioning perspective, there are a number of challenges which present at the level of commissioning services for alcohol users. To give some historical context to commissioning responsibilities, a new executive agency, Public Health England, was formed in 2013 to take the national lead on public health issues. The National Treatment Agency for Substance Misuse was abolished and its key functions taken over by Public Health England. Most of the budget for drug and alcohol services was transferred to Directors of Public Health, who became statutory members of Health & Well-being Boards alongside NHS Clinical Commissioning Groups. These changes were to significantly affect the commissioning of services for alcohol users in a number of ways, in combination with other social and economic factors.

Conversations with some current commissioners of drug and alcohol services have identified key challenges facing commissioning in 2019, as well as some areas of good practice and innovation in response to these challenges.

A number of issues will be discussed as identified by commissioners: changing patterns of service configuration; challenging stigma experienced by alcohol users; health inequalities; communication between diverse service providers; service user involvement and difficulties in establishing prevalence data. In addition, good practice was highlighted and encouraged, including effective hospital liaison teams and cross-sector working with mental health services.

The configuration of services for those with alcohol problems has shifted. A recent study by Public Health England into the fall in numbers of people in alcohol treatment (PHE, 2018b) highlighted that many areas which previously had separate services for alcohol and other drug users, have now integrated services to provide for both treatment populations. Whilst this shift has provided economies of scale, a number of challenges have arisen. Where drug services began to incorporate provision for alcohol users, some alcohol users have become less likely to approach an integrated service and commissioning guidance recommends alcohol-specific pathways within these services (PHE, 2018a, 2018b). Traditionally this service may have been associated with users of illegal drugs, perceived by many alcohol users as different from themselves. Association with this service may be perceived by the alcohol user as potentially stigmatising. In addition, the merging of services into larger more centralised buildings may be a barrier to engagement. This is particularly so where services were previously situated in more anonymised community settings such as GP practices.

Another aspect of the integration of services has been the challenge to staff competence. A drug treatment workforce with specific skills, has very rapidly needed to develop knowledge and skills in working with alcohol users, when moved into an integrated drug and alcohol service. Alcohol users may face different challenges to users of illicit substances, due to the prevalence of alcohol in our society. Additional specialist knowledge is required, such as risks of alcohol withdrawal and the process of alcohol detoxification. An increased focus not only on staff training, but regular supervision to maintain competence in an ever more demanding work situation is crucial if we are to provide effective and evidence-based services for such a wide range of people.

A related issue is that of stigma experienced by those with alcohol problems, which is in juxtaposition with a confused attitude to alcohol within our society – street drinking of cheap alcohol is perceived in a very different light to the more hidden binge drinking of professionals (NHS, UK, 2013). Commissioners need to obtain evidence-based services for a range of people with differing needs, yet services may not have the range of provision required for such a diverse population. Social acceptability of alcohol use differs between cultural groups and this may affect whether or how people engage with treatment. Services often find it difficult to attract people from a range of ethnic backgrounds and ages. Cultural and religious beliefs may increase the stigma attached to seeking treatment and it has often been difficult to attract older adults into traditional treatment services, for example. Interestingly, such groups are often labeled as 'hard to reach'. It would be more accurate to suggest that the onus is on the treatment provider to be sufficiently attuned to the needs of a diverse population.

A way of doing this is to work with people where they are already participating, for example in arts and community projects, to better understand their needs and cultural context, rather than to expect them to self-identify as a potential 'service user' of a drug and alcohol service. With treatment populations which are traditionally less likely to be attracted to traditional drug and alcohol services (for example, older adults and women) we need to be more proactive and creative in meeting people where they already are (at community projects and activities for example) as a venue for introducing the topic of alcohol use in a less 'treatment-focussed' way. One example of this is a treatment service working with Age Concern to visit day centers and invite attendees to informal discussions about alcohol use in a non-threatening and engaging way.

Traditionally, treatment services have operated on a working week 9-5 basis, whereas support needs can occur at any hour of any day and the emphasis on provision previously seen as 'out of hours' is increasing.

Some of the responses to this need for increased flexibility come from service providers with good partnership working, for example with emergency services, social care services and crisis provision. Other helpful responses are in the flexibility of services in how they provide support – not always face to face, but by telephone, online video conferencing and digital interventions which are based on NICE Guidance (NICE, 2011).

In conversation with commissioners, a significant challenge to this more 'joined-up' way of working is the commissioning system which does not always encourage communication or seeing the person as a whole being in a social context. Separate services are commissioned for homelessness, mental health, physical health and substance use, for example and providers struggle to communicate quickly and effectively with each other. When multiple interventions with one person can be ongoing in different services, cohesive and planned communication can be a challenge.

One example of a way to combat this fragmentation has been work on creating information networks, such as a terminal for GPs to increase knowledge of which service to refer a person to. Other examples of good practice include hospital liaison services which aim to encourage people with alcohol-related physical health problems in general medical environments, to engage with alcohol treatment services. Those commissioners interviewed, welcomed the reference to hospital liaison teams in the NHS Long-term Plan (NHS, 2019) with plans for more NHS funding to support them. Whilst such services have a very good evidence base (Health Innovation Network, 2018) and make good sense for the person using alcohol, commissioning structures can make them difficult to commission. Having external providers working in an NHS Trust can be difficult on all kinds of levels, which include sharing of patient data and funding streams. This is an interesting example of where what makes good sense for the person (or patient) can be a struggle to commission due to inflexible structures and budgets.

The involvement of people with alcohol problems in planning and contributing to service provision is increasing and reference made to 'co-production' in a number of key guidance documents (PHE, 2015). Attempts are made by commissioners to gain feedback from the people using services, for instance through questionnaires, focus groups and consultation. A challenge here is in involving people who may be in services for short periods of time or in and out of services. Again, meeting users of services outside treatment settings would be helpful but there are limitations in terms of reduced size of commissioning teams and their being based often in large centralised buildings which lend themselves less to direct community involvement and feedback systems.

A further challenge identified by commissioners, which relates to all the topics previously mentioned, is that of being able to draw on accurate and current prevalence data of alcohol problems in their geographical area. Whether relating to patterns of alcohol use or local population data in terms of ethnicity, since 2012, data has been estimated from intelligence about small samples and there has been a significant gap in terms of needs assessment. Such a fundamental issue has made it difficult for commissioners to identify priority areas based on evidence rather than estimates.

Clearly, many commissioners are experienced in the field of commissioning alcohol services and passionate about obtaining good quality evidence-based services for those with alcohol problems. The people we interviewed expressed a number of ways in which commissioning could be more effective. More accurate prevalence data would enable them to commission locally relevant and responsive services. It would help commissioners to develop relevant performance indicators based on local needs, for example, numbers of affected others being supported, numbers of children at risk or in need, re-engagement of people with alcohol problems with education or employment. Research indicates that recovery from alcohol dependence is a long process. Commissioners would like to see more performance indicators related to long-term recovery, rather than short-term treatment outcomes, which may not predict future well-being. Fundamental to improvement in commissioning would be for money to be ring fenced for providing alcohol and drug services. In addition, services could be commissioned every 10 years, rather than more frequently, which is expensive and disruptive to both service users and staff.

In straitened economic circumstances and a challenging commissioning environment, examples of good practice are often hard-won but significant. These include: partnership and community-based service provision, embedding of Brief Interventions for alcohol in primary care and pharmacies and moving away from a 'one size fits all' service provision for alcohol users. Commissioning does not occur in a vacuum and clearly wider issues impinge on effectiveness of treatment, such as alcohol labeling, pricing and advertising. Perhaps shifts in the wider availability of alcohol and laws regulating its use, could significantly contribute to prevention of further alcohol problems and change societal attitudes. This has been demonstrated in relation to tobacco regulation (Levy, Currie, & Clancy, 2013). Meanwhile, commissioners and service providers often continue to work together to innovate and be responsive in the attempt to provide high quality and effective approaches to alcohol misuse.

An academic perspective

We turn now, to focus on those who are actively contributing to the alcohol evidence base, through their work as academics. A number of issues will be discussed, as raised by the academics we spoke with. The first issue encountered was with the term 'academic' and those who may be carrying out research. Not everyone within academia would consider themselves to be an academic. One PhD student considered herself to fundamentally be a clinician, having had a career within a clinical setting; a penchant for research, brought her in to the arena of academia. Interestingly, this may be unusual, with many academics behind the evidence base, never having a clinical role within a drug and alcohol service. It was thought that this could make it more difficult for those doing research to make theory to practice links and their research easily implementable within current services.

As discussed, evidence based practice is there to improve standards and ensure that the treatment and interventions received by service users, will lead to the best possible outcomes. However, this comes at a price as research can be expensive. In 2017, PHE published over 910 articles, and £19.4 million was acquired in external research funding (PHE, 2019); on average £21,000 per publication The PHE '2016–17 Alcohol and Drugs

Treatment Commissioning Tool' estimated expenditure of adult drug treatment services at £481 million; an additional £222 million was estimated to have been spent on adult alcohol services (PHE, 2017a). Within the period of 2016–2017, 589,101 adults were estimated to have an alcohol dependency across the 151 local authorities within England (PHE, 2017b); 80,454 adults had contact with treatment services for support with alcohol and it took clients, on average, 202.7 days to complete treatment (PHE, 2017c). It is difficult to calculate the exact commissioning costs of treatment per individual, but these figures would indicate that treatment cost in the region of £2759 per person; £13.61 per day. This puts the cost of research in to perspective. Thinking about alcohol research specifically, Project MATCH was commissioned by the National Institute on Alcohol Abuse and Alcoholism, set out to ascertain which treatment interventions were most effective in treating people mostly struggling with alcohol dependency. The study ran from 1989 to 1997, involved 1726 clients and tested 504 hypothesis (Longabaugh & Wirtz, 2001); It was considered the largest and most expensive clinical trial of its kind at $27 million. With inflation in today's economy this would cost in the region of $43 million.

The cost and revenue from research can mean that emphasis is placed on funding and publication at the expense of the research itself. Stakeholders may only be interested in funding specific research projects which skews what is researched or how it is researched. Practices such as 'publication bias' (Guy, Davies, & Rizq, 2019) where emphasis is placed only on significant results, and the 'file drawer problem' (Rosenthal, 1979) where research supporting the null hypothesis is never published, have been well documented. Some academics may only be interested in projects which are likely to lead to publication in high profile journals or are likely to have demonstrable quickly realised impact. At the opposite end of the spectrum, 'bottom up' influences, like commissioners' priorities, can impact on what is researched, but often only when these ideas are associated with access to funding. All these factors can narrow the evidence base and even affect the direction of future research.

Just as staff within services may not have a contextualized sense of what evidence based practice is due to time constraints, academics described how time pressures can affect them. Keeping up to date can be difficult as can expanding knowledge in relevant areas beyond their chosen fields, which are often fairly tightly defined. It could be argued that the research is only as good as the researchers' knowledge. However, it may be even more complicated. A further problem that the academics face is making the research relevant by answering the questions which clinicians need answering (Orford, 2008). Within academia, funding streams may influence the focus to be on the causation of alcohol problems. The clinicians' focus may be more centered on what will help them work with the client.

If the research is unhelpful in a clinical setting, clinicians can be more inclined to do what they feel works; practice-based evidence. There is some overlap between evidence- based practice and practice-based evidence. We could question whether we are learning from observation and measurement or applying knowledge to the individual and measuring the consequences, or indeed doing both. Practice-based evidence can be harder to quantify as it is not necessarily standardised. However even when people say that they are using a theoretical underpinning how do we truly know that this is what they are doing?

The social stigma that surrounds alcohol addiction, was also touched upon by an academic, who spoke of the social bias and social power at play within substance misuse, in particular the shame and blame felt by those who become dependent on alcohol. There is a common misconception that someone within treatment services for alcohol addiction has to announce that "I am an alcoholic". This is a peculiarity which is not seen within other sectors, for instance you do not commonly hear of someone struggling with depression standing up and saying, "I'm a depressive", or even blaming themselves for feeling depressed. This may have something to do with the availability of alcohol and its social prevalence and acceptability. Media portrayal of 12 step fellowships may also yield unhelpful stereotypes that deter people from accessing support. Ironically, research which could perhaps support in educating and informing societal attitudes can confound issues. The language and style in which research is written can make it inaccessible to staff and the lay person (Salita & Germany, 2015). Words such as 'substance misuse', 'substance abuse', 'alcohol use disorder' and 'alcoholism' have a negative connotation, presenting individuals as problematic or to blame. Such terms can be dehumanizing and reductionist, alienating the people that the evidence base is attempting to understand and support.

It is clear from academics' perspective that there are many agendas which influence the evidence base, including the 'academic' themselves, commissioner, clinician and service-user. In order for evidence-based practice to be truly beneficial, these agendas with their different voices need to link up. There are some good examples within current practice, where such collaboration is happening in order to produce meaningful evidence based practice. For instance, within the development of digital interventions within services. Where it has been recognized that people with alcohol problems are finding it increasingly difficult to access alcohol treatment, service users, academics and treatment providers have come together to develop and test digital the efficacy of digital interventions (Dugdale, Elison, Davies, Ward, & Jones, 2016; Stefanopoulou, Lewis, Taylor, Broscombe, & Larkin, 2019).

Themes from these different perspectives

In conclusion, the pathways from the evidence to practice or from practice to evidence can be viewed through different lenses, depending on the role of the observer and their attitudes and beliefs. However, all the perspectives discussed in this chapter share a common goal in aiming for better and more effective approaches to alcohol misuse. A number of challenges have been identified in achieving this goal. These include most readily perceptible challenges of reduction in time and resources available to meet the demand of supporting people who misuse alcohol, which is arguably the most pervasive substance in UK society. Some more abstract but nevertheless important challenges relate to the nature of the guidance on what works and the subjectivity in its interpretation, within the context of changing service and commissioning structures and national funding priorities. Some of the more creative ways to face these challenges include the use of technology to create readily available and updated resources for people and a range of types of service provision with flexibility in where and how to access support, involving working across systems and treatment providers. The need to deal with and challenge the stigma associated with alcohol misuse pervades all of these creative solutions and the importance of co-production of services is paramount if we are to truly offer person-centered approaches.

Challenges to good quality treatment, based on best available evidence are unlikely to diminish and will inevitably change. Our recommendations for meeting these challenges, based on the people we have interviewed and on our own experience of working in this field, rest on some key principles. There needs to be true co-production of services from their inception, involving people who misuse alcohol and others affected by that use. A 'one size fits all' approach is likely to be ineffective and misses the complexity of individuals, their social networks and communities – we need variation in types, locations and modes of treatment. Fundamental to any effective approach to alcohol misuse is the people who work in services – recruitment of staff based on their values and attitudes is essential to address stigma associated with alcohol misuse and communication within services needs to be not only 'top-down' but 'bottom-up'. Longer commissioning cycles for these services and the development of place-based commissioning which focusses on the needs of the whole person, rather than specific problem areas, would provide a healthier context for addressing alcohol use and misuse. This theme of joining up and working across different types of services is also manifest in the need to link evidence-based practice with practice-based evidence and to link frontline provision with academic research and lived experience.

These are difficult times for working in the alcohol misuse treatment field, yet honest recognition of challenges, innovation, creativity and hard work can all provide some direction for effecting real changes and improvement in service provision.

References

Adfam. (2012). *Challenging stigma: Tackling the prejudice experienced by the families of drug and alcohol users.* Retrieved from https://adfam.org.uk/files/docs/adfam_challenging_stigma.pdf.

Adfam. (2013). *Out of focus: How families are affected by problem drinking, and how they look for help*. Retrieved from https://adfam.org.uk/files/docs/adfam_alcoholreport_2013.pdf.

Adfam. (2017). *Making it happen – Support for families and carers affected by someone else's drug or alcohol use*. Retrieved from https://adfam.org.uk/files/docs/Making_it_happen_final_PDF.pdf.

Al-Anon Family Groups. (n.d.). *Al-Anon family groups UK & EIRE*. Retrieved from https://www.al-anonuk.org.uk/.

Alcohol Change UK. (n.d.). *Alcohol change UK*. Retrieved from https://alcoholchange.org.uk/.

Bowen, S., Chawla, N., & Marlatt, G. A. (2011). *Mindfulness-based relapse prevention for addictive behaviors: A clinician's guide*. London: Guilford Press.

Cook, S., Heather, N., McCambridge, J., & United Kingdom Alcohol Treatment Trial Research Team. (2015). The role of the working alliance in treatment for alcohol problems. *Psychology of Addictive Behaviors*, *29*(2), 371–381.

Copello, A., Templeton, L., Orford, J., & Velleman, R. (2010). The 5-step method: Evidence of gains for affected family members. *Drugs: Education, Prevention and Policy*, *17*(S1), 100–112.

Critchlow, N., MacKintosh, A., Hooper, L., Thomas, C., & Vohra, J. (2019). Participation with alcohol marketing and user-created promotion on social media, and the association with higher-risk alcohol consumption and brand identification among adolescents in the UK. *Addiction Research & Theory*, *27*(6), 515–526. Available from https://doi.org/10.1080/16066359.2019.1567715.

Dubois, C. A., Bentein, K., Mansour, J. B., Gilber, F., & Bédard, J. L. (2014). Why some employees adopt or resist reorganization of work practices in health care: Associations between perceived loss of resources, burnout, and attitudes to change. *International Journal of Environmental Research and Public Health*, *11*(1), 187–201.

Dugdale, S., Elison, S., Davies, G., Ward, J., & Jones, M. (2016). The use of digital technology in substance misuse recovery. *Cyberpsychology: Journal of Psychosocial Research on Cyberspace*, *10*(4). Available from https://doi.org/10.5817/CP2016-4-5, Article 5.

Grandparents Plus. (n.d.). Retrieved from https://www.grandparentsplus.org.uk/.

Greenhalgh, T., Snow, R., Ryan, S., Rees, S., & Sailsbury, H. (2015). Six 'biases' against patients and carers in evidence-based medicine. *BMC Medicine*, *13*, 200. Available from https://doi.org/10.1186/s12916-015-0437-x.

Guy, A., Davies, J., & Rizq, R. (Eds.), (2019). *Guidance for psychological therapists: Enabling conversations with clients taking or withdrawing from prescribed psychiatric drugs*. London: APPG for Prescribed Drug Dependence.

Guy, A., Thomas, R., Stephenson, S., & Loewenthal, D. (2011). *NICE under scrutiny: The impact of the National Institute for Health and Clinical Excellence guidelines on the provision of psychotherapy in the UK. UK Council for Psychotherapy Research Unit*. UK: Research Centre for Therapeutic Education, Roehampton University.

Health Innovation Network. (2018). *Annual report 2018/19*. Retrieved from https://healthinnovationnetwork.com/annual-report-18-19/.

Levy, D. T., Currie, L., & Clancy, L. (2013). Tobacco control policy in the UK: Blueprint for the rest of Europe? , Retrieved from*European Journal of Public Health*, *23*(2), 201–206. Available from https://doi.org/10.1093/eurpub/cks090.

Miller, W. R., & Rollnick, S. (2013). *Applications of motivational interviewing. Motivational interviewing: Helping people change* (3rd ed.). London: Guilford Press.

National Health Service [NHS]. (2019). *Long term plan, 2019*. Retrieved from https://www.longtermplan.nhs.uk/.

National Institute for Health and Care Excellence [NICE]. (2011). *Alcohol-use disorders: Diagnosis, assessment and management of harmful drinking (high-risk drinking) and alcohol dependence [CG115]*. Retrieved from https://www.nice.org.uk/guidance/cg115.

NHS UK. (2013). *Are the middle classes in denial about alcohol use?* Retrieved from https://www.nhs.uk/news/lifestyle-and-exercise/are-the-middle-classes-in-denial-about-alcohol-use/.

NICE. (2018a). *Developing NICE guidelines: The manual. Process and methods [PMG20]*. Retrieved from https://www.nice.org.uk/process/pmg20/chapter/introduction-and-overview.

NICE. (2018b). *Principles for putting evidence-based guidance into practice*. Retrieved from https://www.nice.org.uk/Media/Default/About/what-we-do/Into-practice/Principles-for-putting-evidence-based-guidance-into-practice.pdf.

Orchowski, L. M., & Johnson, J. E. (2012). Efficacy of group treatments for alcohol use disorders: A review. *Current Drug Abuse Reviews*, *5*, 148–157.

Orford, J. (2008). Asking the right questions in the right way: The need for a shift in research on psychological treatments for addiction. *Addiction*, *103*(6), 875–885.

Orford, J. (2013). Addiction in the family is a major but neglected contributor to the global burden of adult ill-health. *Social Science & Medicine*, *78*, 70–77.

Orford, J., Copello, A., Velleman, R., & Templeton, L. (2010). Family members affected by a close relative's addiction: The stress-strain-coping-support model. *Drugs: Education, Prevention and Policy*, *17*(S1), 36–43.

Oxford Centre for Evidence-Based Medicine [OCEBM] Working Group. (2011). *The Oxford 2011 levels of evidence* . Retrieved from http://www.cebm.net/ocebm-levels-of-evidence/.

Project MATCH hypotheses: Results and causal chain analyses. In R. Longabaugh, & P. W. Wirtz (Eds.), *NIAAA Project MATCH monograph series* (Vol. 8). Rockville, MD: NIAAA.

Public Health England. (2015). *A guide to community-centred approaches for health and wellbeing*. Retrieved from https://assets.publishing.service.gov.uk/government/uploads/system/uploads/attachment_data/file/768979/A_guide_to_community-centred_approaches_for_-health_and_wellbeing__full_report_.pdf.

Public Health England. (2017a). *2016–17 Alcohol and drugs treatment commissioning tool: Guidance document*. Retrieved from https://assets.publishing.service.gov.uk/government/uploads/system/uploads/attachment_data/file/670959/Alcohol-and-drugs-treatment-commissioning_tool-guidance-document.pdf.

Public Health England. (2017b). *Research and analysis: Alcohol dependence prevalence in England; Estimates of the number of alcohol dependent adults in each local authority in England*. Retrieved from https://www.gov.uk/government/publications/alcohol-dependence-prevalence-in-england.

Public Health England. (2017c). *Adult substance misuse statistics from the National Drug Treatment Monitoring System (NDTMS), 1 April 2016 to 31 March 2017*. Retrieved from https://assets.publishing.service.gov.uk/government/uploads/system/uploads/attachment_data/file/658056/Adult-statistics-from-the-national-drug-treatment-monitoring-system-2016-2017.pdf.

Public Health England. (2018a). *Alcohol commissioning support: Principles and indicators*.

Public Health England. (2018b). *Research and analysis: PHE inquiry into the fall in numbers of people in alcohol treatment: findings*. Retrieved from https://www.gov.uk/government/publications/alcohol-treatment-inquiry-summary-of-findings/phe-inquiry-into-the-fall-in-numbers-of-people-in-alcohol-treatment-findings.

Public Health England. (2018c). *Innovation fund open to help children of dependent drinkers Scottish families affected by alcohol & drugs*. Retrieved from https://www.sfad.org.uk.

Public Health England. (2019). *Corporate report PHE research 2017 to 2018: Annual review [online]*. Gov.UK. 16 January 2019. [viewed 03 January 2020]. Retrieved from https://www.gov.uk/government/publications/phe-research-annual-review/phe-research-annual-review-2017-to-2018.

Rosenthal, R. (1979). The "file drawer problem" and tolerance for null results. *Psychological Bulletin*, *86*(3), 838-641.

Salita, J. T., & Germany, B. (2015). Writing for lay audiences: A challenge for scientists. *Medical Writing*, *24*(4), 183–189.

SMART Family & Friends. (n.d.). *UK SMART Recovery, self-managementand recovery training*. Retrieved from https://smartrecovery.org.uk/smart_family__friends.

Stefanopoulou, E., Lewis, D., Taylor, M., Broscombe, J., & Larkin, J. (2019). Digitally delivered psychological interventions for anxiety disorders: A comprehensive review. *The Psychiatric Quarterly*, *90*(1), 197–215.

Swisher, A. (2010). Practice-based evidence. *Cardiopulmonary Physical Therapy Journal*, *21*(2), 4.

UK-Rehab. (n.d.). Retrieved from https://www.uk-rehab.com/about-uk-rehab/.

Velleman, R., & Templeton, L. (2018). *Impact of parents' substance misuse on children: An update*. Published online by Cambridge University Press. Available from https://doi.org/10.1192/apt.bp.114.014449.

Wendt, D. C., & Gone, J. P. (2017). Group therapy for substance use disorders: A survey of clinician practices. *Journal of Groups in Addiction & Recovery*, *12*(4), 243–259. Available from https://doi.org/10.1080/1556035x.2017.1348280.

Chapter 24

Transdermal alcohol monitors: Research, applications, and future directions

Catharine E. Fairbairn and Dahyeon Kang
Department of Psychology, University of Illinois at Urbana-Champaign, Champaign, IL, United States

Developing a reliable alcohol biosensor has become a major public health priority (Leffingwell et al., 2013). Approximately 4.5% of the global burden of disease and injury is attributable to alcohol (WHO, 2018) with alcohol-related traffic accidents taking approximately 10,000 lives each year in the U.S. alone (National Highway Traffic Safety Administration, 2017). An alcohol biosensor could represent a tremendous advance towards helping people make informed decisions about their drinking and, ultimately, towards curbing alcohol-related mortality.

Devices for the objective quantification of behaviors have long been of interest to researchers and consumers across health domains (e.g., wearable exercise trackers such as 'fitbit'), but, due to alcohol's neurocognitive effects and also cultural conventions surrounding drinking, the need for a biosensor to measure drinking behavior has loomed particularly large. More specifically, heavy alcohol consumption is associated with profound memory and cognitive disruptions that impair awareness of consumption (Weissenborn & Duka, 2003; White, 2003). Further, standard drink sizes and quantities can vary widely so that the consumer is not always conscious of the quantity of alcohol consumed (Barnett, Wei, & Czachowski, 2009; Kerr, Greenfield, Tujague, & Brown, 2005; Kerr, Patterson, Koenen, & Greenfield, 2008). Finally, substantial societal stigma can accompany alcohol consumption for many individuals (e.g., women, underaged individuals, members of certain religious and ethnic groups) such that, even given an awareness of their own drinking practices, some might be reluctant to share information about their drinking with others (Davis, Thake, & Vilhena, 2010; George, Gournic, & McAfee, 1988; Zapolski, Pedersen, McCarthy, & Smith, 2014). Continuous

The Handbook of Alcohol Use - Understandings from Synapse to Society.
DOI: https://doi.org/10.1016/B978-0-12-816720-5.00014-1

objective monitoring of alcohol consumption is likely to prove a valuable tool for prevention and intervention, where awareness of problematic behavior has been identified as a key factor in behavioral change (DiClemente & Prochaska, 1998; Miller, Zweben, DiClimente, & Rychtarik, 1994), and could also help us move towards a better understanding of drinking behaviors by improving the measurement of alcohol consumption in empirical research studies (Leffingwell et al., 2013). Thus, the development of a reliable alcohol biosensor could represent a major advance in our ability to understand, prevent, and treat problem drinking.

In pursuit of a reliable alcohol biosensor, researchers have explored a variety of different methods, each of which has presented with its own distinct set of strengths and limitations. Breathalyzers are a reliable method for estimating BAC that will doubtless continue to be valuable moving forward (Jones, 1996). But breathalyzers require a motivated episode by the user, may be inconvenient/embarrassing to use in some settings, and further can be contaminated by mouth alcohol when used in close proximity to drinking. Techniques assessing alcohol use indirectly through metabolites may involve a significant delay and/or be alcohol nonspecific (Dougherty et al., 2014; Swift, 2003). Finally, it is possible that future biosensors will have the capability of directly assessing alcohol in tissue using optics (e.g., Near-infrared spectroscopy). However, such devices currently take the form of large table-top machines, and the sensors they require to detect alcohol put them out of the price range of most consumers. Currently, transdermal devices are the technology with the most promise for the continuous, noninvasive assessment of alcohol consumption.

Transdermal alcohol sensors

Three decades ago, scientists produced some of the first evidence that transdermally detected alcohol, measured by a device that rested on the surface of the skin, was highly correlated with Blood Alcohol Concentration (r's .94–.99; Giles et al., 1987; Swift, Martin, Swette, Laconti, & Kackley, 1992). Approximately 1% of alcohol consumed is diffused transdermally in the form of sweat and insensible perspiration. So, similar to the manner in which a breathalyzer estimates BAC by measuring the quantity of alcohol in expired air, transdermal sensors estimate drinking by examining the content of alcohol in water vapor emitted from the skin's surface.

Several transdermal devices have been developed, and these devices vary substantially in their features and design. Currently, the most widely used transdermal device is the Secure Remote Alcohol Monitoring System (AMS SCRAM) transdermal bracelet. SCRAM is a relatively large/bulky device (164.4 g/5.8 oz) that is worn around the ankle, employing fuel cell technology to detect alcohol in insensible perspiration. SCRAM incorporates technology within the sensor itself, as well as within the sensor strap, that detects when the bracelet has been tampered with or removed—technology that is necessary given the SCRAM's use within criminal justice-involved populations (see below).

Transdermal sensors have also taken more compact forms. The WrisTAS—which was among the first of the transdermal monitors—is a relatively compact watch-like device warn around the wrist. SCRAM and WrisTAS are the devices that have most commonly been examined in research to date. More recent devices, all of which are currently under development, include the BACtrack Skyn, Milo Proof, and Quantac Tally (Fairbairn & Kang, 2019; Fairbairn, Kang & Bosch, 2020). Similar in size/appearance to a fitbit, these devices feature smartphone/smartwatch integration, allowing users to examine real-time estimates of their blood alcohol concentration (BAC) directly from their phones/watches. However, although several transdermal monitors are under development and/or have been made available to researchers, none are currently available to consumers.

Research and treatment applications of transdermal monitors

A range of potential applications have been proposed for transdermal alcohol monitors. Conversion factors for translating transdermal alcohol concentration (TAC) into precise estimates of BAC are still currently under development (see below), and so transdermal devices are used primarily as abstinence monitors (i.e., to detect whether any alcohol consumption has occurred), and not as a means for estimating the quantity of alcohol consumed or of quantifying BAC. Nonetheless, even as abstinence monitors, these sensors have proven useful across several domains, including within the criminal justice system, alcohol interventions, and also more basic alcohol research.

At the present time, the criminal justice system offers one of the largest markets for transdermal sensors. Individuals who have committed alcohol-related offenses (e.g., driving while intoxicated, etc.) may be assigned a transdermal alcohol monitor with the requirement that they abstain from alcohol as a condition of probation or parole. SCRAM is currently the most widely used transdermal monitor in such contexts. The SCRAM system issues "alcohol alerts," employing formulas that examine the precise rate of TAC increase and decrease to distinguish environmental alcohol (e.g., alcohol-based perfume applied to the skin) from ingested alcohol. SCRAM has been shown to detect approximately 57% of episodes of true alcohol consumption, with the rate of alcohol detection increasing with the amount of alcohol ingested, and research further indicates that rates of false positives using SCRAM are likely to be quite low (Marques & McKnight, 2009). Criminal justice applications of SCRAM have now spread across 6 countries and over 600,000 users (Alcohol Monitoring Services, 2018)

Transdermal monitors are also now beginning to be applied within intervention programs aimed at helping individuals with alcohol use disorder

(AUD) achieve abstinence. Transdermal sensors have proven particularly useful within the context of contingency management programs, approaches in which patients have the opportunity to gain incentives—e.g., food items, gift vouchers, or other items consistent with a drug-free lifestyle—in exchange for proof of abstinence from substances (Prendergast, Podus, Finney, Greenwell, & Roll, 2006). Contingency management interventions have proven highly effective when applied to illicit substances such as cocaine or opiates, but, in applications to AUD, some researchers have pointed to challenges associated with the measurement of alcohol biomarkers including a short half-life and, in the case of indirect alcohol metabolites, non-specificity to alcohol (Dougherty et al., 2014). The use of transdermal alcohol sensors within contingency management interventions appears to be effective, with initial research indicating that participants assigned to wear transdermal ankle monitors, and receiving incentives on the basis of transdermal data, significantly reduce their alcohol consumption compared with control participants (Barnett, 2015; Barnett, Tidey, Murphy, Swift, & Colby, 2011; Dougherty et al., 2014, 2015).

More recently, scientists have begun using transdermal alcohol sensors within basic alcohol research, including studies seeking to understand contexts and correlates of acute alcohol reinforcement as a means of understanding the roots of problematic drinking. For example, our team employed transdermal sensors to better understand the role of social factors in the emotional rewards that heavy drinkers gain from alcohol (Fairbairn et al., 2018). Participants in this study wore the SCRAM transdermal sensor in their daily lives over the course of a week while self-reporting on their mood and also taking photographs of their social surroundings. Since the relationship between TAC and BAC is thought to be moderated in part by individual difference factors, each participant in the study attended an alcohol-administration session, the data from which was used to convert that individual's TAC collected outside the laboratory into estimates of BAC (see below). Using these individualized equations to estimate the timing of alcohol episodes, we found that individuals gained more emotional reward from drinking alcohol in social settings than when drinking alone and, further, that alcohol boosted mood to a greater extent when individuals drank among strangers vs. among friends. We also conducted analyses using calibrated transdermal sensors to show that estimated BAC's were significantly higher when individuals were drinking with strangers vs. friends although, given complexities associated with creating continuous estimates of BAC from transdermal data, these results should be considered preliminary.

In sum, use of transdermal sensors is increasing across domains, with the most widespread current application of these sensors being within the criminal justice system. Other more recent applications include contingency-management alcohol interventions and also basic alcohol research. The current primary function of transdermal sensors as abstinence monitors, rather than as devices permitting the continuous estimation of BAC, lends itself mainly to applications within non-voluntary populations and/or those whose motivation for abstention might vary over time (i.e., those in treatment for AUD). Studies are also being conducted that seek to convert transdermal alcohol data into continuous, real-time estimates of BAC—a field of research that, if successful in its aims, would greatly expand the range of potential applications for transdermal technology.

Converting TAC into estimates of BAC

Unlike the relationship between BAC and the alcohol content of expired air, which can be characterized by a relatively straightforward conversion factor (Jones, 1996), the relationship between BAC and transdermal alcohol concentration (TAC) is believed to be complex (Anderson & Hlastala, 2006; Brown, 1985; Fairbairn, Rosen, Luczak, & Venerable, 2019). In particular, researchers have pointed to the following factors that complicate the transdermal estimation of alcohol consumption: (1) The relationship between BAC and TAC may vary depending on individual difference factors that covary with physical properties of the skin (e.g., gender; Hill-Kapturczak et al., 2015; Marques & McKnight, 2009). (2) The TAC-BAC relationship may vary depending on within-person/contextual factors (e.g., the temperature of the skin, the amount of sensible perspiration; Anderson & Hlastala, 2006); and finally (3) Some studies suggest TAC lags behind BAC by as much as 3–4 hours, a lag that would impact the utility of TAC as a proxy for BAC in real time (vs. as a record of past drinking; Swift, 2003).

Several groups have conducted research aimed at creating formulas that account for these complexities and so allow for the conversion of TAC into estimates of BAC. For example, studies conducted by researchers Dougherty and colleagues employ laboratory drinking paradigms and relatively straightforward regression models to predict BAC from TAC (Dougherty et al., 2012; Hill-Kapturczak et al., 2014, 2015). Note, however, that these regressions include parameters as predictors that are typically only known post-hoc (e.g., time to peak TAC) and so are not appropriate for the conversion of real time TAC data. Researchers Rosen and Luczak have created a sophisticated model for the estimation of BAC from TAC data via formulas reflecting the physiological process through which alcohol is transported from the blood through the skin and then measured by the transdermal sensor. While earlier applications of these formulas required individual calibration of transdermal sensors to each participant via a laboratory alcohol-administration (Luczak & Rosen, 2014)—thereby allowing for adjustment for individual differences (e.g., skin thickness; see Fairbairn et al., 2018 for example application)—recent work by this group indicates that estimates of BAC may be created using non-calibrated, generic models as well (Fairbairn et al., 2019; Sirlanci et al., 2018). Various research groups are also exploring the utility of machine learning algorithms—methods that use artificial intelligence to learn complex patterns in data—for translating TAC into BAC estimates (Fairbairn, Kang, & Bosch, 2020).

In sum, several statistical/computational frameworks have been proposed for the conversion of TAC into estimates of BAC, and so the field is not lacking potential analytic methods that might be used to convert data from transdermal monitors. While rich in analytic theory, however, the field has tended to be poor in data, as there has been a relative paucity of human subjects research that examines the TAC-BAC relationship using empirical methods.

Given the complex nature of the TAC-BAC relationship, studies employing large samples of participants as well as those examining the same participants across a range of contexts would be indicated. To date, to our knowledge, only 11 studies have examined TAC in relation to objectively assessed BAC (i.e., breathalyzer or direct blood/plasma measure). Of these studies, 7 have featured only laboratory methods (Davidson, Camara, & Swift, 1997; Dougherty et al., 2012; Giles et al., 1987; Hill-Kapturczak et al., 2014, 2015; Swift et al., 1992; Wang, Fridberg, Leeman, Cook, & Porges, in press) and 4 studies combined laboratory and ambulatory methods (Fairbairn et al., 2018; Luczak & Rosen, 2014; Marques & McKnight, 2009; Sakai, Mikulich-Gilbertson, Long, & Crowley, 2006). Of note, none of these studies were well powered to examine individual differences in the TAC-BAC relationship. The average sample size across all studies was 19, with the largest study involving just 48 participants (Fairbairn et al., 2018). Of the four studies to employ ambulatory methods (i.e., examining drinking in everyday contexts outside the lab), two focused on validating transdermal devices as abstinence monitors and so contain little information on the continuous TAC-BAC relationship (Marques & McKnight, 2009; Sakai et al., 2006) while a third featured a sample size of one expert user (Luczak & Rosen, 2014). Our own ambulatory study involved objective (breathalyzer) transdermal validation only in the lab, and not in everyday contexts (Fairbairn et al., 2018). None of these ambulatory studies have examined contextual factors (e.g., humidity level, degree of physical exertion, etc.) as moderators of the BAC-TAC relationship.

While deficiencies in the size and quantity of prior studies (particularly ambulatory studies) is notable, also notable are the limitations of the transdermal devices employed in these studies. Studies conducted to date report lags between BAC and TAC varying from 30 minutes (Swift et al., 1992) to 270 minutes (Marques & McKnight, 2009), and correlation coefficients (*r*'s) ranging as low as .49 (Sakai et al., 2006) and as high as .99 (Giles et al., 1987). One possibility is that these results reflect true variability in the TAC-BAC relationship. However, a close look at this research suggest that at least some of this variation is likely attributable to limitations of the transdermal devices themselves. Three of these studies (Luczak & Rosen, 2014; Marques & McKnight, 2009; Swift et al., 1992) employed the WrisTAS sensor, a device that is notorious for nonresponse and extreme data noise, with the largest WrisTAS study yielding a remarkable 67% failure rate (Marques &

McKnight, 2009). Of note, however, the device most commonly used in prior research is the SCRAM ankle bracelet (Dougherty et al., 2012; Fairbairn et al., 2018; Hill-Kapturczak et al., 2014, 2015; Marques & McKnight, 2009; Sakai et al., 2006). The ankle positioning of the SCRAM device is ideal for the minimization of tampering and removal among criminal-justice populations but may interfere with the measurement of BAC transdermally. Specifically, the precise positioning of the transdermal device relative to the skin has been identified as an important factor impacting the transdermal detection of alcohol (Anderson & Hlastala, 2006), and the ankle positioning of the SCRAM might introduce variability into this position (e.g., SCRAM might slip from sitting snug against the calf to hanging loose around the ankle as the user walks). Further, the relationship between TAC and BAC can vary significantly depending on the positioning of the TAC device on the body—e.g., measurement from forearm vs. forehead produce different TAC-BAC relationships (Swift, 2000). Importantly, the notion that TAC lags behind BAC by many hours is derived primarily from studies employing the SCRAM ankle bracelet (e.g., 130 min lag in Fairbairn et al., 2018; 129 min lag in Hill-Kapturczak et al., 2015; 150 min lag in Sakai et al., 2006), with wrist-worn devices typically estimating 50%, or less, the delay of ankle worn devices (e.g., 30 min lag in Swift et al., 1992; average 65 min lag in Wang et al., in press)—see also Marques and McKnight (2009) and Fairbairn and Kang (2019) for research capturing this lag differential within a single participant sample.

In sum, the relationship between TAC and BAC is complex, likely varying based on contextual and individual factors and also involving some degree of lag. Although a number of mathematical models have been developed to characterize the relationship between BAC and TAC, human subject studies, particularly those examining transdermal sensors in everyday contexts, have been scarce and underpowered, and the devices examined in these studies (SCRAM and WrisTAS) have been suboptimal. As a result, the precise relationship between transdermal alcohol concentration and blood alcohol concentration is unknown. Further, it is possible that the extent of the complexity of this relationship may have been overestimated on the basis of noisy and otherwise suboptimal transdermal monitoring devices employed in extant human subjects research.

Future research directions and applications

Moving forward, to produce a transdermal device capable of creating precise estimates of BAC, the field is in need of human subject research that is improved across several different areas. In particular, given that the relationship between TAC and BAC is theorized to vary based on individual-difference factors, research with much larger samples of participants would be required to create BAC estimates with a high likelihood of generalizing across people. Further, in light of the potential influence of contextual factors on the transdermal measurement of BAC (e.g., humidity, temperature, etc), more research examining individuals across contexts is needed, including research in everyday drinking settings and research that attempts to explicitly measure and/or manipulate contextual factors. Finally, given the limitations of prior devices, transdermal devices for use in research that are better suited to producing precise estimates of BAC in near real time would be required. It is possible that some of the wrist-worn smartphone-integrated devices currently under development would serve this purpose, although none are currently widely available to researchers.

Current transdermal technology does appear to serve the purpose of monitoring whether or not any alcohol consumption is taking place, a purpose that serves key functions in criminal justice settings as well as abstinence-oriented alcohol interventions. Such abstinence-monitoring devices might also ultimately be useful to researchers seeking to understand frequency of drinking across longer spans of time. However, since individuals' awareness/memory for abstinence vs. non-abstinence tends to be relatively good, at least over brief time intervals, such applications are likely to be specifically useful among populations who are unmotivated and/or sporadically motivated to accurately report on their alcohol consumption. In other words, among consistently motivated, voluntary populations, abstinence monitors have limited utility above and beyond self-report.

In contrast, were alcohol biosensors to be developed with the capability of producing relatively precise estimates of BAC, a range of additional applications for these devices seem plausible. In the realm of prevention, a discreet, wearable alcohol monitor could prove attractive to individuals interested in monitoring and improving their overall health and wellbeing, as has been the case with other health biosensors such as the fitbit. This widespread use of alcohol monitoring devices among social drinkers might stem the development of alcohol use disorder as well as various medical disorders associated with drinking (Centers for Disease Control & Prevention, 2010). In the realm of motor vehicle safety, continuous passive monitoring of BAC might reduce drunk driving fatalities, which are currently estimated at 10,000 annually (National Highway Traffic Safety Administration, 2017). Users might link transdermal sensors to automated prompts or alarms which would indicate when BAC is approaching unsafe levels, thus potentially reducing alcohol-related accidents and injuries. They might also be programmed to send alerts to notify a designated driver or ride-sharing service. In the medical realm, interventions for some of the U.S.'s most common health conditions (i.e., diabetes, high blood pressure) require that patients moderate their alcohol intake, while not necessarily requiring abstinence (Howard, Arnsten, & Gourevitch, 2004; Puddey & Beilin, 2006). A continuous BAC monitor could help patients maintain healthy levels of alcohol consumption. The information provided by these monitors might also be useful to their healthcare providers in assessment and intervention.

In the clinical realm, transdermal sensors could be integrated into the assessment phase of alcohol interventions, thereby increasing motivation for change at intake by providing patients with objective information about their current drinking patterns (Miller et al., 1994; Vasilaki, Hosier, & Cox, 2006). Furthermore, within moderation management and harm reduction approaches to treating alcohol problems, transdermal sensors might be used as a means by which to track alcohol consumption and aid in the reduction of unsafe drinking practices (Marlatt & Witkiewitz, 2002). Finally, in the realm of research, an alcohol biosensor could revolutionize alcohol studies by providing an objective means of tracking drinking over time, thus improving science aimed at examining the causes and correlates of alcohol consumption, as well as research evaluating the success of intervention and prevention programs.

Conclusions

In sum, transdermal sensors show promise for the discreet, continuous assessment of alcohol consumption in real time. Currently, these devices are well validated for use as abstinence monitors among populations likely to produce unreliable reports of drinking episodes. The human subjects literature examining the relationship between TAC and BAC is currently small, underpowered, and inadequate to modeling contextual effects, and so continuous estimates of BAC from transdermal data may be imprecise and applications of transdermal sensors are somewhat limited. However, with improved human subjects research and a more precise understanding of the TAC-BAC relationship, transdermal sensors might serve health needs across a variety of domains, including aiding prevention of alcohol-related disorders, improving outcomes in harm reduction alcohol interventions, refining outcome assessment in alcohol research, and reducing the number of alcohol-related motor vehicle fatalities.

Acknowledgment

This research was supported by grant R01AA025969 to Catharine Fairbairn.

References

Alcohol Monitoring Services. (2018). About SCRAM systems. Retrieved from https://www.scramsystems.com/about/.

Anderson, J. C., & Hlastala, M. P. (2006). The kinetics of transdermal ethanol exchange. *Journal of Applied Physiology*, *100*(2), 649–655.

Barnett, N. P. (2015). Alcohol sensors and their potential for improving clinical care. *Addiction*, *110*(1), 1–3.

Barnett, N. P., Tidey, J., Murphy, J. G., Swift, R., & Colby, S. M. (2011). Contingency management for alcohol use reduction: A pilot study using a transdermal alcohol sensor. *Drug and Alcohol Dependence*, *118*(2), 391–399.

Barnett, N. P., Wei, J., & Czachowski, C. (2009). Measured alcohol content in college party mixed drinks. *Psychology of Addictive Behaviors*, *23*(1), 152–156.

Brown, D. J. (1985). The pharmacokinetics of alcohol excretion in human perspiration. *Methods and Findings in Experimental and Clinical Pharmacology*, *7*(10), 539–544.

Centers for Disease Control and Prevention. (2010). Alcohol and public health: Alcohol-related disease impact (ARDI). Average for United States 2006–2010 alcohol-attributable deaths due to excessive alcohol use. Available from https://nccd.cdc.gov/DPH_ARDI/default/default.aspx.

Davidson, D., Camara, P., & Swift, R. (1997). Behavioral effects and pharmacokinetics of low-dose intravenous alcohol in humans. *Alcoholism: Clinical and Experimental Research, 21* (7), 1294–1299.

Davis, C. G., Thake, J., & Vilhena, N. (2010). Social desirability biases in self-reported alcohol consumption and harms. *Addictive Behaviors*, *35*(4), 302–311.

DiClemente, C. C., & Prochaska, J. O. (1998). Toward a comprehensive, transtheoretical model of change: Stages of change and addictive behaviors. In W. R. Miller, & N. Heather (Eds.), *Treating addictive behaviors* (pp. 3–24). New York, NY: Plenum Press.

Dougherty, D. M., Charles, N. E., Acheson, A., John, S., Furr, R. M., & Hill-Kapturczak, N. (2012). Comparing the detection of transdermal and breath alcohol concentrations during periods of alcohol consumption ranging from moderate drinking to binge drinking. *Experimental and Clinical Psychopharmacology*, *20*(5), 373–381.

Dougherty, D. M., Hill-Kapturczak, N., Liang, Y., Karns, T. E., Cates, S. E., Lake, S. L., ... Roache, J. D. (2014). Use of continuous transdermal alcohol monitoring during a contingency management procedure to reduce excessive alcohol use. *Drug & Alcohol Dependence*, *142*, 301–306.

Dougherty, D. M., Karns, T. E., Mullen, J., Liang, Y., Lake, S. L., Roache, J. D., & Hill-Kapturczak, N. (2015). Transdermal alcohol concentration data collected during a contingency management program to reduce at-risk drinking. *Drug & Alcohol Dependence*, *148*, 77–84.

Fairbairn, C. E., Bresin, K. W., Kang, D., Rosen, I. G., Ariss, T., Luczak, S. E., ... Eckland, N. S. (2018). A multimodal investigation of contextual effects on alcohol's emotional rewards. *Journal of Abnormal Psychology*, *127*(4), 359–373. Available from https://doi.org/10.1037/abn0000346.

Fairbairn, C. E., Rosen, I. G., Luczak, S. E., Venerable, W. J. (2019). Estimating the quantity and time course of alcohol consumption from transdermal alcohol sensor data: A combined laboratory-ambulatory study. *Alcohol, 81*, 111–116.

Fairbairn C.E., & Kang, D. (2019). Temporal dynamics of transdermal alcohol concentration measured via new-generation wrist-worn biosensor. *Alcoholism: Clinical and Experimental Research, 43*(10), 2060–2069.

Fairbairn C. E., Kang, D., & Bosch, N. (2020). Using machine learning for real-time BAC estimation from a new-generation transdermal biosensor in the laboratory. *Drug and Alcohol Dependence, 216*, 108205.

George, W. H., Gournic, S. J., & McAfee, M. P. (1988). Perceptions of postdrinking female sexuality: Effects of gender, beverage choice, and drink payment. *Journal of Applied Social Psychology*, *18*(15), 1295–1316.

Giles, H. G., Meggiorini, S., Renaud, G. E., Thiessen, J. J., Vidins, E. I., Compton, K. V., ... Israel, Y. (1987). Ethanol vapor above skin: Determination by a gas sensor instrument and relationship with plasma concentration. *Alcoholism: Clinical and Experimental Research, 11* (3), 249–253.

Hill-Kapturczak, N., Lake, S. L., Roache, J. D., Cates, S. E., Liang, Y., & Dougherty, D. M. (2014). Do variable rates of alcohol drinking alter the ability to use transdermal alcohol monitors to estimate peak breath alcohol and total number of drinks? *Alcoholism: Clinical and Experimental Research*, *38*(10), 2517–2522.

Hill-Kapturczak, N., Roache, J. D., Liang, Y., Karns, T. E., Cates, S. E., & Dougherty, D. M. (2015). Accounting for sex-related differences in the estimation of breath alcohol concentrations using transdermal alcohol monitoring. *Psychopharmacology*, *232*(1), 115–123.

Howard, A. A., Arnsten, J. H., & Gourevitch, M. N. (2004). Effect of alcohol consumption on diabetes mellitus: A systematic review. *Annals of Internal Medicine*, *140*(3), 211–219.

Jones, A. W. (1996). Measuring alcohol in blood and breath for forensic purposes: A historical review. *Forensic Science Review*, *8*, 13–44.

Kerr, W. C., Greenfield, T. K., Tujague, J., & Brown, S. E. (2005). A drink is a drink? Variation in the amount of alcohol contained in beer, wine and spirits drinks in a US methodological sample. *Alcoholism: Clinical and Experimental Research*, *29*(11), 2015–2021.

Kerr, W. C., Patterson, D., Koenen, M. A., & Greenfield, T. K. (2008). Alcohol content variation of bar and restaurant drinks in Northern California. *Alcoholism: Clinical and Experimental Research*, *32*(9), 1623–1629.

Leffingwell, T. R., Cooney, N. J., Murphy, J. G., Luczak, S., Rosen, G., Dougherty, D. M., & Barnett, N. P. (2013). Continuous objective monitoring of alcohol use: Twenty-first century measurement using transdermal sensors. *Alcoholism: Clinical and Experimental Research*, *37*(1), 16–22. Available from https://doi.org/10.1111/j.1530-0277.2012.01869.x.

Luczak, S. E., & Rosen, I. G. (2014). Estimating BrAC from transdermal alcohol concentration data using the BrAC estimator software program. *Alcoholism: Clinical and Experimental Research*, *38*(8), 2243–2252. Available from https://doi.org/10.1111/acer.12478.

Marlatt, G. A., & Witkiewitz, K. (2002). Harm reduction approaches to alcohol use: Health promotion, prevention, and treatment. *Addictive Behaviors*, *27*(6), 867–886.

Marques, P. R., & McKnight, A. S. (2009). Field and laboratory alcohol detection with 2 types of transdermal devices. *Alcoholism: Clinical and Experimental Research*, *33*(4), 703–711.

Miller, W. R., Zweben, A., DiClimente, C., & Rychtarik, R. (1994). *Motivational enhancement therapy manual: A clinical research guide for therapists treating individuals with alcohol abuse and dependence*. Bethesda, MD: NIAAA.

National Highway Traffic Safety Administration. (2017). Traffic Safety Facts 2016 data: Alcohol-impaired driving. U.S. Department of Transportation. DOT HS 812, 450s. Retrieved from https://crashstats.nhtsa.dot.gov/Api/Public/ViewPublication/812450.

Prendergast, M., Podus, D., Finney, J., Greenwell, L., & Roll, J. (2006). Contingency management for treatment of substance use disorders: A meta-analysis. *Addiction*, *101*(11), 1546–1560.

Puddey, I. B., & Beilin, L. J. (2006). Alcohol is bad for blood pressure. *Clinical and Experimental Pharmacology and Physiology*, *33*(9), 847–852.

Sakai, J. T., Mikulich-Gilbertson, S. K., Long, R. J., & Crowley, T. J. (2006). Validity of transdermal alcohol monitoring: Fixed and self-regulated dosing. *Alcoholism: Clinical and Experimental Research*, *30*(1), 26–33.

Sirlanci, M., Rosen, I. G., Luczak, S. E., Fairbairn, C. E., Bresin, K., & Kang, D. (2018). Deconvolving the input to random abstract parabolic systems: A population model-based approach to estimating blood/breath alcohol concentration from transdermal alcohol biosensor data. *Inverse Problems*, *34*(12), 125006.

Swift, R. M. (2000). Transdermal alcohol measurement for estimation of blood alcohol concentration. *Alcoholism: Clinical and Experimental Research*, *24*(4), 422–423.

Swift, R. M. (2003). Direct measurement of alcohol and its metabolites. *Addiction, 98*(s2), 73–80.

Swift, R. M., Martin, C. S., Swette, L., Laconti, A., & Kackley, N. (1992). Studies on a wearable, electronic, transdermal alcohol sensor. *Alcoholism: Clinical and Experimental Research, 16*(4), 721–725.

Vasilaki, E. I., Hosier, S. G., & Cox, W. M. (2006). The efficacy of motivational interviewing as a brief intervention for excessive drinking: A meta-analytic review. *Alcohol and Alcoholism, 41*(3), 328–335.

Wang, Y., Fridberg, D.J., Leeman, R.F., Cook, R.L., & Porges, E.C. (in press). Wrist-worn alcohol biosensors: Strengths, limitations, and future directions. *Alcohol.*

Weissenborn, R., & Duka, T. A. (2003). Acute alcohol effects on cognitive function in social drinkers: Their relationship to drinking habits. *Psychopharmacology, 165*(3), 306–312.

White, A. M. (2003). What happened? Alcohol, memory blackouts, and the brain. *Alcohol Research and Health, 27*(2), 186–196.

WHO. (2018). *Global status report on alcohol and health.* Geneva, Switzerland: World Health Organization.

Zapolski, T. C. B., Pedersen, S. L., McCarthy, D. M., & Smith, G. T. (2014). Less drinking, yet more problems: Understanding African American drinking and related problems. *Psychological Bulletin, 140*(1), 188–223.

Chapter 25

Recovery from addiction: A synthesis of perspectives from behavioral economics, psychology, and decision modeling

Amber Copeland, Tom Stafford and Matt Field
Department of Psychology, University of Sheffield, Sheffield, United Kingdom

Alcohol-related harm and addiction

Alcohol consumption is one of the leading preventable causes of poor health and death on a global scale (Forouzanfar et al., 2016). Statistics from the World Health Organization (WHO) demonstrate that three million deaths per year are attributable to harmful alcohol consumption, representing 5.3% of all deaths worldwide (WHO, 2018). Consequently, harmful alcohol consumption and dependence are significant public health concerns (Rehm & Imtiaz, 2016).

There are two important tools for diagnosing 'addiction' (substance use disorder). These are *The Diagnostic and Statistical Manual of Mental Disorders, version 5* (DSM-5), published by the American Psychiatric Association in 2013 and the *International Classification of Diseases, version 11* (ICD-11), which is due to be finalized by the WHO in 2022. Both recognize that addictions operate on a continuum of severity. For example, the DSM-5 characterizes people based on the number of symptoms of substance use disorder (SUD) that they exhibit. A diagnosis of alcohol use disorder (AUD) can be mild (2–3 symptoms from 11), moderate (4–5 symptoms), or severe (6 or more symptoms).

Alcohol-related behavior change and recovery from addiction

There is no universally-accepted definition of 'recovery' from addiction (Ashford et al., 2019), which is reflective of the heterogeneous pathways and outcomes that are associated with recovery (White, 2007). People recover with

The Handbook of Alcohol Use - Understandings from Synapse to Society.
DOI: https://doi.org/10.1016/B978-0-12-816720-5.00002-5

and without treatment, and outcomes vary from complete abstinence to moderation of alcohol consumption (Witkiewitz, 2013; Witkiewitz et al., 2019).

Influential theoretical accounts of addiction depict it as a chronic and irreversible brain disease that promotes compulsive substance use and recurrent cycles of treatment and relapse (Everitt & Robbins, 2016; Leshner, 1997; Volkow, Koob, & McLellan, 2016). This framing is contradicted by evidence that most people with addiction eventually recover, often without treatment (Dawson et al., 2005; Heyman, 2013; Lopez-Quintero et al., 2011). A convincing line of evidence comes from nationally representative surveys in the USA (Heyman, 2013). Among all people who had previously met DSM criteria for SUD, between 76% and 83% were in remission (defined as the absence of dependence symptoms in the previous year) at the time of the surveys. Latency to remission varied by substance, with recovery taking longer for AUD than for cocaine use disorder, for example. 'Brain disease' theories of addiction posit that the duration of addiction is an important predictor of recovery: the longer a person is addicted, the less likely they are to recover. However, in contrast to this, Heyman's (2013) work indicates that the likelihood of recovery *increases* with increasing duration of SUD. Overall, around three quarters of people who have ever had SUD will eventually recover.

Recovery without treatment – often labeled as *natural recovery*, *unassisted recovery*, and *self-change* – is surprisingly common (Dawson et al., 2005; Klingemann, Sobell, & Sobell, 2010). Epidemiological data clearly show a pattern of age-related decline in alcohol consumption (Britton, Ben-Shlomo, Benzeval, Kuh, & Bell, 2015) typically referred to as "maturing-out" (O'Malley, 2004). This process is often explained through the role incompatibility theory (Yamaguchi & Kandel, 1985) whereby the acquisition of adult roles and responsibilities is in direct conflict with heavy drinking. For example, regular employment or parenthood are likely to require a structured daily waking routine which is incompatible with heavy drinking. Although "maturing-out" of heavy drinking is commonly associated with emerging adulthood, it is not limited to this period of life because people reduce their alcohol consumption and recover from AUD during transitions into roles such as parenthood, marriage, and employment, regardless of age (Dawson, Grant, Stinson, & Chou, 2006; Staff, Greene, Maggs, & Schoon, 2014; Vergés et al., 2013). Acquiring adult roles is related to establishing a sense of meaning and purpose in life (Negru-Subtirica, Pop, Luyckx, Dezutter, & Steger, 2016). Meaning in life has an inverse association with alcohol consumption (Csabonyi & Phillips, 2017) and increased meaning in life is associated with recovery from AUD (Krentzman, Cranford, & Robinson, 2015).

For people who receive treatment, some of the effective psychological interventions for SUD include alcoholics anonymous (AA), motivational interviewing (MI) or motivational enhancement therapy (MET), and cognitive behavioral therapy (CBT). The efficacy and psychological mechanisms of action of these treatments have been intensively studied (Dutra et al., 2008; Magill & Hallgren, 2019; Magill, Kiluk, McCrady, Tonigan, & Longabaugh, 2015). AA is a non-professional organization whereby group meetings promote complete abstinence from alcohol through adherence to a twelve-step program. People who were formerly dependent on alcohol but are now abstinent are referred to as '*sponsors*' and help to run the program. AA has been shown to enhance recovery via numerous mechanisms, the most prominent being the facilitation of social network changes (Brooks, Lòpez, Ranucci, Krumlauf, & Wallen, 2017; Kelly, 2017) and boosting abstinence self-efficacy (Kelly, Hoeppner, Stout, & Pagano, 2012; Kelly, Magill, & Stout, 2009). MI or MET is a client-centered method used to enhance intrinsic motivation to change by exploring and resolving ambivalence, particularly through "change-talk" techniques, which may be effective in moving people into recovery (Magill et al., 2016). CBT is a type of talking therapy aimed at changing the way a person thinks and behaves. It tackles thought processes with the goal of increasing coping skills involved in resisting the temptation to drink. Improvements in alcohol-specific coping skills mediate the effects of CBT on post-treatment drinking outcomes (Roos, Maisto, & Witkiewitz, 2017).

Improvements in mental health, perceived social support and employment status facilitated coping behaviors related to recovery after treatment for SUD (Johannessen, Nordfjærn, & Geirdal, 2019). These findings demonstrate how different types of treatment and life changes may facilitate recovery from addiction in different ways. For example, AA is particularly effective at facilitating and supporting social changes, employment is a social role that may enable a person to experience meaning in life through structure, and these both facilitate coping behavior which is the aim of CBT. Furthermore, they are in line with the conceptualization of recovery as a period of changes in social networks and related meaningful activities (Best et al., 2016). Therefore, although different types of treatment are philosophically diverse in nature, perhaps what they share are psychosocial mechanisms that facilitate changes that play a crucial role in sustaining recovery from addiction, such as self-efficacy, social support, responsibility, and structure in life (Moos, 2007a, 2007b). The overall effect may be to increase the value of alcohol-free alternatives and place emphasis on the capacity a person has to change (Heyman, 2017). In the following sections, we consider different perspectives that attempt to explain the psychological underpinnings of how these changes come about. Reconciliation of these differing perspectives will enable a better understanding of the recovery process.

The molar perspective: behavioral economics

Behavioral economics is a discipline that combines economics and psychology in order to understand long-term patterns of human behavior, referred to as a *molar* perspective (Ainslie, 2005; Bickel, Johnson, Koffarnus, MacKillop, & Murphy, 2014; Rachlin, 1995). Behavioral economic theories explore patterns of substance use as they develop and change over time in the context of changes in access (e.g. availability and price) to substance use and alternative sources of substance-free reinforcement (Bickel, Johnson et al., 2014; MacKillop, 2016). The central claim is that, over extended periods of time, the amount of substance use is a function of the benefit/cost ratio of substance use in relation to the benefit/cost ratios of alternative sources of substance-free reinforcement (Murphy, MacKillop, Vuchinich, & Tucker, 2012).

"Behavioral economic demand" is a term that captures the reinforcing value of a substance (MacKillop, 2016). It is typically assessed with hypothetical purchase tasks (Murphy & MacKillop, 2006) and concurrent choice tasks (Hardy, Parker, Hartley, & Hogarth, 2018). For example, the alcohol purchase task (Murphy & MacKillop, 2006) assesses a person's hypothetical consumption of alcohol across a range of prices. In concurrent choice tasks (Hardy et al., 2018) participants repeatedly choose between alcohol and alternative reinforcers (e.g. food), and the percentage of alcohol choice captures the demand for, or relative value of, alcohol. Responses on hypothetical purchase tasks and concurrent choice tasks are correlated (Chase, MacKillop, & Hogarth, 2013).

According to behavioral economic theories, addiction is characterized by 'reinforcement pathologies' whereby valuation processes are distorted (Bickel, Johnson, et al., 2014; Murphy, MacKillop, et al., 2012; Redish, Jensen, & Johnson, 2008): the value of alcohol increases, and the value of alternative reinforcers declines. For example, increased behavioral economic demand for alcohol is associated with the quantity and frequency of alcohol consumption (Murphy & MacKillop, 2006), AUD severity (MacKillop et al., 2010), and preference for alcohol over food rewards in people who are dependent on alcohol (Hardy et al., 2018). A further reinforcement pathology is delay discounting (DD; also referred to as temporal discounting), which refers to the subjective devaluation of rewards that are delayed (MacKillop et al., 2011). This is often understood as a measure of impulsivity or self-control (Ainslie, 1975). DD is typically measured with experimental tasks whereby people choose between smaller-sooner rewards that are available immediately and larger-later rewards that are available after a delay (Amlung, Vedelago, Acker, Balodis, & MacKillop, 2017). Elevated DD is robustly associated with addiction (Bickel, Koffarnus, Moody, & Wilson, 2014; MacKillop et al., 2011).

Behavioral economic accounts of addiction posit that recovery is dependent on repair of these reinforcement pathologies (Bickel, Johnson, et al., 2014). Specifically, in order for recovery to occur, alcohol must reduce in value whereas alternative reinforcers must increase in value, and people must learn how to mitigate or counteract the influence of DD on decision-making. As detailed below, several sources of evidence point to the importance of these changes for successful treatment of addiction and for the maintenance of long-term recovery.

Contingency management (CM) is a behavior modification technique that aims to reinforce desired behaviors (e.g. reductions in substance use) through the use of incentives (Petry, Alessi, Olmstead, Rash, & Zajac, 2017). These incentives can vary but typically include things such as small cash rewards, vouchers, prize-draws, and clinic privileges. By reinforcing abstinence, CM should rebalance reinforcement pathologies by increasing the subjective value of substance-free activities at the same time as reducing the value of drinking alcohol. Alternatively, CM may work through increasing deliberative processes when people are faced with an opportunity to use the substance (Regier & Redish, 2015). There is robust evidence that CM is an effective treatment for AUD (Benishek et al., 2014; Petry, Martin, Cooney, & Kranzler, 2000; Prendergast, Podus, Finney, Greenwell, & Roll, 2006).

Many people with AUD might not have access to substance-free reinforcement that could compete with alcohol reinforcement. Anhedonia refers to the inability to show interest or enjoy substance-free activities that would typically be enjoyed (Sussman & Leventhal, 2014) and is a common consequence of addiction (Garfield, Lubman, & Yücel, 2014). Additionally, years of addiction may have resulted in a number of adverse consequences, including breakdowns in social relationships and/or declines in meaningful activities that provide a sense of meaning or purpose in life (McKay, 2017). Consequently, for people with addiction, increasing the availability of substance-free reinforcement is recognized as an important treatment target (McKay, 2017). Indeed, a number of novel treatments such as behavioral activation (Daughters et al., 2018; Martínez-Vispo, Martínez, López-Durán, Fernández del Río, & Becoña, 2018) and substance free activity sessions (Murphy et al., 2019; Murphy, Skidmore et al., 2012) aim to increase a person's engagement with substance-free activities, and there is emerging evidence for their effectiveness as treatments for SUD.

Broadly speaking, when people recover from addiction they experience an increase in substance-free reinforcement (Tucker, Vuchinich, & Pukish, 1995; Tucker, Vuchinich, & Rippens, 2002). Many of the psychosocial mechanisms through which people recover (with or without treatment) may increase the value of alcohol-free alternatives, such as adopting new social roles that give meaning and structure in life, and access to social networks that support substance-free activities. Finally, DD has been found to be a malleable construct that is context dependent and can be overcome by techniques that enhance the incentive salience of long-term goals and rewards (Scholten et al., 2019). This is in line with observations that self-control is as an important predictor of recovery after treatment for AUD (Stein & Witkiewitz, 2019).

Overall, recovery from addiction can be understood from the perspective of behavioral economics: people recover from addiction when 'reinforcement pathologies' are corrected, and diverse forms of formal treatment and changing life circumstances might work through these mechanisms. However, although behavioral economics attempts to explain how people make patterns of choices over time (the molar perspective), it does not attempt to explain individual choices or instances of behavior or the internal or cognitive processes that precede individual choices (the molecular perspective). It is important to understand this, because the first concrete step to recovery will always be an individual's decision to refrain from drinking alcohol in a situation in which they would otherwise have consumed it. In the next sections we contrast two accounts of the internal processes that determine individual choices or decisions and discuss their implications for the development of addiction and recovery from it.

The molecular perspective: value-based decision-making (VBDM)

VBDM describes a set of experimental tools and data analytic techniques that model the internal processes that occur during decision-making, specifically when choosing between one or more items on the basis of their value. According to this framework, the subjective value of a response option is the weighted sum of choice-relevant attributes (Berkman, Hutcherson, Livingston, Kahn, & Inzlicht, 2017) such as anticipated gains and costs, effort required to obtain it, delay to its receipt, and so on (Berkman, 2018; Berkman et al., 2017). These attributes are then translated into a common metric of the overall subjective value that is essential for comparison of response options (Levy & Glimcher, 2012). The response option with the highest subjective value on average is acted upon through a value-to-action evidence accumulation process that is demonstrated through computational modeling, such as with drift diffusion models (DDM; Forstmann, Ratcliff, & Wagenmakers, 2016; Ratcliff & McKoon, 2008). These models assume that neurons track subjective value in a noisy probabilistic manner, and so take fluctuating signals as evidence for or against a particular choice, accumulating them over time until the accumulated evidence passes some response threshold for committing to a decision.

In a typical VBDM task (e.g. Polanía, Krajbich, Grueschow, & Ruff, 2014) participants initially make value judgments about a set of pictorial stimuli so that they can be rank ordered from the most valued to the least valued. They then complete a computerized task in which two of those images appear side-by-side on a computer screen and participants are asked to indicate their preference, as quickly as possible. Behavioral data (response time (RT) and accuracy) can then be fitted using a DDM. The underlying decision model is able to provide a principled reconciliation of RT and accuracy data, so that the confounding effects of differential sensitive and speed-accuracy trade-offs are disambiguated and the underlying processes – reflected in the model parameter estimates – are revealed (Roberts & Hutcherson, 2019). The model parameters that underlie decision-making of most interest are, the *drift rate* (the rate of evidence accumulation), and *response threshold* (how conservative a person is when responding). The key distinction between conventional forced choice tasks (e.g. Hardy et al., 2018) and VBDM tasks (e.g. Polanía et al., 2014) is that only VBDM tasks purport to capture the internal processes that *precede* decision-making—specifically, the subjective value of different stimuli.

A recent conceptual model (Field et al., 2020) speculatively applied VBDM to provide a novel account of the changes in decision-making that may underlie addiction and recovery. Specifically, when a person is faced with a choice between drinking alcohol versus engaging in an alternative alcohol-free activity (e.g. spending time with their family), hypervaluation of alcohol would be reflected in enhanced evidence accumulation and lower response thresholds for the alcohol option. Additionally, hypovaluation of alcohol-free alternatives would be reflected in blunted evidence accumulation and raised response thresholds for the alcohol-free alternative option. As a consequence, this person would be more likely to choose to drink alcohol rather than choose the alcohol-free option. By contrast, in a recreational drinker for whom alcohol and alcohol-free activities are valued relatively equally, the 'race' between evidence accumulation and the response thresholds would be relatively evenly balanced, and this person would be equally likely to choose either option.

This model was extended to model the changes in decision-making that underlie recovery from addiction by building on the work from behavioral economics that was discussed in the previous section (Field et al., 2020). Specifically, changes in VBDM parameters during decisions that involve the addictive substance are hypothesized to underlie recovery. According to this account, when a person is faced with the opportunity to drink alcohol versus engage in an alcohol-free activity, the following changes characterize a person who is in recovery in comparison to a person with AUD who is not seeking treatment: (1) evidence accumulation for alcohol is suppressed; (2) evidence accumulation for alcohol-free alternatives is amplified; and (3) the response threshold increases. These changes are depicted in Fig. 25.1. The application of VBDM to addiction and to recovery from it awaits empirical testing, but the conceptual model described in Field et al. (2020), and briefly reiterated here, provides some testable hypotheses that could be investigated in future research.

Dual-process theories: automatic and controlled processes

In contrast to dynamical accounts such as VBDM (e.g. Berkman et al., 2017), dual-process theories (Kahneman, 2011; Strack & Deutsch, 2004) propose that behavior is determined by the interplay between two cognitive systems; one that is *automatic* and another that is *controlled*. Dual-process theories of addiction (McClure & Bickel, 2014; Stacy & Wiers, 2010) postulate that addiction is characterized by an imbalance between these cognitive systems, in that automatic processes (that favor substance use) overcome controlled processes (that favor not using the substance). Evidence is broadly consistent with these claims: automatic processes include things such as attentional biases for, and automatic approach tendencies evoked by substance-related cues, and automatic substance-related memory associations, all of which are apparent in people with addiction

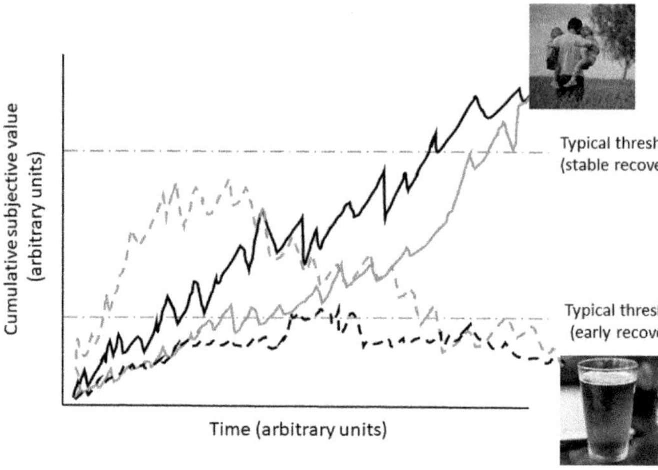

FIGURE 25.1 Schematic depiction of the parameters of VBDM (evidence accumulation and response thresholds) that may underlie recovery from addiction. When a person has recovered from addiction and is faced with the opportunity to drink alcohol versus engage in an alcohol-free activity, they may experience gradual increases in their response thresholds through the ability to take time to consider their decision carefully (the shift from the lower to the upper horizontal response threshold line). Furthermore, evidence accumulation for alcohol is blunted or suppressed (the shift from the gray dashed line to the black dashed line), whilst evidence accumulation for alcohol-free alternatives is amplified (the shift from the gray solid line to the black solid line). These hypothesized changes can occur in combination or isolation. These changes in VBDM parameters increase the probability that the alcohol-free alternative will cross the response threshold first and be the action that is acted upon when a person has recovered from addiction. *Schematics are adapted from Field, M., Heather, N., Murphy, J. G., Stafford, T., Tucker, J. A., & Witkiewitz, K. (2020). Recovery from addiction: behavioral economics and value-based decision-making. Psychology of Addictive Behaviors, 34(1), 182–193. https://doi.org/10.1037/adb0000518. and Berkman, E. T., Hutcherson, C. A., Livingston, J. L., Kahn, L. E., & Inzlicht, M. (2017). Self-control as value-based choice. Current Directions in Psychological Science, 26(5), 422–428. https://doi.org/10.1177/0963721417704394. Images are reproduced from Unsplash.com. https://unsplash.com/photos/M44ppvVbnEQ, https://unsplash.com/photos/dmkmrNptMpw.*

(Stacy & Wiers, 2010). Alongside this, people with addiction show deficits in controlled processes, such as executive control functions and response inhibition (Smith, Mattick, Jamadar, & Iredale, 2014). Therefore, in a person with AUD, the incentive salience of an alcohol cue (e.g. a pub) is likely to evoke appetitive motivation by capturing attention and eliciting approach behavior (Robinson & Berridge, 1993). This is alongside the impaired ability to control or reflect upon behavior (e.g. consider the long-term negative outcomes) when alcohol-related cues are present. Consequently, addiction is proposed to be accompanied by increasing automaticity of substance use in specific environmental contexts where alcohol is readily available, and the inability to consider long-term goals when exposed to short-term temptations (Munakata et al., 2011).

The notion that behavior in people with addiction becomes dominated by automatic rather than controlled cognitive processes is compatible with other theoretical accounts that characterize it as a disorder of compulsion, in which drug use becomes largely driven by environmental stimuli and increasingly decoupled from subjective intentions to behave otherwise (Everitt & Robbins, 2005, 2016; Volkow et al., 2016). However, an important difference is that dual-process theories paint a more optimistic picture of the prospects of recovery, because in principle, it may be possible to rebalance the influence of automatic and controlled processes. For example, novel interventions that aim to suppress automatic processes that favor substance use such as cognitive bias modification (CBM) may be effective in some circumstances (Wiers, Eberl, Rinck, Becker, & Lindenmeyer, 2011), although this is contentious (Cristea, Kok, & Cuijpers, 2016). Furthermore, other established psychological interventions such as motivational interviewing and CBT may work because they strengthen controlled processes that favor abstinence (Stacy & Wiers, 2010).

Despite the evidence in support of dual-process theories as applied to behavior in general, and addiction in particular, objections have been raised to some specific predictions that are derived from these theories. For example, the notion that choices between immediate gratification versus the pursuit of longer-term goals must involve a tug of war between automatic and controlled processes (Berkman et al., 2017), is contradicted by recent imaging studies (e.g., Cosme, Ludwig, & Berkman, 2019).

Resolving competing predictions derived from dual-process theories and VBDM by modeling conflict during decision-making

According to dual-process theories, when a person with AUD is faced with the choice between drinking alcohol versus engaging in an alcohol-free activity, this choice represents a conflict between automatic processes (that favor drinking alcohol) and controlled processes (that favor the alcohol-free activity). Recovery from addiction arises when the person is able to consistently resolve that conflict in favor of the alcohol-free activity, either by bolstering controlled processes or weakening automatic processes. By contrast, a VBDM account of addiction does not require the existence of qualitatively distinct cognitive processes (automatic and controlled) to explain addiction and recovery from it. This account assumes that the influences of 'controlled' and 'automatic' processes are incorporated into the valuation processes that determine overt behavior. One way to resolve these competing theoretical predictions is to assess the conflict that occurs when people are faced with a difficult decision, such as between consuming alcohol or engaging in an alternative behavior.

Resolution of conflict is a core component of decision-making, particularly when people are faced with a choice between two options, one of which is associated with immediate gratification whereas the other is associated with longer-term gain (Stillman, Shen, & Ferguson, 2018). For example, alcohol-related decisions can be especially difficult because of the conflict between immediate (e.g. intoxication) versus delayed (e.g. health benefits) gratification. Mouse-tracking offers a real-time technique that can directly tap into the processes underlying conflict, by measuring computer mouse movements made by a person as they deliberate between response options (Stillman et al., 2018).

In a typical mouse-tracking task (e.g. Stillman, Medvedev, & Ferguson, 2017), participants begin by clicking a start box at the bottom center of the computer screen. Subsequently, two response options appear in the upper left and upper right corners (e.g. healthy versus unhealthy food). The participant is asked to move the mouse to select their preferred image and during this process the computer samples their cursor location hundreds of times per second. People with enhanced self-reported self-control experience a lesser magnitude of conflict, and a greater ability to resolve conflict, when selecting the image consistent with long-term goals, compared to those with lower levels of self-control (Gillebaart, Schneider, & de Ridder, 2016; Stillman et al., 2017).

Looking at the nature of mouse trajectories could provide important insights into the processes that underlie recovery from addiction, by examining whether the nature of conflict resolution in decision-making is consistent with dual-process theories or a dynamical VBDM approach (Fig. 25.2). Dual-process approaches assume that successful self-control requires inhibiting impulses

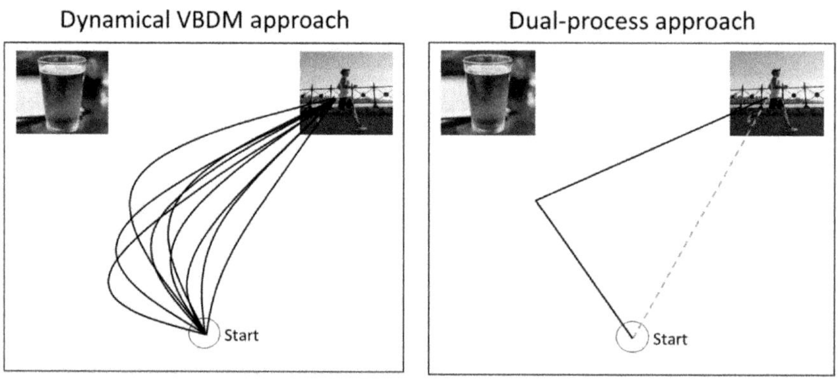

FIGURE 25.2 Schematic comparison of a dual-system and a dynamical system approach (e.g. VBDM) of conflict resolution (e.g. successful self-control) on a typical trial involving the choice between an immediate temptation (e.g. a pint of beer) and an alcohol-free alternative (e.g. going for a run). When choosing between alcohol and a competing alcohol-free alternative, dynamical models predict that information from both response options compete against each-other dynamically over time until a final response emerges, reflected in smooth mouse trajectories (left panel). In contrast, dual-process models predict that the mouse will initially move towards alcohol (automatic process), but that there will be a mid-flight correction in favor of the alcohol-free alternative (controlled process), reflected in abrupt mouse trajectories (right panel). *Schematics are adapted from Stillman, P. E., Medvedev, D., & Ferguson, M. J. (2017). Resisting temptation: tracking how self-control conflicts are successfully resolved in real time. Psychological Science, 28(9), 1240–1258. https://doi.org/10.1177/0956797617705386. Images are reproduced from Unsplash.com. https://unsplash.com/photos/z4WH11FMfIQ, https://unsplash.com/photos/W9WN_cIR9JM.*

toward temptations, in that controlled processes inhibit automatic processes (Fig. 25.2, right panel). By contrast, dynamical-approaches such as VBDM posit that decisions unfold with input from two evidence accumulators that compete with each other over time until a final response emerges (Fig. 25.2, left panel).

Outside of the addiction domain, research is broadly supportive of a dynamical VBDM approach. For example, during successful self-control choices (e.g. choosing healthy versus unhealthy food), mouse trajectories were smooth, indicating dynamic competition between goals and temptations rather than sequential unfolding between automatic and controlled processes (Stillman et al., 2017). Furthermore a recent imaging study (Cosme et al., 2019) that found that a dynamical VBDM theory predicted neural activity during self-control choices better than dual-process theory.

These findings could have important implications for our understanding of the internal processes that characterize recovery from addiction. For example, when a person who has recovered is faced with the decision between alcohol and an alcohol-free alternative, if the trajectory of the mouse movement towards the alcohol-free alternative is dynamical and smooth, this would be consistent with a VBDM account. On the other hand, if mouse trajectories were abrupt with a mid-flight correction, this would be consistent with dual-process models of addiction. These competing predictions await empirical testing.

Summary and conclusion

Recovery from AUD occurs when there are decreases in the value of alcohol, increases in the value of alcohol-free alternatives, and/or improvements in self-control. Behavioral economics provides a clear account of how these changes happen over-time (the molar perspective). However, this does not attempt to explain the internal processes that determine individual behaviors (the molecular perspective). VBDM and dual-process theory yield competing predictions about how internal processes develop and change during the transition from addiction to recovery. Conflict resolution provides an exciting opportunity to empirically distinguish between these competing accounts. Research to date appears to be supportive of a dynamical VBDM approach whereby choices are made based on the integration of diverse sources of information, rather than dual-process models, which propose distinctions between the roles of automatic and controlled processes. However, this has not been applied to the study of addiction and recovery. Further empirical research in this area could characterize the changes in decision-making that underlie recovery from addiction, and identify novel targets for treatment.

References

Ainslie, G. (1975). Specious reward: A behavioral theory of impulsiveness and impulse control. *Psychological Bulletin*, *82*(4), 463–496. Available from: https://doi.org/10.1037/h0076860.

Ainslie, G. (2005). Précis of breakdown of will. *Behavioral and Brain Sciences*, *28*(5), 635–650. Available from: https://doi.org/10.1017/S0140525X05000117.

Amlung, M., Vedelago, L., Acker, J., Balodis, I., & MacKillop, J. (2017). Steep delay discounting and addictive behavior: A meta-analysis of continuous associations. *Addiction*, *112*(1), 51–62. Available from: https://doi.org/10.1111/add.13535.

Ashford, R. D., Brown, A., Brown, T., Callis, J., Cleveland, H. H., Eisenhart, E., ... Whitney, J. (2019). Defining and operationalizing the phenomena of recovery: A working definition from the recovery science research collaborative. *Addiction Research & Theory*, *27*(3), 179–188. Available from: https://doi.org/10.1080/16066359.2018.1515352.

Benishek, L. A., Dugosh, K. L., Kirby, K. C., Matejkowski, J., Clements, N. T., Seymour, B. L., & Festinger, D. S. (2014). Prize-based contingency management for the treatment of substance abusers: A meta-analysis. *Addiction*, *109*(9), 1426–1436. Available from: https://doi.org/10.1111/add.12589.

Berkman, E. T. (2018). Value-based choice: An integrative, neuroscience-informed model of health goals. *Psychology & Health*, *33*(1), 40–57. Available from: https://doi.org/10.1080/08870446.2017.1316847.

Berkman, E. T., Hutcherson, C. A., Livingston, J. L., Kahn, L. E., & Inzlicht, M. (2017). Self-control as value-based choice. *Current Directions in Psychological Science*, *26*(5), 422–428. Available from: https://doi.org/10.1177/0963721417704394.

Best, D., Beckwith, M., Haslam, C., Alexander Haslam, S., Jetten, J., Mawson, E., & Lubman, D. I. (2016). Overcoming alcohol and other drug addiction as a process of social identity transition: The social identity model of recovery (SIMOR). *Addiction Research & Theory*, *24*(2), 111–123. Available from: https://doi.org/10.3109/16066359.2015.1075980.

Bickel, W. K., Johnson, M. W., Koffarnus, M. N., MacKillop, J., & Murphy, J. G. (2014). The behavioral economics of substance use disorders: Reinforcement pathologies and their repair. *Annual Review of Clinical Psychology*, *10*, 641–677. Available from: https://doi.org/10.1146/annurev-clinpsy-032813-153724.

Bickel, W. K., Koffarnus, M. N., Moody, L., & Wilson, A. G. (2014). The behavioral- and neuro-economic process of temporal discounting: A candidate behavioral marker of addiction. *Neuropharmacology*, *76*, 518–527. Available from: https://doi.org/10.1016/j.neuropharm.2013.06.013.

Britton, A., Ben-Shlomo, Y., Benzeval, M., Kuh, D., & Bell, S. (2015). Life course trajectories of alcohol consumption in the United Kingdom using longitudinal data from nine cohort studies. *BMC Medicine*, *13*(1), 47. Available from: https://doi.org/10.1186/s12916-015-0273-z.

Brooks, A. T., Lòpez, M. M., Ranucci, A., Krumlauf, M., & Wallen, G. R. (2017). A qualitative exploration of social support during treatment for severe alcohol use disorder and recovery. *Addictive Behaviors Reports*, *6*, 76–82. Available from: https://doi.org/10.1016/j.abrep.2017.08.002.

Chase, H. W., MacKillop, J., & Hogarth, L. (2013). Isolating behavioural economic indices of demand in relation to nicotine dependence. *Psychopharmacology*, *226*(2), 371–380. Available from: https://doi.org/10.1007/s00213-012-2911-x.

Cosme, D., Ludwig, R., & Berkman, E. T. (2019). Comparing two neurocognitive models of self-control during dietary decisions. *Social Cognitive and Affective Neuroscience*, *14*(9), 957–966. Available from: https://doi.org/10.1093/scan/nsz068.

Cristea, I. A., Kok, R. N., & Cuijpers, P. (2016). The effectiveness of cognitive bias modification interventions for substance addictions: A meta-analysis. *PLoS One*, *11*(9), e0162226. Available from: https://doi.org/10.1371/journal.pone.0162226.

Csabonyi, M., & Phillips, L. J. (2017). Meaning in life and substance use. *Journal of Humanistic Psychology*, *57*, 1–17. Available from: https://doi.org/10.1177/0022167816687674.

Daughters, S. B., Magidson, J. F., Anand, D., Seitz-Brown, C. J., Chen, Y., & Baker, S. (2018). The effect of a behavioral activation treatment for substance use on post-treatment abstinence: A randomized controlled trial. *Addiction*, *113*(3), 535–544. Available from: https://doi.org/10.1111/add.14049.

Dawson, D. A., Grant, B. F., Stinson, F. S., & Chou, P. S. (2006). Maturing out of alcohol dependence: The impact of transitional life events. *Journal of Studies on Alcohol*, *67*(2), 195–203. Available from: https://doi.org/10.15288/jsa.2006.67.195.

Dawson, D. A., Grant, B. F., Stinson, F. S., Chou, P. S., Huang, B., & Ruan, W. J. (2005). Recovery from DSM-IV alcohol dependence: United States, 2001-2002. *Addiction*, *100*(3), 281–292. Available from: https://doi.org/10.1111/j.1360-0443.2004.00964.x.

Dutra, L., Stathopoulou, G., Basden, S. L., Leyro, T. M., Powers, M. B., & Otto, M. W. (2008). A meta-analytic review of psychosocial interventions for substance use disorders. *American Journal of Psychiatry*, *165*(2), 179–187. Available from: https://doi.org/10.1176/appi.ajp.2007.06111851.

Everitt, B. J., & Robbins, T. W. (2005). Neural systems of reinforcement for drug addiction: From actions to habits to compulsion. *Nature Neuroscience*, *8*(11), 1481–1489. Available from: https://doi.org/10.1038/nn1579.

Everitt, B. J., & Robbins, T. W. (2016). Drug addiction: Updating actions to habits to compulsions ten years on. *Annual Review of Psychology*, *67*(1), 23–50. Available from: https://doi.org/10.1146/annurev-psych-122414-033457.

Field, M., Heather, N., Murphy, J. G., Stafford, T., Tucker, J. A., & Witkiewitz, K. (2020). Recovery from addiction: Behavioral economics and value-based decision-making. *Psychology of Addictive Behaviors*, *34*(1), 182–193. Available from: https://doi.org/10.1037/adb0000518.

Forouzanfar, M. H., Afshin, A., Alexander, L. T., Anderson, H. R., Bhutta, Z. A., Biryukov, S., ... Murray, C. J. L. (2016). Global, regional, and national comparative risk assessment of 79 behavioural, environmental and occupational, and metabolic risks or clusters of risks, 1990–2015: A systematic analysis for the Global Burden of Disease Study 2015. *The Lancet*, *388*(10053), 1659–1724. Available from: https://doi.org/10.1016/S0140-6736(16)31679-8.

Forstmann, B. U., Ratcliff, R., & Wagenmakers, E. J. (2016). Sequential sampling models in cognitive neuroscience: Advantages, applications, and extensions. *Annual Review of Psychology*, *67*, 641–666. Available from: https://doi.org/10.1146/annurev-psych-122414-033645.

Garfield, J. B. B., Lubman, D. I., & Yücel, M. (2014). Anhedonia in substance use disorders: A systematic review of its nature, course and clinical correlates. *Australian & New Zealand Journal of Psychiatry*, *48*(1), 36–51. Available from: https://doi.org/10.1177/0004867413508455.

Gillebaart, M., Schneider, I. K., & de Ridder, D. T. D. (2016). Effects of trait self-control on response conflict about healthy and unhealthy food. *Journal of Personality*, *84*(6), 789–798. Available from: https://doi.org/10.1111/jopy.12219.

Hardy, L., Parker, S., Hartley, L., & Hogarth, L. (2018). A concurrent pictorial drug choice task marks multiple risk factors in treatment-engaged smokers and drinkers Pavlovian-instrumental transfer. *Behavioural Pharmacology*, *29*(8), 716–725. Available from: https://doi.org/10.1097/FBP.0000000000000421.

Heyman, G. M. (2013). Quitting drugs: Quantitative and qualitative features. *Annual Review of Clinical Psychology*, *9*, 29–59. Available from: https://doi.org/10.1146/annurev-clinpsy-032511-143041.

Heyman, G. M. (2017). Do addicts have free will? An empirical approach to a vexing question. *Addictive Behaviors Reports*, *5*, 85–93. Available from: https://doi.org/10.1016/J.ABREP.2017.02.001.

Johannessen, D. A., Nordfjærn, T., & Geirdal, A. Ø. (2019). Change in psychosocial factors connected to coping after inpatient treatment for substance use disorder: A systematic review. *Substance Abuse Treatment, Prevention, and Policy, 14*(1), 16. Available from: https://doi.org/10.1186/s13011-019-0210-9.

Kahneman, D. (2011). *Thinking, fast and slow.* New York, NY: Farrar, Straus and Giroux.

Kelly, J. F. (2017). Is alcoholics anonymous religious, spiritual, neither? Findings from 25 years of mechanisms of behavior change research. *Addiction, 112*(6), 929–936. Available from: https://doi.org/10.1111/add.13590.

Kelly, J. F., Hoeppner, B., Stout, R. L., & Pagano, M. (2012). Determining the relative importance of the mechanisms of behavior change within alcoholics anonymous: A multiple mediator analysis. *Addiction, 107*(2), 289–299. Available from: https://doi.org/10.1111/j.1360-0443.2011.03593.x.

Kelly, J. F., Magill, M., & Stout, R. L. (2009). How do people recover from alcohol dependence? A systematic review of the research on mechanisms of behavior change in alcoholics anonymous. *Addiction Research & Theory, 17*(3), 236–259. Available from: https://doi.org/10.1080/16066350902770458.

Klingemann, H., Sobell, M. B., & Sobell, L. C. (2010). Continuities and changes in self-change research. *Addiction, 105*(9), 1510–1518. Available from: https://doi.org/10.1111/j.1360-0443.2009.02770.x.

Krentzman, A. R., Cranford, J. A., & Robinson, E. A. R. (2015). Long-term increases in purpose in life are associated with remission from alcohol dependence. *Alcoholism Treatment Quarterly, 33*(3), 252–269. Available from: https://doi.org/10.1080/07347324.2015.1050924.

Leshner, A. I. (1997). Addiction is a brain disease, and it matters. *Science, 278*(5335), 45–47. Available from: https://doi.org/10.1126/science.278.5335.45.

Levy, D. J., & Glimcher, P. W. (2012). The root of all value: A neural common currency for choice. *Current Opinion in Neurobiology, 22*(6), 1027–1038. Available from: https://doi.org/10.1016/j.conb.2012.06.001.

Lopez-Quintero, C., Hasin, D. S., de Los Cobos, J. P., Pines, A., Wang, S., Grant, B. F., & Blanco, C. (2011). Probability and predictors of remission from life-time nicotine, alcohol, cannabis or cocaine dependence: Results from the National Epidemiologic Survey on Alcohol and Related Conditions. *Addiction, 106*(3), 657–669. Available from: https://doi.org/10.1111/j.1360-0443.2010.03194.x.

MacKillop, J. (2016). The behavioral economics and neuroeconomics of alcohol use disorders. *Alcoholism: Clinical and Experimental Research, 40*(4), 672–685. Available from: https://doi.org/10.1111/acer.13004.

MacKillop, J., Amlung, M. T., Few, L. R., Ray, L. A., Sweet, L. H., & Munafò, M. R. (2011). Delayed reward discounting and addictive behavior: A meta-analysis. *Psychopharmacology, 216*(3), 305–321. Available from: https://doi.org/10.1007/s00213-011-2229-0.

MacKillop, J., Miranda, R., Monti, P. M., Ray, L. A., Murphy, J. G., Rohsenow, D. J., ... Gwaltney, C. J. (2010). Alcohol demand, delayed reward discounting, and craving in relation to drinking and alcohol use disorders. *Journal of Abnormal Psychology, 119*(1), 106–114. Available from: https://doi.org/10.1037/a0017513.

Magill, M., & Hallgren, K. A. (2019). Mechanisms of behavior change in motivational interviewing: Do we understand how MI works? *Current Opinion in Psychology, 30*, 1–5. Available from: https://doi.org/10.1016/J.COPSYC.2018.12.010.

Magill, M., Kiluk, B. D., McCrady, B. S., Tonigan, J. S., & Longabaugh, R. (2015). Active ingredients of treatment and client mechanisms of change in behavioral treatments for alcohol use disorders: Progress 10 years later. *Alcoholism: Clinical and Experimental Research, 39*(10), 1852–1862. Available from: https://doi.org/10.1111/acer.12848.

Magill, M., Walthers, J., Mastroleo, N. R., Gaume, J., Longabaugh, R., & Apodaca, T. R. (2016). Therapist and client discussions of drinking and coping: A sequential analysis of therapy dialogues in three evidence-based alcohol use disorder treatments. *Addiction, 111* (6), 1011–1020. Available from: https://doi.org/10.1111/add.13313.

Martínez-Vispo, C., Martínez, Ú., López-Durán, A., Fernández del Río, E., & Becoña, E. (2018). Effects of behavioural activation on substance use and depression: A systematic review. *Substance Abuse Treatment, Prevention, and Policy, 13*(1), 36. Available from: https://doi.org/10.1186/s13011-018-0173-2.

McClure, S. M., & Bickel, W. K. (2014). A dual-systems perspective on addiction: Contributions from neuroimaging and cognitive training. *Annals of the New York Academy of Sciences, 1327*, 62–78. Available from: https://doi.org/10.1111/nyas.12561.

McKay, J. R. (2017). Making the hard work of recovery more attractive for those with substance use disorders. *Addiction, 112*(5), 751–757. Available from: https://doi.org/10.1111/add.13502.

Moos, R. H. (2007a). Theory-based active ingredients of effective treatments for substance use disorders. *Drug and Alcohol Dependence, 88*(2–3), 109–121. Available from: https://doi.org/10.1016/j.drugalcdep.2006.10.010.

Moos, R. H. (2007b). Theory-based processes that promote the remission of substance use disorders. *Clinical Psychology Review, 27*(5), 537–551. Available from: https://doi.org/10.1016/j.cpr.2006.12.006.

Munakata, Y., Herd, S. A., Chatham, C. H., Depue, B. E., Banich, M. T., & O'Reilly, R. C. (2011). A unified framework for inhibitory control. *Trends in Cognitive Sciences, 15*(10), 453–459. Available from: https://doi.org/10.1016/j.tics.2011.07.011.

Murphy, J. G., Dennhardt, A. A., Martens, M. P., Borsari, B., Witkiewitz, K., & Meshesha, L. Z. (2019). A randomized clinical trial evaluating the efficacy of a brief alcohol intervention supplemented with a substance-free activity session or relaxation training. *Journal of Consulting and Clinical Psychology, 87*(7), 657–669. Available from: https://doi.org/10.1037/ccp0000412.

Murphy, J. G., & MacKillop, J. (2006). Relative reinforcing efficacy of alcohol among college student drinkers. *Experimental and Clinical Psychopharmacology, 14*(2), 219–227. Available from: https://doi.org/10.1037/1064-1297.14.2.219.

Murphy, J. G., MacKillop, J., Vuchinich, R. E., & Tucker, J. A. (2012). The behavioral economics of substance use and abuse. In S. T. Walters, & F. Rotgers (Eds.), *Treating substance abuse: theory and techniquesubstance abuse:* (3rd ed.). New York, NY: Guilford Press.

Murphy, J. G., Skidmore, J. R., Dennhardt, A. A., Martens, M. P., Borsari, B., Barnett, N. P., & Colby, S. M. (2012). A behavioral economic supplement to brief motivational interventions for college drinking. *Addiction Research & Theory, 20*(6), 456–465. Available from: https://doi.org/10.3109/16066359.2012.665965.

Negru-Subtirica, O., Pop, E. I., Luyckx, K., Dezutter, J., & Steger, M. F. (2016). The meaningful identity: A longitudinal look at the interplay between identity and meaning in life in adolescence. *Developmental Psychology, 52*(11), 1926–1936. Available from: https://doi.org/10.1037/dev0000176.

O'Malley, P. (2004). Maturing out of problematic alcohol use. *Alcohol Research & Health, 28* (4), 202–204.

Petry, N. M., Alessi, S. M., Olmstead, T. A., Rash, C. J., & Zajac, K. (2017). Contingency management treatment for substance use disorders: How far has it come, and where does it need to go? *Psychology of Addictive Behaviors, 31*(8), 897–906. Available from: https://doi.org/10.1037/adb0000287.

Petry, N. M., Martin, B., Cooney, J. L., & Kranzler, H. R. (2000). Give them prizes and they will come: Contingency management for treatment of alcohol dependence. *Journal of*

Consulting and Clinical Psychology, *68*(2), 250–257. Available from: https://doi.org/10.1037/0022-006X.68.2.250.

Polanía, R., Krajbich, I., Grueschow, M., & Ruff, C. C. (2014). Neural oscillations and synchronization differentially support evidence accumulation in perceptual and value-based decision making. *Neuron*, *82*(3), 709–720. Available from: https://doi.org/10.1016/J.NEURON.2014.03.014.

Prendergast, M., Podus, D., Finney, J., Greenwell, L., & Roll, J. (2006). Contingency management for treatment of substance use disorders: A meta-analysis. *Addiction*, *101*(11), 1546–1560. Available from: https://doi.org/10.1111/j.1360-0443.2006.01581.x.

Rachlin, H. (1995). Self-control: Beyond commitment. *Behavioral and Brain Sciences*, *18*(1), 109–121. Available from: https://doi.org/10.1017/S0140525X00037602.

Ratcliff, R., & McKoon, G. (2008). The diffusion decision model: Theory and data for two-choice decision tasks. *Neural Computation*, *20*(4), 873–922. Available from: https://doi.org/10.1162/neco.2008.12-06-420.

Redish, A. D., Jensen, S., & Johnson, A. (2008). A unified framework for addiction: Vulnerabilities in the decision process. *Behavioral and Brain Sciences*, *31*(4), 415–487. Available from: https://doi.org/10.1017/S0140525X0800472X.

Regier, P. S., & Redish, A. D. (2015). Contingency management and deliberative decision-making processes. *Frontiers in Psychiatry*, *6*, 76. Available from: https://doi.org/10.3389/fpsyt.2015.00076.

Rehm, J., & Imtiaz, S. (2016). A narrative review of alcohol consumption as a risk factor for global burden of disease. *Substance Abuse Treatment, Prevention, and Policy*, *11*(1), 37. Available from: https://doi.org/10.1186/s13011-016-0081-2.

Roberts, I. D., & Hutcherson, C. A. (2019). Affect and decision making: Insights and predictions from computational models. *Trends in Cognitive Sciences*, *23*(7), 602–614. Available from: https://doi.org/10.1016/j.tics.2019.04.005.

Robinson, T. E., & Berridge, K. C. (1993). The neural basis of drug craving: An incentive-sensitization theory of addiction. *Brain Research Reviews*, *18*(3), 247–291. Available from: https://doi.org/10.1016/0165-0173(93)90013-P.

Roos, C. R., Maisto, S. A., & Witkiewitz, K. (2017). Coping mediates the effects of cognitive-behavioral therapy for alcohol use disorder among out-patient clients in Project MATCH when dependence severity is high. *Addiction*, *112*(9), 1547–1557. Available from: https://doi.org/10.1111/add.13841.

Scholten, H., Scheres, A., de Water, E., Graf, U., Granic, I., & Luijten, M. (2019). Behavioral trainings and manipulations to reduce delay discounting: A systematic review. *Psychonomic Bulletin & Review*, 1–47. Available from: https://doi.org/10.3758/s13423-019-01629-2.

Smith, J. L., Mattick, R. P., Jamadar, S. D., & Iredale, J. M. (2014). Deficits in behavioural inhibition in substance abuse and addiction: A meta-analysis. *Drug and Alcohol Dependence*, *145*, 1–33. Available from: https://doi.org/10.1016/J.DRUGALCDEP.2014.08.009.

Stacy, A. W., & Wiers, R. W. (2010). Implicit cognition and addiction: A tool for explaining paradoxical behavior. *Annual Review of Clinical Psychology*, *6*, 551–575. Available from: https://doi.org/10.1146/annurev.clinpsy.121208.131444.

Staff, J., Greene, K. M., Maggs, J. L., & Schoon, I. (2014). Family transitions and changes in drinking from adolescence through mid-life. *Addiction*, *109*(2), 227–236.

Stein, E., & Witkiewitz, K. (2019). Trait self-control predicts drinking patterns during treatment for alcohol use disorder and recovery up to three years following treatment. *Addictive Behaviors*, *99*, 106083. Available from: https://doi.org/10.1016/J.ADDBEH.2019.106083.

Stillman, P. E., Medvedev, D., & Ferguson, M. J. (2017). Resisting temptation: Tracking how self-control conflicts are successfully resolved in real time. *Psychological Science*, *28*(9), 1240–1258. Available from: https://doi.org/10.1177/0956797617705386.

Stillman, P. E., Shen, X., & Ferguson, M. J. (2018). How mouse-tracking can advance social cognitive theory. *Trends in Cognitive Sciences*, *22*(6), 531–543. Available from: https://doi.org/10.1016/J.TICS.2018.03.012.

Strack, F., & Deutsch, R. (2004). Reflective and impulsive determinants of social behavior. *Personality and Social Psychology Review*, *8*(3), 220–247. Available from: https://doi.org/10.1207/s15327957pspr0803_1.

Sussman, S., & Leventhal, A. (2014). Substance misuse prevention: Addressing anhedonia. *New Directions for Youth Development*, *2014*(141), 45–56. Available from: https://doi.org/10.1002/yd.20085.

Tucker, J. A., Vuchinich, R. E., & Pukish, M. M. (1995). Molar environmental contexts surrounding recovery from alcohol problems by treated and untreated problem drinkers. *Experimental and Clinical Psychopharmacology*, *3*(2), 195–204. Available from: https://doi.org/10.1037/1064-1297.3.2.195.

Tucker, J. A., Vuchinich, R. E., & Rippens, P. D. (2002). Predicting natural resolution of alcohol-related problems: A prospective behavioral economic analysis. *Experimental and Clinical Psychopharmacology*, *10*(3), 248–257. Available from: https://doi.org/10.1037/1064-1297.10.3.248.

Vergés, A., Haeny, A. M., Jackson, K. M., Bucholz, K. K., Grant, J. D., Trull, T. J., ... Sher, K. J. (2013). Refining the notion of maturing out: Results from the national epidemiologic survey on alcohol and related conditions. *American Journal of Public Health*, *103*(12), e67–e73. Available from: https://doi.org/10.2105/AJPH.2013.301358.

Volkow, N. D., Koob, G. F., & McLellan, A. T. (2016). Neurobiologic advances from the brain disease model of addiction. *New England Journal of Medicine*, *374*(4), 363–371. Available from: https://doi.org/10.1056/NEJMra1511480.

White, W. L. (2007). Addiction recovery: Its definition and conceptual boundaries. *Journal of Substance Abuse Treatment*, *33*(3), 229–241. Available from: https://doi.org/10.1016/j.jsat.2007.04.015.

Wiers, R. W., Eberl, C., Rinck, M., Becker, E. S., & Lindenmeyer, J. (2011). Retraining automatic action tendencies changes alcoholic patients' approach bias for alcohol and improves treatment outcome. *Psychological Science*, *22*(4), 490–497. Available from: https://doi.org/10.1177/0956797611400615.

Witkiewitz, K. (2013). "Success" following alcohol treatment: Moving beyond abstinence. *Alcoholism: Clinical and Experimental Research*, *37*(Suppl.1), E9–E13. Available from: https://doi.org/10.1111/acer.12001.

Witkiewitz, K., Falk, D. E., Litten, R. Z., Hasin, D. S., Kranzler, H. R., Mann, K. F., ... Anton, R. F. (2019). Maintenance of World Health Organization risk drinking level reductions and posttreatment functioning following a large alcohol use disorder clinical trial. *Alcoholism: Clinical and Experimental Research*, *43*(5), 979–987. Available from: https://doi.org/10.1111/acer.14018.

World Health Organization. (2018). Alcohol. Retrieved August 17, 2019, from <https://www.who.int/news-room/fact-sheets/detail/alcohol>.

Yamaguchi, K., & Kandel, D. B. (1985). On the resolution of role incompatibility: A life event history analysis of family roles and marijuana use. *American Journal of Sociology*, *90*(6), 1284–1325. Available from: https://doi.org/10.1086/228211.

Section 7

Future directions

Chapter 26

Alcohol addiction: A disorder of self-regulation but not a disease of the brain

Nick Heather
Department of Psychology, Northumbria University, Newcastle upon Tyne, United Kingdom

Introduction

In this chapter I outline a perspective on addiction to alcohol that derives from a more general perspective on addiction as a whole. This general perspective is that addiction is essentially a disorder of self-regulation. This applies to the entire range of substance addictions and those non-substance problem behaviors to which the term addiction may legitimately be applied (see Heather, 2017a). There are doubtless many important distinctions to be made between the ways what is called addiction shows itself in different substances and activities but it is also possible to describe addiction at a level of abstraction that subsumes those more specific manifestations. Because this Handbook is about alcohol I have referred to 'alcohol addiction' in the title of the chapter and illustrate my arguments with reference to drinking behavior wherever appropriate. However, it is the wider perspective on addiction, and not the more local one on alcohol addiction *per se*, that I am primarily interested in here. I do not claim to present anything like a theory of addiction, merely the 'direction of travel' I believe the development of a fully-formed theory of addiction should take.

The chapter is divided into two main parts. In the first, I set out the main theoretical and empirical grounds for suggesting that addiction can profitably be seen as a disorder of self-regulation. In the second, I discuss research on the neurobiological correlates of impaired self-regulation and show that this view of addiction has much in common with elements of theory and research from the perspective of addiction as a brain disease. I also note that there exists an important obstacle to the integration of the present perspective with that of the brain disease model of addiction, as represented by typical presentations of it. I argue that addiction, including alcohol addiction, can be

The Handbook of Alcohol Use - Understandings from Synapse to Society.
DOI: https://doi.org/10.1016/B978-0-12-816720-5.00003-7

usefully seen as a disorder of self-regulation without the added implication that it is thereby a disease of the brain.

Addiction is a disorder of self-regulation[1]

Addiction is a multi-faceted phenomenon and can plausibly be seen in many ways, with many corresponding attempts at explanation (Ainslie, 2017). It is therefore important to ask, what is the crucial puzzle of addiction; what is the feature of addicts' behavior that most demands our theoretical attention, our best scientific endeavors to explain it, and our best therapeutic and preventive attempts to ameliorate it? My answer to these questions is that addicts repeatedly behave in ways they *know* are bad for them – not merely ways that we, as outside observers, believe to be bad for them but ways that they themselves recognize as bad for them. We can be sure of this because addicts persistently try to desist from addictive behavior but repeatedly fail. Thus, from the present viewpoint, and in terms of Frankfurt's (1971) classic delineation of ways of being addicted, there are only 'unwilling addicts';[2] the existence of 'willing addicts' is an oxymoron (cf. Flanagan, 2017).

It is often said that addiction is a relapsing condition. It is relatively easy to bring about an initial change in behavior, either in treatment or by the person's own resources, but much harder to maintain that change over time (e.g., Marlatt & Donovan, 2007). To take the example of cigarette smoking, it has recently been estimated that the average number of attempts that are made before successful quitting occurs ranges, depending on various assumptions, from 6 to 30 (Chaiton et al., 2016). A similar situation applies to alcohol addiction (Chiapetta, Garcia-Rodriguez, Jin, Secades-Villa, & Blanco, 2014). Indeed, I argue that, were it not a relapsing condition, there would be no need for the term 'addiction', at least in its modern sense as applying to harmful drug consumption and other forms of repetitive, harmful behavior. If someone engaging, for example, in harmful or risky alcohol consumption had those harmful consequences brought to her attention, by a medical practitioner or in some other way, and immediately gave up drinking or reduced her consumption to less risky levels, going on permanently to maintain those behavioral changes over time, there would obviously be no continuing problem to be addressed. The fact that some people do not respond to knowledge

1. I prefer the term 'self-regulation' to 'self-control' in the present context, mainly because the latter is conventionally interpreted to refer to an effort to inhibit and suppress thoughts, feeling and behavior that conflict with one's primary goals, whereas 'self-regulation' includes a wider range of ways in which goal-directed behavior is achieved (cf. Fujita, Carnevale, & Trope, 2018). However, I will sometimes refer to 'self-control' where appropriate and when discussing the work of authors who use that term.

2. To this might be added Kennett's (2013) concept of 'the resigned addict' (pp. 160-2). However, the resigned addict is an unwilling addict who has given up trying, at least temporarily, to change behavior.

of harmful consequences from their behavior in this way is precisely why we need the concept of addiction and why it arose in its modern meaning.

Defining addiction

How then should addiction be defined? I have previously suggested that it be defined thus: "A repeated and continuing failure to refrain from or radically reduce a specified behavior despite prior resolutions to do so" (Heather, 2017a). On reflection, this definition might be considered over-inclusive because it does not rule out obsessional rituals and other kinds of behavior that are unwanted and difficult to break free from but not reasonably called addictions. Another hallmark of addictive behavior frequently remarked on in the literature is that it gives rise to short-term rewards but longer-term punishments (e.g., Ainslie, 2001). Thus an amended definition is: "A repeated and continuing failure to refrain from or radically reduce a behavior that gives short-term rewards but longer-term punishments despite prior resolutions to do so." Advantages of defining addiction in this way have been discussed by Heather (2017a). They include the possibility of distinguishing those repetitive and harmful behaviors, like problem gambling, gaming, shopping, internet use, etc., that are legitimately called behavioral addictions from those that are not.

The compulsion view of addiction

A familiar attempt to solve the puzzle that some people, conventionally called addicts, continue to behave in ways they know are bad for them is the idea that they are *compelled* to do so. This idea has formed the cornerstone of the disease theory of addiction for the last 200 years (Levine, 1978) and continues to be the underpinning of the brain disease model of addiction (BDMA), as shown by this quotation from what might be called Leshner's (1997) manifesto for the BDMA:

> *That addiction is tied to changes in brain structure and function is what makes it, fundamentally, a brain disease. A metaphorical switch in the brain seems to be thrown as a result of prolonged drug use. Initially, drug use is a voluntary behavior, but when that switch is thrown, the individual moves into the state of addiction, characterized by compulsive drug seeking and use (p. 46).*

Elsewhere Leshner (2001) equates addicts' uncontrollable addictive behavior to the hallucinations and delusions of schizophrenics and the trembling of Parkinson's patients. Compulsion, in various manifestations, is also the kernel of the leading neuroscientific accounts of addiction in existence today (Everitt & Robbins, 2016; Goldstein & Volkow, 2011; Koob, 2009; Robinson & Berridge, 1993; see Heather, 2017b).

The trouble is that it is not at all clear what exactly compulsion is supposed to mean in relation to addiction; different authors and institutions mean different things by it (Heather, 2017b). However, it is possible to discern at least three distinct meanings of the term in BDMA writings (see Heather, 2018a).

The minimal version of compulsion: repeated, persistent (drug) use causes harm; addicts know that it causes harm but continue to do it; no rational person would choose to behave that way; therefore, they must be compelled to do it.

This version is best illustrated in an article by (Hyman 2007, p. 9). However, although it has some face validity as a description of addictive behavior, it is merely a restatement of the central puzzle of addiction and does nothing to further our understanding of it. The danger here is of assuming that, by calling addictive behavior compulsive in this way, something *has* been explained when it has not (see Heather, 2018a).

Automaticity - the strong version of compulsion: This rests on the idea that addictive behavior is the result of automatic processes over which the addict has no control. I call it 'strong' because automatic processes are considered both necessary and sufficient for the occurrence of addictive behavior (Heather, 2017b, 2018a).

A prime example of a theory of addiction along these lines is Everitt and Robbins' (2005) *aberrant learning theory* in which addiction is seen as the culmination of a series of transitions from voluntary behavior, through habitual use, to compulsive use. This version of compulsion does potentially have explanatory power but is flatly contradicted by evidence (to be summarized below).

"Irresistible" desires - the weak version of compulsion: This refers to the effects on behavior of powerful desires, urges, cravings, or impulses; these powerfully motivating feelings or sensations cause addicts compulsively to carry out addictive behavior against their wills. I call it 'weak' because, in contrast to the 'strong' version above, although powerful motivations may be thought necessary for addictive behavior to occur, they are not sufficient. This is shown simply by the fact that addicts do occasionally resist such motivational forces and refrain from addictive behavior.

Although inherited from 19th Century portrayals of addiction, the best modern example of this motivational kind of account of compulsion is found in Robinson and Berridge's (1993) *incentive-sensitization theory*. In particular, the distinction in this theory between 'wanting' and 'liking' drug effects can make sense of several irrational aspects of addictive behavior (see Heather, 2018a). Unfortunately, it is still embarrassed by evidence which will now be summarized.

Evidence on the nature of addictive behavior in humans

Much of the evidence on compulsion in addiction derives from experimental studies of non-human animals, chiefly chimpanzees and rats (see Ahmed, 2019;

Heather, 2019). When researchers have turned their attention to addictive behavior in humans, however, a very different picture emerges. The following are summaries of bodies of evidence that are difficult for the compulsion view of addiction to accommodate (see Heather, 2018b; for more extended discussion, see Heather, 2017b):

i. A large number of laboratory investigations in the 1960s and 1970s showed conclusively that the drinking of the most chronic and severe alcohol addicts found in institutional settings was 'operant behavior', i.e., behavior that was largely determined by its environmental consequences. Thus, rather than being compelled in any useful sense, alcohol addicts' drinking was subject to the same general laws that govern normal, goal-directed, voluntary behavior of any sort (see Heather, 2017b for summary).

ii. In similar fashion but more recently, Carl Hart and colleagues (2000) demonstrated that alternative reinforcers (money or merchandise vouchers) could modify cocaine use in experienced cocaine smokers recruited from the community. These were individuals who would be regarded as hopelessly addicted to crack cocaine in the mainstream media and by many scientists and professionals, but could be persuaded by the offer of a relatively small amount of money or equivalent goods to reject the choice of cocaine.

iii. Contingency management (CM), which provides tangible rewards for engaging in desired behaviors and is based on the principles of operant conditioning, is widely recognized as the most efficacious method of treatment for addictive behavior (Zajac, Alessi, & Petry, 2018), further supporting the conclusion that addictive behavior is goal-directed and responsive to its consequences.

iv. The notion of compulsion implies that addictive behavior is inflexible and stereotyped. However, in her qualitative study of drug (mostly heroin) users in Scotland, Joanne Neale (2002) was unable to confirm this depiction. Far from helpless victims of forces over which they had no control, Neale's respondents were typically self-respecting and self-determining individuals "who actively confronted and purposefully responded to external constraints and life opportunities" (p. 35). Neale's observations are consistent with a long tradition of ethnographic research with addicts, including the classic study by Preble and Casey (1969).

v. Heyman (2013) reported a reanalysis of data from four large-scale, longitudinal surveys of the general population in the USA carried out at various times since 1980. If addictive behavior is compulsive, one would expect that addicts would take a long time to recover and that many would fail to do so. This was not what was found in these data. Of all those individuals who had ever in their lifetimes met criteria for 'substance dependence' laid down in the fourth edition of the *Diagnostic and Statistical Manual of Mental Disorders* (DSM-IV: American Psychiatric Association, 1994), between 76% and 83% were 'in remission' (i.e., showed no evidence of dependence in the past year) at the time of the survey. For the great majority of these respondents, remission was achieved without benefit of treatment.

vi. In assessing the validity of the compulsion concept, it is also relevant to consider the nature of recovery from addiction: what are the main factors influencing addicts' changes in behavior when they give up or radically reduce substance use or other harmful activities? If addiction were compulsive due to a brain disease, we would expect that recoveries would mainly come about through treatment, directed presumably at correcting the neurobiological basis of the compulsion. But we have seen that this is not the case for the majority of recovered addicts. Instead, it has long been established that in most cases recovery from, for example, alcohol addiction appears due to changes in life circumstances, involving marriage, employment, health, and finance (Tuchfeld, 1981). From a psychological stance, the typical way in which self-change occurs is by a 'cognitive appraisal', which involves a process of weighing up the advantages and disadvantages of changing addictive behavior and becoming committed to change (Klingemann et al., 2007).

vii. Perhaps the most influential body of evidence that casts doubt on the compulsion idea comes from a follow-up of Vietnam War veterans. Toward the end of the war, the US government became alarmed by reports that a large proportion of American servicemen in Vietnam were addicted to heroin or other drugs; the government commissioned research to conduct interviews with a large sample of soldiers in Vietnam and determine the extent and characteristics of their drug use, and then to follow them up on their return to the US after discharge in 1971 (Robins, Davis, & Goodwin, 1974; Robins, Helzer, & Davis, 1975). Against all expectations based on a compulsion account of addiction, it was found that, in the first year after return, only 5% of those who had been addicted in Vietnam were addicted in the USA. And despite reports of withdrawal symptoms, 88% had not resumed regular use of opiates at a 3-year follow-up. This did not happen because drugs were unavailable; interviewees said that they knew how to get heroin and some had occasionally but not regularly used. It is difficult to see how these findings could have been obtained if addictive behavior were compulsive in any straightforward sense.

Other stands of evidence causing embarrassment to the compulsion view of addiction may be found in Heather (2017b). It should be made clear, however, that there are some ways in which it might be valid to describe addictive behavior and/or experience as compulsive (see Heather, 2017b). While the evidence contradicts compulsion in the strong sense of automatic behavior elicited involuntarily by drug-related cues independently of the person's motivational status, it may have some useful meaning in the weaker sense of the addict's experience of feeling unable to resist powerful temptations, although this cannot be a sufficient condition for use to occur. It is also possible that addicts report addictive behavior to be compulsive because they cannot understand why their resolutions to change behavior keep breaking down; they cannot give reasons for their repeated relapses and therefore feel that their behavior must be driven by some extrapersonal force over which they have no control (Heather & Segal, 2013). Nevertheless, the key point for present purposes remains that the evidence shows addictive behavior to be voluntary rather than compelled *at the time it is carried out.*

Addiction as a form of akrasia

If addictive behavior is voluntary at the time it is carried out, an obvious problem immediately arises: how can addiction be said to exist? There are, indeed, some writers and researchers on addiction who declare that it does not exist, that addiction is a myth (Davies, 1997) and that what is called addictive behavior represents a free choice just like any other (Schaler, 2000).[3] But surely, when we refer to someone as an addict, we imply that there must be some limits to that individual's autonomy, some kind of constraint on their ability to choose what to do? If there were no such constraint, addicts would presumably not complain that their behavior was out of their control, or at least not fully within it. If we rule out the possibility, on the basis of good evidence and sound reasoning, that the constraint arises because of something called 'compulsion', how can we begin to explain the addict's predicament?

A possible solution to this conundrum lies in the ancient philosophical concept of *akrasia.* This is the term Aristotle used for 'acting against one's best judgement' or 'contrary to what one judges it is in one's best interests to do' (see Heather, 2017c). A frequently-used synonym for akrasia is 'weakness of will'. There is disagreement among philosophers about what is usually meant by weakness of will but most would agree that it implies failing to act on one's intention to do what one considers best to do (Holton, 2009). In this sense, what we might call 'ordinary akrasia' (or ordinary weakness of will) is something we are all familiar with and an everyday occurrence (e.g., Hofmann, Baumeister, Forster, & Vohs, 2012).

The relevance to addiction of all this is simply the proposition that addictive behavior represents an extreme form of akrasia. The intentions that fail to be carried out in addiction are somewhat different to those in ordinary akrasia; Holton (2009) calls them 'contrary-inclination-defeating intentions',

3. See Heather, and Segal (2017) for a rejection of such views.

i.e., resolutions made "in the attempt to overcome contrary desires that one believes one will have when the time comes to act" (p. 77); in other words, attempts to forestall the temptation to break the resolution that one knows will arise. This clearly relates to what was argued above to be the characteristic of addiction most urgently in need of understanding – its relapsing nature. There may be other differences between ordinary akrasia and addictive behavior – the strength of the resolution broken in the latter is typically much stronger, it involves many more repetitive breakdowns of resolutions, and the consequences of such breakdowns may be much more troublesome and painful to the individual than those from ordinary akrasia – but these are not crucial obstacles to seeing addiction usefully as an extreme form of akrasia.

One further point should be stressed before moving on. In arguing that addictive behavior is an extreme form of akrasia or weakness of will, no claim is being made that anything has thereby been explained. Even if the akrasia perspective on addiction were favored, it still remains to be explained *why* addicts persistently choose to behave in ways they know to be against their best interests. What has been achieved in describing addiction in this way is to clarify what *needs* to be explained.

Addiction as temporal inconsistency

Addicts often tell us that they drink alcohol, take illicit drugs, smoke cigarettes, gamble, etc. 'against their will'. But in what sense can this be true? We have seen that, if someone makes a strong resolution to refrain from behaving in a certain way but fails to carry out that resolution, and if this happens repeatedly and distressingly, we are entitled to describe this pattern of behavior as addiction. If we then take the further step of identifying the addict's resolution with their will, on the ground that this reflects that set of considerations which the addict "in a cool and non-deceptive moment articulates as definitive of the good, fulfilling and defensible life" (Watson, 1975, p. 215), it is in this sense that addictive behavior can be described as against the will.[4]

It follows that, although addicts respond to incentives and are free to choose to engage or not engage in addictive behavior at any one time, their autonomy is impaired when their pattern of choices is considered over time. In other words, in respect of their addictive behavior, addicts are unable effectively to extend their will over time. This view of addiction has been articulated by Neil Levy (2006), who writes: "It is because addiction undermines extended agency, so that addicts are not able to integrate their lives and pursue a single conception of the good, that it impairs autonomy" (p. 427).

4. There are other ways of seeing people's resolutions to change behavior as equivalent to their will. See Center on Addiction (2018).

What kind of disorder then is addiction?

A popular alternative to the position that addiction is a brain disease is the idea that it is a disorder of choice (Heather, 2017d; Heyman, 2009). And so far in this chapter I have variously described addiction as a form of akrasia or weakness of will and a disorder of self-regulation. There is nothing inconsistent in these descriptions and they are all valid ways of regarding addiction, with much in common between them. However, a disorder of self-regulation is preferred here as the more useful description; it specifies more precisely what kind of disorder of choice is involved in addiction - a disorder of choice over time - and clarifies what are the important consequences of akrasia or weakness of will - that it impairs the addict's regulation of her behavior over time[5].

Advantages of seeing addiction as a disorder of self-regulation

In addition to clarifying the essential nature of addiction, seeing it as a disorder of self-regulation has the advantage of being consistent with several important bodies of theory and research that, in combination, may help to achieve a coherent scientific understanding of addiction. These are briefly as follows:

i. *Hyperbolic delay discounting.* A disorder of self-regulation is consistent with an influential account of impulsive behavior in general and addictive behavior in particular developed over the years by George Ainslie (e.g., Ainslie, 1975, 1992, 2001, 2017, 2019). This may be crudely summarized as proposing that, because of the way the value of rewards is discounted over time (hyperbolically and not exponentially), our preferences reverse from larger, later rewards to smaller, sooner rewards as the latter are approached. To establish self-control over behavior, we must find ways to resist the temptation of smaller, sooner rewards, chiefly by 'bunching' the value of a series of later, larger rewards. This bunching process is equivalent to 'willpower'. Ainslie's theory may also be seen as one of several accounts of addiction from the perspective of behavioral economics (see Vuchinich & Heather, 2003), all of which are consistent with addiction as a disorder of self-regulation.
ii. *Delay of gratification.* In a renowned series of experiments conducted at Stanford University in the 1960s, Walter Mischel and his colleagues gave preschool children a choice of eating one marshmallow now or waiting and enjoying two later (see, e.g., Mischel, 2014; Mischel & Ebbeson, 1970).

5. During an episode of the BBC program, *Desert Island Disks* broadcast on May 29, 2009, the comedian Barry Humphries, who had suffered for 15 years of his life from severe alcohol addiction, said that he thought alcoholism must be 'a disorder of the memory'. This was because he repeatedly woke up in the morning groaning and vowing 'never again' but by lunchtime invariably found himself on to his second glass of beaujolais.

Remarkably, at a follow-up a decade later, adolescents who had shown delay behavior as children were, as rated by parents, more academically and socially competent, verbally fluent, rational, attentive, and able to deal well with frustration and stress (Mischel, Shoda, & Peake, 1988). The predictive validity of the marshmallow test has recently been thrown in doubt by an attempt at replication that showed a much weaker predictive effect than had previously been reported (Watts, Duncan, & Quan, 2018). Nevertheless, this body of work is valuable in increasing our understanding of how children, and adults too, manage to resist temptation and achieve control over behavior, as well as the wider consequences of such abilities. It also helps to relate the study of addiction to the ordinary, everyday practice of self-regulation.

iii. *Ego-depletion.* Another prominent body of work with clear implications for addiction as self-regulation is research on so-called 'ego-depletion' carried out by Roy Baumeister and colleagues over the last 30 years (see, e.g., Baumeister, 2017; Baumeister, Bratlavsky, Muraven, & Tice, 1998; Baumeister, Heatherton, & Tice, 1994). This refers to the idea that active choices, attempts at self-regulation and other volitional efforts draw on a common but limited reserve of mental resources. Acts of self-control deplete the pool of resources and make successful control less likely on subsequent tasks, even if the contents of those tasks are unrelated to the prior task. In this way, self-regulation works like a muscle that tires through repetition but can be strengthened through practice over time. The relevance to addiction is that ego-depletion impairs the maintenance of behavior change over time and makes relapse more likely as a response to tempting situations. There is also the theoretical deduction that practice at resisting temptation builds up volitional resources and this has been applied to the treatment of smoking cessation by Muraven (2010).

Again, an attempt to replicate the ego-depletion phenomenon across numerous laboratories by Hagger and Chatzisarantis (2016) found a smaller effect than had previously been reported, and Baumeister and Vohs (2016) have responded to this evidence. There has also been an attempt to explain the ego-depletion effect from a different theoretical perspective than the resource-strength model (e.g., Inzlicht & Schmeichel, 2012) but this does not affect the reliability of the basic finding that exerting self-control on one task impairs self-control on subsequent tasks (see Dill and Holton (2014) for discussion). Despite these complexities, however, the large body of research and theorizing stimulated by the concept of ego-depletion is highly relevant to seeing addiction as a failure of self-regulation (see, e.g., Levy, 2011).

iv. *Other research on temptation, self-control and self-regulation.* In addition to the above, the last 50 years has witnessed a very large amount of theory and research on self-control and self-regulation, increasing in frequency to the point where it is now one of the most common topics for research in psychology and related sciences. This applies to the self-regulation of human behavior in general (e.g., Berkman, Hutcherson, Livingstone, Kahn, & Inzlicht, 2017; Duckworth, Gendler, & Gross, 2016; Logue, 1988; Lord & Levy, 1994; Nigg, 2000; Norman & Shallice, 1986; Oaten & Cheng, 2006; Rachlin, 1974, 2000) and more specifically in relation to addiction (e.g., Bickel, Quisenberry, Moody, & Wilson, 2015; Heather, Miller, & Greeley, 1991; Heatherton & Wagner, 2011; Hofmann et al., 2012; Koepetz, Lejuez, Wiers, & Kruglanski, 2013; Maisto & Caddy, 1981; O'Donoghue & Rabin, 1999; Oettingen, Mayer, & Thorpe, 2010; Palfai, 2006).

To attempt to summarize and integrate this enormous body of work, together with the lines of theory and research briefly noted above, is beyond the scope of this chapter. The point being made is that there exists a large amount of evidence and ideas that could help to develop a self-regulation theory of addiction.

Self-regulation and dual-systems theory

There is another body of work that is consistent with the idea of addiction as a disorder of self-regulation. This is based on the proposal that addiction can be explained within the overall framework of a dual-systems (or dual-process) theory of human behavior and experience (Evans & Frankish, 2009) and this will be expanded on below. However, the reason for devoting a separate section to this proposal is that, while I have so far avoided the claim that seeing addiction as a disorder of self-regulation has explanatory value, I make an exception here; the claim is that the difficulties of self-regulation seen in addiction *can* potentially be explained under a dual-systems framework and, moreover, that this framework might be able to bring together the various strands of research and theory briefly summarized in the preceding section.

There are different versions of dual-systems theory but they all offer accounts of how human behavior can be viewed as the result of one of two different kinds of information processing and of their interaction— implicit, automatic and mainly non-conscious processes and explicit, controlled, and mainly conscious processes. The distinction between dual-process and dual-system theories is that, while the former are based on the assumption that two distinct processes of thinking compete for control of behavior, the latter go further in ascribing the origin of these dual processes "to biologically distinct cognitive systems with sharply differing evolutionary histories" (Evans & Coventry, 2006, p. 30). In one of the most influential dual-system models, Strack and Deutsch (2004) posit that behavior is a joint function of two parallel and interacting processing systems that follow different operating principles: a *reflective* system that generates behavioral decisions based on knowledge about facts and values, and an *impulsive* system that elicits behavior through associative links and motivational orientations. This model has been applied to addiction by Deutsch and Strack (2006), thus providing one example of the application of dual-systems theory to addiction that is under discussion here.

Roughly, the proposal is that, in addiction, the balance between the two systems has become disturbed. Automatic processes, such as memory associations and cognitions, promote addictive behavior while, at the same time, poor goal-directed planning, distorted judgements and evaluations result in impaired self-control capacity that undermines attempts to resist it. Thus, a dual-systems theory of addiction is an attempt to understand what Borland (2014) has called "the constraints on and the potential of volitional attempts to change behavior patterns that are under the moment-to-moment control of non-volitional processes" (p. 1).

The main practical implication of this for the treatment of addictive behaviors is that improvements in treatment would rely on research to strengthen self-control, including techniques both to modify bottom-up automatic processes and to improve top-down executive functions (see Wiers & Stacy, 2006). The main Implication for prevention is that interventions should modify the environmental architecture of choice by framing behavioral options in a way that helps people choose in their best interests (see, e.g., Tucker, Chandler, & Cheong, 2017).

It should be pointed out in fairness that there have been recent criticisms of dual-systems/process models of addiction (Berkman et al., 2017; Fujita et al., 2018; Hommel & Wiers, 2017). Whether or not these criticisms lead to the downfall of the dual- systems account of self-regulation disorders remains to be seen but is in my view unlikely.

Commonalities with neuroscientific research on addiction

It may first be important to clarify that the disorder of self-regulation perspective is by no means inimical to neuroscientific research and to identifying the neurobiological correlates of self-regulation deficits in addiction. More specifically, despite their apparently very different portrayals of addiction, there is common ground between theory and research on addiction as a disorder of self-regulation and as a brain disorder, and these commonalities might eventually provide the basis for an integration of the two perspectives.

Neuroscience and self-regulation

As but one example from cognitive neuroscience research, Heatherton and Wagner (2011) suggest that successful self-regulation depends on top-down control by the prefrontal cortex over subcortical brain regions implicated in reward and emotion. They describe a balance model of self-regulation in which failures take place when the balance is tipped in favor of subcortical areas, due either to strong temptations or impairment to prefrontal functioning. Such a model is supported by neuroimaging research on self-regulatory failure and is consistent, say the authors, with findings on the cognitive neuroscience of addictive behavior.

Heatherton and Wagner's (2011) article is written mainly within the tradition of Baumeister and colleagues' ego-depletion theory (see above) but could also be cast as a dual-systems model. Similarly, from the viewpoint of hyperbolic delay discounting (see above), McClure, Laibson, Loewnestein, and Cohen (2004) posit separate neural systems responsible for valuing immediate and delayed rewards, while Metcalfe and Mischel (1999) hypothesize the neural underpinnings of 'hot' and 'cool' systems involved in delay of gratification (see above). Other notable publications exploring the neurobiological basis of self-regulation deficits in addiction from a dual-systems stance are Jentsch and Taylor (1999), Bechara (2005), Bickel and Li (2010), and Lindgren et al. (2019). Many more examples of research and theory on the links between self-regulation, dual systems theory and addiction could be provided. Note that researchers in this category do not necessarily subscribe to a brain disease model of addiction; whether difficulties in self-regulation can be usefully seen as due to a putative brain disease is either denied or left moot.

Incentive salience and self-regulation

In an important theoretical paper, Dill and Holton (2014) show how many of the puzzling features of addiction, including the deficits in self-regulation of interest in this chapter, can be explained by Robinson and Berridge's (1993) incentive sensitization theory of addiction. This theory assumes that addictive drugs artificially increase dopamine transmission in the brain system (the mesolimbic dopamine system) involved in reward and motivation for natural rewards. This system attributes 'incentive salience' to stimuli associated with reward, making them attractive and sought-after. The repeated use of addictive substances results in incremental neuro-adaptations in this system, rendering it increasingly and persistently 'sensitized' to drugs, and this is one meaning of the common claim that in addiction the brain has been 'hijacked' by the effects of drugs.

An essential part of the theory is the distinction between 'wanting' and 'liking' drugs and drug experiences. The sensitization of incentive salience is called drug 'wanting' but the accompanying changes in neural systems can occur independently of changes in other neural systems responsible for the pleasurable effects of drugs, called drug 'liking'. Thus, incentive sensitization can lead to drug-seeking and -taking even when the expectation of pleasure is low and even in the face of strong personal and social disincentives to use (see Berridge & Robinson, 2016).

The contribution made by Dill and Holton (2014) is to argue that, within the terms of incentive salience theory, addictive temptations and desires are not fundamentally different from many of the desires experiences by non-addicts; the differences lie in the 'unnatural' manner in which addictive desires are acquired and their greater strength and difficulty to resist. For Dill and Holton, the self-control challenge faced by addicted persons is essentially the same as that faced by the non-addicted and, on this basis, they construct a general model of self-control embracing three different stages in the passage from thought to action.[6] The immediate point is that, as interpreted by Dill and Holton (2014), a leading neurobiological theory of addiction is helpful in understanding how addiction may be seen as a disorder of self-regulation and is perfectly consistent with a view of addiction based on notions of akrasia, temporal behavioral inconsistency, and dual-systems theory.

It is relevant here that Berridge (2017) is equivocal about whether or not addiction should be termed a brain disease. He says that, although the term was never used by the theory, the changes in neural sensitization underlying addiction are "arguably extreme enough and problematic enough to be called pathological. This implies that 'brain disease' can be a legitimate description of addiction, though caveats are needed to acknowledge roles for choice and active agency by the addict" (p. 29).

Involvement of the frontal cortex in addiction

In comparison to Berridge's (2017) somewhat equivocal endorsement of the BDMA, we turn now to work in which addiction is seen unequivocally as a brain disease. Much neuroscience research on addiction, including that associated with Robinson and Berridge's (1993) incentive sensitization theory (see above), is concerned with how the mesolimbic dopamine reward system is said to 'hijacked' by the effects of drug-taking or other potentially addictive activities. But there is another important body of neuroscience research, associated with the neuroimaging work of Nora Volkow and her colleagues, on impairments to self-regulation involving dysfunction in the frontal cortex and related neurocircuitry (e.g. Goldstein & Volkow, 2002, 2011; Kalivas & Volkow, 2005).

Based on findings from neuroimaging, Goldstein and Volkow (2002) report that the orbitofrontal cortex (OFC) and the anterior cingulate gyrus (ACC), regions connected neuro-anatomically with subcortical, limbic structures, are the frontal cortical areas that are most frequently implicated in drug addiction. The OFC is thought to be involved primarily in emotion and reward in decision-making whereas the ACC is involved in the allocation of attention, the anticipation of reward, response inhibition and decision-making. On this basis, Goldstein and Volkow (2002) propose that "the behaviors and associated motivational states that are at the core of drug addiction are distinctly the processes of loss of self-directed/willed behaviors to automatic sensory-driven formulas

---

6. There will not be space to consider this model of self-control in any detail but the reader is encouraged to consult the original source (Dill & Holton, 2014).

and attribution of primary salience to the drug of abuse at the expense of other available rewarding stimuli" (p. 1643). These states are hypothesized to be evoked first in the initiation of drug use in the presence of drug-related stimuli but then become 'chronic action tendencies' that contribute to craving, bingeing and relapse. In this way, addiction is seen as a syndrome of 'impaired response inhibition and salience attribution' or iRISA for short.

It is clear that this research and accompanying theory, which is far more extensive and complex that there is space to convey here (see, e.g., Goldstein & Volkow, 2011), has much to offer the development of a full theory of addiction as a disorder of self-regulation. In particular, the impairments to the top-down regulation of automatic processes involved in addiction, as revealed by neuroimaging, promise to fill in some of the picture of the neurobiological correlates of behavioral dysregulation in a dual-systems model of addiction. Unfortunately, there is one crucial issue that threatens to undermine this convergence of theory and research.

The key issue is that, in typical writings on the BDMA, control over addictive behavior is not described merely as impaired or compromised in some way, it is said to be *lost*. We saw earlier in this chapter that Alan Leshner (1997), the first to attempt the widespread promotion of the BDMA, believed that in addiction drug use has ceased to be voluntary behavior, similar to the shaking of sufferers from Parkinson's disease. Similarly, in the quotation from Goldstein and Volkow (2002) given above, there is said to be a loss of self-directed/willed behaviors in addiction. Volkow and Li (2004) write: "... recent studies have shown that repeated drug use leads to long-lasting changes in the brain that undermine voluntary control" (p. 963). The same authors (Volkow & Li, 2005) complain that "addicted individuals continue to be stigmatized by the pernicious yet enduring popular belief that their affliction stems from voluntary behavior" (p. 1430). It is difficult to make sense of the idea that addiction 'stems' from voluntary behavior but, as research briefly summarized earlier in this chapter clearly showed, addictive behavior is voluntary at the time it is carried out.

It is true that, in other writings from the BDMA perspective, control over drug use is said to be 'decreased' or 'reduced' (see, e.g., Kalivas & Volkow, 2005) but it is perhaps in communications intended for non-specialists and the general public that the complete elimination of choice in addiction is more likely to be suggested. For example, in an article in the *Huffpost* entitled *Addiction is a disease of free will*, Nora Volkow (2016) writes that "the person who is addicted does not choose to be addicted; it's no longer a choice to take the drug". These are very different statements; nobody, of course, chooses to be addicted but, again, evidence clearly shows that addicts choose to take drugs at the time they take them (cf. Rachlin, 2000,[7] p. 4). Apart from the

7. "The alcoholic does not choose to be an alcoholic. Instead he chooses to drink now, and now, and now." (Rachlin, 2000 p. 4).

appeal to neuroimaging, Volkow's view of addiction here seems a reversion to Benjamin's Rush's (1812) characterization of 'habitual drunkenness' as a 'disease of the will' in the early 19th Century. It may be that, in her role as Director of the *National Institute on Drug Abuse* in the USA, Volkow believes that such oversimplifications and distortions are necessary to persuade the general public that addiction is a disease of the brain but that is another matter. From a scientific and scholarly viewpoint, there seems little hope of a *rapprochement* between the BDMA and the criticisms made in this chapter of the compulsion view of addiction as long as this all-or-none conception of choice in addiction versus non-addiction is maintained. At the very least, it is a probabilistic understanding of impaired control in addiction, in which the addict cannot be sure that she will be able to maintain control over temptation in the future, that is required if progress is to be made.[8]

Concluding remarks: addiction is not a disease of the brain

We have just seen that a version of the BDMA that depicts control over addictive behavior as completely lost is unhelpful. Earlier in the chapter, evidence was presented to show that addiction does not result in the compulsive, automatic behavior that is required under the BDMA but is rather manifested as a disorder of self-regulation over time. Various strands of evidence were described which conspire to demonstrate that, at the time it is carried out, addictive behavior is operant, goal-directed behavior and thus voluntary in nature. All this evidence suggests that the BDMA is fundamentally mistaken in its account of addictive behavior. Moreover, if addiction is a brain disease, it must be a very odd kind of disease if a clear majority of sufferers from it can eventually make a *choice* to abandon its leading symptom, excessive and harmful drug consumption, without benefit of treatment (Heyman, 2009, 2013). Could the same be said of other chronic diseases with which the brain disease of addiction is frequently compared, such as diabetes, cancer and heart disease (e.g., Center on Addiction, 2018)?

There are other criticisms of the BDMA that are relevant to the main thrust of this chapter, that addiction can usefully be seen as a disorder of self-regulation without the implication that it is thereby a disease of the brain. Unfortunately, there will not be space to cover these criticisms here and the interested reader is encouraged to consult original sources (e.g., Borsboom, Cramer, & Kalis, 2019; Hall, Carter, & Forlini, 2014; Heather, 2018b; Heather et al., 2018; Levy, 2013; Lewis, 2017; Satel & Lilienfeld, 2014; Wakefield, 2019).

---

8. Such a probabilistic view of impaired control in alcohol addiction can be found in earlier writings on alcoholism as a disease. Thus, Mark Keller (1972) proposed that alcoholics had not lost control over drinking but could never be sure that, once started, they would be able to stop; Ludwig and Wikler (1974) referred to a relative inability to control alcohol consumption; and in describing the alcohol dependence syndrome, Griffith Edwards (1982) stated that control was "variably or intermittently impaired rather than 'lost'" (p. 29).

Acknowledgments

This chapter is based on a presentation at the Deutscher Suchtkongress, Hamburg, Germany, September 18, 2018. I am grateful to the congress organizers for inviting me to speak and to participants for useful discussions following my presentation.

References

Ahmed, S. (2019). "A walk on the wild side" of addiction: The history and significance of animal models. In H. Pickard, & S. Ahmed (Eds.), *The Routledge handbook of philosophy and science of addiction* (pp. 192–203). Abdingdon, UK: Routledge.

Ainslie, G. (1975). Specious reward: A behavioral theory of impulsiveness and impulse control. *Psychological Bulletin*, *82*, 463–496.

Ainslie, G. (1992). *Picoeconomics: The strategic interaction of successive motivational states within the person.* Cambridge: Cambridge University Press.

Ainslie, G. (2001). *Breakdown of will.* Cambridge, UK: Cambridge University Press.

Ainslie, G. (2017). Palpating the elephant: Current theories of addiction in the light of hyperbolic delay discounting. In N. Heather, & G. Segal (Eds.), *Addiction and choice: Rethinking the relationship* (pp. 227–244). Oxford UK: Oxford University Press.

Ainslie, G. (2019). The picoeconomics of addiction. In H. Pickard, & S. Ahmed (Eds.), *The Routledge handbook of philosophy and science of addiction* (pp. 34–44). Abingdon, UK: Routledge.

American Psychiatric Association. (1994). *Diagnostic and statistical manual of mental disorders* (4th ed.). Washington, DC: Author.

Baumeister, R. (2017). Addiction, cigarette smoking, and voluntary control of action: Do cigarette smokers lose their free will? *Addictive Behavior Reports*, *5*, 67–84.

Baumeister, R., Bratlavsky, E., Muraven, M., & Tice, D. (1998). Ego depletion: Is the active self a limited resource? *Journal of Personality & Social Psychology*, *74*, 1252–1265.

Baumeister, R., Heatherton, T., & Tice, D. (1994). *Losing control: Why people fail at self-regulation.* San Diego, CA: Academic Press.

Baumeister, R., & Vohs, K. (2016). Misguided effort with elusive implications. *Perspectives on Psychological Science*, *11*, 474–475.

Bechara, A. (2005). Decision making, impulse control and loss of willpower to resist drugs: A neurocognitive perspective. *Nature Neuroscience*, *8*, 1458–1463.

Berkman, E., Hutcherson, C., Livingstone, J., Kahn, L., & Inzlicht, M. (2017). Self-control as value-based choice. *Current Directions in Psychological Science*, *26*, 422–428.

Berridge, K. (2017). Is addiction a brain disease? *Neuroethics*, *10*, 29–33. Available from: https://doi.org/10.1007/s12152-016-9286-3.

Berridge, K., & Robinson, T. (2016). Liking, wanting, and the incentive-sensitization theory of addiction. *American Psychologist*, *71*, 670–679.

Bickel, W., & Li, R. (2010). Neuroeconomics of addiction: The contribution of executive dysfunction. In D. Ross, H. Kincaid, D. Spurrett, & P. Collins (Eds.), *What is addiction?* (pp. 1–26). Cambridge, MS: MIT Press.

Bickel, W., Quisenberry, A., Moody, L., & Wilson, A. (2015). Therapeutic opportunities for self-control repair in addiction and related disorders: Change and the limits of change in trans-disease processes. *Clinical Psychological Science*, *3*, 140–153.

Borland, R. (2014). *Understanding hard to maintain behaviour change: A dual process approach.* Chichester, UK: John Wiley.

Borsboom, D., Cramer, A., & Kalis, A. (2019). Brain disorders? Not really... Why network structures block reductionism in psychopathology research. *Behavioral & Brain Sciences*, in press.

Center on Addiction. Addiction as a disease. (2018). <https://www.centeronaddiction.org/what-addiction/addiction-diseaseion>. Accessed 06.12.18.

Chaiton, M., Diemert, L., Cohen, J., Bondy, S., Selby, P., Philipneris, A., & Schwartz, R. (2016). Estimating the number of quit attempts it takes to quit smoking successfully in a longitudinal cohort of smokers. *BMJ Open*, *6*, e011045. Available from: https://doi.org/10.1136/bmjopen-2016-011045.

Chiapetta, V., Garcia-Rodriguez, O., Jin, C., Secades-Villa, A., & Blanco, C. (2014). Predictors of quit attempts and successful quit attempts among individuals with alcohol use disorders in a nationally representative sample. *Drug & Alcohol Dependence*, *141*, 138–144.

Davies, J. (1997). *The myth of addiction* (2nd ed.). Reading, UK: Harwood Academic Press.

Deutsch, R., & Strack, F. (2006). Reflective and impulsive determinants of addictive behavior. In R. Wiers, & A. Stacy (Eds.), *Handbook of implicit cognition and addiction* (pp. 45–58). Thousand Oaks, CA: Sage.

Dill, B., & Holton, R. (2014). The addict in all of us. Frontiers in Psychiatry, *5*,139. <https://www.ncbi.nlm.nih.gov/pmc/articles/PMC4191137/pdf/fpsyt-05-00139.pdf> Accessed 10.12.18.

Duckworth, R., Gendler, T., & Gross, J. (2016). Situational strategies for self-control. *Perspectives on Psychological Science*, *11*, 35–55.

Edwards, G. (1982). *The treatment of drinking problems: A guide for the helping professions*. London: Grant McIntyre.

Evans, J., & Coventry, K. (2006). A dual-process approach to behavioral addiction: The case of gambling. In R. Wiers, & A. Stacy (Eds.), *Handbook of implicit cognition and addiction* (pp. 29–44). Thousand Oaks, CA: Sage Publications.

Evans, J. S. B., & Frankish, K. (Eds.), (2009). *In two minds: Dual process and beyond*. New York, NY: Oxford University Press.

Everitt, B., & Robbins, T. (2016). Drug addiction: Updating actions to habits to compulsions ten years on. *Annual Review of Psychology*, *67*, 23–50.

Flanagan, O. (2017). Willing addicts? Drinkers, dandies, druggies, and other Dionysians. In N. Heather, & G. Segal (Eds.), *Addiction and choice: Rethinking the relationship* (pp. 66–81). Oxford, UK: Oxford University Press.

Frankfurt, H. (1971). Freedom of the will and the concept of a person. *Journal of Philosophy*, *68*, 5–20.

Fujita, K., Carnevale, J., & Trope, Y. (2018). Understanding self-control as a whole vs. part dynamic. *Neuroethics*, *11*, 283–296.

Goldstein, R., & Volkow, N. (2002). Drug addiction and its underlying neurobiological basis: Neuroimaging evidence for the involvement of the frontal cortex. *American Journal of Psychiatry*.

Goldstein, R., & Volkow, N. (2011). Dysfunction of the prefrontal cortex in addiction: Findings and clinical implications. *Nature Reviews Neuroscience*, *12*, 652–669.

Hagger, M., & Chatzisarantis, N. (2016). A multilab preregistered replication of the ego-depletion effect. *Perspectives on Psychological Science*, *11*, 546–573.

Hall, W., Carter, A., & Forlini, C. (2014). The brain disease model of addiction: Is it supported by the evidence and has it delivered on its promises? *Lancet Psychiatry*, *2*, 105–110.

Hart, C., Haney, M., Foltin, R., & Fischman, F. (2000). Alternative reinforcers differentially modify cocaine self-administration by humans. *Behavioural Pharmacology*, *11*, 87–91.

Heather, N. (2017a). On defining addiction. In N. Heather, & G. Segal (Eds.), *Addiction and choice: Rethinking the relationship* (pp. 3–25). Oxford, UK: Oxford University Press.

Heather, N. (2017b). Is the concept of compulsion useful in the explanation or description of addictive behaviour and experience? *Addictive Behavior Reports*, *6*, 15–38.

Heather, N. (2017c). Addiction as a form of akrasia. In N. Heather, & G. Segal (Eds.), *Addiction and choice: Rethinking the relationship* (pp. 133–150). Oxford, UK: Oxford University Press.

Heather, N. (2017d). Overview of addiction as a disorder of choice and future prospects. In N. Heather, & G. Segal (Eds.), *Addiction and choice: Rethinking the relationship* (pp. 463–482). Oxford, UK: Oxford University Press.

Heather, N. (2018a). Is addictive behavior compulsive? *Science Trends*. 17 May, <https://scien-cetrends.com/is-addictive-behavior-compulsive/>.

Heather, N. (2018b). Rethinking addiction. *The Psychologist*, 24–28.

Heather, N. (2019). Is addiction uniquely human? *Psychology Review*, *24*, 8–11.

Heather, N., Best, D., Kawalek, A., Field, M., Lewis, M., Rotgers, F., & Heim, D. (2018). Challenging the brain disease model of addiction: European launch of the Addiction Theory Network (Editorial). *Addiction Research & Theory*, *26*(4), 249–255. Available from: https://doi.org/10.1080/16066359.2017.1399659.

Heather, N., Miller, W., & Greeley, J. (Eds.), (1991). *Self-control and the addictive behaviours*. Sydney, Australia: Maxwell Macmillan.

Heather, N., & Segal, G. (2013). Understanding addiction: Donald Davidson and the problem of akrasia. *Addiction Research & Theory*, *21*, 445–452.

Heather, N., & Segal, G. (Eds.), (2017). *Addiction and choice: Rethinking the relationship*. Oxford, UK: Oxford University Press.

Heatherton, T., & Wagner, D. (2011). Cognitive neuroscience of self-regulation failure. *Trends in Cognitive Science*, *15*, 132–139.

Heyman, G. (2009). *Addiction: A disorder of choice*. Cambridge, MS: Harvard University Press.

Heyman, G. (2013). Quitting drugs: Quantitative and qualitative features. *Annual Review of Clinical Psychology*, *9*, 29–59.

Hofmann, W., Baumeister, R., Forster, G., & Vohs, K. (2012). Everyday temptations: An experience sampling study of desire, conflict and self-control. *Journal of Personality & Social Psychology*, *102*(6), 1318–1335.

Holton, R. (2009). *Willing, wanting, waiting*. Oxford, UK: Oxford University Press.

Hommel, B., & Wiers, R. (2017). Towards a unitary approach to human action control. *Trends in Cognitive Science*, *12*, 940–949.

Hyman, S. E. (2007). The neurobiology of addiction: Implications for the voluntary control of behavior. *American Journal of Bioethics*, *7*, 8–11.

Inzlicht, M., & Schmeichel, B. (2012). What is ego depletion? Toward a mechanistic revision of the resource model of self-control. *Perspectives on Psychological Science*, *7*, 450–463.

Jentsch, J., & Taylor, J. (1999). Impulsivity resulting from frontostriatal dysfunction in drug abuse: Implications for the control of behavior by reward-related stimuli. *Psychopharmacology*, *146*, 373–390.

Kalivas, P., & Volkow, N. (2005). The neural basis of addiction: A pathology of motivation and choice. *American Journal of Psychiatry*, *162*, 1403–1413.

Keller, M. (1972). On the loss-of-control phenomenon in alcoholism. *British Journal of Addiction*, *67*, 153–166.

Kennett, J. (2013). Just say no? Addiction and elements of self-control. In N. Levy (Ed.), *Addiction and self-control* (pp. 144–164). Oxford, UK: Oxford University Press.

Klingemann, H., Sobell, L., Barker, J., Blomqvist, J., Cloud, W., Ellinstad, T., & Tucker, J. A. (Eds.), (2007). *Promoting self-change from addictive behaviors: Practical implications for policy, prevention and treatment*. New York: Springer.

Koepetz, C., Lejuez, C., Wiers, R., & Kruglanski, A. (2013). Motivation and self-regulation in addiction: A call for convergence. *Perspectives in Psychological Science*, *8*, 3–24.

Koob, G. (2009). Neurobiological substrates for the dark side of compulsivity in addiction. *Neuropharmacology*, *56*, 18–31.

Leshner, A. I. (1997). Addiction is a brain disease, and it matters. *Science*, *278*, 45–47.

Leshner, A. (2001). Addiction is a brain disease. *Issues in Science and Technology*, *17*. <https://issues.org/leshner/>.

Levine, H. (1978). The discovery of addiction: Changing conceptions of habitual drunkenness in America. *Journal of Studies on Alcohol*, *39*, 143–174.

Levy, N. (2006). Addiction and autonomy. *Canadian Journal of Philosophy*, *36*, 427–447.

Levy, N. (2011). Addiction, responsibility, and ego depletion. In J. Poland, & G. Graham (Eds.), *Addiction and responsibility* (pp. 89–112). Cambridge, MA: MIT Press.

Levy, N. (2013). Addiction is not a brain disease (and it matters). Frontiers in Psychiatry, 4, 24. Available from: https://doi.org/10.3389/fpsyt.2013.00024.

Lewis, M. (2017). Addiction and the brain: Development, not disease. *Neuroethics*, *10*, 7–18.

Lindgren, K., Hendershot, C., Ramirez, J., Bernat, E., Rangel-Gomex, M., Peterson, K., & Murphy, J. (2019). A dual process perspective on advances in cognitive science and alcohol use disorder. *Clinical Psychology Review*, *69*, 83–96.

Logue, A. W. (1988). Research on self-control: An integrating framework. *Behavioral & Brain Sciences*, *11*, 665–709.

Lord, R., & Levy, P. (1994). Moving from cognition to action: A control theory perspective. *Applied Psychology: An International Review*, *43*, 335–398.

Ludwig, A., & Wikler, A. (1974). "Craving" and relapse to drink. *Quarterly Journal of Studies on Alcohol*, *35*, 108–130.

Maisto, S. A., & Caddy, G. R. (1981). Self-control and addictive behavior: Present status and prospects. *International Journal of the Addictions*, *16*, 109–133.

Marlatt, G., & Donovan, D. (Eds.), (2007). *Relapse prevention: Maintenance strategies in the treatment of addictive behaviors* (2nd ed.). New York, NY: Guilford Press.

McClure, S., Laibson, D., Loewnestein, G., & Cohen, J. (2004). Separate neural systems value immediate and delayed monetary rewards. *Science*, *306*, 503–507.

Metcalfe, J., & Mischel, W. (1999). A hot/cool-system analysis of delay of gratification: Dynamics of willpower. *Psychological Review*, *106*, 3–19.

Mischel, W. (2014). *The marshmallow test: Mastering self-control*. New York: Little Brown.

Mischel, W., & Ebbeson, E. B. (1970). Attention in delay of gratification. *Journal of Personality & Social Psychology*, *16*, 329–337.

Mischel, W., Shoda, Y., & Peake, P. (1988). The nature of adolescent competencies predicted by preschool delay of gratification. *Journal of Personality & Social Psychology*, *54*, 687–696.

Muraven, M. (2010). Practicing self-control lowers the risk of smoking lapse. *Psychology of Addictive Behaviors*, *24*, 446–452.

Neale, J. (2002). *Drug users in society*. Basingstoke: Palgrave.

Nigg, J. (2000). On inhibition/disinhibition in developmental psychopathology: Views from cognitive and personality psychology and a working inhibition taxaonomy. *Psychological Bulletin*, *126*, 220–246.

Norman, D., & Shallice, T. (1986). Attention to action: Willed and automatic control of behaviour. In R. Davidson, G. Schwarz, & D. Shapiro (Eds.), *Consciousness and self-regulation: Advances in research* (pp. 1–18). New York, NY: Plenum.

Oaten, M., & Cheng, K. (2006). Improved self-control: The benefits of a regular program of academic study. *Basic & Applied Social Psychology*, *28*, 1–16.

O'Donoghue, T., & Rabin, M. (1999). Addiction and self-control. In J. Elster (Ed.), *Addiction: Entries and exits* (pp. 169–206). New York: Russell Sage Foundation.

Oettingen, G., Mayer, D., & Thorpe, J. (2010). Self-regulation of commitment to reduce cigarette consumption: Mental contrasting of future with reality. *Psychology & Health, 25*(8), 961–977.

Palfai, T. (2006). Automatic processes in the self-regulation of addictive behaviors. In R. Wiers, & A. Stacy (Eds.), *Handbook of implicit cognition and addiction*. Thousand Oaks CA: Sage Publications.

Preble, E., & Casey, J. (1969). Taking care of business: The heroin users' life on the streets. *International Journal of the Addictions, 4*, 1–24.

Rachlin, H. (1974). Self-control. *Behaviorism, 2*, 19–74.

Rachlin, H. (2000). *The science of self-control*. Cambridge, MA: Harvard University Press.

Robins, L., Davis, D., & Goodwin, D. (1974). Drug use by army-enlisted men in Vietnam: A follow-up on their return home. *American Journal of Epidemiology, 99*, 235–249.

Robins, L., Helzer, J., & Davis, D. (1975). Narcotic use in Southeast Asia and afterward: An interview study of 898 Vietnam returnees. *Archives of General Psychiatry, 32*, 955–961.

Robinson, T., & Berridge, K. (1993). The neural basis of drug craving: An incentive-sensitization theory of addiction. *Brain Research Reviews, 18*, 247–291.

Rush, B. (1812). *Medical inquiries and observations, upon the diseases of the mind* (1st ed.). Philadelphia: Kimber & Richardson.

Satel, S., & Lilienfeld, S. (2014). Addiction and the brain-disease fallacy. *Frontiers in Psychiatry, 4*(141). Available from: https://doi.org/10.3389/fpsyt.2013.00141.

Schaler, J. A. (2000). *Addiction is a choice*. Chicago, IL: Open Court Publishing.

Strack, F., & Deutsch, R. (2004). Reflective and impulsive determinants of social behavior. *Personality & Social Psychology Bulletin, 8*, 220–247.

Tuchfeld, B. (1981). Spontaneous remission in alcoholics: Empirical observations and theoretical implications. *Journal of Studies on Alcohol, 42*, 626–640.

Tucker, J., Chandler, S., & Cheong, J. (2017). Role of choice biases and choice architecture in behavioral economic strategies to reduce addictive behaviors. In N. Heather, & G. Segal (Eds.), *Addiction and choice: Rethinking the relationship* (pp. 346–364). Oxford, UK: Oxford University Press.

Volkow, N. (2016). Addiction is a disease of free will. *Huffpost*. Updated 12 June. <https://www.huffingtonpost.com/nora-volkow/addiction-is-a-disease-of_b_7561200.html?ec_carp = 8036785529832207068&guccounter = 1>.

Volkow, N., & Li, T. (2004). Drug addiction: The neurobiology of behavior gone awry. *Nature Reviews - Neuroscience, 5*, 963–970.

Volkow, N., & Li, T.-K. (2005). The neuroscience of addiction. *Nature Neuroscience, 8*, 1429–1430.

Vuchinich, R., & Heather, N. (Eds.), (2003). *Choice, behavioural economics and addiction*. Oxford, UK: Elsevier Science.

Wakefield, J. (2019). The harmful dysfunction analysis of addiction: Normal brains ad abnormal states of mind. In H. Pickard, & S. Ahmed (Eds.), *The Routledge handbook of philosophy and science of addiction* (pp. 90–101). Abingdon, UK: Routledge.

Watson, G. (1975). Free agency. *Journal of Philosophy, 72*, 205–220.

Watts, T., Duncan, G., & Quan, H. (2018). Revisiting the marshmallow test: A conceptual replication investigating links between early delay of gratification and later outcomes. *Psychological Science, 29*, 1159–1177.

Wiers, R., & Stacy, A. (Eds.), (2006). *Handbook of implicit cognition and addiction*. Thousand Oaks, CA: Sage.

Zajac, K., Alessi, S., & Petry, N. (2018). Contingency management approaches. In H. Pcikard, & S. Ahmed (Eds.), *The Routledge handbook of philosophy and science of addiction* (pp. 455–463). London, UK: Routledge.

Further reading

Carver, C., & Scheier, M. (1998). *On the self-regulation of behavior.* Cambridge, UK: Cambridge University Press.

de Kenessey, B. (2018). *People are dying because we misunderstand how those with addiction think.* Vox, 17 April. <https://www.vox.com/the-big-idea/2018/3/5/17080470/addiction-opioids-moral-blame-choices-medication-crutches-philosophy>. Accessed 10.12.18.

Farah, M. (2014). Brain images, babies, and bathwater: critiquing critiques of functional neuroimaging. In: *Interpreting neuroimages: An introduction to the technology and its limits* (pp. S19–S30). Hasting Center special report #45. Available from: https://doi.org/10.1002/hast.295.

Ioannides, J. (2011). Excess significance bias in the literature on brain volume abnormalities. *Archives of General Psychiatry, 68*, 773–780.

Maguire, E., Gadian, G., Johnsrude, I., Good, C., Ashburner, J., Frackowiak, R., & Frith, C. (2006). Navigation-related structural change in the hippocampi of taxi drivers. *Proceedings of the National Academy of Sciences of the United States of America, 97*, 4398–4403.

Miller, W., & Brown, J. (1991). Self-regulation as a conceptual basis for the prevention and treatment of addictive behaviors. In N. Heather, W. Miller, & J. Greeley (Eds.), *Self-control and the addictive behaviors* (pp. 3–79). Sydney, Australia: Maxwell-Macmillan.

Author Index

Note: Page numbers followed by "*f*" and "*t*" refer to figures and tables, respectively.

A

B

C

D

E

F

G

I

L

M

N

O

P

Q

R

S

T

W

X

Y

Z

Subject Index

Note: Page numbers followed by "*f*" and "*t*" refer to figures and tables, respectively.

B

C

D

S

T

U

V

W

Y

Z

CPI Antony Rowe
Chippenham, UK
2021-01-31 14:00